Islam without Europe

Islamic Civilization and Muslim Networks

Carl W. Ernst and Bruce B. Lawrence, editors

Highlighting themes with historical as well as contemporary significance, Islamic Civilization and Muslim Networks features works that explore Islamic societies and Muslim peoples from a fresh perspective, drawing on new interpretive frameworks or theoretical strategies in a variety of disciplines. Special emphasis is given to systems of exchange that have promoted the creation and development of Islamic identities—cultural, religious, or geopolitical. The series spans all periods and regions of Islamic civilization.

A complete list of titles published in this series appears at the end of the book.

Islam without Europe

Traditions of Reform in Eighteenth-Century Islamic Thought

AHMAD S. DALLAL

The University of North Carolina Press
Chapel Hill

This book was published with the assistance of the Anniversary Fund of the University of North Carolina Press.

Manufactured in the United States of America
Set in Adobe Text Pro by Tseng Information Systems, Inc.
The University of North Carolina Press has been a member of the Green Press Initiative since 2003.

Cover illustrations from *Persian Designs* (Amsterdam: The Pepin Press / Agile Rabbit editions, 2007), www.pepinpress.com.

Library of Congress Cataloging-in-Publication Data
Names: Dallal, Ahmad S., author.
Title: Islam without Europe : traditions of reform in eighteenth-century Islamic thought / Ahmad S. Dallal.
Description: Chapel Hill : The University of North Carolina Press, [2018] | Series: Islamic civilization and Muslim networks | Includes bibliographical references and index.
Identifiers: LCCN 2017054850| ISBN 9781469640341 (cloth : alk. paper) | ISBN 9781469641409 (pbk : alk. paper) | ISBN 9781469640358 (ebook)
Subjects: LCSH: Islam—18th century. | Islamic countries—Intellectual life.
Classification: LCC BP55 .D35 2018 | DDC 297.09/033—dc23
LC record available at https://lccn.loc.gov/2017054850

To my gracious and charming daughters,

Shezza and Kinda,

and their inspired and kindhearted brother,

Millal

اقرأ كتابك كفى بنفسك اليوم عليك حسيبا

(الإسراء، 14)

Read your own book. Suffice it today that you be accountable to yourself.

—Qur'ān 17:14

Contents

Acknowledgments, ix

Introduction, 1
Reimagining the Eighteenth Century

Chapter 1 The Boundaries of Faith, 20

Chapter 2 *Ijtihād* and the Regional Origins of a Universal Vision, 56

Chapter 3 Sufism, Old and New, 94
The Multiple Faces of the Spirit

Chapter 4 Genealogies of Dissent and the Politics of Knowledge, 140

Chapter 5 Humanizing the Sacred, 219

Conclusion, 280
The Limits of the Sacred

Notes, 323

Index, 415

Acknowledgments

I worked on this book intermittently over two decades, while based at different institutions. A significant part of the research was facilitated by a Yale University Morse Fellowship in the Humanities (1996–97) and a National Endowment for the Humanities Fellowship (2003–4). Sections of this work were presented at different forums at Yale University, Stanford University, Georgetown University, and the American University of Beirut, and at different conferences and workshops. I am grateful for all the valuable insights and ideas I received from colleagues and students on these and other occasions. I am especially indebted to my dear friends and colleagues Joel Beinin and Mary Wilson for their penetrating feedback, and for their unwavering friendship. I owe a huge thanks to Rosemary Stanfield and Rochelle Davis for their scholarly counsel and friendly sympathy and encouragement; they read earlier versions of the evolving book manuscript and offered valuable advice on its content and format. I am also grateful to the two manuscript reviewers for their very useful suggestions and comments. Needless to say, while I benefited greatly from this input, the views expressed in this book do not necessarily represent those of the above individuals or institutions, and I alone am responsible for any errors and shortcomings that may appear in the book.

At the early stages of working on this book, I used to discuss it with the late Eqbal Ahmad. Eqbal often pressed me to finish writing this book and told me that he would like to translate it to Urdu. He stayed with me throughout the writing of this book, as an inspiration and motivation for continuing to improve my knowledge and move this project forward. He, for one, would have appreciated the attraction of a tradition of dissent that perseveres for centuries and finally prevails, a tradition that, even when in power, does not shed its own memory of struggle.

I cannot adequately express my gratitude to my family. I learned much from Dalal about resilience and courage. For her intellectual and emotional companionship, and for our beautiful daughter, Kinda, I will always be in her debt. I dedicate this book to my wonderful children: Shezza, Millal, and Kinda. My life would not be as full and as rich as it has been without them. I look forward to the day when they can read and enjoy this book.

Islam without Europe

Introduction

Reimagining the Eighteenth Century

Sometime around the middle of the nineteenth century, the intellectual world of Muslims began to crumble and the great traditions of the past were forgotten. Contrary to common modern assertions, the recession of these traditions was sudden and unexpected. Throughout the eighteenth century and the early decades of the nineteenth, the Muslim world had witnessed one of the most lively and creative periods in its intellectual history. Echoes of this intellectual activity could still be felt in the late nineteenth and early twentieth centuries, yet nothing in this latter period approximated the erudition and depth of eighteenth-century thought. In the eighteenth century, enormous energies were devoted to a systematic and comprehensive restructuring of Islamic thought. The erudition of eighteenth-century thinkers and their honed historical consciousness enabled them to mold the past and fully appropriate its legacies. Classical styles of thinking were preserved, despite a great awareness of the need to reorganize religious knowledge and identify those aspects of Islam that were shared by all. From within the framework of classical learning, these thinkers dramatically restructured the intellectual world of Muslims. Diverse Islamic ideologies were forged and employed in Islamic sociopolitical as well as intellectual movements. Eighteenth-century models of Islamic activity ranged from political mobilization under the banner of classical Islamic ideology to the creation of a centralized network of Sufi settlements to purely intellectual reform embodied in new approaches to the study of traditional Islamic disciplines.

From the banks of the Ganges to the shores of the Atlantic, masses and elites alike embraced the relentless appeals of eighteenth-century Muslim thinkers. No other earlier period in Islamic history can boast of intellectual activities as self-consciously transformative and inclusive in their conception. Eighteenth-century thinkers were fully aware of the intellectual and political significance of their undertakings, and they embarked upon them with great self-confidence and optimism. Despite their alarmist tone, eighteenth-century thinkers had great hopes for the future: they asserted the potential superiority of later generations of Muslims over earlier ones and then proceeded to demonstrate this superiority; they articulated and espoused an Islam that transcends the boundaries of the schools of law and eradicates sectarian and legal differences; and they advocated the active participation of all Muslims in the definition of Islam and set out meticulously to chart the practical venues for this participation. From the perspective of the late nineteenth century, the intellectual ventures of the eighteenth century had failed to stand the test of time. Yet, judging by the record of the eighteenth century and its immediate aftermath, and not from later, hazy perceptions of this century, these ventures were quite successful and influential. The cultural vitality of the eighteenth century was not limited to certain regions but was spread over most of the Muslim world. The distinguished thinkers of this period came from India and Arabia, North Africa and West Africa, as well as Syria and Yemen. The diverse and rich legacies of this period—the vibrant eighteenth-century intellectual activities in the Muslim world that developed independent of European influence—are the subject of this book.

The choice of period and subject matter is justified primarily in light of the scope of this cultural activity and its contrast to cultural activities in the age of colonialism. Chronologically, it is easier to demarcate the end of this period than its beginnings. What I call the eighteenth century extends to the beginnings of the modern period, a period that is marked, above all, by European political, economic, and cultural domination over the Muslim world, and by an Islamic discursive culture largely articulated in reaction to this European challenge. Naturally, therefore, no single date can mark the end of the eighteenth century and the beginning of the modern period, as European penetration and domination took hold at different dates in different places. While, for example, the modern era in Egypt arguably starts in the early nineteenth century, European modernity in sub-Saharan Africa does not commence till after the middle of this century. Moreover, since the extent and significance of European hegemony was not simultaneously appreciated in all parts of the Muslim world, the cultural eighteenth century, defined here in terms of cultural production that was not articulated in response to Europe, sometimes lingered past the colonial takeover. As such, my approach is opposed to the traditional Orientalist view that marks the 1798 French invasion of Egypt as the beginning of the modern history of the Middle East and the Muslim world not just because many social, economic, political, and cultural continuities in large parts of the Muslim world were not affected by this invasion, but primarily because this periodization assumes generalized stagnation and decline in the eighteenth-century Muslim world. This idea of economic and political decline has been largely discredited in a substantial number of studies, especially by historians of the Ottoman Empire and the Ottoman provinces.[1] This study will undermine the decline thesis in the cultural sphere.

For the purposes of this study, the beginnings of the period under examination are also defined primarily in cultural terms. As I will demonstrate in the chapters that follow, the eighteenth century was characterized by intensive intellectual activities of great cultural significance. These activities continued traditional patterns of thinking[2] but were nonetheless very original and transformative. Eighteenth-century thought was the creative culmination of traditional Islamic traditions and epistemologies, but it was also the end of these traditions. And despite continuities between eighteenth-century thought and earlier traditional patterns of knowledge production, the intellectual constructs of the eighteenth century were unique and, in the case of hadith and legal theory (arguably two of the most important Islamic traditions), had radical transformative implications that far exceeded the scope and impact of earlier Islamic intellectual activities. The ubiquity in Orientalist historiography of the faulty paradigm of eighteenth-century decline further underscores the need for a different and more accurate understanding of eighteenth-century Islamic culture. The appropriateness of treating the Islamic eighteenth century as a unit is further corroborated by political and economic developments in this century. Already in the seventeenth century and through the eighteenth century, the central governments of the three major empires of the Muslim world—the Ottomans, Safavids, and Moghuls—often referred to as the gunpowder empires, were losing some of their control over their provinces and subjects. Changes in the structures of society and economy in each of these states were also coupled with military vulnerability and loss of territory. These gradual, and in no way irreversible, changes culminated in the eighteenth century in a number of dramatic events that underscore the historical distinctiveness of this period. In 1718, the Ottomans signed a treaty that forced them to surrender parts of the Balkans. Mindful of the weakening of its military position relative to Europe, the Ottoman state attempted to reform its bureaucracy and military by importing some of the practices of its European rivals. Around the same period, an Afghan invasion of Iran ended the Safavid dynasty in 1722 and, in 1739, Nāder Shāh, the new ruler of Iran, sacked Delhi and sealed the fate of an already weakened Moghul dynasty. Of course, the weakening or even demise of these centralized and centralizing states did not plunge the Muslim world into a period of irreversible stagnation. In the Ottoman Empire, for example, autonomous local powers, with vibrant and revived economies, emerged in several provinces including Mount Lebanon, Syria, Iraq, Palestine, and Egypt.[3] While significant research has already established the viability and vitality of several emerging eighteenth-century economies and polities of this period, eighteenth-century culture remains largely unexamined. This book explores the exceptional cultural achievements of the eighteenth century.

While offering general signposts for demarcating the boundaries and characteristics of the eighteenth century, political history does not determine the beginning or end of the eighteenth-century cultural activities that are studied in this book.[4] For similar reasons, I do not limit the geographical scope of inquiry to the regions examined in traditional histories of this period. A political or economic history of the period may legitimately limit its scope to regions that have similar state structures or economic patterns of production and circulation. Studies of the eighteenth century usually focus on the territorial domains of one or more of the three gunpowder empires, or on other parts of the Middle East or the Muslim world with comparable polities and economies. Since the primary focus of this study, however, is on trends of Islamic cultural production that were developed independent of European influence, the inclusion of ʿUthmān Ibn Fūdī of West Africa, or Muḥammad Bin ʿAlī al-Sanūsī of North and sub-Saharan Africa, is justified by the intellectual merits of these reformers and the social significance of the movements they led, even if their base territories fell outside the domains of the recognized powers of the time.

Remembering the past is hardly an innocent or objective act. Modernists all too often collect the debris of past cultures and labor in order to turn the deposits of nonsocieties into redeeming social realities in the present. This is not the purpose of this book. Rather, the object of this study is the cultural and social import of the intellectual achievements of the premodern period in the Muslim world, which, depending on the region, ends sometime between the beginning and the middle of the nineteenth century. The working hypothesis of this book is that the eighteenth century was a period of intellectual vitality rather than decadence. The focus on decline is deliberately avoided not least because it distills and distorts the view of the eighteenth century through the prism of later events. To avoid the retrospective use of modernist criteria in establishing the intellectual trends of the premodern period, the testimonies of eighteenth- and nineteenth-century sources are used to identify the major thinkers of the time. In the absence of an established canon for the intellectual achievements of this period, it is important to justify why certain works are deemed more significant than others. Once again, my purpose is not to canonize the works of unknown individuals but simply to study the contents of the works of scholars who have already been recognized in traditional scholarship. I used two criteria in selecting eighteenth-century authors and writings. First, the works examined in this book are all from prolific writers who were celebrated by their contemporaries and later generations of Muslims as the leading intellectuals of the century. Some enjoyed only regional recognition, whereas the reputation of others spread widely in the Muslim world. These writers often thought of themselves, and were portrayed in contemporary and later sources, as the *mujtahid*s (independent thinkers) of the time. They contributed to more than one field of study, and, as leaders of political movements or intellectual schools of thought, they had substantial influence and popularity. Their works were widely circulated, often far beyond their own countries, and became the subject of commentaries by later scholars. Although their views did not represent all or even most Muslim intellectual activity, these eighteenth-century reformers were the most celebrated among their contemporaries, and their thought prevailed, already during their own lifetime, as the best thought of the period. The second factor that informed my choice of themes to examine was my objective of providing a corrective to prevalent assumptions in current scholarly accounts of the history of the eighteenth century. In particular, I focus on the kinds of cultural production that undermine the thesis of Islamic decline as well as the various revisionist attempts to qualify this thesis.

The earliest and most widely accepted scholarly view asserts that the eighteenth century is a century of political and economic decline and of intellectual stagnation. According to this view, an era of political and intellectual revival and reform ensues in the nineteenth century primarily as a result of the growth of European influence in, and the resulting intellectual challenges to, the Muslim world. The reaction or response to Europe became the central criterion for defining Islamic reform, as is clearly stated, for example, in Albert Hourani's introduction to his *Arabic Thought in the Liberal Age, 1798–1939*.[5] This approach has privileged one particular kind of intellectual activity, namely, that which responded to the "European challenge" by adapting itself to it. Such, for example, is the disproportionate interest in modern scholarship in the views of the Egyptian historian ʿAbd al-Raḥmān al-Jabartī (1756–1825), who commented on the French in the aftermath of their occupation of Egypt,[6] or in the thought of the Egyptian writer Rifāʿa al-Ṭahṭāwī (1801–73), who, among other things, tried to provide an Islamic rationale for Egyptian nationalism.[7]

Later historians have looked at ways in which traditional sectors of Muslim society did in fact participate in the modernization efforts. Other kinds of intellectual activity, however, were deemed "traditional" and, it would seem, not worthy of study. Today, although many of the writings of eighteenth-century thinkers have been published, these writings are often presented as exceptional achievements in an age characterized by intellectual stagnation; as such, scholars see the significance of these writings chiefly as laying the foundation for the more substantial reforms of the nineteenth and twentieth centuries.

Historians who adopt the paradigm of decline almost invariably treat the Wahhabi movement as the representative trend of the eighteenth century, thus compounding, in my view, the misunderstanding of this century. The Wahhabi movement, which is recognized as the one example of Islamic success in the eighteenth century, is in fact its biggest intellectual exception. Also,

Wahhabi thought, though manipulated toward political ends, is extremely apolitical. The limited works of Muḥammad Ibn ʿAbd al-Wahhāb focus exclusively on creedal issues, whereas the majority of eighteenth-century thinkers and leaders, in contrast to Wahhabism, were primarily concerned with larger social and political problems, both in theory and in practice.

Although my views on the eighteenth century were articulated before the protracted events unleashed on September 11, 2001, and are in no way a response to them, arguments about the eighteenth century have some relevance to the current debate about the roots of contemporary Islamic radicalism. This relevance, however, is contrary to what has been adduced in most discussions about the so-called Wahhabi brand of Islam that, according to many contemporary commentators, triggered the wave of fundamentalism that culminated in the September 11 attacks. Many scholars and observers contend that modern fundamentalism is rooted in the legacy of the eighteenth-century as represented in the Wahhabi ideology. In the chapters that follow I demonstrate the inadequacy of the use of Wahhabism as a paradigm for understanding the eighteenth century; moreover, I argue that there is a fundamental rupture between the legacies of the long eighteenth century and those of the twentieth century. As such, eighteenth-century Wahhabism is quite distinct from twentieth-century radicalism, whether Wahhabi or otherwise. Eighteenth-century Wahhabism emerged out of Najd, the desert region of Arabia, as an isolated phenomenon and managed to overrun Mecca and Medina, the cultured cities of the Hejaz, due to declining Ottoman control over this region. This brief expansion of Wahhabi power, however, was reversed through the intervention of the armies of Muḥammad ʿAlī, the autonomous Ottoman governor of Egypt. Both politically and ideologically, Wahhabism was checked by local and regional actors and was forced to retreat to Najd, where it had no strategic regional significance. In addition to being a political exception, Wahhabism was not representative of eighteenth-century intellectual trends. Numerous countertrends emerged in the eighteenth century and, in contrast to Wahhabism, these more influential movements were thwarted only after the encounter with Europe. The twentieth-century reemergence of Wahhabism as a regional power in Arabia resulted largely from a new balance of power in the region marked by both a decline of the Ottomans and a rise of British influence in Arabia, which was favorable to the Wahhabis. Furthermore, the Wahhabi regional influence in the twentieth century was dramatically bolstered by the discovery of oil in Arabia. The sway of contemporary Wahhabism is a function of the legacies of postcolonialism. In fact, European influence not only shaped twentieth-century Wahhabism and allowed it to reemerge despite its limited popular appeal, but it also aborted the rich, non-Wahhabi traditions of the eighteenth and early nineteenth centuries that had previously managed to contain Wahhabi ideology and provide alternatives to it. Twentieth-century radicalism, therefore, is better explained by reference to modernity than by reference to the eighteenth-century or the Wahhabi movement that represented the exception of this century. Neither Wahhabism nor decline is emblematic of Muslim intellectual life in the eighteenth century.

In recent years, scholars have proposed several critiques of the notion of decline and have attempted to construct alternative accounts of the Islamic eighteenth century.[8] None of the revisionist approaches to the eighteenth century, however, questions the validity of using Wahhabism as a model for representing eighteenth-century Islamic movements and intellectual activity. Instead, these accounts generally suggest that both nineteenth-century Islamic reform and twentieth-century fundamentalism are rooted in the legacy of the eighteenth century.[9] Such estimations of eighteenth-century thought presuppose that its main value was in laying the foundations of later, socially significant reforms.[10] Revisionist accounts of the eighteenth century have placed much emphasis on a Sufism (Islamic mysticism) void of intellectual or spiritual rigor, and on the so-called socio-moral use of hadith (the traditions of the Prophet Muhammad), that is, on hadith as the source providing standards of individual and collective codes of conduct.[11] This emphasis has shifted the focus of examination from the intellectual content of eighteenth-century writings on Sufism or hadith to the social uses of these two disciplines. Although a large amount of the writings of eighteenth-century thinkers has been published, revisionist historiography continues to focus on practical and social aspects of eighteenth-century activity in a move that confirms the earlier notion that the intellectual value of eighteenth-century thought is minimal.[12]

The distinction between culture and social reality is implied in studies that argue that a political economy approach to the study of the eighteenth century would undermine traditional Orientalist views and would yield a radically different understanding of this period.[13] While these works convincingly criticize notions of social and economic decline in the eighteenth century, they suffer, in my view, from two related shortcomings. First, in advocating that historians ought to "leave what is still basically the intellectual world of culture history (with its typical concern for the transmission of ideas) for the world of political economy,"[14] they posit a problematic dichotomy between the "unreal" ideas and the "real" material forces at work in society. Such a dichotomy seriously underestimates the role of Islamic discursive culture and ideology in society. Second, the invitation to shift the focus of research presumably implies that although there might be cultural stagnation in the eighteenth century, we are likely to reach different conclusions if we focus our attention on political economy. While this is meant as a critique of the Orientalist notion that equates "the high point of 'Islamic' creativity" with "Islamic culture," it fails to provide a corrective to the long-standing Orientalist assumption that the eighteenth century is, nevertheless, a low point in Islamic culture. This assumption, it must be added, is central to the crude Orientalist scheme of periodization that not only asserts essentialist distinctions between the Islamic world and the West but also posits a European monopoly over humanistic cultural production since the beginnings of European awakenings in the eleventh century. Abandoning the study of ideas in the Muslim world when our knowledge of the world of culture or even ideas is so impoverished can only reinforce this flawed paradigm.[15]

Sharing the underlying assumption that eighteenth-century *movements* are more interesting than eighteenth-century *thought,* both Orientalist and revisionist accounts presuppose that the eighteenth century did not contribute anything of value at the intellectual level. As such, what is implied in this notion of *indigenous* revivals is an *indigenous but intellectually impoverished* eighteenth-century revival. One reason that the older account of eighteenth-century decline still prevails is the many weaknesses of the proposed revisionist explanations. Perhaps the weakest point in all of the alternative accounts is that they have yet to identify the elements of eighteenth-century innovation.[16]

To undermine the thesis of decline, I start by revisiting Wahhabism and its place in the intellectual landscape of the eighteenth century. In the chapters that follow I explore the adequacy of revisionist conceptions of eighteenth-century reform. One such conception that I examine is *ijtihād,* the exercise of independent legal reasoning, a concept commonly considered as the hallmark of Islamic reform. Muslim intellectuals of the twentieth century as well as modern scholars of Islam have given much attention to the subject of *ijtihād.* Earlier scholarly accounts of modern Islamic history contend that the "gates of *ijtihād*" were closed in the classical period and were reopened in the late nineteenth century, as a result of the redeeming encounter with Europe.[17] Revisionist historians, however, cite the proliferation of writings on *ijtihād* in the eighteenth century and hence move back the starting date of reform to the eighteenth century. Yet, in contrast to the revisionist reference to *ijtihād,* I argue that works on *ijtihād* were composed throughout earlier periods and, as far as legal theory is concerned, can hardly be considered exclusively characteristic of eighteenth-century thought. What is new about these discussions, however, is the way *ijtihād* is deployed within the larger projects of their authors. Furthermore, during their lifetime, as the *mujtahid*s (independent legal scholars as well as thinkers) of their times, the writers examined in this book were celebrated primarily for their ability to exercise *ijtihād.*

Several Muslim intellectuals of the nineteenth and early twentieth centuries attempted to identify the *mujtahid*s or *mujaddids* (renewers) of the previous century. The nineteenth-century Indian author Ṣiddīq Khān al-Qanūjī lists among the *mujtahid*s of the end of the eighteenth and beginning of the nineteenth centuries Shāh Walī Allāh al-Dihlawī and his grandson Muḥammad Ismāʿīl; Muḥammad Ibn Ismāʿīl al-Ṣanʿānī; Muḥammad Ibn ʿAlī al-Shawkānī; Ṣāliḥ Ibn ʿUmar al-Fulānī; Muḥammad Ḥayāt al-Sindī; Muḥammad Fākhir al-Ilāh Ābādī; and Muḥammad Ibn Nāṣir al-Ḥāzimī.[18] These names appear in many other biographical sources, and all but the last two will be examined in this book.[19] Rashīd Riḍā, the famous reformer of the early twentieth century, also tried to identify the *mujaddid*s of the past. Riḍā repeats many of the same names, but he also provides a general rule for identifying these *mujaddid*s. These, he argues, are individuals who not only combine a solid scholarly reputation and an aura of leadership but also offer ideas that satisfy their time's needs for *tajdīd* (renewal). This definition of *mujaddid*s would be satisfactory if the records of the eighteenth century indicated what the period's needs for renewal might have been. But in most instances, including that of Riḍā himself, twentieth-century writers analyzed and defined these needs retrospectively, and the resulting definitions may better represent the perceived needs for renewal in the writers' eras than any objective assessment of the needs of the eighteenth century. Even if the explanatory value of later accounts of eighteenth-century reform are in question, the convergence of these accounts provides grounds for identifying the key thinkers of the eighteenth and early nineteenth centuries.

This study is a partial reconstruction of the thought-world of the main thinkers of the eighteenth century, and an attempt to assess their intellectual achievements. Because the cultural achievements of the eighteenth century remain largely neglected, some preliminary descriptive work must be done, and the story needs to be told before we can move to the explanatory level of analysis. This study will survey and compare the works and activities of several major thinkers of the eighteenth century whose ideas, I will argue, comprise distinct intellectual trends of Islamic thought in the premodern period, rather than one general trend as suggested by scholarly literature. These thinkers were the most famous scholars or activists of the period in question. They include Muḥammad Ibn Ismāʿīl al-Amīr al-Ṣanʿānī (1688–1769) of Yemen, Shāh Walī Allāh al-Dihlawī of India (1703–62), Muḥammad Ibn ʿAbd al-Wahhāb of Arabia (1703–87), ʿUthmān Ibn Fūdī of West Africa (1754–1817), Muḥammad Ibn ʿAlī al-Shawkānī (1759–1834) of Yemen, and Muḥammad Bin ʿAlī al-Sanūsī of North Africa (1787–1859). Modern studies that draw parallels between their respective backgrounds and ideas have consistently lacked an in-depth account or analysis of their thought.

Muḥammad Ibn Ismāʿīl al-Amīr al-Ṣanʿānī (1688–1769) was one of the central figures in the tradition of Yemeni reform. He grew up in a Zaydi[20] environment, but early in his life he claimed to have become an independent thinker (*mujtahid*). For this he came under constant attack by other Zaydis accusing him of trying to undermine their school. In auspicious times, he served as the imam (religious leader) of the great mosque of Sanaa, but during less fortunate times he was imprisoned by the rulers of the city after his enemies accused him of dropping the name of the Zaydi imams (in this context, rulers) from the Friday *khuṭba* (sermon). Later, he left his hometown and country and traveled to Mecca and Medina, where he became more steeped in traditional Sunni scholarship, especially in the study of the traditions of the Prophet Muhammad (hadith). However, his independent thinking aroused hostility even there, and eventually he went back to northern Yemen, where he spent the rest of his life in relative shelter from public criticism.[21]

Shāh Walī Allāh al-Dihlawī (1703–62) lived and worked in Delhī.[22] During his lifetime he witnessed the final breakup of the Mughal Empire and the rise in its place of a number of smaller and weaker states. The invasion by Nādir Shāh in 1739 and the sack of Delhi further weakened the Muslims and left them vulnerable to aggression from India's numerous non-Muslim communities. It is not surprising that Walī Allāh's thought was in some measure a response to his perception of the crisis of the time.[23] Since most scholars have defined it simply in terms of their perceptions of the political situation of Walī Allāh's time, it would be instructive to examine his own understanding of this crisis, an understanding that is the basis of his intellectual project.[24]

Muḥammad Ibn ʿAbd al-Wahhāb was born in the village of ʿUyayna in Najd in the year 1703. There is little reliable information on his activities during the first four decades of his life. His longest journey was to Basra, from which he was eventually expelled. In the early 1740s, after the death of his father, he started preaching his doctrine of *tawḥīd* (oneness of God). Five years later he gained the political support of the head of the Saʿūd family residing in Darʿīya, and together they gradually gained control over different parts of Arabia. Ibn ʿAbd al-Wahhāb reportedly retired after the conquest of Riyadh and devoted the last two decades of his life to worship and meditation.[25]

ʿUthmān Ibn Fūdī[26] was born in Gobir (in northern Nigeria) in the year 1754. His father was a learned man, and Ibn Fūdī studied with him and with several renowned scholars of the region. He started his career as a wandering teacher in the 1770s, and through the mid-1790s he instructed people on the proper practice of Islam. By the end of this period he had acquired a wide reputation, and his following had increased considerably. Around the year 1795 the emphasis of his teachings and writings gradually shifted from personal instruction to a broader concern with social and political questions and a jihad,[27] which was declared in 1804 and culminated in 1806 in the establishment of the Sokoto caliphate in present-day northern Nigeria. He died in 1817 in the newly established capital, Sokoto, but the caliphate he built continued to flourish under his successors and to inspire many other movements in West Africa.[28]

Muḥammad Ibn ʿAlī al-Shawkānī (1759–1834) was another Yemeni scholar who served as chief judge under three of the imams of Sanaa. He belonged to a long tradition of Zaydism in Yemen that was open to Sunni Islam, not in politics alone but also in serious efforts to rework the doctrines and the laws of the school. In this Zaydi tradition, four major figures stand out as the most distinguished scholars of Yemen after the fifteenth century and had great influence on al-Shawkānī: Muḥammad Ibn Ibrāhīm al-Wazīr (d. 1436), Al-Ḥasan al-Jalāl (d. 1673), Ṣāliḥ Ibn Mahdī al-Maqbalī (d. 1738), and Muḥammad Ibn Ismāʿīl al-Amīr (d. 1768).[29] Al-Shawkānī witnessed the changes in the international and regional political scene of his time and was directly involved in dealing with the political and intellectual ramifications of these changes. Al-Shawkānī's work is consistently of a high caliber. He was an erudite, prolific, and original writer who composed more than 150 books (many of which are multivolume works). Despite this illustrious intellectual career, there is hardly any mention of al-Shawkānī in studies of the eighteenth century in European languages.[30] The influence of al-Shawkānī's thought extended beyond Yemen and his own lifetime. His professed followers include al-Qanūjī in India and al-Sanūsī in North Africa.

The writings of Muḥammad Bin ʿAlī al-Sanūsī[31] represent yet another distinct project of revival. Al-Sanūsī was born in 1787 in Mustaghānim, Algeria. He received his early education in his hometown and later in Fez before he went on pilgrimage to Mecca. There he met and became a loyal disciple of Aḥmad Ibn Idrīs al-Fāsī, founder of the Idrīsīya (or Aḥmadīya) order. After al-Fāsī's death in 1836, al-Sanūsī founded his first *zāwiya* (Sufi lodge) on Mount Abū Qubays just outside Mecca, but opposition and pressure from local scholars and politicians forced him to leave. In 1840 he headed back to North Africa. In 1842 he established his first headquarters on Al-Jabal al-Akhḍar, halfway between Tripoli and the Egyptian border. From this *zāwiya*, al-Sanūsī dispatched missionaries to the southern and western parts of Libya, where the presence of Ottoman and French authorities, the strong Sufi orders of North African cities,[32] and the influence of the Azharite scholars were minimal. Between 1846 and 1853 he went on a second long pilgrimage to Mecca, and soon after his return he moved his headquarters farther south to Jaghbūb, where he spent the final years of his life. Upon his death in 1859, dozens of *zāwiya*s were already established throughout Libya and elsewhere in Egypt, Algeria, and the Sahara. The spread of the Sanūsīya continued under the leadership of the founder's two sons and was halted only by the expanding French powers.

Later the followers of the order were active in the resistance against the Italian occupation, and the head of the order became the first king of Libya after independence.

These eighteenth-century thinkers, along with others not dealt with here, were famous both within and outside their respective regions and were considered the intellectual ancestors of later generations in these regions. The recognition of these thinkers' intellectual credentials by later historians and Muslims resulted from the success of their influential political movements and innovative intellectual traditions. In India, Shāh Walī Allāh is recognized as the most distinguished Muslim scholar that India ever produced, and mutually opposed schools claim to derive and best represent his true thought. Similarly, in Yemen, nationalists, Zaydis, and Sunnis alike claim al-Shawkānī, who was, already during his own lifetime, counted as one of the leading Muslim scholars of Yemen.[33] Ibn Fūdī is also considered the most central figure in the legacy of Islamic Nigeria and in the Islamist discourse of West Africa, partly as a result of his political success in establishing the Sokoto Caliphate. Generally, all of these thinkers were intellectually assertive even when they were not in positions of power.

The ideas developed by these thinkers were decidedly diverse; however, all of them undertook bold and self-consciously transformative intellectual projects. Furthermore, these intellectual projects were coupled with active social and political engagements, a fact that implies a high level of self-confidence and ambition rather than utopian idealism. This is further confirmed by the high quality and quantity of the works of eighteenth-century thinkers and the dual role they assumed as both reformers of tradition and teachers responsible for guiding an Islamic community and effecting changes of great consequence. Their confidence was manifest, among other things, in the grand intellectual synthesis of Shāh Walī Allāh, al-Ṣanʿānī's bold confrontations with political and intellectual authorities, the successful expansion of Islam into sub-Saharan Africa by al-Sanūsī, the building of a centralized state in West Africa by Ibn Fūdī, and al-Shawkānī's attempt to illustrate, via theoretical analysis and historical documentation, the superiority and hence authority of later generations of Muslims over the Prophet's Companions. Viewed from within their own chronological and spatial boundaries, the undertakings of eighteenth-century thinkers were quite successful. These intellectual and political successes suggest that the reasons for the Islamic nineteenth-century crisis are not exclusively endogenous, and that they are rooted in the stifling effect of the events that took hold of the Muslim world during the colonial period. Subsequently, the political and intellectual scenes throughout the Muslim world were characterized by severe crisis, yet the endogenous as well as exogenous factors that contributed to this decline fall outside the scope of this book and will not be addressed here. Instead, the book charts the historical and epistemological foundations of the reformative traditions of the eighteenth century.

The scholars examined in this book reflect on the subject of *ijtihād*; yet, the pamphlets they wrote on the topic, attractive as they may be to modern viewers obsessed by Islamic innovation or decline, were minor works in comparison to their other works. The erudition and originality of eighteenth-century Islamic thought lies more in such disciplines as Qurʾānic exegesis, theory of hadith, and jurisprudence. This rich literature in the core disciplines of the Islamic cultural tradition provides the basis for the present study.

While earlier studies of the eighteenth century did not recognize an Islamic intellectual tradition worthy of study, revisionist historians have focused on social and political developments with only a cursory and formal exploration of culture. One aspect of Islamic culture that has been commonly invoked in revisionist histories of the eighteenth century is so-called neo-Sufism: a kind of Sufism characterized by the tendency to emphasize a Muhammad-oriented mysticism (involving an association with the figure of the Prophet) and to harmonize Sufism with the formal, legal teachings of Islam.[34] The earliest uses of the term *neo-Sufism* were introduced in matter-of-fact fashion without any attempt to define this usage.[35] It denotes a demysticized Sufism that, in the words of Fazlur Rahman, is "nothing else but the postulates of the orthodox religion."[36] Following Rahman, numerous historians have asserted that this neo-Sufism is central to all premodern reform movements.[37] Various studies characterize neo-Sufism in terms of the rejection of popular Sufi practices, the rejection of the philosophical mysticism of the great Sufi thinker Ibn ʿArabī, the rejection of the strict Sufi hierarchy (the *murshid-murīd* or teacher-disciple relationship), and the rejection of imitation (*taqlīd*) in legal matters. Furthermore, this neo-Sufism supposedly is characterized by an emphasis on mass organization and initiation into social organizations, union with the Prophet and a Muhammad-oriented mysticism (*Ṭarīqa Muḥammadiyya*), legitimation through chains of authority (*silsilas*) going all the way to the Prophet, willingness to take political and military action in defense of Islam, emphasis on hadith, and the right to exercise independent legal reasoning (*ijtihād*). In short, the term *neo-Sufism* is used to refer to Sufi movements that make deliberate effort to distance themselves from excessive Sufi practices and to conform to "orthodox" beliefs and practices. As such, eighteenth-century Sufism is often viewed by historians as void of spiritual dimensions, and as merely a mass movement in the service of legalistic Islam.

While this scholarly coinage is not grounded in evidence,[38] several elaborate studies have been written to illustrate the inadequacy of the paradigm of neo-Sufism for understanding actual developments in eighteenth-century

Sufism, both at the social and the intellectual levels.[39] Among the many criticisms leveled against this concept is that Ibn ʿArabī's influence continued to be pervasive in both high and popular Sufism. These studies also point out that the ascribed anthropocentric tendencies of Muhammad-oriented Sufism (*Ṭarīqa Muḥammadiyya*) were already introduced by Ibn ʿArabī himself in the thirteenth century, and that this kind of Sufism can be, and in fact most of the time is, a deeply mystical principle that reinforces rather than undermines the spiritual, imaginative dimension of Sufism.[40] Critics of the concept of neo-Sufism have also noted that the rejection of imitation (*taqlīd*) and of legal schools or *madhhab*s that is emphasized in *Ṭarīqah Muḥammadiyya* is not replaced by an advocacy of personal legal judgment that would have recourse to reason. Therefore, these critics argue, Muhammad-oriented mysticism does not represent a shift from a notion of authority that stands above individual reason to one that is personal; rather, the alternative is the notion of personal access to God.[41]

Of all the paradigms deployed by the revisionist historians of the eighteenth century, the concept of neo-Sufism has received the most criticism. Critiques of this concept, however, do not account for the whole range of eighteenth-century discourse on Sufism, both by Sufis and critics of the Sufi tradition. Most notably, there were eighteenth-century critics of Sufism who did not replicate the Wahhabi attitude toward it, and who managed instead to produce a nuanced criticism of Sufi thought and practice. Moreover, valid as the critiques of the concept of neo-Sufism are, they do not situate Sufism within the context of the main trends of eighteenth-century intellectual reform. In chapter 3, I offer a more nuanced discussion of aspects of eighteenth-century Sufism.

One of the most central assertions of revisionist historians of the eighteenth century is that of the continuity between the eighteenth century and the nineteenth and twentieth centuries.[42] One prominent view argues that eighteenth-century reform and modern fundamentalism are linked by virtue of a shared "fundamentalist mode of Islam" that presumably had its latest formulation in the eighteenth century and continues to unfold in the modern period. Proponents of this thesis maintain that several Islamic "socio-moral"[43] reform movements were active in the eighteenth century, that these movements were not inspired by the encounter with Europe, and that they laid the foundation for an indigenous "fundamentalist" tradition that continues today.[44] Several studies of eighteenth-century Islamic thought have already been produced with the explicit intention of establishing its connection to later developments in Islamic thought.[45] To be sure, advocates of this view do not deny the effect of the encounter with the West on modern reform, but they still maintain that the eighteenth century had its autonomous agents of innovation and its own brand of original renovation and renewal, and that this indigenous tradition is partly responsible for modern renewal and fundamentalism.[46] This serious scholarly attempt to trace continuities between eighteenth-century reform and modern fundamentalism is not to be equated with nationalist efforts to construct genealogies that root modern regimes in the past of the nation. Yet despite the important differences between these two approaches, both fail to recognize that the problems that informed the reform ideas of the eighteenth century bear no resemblance whatsoever to those that inspired and drove later reforms. The most noticeable absence from the thought of all the major Muslim intellectuals of the eighteenth century is Europe. Even when some of these thinkers were aware of colonial encroachments on Muslim lands, they did not appreciate the extent of the threat these infringements presented, nor did such events influence their thought: Europe, as a politico-cultural challenge, was completely absent. Of course, the exact opposite is true of later Islamic thought, where the challenge of Europe drives all the famous thinkers of the late nineteenth and early twentieth centuries. Their responses to Europe ranged from rejecting Europe in all of its political and intellectual dimensions, to striking a compromise and adopting some European institutions, to embracing these institutions wholeheartedly. In all cases, these were responses or reactions to what became the ever-present reality of European hegemony.

To substantiate the continuity thesis, reference is often made to an informal network of teachers and students in the Ḥaramayn (Mecca and Medina). Advocates of this view further maintain that although there were no formal organizational links between eighteenth-century movements, the ideas of the scholars in this network were preached in various parts of the Muslim world, providing a measure of intellectual coherence and family resemblance among these movements. Aside from tracing possible links and contacts between the known thinkers of the presumed network of scholars, the only attempt to verify this view is simply to assert that most, if not all, of these movements promoted neo-Sufism and championed hadith scholarship as the means for "socio-moral reconstruction."[47]

This idea of an informal intellectual network has had strong appeal among historians of the eighteenth and nineteenth centuries; several students of eighteenth-century Islam have attempted to trace the links between the Ḥaramayn scholars and various regional traditions of the period.[48] When it comes to the specific research methodologies, the primary sources privileged for this kind of analysis are the biographical dictionaries, and even then, the parts of biographical entries primarily examined are the names of teachers and students that a certain eighteenth-century scholar studied with. The most serious drawback of this approach is that the actual content of the thought of various members of the network in question does not figure into the analysis before affinities are posited between these scholars. For example, an examination of the writings of Ibn ʿAbd al-Wahhāb, who asserts that Sufis are unbelievers punishable by death, and those of Walī Allāh, who wrote extensively on Sufism, renders the notion of a common intellectual network meaningless.

In opposition to focusing on transregional networks of scholars, I trace the development of regional reform traditions that drew heavily on local learning and canons. The primary concerns of this study are the generation of new traditions and epistemologies, their local adaptations, and the distinct characteristics they acquired at the local levels. However, I make no attempt to provide thorough explanations of the local peculiarities, or to delineate the regionally specific social organization of shared theoretical knowledge in local contexts. In other words, this is not a study of local forms of Islam or of the role of Muslim scholars as cultural brokers. I focus instead on conceptual discussions that, despite their reliance on and awareness of universal, transregional Islamic traditions, took different forms in different regions.[49] Nonetheless, once these new ideas were articulated locally, they triggered other reforms beyond the local level. As such, despite their utility in partially explaining developments in the thought of individual eighteenth-century thinkers, the local sociopolitical contexts of each man's thought have little bearing on intellectual developments in the larger Muslim world, or on the influence of this author outside his particular region of activity.[50] Within any geographical region, particular traditions often emerge over long periods of time and encompass several figures working under radically different social and political conditions. The history of a tradition, therefore, cannot be mechanically reduced to the history of its context; from the perspective of the comparative study of intellectual traditions in the eighteenth century, context is secondary to content.[51]

The various universal visions of eighteenth-century thinkers had their roots in earlier regional traditions. While many peripatetic scholars traveled in that century in pursuit of knowledge, the era's major thinkers either traveled after their ideas matured and their views were articulated or they did not travel at all. They also recognized the peculiarities of their own traditions and set out to transform them by deliberately importing ideas and theories from other regional traditions and schools of thought. It is thus possible to speak of an Indian school of thought and a Yemeni one. It is perhaps even possible to claim that groundbreaking intellectual contributions were made within the context of mature and erudite regional traditions, whereas the intellectual contributions of traveling apprentice scholars, important as they were from a social perspective, were derivative. The regional rootedness of the main reform traditions, however, does not imply that their intellectual horizons were limited or parochial. Quite the contrary, regional traditions were revitalized by opening them up to the legacies of other Muslim regions and schools of thought. The regional character of their thought was simply a reflection of the concern of eighteenth-century thinkers with the problems of their societies and their attempts to provide real solutions for these problems. This regional character, however, did not amount to the formation of national identities. Contrary to many contemporary assertions in both scholarly works and nationalist discourse, the reformers of the eighteenth century were not national heroes, nor were they the precursors of the later ideologues of the nationalist movements.[52]

Perhaps paradoxically, the strong emphasis in eighteenth-century writings on the legitimacy of the present was firmly rooted in tradition and the cultural legacies of the past. The deep import of eighteenth-century rejection of imitation (*taqlīd*) was that imitation undermines the authority of the present. This focus on the present, however, did not come at the expense of tradition. Although from the perspective of the late nineteenth century the adoption of hybrid, non-Islamic cultural legacies seemed inevitable, in the eighteenth century it was not an option. Thus, radical as they were, the reformative projects of the eighteenth century did not involve a complete break with the past. This is why I use the term *traditional* to describe these reform projects. The ability of eighteenth-century thinkers to re-form knowledge was facilitated by a critical awareness of the historicity of the received traditions. Through a systematic delineation of multiple past legacies, these thinkers were able to provide fresh readings of these legacies. Established canons were thus opened up to new interpretations, and, through a process of inter-Islamic hybridization, the contours of canonical Islamic knowledge were expanded. Although eighteenth-century thought introduced significant departures from traditional epistemologies, these departures were generated from within the tradition and were not derived from alternative cultural systems.

The focus on the comparative, transregional study of traditions is further justified by the nature of the writings of the period under examination. None of the regional traditions examined in this book was intellectually marginal. To be sure, most modern scholars would contend that the examples studied in this book belong to peripheral traditions and would limit the center to those areas first influenced by Europe, that is, Anatolia, Egypt, and Greater Syria. The definition of an intellectual center on the basis of exposure to Europe is a later historical creation that was not prevalent in the eighteenth century. Since this assumed center has been the subject of numerous studies, in this book I will explore intellectual developments in other parts of the Muslim world. The regions under examination here were, in their own right, centers of highly original Islamic scholarship and were in no way marginal or peripheral. Quite the contrary, some of the most interesting intellectual activities in the Muslim world took place in these regions. The centrality of innovativeness in these regional traditions was coupled with a great ability to exert influence locally and beyond. My focus, therefore, is on central reformative textual traditions, and not on marginality or a pristine "primitiveness" that preserves unchanged age-old patterns of thinking or behavior.[53] Moreover, textual traditions are socially embedded phenomena and as such are constituent of, and not distinct from, social reality.

The objective of this book, however, is not simply to question the current historians' accounts of the eighteenth century but also to reconstruct the thought-world of this period. The writings produced in the eighteenth century were preoccupied with two themes. The first was the value of the present and its legitimacy. The second was the study of hadith, with an emphasis on the importance of scrutinizing the circumstances of the reports and the biographies of the reporters (*ʿilm al-rijāl*), that is, the process of reporting and the validity of this process. Thus a dialectic relationship between knowledge (the content of reports) and history (the reporters and their conditions) and between content and environment was set up and rigorously tested. There was also an emphasis on understanding the sciences and their precepts and rules in light of the historical conditions under which they were formed,[54] and on the role of intellectual authority and its connection to political authority in generating rigid and elitist interpretations of knowledge. For eighteenth-century writers, the undermining of these rigid interpretations in effect liberates knowledge from the hegemony of political authority through understanding the history of this authority. One expression of the historicity of eighteenth-century thought was the recognition of regional histories (in Yemen and in India, for example). Furthermore, the emphasis on the role of the free intellectual scholar in contrast to official scholars (*fuqahāʾ al-sulṭān*) underscores the subversive nature of knowledge in the minds of eighteenth-century thinkers.

The Islamic eighteenth century was a period of great intellectual vitality comparable in its scope, intensity, and quality to the cultural activities of the classical period. Intellectuals from virtually all the regions of the Muslim world systematically attempted to scrutinize the epistemological foundations of inherited knowledge and to reformulate the traditional Islamic disciplines of learning. No other fields of study received more scrutiny than the fields of *uṣūl* (theoretical principles), in particular *uṣūl al-fiqh* (literally principles of jurisprudence, or legal theory) and *uṣūl al-ḥadīth* (the theory of hadith). Orientalists have for long maintained, without any dissent by the revisionist historians, that the fields of *uṣūl* are by definition apologetic; that *uṣūl al-fiqh*, for example, is an attempt by legal scholars to theorize and hence justify older legal practices, and that political theory is a retrospective attempt to justify existing political orders, and so on. However, in contrast to the perceived conservative nature of these disciplines, the most radical rethinking of traditional Islamic thought, and hence the most original thought of the eighteenth century, was in fact in these same fields of *uṣūl*. Chapter 5 and the conclusion of the book discuss these fields.

Chapters 1, 2, 3, and 4 deal with the historical and epistemological foundations of the various reformative traditions of the eighteenth century and the social and intellectual mechanism employed to introduce these reforms. Against this background, the current historiography of the eighteenth century is assessed. In particular, I revisit both the notions of decline and the alternate view that argues for intellectual conformity and continuity. I also revisit three widely accepted claims commonly used to substantiate these notions. These are the assertions that the thought of Ibn ʿAbd al-Wahhāb is representative of premodern Islamic thought; that a new kind of puritanical Sufism emerged in this period; and that this period witnessed a resurgent insistence on *ijtihād* and rejection of *taqlīd*. Chapter 5 and the conclusion focus on the intellectual content of eighteenth-century reform. In particular, I examine the original contributions of eighteenth-century thinkers in the traditional disciplines of hadith and legal theory, and I demonstrate an originality and radicalism in eighteenth-century Islamic thought that was hardly equaled in any other period of Islamic history.

Chapter 1

The Boundaries of Faith

The new generation of eighteenth-century scholars was purposeful about the need for change. Although their diagnoses of the ills of their times largely overlapped, their proposed solutions differed significantly. The crisis of choice for most eighteenth-century thinkers was *tamadhhub*: zealous partisanship to the schools of law (*madhāhib*, sing. *madhhab*). *Tamadhhub* was considered the main problem of Muslims and the primary cause of weakness and strife in Muslim societies. It was tied to pressing problems, such as the imposition of illegal taxes and religious degeneration reflected in the supplication to human intermediaries and ignorance. Another main problem identified by almost all eighteenth-century scholars in connection with *madhhab* partisanship was *takfīr*, the condemnation of fellow Muslims as unbelievers.[1] A unifying theme, as it were, *takfīr* was often considered the hallmark of Muḥammad Ibn ʿAbd al-Wahhāb's teachings and was usually brought up in criticism of the Wahhabi discourse.

In contrast to the dominant anti-Wahhabi trend in eighteenth-century thought, both old-fashioned and revisionist historiography converge in the view that Wahhabism was a prototype of eighteenth-century thought and movements.[2] This emphasis on Wahhabism correlates with a common assumption underlying most studies of modern and contemporary Islamic activism, namely, that it is socially interesting but intellectually impoverished. Typically, traditional Orientalist historiography maintains that interesting intellectual developments in Islamic thought belong to the classical period (however defined), that the postclassical period is decidedly a period of political and economic decline and intellectual stagnation, and that Islamic creative thinking was rekindled after, and as a result of, the encounter with Europe.[3] According to this view, the decline, which set in some time after the eleventh century and no later than the thirteenth or fourteenth centuries, culminated in the eighteenth century, the darkest period in Islamic history. The subsequent political and intellectual revivals and reforms of the nineteenth century were triggered by the encounter with Europe. Presumably inspired by Europe, the activities of the Muslim reformers of the late nineteenth century partially checked the steady degeneration in Islamic thought.[4]

Historians of the modern Muslim world have thus defined reform in terms of the reaction or response to Europe. For example, in his *Arabic Thought in the*

Liberal Age, 1798–1939, Albert Hourani maintains that the thinkers he studies in his book are chosen not on account of their intellectual excellence, for, in his words, their work was not "of the highest caliber," but rather for their ability to "express the needs of their society," and the extent to which "their ideas served as forces in the process of change." Furthermore, although "more than one kind of reaction [to the European challenge] was possible," Hourani chose to focus on the thought of those thinkers who responded to the European challenge by arguing for societal change "through the acceptance of some of the ideas and institutions of modern Europe."[5]

Based on a similar criterion, most studies of the history of the early modern Islamic world have privileged intellectual activities that responded to the European challenge.[6] As a result, only a few eighteenth-century political and intellectual developments have been considered seriously and, even then, these developments have almost always been examined from the vantage point of the "reforming elites." There is of course no doubt that this historical perspective is important for understanding developments that started in the nineteenth century. The emphasis on modernization and reform, however, has come at the expense of other kinds of intellectual activity deemed "traditional" and thus excluded as not worthy of study.[7]

In recent years, several critiques of the notions of decline have been proposed and attempts to construct alternative accounts of the Islamic eighteenth century have been undertaken. These accounts generally suggest that both nineteenth-century Islamic reform and twentieth-century fundamentalism are rooted in the legacy of the eighteenth century.[8] Such estimations of eighteenth-century thought presuppose that its main value was in laying the foundations of later, socially significant reforms. Revisionist accounts also often utilize notions of neo-Sufism, socio-moral reconstruction, and the use of hadith, the traditions of the Prophet Muhammad, as a blueprint for organizing society. Although many of the writings of eighteenth-century thinkers have been published, revisionist historiography continues to focus on practical and social aspects of eighteenth-century activity in a move that confirms the earlier notion of the poor quality of eighteenth-century thought.

For Orientalists and revisionists alike, Wahhabism provided an accurate illustration of the model of social activism and intellectual impoverishment and was treated as the paradigmatic Islamic movement of the eighteenth century. With its exclusive focus on the single issue of *takfīr*, Wahhabism lacks intellectual complexity and thus does not lend itself to extensive intellectual analysis. Attempts to make political and intellectual sense of the Wahhabi use of the concept of *tawḥīd* (the unity or oneness of God) have not invalidated the fact that the thought of Ibn ʿAbd al-Wahhāb himself was far narrower than the movement he initiated. Yet Wahhabism, both in its social manifestation and intellectual content, was the exception rather than the norm of eighteenth-century Islamic thought. Eighteenth-century thinkers probed the boundaries of faith in varying ways and provided critical evaluations of Sufi thought and practice. But, despite the diversity of their views, all of these thinkers concurred in their rejection of Wahhabi views, as well as the political movement these views inspired. One of the most pervasive discourses of the eighteenth century was a discourse against *takfīr*. In fact, discussions of this subject, as will be shown, predate and, in a sense, anticipate and preempt Wahhabi dogma. In contrast to the crude doctrinal concerns of Ibn ʿAbd al-Wahhāb, the primary focus of most eighteenth-century thinkers was on social and political issues.

Early studies of Islamic thought in the eighteenth century argue that there was Wahhabi influence on contemporaneous Islamic thought and movements in the later periods.[9] In these studies, Wahhabism is seen as a puritanical political movement that served at once as a precursor to later reform and as a reactionary obstruction to it. Similarly, almost all of the revisionist histories of eighteenth-century Islamic thought continue to invoke the example of Wahhabism without questioning the validity of using it as a model for other eighteenth-century Islamic movements and intellectual trends. Most such studies fail to account for intellectual and ideological content and focus instead on the political and organizational history of their development. Following a cursory account of Ibn ʿAbd al-Wahhāb's thought, these studies frequently conclude that he was an indigenous predecessor of modern reform. And yet, a majority of Muslim thinkers who were contemporaries of Ibn ʿAbd al-Wahhāb either opposed Wahhabism indirectly by articulating ideas that rebutted basic Wahhabi doctrine or condemned Wahhabism directly. Aside from polemics directed against Wahhabis and their views on Sufism, the main ideological divide between Ibn ʿAbd al-Wahhāb and the leading intellectuals of the eighteenth century pertains to the delineation of the boundaries of faith. The exclusive concern of Wahhabi thought (and practice) is the determination of who is a true Muslim and, consequently, of unbelief and unbelievers. The Wahhabi attempts to clearly demarcate the divide between Islam and unbelief, and the actual large-scale exercise of *takfīr* was perceived by the main intellectuals of the eighteenth century as a fundamental problem of Muslim societies, a problem they attempted to address and solve in a variety of ways. In marked contrast to the simple and direct Wahhabi use of the concept *kufr* (unbelief or disbelief), and despite the diversity of proposed solutions to this problem, eighteenth-century thinkers concurred in problematizing the concept of *takfīr* and ultimately curtailed or undermined it altogether.

The discrepancy between the historical Wahhabis and the Wahhabism of modern scholarship is a consequence of modern scholars' privileging and elevating the thought of the "modernizing reformers," such as Jamāl al-Dīn al-Afghānī and Muḥammad ʿAbdu, not just in overrating their importance and historical role at the expense of other writers but also in interpreting and recording the past through their eyes. Modern Muslim reformers are equally responsible for this reading of Wahhabism. Rashīd Riḍā (Egypt, 1865–1935), Muḥammad ʿAbdu's (Egypt, 1848–1905) main student and the powerhouse of the *Al-Manār* circle and its influential publications, tried to make a case for the compatibility of Islam with the institutions of the modern nation-state, as well as with values and norms underlying these new institutions. To do this, he invoked and reinterpreted traditional Islamic sources, but he also tried to authenticate his interpretations by positing a continuous tradition of Islamic political reform and by attempting to revive this reconstructed tradition. Riḍā published the works of several eighteenth-century Muslim thinkers, who, he argued, promoted the ideals of liberty, justice, equality, and the like. Ibn ʿAbd al-Wahhāb was one of the authors invoked by Riḍā, and his simple idea of *tawḥīd* (professing the unity of God) was reconstituted and understood to mean a rejection of despotism and human tyranny. Similarly, Riḍā published a number of the works of eighteenth-century thinkers, whose emphasis on *ijtihād* (independent legal reasoning) and rejection of *taqlīd* (imitation in legal matters) was used to corroborate Riḍā's (and before him ʿAbduh's) calls for *ijtihād*. It is worth noting that Ibn ʿAbd al-Wahhāb's only reference to *ijtihād* is to deny that he himself was a *mujtahid* or that *ijtihād* is a prerequisite for his doctrine; nowhere in his meager and simple writings does he discuss *ijtihād* or call for its reintroduction.[10]

Ibn ʿAbd al-Wahhāb's writings are almost entirely devoted to a discussion of the concept of *tawḥīd* (professing the oneness of God). Before trying to characterize his thought, however, it might be useful to outline some of his views and to compare them to those of other thinkers of the same period. Most eighteenth-century thinkers would have disagreed with Ibn ʿAbd al-Wahhāb on almost all of the issues he addressed. To start with, Ibn ʿAbd al-Wahhāb had no interest in intellectual accommodation or reconciliation. He strove to classify people on the basis of their creed into believers and unbelievers, and his subsequent actions were all predicated on this classification.[11] Political and social concerns were marginal to his agenda. He made a distinction between politics and creed, and although he recognized that in promoting his cause he needed the support of local rulers,[12] he neither couched his teachings in political language nor considered the seizure of power an aim of his movement. The only tolerance he exhibits is in his attitude toward rulers who, he says, should be advised gently, and in the event they fail to heed this advice, their injustice should be tolerated patiently. Rulers should be obeyed despite the harm and injustice they cause.[13] Zealotry, in contrast, upon which Wahhabism has many obvious claims, is defined only in terms of the intolerant attitude of Muslims toward political authority.[14] Ibn ʿAbd al-Wahhāb even distinguishes between what may be termed as injustice because of social and economic inequities (*ẓulm al-amwāl*) and creedal injustice (*ẓulm al-shirk*, the injustice of association of others with God).[15] Needless to say, Wahhabi thought is focused on the second kind, whereas the first is tolerable as long as it is accompanied by *tawḥīd*.

Immediate concern for the social is largely absent from the writings of Ibn ʿAbd al-Wahhāb. Not only are tyranny[16] and social injustice minor problems in his view, but also numbers are irrelevant and of no merit.[17] In his view, the community may very well be represented by one man,[18] and the Qurʾānic injunction to abide by the community (*jamāʿa*) may refer to an earlier generation of Muslims, rather than to Muslims' contemporary consensus.[19] As such, unity is of no importance, and neither are the venues that guarantee the empowerment and participation of the community in deciding its future. Withholding knowledge from the masses is permissible.[20] Similarly, *ijtihād* is not an issue that Ibn ʿAbd al-Wahhāb seriously addresses. In a couple of instances he denies that he himself is a *mujtahid*, and he asserts that in every case where he diverges from a scholar, he relies on the authority of an earlier one.[21] He also rejects the notion that a *mujtahid* is needed to bypass the authoritative works of the later jurists, in order to go back directly to the tradition of the first generation of Muslims.[22] The Qurʾān, he argues, has ambiguous and unambiguous verses; the latter require neither the explanation of earlier jurists, nor the interpretations of contemporary *mujtahids*.[23] He thus reduces the operativeness of the Qurʾān to its unambiguous verses, and he dismisses the need for the intermediary traditions but does not replace them with the empowering tool of *ijtihād*. The closest Ibn ʿAbd al-Wahhāb comes to rejecting *taqlīd* is when he blames it, together with the excessive veneration of scholars and saints, for much of the unbelief of his contemporaries.[24] His opposition to *taqlīd* is used only to undermine traditional authority and is not contrasted with its logical opposite, *ijtihād*. Elsewhere Ibn ʿAbd al-Wahhāb does not hide his scorn for scholarship that disagrees with his positions and adds that the enemies of God may have a lot of knowledge and many books.[25]

Ibn ʿAbd al-Wahhāb shared none of the concerns of other eighteenth-century thinkers. His enemies were Muslims who held wrong beliefs about God, not tyrants who oppress Muslims. He separates the creedal and the political, but unlike with other eighteenth-century thinkers, this separation ultimately benefits the political and fails to produce alternatives to it. His ideology was generally intolerant of many practices and beliefs of individual Muslims. In his extensive discussion of what constitutes unbelief (*kufr*) and the belief in more than one God (*shirk*), he lists numerous convictions and acts. *Shirk* includes supplicating pious people, living or dead,[26] seeking their intercession,[27] making vows to them,[28] offering sacrifices and praying at their tombs,[29] and attributing to the dead the power to harm or benefit.[30] *Shirk* also includes the belief in, practice, teaching, and learning of magic, astrology, and divination;[31] the use of amulets and talismans;[32] the provision of shelter to innovators and the befriending of unbelievers;[33] the treatment of rabbis and monks as lords by offering them unquestioning obedience;[34] and the worship of God through intermediaries.[35] A person who knows both the Ashʿarī school and the school of the first generation and gives preference to the former over the latter is also considered an unbeliever by Ibn ʿAbd al-Wahhāb.[36] In addition, someone who says, for example, "Take note my brother, may you never know evil," will also qualify as a *kāfir* (unbeliever), since without knowledge of evil one cannot know *tawḥīd*.[37]

It is through this emphasis on *shirk* and *kufr* that Ibn ʿAbd al-Wahhāb introduces his theory of *tawḥīd*. *Tawḥīd*, he argues, is the exclusive dedication of worship to God; it is worshipping God without *shirk*.[38] The mere profession of faith is not sufficient for Islam[39] because there is a difference between knowing the truth about God (*ʿilm*), actively affirming this truth (*taṣdīq*), and believing in it (*īmān*).[40] The first two kinds of recognition are possible for unbelievers, whereas *īmān* involves full reliance on and fear of God; it also involves loving, hating, and making friends or enemies in the way of God.[41] Ibn ʿAbd al-Wahhāb's cautious attempt to develop a positive definition of *tawḥīd* in terms of *īmān* suffers a great setback when he argues that even someone with great love for God may be an unbeliever.[42]

There are, according to Ibn ʿAbd al-Wahhāb, two kinds of *tawḥīd*. The first is the *tawḥīd rubūbī* (professing the Lordly unity), the belief that God is the creator and administrator of the universe.[43] This belief is held by most people and was even held by the Arabs before the advent of Islam.[44] The unbelievers in the pre-Islamic *jāhilīya* knew God, glorified Him, and believed that He was the only creator and that He alone could grant sustenance and bring life and death. They were followers of Ibrāhīm and performed the pilgrimage to Mecca, but they were still guilty of *shirk* because they associated partners with God in worship and supplicated and sought the intercession of prophets, angels, and pious people.[45] They did not oppose the message of Muhammad until he initiated hostilities against them and cursed their religion and scholars.[46] The second kind of *tawḥīd* demanded of humanity, and required for true Islam, is the *tawḥīd ulūhī*[47] (professing the Godly unity). It entails bearing witness that there is one God and that Muhammad is His messenger, ridding oneself of *shirk*, abandoning the worship of anything but God, devoting all worship exclusively to God, and disowning the nonbelievers and taking them for enemies.[48] Recognizing *shirk* is a prerequisite for this second kind of belief,[49] and so is *barā'a*,[50] dissociating oneself from unbelievers and disbelief in words and deeds. The concept of *tawḥīd* is thus linked in the thought of Ibn ʿAbd al-Wahhāb to an act of repudiation, which functions as a rite of initiation into Wahhabism. The noninitiated remain guilty of *shirk*.

Armed with this concept of *tawḥīd*, Ibn ʿAbd al-Wahhāb was able to change his discourse *on* practice to a discourse *in* practice. He argued that the first battle in Islam after the death of Muhammad was fought by Abū Bakr against people who claimed to be Muslims.[51] They believed in God and in the prophethood of Muhammad, but they refused to pay taxes. This act of disobedience was reason enough to fight them.[52] The *shirk* of the time of Ibn ʿAbd al-Wahhāb, in contrast, is graver than the *shirk* of the first *jāhilīya*: the people who are supplicated are neither pious people nor inanimate objects that are by their very nature obedient to God, and the *shirk* of the later generations persists in times of plenitude and hardship alike.[53] In this framework, the Wahhabi war against the hidden unbelievers of Islam is not only justifiable but is itself a condition for proper belief.

Far from the tolerant and sophisticated thought of the vast majority of eighteenth-century thinkers, Ibn ʿAbd al-Wahhāb provides a grim and narrow theory of unbelief, which fails to link the creedal to the political or the social, or to generate a meaningful discourse that could justify its perpetuation as a legitimate theoretical reading of Islam. Many, if not all, the issues discussed by Ibn ʿAbd al-Wahhāb were also taken up by other eighteenth-century thinkers in more complex and nuanced discussions. A diverse range of views were articulated in the course of either responding to Ibn ʿAbd al-Wahhāb directly or discussing issues similar to those he addressed. Invariably, however, these views contradicted Wahhabi ideas both in their details and overall spirit. In the next section I will survey selected samples of these views. Since the main purpose of this book is to identify the major trends in eighteenth-century Islamic thought, however, I will not attempt to provide a comprehensive survey of how these views differed from Wahhabi thought, or discuss all the eighteenth-century responses to Wahhabism. Such differences will be highlighted only inasmuch as they pertain to the identification of salient features of eighteenth-century thought.

Wahhabism: The First Impulse of Revival?

In "Islamic Movements: One or Many?," William Roff compares four eighteenth-century Wahhabi or Wahhabi-like movements: the Wahhabi Movement; the Padri movement of Minangkabau, Central Sumatra (1784–1847);[54] the Farā'iḍī Movement in East Bengal led by Hajji Shariat Allah and later by his son Dudhu Miyan, started in 1821;[55] and the Fulani jihad led by Ibn

Fūdī and his brother and son.[56] Roff argues that although one may question the accuracy of calling these movements Wahhabi, still there is a "repertory of principles of individual and collective action" that underlies "the intelligibility of Islamic imperatives for Muslims" and "the comparability of the social dynamics that result."[57] To Roff, the fundamental question is, "In what ways can it make sense to see 'Islam' as constituting social relations in Muslim societies?"[58] Although the question is valid, Roff attempts to answer it by comparing four movements often referred to as Wahhabi; the first problem that arises here is that, by definition, Wahhabism is a special case within Islam, and although we can refer to diverse movements as Islamic, it is not clear that we can refer to them as Wahhabi.

In his detailed analysis, Roff argues that even though there seems to be a "presumption among scholars that something called 'Wahhābism' played a significant part in violent social upheavals occurring in many scattered regions of the 'Muslim world' in the late eighteenth and early nineteenth centuries, it is actually not at all clear what, if anything, they truly had in common, in their impulse and content."[59] Roff then attempts to show where the "true" parallels among the movements lie. Invariably, he approvingly refers to study and teaching links,[60] and to similar emphasis on hadith and "purified" Sufism; he argues that these have explanatory usefulness but that more needs to be done to understand the context out of which the various movements grew in order to see real parallels in the dialectic between ideals and realities.[61] This, however, is not the primary concern. Roff maintains that a more important question to resolve is that of an intellectual or ideational affinity between the four or other movements of this period. But although Roff insists that one needs to seriously account for what eighteenth-century thinkers actually say, he does not address the extensive differences in the articulations of the actors in these movements. Instead of engaging with the textual materials, Roff takes the Wahhabi influence for granted.[62] He then maintains that the real task is to find out why the Wahhabi ideas worked and why they had influence. The fact, however, is that they did not.

This last assertion can be easily proved. To start with, the writings of Ibn ʿAbd al-Wahhāb are very limited.[63] For example, Roff provides short overviews of the backgrounds and ideas of the movements. The Padri movement, according to Roff, propagated Wahhabi doctrines, "urging adherence in all respects to a shariʿa derived solely from the Qurʾān, requiring the substitution of plain white clothing (and the veiling of women) for native dress, strict performance of the salat and other *ʿibadat*, and the prohibition against cock-fighting, tobacco and opium smoking, and *tuak* (rice wine) drinking."[64] None of these imperatives, however, are characteristic of the Wahhabi doctrine. The thought of Ibn ʿAbd al-Wahhāb addresses issues of *tawḥīd*, *shirk*, and *kufr*, not practical issues of this sort, and there is no similarity in either discourse or socioeconomic context between the two aspects of Roff's dialectic. Roff then asserts that although it is not always helpful to see the Padri movement as Wahhabi, "there can be little doubt that despite the great contextual differences it was *remarkably similar to that of the muwahhidun in its impulses and argument, in its capacity to create and convey meaning for its followers through Islamic imperatives,* and can best be understood, in a comparative way, in such terms" (emphasis mine).[65] If there is a "great contextual difference" (which is the case for all the movements considered by Roff) and if there is a great difference in doctrines and ideas, what then remains to be deemed Wahhabi in the movements Roff cites? The "capacity to create and convey meaning" is something that fuels all ideologies, Islamic or otherwise, be these of radical revolutionary movements, states, quietist groups, and so on. Though it pledges not to, Roff's argument slips into treating these considered movements as the social and literary expressions of an undifferentiated mass of Muslims.

The case of the Farāʾiḍī movement is even more striking. To start with, Shariat Allah, the founder of the movement, was a Sufi who was initiated into the "Qadiriya tariqa" during his stay in Mecca;[66] moreover, the Sufi practice and discipline (including the performance of *dhikr*) was central to the organization and effectiveness of the movement.[67] It is striking that one would even consider using the title *Wahhabi* to describe such a movement when Sufism was simply anathema to Wahhabis. Another difference is that the Farāʾiḍī movement passed through two stages and turned into a more militant expression of discontent (though not jihad) under the son of the founder. There is no evidence whatsoever that the movement was conceived as a militant movement, or that it actually became one beyond a few minor and small-scale acts of resistance. More important, the movement was directed not against heretical acts and unbelievers, as in the case of the Wahhabis, but against exploitation by landlords, economic hardship, and so on. Unlike the Wahhābiyya, it was an organization concerned primarily with social issues. A higher Islamic discipline was obviously desirable to consolidate Muslims in the face of imminent dangers, but the latter was the objective, not the former. Wahhabi thought, in contrast, was totally divorced of any such social or political vision, as analysis of this thought clearly illustrates.[68]

Pre-Wahhabi Rejection of *Takfīr*: The Thought of al-Nābulsī

Long before Muḥammad Ibn ʿAbd al-Wahhāb, ongoing lively debates on matters of creed and on Sufi practices were conducted among Muslims. ʿAbd al-Ghanī al-Nābulsī (1050–1143/1641–1731), one of the leading Sufis of his time, addressed the question of belief and the meanings of hidden and manifest association (*shirk khafī* and *shirk jalī*) and defended Sufi practices and knowledge.

In addition to Sufism, al-Nābulsī was well versed in the traditional Islamic sciences; he wrote on most of the traditional disciplines, including hadith, *tafsīr*, law, theology, medicine, and agronomy/agriculture. One of his most useful and widely circulated works is a comprehensive index of the hadiths of the seven canonical books of hadith (including Mālik Ibn Anas's *Muwaṭṭa'* as well as Ibn Māja's *Sunan*).[69] Most of al-Nābulsī's works, however, are on Sufism, and many of them were devoted to the defense of Muḥyī al-Dīn Ibn al-ʿArabī, the doctrine of "unity of being [*waḥdat al-wujūd*]," and various other Sufi doctrines and practices. In many of these works al-Nābulsī takes up the issue of unbelief (*kufr*) and spells out his theoretical views on the subject. Al-Nābulsī's views are relevant here because they reveal the widespread rejection of Wahhabi-like doctrines, long before Ibn ʿAbd al-Wahhāb, and the circulation of ideas that bear great resemblance to those articulated by many earlier and later eighteenth-century thinkers on the issue of *takfīr*.[70] To be sure, other thinkers may have overlapped with al-Nābulsī only on the particular question of belief and unbelief, and there is no necessary direct link or influence between them. However, the preponderance of ideas antithetical to Wahhabi-like doctrines among the leading thinkers of the periods before, during, and after the time of Ibn ʿAbd al-Wahhāb is a telling indicator of the general character of Islamic thought in this period.

Starting with the interpretation of his own writings, al-Nābulsī urges his readers not to distort his view and assign to his words meanings that contradict the outward requirements of Islam.[71] Al-Nābulsī preemptively declares that his intention is to pass on knowledge granted to him by God; this knowledge, according to al-Nābulsī, is always "in harmony with the noble law." If any misunderstanding arises, it is on account of the equivocal nature of language, and not any intention on al-Nābulsī's part to diverge from the formal requirements of the law.

Al-Nābulsī's prescribed rules of engagement do not apply only to those who are reading his works but extend equally to all Muslims, living or dead. While a Muslim should always be cautious when assessing his or her own actions, he or she should be generous in thinking about other Muslims. In fact, a positive judgment of other Muslims derives from a person's trust in God, both by entrusting God with the final judgment rather than taking matters into one's own hands and by believing that "in the same way that God has bestowed beneficence on good doers during their life, He would extend the same benefits to them upon death."[72] In contrast to the Wahhabi stance, therefore, al-Nābulsī advises Muslims to be demanding of themselves but generous toward others. Damnation to hell, al-Nābulsī asserts, is guaranteed for people who unequivocally deny the existence of God or one of the prophets. Dwellers of hell also include "tyrants and their accomplices," "as well as hypocrites who display Islam and belief while in their hearts there exists either unbelief in God, association [*shirk*], or some kind of denial of the necessary beliefs of sharia or contempt of one of its branches." "The sign of a hypocrite," adds al-Nābulsī, "is that God removes mercy from his heart."[73]

While al-Nābulsī does not rule out the possibility of identifying those who will suffer punishment on account of their sins or unbelief, he includes in this category people who either make an unequivocal profession of unbelief or who are oppressors and hypocrites who have no mercy in their hearts. It would seem, therefore, that al-Nābulsī is more willing to condemn Muslims on account of their intolerance than on account of suspected doctrinal or practical flaws. Al-Nābulsī's argument clearly minimizes the ability to condemn people on creedal grounds and shifts the emphasis to social concerns.

Elsewhere al-Nābulsī refines this argument by adding a legal component to it. He asserts that issuing legal rulings (*iftāʾ*) is not permissible in a generalized manner without any kind of particularization, and that a mufti must be a *mujtahid* who knows the proofs and legal indicants of the matter under examination.[74] Al-Nābulsī proposes this general rule in the introduction to an elaborate examination of whether singing and music (or listening to both) is permissible or forbidden. Al-Nābulsī argues that the scriptural basis for the prohibition against singing and music is operative in the particular cases when they are accompanied with forbidden, heedless pleasures (*lahū*, *malāhī*); these include, for example, drinking wine or illegal sexual intercourse.[75] Al-Nābulsī adds that when "virtuous people listen to enchanting instruments, this particularization does not apply to them, nor do the views of the thorough [*kāmil*] jurists refer to them. The basic judgment is that people are virtuous and religious, unless sinfulness and debauchery are known to prevail [among them] with certainty and without any doubt" (29). Al-Nābulsī explains further that "what is meant by [*lahū*] is that which is prohibited, and by forbidden entertainment that which distracts from the performance of obligations and duties, and which is accompanied by debauchery, sinfulness, and forbidden acts like illegal sexual intercourse, and wine-drinking." Otherwise, "entertainment, generally understood, is not forbidden" (35). Moreover, since eavesdropping and spying are forbidden in Islam, al-Nābulsī adds that in the absence of obvious evidence to the contrary, one ought to assume that people are decent and that their entertainment is not accompanied by forbidden acts.

Al-Nābulsī lashes out at "ignorant people [who] give free rein to their tongues in prohibiting [singing and musical instruments] without discernment of the [legal] details [of the matter], and with knowledge of neither proof nor evidence regarding it."[76] According to al-Nābulsī, therefore, a generalized prohibition against singing and music is based on imitation by ignorant people who, despite their incompetence, allow themselves to "violate the religion and honor" of Muslims who disagree with them. Al-Nābulsī maintains that there are two kinds of jurists: first, thorough (*kāmil*) jurists[77] who know the principles as well as the branches (of the law), and who know the particular situations and categories that determine the legal status of various beliefs and acts.[78] Jurists of the second kind are incompetent: "They reproduce questions from the books of applied law, despite the differences between the four schools of law, and without understanding what these [laws] really meant to the scholars who spelled them out. They only reproduce them by imitating each other in their deficient understandings." Competent and thorough jurists, therefore, are careful because they are aware of the complexity of legal questions and the factors that need to be considered before issuing a ruling. Ignorant people, however, are reckless; they apply the rulings of earlier jurists without knowing what constitutes valid evidence in these rulings, or how to apply these general rules to new situations.[79] Al-Nābulsī refers to such people as "lay jurists [*fuqahāʾ al-ʿawām*]"[80] and states that most of them come from villages or are craftsmen (*ahl al-qurā wa-l-ḥiraf*).[81]

The readiness to condemn fellow Muslims, according to al-Nābulsī, is associated with lack of urban sophistication or of professional legal training. Al-Nābulsī provides a general rule that draws the line between the crude slurs of unqualified imitators and the fair rulings of competent jurists. "Know that the [negative] statements of jurists in their books are always directed against corrupt doings and evil intentions, without judging a specific person or a particular group of people. [They make these general statements] so that the believer may avoid and guard himself against evil predicaments. You should thus not understand law as it is understood by the lay jurists of our time; these have turned it [the law] into mere statements that are enacted in places where they do not apply."[82]

Al-Nābulsī goes on to assert that competent jurists and scholars would not think ill of individual members of the community of Muhammad.[83] During periods of prevalent corruption, such scholars may issue general warnings against certain kinds of belief or action. However, "no particular individual can be accused of this corruption except through the [appropriate] legal procedures, which is a very difficult thing to do." There is a very clear divide, then, between assessing an act and judging a particular individual performing this act. This same distinction is invoked by many eighteenth-century thinkers in their final assessment of Wahhabi thought (see below).

Al-Nābulsī's contempt for the "lay jurists" contrasts with his respectful attitude toward the "common" Muslim. In reference to "God's commands [*aḥkām Allāh*]," he argues that it is forbidden to withhold knowledge from Muslims.[84]

Withholding knowledge, he adds, is premised on the assumption that, because of the way they look or dress, certain Muslims are incapable of rationalizing or understanding and are generally undiscerning. Such assumptions, al-Nābulsī maintains, are prohibited "because thinking ill of Muslims is prohibited." In response to objections raised against his uncensored teaching of ordinary Muslims in public and private lessons, al-Nābulsī invokes the example set by the Prophet Muhammad, who, he maintains, "used to address people with things which were perceivable to them as well as with others which were not, such as the accounts of the night trip [to heaven] and the like."[85] Moreover, according to al-Nābulsī, Islam is not based on the rational designation of goodness and badness; as such, scholars are obliged to inform Muslims of the requirements of the law even if these Muslims cannot always rationally discern the inherent value of these requirements. Al-Nābulsī even suggests that adherence to the scriptural injunctions of the Qurʾān and the Sunna are in fact licenses granted that work in favor of ordinary Muslims; the difference between right and wrong is spelled out in the scripture, saving Muslims the difficulty of having to resort to uncertain speculation.[86] Al-Nābulsī also maintains that there is no evidence whatsoever that the lawgiver (Muhammad) has ever concealed any legal knowledge (*ʿilm al-sharīʿa*).[87] Injunctions by later scholars to conceal certain kinds of knowledge refer to the science of the truth of sharia (*ʿilm ḥaqīqat al-sharīʿa*), which is acquired through taste and experience.

Al-Nābulsī's refined mystical thought finds common cause with ordinary Muslims in the face of mediocre jurists. The latter's claim to exclusive scholarly authority is particularly troubling to al-Nābulsī. Equally objectionable are the exclusive claims of theologians. Criticizing people who define God in terms of mental constructs, al-Nābulsī exclaims, "Until when will you worship the progenies of your minds, although you know that He has begotten no one and is begotten by none, and there is no one comparable to Him? Until when will you make Him the outcome of mental proofs and rational demonstrations?"[88]

Al-Nābulsī thus identifies theologians (*mutakallimūn*) as the opponents of Sufi knowledge and goes on the offensive against the basic premise of their discipline. "Salvation," he argues, "is attainable only by adhering to the way of the elite, the people of sincere devotion. . . . This [is the way to achieve] truthfulness in worship [*al-sidq fī al-ʿubūdiyya*] as well as the profession of unity in lordship [*tawḥīd al-rubūbiyya*] which guards against association [*ishrāk*]."[89] The language used here by al-Nābulsī is strikingly similar to that used later by Ibn ʿAbd al-Wahhāb. However, the superficial linguistic similarities between the two thinkers can hardly conceal their complete and unqualified contrariety. As is manifested in al-Nābulsī's response to them, Wahhabi-like ideas existed long before Ibn ʿAbd al-Wahhāb. Al-Nābulsī is clearly aware of attacks on fellow Sufis, and his writings are partly motivated by his desire to respond to these attacks. Such exchanges are not new; what is interesting, however, is al-Nābulsī's appropriation of the same language used by his opponents. Al-Nābulsī employs the categories of hidden and manifest association (*shirk khafī* and *jalī*) to defend Sufism; manifest association, he maintains, is that which includes a belief that compromises the principle of absolute oneness of God (*tawḥīd*), the latter being the most central of all Sufi beliefs.[90] A Muslim, according to al-Nābulsī,

> does not rid himself of the two kinds of association, the hidden and the manifest one, and does not achieve complete belief both inwardly and outwardly . . . unless he tastes the meanings of divine theophany. . . . This way [the Muslim] would discover the One, the Singular, who, from the perspective of His traits and names, is manifest in the image of every being, without becoming incarnate or uniting with any object. . . . Thus, from the perspective of His traits and names, He is similar to anything that occurs to your mind, yet from the perspective of His exalted essence He is different [*kullu mā yakhṭuru fī bālika fa huwa min ḥaythu ṣifātihī wa asmāʾihi kadhālika, wa huwa min ḥaythu dhātihi bi-khilāfi dhālika*].[91]

Al-Nābulsī adds that through their rational reflection the theologians arrive at only part of the truth and fail to grasp its totality. A theologian "errs when he abandons religious [*sharʿī*] knowledge and adheres instead to speculative meanings; when he follows the way of proofs and demonstrations, and disregards admission of certain religious texts and submission to them . . . claiming to be self-sufficient in knowledge and making this [self-sufficiency] obligatory for all legally responsible [Muslims]."[92]

The trait common to "lay jurists" and theologians in al-Nābulsī's portrayals is their creedal exclusivity. The formulations of the former are ill-informed, whereas those of the latter are the result of excessive speculation. Both, however, wrongly impose their formulations on Muslims and readily condemn any divergence from them. The advantage of Sufism is that, while it is in closer conformity with the apparent injunctions of the divine law than theology, it is not used as a weapon to condemn Muslims and violate their sanctity.

Had they been contemporaries, al-Nābulsī's reflections on belief and creedal propriety would have easily qualified as responses to Ibn ʿAbd al-Wahhāb. Even in the case of such contemporaries, many of the ideas seem to be rebuttals of Wahhabi-like beliefs but do not mention Ibn ʿAbd al-Wahhāb by name. In many cases, however, we have direct assessments of Wahhabi ideas and practices and clear reactions to them. Muḥammad Ibn Ismāʿīl al-Amīr al-Ṣanʿānī (1688–1769) is one of the major thinkers of the eighteenth century who struggled with the problems posed by Wahhabi thought.

Al-Ṣanʿānī's Direct Response to Wahhabism

As already mentioned, al-Ṣanʿānī is one of the celebrated *mujtahids* of Yemen. He was born into the Zaydi school but soon acquired the tools of *ijtihād* and declared himself to be an independent scholar. In practice this meant that al-Ṣanʿānī did not follow one particular school but relied instead on his independent reasoning on the basis of his own assessment of legal indicants and their applicability in particular situations. One of the consequences of this independence was al-Ṣanʿānī's willingness to diverge from the established rulings of the various schools of law, no matter what symbolic value some of these rulings may have had. Because he was not bound by any particular school of law, al-Ṣanʿānī did not observe the self-imposed limits that regulated the normalized relationships among these schools. Al-Ṣanʿānī felt free to pick and choose from all schools; at the same time, he did not refrain from criticizing their rulings whenever he disagreed with them. More important, he adamantly opposed the adherence of individual Muslims to particular schools to the exclusion of others.

Several attempts on al-Ṣanʿānī's life were made in Yemen.[93] He was once accused of dropping the names of the Zaydi imams from the sermon (*khuṭba*) at the Friday congregational prayer in the mosque of Sanaa. Several Zaydi scholars and government officials then conspired to kill him, and he was spared only when the imam learned of the plot and imprisoned or banished the plotters. But in order to appease the angry mob, al-Ṣanʿānī was banned from teaching or preaching at the mosque and was imprisoned for two months. On another occasion, the tribes of the Barṭ Mountains of northern Yemen marched toward Sanaa allegedly because al-Ṣanʿānī was trying to undermine the Zaydi school with the complacency of the imam. The latter tried but failed to convince the tribes that he was a devout Zaydi and was able to stop them from attacking the capital only by offering to increase their yearly allowances. In every sense, therefore, al-Ṣanʿānī was a persecuted intellectual and social reformer who repeatedly managed to antagonize political as well as intellectual authorities. This is why upon receiving news of Ibn ʿAbd al-Wahhāb's antiestablishment activities, he felt sympathy toward him and his ideas. Al-Ṣanʿānī's initial impressions were based on both positive and negative accounts of Ibn ʿAbd al-Wahhāb's fight against religious corruption in the form of cults of saints, tomb worshiping, and so on.[94] Al-Ṣanʿānī also detected resistance from the religious and political establishments of Arabia to Ibn ʿAbd al-Wahhāb and assumed that such resistance stemmed from the latter's rejection of *taqlīd* and promotion of *ijtihād*. Since these were the main causes that he himself championed, and for which he suffered persecution, al-Ṣanʿānī also assumed that, as in his own case, the charges leveled against Ibn ʿAbd al-Wahhāb were fabricated by zealous partisans of the schools. The main sentiment expressed by al-Ṣanʿānī during this first stage was one of self-assuring relief at finally finding someone who preached what he himself had preached for years.

Contrary to al-Ṣanʿānī's first impressions, however, Ibn ʿAbd al-Wahhāb's political views were far from radical. As we have already seen, concern for social and political issues was completely absent from the thought of Ibn ʿAbd al-Wahhāb; instead, he launched a crude creedal crusade directed primarily against Muslims. Moreover, he was far more successful in condemning individual Muslims than in providing a clear, positive definition of *tawḥīd*, the central concept or slogan of his movement. In contrast, al-Ṣanʿānī's teachings had strong social and religious overtones. Al-Ṣanʿānī's political involvement ranged from indirect criticism of the religious establishment working in conjunction with the state to direct criticism of the rulers of Yemen. On one occasion, al-Ṣanʿānī wrote to Imam al-Mahdī al-ʿAbbās Ibn al-Ḥusayn to reprimand him for buying *waqf* property which, according to Islamic law, is inalienable. In his *Diwān*, al-Ṣanʿānī ridicules another imam of Sanaa, al-Manṣūr Ḥusayn (1161–1748) for turning the imamate into a plaything in the hands of the tribes. Elsewhere, he calls the Yemeni rulers "a band that strayed from truth and guidance and drifted toward tyranny and corruption."[95] Al-Ṣanʿānī adds that these rulers surpassed the worst kings in their corruption, and that Satan rested assured upon witnessing their actions. The evil-doings of these latter-day rulers, according to al-Ṣanʿānī, included turning public lands into *kharāj* lands in order to extort illegal taxes from Muslims. Al-Ṣanʿānī blames complacent judges for accepting bribes from rulers and for sanctioning their actions or remaining silent rather than speaking out against them. He then resumes his criticism:

> O you, the band from the Qāsimī branch of Banū Ḥāshim
> how long will you continue to brag about tyranny
> You have flagrantly made lawful what God has forbidden
> and the worst kind of sin is that which is done in the open
> You also permitted the collection of the *mukūs*[96] taxes in our lands
> and unjustly imposed them on every merchant[97]

Needless to say, nowhere in all of his writings does Ibn ʿAbd al-Wahhāb express such concern for social justice or the welfare of the people. Neither does he ever attack rulers for their social and economic policies, nor does he even conceive of assuming the role of a moral authority in relation to them. In contrast to the radical political stance of al-Ṣanʿānī, Ibn ʿAbd al-Wahhāb was essentially apolitical.[98]

Yet, as al-Ṣanʿānī was soon to realize, these were not the only differences between the two men. Many of al-Ṣanʿānī's views are preserved, among other places, in his collection of poetry. An accomplished poet with a sizeable *dīwān*, al-Ṣanʿānī often used poems instead of letters to correspond with contemporaries and to discuss with them the pending issues of the day. As evident above, this use of the medium of poetry to reflect on events, as well as the appreciation and love of poetry, was not unique to al-Ṣanʿānī. Equally beautiful and expressive poetry was also written by al-Shawkānī, to name only one other example. No trace of such poetic spirit can be detected in the austere writings of Ibn ʿAbd al-Wahhāb.

Al-Ṣanʿānī composed poems on diverse themes ranging from stylized formal responses to friends and acquaintances, elaboration on his love of hadith and allegiance to the family of Muhammad (*ahl al-bayt*), and moving descriptions of his anguish at the hostility of his friends and kinsmen, his longing for home, and the difficulties of life in exile. Two of al-Ṣanʿānī's long poems are about Ibn ʿAbd al-Wahhāb.[99] In the first poem, al-Ṣanʿānī starts by expressing his inclination to give Ibn ʿAbd al-Wahhāb the benefit of the doubt. He maintains that, based on what he heard, the teachings and practices of the "Najdi" are ones that he himself promotes. Al-Ṣanʿānī then uses the occasion to express his own views on the doctrinal matters in question. He maintains that extreme practices like making offerings and sacrificing animals at shrines are tantamount to idolatry; shrines where such acts are practiced, al-Ṣanʿānī adds, ought to be destroyed. Al-Ṣanʿānī also maintains that the ultimate authority in Islam should be the hadith, and that imitators are wrong to invest such authority in fellow Muslims rather than in God. Al-Ṣanʿānī also attacks Sufis like Ibn al-ʿArabī who argue for the unity of all beings and, therefore, equate themselves to God. Al-Ṣanʿānī then goes back to Ibn ʿAbd al-Wahhāb, whom he urges to have patience if he is misunderstood by people. Estrangement because of religious stance, al-Ṣanʿānī adds, is something that he himself suffers from: "For I too am a stranger although my friends are countless."

This poem says very little about Ibn ʿAbd al-Wahhāb, who was simply the pretext for the poem. The controversy over Ibn ʿAbd al-Wahhāb triggers the discussion, but the substance of this discussion is provided by al-Ṣanʿānī himself, and the bulk of the poem is about al-Ṣanʿānī's own views. Al-Ṣanʿānī also allows for the possibility that just as he himself is maligned by his enemies, so it could be that Ibn ʿAbd al-Wahhāb is vilified by his. This possible affinity accounts for the sympathy expressed by al-Ṣanʿānī toward the Najdi leader. As time passed, however, al-Ṣanʿānī learned more about Wahhabi thought, and his initial sympathy gave way to cynicism. Al-Ṣanʿānī's additional information was filtered through many channels, including non-Wahhabi sources. Insider information was also provided by a Najdi scholar who used to be a student of Ibn ʿAbd al-Wahhāb. This scholar visited Yemen and brought along some of his teacher's writings. The accounts amassed by al-Ṣanʿānī on the Wahhabi movement were more reliable than the initial hearsay, and they were also alarming. For a period of time, al-Ṣanʿānī was uncertain and did not know whether rumors about Wahhabi deeds were fabricated to slander Ibn ʿAbd al-Wahhāb, or whether they were true.[100] When the Wahhabi shaykh arrived in Yemen, al-Ṣanʿānī had firsthand access to Ibn ʿAbd al-Wahhāb's writings where he argues that Muslims who pray and pay their taxes are in fact unbelievers who should be killed and whose wealth should be confiscated. Al-Ṣanʿānī thus realized that Ibn ʿAbd al-Wahhāb was "a man who knew a portion of sharia but did not examine it carefully. Neither did he study under someone who would guide him to the right path, point out to him the useful sciences, and make him understand them. In fact he read some of the writings of Abū al-ʿAbbās Ibn Taymiyya and his student Ibn Qayyim al-Jawziyya and imitated them incompetently, even though they have prohibited imitation."[101]

Al-Ṣanʿānī reports that the poem in which he praised Ibn ʿAbd al-Wahhāb was widely circulated, and that he received considerable criticism for what he said in it from people in Mecca, Basra, and elsewhere. Some of this criticism, al-Ṣanʿānī tells us, was not totally fair. Yet after realizing what the Wahhabis were doing, al-Ṣanʿānī felt that he was morally obliged to dissociate himself from their beliefs and acts, though not from the principles outlined in his earlier poem/letter. He thus composed a second poem that he opens by saying: "I withdraw the poem that I wrote about the Najdi, for I realized that he is different from what I thought him to be."[102] What is disappointing, al-Ṣanʿānī asserts, is the man he praised, not the advice he proffered in his early poem. He then goes on to chastise Ibn ʿAbd al-Wahhāb for committing atrocities that have no excuse or legal justification whatsoever. These include violating the souls and wealth of Muslims that God made inviolable, killing Muslims even by assassination, and—most outrageous of all—accusing the whole Muslim community across different lands of unbelief.

Explain to me, explain to me, why did you shed their blood,
  why did you plunder their wealth deliberately, with full intention,
When both have been made inviolable by their profession that
  there is no God but the glorious all-powerful God?
In shedding blood you have no justification whatsoever.
  Fear God and beware what you hide and what you show
Treat the worshippers of God gently and invite them
  to do what will lead them to the paradise of eternity.
Return to them what you stole from them, for your theft is
  unlawful, do not be conceited by might and good fortune.

Al-Ṣanʿānī then reiterates his belief that innovations are unlawful and insists that he is not changing his view regarding the substance of the argument he made in the first poem to Ibn ʿAbd al-Wahhāb. His problem with Wahhabi dogma and practice is that they sanction the outrageous shedding of blood and judge Muslims of all lands as unbelievers. Because of this, al-Ṣanʿānī declares to Ibn ʿAbd al-Wahhāb: "I hereby dissociate myself from the acts you committed against people; for in these you are neither right nor guided."[103] In the remainder of the poem al-Ṣanʿānī distinguishes between two kinds of unbelief. First, convictional or creedal unbelief (*kufr iʿtiqād*), in which a person professes to be an unbeliever. This kind of unbelief is punishable by death, enslavement, and confiscation of wealth until the unbeliever either becomes Muslim or enters into an agreement with Muslims. The second kind of unbelief is one that results from committing certain grave sins, such as deliberate neglect of prayer or accusing another Muslim of unbelief. Al-Ṣanʿānī then asserts that this kind of unbelief does not automatically cast the person who commits it outside the pale of religion (*khārij ʿan al-dīn*).[104] A difference is thus made between *kufr*, which is a matter of judgment with no automatic legal consequence, and *khurūj ʿan al-Dīn*, which entails all the penalties prescribed by the law.[105]

Walī Allāh's Intellectual Synthesis: An Indirect Response to Wahhabism

Al-Ṣanʿānī's thought was decidedly and diametrically opposed to that of Ibn ʿAbd al-Wahhāb, both in its content and scope. For a period of time, al-Ṣanʿānī may have been uncertain of what to make of the person of Ibn ʿAbd al-Wahhāb, but he never had doubts on creedal matters. His final verdict against Wahhabism provides conclusive evidence of this fact. At first glance, the relationship between other eighteenth-century thinkers and Wahhabism may seem more difficult to untangle. For example, in view of the absence of any direct mention of Ibn ʿAbd al-Wahhāb or Wahhabism in the works of Shāh Walī Allāh al-Dihlawī,[106] scholars have argued that informal links and influences existed between the two figures.[107] Yet the inadequacy of such assertions can be easily verified simply by reading what Walī Allāh writes in any of his many books. To be sure, like most of the other eighteenth-century thinkers, Walī Allāh writes on many subjects unrelated to the issues raised by Ibn ʿAbd al-Wahhāb. I will examine many of Walī Allāh's ideas later in this book. Here, however, I will consider only those views that situate Walī Allāh relative to Wahhabism.

There is, of course, a most obvious difference between Walī Allāh and Ibn ʿAbd al-Wahhāb that should disprove any suggestion of similarity or parallelism between the two: Walī Allāh is a Sufi, and it is hard to conceive of a more hostile attitude toward Sufism than that of Ibn ʿAbd al-Wahhāb. It could be argued that the intensity of this difference is diluted due to a presumed special brand of purified Sufism espoused by Walī Allāh. One of the prevalent errors in studies of the eighteenth century is the contention that this century witnessed the spread of a "neo-Sufism" that struggled to rid itself of innovations that contradict the formal requirements of Islamic law. We will consider this view at length in chapter 3. Suffice it to say here that Walī Allāh was a traditional Sufi and a loyal admirer of Ibn al-ʿArabī; in the eyes of Ibn ʿAbd al-Wahhāb, however, the latter embodied all the evils of Sufism. Ibn ʿAbd al-Wahhāb went as far as to condemn as an unbeliever anyone who failed to denounce Ibn al-ʿArabī.

Unlike Ibn ʿAbd al-Wahhāb, Walī Allāh had serious social concerns. He was primarily interested in unity, not just as a doctrinal issue but also as a social reality. He was thus careful not to antagonize the majority of Muslims or to pose as a radical reformer crusading against mainstream social trends. In several places in his writings he conveys his belief that renewal does not necessarily mean going against the trend. In one of his visionary dreams[108] he sees the Prophet, who informs him that God wants "to bring about some unity to the blessed community through you [*yajmʿ shamlan min shaml al-umma al-marḥūma bika*]; so beware of the common claim that a truthful person is not truthful unless a thousand friends accuse him of heresy; beware also not to oppose people in the branches [of the law] for this contradicts what the Truth wants [for you]."[109] Walī Allāh's purpose, then, is to unify not to antagonize. In fact, in this secure and optimistic attitude, Walī Allāh differs not just from Ibn ʿAbd al-Wahhāb but also from al-Ṣanʿānī. The latter's reflections on the social estrangement (*ghurba*) of the virtuous scholar is completely absent from the writings of Walī Allāh, who, despite all the setbacks for the Muslim community in India, has more faith in the potential for a moral and political recovery of Muslim societies. In addition to trusting fellow Muslims, Walī Allāh also cares for them; in the same visionary dream just mentioned, he is urged to exhibit "sympathy toward the common people, by teaching them, guiding them, striving for their well-being, and seeking what is directly or indirectly beneficial to them."

Whereas Wahhabi doctrine functioned as an Inquisition-like ideology used against ordinary Muslims, Walī Allāh's thought was meant to further the interests of these Muslims. This is clearly manifest in Walī Allāh's definition of belief (*īmān*), where he makes a distinction between a this-worldly *īmān* and an otherworldly one.[110] Worldly belief is the profession of faith on the basis of which worldly action is decided, whereas a person's status in the hereafter is decided on the basis of otherworldly faith. In the hereafter, cardinal hypocrisy may entail eternal residence in hell, yet this-worldly *takfīr* cannot be predicated on a person's intention.[111] *Takfīr* is only possible on the basis of an unambiguous scriptural statement. Actions as extreme as prostration[112] to trees, stones, idols, and stars, although strictly forbidden, are not final evidence of disbelief because no text explicitly defines them as such.[113] The accusation of disbelief is valid only when the person performing such forbidden acts declares them to be acts of worship, or professes his or her belief in, and obedience to, creators other than God.[114] Walī Allāh even uses his own reading of certain historical classifications to support a conciliatory distinction between sin and disbelief. He distinguishes between the first and the second *jāhiliyas*: while in the first people denied that God is the creator, in the second they simply turned away from Him, and failed to obey Him as they should.[115] In contrast to Ibn ʿAbd al-Wahhāb, who asserts that the second *jāhiliya* is far more serious than the first pre-Islamic one, Walī Allāh clearly downplays the graveness of the errors of later generations of Muslims and rules out the possibility of indiscriminately accusing them of unbelief. In one of many references to the problem of *takfīr*, Walī Allāh maintains that

> every human is charged according to his capacity. This is the meaning of what the truthful and veracious one, peace be upon him, said about the salvation of the man who was excessive toward himself, and who ordered his family to burn him and scatter his ashes, fearing that God would resurrect him and have power over him. This man was sure that God was characterized by complete power, but that this power was only over possible things and not over the impossible. He thought that the reconstitution of his ashes, half of which were scattered on the land and half in the sea, would be impossible. This was not deemed to be a fault on his part so that he was held responsible according to the extent of the knowledge that he had, and was not considered to be an unbeliever.[116]

Walī Allāh then adds that

> since the basis of divine legislation is establishing an anticipated source [*maẓinna*] in the place of the principle; tangible things that are anticipated sources of association are considered to be infidelity [*kufr*]. Examples are prostrating to idols, sacrificing to them, making oaths in their names, and the like. The first disclosure of this knowledge to me was a vision I had of a group of people prostrating before a small poisonous fly that kept moving its tail and limbs continuously. Then it was uttered in my heart, "Do you find in them the evil of polytheism, and has vice encompassed them as you find among idol worshippers?" I said, "I do not find it in them, for I find that they have made the fly a direction of worship [*qibla*] and they do not confuse the degree of humbleness with the other [of worship]." It was then revealed to me: "You have been guided to the secret," and on that day my heart was filled with this knowledge and I became possessed of

> insight into the matter, and came to know the true nature of the belief in God's unity and association [*shirk*], and those things which the divine law has set as anticipated sources for these two. I realized the connection of worship to divine management, and God knows better.[117]

In these passages Walī Allāh goes so far as to distinguish between unbelief, on the one hand, and rebellion and association, on the other. According to Walī Allāh, prostration to flies is definitely forbidden, but what the people who prostrated did is not real polytheism. Even *shirk*, he maintains, does not rule out the belief that God is the ultimate source from which emanates the mantle of divinity onto other created objects of worship.[118]

> This [kind of association has various manifestations and forms [*ashbāḥ wa qawālib*]. The divine law only discusses its embodiments and forms that people get into with the intention of association, so that they become anticipated sources of association and customarily inseparable from it. This is similar to the custom of the divine law in substituting the causes that entail good or evil actions in the place of the actions themselves. We want to alert you to things that God, may He be exalted, has made anticipated sources of association in the Muhammadan divine law . . . and thus He forbade them.[119]

Walī Allāh then lists a number of embodiments and formal manifestations of association including prostrating before idols, requesting assistance from other than God, calling some people partners or sons of God, treating rabbis and monks as lords beside God, sacrificing to idols and stars, performing pilgrimage to anyone but God, and so on.[120] What is noteworthy here is the circumspect way Walī Allāh argues for the prohibition of standard association practices but leaves the question of the final verdict on the doer open. These actions are considered casts or formal manifestations (*qawālib*) of association (*shirk*), signs by which it can be anticipated (*maẓān*), rather than expressions of its actuality. Thus, because these suggest the possibility of association, and because the law is concerned with formal considerations, not the reality of things, these acts were prohibited. Once again, although Walī Allāh does not question the prohibition of these acts, the final verdict on the person who commits them remains open.

Ibn Fūdī: Political *Takfīr* and Social Tolerance

A slightly more complex set of problems arises when we attempt to draw parallels between the Wahhabis' ideology and that of other militant movements of the premodern period. It has been argued, for example, that the jihad movements of West and East Africa share many of the concerns and strategies of Wahhabism.[121] In addition to adducing structural parallels, studies of these movements often posit direct or indirect influence through the Ḥaramayn network of scholars. Without providing actual evidence for contact or influence, such as direct mention of Ibn ʿAbd al-Wahhāb or Wahhabism in any of the abundant writings of West African activists, these studies typically assert that "it is impossible that they [leaders of West African jihad] can have remained unaware of the 'innovations' in Arabia in their day."[122] The most cited and best studied of these movements is the one led by ʿUthmān Ibn Fūdī (1754–1817) (and his brother and son) that culminated in the establishment of the Sokoto Caliphate in present-day northern Nigeria. Ibn Fūdī's jihad was often directed against fellow Muslims whose beliefs, he argued, were tainted with innovation and heresy; this combination of militancy and an attempt to "restore" a pristine Islam has led many scholars to assume some sort of affinity between the Fulani jihad and the Wahhabi movement.[123] To examine the validity of this thesis, it is more useful to examine the ideas of Ibn Fūdī rather than those of Ibn ʿAbd al-Wahhāb; this task is significantly enhanced by the wealth of written sources by Ibn Fūdī, which provide a fairly clear outline of his thinking in the various stages of his career.[124]

As a young man ʿUthmān Ibn Fūdī studied the classical works of medieval Muslim writers, whose views informed his notions of an ideal society.[125] His experience, however, brought him into contact with a reality that did not conform to his ideals. The communities of Muslims were plagued by two sets of problems that are interrelated in the thought of Ibn Fūdī: improper practice of Islam and social injustice. Islam, Ibn Fūdī noted, was injected with non-Islamic practices by ordinary Muslims.[126] It was not uncommon for Muslims to glorify stones and trees, offer sacrifices to them, and seek them for the fulfillment of one's needs.[127] Some people claimed to be Muslims while they consulted magicians and soothsayers, claimed knowledge of the hidden, made vows at the tombs of pious people, and mocked Islam and Muslims.[128] They neglected performance of religious obligations and participated in corrupting and forbidden ceremonies.[129] Ibn Fūdī also decried the corruption that crept into families: men married far more than the four wives allowed by the law, and the first and oldest of these wives was allowed full control of the others;[130] inheritance was usurped by the strongest heir among the descendants of the diseased;[131] Muslims cheated in their commercial transactions;[132] and moral laxity and decadence prevailed.[133] In short, Ibn Fūdī concluded, Muslims emulated the customs of unbelievers in their private and public lives.[134]

Clearly, then, Ibn Fūdī attacked what he considered non-Islamic practices. It is important to note that despite his emphasis on the proper practice of Islam and on rejecting non-Islamic practices that lead to *kufr*, Ibn Fūdī's primary concern was social. In contrast to Ibn ʿAbd al-Wahhāb, creed for Ibn Fūdī was not an aim in itself but an integral part of his larger scheme of social reform. Ibn Fūdī's main objective was to create the kind of Muslim defined by this creed. He called upon Muslims to order their lives on the basis of Islam and to resist the influences of the prevailing non-Islamic religious and social practices. At this first stage, Ibn Fūdī envisioned a solution for the problems of Muslims by modeling a society after the Islamic ideal. His concern for the community and his tolerance in dealing with individual Muslims fuels the positive and constructive articulation of notions of belief and *kufr*. He insists that disbelief can be discerned only through deeds, and not through what is in the heart.[135] On numerous occasions he warns of the great danger in accusing Muslims of disbelief on account of sins[136] and implies that it is definitely *kufr* to accuse the whole community of unbelief.[137] The sanctity of a Muslim's blood and dignity is unequivocally protected by the law,[138] and judgment about disbelief can only be made on the basis of a transmitted tradition that is not the subject of speculation or analogy.[139] He further distinguishes between prohibited and reprehensible innovations. Muslims are discouraged but not prohibited from the latter. Reprehensible innovations include, among other things, planting trees and building mosques at gravesites and seeking intercession by praying at a tomb or rubbing oneself against it.[140] In fact, he strongly condemns denying the blessings (*karāmāt*) of pious people and argues that such denials are themselves prohibited innovations.[141] He maintains that it is permissible to seek these blessings by visiting the tombs of saints,[142] and that this permission is confirmed by the actions of the Companions of the Prophet.[143] Ibn Fūdī thus defends actions that are tantamount to dissociation and unbelief in the thought of Ibn ʿAbd al-Wahhāb.

The stark differences between Ibn Fūdī's social agenda and Ibn ʿAbd al-Wahhāb's exclusively doctrinal agenda are further magnified in the second stage of Fulani jihad. Ibn Fūdī's initial move to institute an alternative order based on Islam was at least partly successful; it clearly alarmed the authorities and provoked them to take measures against the growing autonomous communities of Fulani Muslims.[144] Restrictions were imposed on the freedom of Muslims to practice their religious rituals. Rather than succumb to pressure, Ibn Fūdī led his community in a confrontation from which he emerged victorious. The ideological position of Ibn Fūdī was also transformed in conjunction with changes in his political strategies.[145] He considered the gravest problem facing Muslims in this new stage to be the hegemony of un-Islamic rule. It became apparent to him that, to lead an Islamic life, Muslims had to seize power. His ideas were increasingly influenced by the belief that social ills were exacerbated by the rule of unbelievers,[146] who forced Muslims to abide by un-Islamic customs and laws.[147] The targets of Ibn Fūdī's attacks included, as before, what he considered to be unjust laws and customs that sharply contradict Islamic norms. What is distinctive in this formulation is that the rulers are held responsible for the perpetuation of this corruption. The status of a town, Ibn Fūdī added, is the status of its rulers,[148] and it is obligatory for Muslims to leave towns ruled by unbelievers for a land where Islam prevails.[149] A Muslim should also refrain from commercial exchange with these towns,[150] should not support them in any way against other Muslims,[151] and, if possible, should participate in the obligatory jihad against them.[152] A capable Muslim who fails to emigrate from a land of unbelief chooses to belong to that land and must bear the consequences of his or her choice.[153]

The apparent contradiction between Ibn Fūdī's early tolerance and his later sweeping vision of *takfīr* is an issue that he confronted and creatively resolved. *Takfīr* on the basis of the ruler is a political *takfīr*,[154] which is not equated to individual unbelief. Ibn Fūdī wrote extensively on the difference between the laws that apply to a genuine unbeliever in enemy territories and a Muslim residing therein.[155] These laws addressed such questions as whether it is permissible to continue fighting a retreating Muslim as opposed to a retreating unbeliever, and the status of the person, his family and wives, and his wealth once captured by Muslims. It is significant that, legally, Ibn Fūdī's treatment of Muslims guilty of political *kufr* or loyalty to the unbelievers is similar to the treatment of Muslim criminals, and not apostates.[156] In fact, political *takfīr* was needed to justify a jihad that Ibn Fūdī believed was unavoidable, and which ultimately served the interests of the Muslim individual as well as society.

The incorporation of tolerant and inclusive formulations from the first stage of his career into the ideological scheme of a radically different stage clearly reflects the seriousness with which Ibn Fūdī treated ideology, and how his early thoughts, together with the transformed conditions of the later phase of his struggle, were important in shaping his later ideas about society and politics.[157] In contrast to Wahhabi political neutrality and social inflexibility, both Ibn Fūdī's thought and his actual practice exhibit a model of political radicalism and social tolerance.

Ibn Fūdī was a Sufi, yet Sufism was not part of his intellectual discourse. His few references to Sufism were part of larger discussions of proper Islamic practice for individuals and had nothing to do with Sufism's intellectual merits. He did, however, write enough on Sufism to indicate that his position was radically opposed to that of Ibn ʿAbd al-Wahhāb.[158]

Al-Shawkānī's Preemptive Engagement with Wahhabism

Throughout the eighteenth century and long into the nineteenth, Muslim thinkers advocated ideas and programs for social action that differed radically, each in its own way, from the Wahhabi model. In addition to al-Nābulsī, al-Ṣanʿānī, Walī Allāh, and Ibn Fūdī, the thought of Muḥammad Ibn ʿAlī al-Shawkānī represents another example of divergence. Like al-Ṣanʿānī before him, al-Shawkānī had initial sympathy for some puritanical Wahhabi doctrines. He eventually realized, however, the destructive and divisive potential of Wahhabism and wrote a poem criticizing Wahhabis for accusing Muslim sinners, including the builders of shrines, of *kufr*, and proceeded to say that the "Khawārij had maintained such a position, and the likes of the Khawārij are not fit to lead."[159] Elsewhere, in a response al-Shawkānī composed on behalf of a Yemeni governor who was invited to join the Wahhabis, al-Shawkānī refers to Wahhabism as a sedition that makes Satan rejoice, for he never fathomed that an individual would come out from among the ranks of Muslims and accuse them all of *kufr*.[160] Indiscriminately accusing good or bad Muslims of *kufr*, al-Shawkānī maintains, stifles religion and breaks its back, and would abrogate sharia altogether (*yastalzim ṭayy bisāṭ al-sharīʿa al-islāmiyya bi-asrihā*).[161]

Al-Shawkānī was aware of Wahhabism and of the unfavorable responses to it. He was also aware of al-Ṣanʿānī's position both on the Wahhabis and on the legal distinction he makes between unbelief (*kufr*) and breaking away from religion (*khurūj ʿan al-Dīn*). Despite his tentative willingness to entertain some Wahhabi ideas, and even to take a stricter position than al-Ṣanʿānī on the issue of unbelief, al-Shawkānī ultimately is at radical odds with Wahhabism.[162] In al-Shawkānī's view, the judgment that a person is outside the fold of Islam and is an unbeliever can only be based on indisputable evidence and the unequivocal and deliberate adoption of *kufr*. As such, an act (or utterance) of unbelief (*fiʿl kufrī*) would only count as such if its doer intends through it to withdraw from the fold of Islam and to profess *kufr*. For example, prostrating before any thing other than God counts as an act of *kufr* if the prostrating person understands it to mean the divinity of what he or she prostrates to. Prostration does not count as *kufr* if it is only meant as a sign of respect and glorification.[163] Al-Shawkānī's retraction of his earlier condemnation of Sufis, his reference to the collective condemnation (*takfīr*) of Muslims as a disaster, and, above all, his nuanced and elaborate discourse on *kufr*, easily undermines everything that Wahhabism promoted and stood for.[164]

Al-Shawkānī discusses Wahhabis in several of the biographies collected in *Al-Badr al-Ṭāliʿ* recounting the lives of individuals politically involved in events unfolding in the Hejaz under the Saʿūd family. Significantly, there is no separate entry for Ibn ʿAbd al-Wahhāb in this book, which is devoted to celebrating the virtues of Muslims after the seventh century AH. It would seem that, in al-Shawkānī's assessment, Ibn ʿAbd al-Wahhāb did not merit inclusion in this book. One individual involved in the politics of the Hejaz in the Wahhabi period is Ghālib Ibn Musāʿid, the sharif of Mecca and its governor.[165] Al-Shawkānī maintains that Sharif Ghālib and his father before him cared for the interests of people and exerted themselves to do good deeds to secure the roads and ward off threats from the nomads. Therefore, both father and son performed their executive duties and would qualify, according to al-Shawkānī's model, as good rulers.[166] Ghālib's authority was challenged by "Ṣāḥib Najd," ʿAbd al-ʿAzīz Ibn Saʿūd, who at the time was in control of Najd and adjacent areas. Al-Shawkānī maintains that Ghālib marched on Najd on several occasions only to be defeated by small bands from this peripheral region. Al-Shawkānī adds that "if only he [Ghālib] would give up these [attempts] and busy himself with someone else, that would be better for him. One who fights stronger foes brings disaster to himself. We hear that the leader of Najd has great power for which the subject of this biography [Ghālib] is not a match."[167] Al-Shawkānī then observes that those who come under the control of the Wahhabis observe the rituals of Islam; al-Shawkānī further notes that many of the Syrian nomads living between the Hejaz and Ṣaʿda have pledged obedience to Ibn Saʿūd, either willingly or out of fear, and have since started to observe the religious obligations, whereas before the Wahhabi takeover, they hardly knew anything about Islam, and barely knew how to profess the *shahāda*. These nomads, therefore, who were previously ignorant of the basic principles and requirements of religion, have started to perform their prayers and other obligations in a perfect manner. Clearly, therefore, the Wahhabis are to be credited for this change.

Any positive assessment of the Wahhabis' role implied in this account is quickly undermined as al-Shawkānī abruptly remarks that "they believe that anyone who is not under the authority of the state of the leader of Najd and who does not obey his commands is outside the pale of Islam [*khārij ʿan al-Islām*]."[168] Al-Shawkānī then adds that the nomad followers of Ibn Saʿūd are dedicated and attack neighboring regions that do not submit to him. Al-Shawkānī remarks, however, that despite their success in spreading their control over new territories, he has received disturbing reports about the behavior of Ibn Saʿūd.[169] Foremost among these is that Ibn Saʿūd considers violable the blood of a person who pleads for help from anyone but God, be that person a prophet, saint, or anyone else. Al-Shawkānī agrees that if such pleading comes from someone who truly believes in and worships the dead person to whom he or she supplicates, or from someone who relies on the dead more than God, then this pleading is tantamount to unbelief. Al-Shawkānī further maintains that if a person does not repent, then his blood and wealth are violable like that of other apostates. Yet this seeming confirmation by al-Shawkānī of the Wahhabi stand on intercession in effect amounts to a rejection of this stand: in contrast to the qualifications stipulated by al-Shawkānī, Ibn ʿAbd al-Wahhāb had devoted most of his meager intellectual career to proving that no qualification whatsoever could vindicate a person who invokes the dead, irrespective of the actual intentions and beliefs of this person.

Al-Shawkānī's criticism of Wahhabi ideas takes more direct forms. Immediately following the above discussion, al-Shawkānī reports that the leader of Najd "considers lawful the shedding of the blood of a person who does not attend the congregational prayer; if this is true, then it is not in agreement with the rules of the divine law."[170] All along, it seems that al-Shawkānī tries to maintain a distance from and to air critical views of extreme Wahhabi ideas while avoiding a direct confrontation with the menacing neighboring power of Ibn Saʿūd. Al-Shawkānī, it seems, was trying to disarm the Wahhabis by depriving them of creedal-ideological claims that could be used against the Imamate of Sanaa. At the same time, al-Shawkānī made sure to hint at the problematic ideological claims of the Wahhabis.[171]

Another factor that seems to have tempered al-Shawkānī's response to the Wahhabis is his respect for the legacy of the late Ḥanbalīs, like Ibn Taymiyya and Ibn al-Qayyim, who were also strict in their attacks on saint cults and extreme Sufi practices. Yet his stand was more out of political expediency. Al-Shawkānī judiciously notes the accusation by some that the Wahhabi has the same beliefs as the Khawārij, only to add that this is probably not true. Al-Shawkānī then says that he has seen letters from ʿAbd al-ʿAzīz Ibn Saʿūd and some of the writings of Ibn ʿAbd al-Wahhāb, and found them acceptable.[172] Al-Shawkānī, however, also reports that the people of Mecca accuse the Wahhabis of unbelief. Rather than defending them, al-Shawkānī remarks that it is hard to figure out the truth.

Later, al-Shawkānī describes the Wahhabi takeover of Mecca as a grave event that shook all the Muslim countries, especially after the expulsion of the *ashrāf* of Mecca from their city.[173] Al-Shawkānī tries to balance ideological and political concerns. One of the pressing problems he addresses is the Wahhabi threat posed by an expanding movement under Ibn Saʿūd. Opposed as he may have been to the Wahhabi views on unbelief, his priority was to make sure the Wahhabis had no pretext to initiate hostilities and expand south into Yemen. Thus, al-Shawkānī reports that in the year 1215 the leader of Najd sent two volumes to the imam of Sanaa, including a volume of the treatises of Ibn ʿAbd al-Wahhāb, which were "good treatises full of indicants from the Book and the Sunna"; the other volume was a solid and demonstrated response to some inferior scholars from Sanaa and Ṣaʿda. Al-Shawkānī maintains that these Yemeni scholars have brought shame and disgrace to the people of Sanaa and Ṣaʿda by dealing with subjects they are not fit to handle.[174] To save face, al-

Shawkānī indicates that those local scholars are insignificant and do not represent the official or the general views of Yemeni scholars; and then provides his own guarded and weighed response to the Wahhabi views.

Al-Shawkānī seems to avoid taking a decisive stand on the Wahhabis. In his assessment, Wahhabism can play a positive role with nomads, whose Islam is usually nominal, and whose understanding and practice of Islam can only improve under Wahhabi influence. The Wahhabis, therefore, can help tame the nomads and check their un-Islamic tendencies. A problem arises, however, when Wahhabism is imposed over urban Muslims, as indicated in al-Shawkānī's account of the Wahhabi takeover of Mecca and the expulsion of the *ashrāf* of Mecca from the city.[175] The main objection against Wahhabis is the blanket accusation of unbelief that they level against anyone who does not submit to their political authority. Conversely, al-Shawkānī condones some Wahhabi ideas, but his approval is most guarded. His willingness to go along with Wahhabi judgments is conditional, and the conditions he introduces in fact amount to a rejection of the Wahhabi position. In contrast to the all-out war launched by Wahhabis against all manner of Sufi belief and practice, al-Shawkānī is willing only to condemn an unrepentant Sufi who truly believes in the dead as opposed to God. Al-Shawkānī, therefore, objects to the doctrinal claims of the Wahhabis. From a purely pragmatic point of view, however, neither Ghālib nor his Wahhabi rivals had higher claims to political legitimacy, and while the latter are suitable for the nomads, the former seem to be more appropriate, in al-Shawkānī's assessment, to rule over urban Muslims, especially Mecca. Al-Shawkānī, therefore, was well aware of problems in Wahhabi thought, but his views were conditioned by two considerations: that the opponents of the Wahhabis were not necessarily better than them; and that his response to the Wahhabis must be carefully worded to diffuse the political tension arising from ideological and dogmatic differences.

Political pragmatism aside, al-Shawkānī's willingness to engage with Wahhabi thought is more a reflection of his own experience than it is a positive reflection of this thought. Al-Shawkānī's own tribulations in dealing with the tribes of northern Yemen were responsible for his dislike of nomads, and his positive disposition toward disciplining them. The Wahhabis, therefore, represented to al-Shawkānī a possible means of imposing such discipline over the unruly Najdis. The problem of nomadic disorder, as al-Shawkānī saw it, was not peculiar to Najd, or to the Yemen of his time. Rather, this was an ongoing problem that posed continuous threats to the Islamic order. In his biography of al-Ṣanʿānī, for example, al-Shawkānī highlights the former's suffering at the hands of the clans of Muḥammad and Ḥusayn of Mount Barṭ (in northern Yemen). These, according to al-Shawkānī, were the uncontrollable masses of Yemen; they took advantage of any opportunity to unsettle the prevalent social and political order for no reason other than their own material gain. On one occasion, rumors were spread alleging that al-Ṣanʿānī was trying to undermine the Zaydi school. The elders of the Barṭ tribes met and decided to march massive armies on Sanaa against Imam al-Mahdī. Al-Shawkānī asserts that the claims of these tribes concerning al-Ṣanʿānī's alleged anti-Zaydi views were purely a pretext, and that they were motivated only by the prospect of worldly gain and the desire to extort more money from the authorities. Thus, all the scholarly responses they received were to no avail, and the only thing that finally stopped them was the imam's agreement to raise the yearly tribute paid to them.[176]

Al-Shawkānī lashes out against these tribes, whose knowledge of religion is superficial. In fact, al-Shawkānī asserts, they oppose some of the certain obligations of religion by "disallowing the inheritance of women, seeking the disciplining arbitration of oppressors, and violating the blood and wealth [of people]; they have nothing whatsoever to do with religion." Al-Shawkānī describes the yearly tribal descent on Sanaa: each year, they gathered by the thousands in Sanaa to receive their allotments. Their disorderly behavior included harassing anyone who tried to lead them in prayer. Their mobs also targeted mosques where the books of hadith were taught, and they harassed the scholars who taught these books. This harassment was particularly abhorrent because it came from "vulgar nomads [*al-aʿrāb al-jufāt*], most of whom do not pray, fast, or perform any of the religious duties of Islam aside from professing the two *shahādas*,[177] albeit with a twist in the way they pronounce it."[178]

Al-Shawkānī, like many others whose power was based in urban centers, views nomads as posing a continuous threat to the social order of Muslim cities, as fundamentally alien to urban Islam, and as a source of zeal and social strife. In light of this view, therefore, al-Shawkānī's conditional sympathy with the Wahhabis and their ability to control nomadic tribes is understandable. It is equally understandable that al-Shawkānī should turn against the Wahhabis when it became evident that instead of controlling the hegemony of nomadic zeal and social strife, they were imposing it, albeit clothed in religious beliefs, on urban Islam.[179]

Blanket *Takfīr* and Guilt by Association

In his *Irshād al-Ghabī* (Guiding the fool), which was written in defense of the Companions of the Prophet and to argue that cursing them is prohibited, al-Shawkānī maintains that some ignorant Shiʿis among his contemporaries go beyond cursing the Companions and claim that one who does not curse them is a Nāṣibī (hater of *ahl al-bayt*). This, al-Shawkānī adds, "is even more serious than the question of cursing [the Companions], because such an ignorant accuser would have condemned all of the family of the Prophet, as well as the scholars of earlier and later generations to *naṣb*. Moreover, a Nāṣibī is an unbeliever, so such an assertion implies that all Muslims are unbelievers. *There is no bigger tragedy than this one, and no uglier trait for which the eyes of Islam weep and the faces of unbelief beam*."[180] Clearly, then, al-Shawkānī strongly objects to the attribution of guilt by association. This is in sharp contrast to the Wahhabis, who not only require that Muslims refrain from certain practices but also argue that, to qualify as a Muslim, one should identify unbelief and unbelievers, curse them, and dissociate oneself from them; people who fail to do so belong to the ranks of unbelievers. In other words, a person's Islam is contingent on confessing the negative assessment by some Muslims (in this case the Wahhabis) of others. This way of reasoning, al-Shawkānī asserts, is the greatest tragedy that plagues Muslims.

In one of his poems, al-Shawkānī lists some of the Wahhabi views with which he disagrees; foremost among these is the Wahhabi assertion of the unbelief of those who build elevated and visible tombs, although the early pious Muslim authorities (*al-salaf*) do not level the charge of unbelief even on far more serious innovators including the *rawāfiḍ* (extreme Shiʿis). Al-Shawkānī adds that it is correct to level these tombs; however, building tombs constitutes neither unbelief (*kufr*) nor grave sin (*fisq*); otherwise one would have to accuse a person who commits a sin of unbelief.[181] In a similar manner, after discussions of different arguments in favor of and against accusing one who does not pray of unbelief, al-Shawkānī says that there are "several kinds of *kufr* of which some do not exclude the possibility of forgiveness [by God]. . . . This shows that not every person who neglects to pray will necessarily reside in hell forever."[182] Al-Shawkānī then adds that "the reason for stumbling onto the difficulty of interpretation is because of the false supposition that there is congruity between unbelief [*kufr*] and unforgiveness; this, however, is not a general rule . . . thus the fact that it is not general [*kuliyya*] would absolve you from the need to interpret what has been reported in many of the traditions."[183] Therefore, according to al-Shawkānī, it is possible to simultaneously use several seemingly contradictory traditions simply by limiting the field of their applicability (*taʿyīn* or *takhṣīṣ*); this can be done on the basis of linguistic considerations and does not amount to a free interpretation (*taʿwīl*), which al-Shawkānī clearly wishes to limit. Thus, al-Shawkānī is able to maintain that "whomever the Prophet called an unbeliever we also call an unbeliever, and we do not go beyond this, nor do we interpret any of these [words] because nothing forces us to seek such an interpretation [*li ʿadam al-muljiʾ ilā dhālik*]."[184] In other words, one can apply the appellation *unbeliever* without the legal consequences stipulated by the Wahhabis. In fact, al-Shawkānī quite clearly maintains that it is possible to judge that a person who used to be a

Muslim is no longer a Muslim without applying the death penalty for apostasy (*ridda*) to him.[185]

The theoretical possibility of coexistence of belief and unbelief is even taken up in some of al-Shawkānī's direct responses to Wahhabi pedagogy. On one such occasion al-Shawkānī responded to a scholar from Najd who came to Sanaa and presented him with a set of questions. The first question deals with the relationship between belief (*imān*) and association (*shirk*) as expressed in the Qur'ān (Yūsuf 12:106). The verse reads, "And most of them do not believe [*yu'min*] in God without associating others [*mushrikūn*] [with Him]." It is commonly used by Wahhabis to justify their stringent definition of belief. Al-Shawkānī surveys the interpretations given in the recognized *tafsīr*s (Qur'ānic exegetical works) of this particular verse and adds his own, a total of thirteen interpretations of the juxtaposition in the verse of belief (*imān*) and association (*shirk*).[186] Al-Shawkānī maintains that the differences in the interpretations result from differing interpretations of the occasion of revelation of this verse. "As to the syntax of the Qur'ānic expression, it is valid to construe it to mean that for which the appellation *imān* applies even in the presence of that which is called association. What finally counts is that which is implied by the utterance and not by the determination of the occasion [of revelation]." Al-Shawkānī then concludes that "it is correct that true belief coexists with hidden association in some believers, while belief in the general sense of the word coexists with true association among the people of the Jāhiliyya."[187]

This theoretical analysis by al-Shawkānī is diametrically opposed to the Wahhabi negative definition of faith as the absence of any practical trace of association or unbelief. Thus, despite his pragmatic engagement with Wahhabis, al-Shawkānī unambiguously opposes the central premise of Wahhabi ideology. This opposition applies equally to the evaluation of the living as well as the dead. In contrast to the Wahhabi dissociation from alleged unbelieving Muslims, even after they die, al-Shawkānī maintains,

> One who scrutinizes his own religion and busies himself with his own faults has enough to keep him from slandering dead people and cursing those whose status before the Creator of all creation he does not know. There is no doubt that smearing the honor of one who has done what he has done, and who lies in the hands of the One who knows best the secrets of consciousness—especially when this [criticism] is not justified by [the need of] *jarḥ* [negative assessment of the traits of individual transmitters of hadith] or the like—is a foolish act which would not be committed by a discriminating person, nor is something that would be committed by one who [truly] believes in a religion. . . . may God save us from the slips of the tongue and pen.[188]

As if to contrast the Wahhabi use of the concept of *tawḥīd* (professing the unity of God), al-Shawkānī further ascertains that a person who freely utters the word of *tawḥīd* right before he dies is definitely destined for paradise. This, al-Shawkānī adds, is the result of the "benevolence of God which he assigns to whomever He desires. If anyone denies this, we say to him this has been established to be true on the authority of the Prophet of God . . . despite your nose." Al-Shawkānī then adds that "some people went out of their way to no avail in order to reject this sound Tradition, and the other sound Traditions with similar meanings. . . . Some have tried hard to make it conditional on the absence of an impediment, yet none of these [attempts] have even a trace of knowledge in them."[189]

Mindful of arguments used to dismiss his views, al-Shawkānī rejects the assertion that the promise of paradise applied only at the beginning of Islam, and that once the law was delineated, the early promise of paradise simply on account of belief was abrogated. This claim of abrogation, al-Shawkānī adds, is mere conjecture and has no valid textual proof to corroborate it. Moreover, the promise of paradise is not contradicted by the reports that specify the penalties for discarding any of the obligations prescribed by God, since it is possible to reconcile both sets of texts without the need to dismiss either of them. Al-Shawkānī adds that those who want to discourage Muslims from relying on divine grace without conforming to the law can do so "without driving God's worshippers to despair, and without recklessly claiming the abrogation of God's laws that he legislated through His Prophet."[190] Al-Shawkānī equally rejects as mere speculation the assertions that performing religious obligations is a requisite of the confession of faith, or that uttering this profession is a cause for entering paradise on the condition that one perform religious obligations and avoid prohibitions. All of these speculations, al-Shawkānī adds, amount to being ungrateful for God's bounty. Al-Shawkānī buttresses his theoretical position in actual legal practice. It is perfectly lawful, he argues, to perform the death prayers on a Muslim sinner, even one on whom the death penalty has been imposed. Al-Shawkānī concedes the existence of different views regarding the performance of such prayers on Muslim heretics or those who commit suicide. He adds, however, that even the fact that the Prophet did not pray for such people does not in itself constitute evidence that such prayer is prohibited.[191]

To be sure, al-Shawkānī was strict in delineating what constitutes unbelief, but he was equally adamant in restricting the practical legal implications of this delineation. Put differently, al-Shawkānī exhausted all possible ways of limiting the possibility of taking legal action against a Muslim who may be accused of unbelief or other major religious offenses. The imam, al-Shawkānī argues, is not required to impose the *ḥadd*[192] penalty on a person merely on the basis of reports that he did what is punishable by this penalty. Furthermore, as a general rule, the sanctity of the privacy of a Muslim should deter the imam from the further investigation of alleged violations of the divine law. Moreover, according to al-Shawkānī, textual evidence whose import is to avert the imposition of penalties is stronger than evidence in support of their imposition (*awlawiyyat mā yadraʿ al-ḥadd ʿalā mā yūjibuhu*). Al-Shawkānī also notes that the execution of a *ḥadd* penalty requires both the confession of the doer of the act that is punishable by this penalty, and the legal testimony against him. Therefore, the divine law, as al-Shawkānī reads it, militates against the penalization and condemnation of individual Muslims.[193]

Al-Shawkānī's distinction between the theoretical definitions of sins and the enforcement or implementation of these definitions in real situations is even more applicable in the case of unbelief. After a long discussion of the various views on the status of the Khawārij[194] and renegades, and the conditions under which they are to be fought, al-Shawkānī argues in favor of "the legality of desisting from the application of the death penalty against one who believes in rebellion against the imam unless he actually starts a war because of this belief, or prepares for it."[195] To be sure, al-Shawkānī was aware of the complex views on the subject. He thus maintains that reports regarding the Khawārij, who accused people of unbelief when they were known for certainty to be Muslims, led to the conclusion that the Khawārij were not Muslims. Should this be the case, al-Shawkānī adds, then "their general belief in Islam and their performance of the obligations does not acquit them from the charge of unbelief, just as they do not acquit one who prostrates to an idol." In the same breath, however, al-Shawkānī approvingly states that most legal scholars are of the "opinion that the Khawārij are sinners, and that the laws of Muslims apply to them. . . . They only sinned by accusing Muslims of unbelief on the basis of an erroneous interpretation. . . . Thus intermarrying with them and eating the animals they slaughter are permissible." Al-Shawkānī then quotes Abū Ḥāmid al-Ghazālī to provide the basic principle that guides judgments in these matters, namely, that "what ought to be done is to avoid the charge of unbelief [*takfīr*] by all possible means."[196]

In this same context, al-Shawkānī sides with the standard legal view that Muslim rebels should not be pursued if they are retreating, and that the permission to kill them is an exception contingent on their actual initiation of battle. Whenever they stop fighting, the initial rule is restored, namely, that their blood is sanctified and they are inviolable.[197] In the same spirit also, al-Shawkānī maintains that, after the cessation of hostilities, a rebel cannot be penalized for killing another Muslim during a civil strife, whether he is the oppressor or the oppressed.[198]

Al-Shawkānī himself was capable of engaging in fierce polemics, yet he was acutely aware of the difference between polemics and responsible legal judgments. For example, in reference to the disagreement over whether the *basmala* (the utterance, "In the name of God, the Merciful, the Compassionate") is an integral part of the Qur'ān or simply a recommended addition inserted at the beginning of each of its chapters, al-Shawkānī maintains that one should not be intimidated by the exaggerations of some who treat minor matters as if they were doctrinal issues.[199] Elsewhere, al-Shawkānī lists a number of conditions without which a person is not a Muslim. In conclusion, however, he quotes the hadith that says, "I have been commanded to fight people until they say there is no God but God."[200] Thus, in effect, according to al-Shawkānī, it is possible to pass a theoretical judgment that a certain person is not a Muslim while at the same time desisting from executing the legal implications of this judgment. In fact, according to al-Shawkānī, this is the universal rule that governs the treatment of Muslims unless a particular individual expressly denounces Islam and publicly pronounces his or her unbelief.

One of the most distinguished Muslim scholars to derive inspiration from al-Shawkānī was Muḥammad Bin ʿAlī al-Sanūsī. Al-Sanūsī was a disciple of Aḥmad Ibn Idrīs, the renowned Sufi master who established his order in the Hejaz.[201] Al-Sanūsī's thought and career path were significantly different from those of his master. Like his master, al-Sanūsī avoided political confrontations and did not seek to impose his ideals by force. Yet unlike his master, al-Sanūsī established a network of self-governing communities with characteristic social and political identities. His alternative communities ideally would integrate individuals with a strong sense of responsibility coupled with *madhhab* tolerance; the regimented life that he offered was apparently readily accepted by his followers who established a network of religious and cultural strongholds stretching from North to sub-Saharan Africa.

Early in his life, al-Sanūsī became aware of the hazards of both politics and religious zealotry. In response to the first, he chose withdrawal over confrontation. In response to the second, he adopted, developed, and applied a reading of Islam that is at once authoritative and tolerant. Zealotry, the cause of social strife, was a major ill from which he personally suffered during his formative experience in Mecca. The zealotry of the traditionalists, he argues, is in their claim to a monopoly over truth;[202] that of the Sufis is in their scorn for the law;[203] and that of the masses is in their blind imitation of infallible men.[204] The final manifestation of zealotry concerns the accusation of unbelief. In what sounds like a direct response to Wahhabism, al-Sanūsī quotes none other than Ibn Taymiyya, who warns that the error involved in sparing the life of an unbeliever is far less than the error of spilling the blood of an innocent Muslim.[205] Like al-Shawkānī before him, al-Sanūsī maintains that a ruling of *takfīr* is only applicable to someone who professes *kufr*, unambiguously chooses it as a religion, denies the truthfulness of the two *shahādas*, and apostatizes from the religion of Islam altogether.[206]

Al-Sanūsī was neither an exclusive social reformer nor a simple reviver of the intellectual tradition—he mixed a measure of both in his thought and practice. As opposed to Shāh Walī Allāh, whose intellectual reform had positive but indirect implications for the social order, al-Sanūsī's immediate mission was to model, initiate, and structure an ideal society. Unlike Ibn Fūdī, he managed to avoid conflicts with political authorities by moving into areas of political vacuum, and unlike Ibn ʿAbd al-Wahhāb, the central characteristic of the religion he preached was mercy (*raḥma*).[207] Moreover, in addition to the intrinsic success it enjoyed, the Sanūsiyya movement also illustrates how the ideas of the Yemeni al-Shawkānī were stripped of their regional character as they acquired a life of their own away from their home of origin.

In contrast to Ibn ʿAbd al-Wahhāb, all the major thinkers of the eighteenth century managed to formulate meaningful, often strict, codes of social behavior and religious practice without condemning Muslims and falling into the trap of *takfīr*. Ibn ʿAbd al-Wahhāb was fixated on unveiling the secret sins (*al-shirk al-Khafī*) of multitudes of Muslims and on exposing their hidden unbelief. His was a utopian vision exclusively founded on a doctrinal reading of religion. In contrast, the other eighteenth-century thinkers discussed here were primarily concerned with articulating a social order derived from their understanding of Islam. In contrast to the Wahhabi dogmatic understanding of *tawḥīd*, for these thinkers, the fundamental meaning of unity was encapsulated in the taboo against shedding the blood of fellow Muslims. Despite substantial differences in objectives and projects, the stance against *takfīr* was the main unifying feature of the reformers of the eighteenth century. What they had in common was a deep concern for the Muslim community, which was fundamentally disregarded in the thought of Ibn ʿAbd al-Wahhāb. Most of these thinkers articulated rigorous criticism of practices and beliefs prevalent in Muslim societies, but despite their strictness, the sanctity of Muslim life was a line they were not willing to cross.[208]

Eighteenth-century reformers often viewed religious doctrine through the prism of human interest. This, in a sense, explains the retraction by both al-Ṣanʿānī and al-Shawkānī of their praise poems of Ibn ʿAbd al-Wahhāb. By withdrawing their praise, al-Ṣanʿānī and al-Shawkānī expressed their realization not only that Ibn ʿAbd al-Wahhāb did not provide solutions for the problems of Muslim societies but also that he himself was a symptom of these problems.

Chapter 2

Ijtihād and the Regional Origins of a Universal Vision

Regional Networks

Because the interests of the eighteenth century are not our own, it is easy to misjudge the principle intellectual achievements of this era, or to think that these achievements are related to what we value. Therefore, a main task in the reconstruction of eighteenth-century thought is to identify what its own thinkers perceived to be the problems of their time, how they went about explaining these problems, and the historical and intellectual sources on which alternative visions were founded. Eighteenth-century thinkers were preoccupied with issues of transgression, merit, and identity, and many of them had a shared sense of anxiety, although they proposed different solutions to their perceived problems. These problems included *takfīr* and other forms of social discord, imitation, and intellectual sterility, cultic practices such as tomb worship, and illegal taxation and political oppression. The crisis of choice, however, was what they referred to as *tamadhhub,* which means partisanship to the schools of law and elevating them to the position of sects. *Tamadhhub* and the divisions that result from it were identified as the greatest of all social ills. The critique of school partisanship often started with a historical analysis of the origins of schools and the interest invested in perpetuating them. In contrast, the referential framework for the proposed solutions to these problems included revisiting the disciplines of hadith and legal theory.[1] Indeed, the historical perspectives of eighteenth-century thinkers were largely shaped by their own experiences and conceptions of sectarianism and communal strife among Muslims. *Takfīr,* accusing other Muslims of unbelief, which was so adamantly rejected by most eighteenth-century thinkers, was itself an extreme expression of this sectarian school partisanship. The thought of eighteenth-century thinkers is nowhere clearer than when they reflect on this thorny subject. Such, for example, is al-Shawkānī's warning: "Know that just as partisanship [*tamadhhub*] results in the effacement of the blessings of knowledge, the dissipation of its splendor, and the loss of the reward that derives from it, so too does it cause strife that leads to the shedding of blood, violation of sanctities, vilification of honors, and making violable what is in the protection of the Divine Law."[2]

Underlying the rejection of *takfīr* and of school partisanship is an unmistakable tendency to empower larger sectors of Muslim society and to endow more Muslims with participatory authority. Despite their shared anxieties, the reformers of the eighteenth century proposed to address the problems of their time in diverse ways. Within the context of a shared and universal Islamic intellectual tradition, each of the reform projects of the eighteenth century had its distinct regional character. To be sure, the cultural specificity of various regions of the Muslim world was not a novel development of the eighteenth century. However, acquisition by various intellectual traditions of a specifically regional character reinforced the territoriality and specific political conditions of each geographical region. Moreover, the emerging reform projects as well as ideologies of political reform were shaped by and geared toward the specific traditions of their respective regions of origin. Thus, peculiar and distinct cultural undertakings reinforced the protopolitical identities, starting in the regional states that had developed local traditions of governance as well as set traditions of interacting with their surroundings, and on to local jihad movements that attempted to replace regimes accused of specific kinds of disorder.

The regional character of eighteenth-century thought is often obscured by the exclusive focus on decline in traditional Orientalist historiography. Yet even relatively recent attempts to revisit the eighteenth century seem to concur on the uniformity of its intellectual legacy. This notion of uniformity is reflected in the continuing emphasis on the centrality of the Wahhabi model, as well as the currency of the notion that eighteenth-century intellectual activity was shared in an informal network of scholars converging on the Ḥaramayn (Mecca and Medina). There is, no doubt, a measure of uniformity that characterizes even the most contradictory interpretations of Islam throughout its history; after all, all such interpretations invoke a shared scriptural tradition as well as a limited set of shared, if contested, historical experiences. Yet if the intellectual legacy of the eighteenth century differs from other periods of Islamic history, it does so on account of the diversity, rather than the uniformity, of its emerging regional traditions.

The adjective *Wahhabi* has been applied to such diverse groups as the followers of Sayyid Aḥmad Barelvī of India[3] and the Subbanu al-Muslimin (Association of Young Muslims) of West Africa,[4] despite the recognition that in both of these cases the title *Wahhabi* is a misnomer.[5] Wahhabi thought is considered to belong to a "fundamentalist tradition,"[6] which, despite the diversity in "organizational styles," permeates revivalist movements stretching from the mid-eighteenth to the mid-nineteenth century. Presumably, these movements have produced one rather homogeneous body of thought that belongs to an identifiable "fundamentalist mode of Islam."[7] This mode, which traverses

Islamic history, is defined in terms of such themes as the emphasis on abiding by the Qur'ān and the Sunna, return to origins, revival of *ijtihād* and hadith studies, rejection of innovation and imitation (*taqlīd*) in matters of law, and rejection of the excesses of Sufism.[8] More generally, these themes are said to assert transcendence, unity, and authenticity as opposed to immanence, diversity, and openness.[9] It is thus commonplace to speak of Wahhabi influences on the thought of Shāh Walī Allāh al-Dihlawī of India,[10] ʿUthmān Ibn Fūdī of West Africa,[11] and Muḥammad Bin ʿAlī al-Sanūsī of North Africa.[12] Yet against such assertions, since the thought of Muḥammad Ibn ʿAbd al-Wahhāb deals exclusively with *kufr*, the only meaningful comparison between this thought and other eighteenth-century ideas must pertain to this issue. In chapter 1, we saw the radical differences between Wahhabi and other eighteenth-century ideas on *kufr*. Indeed, both Wahhabi thought and the movement it inspired were the antithesis of everything the Islamic eighteenth century stood for.

The manifold manners in which eighteenth-century thinkers rejected *takfīr* is only one example of the diversity of the intellectual traditions of the eighteenth century. Throughout this book, we will return to the peculiarity of the regional traditions, both in their intellectual contents and their practical applications. To start with, however, a word about the Ḥaramayn network theory is in order.

This theory is founded on the evidence for a common network of teachers with whom most of the renowned champions of the eighteenth century were associated. Overlapping "intellectual family-trees," it is argued, converge on a "small group of teachers of hadith in the holy cities" of Mecca and Medina, thus lending further credibility to the theory of a unified Islamic revivalism.[13] This theory is attractive in many ways, primarily because it allows the student of modern Islam to analyze and understand a complex set of variables in the context of one coherent whole. However, the connections made to achieve this coherence are at best tenuous. Any familiarity with the perception of Wahhabism in the Islamic world would confirm the rather conspicuous status it has among most Muslims, which undermines any parallels between Wahhabis and other movements enjoying general or local recognition outside Arabia. In addition, the general characterizations of modern Islamic revival are not always applicable to specific instances of this revival. What is most inadequate about the theory of a common origin is that the little analysis there is of the substance of the ideologies of Islamic revival has not been comparatively examined. Whether Islamic revival is unified or diverse can only be decided on the basis of analyzing the discursive culture that makes this revival Islamic. It is thus imperative to reconstruct the different intellectual projects of the period in question. Any resolution is contingent upon a comparison of the main features of this body of thought. Even a cursory reading of the work of Shāh Walī Allāh, for example, reveals that, contrary to the accepted paradigm, his reformed "neo-Sufism" is not stripped of its "metaphysical character";[14] this, despite the fact that both Walī Allāh and the ardent anti-Sufi Ibn ʿAbd al-Wahhāb studied under the same Medinese hadith scholar Muḥammad Ḥayā al-Sindī[15] (d. 1750). The "intellectual family-trees" of students and teachers cannot serve as evidence for common origins. Education acquired from the same teacher could be, and indeed was, put to completely different uses by different students, and the commonality of the source does not prove that the outcome is identical or even similar. The only information that can be safely derived from such evidence relates to the pool of prominent teachers of the time with whom a serious student might study. The allegations made in an anti-Wahhabi polemic, in which Muḥammad Ibn Sulaymān al-Kurdī and Muḥammad Ḥayā al-Sindī warned their students against the excesses of Ibn ʿAbd al-Wahhāb, would further corroborate this conclusion.[16]

More important, however, is the fact that the education of the most notable thinkers of the eighteenth century was local. Many of them either did not travel to the Ḥaramayn in pursuit of knowledge or, when they did, it was after the formative years of their careers and after their ideas had matured and become well articulated. Al-Shawkānī, for example, did not travel outside Yemen,[17] and rather than study in the Ḥaramayn, Walī Allāh traveled there as a mature scholar and exchanged information with others.[18] Both thinkers were educated within deeply rooted traditions and, above all, articulated their views in relation to the problems and potentials of these traditions. Furthermore, the teachers of these thinkers were almost exclusively local.[19] Of course, all drew on a shared Islamic intellectual legacy, yet this legacy was vast, and the choices were always informed by local experience even as these thinkers attempted to open up and transform regional traditions.[20] What applied to eighteenth-century thought applied equally to the practical aspects of movements and ideologies. Thus, Ibn Fūdī did not travel outside of a relatively small part of West Africa, and his peculiar mélange of ideas was carefully customized to deal with a specific set of social and political problems. This is not to say that travel and networking did not exist in the eighteenth century as it always had in previous centuries. Rather, what characterized the eighteenth century was that, alongside the age-old pattern of travel for the pursuit of knowledge, there emerged movements and intellectual traditions that were primarily regional in character. The most compelling scholarship of the eighteenth century was produced within these regional traditions.[21] It is thus possible to posit a dichotomy between major traditions, which were mature, self-confident, and decidedly local, and minor traditions, which were promoted by wandering scholars and which, despite their social significance, were intellectually derivative. As we will see in chapters that follow, the groundbreaking intellectual contributions were made within the context of regional traditions. These contributions were made by scholars who, in addition to their direct and deep involvement in the political and social affairs of their own regions, were locally educated;[22] their ideas were definitely hybrid and heavily indebted to diverse elements of the vast Islamic legacy, but they were not the product of a universal pan-Islamic intellectual movement. In other words, the regional character of the reforms introduced by these thinkers were in no way reflections of a narrowness in their intellectual horizons; they were simply an expression of these thinkers' recognition of their societies' real problems and their involvement in attempts to resolve these problems.

While many eighteenth-century thinkers shared the aims of defending and empowering larger sectors of society, their reform ideas, as well as the practical mechanisms employed to effect these ideas, were highly localized. Aware of the radical nature of their interpretations of religious doctrines,[23] these thinkers attempted to spread their innovative ideas by intensely engaging the dominant local traditions of the regions in which they lived and operated. Thus, for example, both al-Ṣanʿānī and al-Shawkānī directed a disproportionate amount of their critical ideas against Zaydism, the dominant tradition of highland Yemen, although the implications of their ideas as far as traditional Sunni thought is concerned were at least as radical. Similarly, the peculiar issues addressed by Walī Allāh are to be explained in terms of intellectual developments specific to Indian Islam.

Some eighteenth-century thinkers also resorted to networking to reinforce their ideas. However, whether their founders traveled or not, all of the established networks were regional. The prime examples of network building are the Sokoto school networks of Ibn Fūdī, the Sanūsī network of settlements stretching from the Mediterranean coast of present-day Libya deep into sub-Saharan Africa, and the network of al-Shawkānī's students who were appointed throughout Yemen to influential positions in courts, schools, and other institutions.

The vital characteristic of the postjihad state of ʿUthmān Ibn Fūdī and its indispensable requisite was the network of schools and administrative centers spread throughout the realm of the Sokoto Caliphate. The jihad led by Ibn Fūdī culminated in the formation of a central state on the ruins of an old social and political order. The interplay of a clear program of social and political change and an effective strategy for the introduction and application of this program resulted in a radical transformation of societal order. The old, fragmented order was meant to be replaced by a model of a centralized Islamic state extracted from the writings of medieval Islamic political theorists.[24] Indeed, the Sokoto state that was established after the successful conclusion of the jihad had all the characteristics of the ideal model; it was a state in which political power was delegated but whose unity was guaranteed by the diffusion of a heterogeneous body of legal and administrative professionals.[25] The key to this uniformity was education, a strategic weapon Ibn Fūdī deployed on several levels.[26] Through his efforts to spread literacy among his followers, Ibn Fūdī sought to forge a common social identity that included and superseded the preceding fragmented identities of the region. He convinced people of the superiority of his literacy program, through which he then implemented and promoted a program of social and political change. As part of this program, he provided training for a group of legal and administrative professionals, who enabled the new state to function in accordance with its ideals.[27] All of the sources of Ibn Fūdī's intellectual inspiration belong to the classical heritage of medieval Islam,[28] which he refers to and quotes extensively and uncritically. Ibn Fūdī did not lack erudition but, unlike other eighteenth-century thinkers, he was not interested in reforming the received intellectual traditions: his emphasis was on reviving or reforming actual Islamic society. He studied classical Islamic political theory not to resolve its contradictions but to derive from it a model for individual and social life. He sought not to reform the content of Islamic education but to employ it in the reformation of the individual and society. It is not surprising, then, that he did not address questions of *taqlīd*, *ijtihād*,[29] or the reconciliation of hadith scholarship and jurisprudence.

Al-Sanūsī's small empire provided yet another example of a unique, regional networking system.[30] Dozens of settlements spread along a trail that started in present-day Libya and extended deep into sub-Saharan Africa.[31] During his lifetime, al-Sanūsī founded some sixty lodges in which the religious and worldly affairs of the community were managed. The religious obligations of the community's members were defined to include, in addition to expected spiritual activities, education, labor, defense, and trade.[32] Typically housing fifty to a hundred members, and often considerably more, the lodges were also integrated into the larger communities in whose midst they were established. Tribes invited the Sanusiyya to establish these orders and donated the lands for the lodges as well as surrounding agricultural land for economic sustenance; they also sent their children to study at the lodges. Equally significant is that authority in each lodge was shared between the Sufi shaykh, who was sent by al-Sanūsī to oversee religion and education, and the *wakīl*, who represented the local tribal authority.[33] In one of his letters, al-Sanūsī sums up this interplay of social and economic well-being with religion: "In the place occupied by the lodge, compassion settles, the country flourishes and settled people and the nomads benefit from it, because it is only founded for the Koraan to be read and the sahria to be spread."[34]

While some eighteenth-century Sufis introduced new ideas into the legacy of Sufi thought, al-Sanūsī's reform of Sufism was primarily at the organizational level.[35] The organizational breakthrough that is responsible for the success of the Sanūsiyya order was an innovation in relation not just to African society but also to earlier Sufi organizations. The lodges themselves were also treated more as inviolable sanctuaries (*ḥaram*) than as endowments (*waqf*), which was "not a formally recognized legal concept in sahria" and was a legal innovation of sorts.[36] The Sanūsī settlements were thus integrated into local communities but also formed a coherent whole that shared economic interests, patterns of social and political organization and authority, as well as religious doctrine and practice.[37] The lodges mediated between tribes and, more important, provided organizational principles that superseded tribal loyalties. Moreover, while accommodating local traditions, the Sanūsiyya order introduced the Islamic model of quasi-urban, settled communities into regions still under tribal sway.[38]

This physical network of settlements bore little resemblance to the intellectual network emanating from the Ḥaramayn or to the educational and administrative network of the Sokoto Caliphate. It is noteworthy that although al-Sanūsī traveled and lived many years in the Hejaz with his teacher Aḥmad Ibn Idrīs, he did not study with the Ḥaramayn scholars.[39] Moreover, although the two never met, al-Sanūsī was greatly influenced by al-Shawkānī's thought, especially his views on *ijtihād* and hadith.[40] In all likelihood, al-Sanūsī became familiar with al-Shawkānī's ideas during his stay in the Hejaz; this however, did not happen through direct contact, or via a Ḥaramayn network of scholars. More important, al-Sanūsī translated al-Shawkānī's intellectual influence into a distinctive social experiment that was not imagined by al-Shawkānī. While al-Shawkānī's only interest in Sufism was critical, al-Sanūsī was primarily a Sufi, and a network of settlements organized along the lines of Sufi orders provided the main vehicle for achieving his reform objectives.[41]

The networks created by both Ibn Fūdī and al-Sanūsī contributed to the emergence of new and distinct forms of collective regional identities. Other models of networking and settlement can also be traced in the cases of several Sufi movements that were active throughout North and sub-Saharan Africa. For example, in the case of the Ṣāliḥiyya order in northern Somalia, no network of settlements was established, and although *ṭarīqa* solidarity cut across lineage lines, it was always subordinate to them. However, a novel social order emerged through the acquisition of rights in land and the mixing of religion and lineage as a basis for a new system of authority.[42] The several branches of the Tījāniyya order, which were established toward the end of the eighteenth century, provided yet another set of models of Sufi organization, sometimes with drastically different social and political profiles. The founder of the order invoked the *Ṭarīqa Muḥammadiyya*, which was not taken to mean purifying Sufism but simply used to claim exclusive mystical authority derived directly from the Prophet. In contrast to the attempts by al-Sanūsī to illustrate the convergence of all chains of transmission of Sufi authority (*silsilas*), and thus of all forms of mystical piety, the Tījāniyya severed connections to all other Sufi orders.[43] This exceptionalist claim, in turn, accentuated the differences between various regional branches of the Tījāniyya. The Algerian branch of the order collaborated with the French colonial authorities, whereas Ḥāj ʿUmar al-Tall (d. 1864) led a branch of the order that undertook jihad in the basins of the Senegal and Niger Rivers to spread Islam among pagans and to resist French expansion east of the Senegal.[44] To be sure, none of these movements was totally detached from outside intellectual currents of the Muslim world. However, their reformative import was primarily of a regional character.

Eighteenth-century regional networks were specific, in their outlook and functions, to the regions in which they operated. Their success had much to do with their ability to speak to the needs of local constituencies and to mobilize local resources in a meaningful way within local power configurations. In fact, the different regional networks were fashioned and introduced to resolve diverse sets of perceived problems specific to their respective regions. At these local organizational levels, a larger Ḥaramayn network, assuming such a network existed, would have been largely ineffectual. Yet the regionalization of these networks was not restricted to organizational structure; it also left its imprints on diverse educational strategies and intellectual traditions of the various regions that came under the networks' influence.

Contingencies of meaning were not restricted to the organizational framework within which reform was introduced, or to the special mechanisms through which this reform could be affected; they also determined which elements of tradition were selected and the way these elements were reconstituted. Eighteenth century Islamic pedagogy was regionalized. The local character of teaching subject matter and methodologies was reflected in the advocacy of regional curriculums and in a tendency to generate, either through translation or new composition, a local corpus of Islamic educational literature written in local languages. In fact, a first step toward the promotion of regional education was the recognition that travel was no longer necessary for the pursuit of knowledge. Such, for example, is al-Ṣanʿānī's argument which avers that, whereas bygone generations had to travel to distant places to acquire knowledge of hadith and language, contemporary students no longer needed to leave their homelands because this knowledge had been compiled in books.[45] Moreover, in a discussion of Ibn al-Wazīr's views on the conditions of *ijtihād*, al-Ṣanʿānī reduces these conditions and argues that a *mujtahid* does not need comprehensive knowledge of all the canonical books written in the fields that are relevant to *ijtihād*; a comprehensive reference book suffices for this task.[46] This subject is systematically treated in al-Shawkānī's

Adab al-Ṭalab, a book that deals exclusively with various aspects of all levels of education. In his discussion of the requisite education of a *mujtahid* who issues rulings, al-Shawkānī lists a number of disciplines and suggests specific books that are useful in this regard.[47] For Arabic grammar, for example, he recommends the study of the poem of Ḥarīrī, the *Kāfiya* of Ibn al-Ḥājib (d. 646) and commentaries on it, and the *Mughnī al-Labīb* of Ibn Hishām, (d. 762) and commentaries on it. Al-Shawkānī is careful, however, to remind his reader that none of these works has authority in and of itself, and that these sources, which are familiar to Yemenis, may have counterparts in other parts of the Muslim world; he further maintains that these books are recommended to the Yemeni student, who is likely to "find experts on these books and not other books of grammar, unless he relies on self-instruction and not on studying with teachers. If this [student] grows up in a region where [scholars] specialize in other than these books, then he ought [to study] what the specialists of this region work on."[48] Elsewhere, al-Shawkānī lists the authoritative sources of various schools that can be consulted by students.[49] However, according to al-Shawkānī, the emphasis on the regional character of various institutions of learning and of canons is not meant to endow any particular set of texts with ultimate authority; rather, the regional character of the tools of learning underscores their relative authoritativeness, or rather utility, while the knowledge deriving from these parochial traditions remains, in al-Shawkānī's view, universal.[50]

To be sure, the curriculum suggested by al-Shawkānī is not exclusively based on books written in Yemen. Rather, it is a mélange of books written both within and outside Yemen with which Yemeni scholars were familiar. A cursory look at al-Shawkānī's curriculum reveals the exhaustiveness of his own education and knowledge, which includes his mastery of all the classical books of hadith and *tafsīr*, their transmission through uninterrupted chains of transmission (*isnād*s), and the major legal works of the Zaydis and the Sunni schools.[51] The transmission of these books from their points of origin to al-Shawkānī was often conducted through scholars associated with the Ḥaramayn network, such as Bābilī, al-Shams al-Ramlī, al-Kurdī, and Muḥammad Ḥaya al-Sindī.[52] Al-Shawkānī maintains that he transmitted a book titled *Al-Amam* by al-Kurdī, the most famous of the Ḥaramayn teachers.[53] This book, like al-Shawkānī's *Itḥāf*, lists all the books studied by its author, and the various chains through which these books were transmitted. This transmission, however, does not imply an intellectual affinity between al-Shawkānī and al-Kurdī; rather, it simply verifies al-Shawkānī's claim to know and be qualified to transmit commonly circulated classics of Islamic learning through their appropriate channels. In fact, in contrast to al-Shawkānī's massive contributions, there is no evidence that al-Kurdī made equally significant intellectual contributions of his own, although he had an outstanding teaching career. Moreover, al-Shawkānī transmitted many other works that do not appear in al-Kurdī's list. Al-Shawkānī refers to the scholars associated with the Ḥaramayn network because they are *isnād* authorities and not because they are sources of intellectual inspiration.

The emergence of regional traditions is also evident from translations into and compositions in vernacular languages. Both Ibn Fūdī and Walī Allāh promoted the study of Arabic as the indispensable requisite for the study of all the other religious sciences.[54] Ibn Fūdī's schools taught Arabic, and competence in the language was a distinguishing trait of the experts that manned the educational and administrative centers of the Sokoto Caliphate. Moreover, all of Ibn Fūdī's numerous treatises in which he advanced his legal and political views were written in Arabic. In addition to these relatively advanced works, Ibn Fūdī also wrote many tracts in Fulfulde, in an attempt to promote basic Islamic education among a population that did not speak Arabic.[55] Many of these texts were written in a rhyming style to facilitate their memorization. Both his Arabic and Fulfulde works were based on and derived from classical Islamic writings in Arabic. However, both kinds of writings acquired peculiar regional characteristics: the Arabic writings on account of their treatment of problems specific to West Africa, and the standard Islamic writings on account of their composition in Fulfulde.

Walī Allāh produced his extensive oeuvre in two languages.[56] He wrote many of his books in a mix of Arabic and Persian, with a paragraph or section in one language alternating with a paragraph or section in the other.[57] More revealing than this alternating style, however, is his translation of what he considered to be the main scriptural sources of Islam into Persian; these are the Qur'ān, Mālik Ibn Anas's *Muwaṭṭa'*, and sections of the *Ṣaḥīḥ* compilation of prophetic traditions by Muḥammad al-Bukhārī.[58] Furthermore, in content as in form, Walī Allāh gave a major impetus to the shaping of a distinct regional Islamic tradition.[59]

The translation of the Qur'ān in particular poses questions that go beyond the problems of language. The sacredness of the Qur'ān is inseparable from the formal linguistic medium of its transmission. In other words, the content and the Arabic language of revelation of the Qur'ān are identical. Initially, there was great reluctance to translate the Qur'ān into other languages and, when undertaken, these translations were considered interpretations rather than renditions in other languages of the sacred text. In Muslim societies where the majority of the population did not speak Arabic, and indeed this is still true today, the identity of form and content of the scripture automatically privileges scholars with knowledge of Arabic, giving them a higher authority to interpret the text. Therefore, the religious authority of such experts was in no small measure a function of their exclusive knowledge of the language of scripture. As such, Walī Allāh's deliberate and systematic attempt to make the Qur'ān, as well as the two fundamental sources of hadith, available in Persian, in effect reduced the expert authority of bilingual scholars and opened the door for the participation of larger sectors of society in determining the meaning of scripture. This deliberate act of linguistic and educational empowerment advocated by the reformers of this period also found expression in the eighteenth-century discourse on *ijtihād*. Writings on *ijtihād* provide stark examples of both reformative thinking and the regional character of this reform.

Ijtihād as a Tool of Intellectual Empowerment

Concerned as they were with the well-being of fellow Muslims, eighteenth-century reformers strove to identify the problems that plagued their societies and propose ways of resolving them. Among the problems they identified are school partisanship (*tamadhhub*), imitation (*taqlīd*), accusation of unbelief (*takfīr*), subservience of scholars to unjust rulers, bedouinity or tribalism, lack of law and order, and the imposition of unjust taxes. Some of these problems are socioeconomic but others belong to the realm of ideas. Following Orientalist constructs, Muslim reformers of the colonial period often conceived of social problems in terms of Islam itself, and its partial or total incompatibility with modernity, rationality, or progress. In contrast, eighteenth-century thinkers argued that Islam provided the blueprint for social order and justice. From their perspective, the problem lay in arbitrary power configurations and unjust authorities, and the solution, therefore, lay in providing Islamic alternatives, in theory and practice, to existing power structures. In the course of providing such alternatives, reformers advanced formulas that would enable large sectors of Muslim societies to assume more authority and play an active role in ordering their lives.[60] Such was the import of the widespread advocacy of *ijtihād*.

Of the vast literature produced in the eighteenth century, only a few texts seem to have gained favor among modern scholars. Reference is often made to works on *ijtihād* (independent legal reasoning) by Shāh Walī Allāh and al-Shawkānī. *Ijtihād*, it should be added, is often considered the hallmark of modern reform, and most studies of late nineteenth- and early twentieth-century reformers highlight their call for a renewed *ijtihād*.[61] Implicit in these studies is the assertion that the gates of *ijtihād*—presumably closed sometime between the ninth and twelfth centuries—were finally reopened in the nineteenth century after some modest beginnings in the eighteenth century.[62] It is important to note here, however, that despite their calls for the exercise of *ijtihād*, none of the reformers of the late nineteenth and early twentieth centuries actually wrote books on the subject. In contrast, many eighteenth-century authors did, and they based their arguments on earlier classics on the subject. Moreover, these eighteenth-century works were part of deeply rooted, uninterrupted traditions of writing books on the subject of *ijtihād*. In Yemen, this tradition can be traced back at least to the fifteenth century, whereas in India it dates back to at least the sixteenth. Among the Yemeni scholars of the Zaydi tradition, which was open to Sunnism, the list of authors of books or commentaries on *ijtihād* before al-Shawkānī includes Muḥammad Ibn Ibrāhīm al-Wazīr (d. 1436), Al-Ḥasan al-Jalāl (d. 1673), Sāliḥ Ibn Mahdī al-Maqbalī (d. 1738), Muḥammad Ibn Ismāʿīl al-Amīr (d. 1768/69), and many others. Their works rely on similar sources and have few differences on the theoretical level, although they vary in details.

While the advocacy of *ijtihād* was a mainstay of Islamic scholarship over the centuries, the scholars of the eighteenth century offered new visions regarding its application. What was radically new about the eighteenth-century writings on the subject was the theoretical arguments about the scope of the exercise of *ijtihād*. These arguments were based on new theories introduced in what are often considered the traditional disciplines of Islamic learning, namely, in hadith and legal theory (*uṣūl*).[63] These "traditional" fields are often ignored by students of modern Islam and are considered unlikely sites of intellectual innovation. The field of legal theory, it is argued, is a conservative discipline that aims to codify traditional legal practices and enshrine existing hierarchies of power.[64] In contrast, modern scholars have noted the revived interest in hadith in the eighteenth century, arguing that this revived interest in hadith was a means toward a "socio-moral reconstruction," that is, for creating a blueprint for reordering society.[65] Seen from this perspective, eighteenth-century intellectual activity offers early signs of a modernity divorced from tradition, as implied in the assertion of a sudden resurgence of *ijtihād*, or early signs of fundamentalism, as suggested by the practical use of hadith for socio-moral regimentation. The focus of all such approaches to the study of eighteenth-century Islam, therefore, has been on social movements, which are of interest in and of themselves, or as preludes to later movements of modernity and fundamentalism. Implicit in all of these approaches, however, is the assumption that the eighteenth century was intellectually impoverished, that it offered little in the way of original thinking, and, as a consequence, that its "traditional" intellectual legacy was not worthy of study.[66]

Studies of modern reformist Islam of the nineteenth and twentieth centuries celebrate its call for an *ijtihād*, which is seen by modern scholars as a response to an outside intellectual challenge, the outcome of an outside stimulus, and a break with, rather than a creative restructuring of, tradition. More recent revisionist histories rightly point out the preponderance of works on *ij-*

tihād in the eighteenth century. These revisions, however, treat the eighteenth century as merely the staging ground for later calls for *ijtihād*. By pushing back the date of origin of the works on *ijtihād* from the nineteenth to the eighteenth century, revisionist studies simply root nineteenth-century calls for *ijtihād* in the earlier momentum of the eighteenth century, without accounting for the difference between the rich discourse of the eighteenth century on *ijtihād* and the impetus for and objectives of nineteenth-century deployment of this concept. A second shortcoming is that the studies of eighteenth-century works on *ijtihād* fail to identify what, if anything, was new in these works, and what distinguishes them from the abundant earlier works on the same subject. Similarly, these studies do not distinguish among various works on *ijtihād* in the eighteenth century itself. Ultimately, there is little analysis of the content of the eighteenth-century writings on *ijtihād*, as if their only significance is their renewed call for independent thinking, and not the new ideas they advance. Eighteenth-century *ijtihād*, however, despite its reference to classical Islamic writings, was envisioned as a tool for undermining existing notions of intellectual authority. This primary objective of the new writings on *ijtihād* represents one of the most radical innovations of eighteenth-century thought, and situates the eighteenth-century discourse on *ijtihād* in marked relief from earlier as well as later writings on the subject.

Eighteenth-century discussions of *ijtihād* invoked many earlier works,[67] but, despite many similarities, the characteristic feature of discussions of the eighteenth century was the focus on widening the scope of *ijtihād* to the point of making it obligatory for all Muslims. Eighteenth-century *ijtihād*, then, was envisioned as a tool for empowering larger sectors of Muslim society and opening up a previously restricted site of authority to broader participation. Although not all eighteenth-century thinkers treated the subject of *ijtihād*,[68] and while those who did often had different views about its scope and purview, it is nevertheless possible to identify two distinct approaches to the question of *ijtihād*, the Yemeni and the Indian approaches, and to subsume other views on the subject under one of these two. These two regional approaches gain added importance because they were tied to larger regional visions of reform.

Following in the footsteps of a long scholarly tradition, al-Ṣanʿānī discussed *ijtihād* in a work devoted specifically to the subject[69] and in many of his other works whenever he had occasion to do so. Al-Ṣanʿānī maintains that *ijtihād* was an easy task that had been performed by bygone generations of Muslims, and that it was even easier to perform for his own generation.[70] The only requisite for the exercise of *ijtihād*, according to al-Ṣanʿānī, is the common ability to understand the simple meanings of the traditions of the Prophet Muhammad. The reason for the increased ease of *ijtihād* is that, in earlier generations, professional knowledge of hadith and the language sciences was in the hearts and minds of people and was as geographically dispersed as the Muslims who mastered these sciences. Thus scholars had to travel widely to acquire hadith and to exercise *ijtihād* based on it. However, when the books of hadith and other allied disciplines were compiled, it became possible to exercise *ijtihād* without having to endure the hardships of travel. Denying this would amount to ingratitude and the denial of God's bounty. But to appreciate the availability of hadith and the consequent ease of *ijtihād*, "one first must purge his thought of the tumors of zealotry, and rid himself of the substance of sectarian delusion."[71] In other words, al-Ṣanʿānī relates the denial of the ease of *ijtihād* to partisanship, thereby attributing an intellectual stand on the question of *ijtihād* to the affiliation with the interest group that is dominant in a particular *madhhab*.

According to this view, *ijtihād* is concomitant with *taklīf*, the state of being legally bound by the rules and regulations of Islamic law. Al-Ṣanʿānī argues that understanding the legal implications of the bare statements of the Qurʾān and the Sunna is a simple matter that does not require exceptional intelligence. Rather, the same level of intelligence that is required for a mature Muslim to be considered a legally responsible individual is sufficient for the understanding of the injunctions of the scriptural sources. Alternatively, al-Ṣanʿānī argues that legal responsibility does not obtain without cognition, and the same reasoning that a Muslim employs to understand the laws as articulated in the rulings of a jurist suffices to enable this Muslim to directly understand the legal implications of the Qurʾān and the Sunna.[72] In fact, al-Ṣanʿānī maintains, to claim that *ijtihād* is not possible for the average Muslim is to deny God's gifts. Moreover, the reasoning on which the claim of the impossibility of *ijtihād* is based is itself a kind of *ijtihād* that is even more difficult than simple *ijtihād* through which laws are derived from the Qurʾān and the Sunna. Scrutinizing the legal views of imams is more involved than the direct derivation of meaning from the basic scriptures.[73] Denying *ijtihād* in effect leads to the denial of legal responsibility because the alternative, *taqlīd* (imitation), ought to be based on some proof (*dalīl*), and such proof can only be derived from the Qurʾān and the Sunna, and thus requires the same amount of reasoning as is needed for *ijtihād*. A person who can furnish or understand the textual proof for *taqlīd* is in effect practicing *ijtihād* and is thus capable of doing the same with other proofs.[74] Al-Ṣanʿānī even argues that the imams of the schools Muslims imitate have themselves forbidden Muslims from imitating them and have clearly instructed their students to always give preference to the scripture over their opinions.[75] Al-Ṣanʿānī adds that a person "who zealously adheres to a particular imam aside from the Prophet, and believes that the former's opinion should be followed under all conditions to the exclusion of other imams, would be treating that imam as a messenger, and this is tantamount to unbelief." According to al-Ṣanʿānī, therefore, *ijtihād* is not just the condition of *taklīf*, but zealous *taqlīd* may even lead to unbelief.[76]

Al-Shawkānī's views on *ijtihād* were similar to those of al-Ṣanʿānī and other earlier Yemeni scholars. Like al-Ṣanʿānī before him, al-Shawkānī was conscious of the radical consequences of the theory of *ijtihād* he was advocating. The kernel of the argument that there can be no legal responsibility (*taklīf*) without *ijtihād* is that understanding is a quality with which God endowed most of His servants;[77] therefore, sane Muslims who have reached the age of reason are qualified to understand God's laws. Thus, for example, al-Shawkānī argues that,

> God has commanded all of this community to worship Him [*taʿabbada kulla hādhihi al-umma*] in accordance with what is in the Book and the Sunna, and He did not privilege the first [Muslim] generation [alone] with the understanding of these [scriptures] to the exception of those of later generations who came after them. Nor did He limit His beneficence regarding the Laws He has granted all His worshippers to the people of one generation or region to the exception of other generations and regions. . . . For He has created for the later generations an understanding similar to that which He created for the earlier ones. . . . Moreover, the Book and the Sunna exist in later times just as they did in earlier ones. Worshipping through them for later [Muslims] is the same as it was for those who passed away. . . . Thus, knowing the truth and becoming aware of what God has legislated for His worshippers has been made easy for later generations by God in such a manner that they only need to devote a fraction of the attention and effort that those who came before needed to devote.[78]

Occasionally, this advocacy of egalitarian *ijtihād* seems to be tempered, and the use of the term seems to be reserved for the traditional process of legal reasoning. Such, for example, is al-Shawkānī's argument that not all Muslims are expected to reach the rank of *mujtahid*; rather, the common Muslim ought simply to ask *mujtahid*s for the indicants (*adilla*, singular *dalīl*) of the law (and not their opinions) and act in accordance with these indicants.[79] Yet although *ijtihād* connotes more than one kind of reasoning about the law, and although these connotations also differ in the views of the different eighteenth-century reformers, all of these reformers argue that *ijtihād*, at all its possible levels, is easier than it was for Muslims of earlier generations. Moreover, requesting the indicants of the law and acting in accordance with them is easier than comprehending the opinions of imams and *mujtahid*s, which are at least one step removed from and more complex than the original sources on which these rulings are based.[80]

While recognizing that there can be different levels in the practice of *ijtihād*, the eighteenth-century reformers opened up all of these levels for broader participation by Muslims by illustrating the ease and facility of this participation. In fact, one of the main characteristics of eighteenth-century writings on *ijtihād*, in contrast to the earlier writings they invoke, is the insistence on the ease of this practice. Al-Ṣanʿānī, for example, summarizes Ibn al-Wazīr's views on the conditions of *ijtihād* and reduces some of them, arguing, among other things, that a *mujtahid* needs knowledge of the sciences of the Arabic language, principles of jurisprudence (*uṣūl al-fiqh*), rhetoric (*al-maʿānī wal-bayān*), and the legal verses of the Qurʾān, which add up to about 200 verses. Al-Ṣanʿānī then argues that there is no need to memorize the relevant knowledge; it is sufficient to be able to identify the reference books to be consulted. It is also possible to write down the relevant information in a concise reference notebook. Similarly, for the collection of hadith needed for *ijtihād*, a comprehensive book of hadith is sufficient.[81]

Similarly, Walī Allāh's extensive discussion of *ijtihād* is also concerned with the ease with which it can be practiced. Walī Allāh defines *ijtihād* as exhausting one's effort in arriving at legal rulings in matters over which there is no explicit statement in the Qurʾān or the hadith[82] and maintains that it is (and will be) a collective obligation until the end of time.[83] The requirements for the different levels of *ijtihād* are attainable without much difficulty.[84] Like al-Ṣanʿānī, Walī Allāh maintains that partial knowledge of a few disciplines suffices for fulfilling these requirements and, even then, this knowledge need not be committed to memory. A *mujtahid* should know the verses of the Qurʾān and the traditions of the Prophet that pertain to the applied law, the instances of abrogation, the difference between ambiguous and unequivocal verses, the legal categories of obligation and prohibition and what falls in between, the principles of hadith authentication, the conditions of legal analogy, and Arabic grammar. A *mujtahid* is also required to know the instances of consensus so as not to contradict them in his ruling. Knowledge of theological disputation (*kalām*) and jurisprudence are not requirements for *ijtihād*.[85] In short, to attain the rank of a *mujtahid* one must know how to extract rulings from traditions and provide their evidence and proof, whether they agree with rulings made by earlier authorities or not.[86]

Walī Allāh maintains that there are different ranks of *ijtihād*:[87] an absolute and independent *mujtahid* (*muṭlaq mustaqill*) is one who has full knowledge of the principles on which he bases his rulings; he should know all the precedent rulings, their proofs in the Qurʾān and the hadith, and the methods of deriving them; he should also be able to handle new questions for which no precedents exist. An absolute and affiliated *mujtahid* (*muṭlaq muntasib*), in contrast, is one who accepts the principles adopted by his teacher, relies on the teacher's arguments in his proofs and derivations of old rulings, and is capable of deducing new rulings on the basis of his teacher's principles; he should also have knowledge of the method of deriving a ruling from evidence. A *mujtahid* within the school (*fī al-madhhab*) is one who follows his teacher or imam wherever there is an existing ruling based on a text (*naṣṣ*); he also knows the general principles upon which his imam's school is based and is capable of independently applying these principles to a limited number of new cases. The plurality of types of *ijtihād* makes this collective obligation accessible, in varying degrees, to any knowledgeable member of the community.

Al-Shawkānī goes further than Walī Allāh in arguing the ease of *ijtihād*. In the context of his advocacy of *ijtihād*, he often argues that knowledge has become much more accessible with the passage of time. He marvels at people who give preference to the sayings of fourth-century scholars over the Qur'ān and the Sunna, even though the command of language and ability to understand the primary sources is better for later generations than it was for scholars of the fourth century.[88] In fact, al-Shawkānī maintains, later generations of Muslims know the language much better than they need to for understanding the scripture. The accumulation of a critical mass of linguistic and grammatical studies has made the interpretation of the Qur'ān and the Sunna more accessible to the contemporaries of al-Shawkānī than it was to earlier generations of Muslims, who had to rely primarily on their intuitive and commonsense knowledge of the language. This advantage notwithstanding, al-Shawkānī argues that ultimate interpretation of the scriptures ought to be based on common usage by ordinary Muslims, and not on technicalities introduced by later generations of Muslims. As far as the understanding of the scripture is concerned, the ability to use Arabic as a living language situates a contemporary of al-Shawkānī on the same footing as a Companion of the Prophet. Thus al-Shawkānī maintains,

> What I believe is that one who knows enough of the language of the Arabs to understand the Book of God, in addition to rectifying his tongue with a little grammar and morphology, and a portion of the essentials of the principles of jurisprudence, has no license to forsake acting in accordance with what he understands from the verses of the glorious Book. If in addition to these, he is familiar with the books of the purified Sunna that have been compiled by the distinguished leading scholars, and which have provided the basis for the action of the earlier and later generations . . . then it is obligatory to act in accordance with what is equally [clear] from the Sunna. It is not permissible [for such a person] to adhere to any opinion that opposes these, whether it is maintained by an individual or a

group of people, or even the majority, since there is nothing in this magnanimous law that indicates that it is obligatory to adhere to opinions which do not contradict the Book or the Sunna, much less when these [opinions] do [contradict them]. . . . In summary, one who reaches such rank of knowledge that he is capable of understanding the expressions of the Book of God, giving preference to different interpretations of the early generations, and handling the books of the Sunna from which one can differentiate between what is sound and what is not, then [this person] is a *mujtahid* and it is not lawful for him to imitate someone else in a religious matter, no matter who this person may be. Rather, he should ask for the reports of the texts from those who specialize in reporting [*yastarwī al-nuṣūṣ min ahl al-riwāya*] and learn to discriminate [between different kinds of reports] from perceptive people. Furthermore, he should restrict himself in each discipline to the amount that is needed. The needed amount of these disciplines is what relates to understanding and discrimination. There is no doubt that the thorough study of all kinds of knowledge and the development of a far-reaching competence in them is invariably valuable. This is especially [true] of acquiring much of the science of the Sunna, memorizing texts, learning the conditions of the men of the chains of transmission, and determining the opinions of the leading scholars on these matters. However, this [process] entails distinction in ranks between different [levels of] *mujtahid*s, but the exercise of *ijtihād* is not predicated on it.[89]

In al-Shawkānī's usage, *ijtihād* assumes several possible meanings. On the one hand, there is the *ijtihād* that is incumbent on all legally responsible Muslims. In contrast, there is the *ijtihād* that admits of various ranks and levels and is thus contingent on the professional acquisition of knowledge. However, in anticipation of notions of partial *ijtihād*, or *ijtihād* within the school, al-Shawkānī argues that this kind of *ijtihād* is not divisible, and that one who is capable of exercising *ijtihād* in some matters would be capable of exercising it in all matters. This is because *ijtihād* is a faculty that hinges on the acquisition of certain kinds of knowledge and the development of certain skills. Once such skills are developed, al-Shawkānī argues, there is no reason to limit the exercise of *ijtihād* to some and not all legal matters.[90] Significantly, however, in discussing either one of these two kinds of *ijtihād*, al-Shawkānī usually delineates the amount of knowledge that would be sufficient, rather than necessary, for the exercise of *ijtihād*. Often, after providing lists of sufficient knowledge in the linguistic and religious sciences, al-Shawkānī adds that one who seeks to practice *ijtihād* does not need to know more than this minimum. For example, he maintains that one who has basic knowledge of the Arabic language will not need to study the books of exegesis [*tafsīr*] with teachers because he would have acquired what he needs to understand the Glorious Book. . . . If one finds differences in the interpretations of the earlier generations which one becomes aware of through reading, then the Qur'ān is in Arabic, and the reference is the language of the Arabs, such that what is closer to it is more correct than what is farther from it. . . . Moreover, this amount that we have mentioned suffices for knowing the meanings of the texts of hadith. As for what suffices for one to know whether a hadith is sound or not . . . we say: if a leading scholar among the scholars of hadith who are renowned for their memorization, probity, and competent knowledge states that he included in his book only sound [traditions], and if he is one who has a broad experience in this subject—as in the case of the compilers of the two *Ṣaḥīḥ*s, and after them the [compilers of the] *Ṣaḥīḥ* of Ibn Ḥibbān, Ibn Khuzayma, and the like—then this statement authorizes acting in accordance with what is in these books, and obligates giving priority to them over imitation. This is not considered imitation because it is action on the basis of the report of a trustworthy person, whereas imitation is action in accordance with this person's opinion. This distinction [between imitation, *taqlīd*, and following, *ittibāʿ*] is more obvious than the sun, even if it may be confusing to many people.[91]

While deeper and more comprehensive knowledge is always recommended for one who has the ability to pursue it, al-Shawkānī is primarily interested in delineating the minimum amount of knowledge that would enable Muslims to act in accordance with the Qur'ān and the Sunna. These levels of *ijtihād* pertain to the active exercise of legal reasoning; however, according to al-Shawkānī, a person who has no firsthand knowledge of what the texts of the Qur'ān and the Sunna say about matters of personal worship and public transactions must ask some trustworthy and knowledgeable Muslim to inform him of the soundest proof texts pertaining to these matters.[92] Again, according to al-Shawkānī, resorting to an intermediary authority is not imitation because it is the report (*riwāya*) and not the opinion of this intermediary that is solicited. In contrast to a person who cannot comprehend the expressions of the Qur'ān and the Sunna, a Muslim who has the basic language skills, and who has access to the basic books of hadith, is obligated to act in accordance with these books without seeking the aid of an intermediary authority. A person who acts on the basis of his own understanding of the scripture is "called a *mujtahid*, whereas a common person who relies on asking is neither an imitator nor a *mujtahid*; rather, he acts on the basis of an evidence [*dalīl*] [that is conveyed to him] through the intermediary agency of a *mujtahid*."[93] Al-Shawkānī adds that the majority of the early pious generations of Muslims (*al-salaf al-ṣāliḥ*) belonged to this last category and were neither imitators nor *mujtahid*s. Rather, they asked the scholars among them to relate to them the proof texts (*yastarwūn nuṣūṣ al-adilla*), and they then acted in accordance with these indicants.

It is clear, therefore, that al-Shawkānī advocates a position between *ijtihād* and *taqlīd*. Like the imitator (*muqallid*), al-Shawkānī's follower (*muttabiʿ*) has to ask a scholar for the information that the follower will then act upon. While there seems to be little difference in the final outcome of these two acts of asking, al-Shawkānī's distinctions are certainly more than symbolic.[94] The main difference is in the kind of authority accorded to the scholar who provides the information—an imitator submits to the scholar's judgment, whereas a follower simply accepts his transmission of a report, a mere function of his technical skills. In the latter case, the scholar reports and explains, but the concerned individual makes the final choice. Thus, the scholar's view is not binding, and the dogmatic belief in the authority of a scholar, or a school of law, is undermined. Equally important is al-Shawkānī's simplification of *ijtihād* and his expansion of its scope. While maintaining a hierarchy of *mujtahid*s, al-Shawkānī also insists that *mujtahid*s of all ranks are prohibited from imitation. These *mujtahid*s, however, are not all the same. Al-Shawkānī clearly distinguishes between transitive *ijtihād*, a kind of *ijtihād* that affects other people, and a passive or personal *ijtihād*, which does not entitle a person to teach, inform, or issue rulings to other Muslims. Al-Shawkānī also posits a middle rank of *ijtihād* that allows a person to engage the scripture in an interpretive manner without issuing rulings to other Muslims. Clearly, the difference between these ranks is a function of knowledge.

Al-Shawkānī delineates the ranks of *ijtihād*, and the requisite quantity of knowledge connected with each of these ranks in his *Adab al-Ṭalab*.[95] A seeker of knowledge, al-Shawkānī maintains, could attempt to achieve the rank of an "imam whom people consult and from whom they benefit and learn, one who teaches, issues fatwas, and composes [books]."[96] The distinctive trait of such a *mujtahid*, according to al-Shawkānī, is that the benefit of his knowledge extends beyond personal use and affects the whole community. A second kind of *mujtahid* seeks to know only those rulings that the lawgiver has requested from him, in order to become independent. A third kind of student, while not aiming at independence, is one who desires to develop the linguistic and intellectual skills needed to understand the law without distorting it; when confronted with apparent contradictions, this kind of *mujtahid* would ask more knowledgeable scholars for additional information and then make his own choice. Finally, a fourth kind of student is the one who, in addition to the basic disciplines for the study of the law, seeks to develop expertise in one or two additional disciplines.[97]

While al-Shawkānī adamantly insists on the ease and facility of the lesser kinds of *ijtihād*, he shows no flexibility whatsoever when it comes to the exercise of transitive *ijtihād*. A student of this kind of *ijtihād* needs to acquire, among other things, a thorough familiarity with different works of Qur'ānic exegesis (*tafsīr*). But knowing only the *tafsīr* works that cover verses having legal import is not sufficient, because "the Qur'ān in its totality, including its parables and aphorisms, does not cease to provide benefits that relate to the legal rulings, in addition to innumerable nuances bearing on religion."[98] Specialized skills are also required when they are indispensable for the study of the religious disciplines. For example, the study of logic is needed to acquire the terminology of the logicians that is used by professional grammarians.[99] The most indispensable and beneficial of all disciplines for the student of transitive *ijtihād* is the science of hadith that, in addition to providing the basis for understanding the Qur'ān, has innumerable additional rulings not found in it. A student of transitive *ijtihād* must study various books treating subsidiary disciplines that examine the hadith texts, their chains of transmission, commentaries on them, the probity of their transmitters, and the technical terminology used in their study.[100]

The requirements for acquiring the next rank of *ijtihād* are considerably less stringent. A *mujtahid* of this rank seeks to develop an independent ability to know the law and deduce its rulings.[101] Like the *mujtahid* of the highest rank, he is capable of deriving the laws from the proof texts and indicants. The epistemic values of both kinds of *ijtihād* are thus comparable. Yet the essential difference between these two ranks lies in their respective consequences as far as other Muslims are concerned. Although both kinds require similar methods of reasoning, much more effort should be exerted, and much more knowledge acquired, when the *mujtahid* is responsible not just for himself alone but for other Muslims as well. One who imitates in his own affairs, al-Shawkānī maintains, endangers only oneself, whereas one who imitates in issuing fatwas is a danger to Islam and Muslims because fatwas based on imitation can lead to the imposition of laws that violate the sanctities of people and turn ignorance into law.[102] A third kind of *mujtahid* resorts to trustworthy scholars whenever confronted by controversial issues on which there is no consensus; as always, however, this *mujtahid* solicits the reports of more knowledgeable scholars and not their opinions.[103] It should be noted that despite a superficial resemblance to those classes of *mujtahid*s who function within the boundaries of the *madhhab*s (as opposed to absolute *mujtahid*s who are not bound by any particular legal school), al-Shawkānī's classification system underscores the independent reasoning that must be exercised by all, and not the adherence to the views of particular *madhhab*s. Other important purposes of his classification system are to illustrate the gravity of transitive *ijtihād* and the facility of the other personal kinds of *ijtihād*.

Al-Shawkānī was not the only eighteenth-century thinker to discuss *ijtihād* in detail. Numerous works from this period approached the question of *ijtihād* from two distinct vantage points. The primary focus of the first approach was to undermine imitation (*taqlīd*) and to introduce the ensuing discussions of the obligation and facility of *ijtihād*. The second approach focused instead on expanding the scope of *ijtihād* without denying the right and need for imitation. Yemeni scholarship generally followed the first of these two approaches.[104] For example, al-Ṣanʿānī summarizes the views of the Indian/Medinese scholar Muḥammad Ḥayāt al-Sindī regarding the necessity of *ijtihād* and the prohibition of *taqlīd*.[105] Al-Sindī, according to al-Ṣanʿānī, argues that after adhering to a school (*iltizām*), a *mujtahid* is not allowed to depart from the teachings of this school on the basis of the judgment of other scholars and can only do so on the basis of his own judgment. In response, al-Ṣanʿānī maintains that adherence (*iltizām*) itself is prohibited, because one who knows how to reflect on textual evidence is prohibited from *taqlīd*. Moreover, adherence without reflection is inconsequential, since a person's whim (*shahwa*) does not constitute proof in legal matters. Al-Ṣanʿānī proceeds to dissect the argument for imitation,[106] especially the use of the verse, "Ask the people of remembrance [*ahl al-dhikr*] if you do not know."[107] He then retorts that one capable of understanding would in fact be a *mujtahid* just by virtue of asking, since in asking, the questioner inquires about the verses and the hadith traditions that he does not know, rather than the personal opinion of the person to whom he or she addresses the inquiry. Al-Ṣanʿānī adds that in the same way a person understands the Qurʾānic injunction "Ask" and infers the ruling from it, so can he or she understand the other verses.[108] Al-Ṣanʿānī responds to another verse used by advocates of *taqlīd*, "And the earliest forerunners among the immigrants and the supporters, and those who follow them [*ittabaʿūhum*] with rectitude,"[109] by arguing that interpreting the word *ittibāʿ* here as "imitation" is a distortion that ascribes the wrong meaning to the word. Rather, it should be read as "following," which means following their path and method, including their prohibition of *taqlīd*, since there is agreement that there are no imitators among the early immigrants and supporters. Those who follow them with rectitude are the scholars, the imams of the Book and the Sunna, who give precedence to these two sources over opinion or analogy. Thus, to follow these scholars is to follow conclusive evidence and to be led by proof.[110]

In his main book on the subject, al-Shawkānī states that his goal is not to adduce evidence in support of *ijtihād* but to examine imitation (*taqlīd*) and determine whether or not it is permissible.[111] He then scrutinizes the evidence of those who argue that *taqlīd* is permissible and refutes them systematically, thus concluding, by process of elimination, that *ijtihād* is obligatory for all Muslims who have reached the age of reason.[112] Like al-Ṣanʿānī before him, al-Shawkānī also refers to the same verse presented as evidence by the advocates of *taqlīd*. He argues that the verse, "Ask the people of remembrance if you do not know," relates to one particular question and is not a general injunction; he further maintains that it was revealed in response to the unbelievers when they denied that the Prophet was human.[113] Al-Shawkānī insists that even if the verse has a general applicability, it is only to command the people to ask those who know the *dhikr*, which is nothing other than the Qurʾān and the Sunna. Thus, for al-Shawkānī, the verse specifically enjoins people to ask the specialists in scripture to inform them on a particular question. Those who are consulted should refer the questioner to the words of God. The questioner is then responsible for acting accordingly. The imitator, in contrast, follows the opinions of the specialists he consults without inquiring about the indicant. The minute a person goes beyond asking for his imam's opinion to asking about the indicant from the Book and the Sunna, he ceases to be an imitator.[114]

After responding in different ways to each of the arguments of the advocates of *taqlīd*, al-Shawkānī goes on the offensive. How, he exclaims, can a scholar argue that imitation is permissible when it is responsible for the division of Muslims? As for those who imitate on the grounds that they are incapable of interpreting the scripture on their own, how can they justify imitating one scholar rather than another, when all of these scholars are knowledgeable?[115] Al-Shawkānī adds that the four imams and other *mujtahid*s did not contrive this innovative practice of *taqlīd*; rather it was the imitators themselves who came up with it, and since there is no authority in the consensus of non*mujtahid*s, there is, therefore, no value in the opinion of those who advocate *taqlīd*. So, no matter what knowledge he possesses, if a scholar advocates *taqlīd* he undermines his authority to say anything.[116]

Influenced by al-Shawkānī, Muḥammad Bin ʿAlī al-Sanūsī also rejected *taqlīd*.[117] According to al-Sanūsī, the argument is not with the great masters of the law but with anyone who follows an opinion against an established hadith. While the imam does not sin by committing an error, the imitator does,[118] and the imitator cannot be excused on the grounds that he lacks knowledge that the imam may possess.[119] The scholar's error to which al-Sanūsī is referring is the opposition to hadith. By definition, al-Sanūsī maintains, a worthy scholar or imam would not deliberately oppose or neglect a hadith, and if he happens to adopt an opinion that contradicts a sound hadith, then he must have an excuse for this oversight. Al-Sanūsī lists ten possible excuses, including being unaware of the existence of the hadith, or simply forgetting it, as well as other excuses of which we are not aware. In all cases, a scholar's opposition to hadith is attributed to human error and not deliberate neglect. However, these excuses only absolve the imam in question, but Muslims are not allowed to follow such an imam's opinion when it contradicts a sound and attested hadith. And just as the imam may have an excuse in failing to act in accordance with hadith, so do Muslims have an excuse in shunning this opinion, although they are forbidden from slandering him and accusing him of prohibiting what God has made lawful or permitting what God has prohibited.[120]

According to al-Sanūsī, *taqlīd*, finally, is a prohibited act, both for a scholar and an ordinary person.[121] A person should refer to scholars to learn from them what the ruling of the Prophet was and should be prepared to abide by their instructions if they provide convincing evidence.[122] The difference between imitating (*taqlīd*) and following (*ittibāʿ*), argues al-Sanūsī, is that the first is blind, whereas the second is based on proof.[123] The first searches for the ruling of God and His messenger, whereas the latter seeks and abides by the rulings of the imam.[124] In following, the follower has a choice, while an imitator by definition has none.[125] Someone who fails to comprehend the scholar's evidence may follow the scholar's opinion because the latter has a reputation for reliability.[126] This too constitutes a case of following and not imitating, because it entails the exercise of some discretion by the follower. Elsewhere, al-Sanūsī seems to allow for the imitation of a commoner in the form of asking scholars to inform them of the requirements of the law. However, the permissible *taqlīd* of a commoner involves a kind of *ijtihād*, which falls short of finding the exact mode of extracting a ruling but entails actively inquiring about proof texts on which the ruling is based.[127] Al-Sanūsī then adds that the real issue is the qualifications of the person who provides the answers and the types of answers he gives. A person who is not conversant with the indicants of the Qurʾān and hadith should not be consulted in the first place; but even if he is conversant in these subjects, his response carries no weight if he does not supply the proof texts with his answer.[128] If a scholar answers a question about the law by saying, "This is my opinion or the opinion of my imam or school," then he ought to be ignored. However, if a credible scholar says, "This is what God or the Prophet commanded," then the follower (*muttabiʿ*) believes him in his reporting (*muṣaddiqan al-ʿālim fī ikhbārihi*), even if this follower cannot infer how a provided indicant leads to a particular ruling.[129] In this manner, the follower simply avails himself of the scholar's understanding, uses it as a guide that leads to something beyond it, and gives it up once he reaches his objective.[130] In all cases, the follower is prohibited from belonging to a legal school, lobbying for it, or arguing against the opinions of other schools,[131] because the knowledge required for these actions cannot be attributed to a person who is ignorant of arguments beyond the immediate opinion in question.[132] Al-Sanūsī further argues that there can be no school in matters that are spelled out by the lawgiver, either in Qurʾān or in hadith, and that *ijtihād* within schools is only permissible in the case of rulings based on uncertain indicants (*dalīluhu madhnūn*).[133]

Al-Sanūsī was well aware of the standard arguments for the permissibility of *taqlīd* for common people. Even Walī Allāh, the ardent defender of *ijtihād*, argues for such permissibility. In response, al-Sanūsī maintains that one cannot make obligatory what God did not,[134] and that there is no explicit command to follow the imam of one legal school over another.[135] Echoing the Yemeni tradition, al-Sanūsī adds that this would be tantamount to treating a member of the community as a prophet.[136] In response to the criticism that common people are incapable of recognizing the exact meanings of hadith, al-Sanūsī argues that the potential for error created by relying on a derived ruling far exceeds the error in relying on the evidence upon which the ruling is built.[137] Al-Sanūsī quotes Shahāb al-Dīn al-Qarāfī's ruling that prohibits an imitator from acting on the basis of hadith or using it as an indicant, and that obligates a person who is not a *mujtahid* to imitate a scholar even if he cannot identify the texts on which this scholar bases his rulings.[138] Al-Sanūsī provides a long overview of various opinions on this matter, and quotes, in greater detail, several opposing views.[139] In response, al-Sanūsī characterizes views similar to those of al-Qarāfī as "dangerous absurdities"[140] and refutes the assumptions behind these views.[141] Elsewhere, al-Sanūsī pushes his argument further and maintains that every Muslim is obliged to exercise a measure of *ijtihād*, or at least try to do so.[142]

In contrast to this stand against *taqlīd*, Shāh Walī Allāh sought not to refute *taqlīd* but to adduce evidence in favor of *ijtihād* and allow for and facilitate its exercise on a large scale. Walī Allāh argues that certain things may be obligatory during one period of time and not obligatory during another. "So, for example, if there were an ignorant person in the region of India or Transoxania, and no Shāfiʿī or Mālikī or Ḥanbalī scholar, or one of the books of these schools there, then he [that person] is obliged to imitate the school of Abū Ḥanīfa, and it is forbidden for him to diverge from this school."[143] Under such conditions, Walī Allāh argues, abandoning the school would be tantamount to completely absolving oneself of the law (*yakhlaʿ rabaqat al-sharīʿa*). In contrast, someone who is in the Ḥaramayn, where it would be easy to know all the schools, may work on the basis of presumptive knowledge alone, without certainty, accepting the opinions of laymen, or even acquiring knowledge from a book that is not famous.[144]

Although he insisted on the ease of engaging in *ijtihād*, Walī Allāh was clearly less strict when it came to *taqlīd*. In addition to making it obligatory in certain locations, he also argues that it is permissible for certain kinds of people. Walī Allāh articulates his views in response to those of Ibn Ḥazm, a major source for the scholars who opposed *taqlīd*. Contrary to Ibn Ḥazm,

Walī Allāh does not deny people the right to resort to *taqlīd* when they are incapable of exercising their own judgment.[145] Still, Walī Allāh adamantly prohibits the belief in an infallible imam and denies that it is obligatory to imitate one.[146] Such blind *taqlīd*, he maintains, is the major reason for disunity and is strictly forbidden.[147] He further argues that *taqlīd* is obligatory for one who is ignorant of the Qurʾān and the hadith, in which case imitation is equivalent to following the tradition.[148] He adds that a commoner who lacks the tools of *ijtihād* has to imitate the scholars and is not allowed to act on the basis of a hadith if it opposes the stand of the school to which he belongs (*bi khilāfi madhhabihi*).[149] However, an imitator does not have to adhere to the opinions of his school as long as he does not oppose or repeal the ruling of a judge, and he does not have to believe in the superiority of his imam for his *taqlīd* to be valid.[150] In fact, such a person cannot belong to a school, and the tradition he follows can only be the ruling of the judge or mufti.[151]

Whether they are opposed to *taqlīd* or not, both groups of scholars provide almost identical definitions and classifications of *ijtihād*, and their conditions for attaining the rank of a *mujtahid* are similar.[152] Al-Sanūsī, for example, emphasizes that the lack of qualified *mujtahids* is due not to the difficulty of *ijtihād* but to the failure to pursue the studies that lead to it.[153] To acquire the expertise needed to exercise *ijtihād*, Muslims could avail themselves of the classics composed by the leading scholars in various fields. Much of this requisite knowledge is easily accessible in well-organized and classified books, and a latter-day *mujtahid* only needs to learn how to use these reference works.[154] Al-Sanūsī adds that it is perfectly acceptable for a *mujtahid* to duplicate the rulings and principles of an earlier imam and still qualify as an absolute *mujtahid*, if he has knowledge of their proofs and methods of extraction.[155] "Accepting a legal opinion together with its indicant is an *ijtihād* that happens to correspond to the *ijtihād* of the person reporting it."[156] Despite the similarities between the discussions of *ijtihād*, these positions understood within the general frameworks of the thinkers' ideologies are considerably different. A key difference is that while one side addresses the question of *taqlīd* in order to articulate a coherent theory of *ijtihād*, the other arrives indirectly at *ijtihād* through the treatment of *taqlīd*. For Walī Allāh, the priority is to revive *ijtihād* in order to revive the Islamic intellectual tradition, while the main concern of al-Ṣanʿānī, al-Shawkānī, and al-Sanūsī is to eliminate *taqlīd*, which is responsible for many divisions among Muslims.

Al-Sanūsī, for example, contends that the difficulties in accepting the obligation of *ijtihād* arise from the failure to realize that *ijtihād* is divisible and can be exercised on different levels.[157] Elsewhere, in illustrating his views on *taqlīd*, he suggests that a scholar whose knowledge is less than a *mujtahid*'s but more than a common person's would be reduced to the lower rank if he were not allowed *ijtihād*.[158] Al-Sanūsī, like al-Ṣanʿānī and al-Shawkānī, thus makes a fundamental distinction between two kinds of *ijtihād*: the personal one that every Muslim ought to exercise in choosing among different rulings, and *ijtihād al-fatwā*, the transitive *ijtihād* exercised by a mufti or *mujtahid* who issues rulings to other people.[159] Al-Sanūsī maintains that these two categories cannot be collapsed, and that it is thus possible to obligate *taqlīd* for one and *ijtihād* for the other without entailing any contradiction.[160] Al-Sanūsī further explains that, in contrast to personal *ijtihād*, which is predicated on basic common sense, transitive *ijtihād* is not just an attribute that appears in a *mujtahid*; rather, it is an acquired skill that requires knowledge of certain disciplines, including those dealing with instances of legal consensus, abrogation, occasions of revelation, conditions of multiple or singular transmission of hadith, and the study of the conditions of its reporters.[161] Elsewhere, al-Sanūsī lists twelve subjects that one needs to know in order to exercise *ijtihād*; he then groups these subjects under two main headings: first, knowledge of the legally relevant parts of the Qurʾān and hadith, and second, basic knowledge of the disciplines of *uṣūl* and the Arabic language.[162] Moreover, the use of hadith requires knowledge of the disciplines of *muṣṭalaḥ* (the convention of hadith, that is, the theory of hadith) and *uṣūl* (principle of jurisprudence) where one learns to identify the legal implications of texts based on the forms of speech used in them.[163]

Depending on the rank of the *mujtahid*, the conditions for the exercise of *ijtihād* vary, but they are generally accessible and relatively easy for all times and ages.[164] Al-Sanūsī adds that all fields of knowledge that were open at the time of Imam Mālik are still open in his own time, and that a scholar does not have to be the most knowledgeable in a certain subject before he can reflect on it.[165] Significantly, al-Sanūsī notes that, because it is nothing other than a scholar's *ijtihād*, the ruling (fatwa) of a *mujtahid* is not binding, whereas the ruling of a judge is.[166] However, in addition to acquiring sound knowledge, the scholar's right to issue fatwas is ultimately contingent on the recognition of the community to whom he addresses his rulings.[167] Al-Sanūsī thus maintains that the elevated rank of an imam is "granted by God only to some individuals to the exclusion of others,"[168] and that religious knowledge "is not merely through profuse transmission or memorization, but it is a light that God instills in whomever He chooses. If someone believes himself qualified to issue fatwas because of what God, may He be exalted and glorified, has granted Him of that light . . . then it is permissible for this person to issue fatwas if he is asked to do so and if people believe that he is qualified. Thus it is only right that a man should not issue fatwas unless he sees himself and people see him as qualified to do so."[169]

Al-Shawkānī also uses the term *ijtihād* to connote different meanings. In a book titled *Al-Darārī al-Muḍiyya Sharḥ al-Durra al-Bahiyya*,[170] he provides a commentary on a summary *fiqh* manual that he had previously written. Included in the commentary is an indication of the soundness of the traditions, the extraction of the indicants for the rulings, the relative authority of the various traditions, and so on. The *fiqh* discussed in this book is based on stated textual evidence that, according to al-Shawkānī, is non*ijtihādī*, which means that deriving the rulings from these texts is straightforward and does not require the exercise of *ijtihād*. Still, al-Shawkānī considers this non*ijtihādī* derivation of the law to be a kind of *ijtihād*. This latter kind of *ijtihād* is based on traditions whose soundness is universally recognized by Muslims. In other words, this kind of *ijtihād*, as exemplified in the book that he composed, provides a lowest common denominator over which there could be no disagreement. The significance of this limited individual *ijtihād* can thus be understood in the context of a general ideology that aims to empower individual Muslims enough to liberate them from the fragmenting effects of *taqlīd* and allow them to have a say by investing communal authority in the persons they choose. This *ijtihād*, however, prohibits these same individuals from judging beyond their persons or on behalf of any collectivity. It gives them the right to choose but not to impose.

While all the thinkers considered here agree that solutions to the question of *ijtihād* should reflect the interests of the Muslim community, they differ over the specific course of action to be taken. Walī Allāh's discussion of the role of imitation in precipitating difference illustrates the common communal concern he shares with those who oppose *taqlīd*.[171] In his response to Ibn Ḥazm's prohibition of *taqlīd*,[172] Walī Allāh takes a positive attitude and almost interprets Ibn Ḥazm against himself. He qualifies his milder stance on *taqlīd* with the insistence that even though imitation is permissible as a special license to Muslims who do not have the skills to practice *ijtihād*, an imitator cannot imitate a school. In other words, an imitator is prohibited from reinforcing school partisanship, while real adherence to a school of law requires more knowledge and entails more responsibilities.[173]

Eighteenth-century notions of *ijtihād*, therefore, were at once different from earlier forms of *ijtihād* and from that which was deployed in the works of the reformers of the late nineteenth and early twentieth century. Despite its wide invocation by scholars and Muslim thinkers alike, the use of *ijtihād* in this late period remains poorly understood.[174] Occasionally, reference is made to the difference between the old and the new *ijtihād*. Brinkley Messick, for example, notes in connection with the "free" *ijtihād* of the early modernist movement and the attempts to codify Islamic law that "while the gate of this new *ijtihād* was being opened, that of the old was finally being shut. Codes such as the Majalla for the first time brought closure to the 'open text' of shariʿa jurisprudence." Messick asserts that "the idea that this new digest of laws would also be accessible to 'anyone' was quite revolutionary."[175] What is missing in Messick's account is an appreciation of the eighteenth-century shifts in theoretical thinking about the law. Notwithstanding the rhetoric of the reformers of the late nineteenth and early twentieth centuries, the theoretical openness of the new *ijtihād* that was codified, abridged, and disseminated was articulated in the context of rigid institutionalization. The new legal code was to be used by the professional lawyers working within the hierarchies of the newly organized and highly regimented nation-state. As such, the claim that these new legal abridgements were accessible to everyone is undermined by the structural constraints of lived reality. In effect, then, the closure of the open text noted by Messick stifled *ijtihād*. In fact, the numerous abridged legal codes that were composed by eighteenth-century scholars like Walī Allāh and al-Shawkānī were much more accessible than the Majalla or other professional codes. Unlike the reformers of the modern period, eighteenth-century thinkers wrote extensively on the subject of *ijtihād*, its ranks, its tools, and the precise manners in which it could be exercised. More than anything else, eighteenth-century discussions of *ijtihād* are distinguished by this deliberate and meticulous delineation of its accessibility to large, if not all, sectors of Muslim society. In a sense, therefore, one can speak of an intellectual movement that rallied around the banner of *ijtihād*. Although the building blocks for the new theories of *ijtihād* had their origins in the works of many earlier scholars, eighteenth-century *ijtihād*, in fact, can be characterized by the primacy given to it by the writers of the period; by the way it was articulated and elevated as the centerpiece of social and intellectual revival projects; and by the systematic delineation of its tools. Together, these features distinguish eighteenth-century *ijtihād* from its antecedents and, most certainly, from later modernist views and uses of *ijtihād*.[176]

The issue of the apparent democratization of *ijtihād* in the eighteenth century cannot be safely settled without further examination of the connection between a scholar's exercise of *ijtihād* and that of a commoner. The individuals who wrote on *ijtihād* were encyclopedic scholars who composed dozens of works on all facets of Islamic learning. Their advocacy of personal *ijtihād* was matched only by their reluctance to allow the transitive kind of *ijtihād* in which they were engaged. Their insistence that a common Muslim is capable of judging the indicants of the law for him- or herself does not, in and of itself, explain how such judgment can be made in reality. For all of these reasons, it seems sensible to ask whether this accessible personal *ijtihād* is not, in fact, an empty and meaningless slogan. In other words, does the continuing insistence on the difficulty of transitive *ijtihād* allow the common Muslim to think that he or she is making a choice while, in reality, this common Muslim has no choice but to adhere to what a narrow circle of scholars presents as the ultimate truth? If this were true, by insisting on the two levels of *ijtihād* eighteenth-century thinkers would have been undermining traditional authority and arrogating this same authority exclusively to themselves. In this manner, *ijtihād* would simply serve as a means for self-empowerment.[177] This, however, was not the case.

Both Walī Allāh and al-Shawkānī boasted scholarly authority on a grand scale. Walī Allāh repeated in many of his works, and in no ambiguous terms, that he had been entrusted with the mission of reviving the whole intellectual legacy of twelve centuries of Islam.[178] He often portrayed this revival in terms of visions in which the highest authority was invested in him by none other than the Prophet himself.[179] "When the cycle of wisdom was perfected in me," Walī Allāh declares, "God donned on me the robe of renewal [*khilʿat al-mujaddidiyya*]."[180] Walī Allāh also maintains that the form of renewal (*ṣūrat al-tajdīd*) differs according to the dominant practices of a people; referring to himself as the member of his generation whom God has entrusted with the duty of renewal (*waṣṣī*), he adds that in his case *tajdīd* is in all three areas of demonstrative, mystical, and transmitted knowledge, so that his duty is to provide an interpretation of sharia through which apparent differences between these three areas of knowledge are resolved.[181] Elsewhere, Walī Allāh asserts that one of God's many gifts to him was to make him "the speaker [*nāṭiq*] and savant [*ḥakīm*] of this cycle, and the leader and chief of this generation," and that God spoke through him (*naṭaqa ʿalā lisānī*).[182]

Al-Shawkānī was not as forthcoming in declaring such authority, although he documented in great detail his scholarly and moral credentials.[183] Even in his discussion of *ijtihād*, he assumes an authority that overshadows all other authorities. Moreover, he maintains that "a *mujtahid* is one who draws the indicants of the divine law from their appropriate sources . . . and, even if he is at the end of time, he assumes himself to have lived during the time of Prophethood when the revelation came down, as if no scholar came before him, and as if he was not preceded by any *mujtahid*."[184] Thus, in this attempt to salvage the present and uphold the right of recent generations to think for themselves, he in fact asserts the authority of his generation of scholars over that of the older generations. Yet, even as he lays the foundations for granting to himself the highest scholarly authority, he systematically undermines individualized authority of all kinds, including his own. A true *mujtahid*, he asserts, is one who pays more attention to the content of a speech than to the person who delivers it. A *mujtahid*'s temptation to conform with the views of the majority and to favor the views of renowned and distinguished scholars on account of their reputation smells of partisanship and *taqlīd*, which suggests that the *mujtahid* has not given *ijtihād* its due. Neither numbers nor reputation should be allowed to inhibit a student's independent thought.[185] This focus on the independent thought of individuals prevails over the discussions of transitive *ijtihād* (*ijtihād al-fatwā*) and its conditions. In fact, the main purpose of the discussion of *ijtihād* in the first place is to solve the crisis of school partisanship, and this can only be achieved, in al-Shawkānī's view, through full participation by all Muslims. Therefore, much as he admired his own scholarly credentials, al-Shawkānī could not pose as an exclusive *mujtahid* of incontestable authority.[186]

Systematic as he was, once al-Shawkānī categorically rejected *taqlīd*, he carefully fashioned his own views and prescriptions in conformity with this same principle. This task was particularly difficult in the context of debating views entrenched in the scholarship of the particular *madhhab*s. Rather than advancing his views in abstract terms, al-Shawkānī often identified the main arguments of various schools and supplied responses or alternative readings from within these schools. In so doing, al-Shawkānī often appears to adopt the views of particular schools. For example, in identifying the scholars of the Shāfiʿī school as the most articulate on the subject of *ijtihād*, al-Shawkānī engages these scholars and scrutinizes their arguments. In particular, he addresses the contention of some Shāfiʿīs that *ijtihād* has ended: in his response to this claim he gives a list of Shāfiʿī *mujtahid*s of later times.[187] However, this recurrent invocation of *ijtihād* within the Shāfiʿī *madhhab* does not in any way mean that al-Shawkānī identifies himself with Shāfiʿīs, or thinks that *ijtihād* is restricted to them.[188] In fact, as discussed above, and in contrast to Walī Allāh, in al-Shawkānī's view the term *mujtahid* within the *madhhab* (*mujtahid fī al-madhhab*) is a contradiction, since a true *mujtahid* is by definition free of *taqlīd* and is, therefore, above school affiliation.

Al-Shawkānī's abidance by the principle of free choice consistently undermined any aspiration he might have had to the rank of the final, unquestioned intellectual authority for Muslim scholars and commoners as well.[189] There is hardly a subject that al-Shawkānī touched about which he did not have strong and definitive views. His tone of speech was so definitive that it often verged on abrasive. And yet, he always reminded his readers to go back to the original sources and make up their minds. Al-Shawkānī's discussion of speculative theology (*kalām*) is a case in point. Since Ibn al-Wazīr, there existed among the Zaydi-born advocates of hadith a tendency to disengage from *kalām*. In a sense, this represented a reversal of the traditional alliance between Zaydism and the Muʿtazilī school of theology.[190] Like his predecessors, he argued that, with the exception of its occasional polemical use to defend Islam and to refute erroneous doctrines,[191] *kalām* is a useless discipline that only contributes to the division of Muslims.[192] Despite his contention that he wasted much time on this useless discipline, he still informs his readers that they too will have to waste their time and study *kalām* so that they can independently verify its futility, and not just take his word for it.

The *Ijtihād* of Scholars and the Scrutiny of Common Sense

Al-Shawkānī reserves his most scathing criticism for scholars who practice *taqlīd*. His attack on jurists and judges who imitate is especially harsh. People who imitate in their own personal affairs endanger only themselves; in contrast, those who issue fatwas and legal rulings in imitation of earlier scholars are a danger to all Muslims because they turn their ignorance into law.[193] In fact, al-Shawkānī's attack on imitating judges and muftis is even harsher than his attack on tomb cultists; in contrast to his stand against the latter, which he tempered at a later, more mature stage of his career, al-Shawkānī sustained his attack on imitating scholars throughout.[194] According to al-Shawkānī, the profession of a mufti or judge has many hazards: it is insecure, as a judge is always subject to whimsical dismissal by rulers; it brings about the enmity of competitive, envious scholars; and it is depressing because a judge or a mufti is continuously occupied with people's trials and tribulations. More than all of these, however, this profession is weighty because of the moral burden and responsibility it entails.[195] Because he does not really know God's law, an imitating mufti, according to al-Shawkānī, is prohibited from issuing a ruling to a person who asks him about this law. Confronted with an ignorant commoner, however, a mufti who practices *taqlīd* may only recount the opinion he himself imitates, or a school opinion that he thinks is wrong. In the latter case, he has to sound his disagreement lest his silence be interpreted as approval.[196]

Despite making a distinction between ranks of *ijtihād*, al-Shawkānī maintains that all *mujtahid*s have to exercise their own *ijtihād* and not follow indiscriminately in the footsteps of earlier schools or scholars. Moreover, a mufti or a judge cannot assume unquestioned authority and has to always provide evidence so other Muslims may judge for themselves. This is especially needed because, no matter how knowledgeable a scholar may be, the possibility of erroneous *ijtihād* can never be ruled out. Al-Shawkānī elaborates his views on this matter in his numerous discussions of the prophetic tradition that states, "Every *mujtahid* is correct." Al-Shawkānī takes issue with a common interpretation of this hadith that understands correctness to mean that every *mujtahid* in fact hits the mark.[197] The problem in this interpretation, al-Shawkānī maintains, is that it attributes contradiction to God's law.[198] In contrast, al-Shawkānī maintains that there can be only one correct ruling that is intended by the Lawgiver; what the hadith refers to is the correctness not of the outcome of the ruling itself but of the exercise of proper *ijtihād*, for which a *mujtahid* would be rewarded irrespective of whether he hits the mark or not.[199] Al-Shawkānī thus prefers to use the term "mistaken but rewarded [*mukhṭiʾ maʾjūr*]" in the place of "correct [*muṣīb*]." On account of this constant propensity to commit errors of judgment, a scholar acts as a reporter (*rāwī*) of texts and indicants, whereas a commoner acts as someone who solicits such reports (*mustarwī*). The latter simply asks for the texts of the Qurʾān and the Sunna that are relevant to a particular religious rule, and for information on the way in which these texts were used (*ṭalab al-dalīl wa istirwāʾ al-naṣṣ*).[200] On the basis of this information the common Muslim can then chose a particular course of action, just as the scholar summons the evidence and makes up his or her own mind. If the scholar makes the wrong judgment, he or she would not be blamed for it, whereas an imitator is blamed for imitating this *mujtahid* in his or her error.

The argument that not every *mujtahid* is correct sets the theoretical grounds for undermining, once and for all, the possibility of absolute authority of individual scholars or corporate schools. *Mujtahid*s are rewarded for the effort of *ijtihād*, which is the considered reflection on the textual evidence of the Qurʾān and the Sunna. Ordinary Muslims as well are required to reflect on this evidence once conveyed to them by trustworthy scholars. By arguing that the ultimate truth cannot be recovered by any individual scholar, al-Shawkānī rules out the possibility of assigning ultimate intellectual authority to any individual, himself included. A *mujtahid* has the right and duty to practice *ijtihād* and thus claims the truthfulness of a certain interpretation of the scripture, but common Muslims also have an equal right, as well as a responsibility, to judge and choose from competing claims of different scholars.[201] This choice is based not on the expert opinion of yet another scholar (like al-Shawkānī himself) who acts as an arbiter of truth but on the simple understanding of ordinary Muslims. No scholar's opinion, including al-Shawkānī's, can escape the scrutiny of common sense.[202]

An added reason for combating scholars' claims to authority is that most of them are corrupt. His own occupation of office notwithstanding, al-Shawkānī fully recognized the corruptive effects of power. Much of the authority claimed by scholars is a function of their proximity to rulers, and to the empty aura of importance that they cultivate. Common people thus tend to rank scholars on the basis of their ornate clothing and headdress, the size of their classes, the number of fatwas they issue, the titles they claim, and so on.[203] The "science of imitation [*ʿilm al-taqlīd*]" thus brings about worldly benefit and is also useful to rulers who recruit such scholars to their service.[204] A true *mujtahid* who summons the courage to oppose the corrupt majority attracts its slander and physical threats.

Al-Shawkānī was opposed to the professionalization of *ijtihād*, and to the exclusive claims to intellectual authority customarily made by small groups of experts. In contrast to the superficial appearances on which such false claims to authority are based, al-Shawkānī argues that true knowledge prevents its owner from making absolute claims to truth. The culture of experts denies ordinary Muslims the right to think and instead thinks on their behalf and demands their silent obedience. In contrast, in al-Shawkānī's view the numerous social functions of the *mujtahid* do not bestow on him the right to claim a monopoly over knowledge and meaning, and they do not place him above the scrutiny of the commonsense understanding of ordinary Muslims. This is not to say, however, that al-Shawkānī conceived of a society free of social hierarchies. In fact, according to al-Shawkānī, society is strictly stratified on the basis of not just its members' intellectual ability but also their social class. And yet, despite this hierarchical vision, al-Shawkānī's views on *ijtihād* underscore his radical restructuring of notions of authority and power relationships within society. The tension between these two perspectives, and the ultimate resolution of this tension, is best manifested in al-Shawkānī's discussion of the status of the commoners in society.

In his advocacy of *ijtihād* by all Muslims, al-Shawkānī dwells at length on the vexed problem of how a layperson can make sense of the often-contradictory indicants (*adilla*) of the Qur'ān and the Sunna. As discussed above, al-Shawkānī's manifold arguments on the *ijtihād* of the commoners add up to the following coherent stand: a commoner who lacks firsthand knowledge of the sources, al-Shawkānī argues, solicits a report from a trustworthy scholar. The scholar provides the textual proofs without embellishment, and the commoner then chooses from and acts upon these proof texts. A layperson may not be qualified to independently extract the proofs from the texts; yet any person with basic understanding is capable of weighing and choosing from the evidence once it is provided to him or her. From a strict legal point of view, a layperson's only obligation is to choose from the reports of various trustworthy scholars by using his common sense. The discriminating faculty of common sense is the requisite for legal responsibility before God (*taklīf*), and it is shared by all sane persons irrespective of their education. Therefore, a Muslim who uses this faculty would be a follower (*muttabiʿ*) and not an imitator (*muqallid*), and would not be bound by the views of any particular scholar, al-Shawkānī included. Just as a scholar who exercises *ijtihād* is procedurally right even if substantively wrong, a commoner who chooses from reliable reports of scholars would have fulfilled his procedural obligations. Since neither scholar nor commoner has access to absolute certain truth, the basis for legitimate action becomes following proper procedure. Al-Shawkānī genuinely trusted the ability of all Muslims to make responsible and religiously legitimate choices by using their commonsense understanding. This, in turn, is the basis of his advocacy of the empowering involvement of commoners in making intellectual choices for themselves.

It is of course difficult to gauge the extent to which al-Shawkānī's vision of public involvement was translated in real life. In fact, we know that the public remained, to al-Shawkānī's dismay, involved in old sectarian and tribal conflicts. Al-Shawkānī even resorted to the support of the imams to ward off the threat of the mob. Yet, we also know that al-Shawkānī managed to create a substantial network of scholars who shared at least some of his views on *ijtihād* and independent reasoning.[205] This network, and, in a different way, the Sokoto network of scholars, considerably loosened the hold over power traditionally exercised by the dominant legal schools and politically sponsored institutions. Moreover, irrespective of the actual manifestations of al-Shawkānī's vision, which he shared to varying degrees with other eighteenth-century thinkers, one of the main objectives of writers such as al-Shawkānī was to undermine social polarization and to reorient the public sense of partisan identity. Throughout the writings of eighteenth-century thinkers, one is confronted with an acute awareness of the severe societal rifts, and the desire to come up with theoretical and conceptual mechanisms that would resituate the public in connection to political, intellectual, and professional sites of power. To be sure, the eighteenth-century concept of the public was different from the modern concepts of nation, people, citizens, or public opinion. Moreover, none of the thinkers of the eighteenth century championed the nation as the ultimate source of power, or public opinion as a source of authority. In fact, even to those scholars who advocated the exercise of *ijtihād* by all, the common people were neglected and despised, and those scholars did not devise tangible mechanisms for channeling their newly conceptualized notions of public authority. Yet despite many differences, the eighteenth-century emphasis on the right (Walī Allāh) or even duty (al-Ṣanʿānī, al-Shawkānī, and al-Sanūsī) to choose for oneself represents a radical break with the practices and concepts of the past.[206] Above all, the right to choose prefigures, albeit at a rudimentary level, a right to political participation by the traditionally marginalized majority, and thus constitutes a rejection of the claim of elite professional groups to monopolize the right to think on behalf of the public.

Al-Shawkānī's argument against *taqlīd* hinges on his ability to justify the participation of the public in *ijtihād* and to reject the unquestioned authority of the select few. While he recognizes the achievements of distinguished scholars and other charismatic figures of the past, al-Shawkānī also steers away from the idealization of men. What makes al-Shawkānī's theoretical gestures all the more remarkable is his strong consciousness of class distinctions. People, he argues, fall into one of three general groups: the common people

(*ʿāmma*), the elites, and a third group in between. Despite his resentment of the mob (*ʿawām*),[207] and the damage it is capable of inflicting, al-Shawkānī does not revert to a traditional division of society into elite and masses. To start with, al-Shawkānī systematically and unequivocally opposes the notion that the masses or ordinary Muslims do not have the ability to understand the law on their own. Al-Shawkānī also perceives the primary role of the scholar to be communicating to ordinary people the knowledge he is privy to, knowledge with which God has privileged him. The authority of the intellectuals in this scheme of things is limited and always contingent. Although these intellectuals, or *mujtahids* in al-Shawkānī's terminology, are portrayed as a force of change, the radical nature of their mission ought to be tempered in practice. Al-Shawkānī maintains that head-on collision with conservative forces and rigid imitators should be avoided.[208] This can be done by appealing to the hearts (*jadhb al-qulūb*) of ordinary Muslims (*ʿāmma*) who, in accordance with their inherent temperament, instinctively desire to learn God's rules. The true *mujtahid*, in contrast, should convey to such people the knowledge of the indicants of the law that God made available to him.

Al-Shawkānī's careful use of language reflects a further distinction he makes between common people (*ʿāmma*) and the mob (*ʿawām*). The former, are instinctively good and, in any event, have the right and obligation to directly engage the law and make their own choices. Receptiveness to truth is the natural disposition of people unless their nature is altered by imitation. Problems arise when a middle group between the common people and the real grounded scholars claims that common people are incapable of understanding the law on their own. Out of ignorance and on the basis of mere speculation, this middle group manipulates ordinary Muslims and convinces them that their only access to knowledge of the divine law is through imitation.[209] The mob, *ʿawām*, is composed of Muslims who have been corrupted by the intervention of incompetent imitators who claim intermediary authority.[210] Left to their own devices, Muslims would do the right thing, whereas the damaging effect of mob zealotry is ultimately a by-product of the entrenched interests of professional imitators.[211]

Al-Shawkānī's ambitious reform agenda was partly inspired by his optimistic assessment of Muslims. Both ordinary Muslims (*ʿāmma*) and real scholars, al-Shawkānī argued, are fair, capable of making the right choices, and likely to side with the truth once they recognize it. Even when they are not free of residues of imitation, it is easy to restore their fairness by exposing them to the truth and providing them with the indicants of the law. The fairness of ordinary Muslims is part of their natural disposition, whereas the professional ethics of true *mujtahids* compels them toward the truth. The way to win over a scholar is to provide her/him with evidence. Ordinary Muslims can be won over by providing them with as much learning as possible. Since the "souls are more inclined to emulate the one who acts rather than the one who just talks," a teacher should also provide an exemplary model out of her or his own practice.[212] Teaching and guidance, however, becomes much more complicated when a middle group intervenes between the commoners and the scholars. Having practiced imitation and speculation for so long, members of this group presume that they are superior to common Muslims. Their only distinction, al-Shawkānī adds, is greed, compounded ignorance, hatred of truth, self-conceit, and egotism.[213]

Both knowledge and common sense, therefore, have redeeming effects in al-Shawkānī's view. However, the intermediaries between ordinary Muslims and true scholars monopolize knowledge by turning it into a profession and a vehicle for reaching positions of power. This power is then manipulated to abuse and oppress Muslims. The majority of public offices are occupied by people who belong to this group. In order to become judges, muftis, mosque preachers, or secretaries, many Muslims of this middle group are willing to endure humiliation and insult by offering their servile loyalty to those in positions of power in the hope that their connections will help them achieve worldly gain.[214] Al-Shawkānī, therefore, argues that unfounded speculation is a by-product of the continuous practice of imitation that, in turn, disables the rational faculties.[215] In characterizing this middle group, al-Shawkānī sometimes invokes social and class considerations. Certain members of the lower classes of society, he maintains, should not frequent scholars and should not be allowed to join their professional ranks. Al-Shawkānī warns of the danger of allowing people of low professions to join the ranks of the ulema class or from pretending to be part of this class.[216] This, however, is simply because such people tend to be more prone to promote narrow and exclusive professional practices and not because of their class. At first sight, al-Shawkānī's hierarchical classification of people seems to be informed by class biases. Contrary to this impression, however, in his critique of the professionalization of knowledge he conceives of a public role for the scholar or intellectual that is distinct from patrician authority. In the latter case, high offices are monopolized by known families (*buyūt*) and are passed on as inheritance with no regard to real knowledge and qualification. Not unlike the butchers and tailors, and despite their considerable power, these family scholars do not necessarily avail themselves of the dignity of knowledge.[217]

The above overview illustrates the existence in the eighteenth century of regional networks of reform and the regional character of the reform ideas that circulated within these networks. Though advocated by most, diverse conceptions of *ijtihād* were articulated by different eighteenth-century reformers. However, despite regional differences, the various conceptions of *ijtihād* concurred on the importance of expanding participation in *ijtihād* by larger sectors of Muslim society. This larger participation implied at least a measure of democratization of knowledge. A similar diversity of views, and an underlying tendency to democratize knowledge and practice, can be traced in eighteenth-century reform views on Sufism, to which we will now turn.

Chapter 3

Sufism, Old and New

The Multiple Faces of the Spirit

Like that of other eighteenth-century thinkers, al-Shawkānī's advocacy of *ijtihād* and his methodical censure of the middle group of pseudo-professional scholars was coupled with a sharp criticism of Sufism. He leveled this dual criticism not just because many jurists became actively involved in Sufism to give themselves added religious legitimacy. Rather, the fundamental reason for his systematic criticism was the rejection by eighteenth-century reformers of all exclusive claims to intermediary intellectual authority, whether in traditional areas of law and the transmission of the authoritative religious texts or in the areas of spiritual knowledge and gnosis. Both Sufis and jurists traditionally shared one end of the spectrum of authority, the social and intellectual, while the other end was occupied by the ruling political elites. Sufis, therefore, shared and competed with jurists over epistemic authority and further claimed access to a kind of knowledge that was superior to formal, legalistic knowledge. Yet in their rejection of intermediaries, eighteenth-century reformers no longer conceived of authority as the exclusive purview of elite circles, whether Sufi or corporate juristic. In fact, intellectual participation in *ijtihād* by larger sectors of society constituted one of the defining features of the eighteenth-century reform project. This participation was portrayed as the way to restore the Muslim unity that had been compromised by the oppression by not just the state but also a scholarly elite that laid exclusive claim to knowledge.

In reaction to social injustices, the focus of eighteenth-century reform was on almsgiving, the lifting of illegal taxes, and on the duty of the rulers to provide for the poor. The notable absence in these reform traditions of any glorification of poverty, or the call for isolation or withdrawal from society, is a clear illustration of the optimism of eighteenth-century reformers, and their trust in the capability of a mobilized Muslim community.[1] Rather than attempting to convert rulers or appropriate their powers, eighteenth-century reformers set out to establish alternative sites of power within the various sectors of society. The reformers who opposed Sufism rejected the claims to intermediary authority that are inherent in Sufi thought and practice. To these reformers, the obligation to practice *ijtihād* is antithetical to the unquestioning obedience to Sufi leaders that is symptomatic of regimented and hierarchical Sufi orders. The reformers argued that, rather than surrendering their wills to presumably infallible Sufi saints with superhuman powers, Muslims are obliged to claim their place in the world by making their own choices and exercising their own *ijtihād*. Yet rejection was not the only reform stand on Sufism. Some eighteenth-century reformers were active Sufis who sought to undermine the hierarchical tendencies within Sufism and to restore its spiritual rigor. Again, these Sufi reformers did not glorify, and hence justify, poverty. Moreover, Sufism to them was not a way to avoid social confrontation by retreat into the safety of the supernatural realm. Some of the Sufi reformers of the eighteenth century availed themselves of the spiritual and organizational potential of Sufism but were not necessarily innovative in their practice of Sufism.[2] Others attempted to resolve internal contradictions within Sufism, and to resituate the Sufi tradition within the full intellectual legacy of Islam. In neither of these two cases, however, was Sufism purged of its spiritual dimensions or turned into a perfunctory practice subservient to formalistic tendencies within Islam.

Generally speaking, all eighteenth-century reformers, whether practitioners or opponents of Sufism, undermined the claim of intermediary intellectual authority to varying degrees, confronted the problems of their societies, and proposed realistic solutions to these problems.[3] To be sure, Sufism continued to thrive in all of its varieties in both popular and elite circles. A wide spectrum of Sufi writings was also produced in this period. Yet, despite some innovation in Sufi thought, there were no radical departures from older patterns of Sufi thinking and practice. Attempts to address and resolve problematic aspects of Sufi thought and practice were, of course, not new. At least as early as Abū Ḥāmid al-Ghazālī (d. 1111 AD), a Sufi discourse that exonerated Sufism by underscoring its Islamic credentials and its harmony with sharia became a mainstay of Sufism. The spectrum of eighteenth-century interest in Sufism generally included four main tendencies, all of which varied in their internal permutations and had counterparts in the classical period of Islam.[4] At one end of this spectrum belongs elite Sufism, spiritual or philosophical. This kind of Sufism did not show much interest in the apologetic exercise of establishing the credentials of Sufism or in defending its legitimacy against the attacks of traditional detractors and focused instead on producing a specialized and highly technical kind of literature that addressed the initiated Sufi.[5] At the same end of the spectrum, but of a radically different nature, were the various populist Sufi groups. These groups were characterized by extreme forms of belief in the supernatural powers of Sufi saints, and by the strict hierarchical structures of authority within their ranks.[6]

These two tendencies within Sufism, the elitist and the populist, evoked, in turn, two general kinds of reactions. One reaction was to criticize and often altogether reject Sufism.[7] Another reaction resulted in the emergence of a popular, reformed Sufism that consciously partook in all aspects of Islamic intellectual life. In a deliberate attempt to distinguish itself from the first two trends, this kind of Sufism affirmed its conformity with the Qurʾān and Sunna as the ultimate sources of its legitimacy, and underscored compliance with the formal obligations of the law as the indispensable prerequisite for deeper forms of Sufi religiosity. By rationalizing Sufi authority on formal, legalistic grounds, this trend in Sufism also contributed to the removal of the aura of unquestioned authority within the Sufi hierarchies. The emphasis on following the Sunna and abandoning innovation sought to secure mainstream, traditional legitimization for Sufism; the ultimate purpose, however, was to salvage the esoteric and spiritual dimensions of Sufism and not to dilute them.[8]

Historically, both the criticism of Sufism and attempts to reform it from within always had dogmatic, social, and spiritual dimensions. Yet, although the reform tendencies in eighteenth-century Sufism had their precedents in the formative experience of Sufism, the peculiarity of eighteenth-century reform was largely a function of its sociopolitical ramifications. As in earlier periods, eighteenth-century reformative attitudes toward Sufism ranged from rejection or disinterest to intellectual reconciliation among various Sufi trends and between Sufism and other understandings of Islam. In all cases, the intermediary authority inherent in traditional Sufism was challenged and diluted, if not totally rejected. Even in a traditionally elitist and hierarchical field, some attempts were made to make Sufi knowledge accessible to all Muslims, and to facilitate their participation in Sufi life. The proliferation of books documenting the chains of authority (*silsilas*) and the prayer litanies (*awrād*) of various Sufi orders served the dual purpose of breaking the exclusive monopoly by any one order over spiritualism and made the basis of Sufi authority readily accessible to anyone who desired to participate.[9] Also notable in the writings of reform Sufis was their attempt to mix Sufi idioms with those of other traditional disciplines, as if to make Sufism understandable in multiple technical languages. Moreover, none of the reformers of the eighteenth century relied on Sufi authority insofar as their reform projects were concerned. In fact, the mainstay of this authority, the principle of intercession, was itself the object of various levels of criticism by most eighteenth-century reformers. The structure of this authority was based on the expectation that intercession by Sufi saints on behalf of their clients would bring about God's amnesty or protection. In extreme cases, the intercessor even takes on divine qualities as his disciples and clients begin to treat him as if he is the grantor of favors, and not just the means for securing them. In either case, however, the dependence on the protection of the Sufi saint and expectation of his or her intercession undermine the authority of intellectuals and jurists, which derives not from intercession but from knowledge. For the reformers of the eighteenth century, knowledge was the basis of all kinds of intellectual authority, whether in the more traditional disciplines of hadith and law or in Sufism itself.[10]

With the exception of Shāh Walī Allāh al-Dihlawī, the attempts of eighteenth-century reformers to resolve the crises of their societies did not rely on a reformulation of Sufi thought. For example, the great Sufi master of the early eighteenth century, ʿAbd al-Ghanī al-Nābulsī, was aware of critiques of Sufism but did not attempt to reformulate it or reform it from within; rather, he defended Sufism and continued to develop it along traditional lines. In one of his treatises, al-Nābulsī argues that commentators should seek not to find fault with earlier scholars and scrutinize their ideas but to interpret them with the best possible intention in order to ward off accusations of unbelief directed against them.[11] At the other end of the long eighteenth century, Muḥammad Bin ʿAlī al-Sanūsī relied on traditional Sufism to mobilize and organize Muslims but reserved his intellectual reformative views for the subject of hadith. At a much later period in the long eighteenth century, ʿAbd al-Qādir al-Jazāʾirī propounded a model of political radicalism and traditional Sufism.[12] The foundations of eighteenth-century reforms, therefore, were not strictly related to Sufism.[13] In this sense, neither the emergence of so-called neo-Sufism[14] nor the Wahhabi rejection of Sufism was characteristic of eighteenth-century reform. In contrast to what is implied in the term *neo-Sufism*, eighteenth-century Sufism was neither void of spiritualism nor subservient to the dry legalistic forms of Islam.[15] Most of the reformers were either active Sufis or had some affinity with Sufism, which they practiced in traditional ways. Walī Allāh even attempted to produce a new and spiritually rich intellectual synthesis of earlier trends within Sufism. Yet those reformers who criticized prevalent Sufi beliefs and practices did not conform to the Wahhabi model for this critique. In fact, as we have seen, despite their different views on the subject, all of the main reformers of the period distanced themselves from Wahhabi-like hostility toward Sufism.

ʿAbd al-Ghanī al-Nābulsī: The Superiority of Mystical Knowledge

Neither attacks on Sufism nor Sufi responses to these attacks were innovations of the eighteenth century. Even before the Wahhabi anti-Sufi crusade, Sufi thinkers were cognizant of and addressed the apparent contradictions between Sufism and legalistic Islam. One of the leading Sufis of the late seventeenth and early eighteenth centuries was ʿAbd al-Ghanī al-Nābulsī.[16] His extensive writings on various aspects of Sufism are characterized by a dual focus: on the one hand, he defends commonly held esoteric beliefs and practices as well as more complex philosophical Sufi concepts; on the other hand, he attempts to reconcile Sufism with orthodox, legalistic understandings of Islam. In a long book on visions and dreams,[17] al-Nābulsī lends credibility to the art of dream interpretation by associating it with the traditional practices of prophets. He also argues that after the passing of the age of prophethood, the only possible access to the world of the unknown is through virtuous dreams.[18] Elsewhere, al-Nābulsī discusses the visions of Sufi saints as one of the special faculties with which they are endowed.[19] In anticipation of the criticism of Sufi intercession, al-Nābulsī argues that the traditional reverence which these Sufi masters enjoy is warranted because of their earned knowledge of the Sufi path, and not because of any presumed infallibility.[20]

One of the controversial Sufi practices that has received sustained criticism from legally minded Muslim scholars is the practice of *samāʿ* (listening to music and religious songs or chanting). Al-Nābulsī maintains that *samāʿ* is a permissible practice that was common among a large number of the Companions of the Prophet, including the caliphs ʿUmar and ʿUthmān, and their successors.[21] He also quotes the views of the imams and other leading scholars of the four schools on the permissibility of both singing and playing musical instruments, and even asserts that one must accept the practice of Companions and their successors on this matter.[22] Aware of the long tradition of criticizing this practice, al-Nābulsī maintains that rather than adopting a general blanket rule either permitting or prohibiting *samāʿ*, one should examine the particular situation in which the issue is raised.[23] *Samāʿ*, he argues, is a general term that encompasses both asceticism and ecstasy, can occur with or without the use of musical instruments, and may or may not be accompanied by dancing and outbursts of passion; it also refers to any of these actions as performed jointly or separately by men and women. The permissibility of *samāʿ*, al-Nābulsī adds quite emphatically, is not predicated on a distinction between any of the above practices.[24] Rather than making such distinctions, al-Nābulsī suggests that the prohibitions issued by some scholars are in fact prohibitions of the possible consequences of *samāʿ*, and not of *samāʿ* itself.[25] Prohibited *samāʿ* is one which is accompanied by forbidden lusts, and what is really forbidden is the latter not the former. Yet even in this case, it is up to individual Muslims to determine for themselves whether they are mixing the permissible practice of *samāʿ* with other damning acts. It is strictly forbidden, however, to spy on other Muslims; political authorities may be allowed to infringe on this privacy only if necessary for the community's public welfare.[26] It is clear from this discussion that al-Nābulsī does not consider the breach of the law that could accompany *samāʿ* to be something that comes under the purview of political authorities; in other words, even in its illegal form, legal authorities are not entitled to prohibit the private practice of *samāʿ*, or to enact penalties for its practice.

In addition to defending Sufi practices, al-Nābulsī adopted key concepts of philosophical Sufism that have been subjects of great controversy since their inception. In particular, he was a strong advocate of the concept of unity of being (*waḥdat al-wujūd*) and strove in several of his works to explain its various meanings. Al-Nābulsī maintains that the concept, adopted by such renowned Sufis as Ibn al-ʿArabī, Ibn al-Fāriḍ, Ibn Sabʿīn, and al-Jīlī, is not at odds with standard Sunni beliefs, or the views of leading imams and scholars. Al-Nābulsī adds that these Sufi masters adhered faithfully to the law, and that those who criticized them did so out of their own deficiency in Sufi terminology and general knowledge.[27] Al-Nābulsī concedes that the attribution of the concept of unity of being to God may be abused by "the people of godlessness and heresy," as well as "the people of denial and rejection."[28] However, al-Nābulsī distinguishes between this possible abuse of the concept and its proper use by the true Sufis, the "people of experience and witness." This proper understanding of the concept of the unity of being, al-Nābulsī adds, is congruent with the meaning intended by the totality of Muslims, elites and masses alike.[29] Other Sufi terms and concepts may be more equivocal, in which case the person who has difficulties with them ought to understand them in agreement with the beliefs of the Muslim community (*Ahl al-Sunna wa-l-Jamāʿa*). Under no circumstances, al-Nābulsī maintains, should one project his own malicious and defective understanding on the language of Sufis, especially that of Ibn al-ʿArabī.[30] Leaving no doubt as to where his own sympathies lie, al-Nābulsī informs his readers that he has composed a book to respond to the detractors of Ibn al-ʿArabī.

Al-Nābulsī maintains that the condemnation by credible jurists of Sufis and their practices is really directed against corrupt and ignorant Sufis and not genuine ones with "sound ecstasy and preponderant taste."[31] These true Sufis, in fact, are superior to the jurists because of their superior knowledge. Whereas the exercise of *ijtihād* by jurists is strictly in the domain of the formal law (sharia), the *ijtihād* of the Sufis is in both sharia and *ḥaqīqa* (gnostic truth), which al-Nābulsī defines as the internal struggle against hidden association (*shirk*).[32] Mandated acquisition of legal knowledge is finite, but the Sufis are commanded to strive for ever-higher forms of knowledge of the science of the truth (*ʿilm al-ḥaqīqa*).[33] The Sufi practice of *ijtihād* in the domain of *ḥaqīqa* exists only with its counterpart in the domain of sharia, whereas the jurists can exercise *ijtihād* in the latter without the former. Furthermore, God holds the Sufis accountable for acting in accordance with the requirements of their *ijtihād* in both domains; as such, the Sufis are superior not only on account of their higher knowledge but also on account of the greater effort they have to exert.[34] "In short," al-Nābulsī maintains, "to God belongs two worlds which were produced from His theophany [*tajallī*] and self-manifestation [*dhuhūr dhātihi li dhātihi*]; the first is called the world of command [*ʿālam al-amr*], and it is one. . . . Knowledge of it is called the science of truth [*ʿilm al-ḥaqīqa*]. The second is called the world of creation [*ʿālam al-khalq*], and it is multiple. . . . Knowledge of it is called the science of divine law [*ʿilm al-sharīʿa*]. What we mean by knowledge of it is the identity with what it is to God; this is knowledge of belief not of reason or sense [perception]. Both worlds belong to God."[35]

Nowhere in his writings does al-Nābulsī compromise the fundamental Sufi belief in the superiority of Sufi spiritual undertakings over all others. Yet at the same time he maintains a very rigorous criticism of the view that this spirituality absolves Sufis from the obligation to adhere to formal aspects of the divine law. Proper knowledge of God, which is the ultimate objective of Sufism, is only possible through abidance by the diverse formal requirements of the divine law.[36] To cultivate the faculties that enable them to experience the divine presence, Sufis must first equip themselves with the legally prescribed codes of behavior (*al-adāb al-sharʿiyya*), in terms of both obligations and prohibitions.[37] In reference to different understandings of the concept of unity of being (*waḥdat al-wujūd*), al-Nābulsī distinguishes between two senses of the word "being [*wujūd*]"; the first, which is identical with God's being, refers to the existence of essences and images, while the second, which is accidental but dependent on God, refers to the material existence of individual objects or their essences.[38] Al-Nābulsī then strongly assails those he calls ignorant and godless heretics who claim that their created beings, essences, and traits are identical to those of God. Such people, al-Nābulsī contends, use these notorious claims to absolve themselves from the legal obligations of sharia and to relieve themselves of any religious responsibility. By so doing, they undermine the whole religion of Islam. For this reason, al-Nābulsī adds, jurists as well as true gnostics concur on the responsibility to denigrate these false Sufis.[39] In contrast to such false interpreters of Sufism, al-Nābulsī prescribes adherence to the positions of the early pious generations of Muslims (*salaf*) on all matters of religious dogma, such as divine attributes and other theological questions. The safest position to adopt, al-Nābulsī contends, is to simply accept the word of the scripture on these matters (*taslīm*), without further exploration of the possible interpretations of these words.[40] Al-Nābulsī recognizes, however, the existence of a legitimate alternative view on this matter, namely, that of the later generations of Muslims (*khalaf*) who accept the words of the scripture but also interpret them.[41]

In addition to his defense of Sufism, al-Nābulsī reiterates fundamental Sufi principles and practices in the language of traditional legal culture, which serves to legitimize Sufism as a form of religiosity superior to that of the jurists. Al-Nābulsī's criticism of Sufi excesses adds to his mainstream credentials although it does not compromise, in any way, the basic tenets of Sufism. Therefore, the Sufism that al-Nābulsī advocates gains legal credibility without losing any of its traditional spirituality. This undertaking by al-Nābulsī was not unique although, as we have seen, it does not represent the whole spectrum of eighteenth-century Sufi thought and practice. Similar attempts to reconcile Islamic legalism and spirituality continued through the eighteenth century and the first half of the nineteenth. Two of the leading intellectuals and activists of this period, Shāh Walī Allāh of Delhi and Muḥammad Bin ʿAlī al-Sanūsī of North Africa, were particularly successful in their efforts. Yet despite their comparable final objectives, each had his own distinct method of recasting Sufism in attempting to vindicate it and establish its legitimacy.

Shāh Walī Allāh: Reconciling the Mystical and the Legal

Walī Allāh's attempt to reconcile Sufism with tradition was as ambitious as that of his predecessor, the eleventh-century scholar al-Ghazālī, although perhaps less universally recognized.[42] Nor did Walī Allāh's defense of Sufism prevent him from criticizing Sufi excesses.[43] His creative interpretations, however, were far more important than his criticism. To start with, he argued that the silence of the law on such subjects as Sufism does not mean they cannot be pursued.[44] Islam, he maintains, prohibits metaphysical speculations on issues beyond the natural order;[45] he adds, however, that the Sufi reflects on these subjects through means that are beyond the intellect, in his capacity as an existing being and not just as a human.[46] The Sufi purification of the hidden faculties is subordinate to the observance of the law and is not achievable without such observance.[47] Moreover, in addition to the legitimacy of its subject matter, Sufism is a fact of life. The common sciences of his time, Walī Allāh maintains, are the demonstrative sciences (*Burhānī*), used especially in theology; the transmitted sciences (*samʿī*), which mark the sciences that are specifically Islamic such as hadith; and the gnostic or mystical sciences (*wijdānī*). This third subject, Walī Allāh adds, is universally accepted among Muslims; it either stands above other sciences in the authority it commands among Muslims, or, when not explicitly recognized, has penetrated the contents and idioms of all other forms of religious knowledge. Walī Allāh also maintains that Sufi influences abound in the sermons of preachers, the beliefs of scholars, and the discussions that take place in the courts of political authorities.[48] Sufism, therefore, is not just legitimate but also unavoidable.

Like al-Nābulsī before him, Walī Allāh asserts that Sufis who maintain that the essence of God and the world are one are unbelievers, and the harm they cause the common people is great.[49] Such an allegation of oneness often results from a misunderstanding of the complex technical terminology used by Sufi writers.[50] Other errors result from the Sufis' neglect of the apparent and real meanings of the Qurʾān and the hadith in favor of the meanings they bring to them.[51] At both the terminological and the conceptual levels, however, basic Sufi truths are reconcilable with the basic tenets of belief.[52] One important concept that Walī Allāh attempts to recover and defend is the unity of being (*waḥdat al-wujūd*), which was systematically advocated by the famous Sufi philosopher Ibn ʿArabī.[53] On the notion that all being is subsumed by the one real existence of God, Walī Allāh writes: "The form of the Real that appeared in the mirror of the fine part of the Supreme Person [*al-Shakhṣ al-Akbar*] also has two aspects. One shows the perfection of *al-Shakhṣ al-Akbar*, counted as a universe, while the other shows the Real and its existence. . . . When a gnostic reaches this Divine Appearance and looks intently at it, he sees in it only corporeality. The mirror does not come to his sight at all, nay, even its presence does not occur to his mind."[54] The unity of existence, therefore, occurs at a level several stages removed from the Creator but still reflects God's all-encompassing nature. Walī Allāh uses a similar approach to reconcile the concepts of unity of being and unity of witness (*waḥdat al-shuhūd*);[55] the latter was promoted by Shaykh Aḥmad Sirhindī (d. 1034/1624), in whose view the notion of unity of being constitutes a denial of God's oneness and transcendence.[56] Walī Allāh maintains that the emergence and polarization of different Sufi sects occurred when people concerned themselves with appearances, and failed to realize that the "Providence of the True One is the same."[57]

Walī Allāh clarifies what he considers a misuse of terminology that partly accounts for the schism over the concepts of the unity of being and the unity of witness. These concepts actually refer to different aspects of the same truth: one meaning of the former is "being absorbed in the knowledge of the encompassing Truth . . . such that the laws of separation and distinction, on which the knowledge of good and evil is based . . . cease to apply"; a meaning of the latter is "to combine the laws of classification and distinction, thus realizing that in one respect multiple things are united in one, and in another respect they are numerous and differentiated."[58]

According to Walī Allāh, the insight of Sirhindī's *waḥdat al-shuhūd* is more profound and hence in some sense superior to the simple notion of unity of being.[59] His defense of Ibn ʿArabī, however, is more persistent and uncritical than his assessment of some of Sirhindī's formulations, with which he takes issue.[60] While Sirhindī is entitled to his interpretations, Walī Allāh argues, his opinions do not necessarily coincide with the normative position of the first generation of Muslims and are not superior to other mystical interpretations of Islam.[61] Moreover, not only are both *waḥdat al-wujūd* and *waḥdat al-shuhūd* expressions of true mystical experience, but it is also wrong to suggest that the latter concept is not embedded in the views of Ibn al-ʿArabī and his followers.[62]

To be sure, Walī Allāh's criticism is not of the veracity of any of the different concepts but only of the modes of their expression and of the use of some of them out of their proper contexts.[63] Ultimately, Walī Allāh aims to reconcile the two concepts on the grounds that each addresses a specific question and correctly articulates an answer to it; these concepts or perspectives are partial truths in themselves but are erroneous only if they claim exclusive monopoly over truth (*ṣaḥīḥ fī al-aṣl, khaṭaʾ bi iʿtibār al-ḥaṣr*).[64] The obvious criticism here is of Sirhindī for advancing the concept of *waḥdat al-shuhūd*, not as one of several legitimate mystical interpretations but as the only one that is valid. In any event, Walī Allāh contends, the errors of Sirhindī are in the realm of the intellectual and not the revelational (*falta ʿilmiyya lā mazalla kashfiyya*) and such intellectual errors do not compromise the mystical status of Sufi masters.[65] Yet Walī Allāh squarely rejects the claim that weds certain mystical views with orthodoxy (*Ahl al-Sunna*), since Sufism is a later development and early generations of Muslims did not articulate a stand on it.[66]

While acknowledging that the last formal link between humanity and God was Muhammad, Walī Allāh grants that a potential experience of the divine can be reclaimed through the spiritually rich Sufi tradition. This allows for a continuous presence of the sacred in the lives of individuals, but it cannot form the basis of community action. A similar accommodating attitude toward individual Muslims characterizes all of Walī Allāh's writings. Thus, for example, visiting tombs, and the accompanying expressions of sadness, cannot be forbidden according to Walī Allāh, as they are by-products of the tenderness of the human heart, which is essential for the proper functioning of society.[67] He also maintains that it is not wrong to believe in and seek the blessing (*baraka*) and intercession (*shafāʿa*) of pious people, as long as this does not involve glorifying them.[68] Strictly speaking, making vows and offering sacrifices at the tombs of saints are not part of proper belief; however, once made, one should not neglect fulfilling vows made in the name of God.[69]

Sufi knowledge, according to Walī Allāh, is ultimately one possible kind of higher knowledge, which is attainable by individual Muslims even when such knowledge cannot be commonly achieved. For example, in reference to the Qurʾānic verse (17:85), "They ask you about the spirit. Say the spirit comes from the order of my Lord and you have been given very little knowledge of it," Walī Allāh maintains that this verse does not unequivocally exclude the possibility that some individuals within the Muslim community may acquire knowledge of "the true nature of the spirit." Similarly, Walī Allāh adds, it is not the case that knowledge of everything on which the religious law is silent is definitely impossible. Rather, religious law is often silent because knowledge of some matters is not suitable for the general community, though it may be achievable by and suitable for certain members of society.[70] Yet despite this argument in defense of the possibility of higher Sufi knowledge, the main purpose of Walī Allāh's general reform project is not just to establish the legitimacy of Sufism and the superiority of mystical knowledge. Rather, the main objective of Walī Allāh's reform project is to resolve conflicts resulting from exclusive claims to intellectual authority. And although Walī Allāh may have had his own preferences, his primary purpose was to reconcile the various intellectual disciplines and to demonstrate the relative legitimacy of each of them.[71] His discourse on Sufism, therefore, was meant neither to establish the superiority of the Sufis over either the jurists or the traditionalists nor to produce a "neo-Sufism" void of spirituality and subservient to legalistic Islam.

Another purpose of Walī Allāh's reform project was to resolve the internal conflicts within Sufism itself. In an account of one of his visions, Walī Allāh describes an encounter with the Prophet Muhammad in which the Prophet informed him that, just like the legal schools, all the Sufi orders (*ṭarīqa*s) are equal.[72] Walī Allāh further describes similar "general provisions" that the Prophet bestowed on him; the translation of these general provisions in specific cases constitutes, according to Walī Allāh, the substance of revival. Walī Allāh also maintains that in this encounter the Prophet appointed him imam and confirmed the theoretical as well as practical validity of both his particular Sufi *ṭarīqa* and his legal school. The Prophet informed Walī Allāh, however, that this new *ṭarīqa* and school of law—which were suitable for all Muslims and not just a select few—were only acceptable if they did not cause additional disagreement and conflict among Muslims.[73] Moreover, Walī Allāh maintains that, in one of his visionary encounters with the Prophet, he sought permission to respond to the criticism of some Sufis by the scholars of Ḥaramayn (Mecca and Medina), but the Prophet did not give his permission. Instead, Walī Allāh realized that scholars who sincerely act in accordance with their knowledge, and who busy themselves with spreading this knowledge, are closer to the Prophet and nobler in his eyes than Sufis, even if the latter occupy the highest ranks of Sufism.[74]

Walī Allāh further qualifies his distinction by transforming the comparison between Sufis and jurists to one between two different kinds of Sufism. He thus maintains that there are two kinds of Sufi paths: the first was revealed to the masses through the intermediary agency of the Prophet himself. In this *ṭarīqa* the physical faculties are disciplined through observance of ritual acts of piety, while the spiritual faculties are disciplined through prayer and remembrance, and through the love of the Prophet. More generally, people are refined through the spreading of knowledge and the cultivation of all that benefits the collectivity of Muslims. In contrast, the second *ṭarīqa* is personal, without intermediaries, and is between God and each individual worshipper. This second path, therefore, is not contingent on the Prophet, and in this respect does not merit the distinction that derives from association with him.[75] It then follows that each of these two *ṭarīqa*s has its merits, and neither is superior to the other in absolute terms. Another way of assessing the relative merits of these two different approaches to Sufism is by evaluating the general benefit (*ʿumūm al-nafʿ*) that results from each. Thus, according to Walī Allāh, the Sufi credentials of Abū Bakr and ʿUmar are better than ʿAlī's, even though ʿAlī is the first Sufi and gnostic. Left to his own nature, Walī Allāh confides, he is instinctively attracted to the character of ʿAlī, and loves him more than the two shaykhs. Yet, in terms of ranking, they come first because of their role in establishing justice and applying the law, which are the prerequisites for the sciences of Sufism.[76]

Elsewhere, Walī Allāh makes it abundantly clear that he elevates Sufi mystical knowledge above all other kinds of religious knowledge. He argues that the teachings of prophets fall under one of three categories: establishing the right creeds, which is the job of theologians; laying out the right course of action in acts of worship and transactions, which is the job of jurists; and cultivating piety (*ikhlāṣ*) and benevolence (*iḥsān*), which are the fundamentals of religion and the most intricate and deepest purposes of the law. Sufis take up the pursuit of this third objective, which is related to other aspects of religion as the soul is to the body or meaning is to words.[77] It is clear, therefore, that Walī Allāh believed in the superiority of certain kinds of knowledge over others, and also in the superiority of his particular understanding of both Sufism and law. However, the overriding objective of his intellectual undertaking was to reveal the relative truth and hence authority of multiple understandings of Islam and not to establish a hierarchical authority of some over others, much as he may have believed in one.

Muḥammad Bin ʿAlī al-Sanūsī and the Superiority of Legal Knowledge

Al-Sanūsī provides a third example of a strong and active commitment to Sufism, although with a much different emphasis than Walī Allāh or al-Nābulsī. Al-Sanūsī led a movement organized largely along Sufi lines. In his extensive writings on Sufism, although he at times discussed the intellectual content of Sufism, he was more interested in formal descriptions of Sufi orders and in defending some Sufi-related notions and practices.[78] In one of his books on Sufism, he describes the rituals of initiation and the prayer formulas of some forty Sufi orders, suggesting that they are equally valid.[79] Unlike Walī Allāh, he does not try to justify or reconcile the differences between the various contradictory Sufi concepts;[80] he attempts instead to resolve contradictions between Sufism and legal Islam.[81]

The Sufis, al-Sanūsī argues, are the friends of God who have certain knowledge through inspiration communicated directly to their hearts. This inspiration is congruent with the content of the law revealed to the Prophet, but lest the literalists object, he terms it inspiration, not revelation.[82] Significantly, however, he defines Sufism as the "way of the elect" on the condition that its practitioners observe and abide by the formal requirements of the law.[83] Moreover, *tajallī* is a form of knowledge that "shines on the heart of the seeker from the lights of the unknown"; however, this inspired knowledge with which the Sufis are endowed is often slippery and may lead the seekers into heresy. The only way to guard against such a risk, and to remain steadfast in the midst of the mystical experience, is to abide by the formal obligations of the law.[84] The Sufis' knowledge is also bound by the Qur'ān and the Sunna,[85] and theirs is a new understanding, not a new legal code.[86]

Al-Sanūsī further argues that it is prohibited for someone who does not know the Sufi conventions to read their books and approvingly quotes Ibn al-ʿArabī on the need to be careful and secretive in discussing Sufi ideas.[87] He also warns common people from denying things that are beyond their mental capabilities. The inability to comprehend Sufi knowledge, he asserts, is a failure of many "scholars who claim to have mastered the rational sciences, while ignorance is better than a rationality which denies the traits that belong to the friends of God." Al-Sanūsī goes on to assert boldly that denying the supernatural powers of saints logically leads to the denial of the powers of the Prophet, which puts the person outside the fold of religion.[88] In addition to his defense of the legality of Sufi practice, al-Sanūsī defends the social status accorded to Sufi masters and confirms the validity of the notion of intercession by asserting that Muhammad was the first intercessor.[89] Furthermore, he justifies the use by such renowned Sufis as Abū Ḥasan ʿAlī al-Shādhilī, Jalāl al-Dīn al-Suyūṭī, ʿAbd al-Wahhāb al-Shaʿrānī, and Ibn al-ʿArabī of expressions like, "My heart reported to me on the authority of my God [*ḥaddathanī qalbī ʿan rabbī*]," as well as their response to questions by saying, "Wait until I ask the angel Gabriel," or more generally, their claim to derive their knowledge directly from the Prophet through a revelatory process. Al-Sanūsī maintains that these Sufis speak of mere revelation (*tanazzul*) and not *tanzīl*; the latter is arrogated only to prophets and is the way through which they receive legal codes from God. This distinction between *tanazzul* and *tanzīl*, al-Sanūsī adds, resolves the problem raised by the literalists.[90]

Clearly, therefore, al-Sanūsī discusses the content of Sufism to a limited extent, mainly responding to criticisms raised by non-Sufis. In his writings, al-Sanūsī does not concentrate on intellectual Sufism and instead focuses on the formal task of legitimizing Sufi practice against Wahhabi-like zealots[91] and on the organizational aspects that formed the backbone of the Sanūsīya enterprise.[92] Al-Sanūsī construes Sufi knowledge by discussing not the substance of the Sufi experience but its system of rationalized conduct.[93] Beyond his organizational ingenuity, however, al-Sanūsī's main reform ideas are in the field of hadith and not intellectual Sufism. It is thus understandable that, despite all of his praise of Sufi knowledge, he does not confer the title "the inheritors of the prophets [*warathat al-anbiyā'*]" on fellow Sufis but bestows it instead on the traditionalist scholars of hadith.[94]

Muḥammad Ibn Ismāʿīl al-Ṣanʿānī and Muḥammad Ibn ʿAlī al-Shawkānī: Non-Wahhabi Criticisms of Sufism

The intellectual spectrum of eighteenth-century reform included diverse Sufi ideas that were diametrically opposed to the Wahhabi brand of anti-Sufism.[95] Yet if Muḥammad Ibn ʿAbd al-Wahhāb was not an intellectual or a reformer by the standards of his time, there were other critics of Sufism who were genuine and original reformers. Of these the most notable are the two Yemeni scholars al-Ṣanʿānī and al-Shawkānī. Both scholars severely criticized Sufi excesses, whether in practice or in belief. In so doing, they continued an old tradition of opposing Sufism in Zaydi Yemen.[96] Generally speaking, Sufism flourished among the Shāfiʿīs of lower Yemen and was opposed by the Zaydis.[97] Both al-Ṣanʿānī and al-Shawkānī refer to and criticize visits to the tombs of saints in Yemen.[98] And although their criticism is articulated in larger theoretical terms, their opposition was clearly rooted in Yemen's Zaydi legacy and was not inspired by Wahhabism or its sources. In fact, both scholars consciously distinguish their opposition to Sufism from that of the Wahhabis. As such, we cannot understand the opposition to Sufism as a point of intersection between Ibn ʿAbd al-Wahhāb and other anti-Sufi reformers of the eighteenth century. The differences between these two kinds of criticism occur not just in the details but also in the overall projects of reform within which these criticisms are situated.

Al-Ṣanʿānī's attack on Sufis was motivated by the same concerns that guided his efforts to undermine the unquestioned authority of the imams of various schools of law. Although, in contrast to his harsh attacks on Sufi excesses, al-Ṣanʿānī did not question the merits of the school imams, his ultimate objective in both instances was to empower the larger community of Muslims and to reject, once and for all, any exclusive claim of intellectual authority to understand scripture and think on behalf of the entire community of Muslims. The only unquestioned authority, according to al-Ṣanʿānī, lies in the textual sources of the Qurʾān and hadith, which are accessible to all Muslims at all times. Al-Ṣanʿānī's arguments served to demystify religious knowledge by treating religion as a science that can be understood, he asserts, by all Muslims who are able to meet the requirements for independent thinking. In a similar manner, al-Ṣanʿānī asserts that mystics have no special powers that privilege them over other Muslims. Although he does not deny the possibility of saintly miracles (*karāmāt*), he maintains that the Qurʾānic term *wilāya* (sainthood) denotes belief and piety. Thus, for example, he responds to Ibrāhīm al-Kurdī's argument in his *Qaṣd al-Sabīl* that there is a level of knowing God that is beyond the powers of the mind and cannot be independently comprehended by normal comprehension and systematic reasoning; it can only be perceived with the light of prophethood and sainthood. Al-Ṣanʿānī rejects al-Kurdī's argument because it considers sainthood (*wilāya*) a part (*qasīm*) of prophethood; this in turn implies that, rather than being the subject of the prophetic mission, the saint partakes in it and can fulfill its objectives without the need for the intervention of the Prophet. Such a conception of sainthood is not acceptable to al-Ṣanʿānī because it presupposes that a particular group enjoys a privileged position of power and authority over the rest of the Muslim community. In contrast, al-Ṣanʿānī maintains that the granting of *karāmāt* to saints, though undeniable, is simply because of their sincere devotion and dedication, and these traits are equally accessible to all Muslims and not restricted to any professional group. Moreover, these *karāmāt* assist in such things as answering the prayers of a pious person, or leading one to an oasis in the middle of a desert, and do not involve, as with prophets, the possibility of a break in the natural order of things, or the performance of supernatural acts.[99]

Unlike earlier critics of Sufism,[100] al-Ṣanʿānī did not believe that the miracles of the Prophet could become *karāmāt* for the saints by proxy. Thus, for example, al-Ṣanʿānī criticizes al-Suyūṭī in his *Al-Qawl al-Jalī fī Taṭawwur al-Walī* for popularizing, on the basis of invalid evidence that contradicts the Qurʾān and the Sunna, the claim that saints are instruments of prophetic miracles. In so doing, al-Ṣanʿānī adds, the erudite scholar al-Suyūṭī has joined the ranks of ignorant commoners who believe in logical and religious impossibilities.[101] Al-Ṣanʿānī, therefore, denies the possibility of serious miracles beyond the age of the prophets. Underlying this denial of Sufi miracles is a more fundamental denial of the validity of all kinds of occult knowledge, such as *ʿilm al-awfāq*, which deals with the spiritual (supernatural) characteristic of letters and numerals. According to al-Ṣanʿānī, this and other similar arts are innovations for which there is no evidence in the Qurʾān, the Sunna, or in the actions of the Companions. In fact, al-Ṣanʿānī adds, these are prohibited arts that are tantamount to magic and have nothing to do with the methods and objectives of religion.[102] In the same manner, al-Ṣanʿānī denies the possibility of having knowledge of the future or making predictions about it.[103]

Al-Ṣanʿānī reserves his sharpest criticism for the cult of saints and the forms of unbelief connected with it. The Sufis, he argues, who call themselves *fuqarāʾ*

(poor) and who maintain that the hand that receives is superior to the hand that gives, are delinquents who find begging appealing and who somehow try to justify their contemptible state.[104] Worse than this social delinquency, however, is the way Sufism often undermines the essential beliefs of Islam. In fact, al-Ṣanʿānī maintains that it is on account of the breach of *tawḥīd* (the profession of God's unity), that he felt obligated to expose the beliefs and practices of Sufis and to condemn that which God commands Muslims to condemn. He adds that the treatment of humans as rivals of God and the attribution of supernatural powers to depraved living or dead humans who are lacking in piety and knowledge, and who do not even perform their basic religious duties, are widespread all over Muslim lands.[105] The fundamental beliefs of Islam, which are compromised by this brand of Sufism, are that all of God's messengers and prophets were sent to call people to profess the unity of God, attribute divinity to and worship only Him, and dissociate from all that is worshiped aside from Him.[106] Al-Ṣanʿānī further elaborates on two meanings of *tawḥīd*. The first is the belief in the oneness of God in His capacity as the creator, provider, and the like. The second kind is the practical profession of the oneness of God as it translates in actual worship. *Tawḥīd* in the second sense entails the devotion of all kinds of worship exclusively to God.[107] Most unbelievers who associate other objects of worship with God (*mushrikūn*) do not deny the first kind of *tawḥīd* and do not attribute the power of creation to deities other than God. Even Christians, who believe in the divinity of Jesus, do not consider him to be a partner to God in the creation of heaven and earth. Rather, the *mushrikūn* to whom most messengers and prophets were sent simply believe that certain objects of worship would bring them closer to God and intercede on their behalf before God;[108] they do not deny that God is the ultimate object of worship, but they do not believe that He is the exclusive object of this worship.[109] In fact, the very act of associating partners with God constitutes an admission of God's lordship.[110] Yet it is exactly this kind of belief in intermediaries that God calls association.

On the basis of this dual categorization of belief, al-Ṣanʿānī identifies several modes of worshipping God:[111] the first is creedal worship, which is the foundation and prerequisite of all other kinds of worship; it includes the belief in the unity of God, belief that He has the power to create and command, and belief that in His hands lies the power to benefit or harm. A second kind of worship is the verbal profession of faith. The utterance of the words of *tawḥīd* is an expression of the willingness to abide by the rules of Islam and to obey God's commands; as such, it is not sufficient to believe in the heart without verbally expressing the willingness to act on this belief. Refusing to utter the words of *tawḥīd* amounts to a kind of *kufr* that is different from unbelief. Conversely, if a person utters the profession of oneness without believing in it, then his wealth and blood become inviolable, and his final reckoning is left to God. A third kind of worship is expressed through bodily acts such as standing or prostrating in prayers, fasting, the ritual circumambulation of the Kaaba during pilgrimage, and so on. A fourth kind of worship is financial, as in tithing in compliance with God's commands. Acts or beliefs that compromise any of the above forms of worship are tantamount to association of other deities with God (*shirk*). Such, for example, is the belief that an object, an angel, a jinn, or a living or dead person is capable of benefiting or harming a person who makes offerings to or supplicates them. *Shirk* also comprises the belief that any of the above objects of worship can bring a person closer to God or intercede on his or her behalf before God.[112] Worse still are those who vow their wealth and even children to a dead or living person they think capable of fulfilling needs that only God can fulfill. It matters little, according to al-Ṣanʿānī, that idol worshippers before Islam used to make their vows and offer sacrificial slaughters to icons or idols, while contemporary Muslims make these offerings at the shrines and tombs of people they call saints, whether dead or alive. The names used to designate such acts as pilgrimage to shrines and calling upon the dead saints in times of hardship do not detract from the fact that these acts amount to idol worship and association.[113] The claim that the offerings are made to God would not do either, since this would not explain away the fact that the sacrifices are made at the gates of shrines.[114] The actions of these idol worshippers belie any claims they make about belief in God,[115] even if they claim not to be aware that their actions amount to *shirk*.[116]

In his discussions of *shirk*, al-Ṣanʿānī's critique of Sufism seems to draw on the same sources invoked in Wahhabism. Al-Ṣanʿānī's critique, however, is fundamentally different from the Wahhabi one. Having outlined the illegal excesses of Sufism, al-Ṣanʿānī advances to the next logical question of what to do with people who are engaged in these excesses. If these people are in fact guilty of association (*shirk*) then, al-Ṣanʿānī asserts, it is legitimate to ask whether they should be treated as the Prophet treated the associators of his own time.[117] This, he maintains, is in fact the opinion of a number of distinguished scholars. However, a few procedures ought to be observed before penalties are administered. First, al-Ṣanʿānī maintains, the associators should be summoned to profess the oneness of God; they should be properly informed that the individuals they think are capable of benefiting or harming them cannot in any way bring them favor with God. They should also be informed that these so-called saints are not different from them, that believing otherwise is a kind of *shirk*, and that belief in the message of Muhammad is incompatible with belief in these saints. Al-Ṣanʿānī adds that providing these explanations is the responsibility of religious scholars. However, this scholarly responsibility ends when the scholars explain the situation to the political authorities. From this point onward, it becomes the responsibility of these authorities to send out preachers to the various realms under their control; these preachers should then call for the unmitigated profession of the oneness of God such that the lives and wealth of those who repent would be spared, whereas those who insist on maintaining their illegal practices would be subject to legal penalties specified by the law.

Al-Ṣanʿānī thus recognizes a procedural imperative that separates the identification of an act as forbidden and the enforcement of penalties on Muslims who commit it. This recognition is what distinguishes al-Ṣanʿānī's critique from the Wahhabi one. Unlike the Wahhabis, who do not differentiate between acts and actors, al-Ṣanʿānī does not collapse the theoretical formulation of the law with its execution. Although adamant in his rejection of what he considers to be illegal Sufi beliefs and practices, al-Ṣanʿānī's theoretical judgment does not translate automatically into tangible penalization or even condemnation of individual Muslims. To be sure, he reiterates over and over again that those involved in the cult of tombs (*qubūriyyūn*) would not be absolved of their acts of unbelief simply on account of the utterance of the profession of faith without adhering to its real meaning.[118] He even asserts that there is consensus among Muslims that a person who denies resurrection, a much lesser crime than association, is punishable by death.[119] Thus while maintaining the toughest possible assessment of Sufi transgressions, al-Ṣanʿānī also manages to provide a whole set of gradations before legal action against individuals is even considered, starting with the scholars telling the rulers, then rulers sending preachers, and on to the exertion of pressure to change the condemned practices.

Although al-Ṣanʿānī maintains that the verbal profession of faith alone does not suffice if accompanied by actions that negate it, he still insists that it is obligatory to leave alone one who openly professes the oneness of God.[120] Unlike the Wahhabi stand, al-Ṣanʿānī makes sure to argue for the legality of a number of practices often associated with the cult of tombs. He maintains, for example, that while it is prohibited to request from living or dead people things only God is capable of doing, it is permissible to ask others to pray to God on one's behalf.[121] Furthermore, after attacking all kinds of innovations connected with the cult of tombs, including such acts as rubbing oneself against the tombstone, al-Ṣanʿānī adds that visiting the tombs and reading the Qurʾān or other kinds of prayers are commendable acts from which the dead person would benefit.[122] Al-Ṣanʿānī also maintains that it is permissible to kiss the black stone and to prostrate before it.[123] Unlike the Wahhabis, therefore, al-Ṣanʿānī does not reject all rituals connected with the visits to tombs; rather, he simply opposes those rituals that invest mystical power and authority in dead or living individuals, and turn their shrines into sites of worship.[124] Significantly, however, at the same time he insists that they ought to be prohibited, al-Ṣanʿānī also maintains that these practices have been going on for long periods of time to the point that people were no longer aware of the gravity of these reprehensible acts.[125] Ultimately, al-Ṣanʿānī contends, "these matters over which we mutter, and the pillars of which we seek to undermine, issue from the commoners whose Islam is the imitation of their forefathers."[126] It is thus the practice of *taqlīd* that is responsible for these innovations. It then follows that the primary solution to this problem will come through not the collective punishment of Muslim innovators but a rigorous public discourse that exposes the innovative nature of the practices themselves. Rather than incriminating Muslims en masse, al-Ṣanʿānī's solution for the problems of innovation presupposes the intellectual ability and willingness of these ordinary Muslims to identify the truth once it is made available to them.

Al-Ṣanʿānī's condemnation of the cult of tombs and other Sufi practices and beliefs was continued by al-Shawkānī. A number of views indirectly implied in al-Ṣanʿānī's writings on the subject were fully developed and articulated by al-Shawkānī. Though equally adamant in his critique of many Sufi practices, al-Shawkānī reflected on his own position regarding individual Sufis and reformulated this position over the course of his intellectual career. In one such instance of self-reflection, al-Shawkānī intimates that earlier in his life, while still in the prime of his youth, he had written an anti-Sufi poem, but that he retracted what he said in that poem in his mature days.[127] In this account, al-Shawkānī attributes his change of heart to the realization that the proper worship of God is not done through accusing other Muslims of unbelief (*lam yataʿabbadnī Allāh bi-takfīr man kān*), and that it is far better to busy oneself with one's own faults than with those of others (*ṭūbā li man shaghalathu ʿuyūbuhu*). However, this moral revelation aside, al-Shawkānī justifies his change of mind by reverting from the criticism of individual actors to the criticism of the committed acts, from the specification (*takhṣīṣ*) to the generalization (*taʿmīm*) of rulings. Nevertheless, al-Shawkānī managed to adopt and defend his moderated position toward Sufism without diluting the substantive criticism launched by al-Ṣanʿānī. In fact, in many instances, al-Shawkānī sounds more radical than his predecessor and even criticizes him for his indecisiveness in identifying the unbelief of the Sufis.

Al-Shawkānī presents his views on Sufism in his analysis of a commentary written by al-Ṣanʿānī on his own poem addressed to the "Najdi," Ibn ʿAbd al-Wahhāb.[128] In his commentary, al-Ṣanʿānī uses the occasion of retracting his own praise of Ibn ʿAbd al-Wahhāb to provide an elaborate analysis of the various levels of disbelief that may result from tomb worship and related practices. Al-Shawkānī notes that al-Ṣanʿānī objects to the undifferentiated attack by Wahhabis on those who believe in intercession. The basis for al-Ṣanʿānī's objection, al-Shawkānī notes, is the classification of this unbelief into practical (*ʿamalī*) and repudiative (*juḥūdī*). The first, al-Ṣanʿānī maintains, results from practice but is not accompanied by conviction, whereas the second is a result of conscious and deliberate disbelief.[129] Al-Shawkānī also notes al-Ṣanʿānī's contention that a person who commits practical disbelief (*kufr ʿamalī*) does not become an unbeliever, nor does he abandon the community of Muslims. It then follows, according to al-Ṣanʿānī, that the blood, family, and wealth of a person do not become violable on account of such a practical act of disbelief.[130] In support of his view, al-Ṣanʿānī quotes Ibn Qayyim al-Jawziyya, who adopts a similar distinction between practical and dogmatic unbelief and maintains that of the former kind some but not all acts may imply the absence of belief.[131] The tomb cultists, al-Ṣanʿānī asserts, commit "prohibited abominations" on account of which "it is necessary to admonish them, make them aware of their ignorance, and chastise them."[132] However, no amount of pressure can compel such people to profess the belief that the saints they supplicate are partners to God; rather, they would insist that these saints are granted the power to help them on account of their intense piety.[133] According to al-Ṣanʿānī, therefore, the tomb cultists are not identical to idol worshippers, and their community does not part away from religion, on account of these practical transgressions (*lā takhruj bihi al-umma ʿan al-milla*).

In his response to al-Ṣanʿānī,[134] al-Shawkānī accepts the basic premise that unbelief is either practical or dogmatic (*kufr ʿamal* or *kufr iʿtiqād*), and that each entails different kinds of legal implications. This is already different from the Wahhabi position that collapses the distinction between the two kinds of unbelief. Yet in contrast to al-Ṣanʿānī, al-Shawkānī argues that this distinction does not apply to the tomb cultists, whose unbelief is not just practical but dogmatic, since they, as al-Ṣanʿānī himself concedes, believe in the supernatural abilities of saints. Al-Shawkānī adds that ignorance of the implications of their actions is not an excuse for these transgressors, and he faults al-Ṣanʿānī for considering only their outward profession of faith while their acts negate their utterances.[135] Al-Shawkānī also takes issue with al-Ṣanʿānī's reading of Ibn Qayyim al-Jawziyya and provides a different way of understanding him.[136] Al-Shawkānī's response clearly positions him at the forefront of the eighteenth-century criticism of Sufism and the cult of tombs. Compared to the other reformers of the time, al-Shawkānī provides the most radical stand on this issue. Yet even in his most radical moments, al-Shawkānī allows for complexities that are totally unrecognized in the Wahhabi view. In particular, the latter's critique of Sufism and its practices does not go beyond the issue of unbelief, whereas al-Shawkānī's assessment is part of a larger project in which critical knowledge plays a constructive social role. Far from being a discourse that seeks to vilify and incriminate individual Muslims, al-Shawkānī's critique recognizes their good intentions and ultimately aims to reveal to them the potentially negative implications of the practices they are engaged in.[137]

If, in comparison to other subjects he wrote on, al-Shawkānī's interest in Sufism was limited, he nonetheless addressed the issue of objectionable Sufi practices in several of his writings. Minor as they were, al-Shawkānī's writings on the subject are perhaps larger than the total output of Ibn ʿAbd al-Wahhāb, much of which was nothing more than a virulent attack on Sufism. In the course of outlining sinful practices wrongly considered part of religion when in fact they subvert it, al-Shawkānī includes the making of vows at the tombs of dead people in order to solicit their help.[138] Al-Shawkānī also discusses the dedication of endowments for the upkeep of tombs rather than for the public interest of Muslims.[139] These and other practices, al-Shawkānī maintains, ought to be denounced; failure to denounce them is a grave vice that can only reinforce the hold of corrupt beliefs and practices on the minds of Muslims, and lead the latter without being aware of it in the direction of association (*shirk*). It is thus the duty of Muslims in positions of power, al-Shawkānī maintains, to refute these practices and to clarify to people that it is prohibited to engage in such acts and beliefs. Should people not heed the official prohibition, al-Shawkānī adds, then the authorities should resort to strict measures to force them to desist. What is noteworthy about this view is the very guarded language in which it is formulated: rather than accusing people engaged in such practices of outright unbelief, al-Shawkānī talks about the possibility that these practices may lead to some kind of unintentional association. This is, no doubt, a far cry from the outright Wahhabi condemnation. Al-Shawkānī is also guarded in the recommendations he makes for official intervention, which, he suggests, ought to be gradual and positive, not aimed at exacting penalties but simply at stopping illegal practices.

In a biographical entry on a contemporary of his who solicited from him a commentary on Sufis, al-Shawkānī indicates that he had responded to the questioner's query, which was written in prose and poetry, with a treatise titled *Al-Ṣawārim al-Ḥidād al-Qāṭiʿa li-Alāʾiq Maqālāt Arbāb al-Ilḥād* (The sharp swords that dissect the associations in the opinions of the people of atheism).[140] In this account, al-Shawkānī includes the poem that he had also composed in response to the query. Although it praises famous Sufis like Abū Dharr al-Ghaffārī and al-Junayd Bin Ḥasan, much of the poem is devoted to severe criticism of such celebrated Sufis as al-Ḥallāj, Ibn Sabʿīn, al-Jīlī, and Ibn al-ʿArabī. Al-Shawkānī adds that the brief condemnatory remarks included in the poem are further elaborated in the treatise, with quotes from the writings of the people concerned, as well as what Muslim scholars have said about them.[141] He then confides that the composition of this response was in the prime of youth. Now, however, I withhold [my judgment] on these [Sufis] and I simply dissociate myself from whatever contradicts the pure and clear divine law in their sayings and doings. . . . God did not command me to worship Him by means of accusing someone who outwardly belongs to the Muslims of unbelief [*lam yataʿabbadnī Allāh bi-takfīr man ṣāra fī dhāhir amrihi min ahl al-Islām*]. Even if we assume that the intended meaning of what is in their books and the reprehensible sayings attributed to them are the apparent meanings, that they correspond to what is literally implied by the Arabic expressions, and that this entails their manifest unbelief and plain falsity; even if [we make these assumptions], how can we ascertain that they did not repent? Even if we belonged to their own generation, and even if we were in their very homes when they were suffering the agony of death, there would be no way we could ascertain that they did not repent; because this could have happened by simply intending it in the heart. . . . Furthermore, should one object to this view by giving the example of unbelievers of all kinds [whom we call unbelievers] despite the possibility [of their repentance], then [in response] we say: there is a difference between one whose origin is Islam and another whose origin is unbelief, for it is obligatory in cases of ambiguity to ascribe a person back to his origin [*ḥaml ʿalā al-aṣl*], especially since converting from unbelief to Islam is not completed without certain words and deeds and by turning to Muslims with an intention that includes remorse and determination not to relapse, and not just by the intention in the heart. These things, however, suffice for the repentance [of a Muslim], but they do not suffice for turning an unbeliever into a Muslim. Moreover, there is a difference between interpretive unbelief [*kufr al-taʾwīl*] and professed unbelief [*kufr al taṣrīḥ*], although, as I have demonstrated elsewhere, I do not accede to [the idea of] interpretive unbelief. . . . Our hearts have much to worry about in way of sins that burden our backs, and blessed is a person who worries about his own sins, for one of the signs of the soundness of the Islam of a person is that he does not interfere in things that are not his business. . . . Moreover, there is no doubt that slandering the honors of those in whose Islam there is doubt, not to mention those whose Islam is not even in doubt, is a reprehensible audacity. . . . Tell me, how can one hope that a dead person whose honor is slandered forgive [this slander], and who would forgive in a situation like this? . . . No doubt, the severest kind of calumny, the most evil and harmful, and the one that is worthy of most retribution and punishment is one that reaches the level of accusation of unbelief and condemnation. It has been established that accusing a Muslim of unbelief is itself unbelief, that the condemnation falls back on the person who issues

> it, that cursing [a Muslim] is a sin, and that all of these are subject to punishments sanctioned by God, may He be exalted. . . . See, then, how the one who accuses of unbelief becomes himself an unbeliever; the one who condemns becomes the condemned; and the curser the sinner. . . . And, in addition to all of this, there is the necessary punishment for the violation of the prohibition [of slandering Muslims], for God has prohibited in His Book and on the tongue of His Messenger all kinds of calumny, and one who violates the prohibition is a doer of a forbidden act which is itself subject to punishment.[142]

The most important characteristic of this passage is that, in the same systematic manner in which he delineates words and deeds that constitute unbelief, al-Shawkānī also delineates the prohibition against taking the extra step of applying this judgment to real individuals. He then withdraws his earlier condemnation of many controversial Sufis like Ḥallāj and Ibn al-ʿArabī. This change of mind was no doubt partly motivated by thinking over the Wahhabi example and the disastrous effects of the identification of heresy and heretics. Despite al-Shawkānī's persistent condemnation of many acts and beliefs associated with Sufism, he resists the easy temptation of attributing unbelief to people who advocate these Sufi ideas and practices. Moreover, he strongly rejects witch hunts in which every word and move can be interpreted as unbelief. Such witch hunts, al-Shawkānī insists, threaten to undermine the whole foundation of Islam and far outweigh the potential damage that may result from Sufi excesses. Once the alternatives are formulated in such terms, there remains no doubt that, unlike Ibn ʿAbd al-Wahhāb, al-Shawkānī does not consider disassociation from potential unbelievers (*barāʾa*) as a prerequisite for Islam.

Al-Shawkānī's hesitation to issue an outright condemnation of Sufism was not just a function of the line he drew between the condemnation of acts and the different issue of condemning individuals. Rather, he seems to have condoned some aspects of Sufi thought and may even have considered himself a Sufi of sorts. It is noteworthy that almost all the main figures who appear in al-Shawkānī's lists of scholars in the chains of transmission of hadith also appear in relation to his study and teaching of major Sufi works. Thus, for example, al-Shawkānī reports the transmission of al-Ghazālī's *Iḥyāʾ ʿUlūm al-Dīn* "on the authority of our shaykh Sayyid ʿAbd al-Qādir Ibn Aḥmad, on the authority of Muḥammad Ḥayāt al-Sindī, on the authority of shaykh Sālim Ibn shaykh ʿAbd Allāh Ibn Sālim al-Baṣrī, the Shāfiʿī, the Makkī, on the authority of his father, on the authority of shaykh Muḥammad Ibn ʿAlāʾ al-Dīn al-Bābulī al-Miṣrī."[143] Al-Shawkānī's transmission of Sufi works is not restricted to mainstream ones such as al-Ghazālī's but also includes the works of controversial

Sufis such as Ibn ʿArabī, whose *al-Futūḥāt al-Makkiyya* al-Shawkānī received through a channel of transmission that includes the famous hadith scholar al-Bābulī.[144] Elsewhere, al-Shawkānī says, "I transmit the works of Muḥyī al-Dīn Muḥammad Ibn ʿAlī Ibn ʿArabī al-Ḥātamī al-Ṣūfī, through the previous chain of transmission to Ibrāhīm al-Kurdī, from his shaykh Aḥmad Ibn Muḥammad al-Madanī."[145] Already in his early career, before relaxing his attitude toward Sufism and other related subjects, al-Shawkānī relates an encounter he had in 1200 AH with a Sufi who came to Yemen from Tunis; al-Shawkānī admires this Sufi for his exceptional skill in the subjects of *ḥurūf* and *awfāq*,[146] and indicates that he studied these subjects with him although, he adds, he did so for the purpose of experimenting and not because he believed in their validity.[147] Yet if al-Shawkānī is reserved in expressing enthusiasm for these subjects, he is less reserved in reporting his formal initiation into Sufism. In one instance, he refers to a certain ʿAbd al-Wahhāb al-Mawṣilī, who was his shaykh in asceticism (*zuhd*).[148] Mawṣilī, who combined diverse kinds of knowledge, came to Sanaa in 1234 AH, and al-Shawkānī reports that he had frequent contacts with him and learned from him (*talaqqaytu*) the prayer litanies (*dhikr*) of the Naqshbandī order.[149]

Throughout his positive references to *taṣawwuf* (Sufism), al-Shawkānī tends to use the words *zuhd* and *zāhid* (ascetic) rather than "Sufism" and "Sufi"; yet this use of words does not change the fact that he often praised Sufis and condoned their practice.[150] On some occasions he would even combine the use of the two terms as in his frequent use of such formulas as "He devoted himself to the matters of the soul"; "He was the ascetic and austere man of his time"; "He practiced Sufism while fulfilling the requirements of the divine law and following the example of the Messenger of God"; and that certain individuals are granted the power to perform *karāmāt* and are said to have *mukāshafāt*.[151] In contrast to the Wahhabi position, al-Shawkānī even asserts the permissibility of seeking the intercession (*tawassul*) of the Prophet as long as the person who does it believes that it is God who ultimately grants or denies a person's request.[152] Al-Shawkānī also composed many works in which he discusses Sufism in a positive light. One such treatise, *Baḥth fī Wujūb Maḥabbat Allāh* (A study on the obligation of loving God),[153] is a simple discussion of a central theme of Sufism, although without much depth or elaboration. Another such work, *Baḥth fī al-Istidlāl ʿalā Thubūt Karāmāt al-Awliyāʾ* (A study seeking evidence that confirms the miracles of saints),[154] asserts that there is no doubt regarding the ability of some pious individuals whom God has privileged with certain powers to perform supernatural acts (*karāmāt*).[155] Interestingly, to provide such evidence, al-Shawkānī refers his skeptical readers to the standard Sufi biographical works compiled by trustworthy scholars. Thus al-Shawkānī not only recognizes the possibility of supernatural powers, and the principle of *karāma*, so central to Sufi claims to authority, but he also recognizes the cultural authority of the reports of Sufi classics. He states in no ambiguous terms that a saint (*walī*) is "qualified for things of which human nature is incapable."[156] In a similar reference, al-Shawkānī approvingly quotes the controversial Sufi Abū Yazīd al-Busṭāmī to support his own condemnation of the attribution of God's exclusive powers to human beings.[157]

Al-Shawkānī wrote one of his major books on the subject of *wilāya* (sainthood).[158] In this book he quotes Ibn Taymiyya, whose ambiguous attitude toward Sufism has already been noted by several scholars.[159] The book was occasioned by the elaborate discussions of the meaning of a sound hadith in which the Prophet reports that

> God, may He be glorified and exalted said, "Whoever makes an enemy of one of my saints [*awliyāʾ*], I hereby declare war on him. Of the acts that bring My servants closer to Me, there is nothing that I like more than what I have required of them. A servant of Mine would persist in approaching Me by performing supererogatory acts until I love him; once I love him I become the hearing through which he hears, the vision through which he sees, the hand through which he strikes, and the leg through which he walks; if he asks Me I give him, and if he seeks refuge in Me I provide it to him; I never hesitate to do anything more than My hesitation in seizing the soul of a believer who hates to die and whom I hate to harm."[160]

Ascribing a high and exclusive rank to saints, al-Shawkānī asserts that although they are different from prophets in that they are not infallible, they do occupy such a unique and elevated rank that it is rare that they do things which oppose the truth and contradict it, and even if this happens, it does not exclude them from the state of being *awliyāʾ*.[161] To be sure, al-Shawkānī holds these saints to the same standards applicable to all Muslims, and adds that they cannot automatically assume that all the inspirations (*mukāshafāt*) they experience are blessings (*karāmāt*) from God, since these may be delusions from Satan. Instead, a *walī* should compare what he experiences with the injunctions of the Book and the Sunna, and only if they are in agreement should he conclude that what he experienced is true and a *karāma* from God. In other words, the *walī* should also subject his gnosticism to the standards of the divine law.[162] In contrast, no one can deny the inspirations (*mukāshafāt*) of saints because this is a gate, which the Prophet has opened for them, as is reported in the two sound collections of hadith.[163] Thus, according to al-Shawkānī, it is not impossible that one who achieves such a high rank of piety is capable of performing supernatural acts, and it is wrong to deny such acts as crossing long distances in short times, knowing hidden things, and doing things that most human powers are incapable of doing. The *karāmāt* of such people are simply God's response to their prayers, and the ultimate supernatural act thus comes from God. In further confirmation of the possibility of supernatural powers, al-Shawkānī maintains that one can only deny that which the law has denied, and that only if one claims to do something that contradicts the law should he be refuted.[164]

To be sure, al-Shawkānī's notion of *wilāya* is tempered and relatively demystified. In addition to his attribution of the ultimate source of supernatural power to God, he also asserts that the best of all saints are the Companions,[165] and that the path to sainthood is that of the practicing scholars and *mujtahids*, *ijtihād* being central to their achievement of this rank.[166] Yet tempered as this concept of sainthood may be, it illustrates in no uncertain terms that al-Shawkānī did not hold an irreversible grudge against Sufis, and that he was willing to recognize their positive traits. In practical terms, he also recognized that Sufism meant different things to different people; thus, in a reference to a Sufi named Ismāʾīl Ibn Ibrāhīm Ibn ʿAbd al-Ṣamad (d. 806 AH), al-Shawkānī states, "His home was a refuge for the people of devotion, indolence, and the needy. The people of devotion would go to him for supplication and prayer; the people of indolence would go for music and entertainment; and the needy would go to him on account of his reputation."[167] Significantly, al-Shawkānī adds, the people who were motivated by devotion would study the works of Ibn al-ʿArabī. Elsewhere al-Shawkānī maintains that, initially, the name *Sufi* was given to people who were extremely pious, followed the guidance of the purified law, and were not deluded by the allure of this world. Later, however, some people made Sufism a way of securing worldly gains, and a pretext for undermining the law and justifying perversion.[168]

In a clear recognition of this variation within the field of Sufism, al-Shawkānī makes an interesting distinction between the lawful acts of the pious Sufis who have no other desire but to purify themselves and the Sufi philosophers (*mutaṣawwifat al falāsifa*) who combine their suspect Sufi views with the opinions of philosophers that are opposed to Islam. When Sufis acquire some knowledge of philosophy, al-Shawkānī asserts,

> they start barking and call this [state] *ḥāl* [a state of mystical intoxication] although, on close examination, it is really an obstacle [*ḥāʾil*] in the way of religion, and the delusion of one who deviates from the path of the Muslims. Against such people I have composed a treatise titled *Al-Ṣawārim al-Ḥidād* [*fī al-Radd ʿalā Ahl al-Ittiḥād al-Qāʾilīn bi-Waḥdat al-Wūjūd*] [The sharp swords in responding to the people of unification who believe in the oneness of being]. This is one of the works that I compiled during

> the days of minority and early youth. After all of what I said [in that treatise, I maintain that] I am not unaware that among the men of this group called Sufis there are some who were enabled by God to combine the adherence to the purified law and to follow the path of Muhammad and the Islamic way, and who, through inward purification . . . achieved a state that many others are inferior to and are incapable of achieving. Yet in this book I take up the task of guiding people to adhere to the Book and the Sunna and discourage them from everything else no matter what it may be. Because of this I would not want a person who seeks to draw closer to God . . . to do so by means outside the two [sources, the Book and the Sunna], be it exercise or self-exertion or observance, or to adopt from the master of some Sufi order some of the conventions which, according to their beliefs, lead to God.[169]

True righteousness, al-Shawkānī asserts, is in accordance with what is laid down in the Qurʾān and the Sunna, and there can be no asceticism in a person who does not follow the Prophet's guidance. One who seeks to obey God in a manner different from what He has decreed for His servants and accepted for them may fall into the category of the Khawārij, who lost while thinking they were the victors.[170] Many Sufis, al-Shawkānī concedes, have good intentions, follow righteous paths, and are capable of remarkable discipline through which they purify their souls from the hidden idols of envy, pride, self-conceit, and hypocrisy.[171] Despite these traits, most Sufis breach the rules of conduct that are sanctioned by the law, a law that is more than sufficient for the achievement of their desired purity. Overstating something does not make it a religious act of obedience. Rather, "pure, complete, blessed, and beneficial acts of obedience [are so designated] simply on account of their agreement with the law and their adherence to the Muhammadan path [*al-ṭarīqa al-Muḥammadiyya*]."[172] Thus after suggesting that his earlier writings on Sufism were rash and impulsive, and after conceding that Sufism is diverse and variant, al-Shawkānī still insists that the surest way of worshiping God and satisfying Him is through the outward adherence to the Qurʾān and the Sunna. It is also not coincidental that al-Shawkānī expresses this view in his pedagogical work *Adab al-Ṭalab,* which addresses a broad audience and aims at outlining the basic requirements for various levels of education. At this basic instructional level, al-Shawkānī had many misgivings about Sufism, but his criticism was deliberately tempered by the recognition of the possibility of superior Sufi piety, and the distinction between the condemnation of acts and that of individuals who commit them. As such, this criticism could be used as a guideline for action, but it cannot be used to issue blanket assessments of individuals.

The view that Sufism is potentially a higher kind of piety but is susceptible to corruption comes after an identification of the partisans of schools and the people who participate in the cult of shrines (*qubūriyyūn*) as the two other problematic groups that undermine, in al-Shawkānī's view, proper adherence to Islam. In this taxonomy of social disorder, al-Shawkānī presents the Sufis as a third group distinct from the tomb cultists, thereby distinguishing between lay practices and the elaborate doctrines of mystics.[173] He further asserts that, problematic as the Sufis may be in his view, their harm is far less than that of the first two groups, both in terms of the content of their views and the scope and extent of this harm. Al-Shawkānī therefore distinguishes between the less harmful, and even possibly worthy, forms of Sufism and the definite harm caused by the people who practice the cult of tomb veneration (*qubūriyyūn*). Despite significant differences in details, al-Shawkānī's criticism of certain aspects of Sufi thought and practice was triggered by a fundamental concern shared with other eighteenth-century reformers, including the Sufis. All of these reformers were keen on identifying and undermining tendencies within the diverse legacies of the Islamic intellectual traditions, as well as the social formations associated with these legacies, that would compromise the unity of Muslims. The main culprit in this process is partisanship, which is itself based on unwarranted claims to absolute, divine-like authority. Thus al-Shawkānī argues that, historically speaking, the veneration of dead people was preceded by the creation of schools of law and a blind adherence to school doctrine that "eroded the vitality of Islam."[174] In al-Shawkānī's view, therefore, although partisanship to schools of law (*tamadhhub*) is less grave in its outward manifestations than the more serious innovation of tomb worship, the two are essentially consequences of imitation and are thus of similar natures. The affinity of the two kinds of error is illustrated in the common reference by imitators to their "imam in the school of law . . . and their shaykh in belief in and love [of God]." This, al-Shawkānī adds, is a further degeneration from earlier forms of imitation in which people would just refer to opinions of scholars without also invoking them after they die. In contrast to later imitation, the earlier imitators do not derive their religion in the manner commanded by God, but neither do they compromise their belief in the unity of God by relying on the intermediary authority of living or dead humans.[175] Al-Shawkānī provides vivid depictions of ways the belief in the oneness of God is compromised in practice: for example, the construction of large shrines for Sufi saints instills a sense of awe that gradually develops into belief in the powers of the shrines themselves or of the saints buried in them.[176]

Al-Shawkānī's unrelenting search for historical and social explanations for religious disorder characterizes his criticism of the cult of tombs and related practices. For example, he argues that the extravagant decoration of mosques is prohibited despite the fact that no such prohibition was voiced in the traditions of the early generations (*salaf*). This is because the building of such mosques is a late innovation that did not exist in the days of the early generations of Muslims and had been introduced along with innumerable other innovations by tyrannical states. These innovations were often introduced without eliciting the condemnation of scholars, either because they were afraid to do so or because they were reduced to servile justification of all the deeds of corrupt kings and rulers.[177] Al-Shawkānī is more virulent when it comes to the construction of shrines, the building of domes and mosques at tombs, and other similar heretical practices prevalent in the Muslim world. Although he argues that the visiting of tombs itself is a legal act,[178] he asserts that much of what goes on in these tombs is tantamount to manifest association not different from the practices of the Arabs before the coming of Islam. Numerous vices for which "Islam weeps" had resulted from the building of shrines, including the belief, similar to that of idol worshippers, that these shrines have power and are capable of bringing about benefit and averting harm; these shrines have thus become pilgrimage sites and people pray to them as they do to God. In fact, al-Shawkānī adds, the belief of some people in the shrine and the person buried in it is often more vivid than their belief in God. And yet, despite all of these "ugly abominations and outrageous beliefs," and the fact that there can be no graver calamity than the disaster of clear unbelief, no anger is stirred among Muslim scholars and rulers, and no one steps up to defend Islam and Muslims.[179]

Despite this seemingly unwavering condemnation of the practice of building shrines, al-Shawkānī seems to concede, albeit indirectly, that the practice itself is not without grounds. Concurring with the opinion of Ibn Ḥanbal and some of the Companions of Mālik and Shāfiʿī, al-Shawkānī maintains that it is only permissible to slightly elevate a tomb, irrespective of the social background of the person buried in it.[180] Al-Shawkānī rejects the view of the Zaydi imam Yaḥyā, as well as al-Mahdī in his legal work *al-Ghayth*, that the building of large tombs is not forbidden because this has been an ongoing practice for generations and has not been denounced by anyone.[181] In response to this view al-Shawkānī argues that silence does not constitute evidence in presumptive matters (*ẓanniyyāt*), and the prohibition against raising tombs is one such matter. It then follows that, being presumptive, the ruling over this matter is not final; and although he opts for the prohibition, the permission is not completely void of legal sanction. The objective of al-Shawkānī's argument, therefore, is to advocate his particular interpretation of the hadith, which attributes to the Prophet the statement that he would level all elevated tombs (*wa lā qabran mushrifan illā sawwaytahu*) as a prohibition against the construction of such tombs. This, in turn, is an argument against the universal permissibility of the construction of elevated tombs and not an attempt to enforce a universal prohibition of this practice.

Al-Shawkānī's discourse on Sufism and the cult of tombs thus fluctuates between two modes. On the one hand, he criticizes the excesses of Sufism, and, on the other, he defends the legitimacy of some fundamental Sufi concepts and practices. In reference to *tawassul* (praying to God through the intercession of some other person), al-Shawkānī argues that this practice was established through the silent consensus of the Companions of the Prophet, who did not object when the caliph ʿUmar prayed to God by invoking another Companion, al-ʿAbbās.[182] Al-Shawkānī adds that the permissibility of *tawassul* through people other than the Prophet is corroborated not just by this silent consensus but also because the invocation of learned men and scholars is in reality an invocation of the good deeds and excellence that distinguishes them. This, he maintains, proves that mediation between humans and God is not just through the Prophet but also through Muslims of established religious credentials. Al-Shawkānī then takes issue with those critics of Sufism who deny any kind of intercession. Such critics, he argues, use verses of the Qurʾān out of context to support their view that intercession is prohibited. In contrast to the Qurʾānic prohibition against worshipping certain people or objects as a way of worshipping God, the invoked scholars and pious Muslims are not themselves the object of worship, and their help is solicited only on account of their knowledge, good deeds, and piety. Furthermore, according to al-Shawkānī, the Qurʾānic verses only state that the ultimate agency belongs exclusively to God, whereas one who invokes prophets or scholars does not necessarily believe that they share this power with God. Al-Shawkānī also responds to those who deny intercession on the basis of the Qurʾānic assertions that none but God has the power to dispense benefit or ward off harm even to oneself, let alone to others.[183] These verses, he maintains, contain no prohibition against invoking either the Prophet Muhammad, other prophets, or other saints or scholars (*awliyāʾ*). In fact, al-Shawkānī adds, textual evidence explicitly states that God has privileged Muhammad by making him the greatest intercessor, and that people in general have been encouraged to seek his intercession.

Having established the validity of the concept of intercession and invocation, al-Shawkānī maintains that the problem is not in the concept but in the identification of the proper objects of these invocations. All too often, commoners and elites alike solicit the help of dead or living pious people to do things that only God is capable of doing. These figures are glorified to the extent of submitting humbly to them and praying to them alongside, or even to the exclusion of, God. Al-Shawkānī asserts that if this kind of action does not amount to association, then nothing would ever count as unbelief.[184] The use of charms and amulets is subsumed under these acts of unbelief because it is accompanied with the conviction that it is within the power of these objects to cure the ill or turn hate into love.[185] Yet even in his condemnation of such acts as the offering of sacrifice to individuals or objects other than God, al-Shawkānī seems to allow for graver forms of "utter association." The offering of such a sacrifice, he maintains, is forbidden because of the presumption that it may entail the glorification (*maẓinnat taʿẓīm*) of the object to which it is offered, while such glorification ought to be exclusively reserved for God.[186] Al-Shawkānī therefore objects to those who assign some of God's exclusive powers to living or dead humans, and who submit to and glorify them. These, however, are forbidden acts but are not necessarily identical with "pure association," in which the created is equated with, or even preferred to, the creator.[187] Acts such as the building of mosques on the tombs of saints and the excessive ornamentation of tombs are, in al-Shawkānī's view, forbidden; this prohibition, however, is not because these acts automatically constitute *shirk* but because they may facilitate it. As such, the prohibition aims to eliminate factors that may occasion the glorification of humans or objects and related corrupt beliefs.[188]

Al-Shawkānī thus classifies certain acts as metaphoric acts of association that are distinct from pure association but may lead to it. These include, in addition to the ones listed above, the practice and belief in soothsaying and magic,[189] as well as hypocrisy and the performance of acts of worship for no other reason than being seen and recognized.[190] Al-Shawkānī also surveys the modes of speech that ought to be avoided in order not to slip into association.[191] Clearly, however, these acts and speech acts are different from, and do not entail the same legal consequences as, the belief in deities besides God. These acts of metaphoric association evoke a whole range of condemnations, from moral censure to various levels of penalties. However, al-Shawkānī leaves no doubt that his unequivocal prohibitions and the penalties that he advocates for committing such prohibited acts are meant to remove the pretexts for association (*qaṭʿ dhrāʾiʿ al-shirk*) and to undermine all that may lead to it.[192] Underlying al-Shawkānī's seemingly strong condemnations and prohibitions is consistent shading that never fails to recognize the different levels of transgression, as well as the fundamental difference between the theoretical condemnation of certain acts and the legal enforcement of penalties against individuals who commit them.[193] This nuanced discourse distinguishes al-Shawkānī's sustained criticism of extreme Sufi actions and beliefs from the Wahhabi discourse that is replete with blanket and undifferentiated charges of unbelief.[194] Once again, al-Shawkānī asserts that "if all that a Muslim does is a simple invocation [of a living or dead Muslim], then it is permissible"; only when this invocation is accompanied by the belief that a dead person has supernatural powers, and by manifest acts of worship that can only result from such a belief, does it become an act of association.[195]

To be sure, al-Shawkānī rejects the argument that differentiates between the unbelievers of pre-Islamic times and the Muslims who believe in tombs on the grounds that the latter think of themselves as Muslims and would rather die than admit they worship anything else, whereas the former believe in certain deities and have no such belief in God.[196] This distinction, al-Shawkānī maintains, is not good enough, since one can be an apostate without being fully conscious of this apostasy. Still, in such cases, the suspected unbeliever ought to be informed of the scriptural evidence on the basis of which his acts are classified as acts of unbelief. "Once [this transgressor] becomes aware of his [transgression] in a manner that leaves no doubt or ambiguity [*ʿilman lā yabqā maʿahu shakkun wa lā shubuha*]," and after further informing him that the insistence on this behavior would subject him to serious penalties, including the violation of his blood and wealth, then, and only then, should the legal penalties for apostasy be enforced.[197]

The imposition of penalties against common Muslims who engage in acts that, in al-Shawkānī's view, may lead to grave forms of unbelief was thus subjected, in practice, to elaborate procedural constraints. In contrast to the Wahhabis, who would issue a general demand of compliance with set norms of belief and conduct and then collectively punish whole regions that fail to comply, al-Shawkānī institutes a complex set of procedures that requires informing and warning, as well as verification in the case of each individual Muslim, before any legal action can even be contemplated. In a sense, therefore, al-Shawkānī introduced elaborate mechanisms to ensure that the theoretical debate over *shirk* does not translate into an inquisition of sorts. When writing on disbelief and association, al-Shawkānī was negotiating, as it were, volatile frontiers. He was fully cognizant of the ideological and physical threat that the Wahhabis posed, in the name of "proper" belief, to their Yemeni neighbors. He also had a genuine interest in undermining practices that may compromise the social unity of Muslims, a unity cemented, in his view, by common religious practices and beliefs. Yet his resolute discourse was always carefully articulated to allow for subtle distinctions and nuances. Thus, unlike Ibn ʿAbd al-Wahhāb, al-Shawkānī always allowed for a positive interpretation of the very practices he wished to undermine, and in so doing, he avoided the grave pitfall of accusing the majority of Muslims of unbelief. In fact, al-Shawkānī even asserts that most of those who in practice commit acts of unbelief do so out of the commendable intention of venerating the prophets and saints. Such people, al-Shawkānī adds, would readily desist from their actions if their errors were pointed out to them. If the source of error inheres in the sayings of some dead Sufi, then all that needs to be done is to point out what is problematic about these sayings, without further need to slander the Sufi who said these things.[198] Again, al-Shawkānī's ultimate objective is to redeem living Muslims and not to malign them or the dead Muslims they venerate.

It is in the interest of Muslims, therefore, and not against them that al-Shawkānī targets practices associated with the cult of tombs. Furthermore, because of this concern for the collective interest of Muslims, al-Shawkānī's dogmatic expositions are invariably grounded in social and historical analysis. In fact, al-Shawkānī maintains that dogmatic blunders are prevalent not because of any ambiguity in the essential creed of Islam but mainly because of the powerful tendency among people to conform to common social practice. Thus Muslims grow up seeing the cult of tombs everywhere around them, and they see many corrupt scholars make a living from this cult rather than denounce it; these Muslims are thus led to believe that this is a legitimate act of worship. So while he does not sanction this cult, al-Shawkānī clearly understands its causes, and this understanding affects the way he attempts to curtail it. Most Muslims who engage in this practice, according to al-Shawkānī, do not do so because of some inherent evil tendencies they have, but out of a genuine, though misguided, desire to worship God. These inherently good Muslims are driven to such acts by social and historical factors for which they are not totally responsible. Left to their own devices, ordinary Muslims would be able to differentiate between permissible and prohibited forms of Sufi practice. The solution to the problem of tomb worship thus lies not in a Wahhabi crusade but in removing the historically specific impediments that prevent ordinary Muslims from directly engaging the scripture. *Taqlīd*, therefore, is the source of all problems, and in this respect there is little difference between the worshippers of saints and the followers of schools who treat these schools as if they are independent religions, and who treat the imams of these schools as if they were infallible prophets.[199]

Taqlīd and the Culture of Experts

Underlying the various critiques by eighteenth-century reformers of extreme Sufi practices and Sufi claims to intercession, as well as school partisanship and the corporate authority of *madhhab*s, is a fundamental rejection of the exclusive agency of intermediaries. The final responsibility for violating the law is always individual, but so is the authority to pronounce final judgment on the meaning of the scripture. Despite frequent emphasis on the role of scholars, no distinguished figures within any particular intellectual trend is accorded exclusive authority, nor is any one discipline held superior to the others. Furthermore, no person or school holds absolute intellectual authority over the masses of Muslims. Hadith, as we will see, was no doubt the favored discipline, but its value was primarily a function of its accessibility to ordinary Muslims and the impossibility of professionalizing or monopolizing the knowledge that derives from it. Eighteenth-century intellectuals had very strong views about many issues, and their discussions were animated and assertive; yet the veracity of whatever views they held was always subject to the final assessment of their audiences, the Muslims who always retained the right to think and choose for themselves. It is particularly significant that on several occasions, eighteenth-century reformers voiced strong and unqualified opposition to some of the Islamic disciplines of learning but then concluded that, to avoid imitation, readers ought to learn about these disciplines and decide for themselves whether the negative assessment is warranted.

Such was, for example, al-Shawkānī's view of the discipline of *kalām* (speculative theology). In view of its subject matter that treats issues of dogma and creed, no kind of expertise could be used to claim more intellectual and even political authority than the discipline of *kalām*. As such, al-Shawkānī's rejection of this field was part of his larger reservation with respect to elitist claims to authority. In addition, however, this rejection of *kalām* stems from an earlier tradition of criticizing theology that prevailed among the traditionalist scholars of Zaydi Yemen, starting with Ibn al-Wazīr. Historically, Zaydis in general were strong advocates of the Muʿtazilī school of theology.[200] In contrast, the traditionalists, starting with Ibn al-Wazīr and on to al-Ṣanʿānī and al-Shawkānī, were opposed to theology, although this opposition was not restricted to the Muʿtazilī school but applied equally to the more orthodox Ashʿarī school.[201] Following the example of the early pious generations of Muslims, al-Shawkānī maintains, one should not waste effort on useless subjects such as *kalām*. This subject, he adds, was introduced after the formative period, whereas the Companions of the Prophet abided by what was reported in the Qur'ān and the Sunna regarding God's attributes and related questions of theology. Al-Shawkānī further asserts that most religious knowledge derives from transmitted evidence, in contrast to the minimal amount of knowledge that derives from rational speculation. As such, the views of the various theological schools that are not grounded in the scripture, and which suffer the added defect of being based on thin rational evidence, are useless and misguided.[202] Yet despite his dislike of *kalām*, al-Shawkānī urges his students to study it and to familiarize themselves with the theology of the Ashʿarīs, Muʿtazila, Māturīdīs, and the Zaydis. He then warns the student not to be discouraged by the frequent criticisms by scholars of *kalām* and their assertions that it has little or no value; one who follows such advice without studying *kalām* himself, al-Shawkānī asserts, would be an imitator, which is especially inappropriate for one who wants to acquire the tools for *ijtihād*. Instead, one should have a sound grasp of the discipline of *kalām* and then formulate his own views about it on the basis of his knowledge.[203]

Al-Shawkānī's view that one should not censor knowledge out of ignorance, and that knowledge of all fields is potentially useful, applies to a variety of disciplines in addition to *kalām*. He argues that a person who has a solid grounding in the religious disciplines can benefit from the acquisition of a share of knowledge in other disciplines that sharpen the mind, develop the intellectual faculties, and add to the happiness of the heart and the openness of the soul. These kinds of knowledge, according to al-Shawkānī, include such disciplines as the mathematical and physical sciences, geometry, astronomy, and medicine. "In general," he adds, "knowledge of every science is far superior to ignorance of it, especially for one who devotes himself to [achieving] the highest rank and the noblest status [of *ijtihād*]."[204] Al-Shawkānī advises his reader to pay no heed to the disparaging remarks of the critics of such fields, because blind rejection is a kind of imitation, which is worse than any potential harm that may derive from these disciplines. He then addresses his reader:

> After you acquire knowledge of any of these sciences, you judge it on the basis of what knowledge you have; you choose for yourself what you prefer without being compelled. There is no fear for one who is steadfast in the religious disciplines; there is only fear for one who is not grounded in the sciences of the Book and the Sunna, for he can be shaken and his confidence may be altered. So if you start by studying the religious science we mentioned, then you can pursue whatever else you desire, add as many disciplines as you wish, and investigate as many details as you can. . . . I really marvel at one who claims to be fair and to love knowledge and at the same time allows his tongue to go on slandering a certain science that he neither knows nor is aware of, whose subject, objective, and benefit he does not know, and of which he cannot perceive in any shape or form. We have seen many a contemporary who pursues scholarship, is fair in legal matters, and who adheres to indicants. Yet if he hears a question in an art that he does not master, such as the disciplines of logic, *kalām*, astronomy, or the like, he has a natural aversion to it and tries to turn people away from it; this while he does not know what that question is, nor does he comprehend it or understand any part of it. It would be more appropriate for such a person to remain silent and confess his inadequate [knowledge] . . . by simply saying, "I do not know." If he must say something either in praise or criticism . . . then he should first start with studying this art until he truly knows it, and then he can say what he wishes.

> . . . Indeed, we have found that many disciplines that are not part of the religious sciences have great benefit and noble utility in refuting falsifiers, those who adhere exclusively to mere opinion, and those who do not comply with indicants.[205]

Elsewhere, al-Shawkānī even defends the study of the philosophical sciences that he was strongly opposed to, since this knowledge in itself does not contradict the religious sciences; rather it makes the jurist who is rooted in the religious sciences more content and happy with his knowledge of the law.[206]

Al-Shawkānī was careful to inform his reader that he did not advocate the views of theologians, and that he found them at fault. Yet, opposed as he was to these views, his rejection of imitation was the overriding principle that led him to sanction the study of *kalām* against critics who blindly accuse those who study it of innovation and heresy without the slightest idea of where they stand and what use they make of this knowledge.[207] This position of al-Shawkānī is different from that of Shāh Walī Allāh, who tried to reconcile the various disciplines on the grounds that elements of truth exist in each. In contrast, al-Shawkānī defended all knowledge on the grounds that the alternative would be ignorance, which rules out the possibility of any informed, independent choice. Ultimately, the choice he advocated was not the partial acceptance of *kalām* but, in effect, its rejection. However, only a person who knows *kalām* is in a position to pass a negative judgment on the theoretical and practical values of this discipline. To be sure, there can be no guarantee that someone who studies *kalām* will conclude that it is a useless discipline. Moreover, al-Shawkānī's sharp criticism could have easily been construed as a blanket condemnation of not just the conclusions of *kalām* but also of the attempts to study it. In fact, in any grand intellectual undertaking such as al-Shawkānī's, it is inevitable that there would be internal contradictions and inconsistencies. This is especially true because of the multiplicity of fundamental principles that he championed. Yet of these, one principle would override every other one in cases of conflict, namely, that every Muslim has to exercise the right and duty of *ijtihād*, and that this can only be done on the basis of knowledge and choice. It is in fact on these very grounds that al-Shawkānī opposes *kalām*, because it further concentrates intellectual authority in the hands of the professional elite. In addition to being a cause of division among Muslims, *kalām* adds political and dogmatic authority to the authority of jurists who claim a monopoly over the right to interpret the scripture and to derive the law from it. On account of its complexity, it also makes the direct understanding of the alleged essentials of religion more obscure and inaccessible to ordinary Muslims. In a sense, therefore, al-Shawkānī's defense of the right to pursue all kinds of knowledge, as well as his informed rejection of certain disciplines, are equally triggered by his rejection of elitism and the profundity (*taʿammuq*) prevalent in all varieties of the culture of experts: legal, spiritual, or theological.

Despite the real differences in their assessment of the various disciplines of learning, eighteenth-century thinkers invariably applied the criterion of antielitism to evaluate the various disciplines both on epistemological grounds and as social practices. This shared antielitism was always coupled with a high regard for scholars and scholarship, an attitude manifested by the these scholars' grand intellectual output. Clearly, therefore, these reformers were not anti-intellectual, but they simply opposed intellectual undertakings closed to the larger Muslim community and used to foster the interests of the select few. Intellectual excellence was no doubt a value to uphold, but it was never considered in isolation from other social considerations and values. Knowledge was not just a means for personal transformation, and its correctness was always discussed in terms of its relation to other members of society. Invariably, the reformers of the eighteenth century maintained a balance between care for the self and the collective responsibility of intellectuals and their situation within society.[208] Although they did deny the unique status of accomplished scholars like themselves, the discussion of *ijtihād* and concurrent rejection of *taqlīd* by these very scholars were in fact expressions of their commitment to the notion that all Muslims are equally predisposed, if they invest the effort, to partake in the knowledge of the elite. This is even true of Walī Allāh, who, despite his argument that not all Muslims are equal in their intellectual abilities, devoted most of his efforts to undermining the basis of exclusive claims to intellectual authority and to making the tools of intellectual participation available to large sectors of Muslims. In their different ways, therefore, the reformers of the eighteenth century were advocates of a democratic notion of knowledge without compromising the quality of this knowledge; they were antielitist without being anti-intellectual.

Being prolific scholars, it was not always possible for eighteenth-century reformers to overcome a sense of intellectual distinction from ordinary Muslims. Not only did many think of themselves as members of the elite community of scholars that, according to a widely circulated hadith, inherit the role and social function of prophets, but they often even thought they were the unmatched leaders of this scholarly community. This certainly was the view of Shāh Walī Allāh, who repeatedly asserted that he was the *mujaddid* (renewer) of his time, and that his mission to revive Islam was inspired by God. Despite this intellectual self-aggrandizement, however, and despite the fact he often grounded his own intellectual authority in privileged forms of knowledge, Walī Allāh's antielitism was real and underscores his whole intellectual project. Walī Allāh's world emerges as one in which the political and the social are separated. This separation, however, is meant not to serve the interests of the political but to provide alternatives to it. The scholars who inherit the role of prophets must not be deterred by the corrupting effects of politics,[209] and if they fail in their endeavor, it is the thought that informs their actions and guides them and the community through them which requires reform.[210] In opposition to the philosophers, Walī Allāh argues that the political imam is not necessarily a real individual but a symbol of the indispensable unity of the community.[211] Moreover, the central role of the ulema may not be restricted to a special elite but should be open to the participation of the community at large.[212] Such participation ensures a program for intellectual as well as social revival, and it is this dialectic between the intellectual and the social that characterizes Walī Allāh's thought.

For the many ills of society, Walī Allāh singles out several sources that he specifies directly in his writings or implicates through the issues he discusses. Disunity is a central theme that occupied him throughout his life.[213] He wrote extensively on differences of opinion within jurisprudence,[214] Sufism,[215] traditionalist hadith scholarship,[216] and among all of these.[217] Although he was concerned with political division and disintegration, the solutions he prescribed were to be found outside the immediate realm of politics. He believed that political authority is important for practical purposes, but what ultimately counts is society. While the outward caliphate (*khilāfat al-ẓāhir*) is in charge of implementing superficial order, the inward one (*khilāfat al-bāṭin*) is responsible for social order in all its details.[218] The guardians of the inward order are the scholars (ulema), and it is their duty to ensure that daily life is conducted in harmony with God's created nature (*fiṭra*).[219] Political corruption is but an outcome of the scholars' neglect in performing their duties properly.[220] Extreme intellectualism or "profundity [*taʿammuq*],"[221] strictness,[222] false consensus,[223] opportunism,[224] and claiming a monopoly on truth[225] are some aspects of this neglect.

The primacy of social revival led Walī Allāh to denounce extreme intellectualism (*taʿammuq*), which he maintains is not obligated by the law,[226] and which he considers to be one of the causes of disagreement and disunity.[227] The law, he maintains, is revealed in the language of common people, not the specialized language of the elite. As such, rather than using a convoluted technical language, jurists ought to articulate the reasons for the various rulings (*ʿilla*, pl. *ʿilal*) in a language ordinary Muslims can understand. To be sure, the reason provided by the jurist is chosen from several sources (*maẓanna*) that anticipate the real reasons for God's satisfaction or wrath.[228] In Walī Allāh's view, therefore, the same truth can be understood on unequal levels. However, in his discussion of the various levels on which the divine utterances can be understood,[229] Walī Allāh maintains that an utterance that requires highly specialized expert knowledge to decipher is not relevant for the derivation of the law (*lā iʿtibāra fīhi*).[230] In fact, Walī Allāh goes so far to assert that "one of the sublime purposes of the divine legislation is to block the gates of profundity in religious matters; so as not to have people holding firmly [to pious practices] who are then followed by others who think that these are among the obligatory heavenly acts of worship, and then yet another generation for whom the doubt becomes certainty. . . . As such, religion would continue to be distorted, as in His saying, may He be exalted: 'And a monasticism they invented which We have not prescribed for them' (Qurʾān, Ḥadīd 57:27)." Walī Allāh then adds, "For the sake of all of these meanings the Prophet asserted to his community that they should be provident in actions and not be excessive to the point that would lead to apathy and confusion in religion, or to the neglect of means for civilizational development."[231]

Of all the reformers of the eighteenth century, Walī Allāh had the grandest regard for his own intellectual undertaking. And yet he persisted in denying any use of knowledge as an exclusive privilege of an elite class. Walī Allāh's formidable attempt to reconcile the conflicts between the different facets of the Islamic intellectual legacy, and to forge a new synthesis of gnostic, inductive, and transmitted forms of knowledge, further illustrates the importance of the antielitist facets of his thought. His attempted intellectual reconciliation was conducted with an eye for the community, its power and well-being. Perhaps the greatest achievement of this intellectual synthesis was in its ability to argue, without being reductive or simplistic, for the community's right to wrench the use of the intellect from the exclusive monopoly of the professional zealots of Islam. Similarly, the manifest erudition of the Yemeni scholars al-Ṣanʿānī and al-Shawkānī did not affect their democratized conceptions of knowledge, and their insistence on the accessibility of knowledge to all ordinary Muslims without exception.

Publicly accessible knowledge was also central to Ibn Fūdī's reform of social disorder. It is through the spread of education that Muslims may recognize and apply the proper Islamic codes of social behavior. Well-educated and committed scholars recognized by Muslims are essential to this project. Ibn Fūdī sharply criticizes those ulema who seek prestige and power in their teaching and are interested only in increasing the number of their students while failing to teach members of their own households the basic tenets of Islam.[232] He is also critical of those scholars who neither study nor teach Arabic and instead dedicate their efforts to justifying the abuses of pagan rulers.[233] Ibn Fūdī evaluates scholarship in terms of its social functions and opposes the establishment of a class of elitist clerics who lack dedication to communal obligations. Ibn Fūdī's life itself was an example of his social commitment; he started his career as a traveling teacher; he also composed numerous works in the local Fulfulde language in a clear attempt to make Islamic education accessible to larger sectors of the community.[234]

Revisionist Histories and the Imperatives of Decline

Eighteenth-century thought teemed with reform projects that, despite significant variances among them, converged on several social and intellectual essentials that animated the reform discourses of this period. All of the reformers of the period were concerned with the question of social unity and the related problem of *takfīr*. They carefully negotiated the volatile relationship between the identification of reprehensible acts and the condemnation of individuals or groups who commit them. They were concerned, each in his separate way, with the problem of social apathy, and they tried to devise ways to increase the social and intellectual participation of ordinary Muslims in decision-making. This in turn led to the reconsideration of accepted notions of intellectual authority and to challenging the claims by corporate schools of law and Sufi saints to exclusive intermediary authority over Muslims. Public knowledge was a key element in all of the proposed reforms, and the right to choose on the basis of this knowledge was elevated by some eighteenth-century reformers into a religious obligation. Yet, all of these similarities notwithstanding, the sense of crisis that triggered the reform efforts of these thinkers was informed by assessments of regional problems afflicting the different areas in which these reformers functioned. Thus, for example, the perceptions of the division endangering Muslims were different in Yemen from what they were in India; in each case, division was perceived in terms peculiar to the specific histories of political and intellectual partisanship, and so were the proposed solutions for this problem of division. Perhaps the main factor that averted the projection of the regional perceptions of crises into one overarching crisis is the absence of a crisis of identity in the eighteenth century. Eighteenth-century reformers did not perceive of a threat to their Muslim identity and, as a result, did not revert to asserting this identity in their attempts to remedy what they thought were the problems of their time. This is notably different from the Islamic reforms of the modern period, starting in the latter part of the nineteenth century; these reforms, as well as other reactions, were primarily triggered by the real material and intellectual challenges to Islamic identity and existence in the colonial and postcolonial periods. In this sense, there is no continuity between the reforms of the eighteenth century and later reforms.

The differences between these two types of reform are not just over the perceived notions of crisis but extend to many other fronts. In particular, the reforms of the eighteenth century are characterized by an intellectual richness and originality notably missing in the later period. This richness remains largely unrecognized in modern scholarship on the eighteenth century. Instead, revisionist historians have underscored the continuity between the reforms of the eighteenth century and those of the modern period and, in some cases, have also noted the seeming modernity of the reforms of the eighteenth century, seeing in them the roots of modern fundamentalism. Yet even when this modernity is noted, most historians concur with traditional Orientalist scholarship on the intellectual impoverishment of the eighteenth century. In chapters that follow I will explore some aspects of the originality and richness of eighteenth-century Islamic thought. In chapter 1 I challenged the notion, prevalent in all historiography on the eighteenth century, that Wahhabism is representative of eighteenth-century Islamic thought. In the remainder of this chapter, I will revisit some other historiographical paradigms prevalent in traditional as well as revisionist studies of the eighteenth century.

In contrast to earlier studies that presented eighteenth-century Islamic thought and movements as reactionary responses to the onslaught of European modernity, recent studies attempting to revisit this period have searched for evidence for an eighteenth-century modernity that anticipates nineteenth-century Islamic reform as well as twentieth-century fundamentalism.[235] The argument for the continuity of the "fundamentalist tradition"[236] encompassing many eighteenth-century thinkers is founded on the assumption that, despite the diversity in their "organizational styles," the revivalist movements stretching from the mid-eighteenth century to the mid-nineteenth have produced a single, more or less homogeneous, body of thought that belongs to an identifiable "fundamentalist mode of Islam."[237] This mode, which traverses Islamic history, is defined in terms of such themes as the emphasis on abiding by the Qur'ān and the Sunna, return to origins, revival of *ijtihād* and hadith studies, rejection of innovation and imitation (*taqlīd*) in matters of law, and rejection of the excesses of Sufism.[238] More generally, these themes are said to assert transcendence, unity, and authenticity as opposed to immanence, diversity, and openness.[239] Along these same lines of argument, many studies of modern Islamic thought assert that the roots of modern Islamic revival originate in the eighteenth century. An intellectual link is postulated between Wahhabi puritanical ideas and later Islamic thought. Wahhabism, it is argued, continues to inspire a growing number of Muslims in their encounter with problems of the modern world.[240]

To be sure, there is nothing unusual about the tendency to transfer the valued aspects of history into a prologue to one's own presentness, or to search for the present in the past. Yet, as we have seen, such notions as *ijtihād*, the exercise of independent legal reasoning, were not new to the eighteenth century, let alone the nineteenth or twentieth. In fact, one of the most noticeable differences between the thought of the eighteenth century and later periods is that the writings on *ijtihād* in the eighteenth century, much like their medieval precursors, were abundant, complex, and systematic, whereas no comparable writings were produced by modern Muslim reformers like Muḥammad ʿAbdu or Rashīd Riḍā to accompany their call for the reopening of the allegedly closed gates of *ijtihād*. Similarly, the notion that the eighteenth century witnessed the emergence of neo-Sufism, the new kind of Sufism characterized by its subservience to legalistic Islam and void of its spirituality, is no longer tenable. The term *neo-Sufism*, first coined by Fazlur Rahman, seems to suggest a rationalistic rethinking of Islamic mysticism, again in the hope of finding signs for rationalist modernity in the eighteenth century. As we have seen, the eighteenth-century discussions of Sufism were manifold and span the whole range of views that existed from much earlier periods of Islamic history. Here too, the Wahhabi hostility to Sufism is an exception, even when compared with contemporary critical attitudes toward it.

The attempts to posit an uninterrupted tradition of reform and activism that starts in the eighteenth century and continues today fails to recognize that while late nineteenth and early twentieth-century Islamic thought is essentially a response to the European challenge, Europe was completely absent in the thought of all the great Muslim thinkers of the eighteenth century. Europe was not part of the eighteenth-century sense of anxiety. In contemporary Islamic political discourse, unity is conceived of as the needed ingredient to resist Western hegemony. In contrast, the dangers that the thinkers of the eighteenth century wanted to ward off were regional and internal, though the traditions they invoked were hybrid and not limited to any one region. The intellectual "outside" of the eighteenth century was not European but Islamic, and it was not threatening but redeeming. Issues of cultural displacement relevant to contemporary Muslims at their present historical remove were not pertinent to the reformers of the eighteenth century, for whom there was no question of identifying the self in relation to the European other. The Islamic eighteenth century was thus characterized by an intense regionalism coupled with a shared intellectual legacy that gave the various regional discourses a universal flavor. The interplay of these two forces produced diverse traditions that claimed universal Islamic authority despite their parochial origins.

For most eighteenth-century thinkers, the Islamic past was still a continuous reality, despite its many mutations, and it was within the framework of this hermetic past that these thinkers proceeded to propose their reforms. The great reformers of the eighteenth century were informed by Islamic history and not by the encounter with Europe. Instead, reformers addressed local issues and the familiar Islamic outside, both of which provided the context for eighteenth-century thought. The possibilities of articulating a response to this Islamic outside were different from later responses to non-Islamic Europe. Unlike later reformers who had a European blueprint for reform and simply put it in Islamic garb, for eighteenth-century reformers the Islamic past was still alive, a continuous past, and not the completed and closed chapter that was purged from the collective consciousness of Muslim elites and replaced with a newly constructed notion of the past.[241] Some of these reformers were aware of European infringements on Muslim lands. Walī Allāh lived during the period in which the East India Company extended its control over India. After spending many years in the Hejaz, al-Sanūsī was not able to return to his homeland in Algeria because of the French occupation. Yet neither Walī Allāh nor al-Sanūsī mention even the military dimension of this colonial penetration in any of their writings.[242] The only reformer who left written expressions of his awareness of the European expansive undertaking and its implications was al-Shawkānī, to whom we shall now turn.

Al-Shawkānī witnessed major changes on the international and regional political scene, and he was directly involved in dealing with the political ramifications of these changes. Of these, three events are of particular significance: the French occupation of Egypt (1798–1801); British attempts to gain a foothold in Yemen and to control Red Sea navigation; and the Wahhabi movement and the threat it represented to the independence of Yemen. Yet although he was aware of the political and military threats posed by European powers, al-Shawkānī did not perceive of Europe as an intellectual challenge to Islam. Moreover, al-Shawkānī's familiarity with both the Wahhabi doctrine and the political movement that championed it left only negative imprints on his thought.[243] An examination of al-Shawkānī's rich and diverse intellectual output suggests no evidence whatsoever for either a Wahhabi or European influence on his thought.

In his capacity as chief judge, al-Shawkānī was in charge, among other things, of the official correspondence between the imam and the rulers of other countries. His duties were not restricted to the drafting of letters but involved a real participation in the articulation of a foreign policy. Upon the French occupation of Egypt, the imam of Sanaa and al-Shawkānī exchanged numerous letters with the Ottoman governors of the neighboring Hejaz and other officials in an attempt to coordinate a defense policy in the face of the French incursion. These exchanges were initiated by the Ottomans, who urged their governors to prepare for a possible confrontation with the French armies. In one of the letters reproduced by al-Shawkānī, the sultan informed Sharif Ghālib of the Hejaz of the potential French threats to Red Sea navigation and the need to fortify the coastal cities of the Hejaz should such threats materialize.[244] Sharif Ghālib then wrote to the imam of Sanaa to urge similar preparations, and a correspondence between him and al-Shawkānī ensued. In these letters, al-Shawkānī speaks of the "enormous disaster, great calamity, and affliction for which the eyes of Islam and Muslims weep, [namely,] the takeover by a group of Franks, called the Farancīs, of all of the Egyptian lands, their arrival in Cairo, and their rule over the Muslims of these lands. This is a tribulation the like of which has not afflicted Islam before; for Egypt has always been in the hands of Muslims since it was conquered in the reign of ʿUmar, may God be pleased with him, and we have not found in any of the historical books any indication that a regime of unbelief ever entered the city of Egypt [Cairo]."[245]

Al-Shawkānī adds that the earlier Franks (Crusaders) did not go beyond Dimyāṭ, and that even the Mongols and the Tatars could not take Cairo. He thus declares that this is a "very serious incident that needs to be acknowledged and publicized."[246] Al-Shawkānī's knowledge of earlier and contemporary foreign infringements on Muslim lands is clearly derivative and has its sources in history books and secondhand accounts, and not in his firsthand experience. However, the universal character of his education compelled him to transcend his parochial political concerns and express solidarity with fellow Muslims. Yet his sense of the gravity of the situation derived from the simple fact that Cairo, which had previously resisted all foreign attacks, had now, for the first time, capitulated before the French. He thus felt it his responsibility to inform Yemeni Muslims of this pending threat to lands of Islam. Al-Shawkānī reproduces the Ottoman sultan's argument in his letter to Sharif Ghālib that the French initially targeted the nomads, the weakest point in the Muslim front, and then gradually spread to the rest of the Muslim society. The French scheme, according to this letter, was to take control of all Muslim lands and wealth, and to covert Muslims to French norms, rules, language, and religion (*uṣūl*, *qawāʿid*, *lisān*, and *dīn*).[247] As such, the French incursion threatened to undermine the foundations of Islam and its laws. This, then, was the basis of the Ottoman demand that the outposts of the Hejaz be fortified in the face of a possible French attack. This was also the basis for the request, voiced in the letter from the sharif of the Hejaz to the imam of Sanaa, to fortify the Yemeni port cities under the latter's control.[248] In this letter, Sharif Ghālib reports that French naval vessels had been sighted in the Red Sea and suggests that the reason for their military success was the apparent failure to fortify the frontiers.[249] Ghālib also blames the nomads who, out of their ignorance, were fooled by French claims that they had the blessings of the Ottoman sultan. The two themes highlighted in Ghālib's letter are the lack of military preparation and the nomads' ignorance. The notion of a French cultural penetration, suggested in the original letter from the sultan, is not echoed in the exchange between Ghālib and al-Shawkānī. In contrast to the Wahhabi problem, which is addressed by al-Shawkānī not just in his diplomatic exchanges but also in his other scholarly works, the French remain a distant military threat and evoke no response from al-Shawkānī at the intellectual level.[250] In fact, after the French withdrawal, al-Shawkānī reports that he was never in doubt of the outcome and was always confident that the Muslims would eventually rid themselves of this infringement on their lands.[251]

Al-Shawkānī, the one eighteenth-century reformer who was aware and wrote of the French threat, did not conceive of this threat in intellectual terms. Put differently, Europe did not represent an intellectual challenge to al-Shawkānī or any of the other reformers of this period. It is thus misleading to suggest, on the basis of his letters about the French, that al-Shawkānī's thought was an early Islamic response to the challenge of Europe. Another common distortion in modern scholarship on the eighteenth century is to represent it as a prelude to the revolutions of the 1960s, the post-Nasser, socialist military coups. For example, the authors of *Ibn al-Amīr wa ʿAṣruhu* provide anachronistic portrayals of Ibn al-Amīr al-Ṣanʿānī as one in a series of isolated rebels combating the corruption of the rulers of Yemen. The authors use such idioms as the "deterministic nature of a Yemeni revolution," in an attempt to construct a genealogy of nationalist struggles that roots the modern regime in the past of the nation. The result is a total distortion of history in the interest of this nationalist agenda. In a similar vein, al-Shawkānī is presented as one of the leaders of "the reform movement of the modern period that started in the Arabian Peninsula, and in particular in Yemen. . . . Thus Imām Shawkānī appeared in the last quarter of the eighteenth century AD, or the twelfth AH; he rebelled against rigidity and imitation, preached the principles of *ijtihād*, attacked tyranny, laxity, and negligence of religion and its values, and called for the need to unify the Arab and Muslim nation in the face of waves of colonial European invasions. Thereafter, this movement spread from Yemen to the countries of the East, then to Egypt, Syria, and the rest of the Islamic and Arab world."[252] This account lists Jamāl al-Dīn al-Afghānī, ʿAbd al-Raḥmān al-Kawākibī, and Muḥammad ʿAbdu as some of the later leaders of this same reform movement. To be sure, al-Shawkānī and al-Ṣanʿānī before him were critical of corruption and advocated notions of authority that undermined the basis of authority in the traditional Zaydi state. Yet the paradigms of modernity, revolution, and nationalism do not apply to these reformers or the thought world in which they operated.

Nationalist historiography at once implicates the past of corruption and decline and claims to be rooted in its exceptional moments of brilliance. This historiography has advanced the view that the great reformers of the eighteenth century were isolated islands of excellence in a sea of stagnation and decadence. Traditional Orientalist historiography concurs on the decadent nature of the eighteenth century. Such, for example, is the assertion that "Islamic intellectual culture in the eighteenth century . . . had fallen so far below even its own medieval standards, and appeared to be quite unconscious of the decline."[253] Both approaches view the eighteenth century as a much-detested historical moment, an exemplar of intellectual defeat that preceded defeat on the battlefield. These historical approaches, in which the lines are blurred between the detection of moments of regression and the grand assertion of an era of total decline, effectively leave a whole century by the wayside in the interest of what comes after it.

The revivals of the eighteenth century were aborted in the nineteenth century, and its legacies were not preserved in any meaningful way. The only legacy that seems to have persisted from the eighteenth century and is echoed among modern and contemporary Islamic movements is that of the Wahhābiyya. Yet even in this case, a distinction needs to be made between contemporary Islamic movements that function in the context of, and are fashioned in response to, the modern nation-state, and the original Wahhabism that developed on the intellectual periphery of the Islamic world and was largely ignorant of and hostile to its civilization. Eighteenth-century reform neither responded to the challenge of Europe nor anticipated future Islamic responses to this challenge. Rather, the various reform projects were rooted in their regional traditions and responded to regional crises. Yet, despite their local origins, they converged in undermining exclusive claims to intellectual authority that marginalized the Muslim community and impeded its ability to reflect and choose.

Chapter 4

Genealogies of Dissent and the Politics of Knowledge

The great reformers of the eighteenth century were fully aware of the radical nature of their intellectual projects. Whether as facilitators of change, or mere interpreters of some perennial truth, these reformers projected an image of themselves as vehicles of change and fashioned their social personas in accordance with this self-perception. In the midst of a sea of change, what was significant was not only the events that shaped the world around these reformers but also how, as actors, they felt about and related themselves to these events.

Eighteenth-century reform, like any intellectual undertaking, involved intensive intellectual activities and could have easily degenerated into elitism. Significantly, the reformers of the eighteenth century were cognizant of this risk and tried hard to remain socially connected and to relate their intellectual projects to their societies. Nevertheless, the most enduring legacies of eighteenth-century reform were first and foremost intellectual and not social; they involved a direct engagement with and a recasting of religious thought and culture, not just social reform movements. And yet, the social and political import of these intellectual reforms was always direct and transparent.

Eighteenth-century reformers were politicized in the sense that they were either directly involved in politics or concerned with political issues, just as they were concerned with other intellectual issues. The one exception was Muḥammad Ibn ʿAbd al-Wahhāb, whose ideas were manipulated toward political ends, while he himself exhibited little interest in either politics or the social well-being of fellow Muslims. In contrast, other reformers were keenly concerned with social and political change. This political and social commitment was founded on their specific perceptions of the nature of the political, social, and intellectual crisis of the time. Direct expressions of the political commitment of eighteenth-century reformers can to be traced in their numerous expressed stands on current political and social issues. The political dimensions of the careers of ʿUthmān Ibn Fūdī and Muḥammad Bin ʿAlī al-Sanūsī, careers that included seizing power and/or state building, as well as formulating the ideologies of these political actions, are obvious and need not be reiterated here. Instead, I will focus on the less apparent cases in which political outlooks are not immediately discernible through direct political actions but are imbedded in the larger intellectual projects of the concerned reformers.[1]

The Multiple Paradigms of Political Action

The intense critique of exclusionist *takfīr*, the rereading of *ijtihād* in a way that empowered larger masses of Muslims and increased societal participation, and the rejection of intermediary authorities are the principal intellectual stands that both underscored the social and political commitment of the eighteenth-century reformers and subverted, and often radically undermined, the established structures of power. In turning now to the multiple connections of eighteenth-century reformers to power we will explore the twin manifestations of this subversive relationship to politics and hegemonic cultural formations.

The paradigms for political action shaped by Ibn Fūdī and al-Sanūsī were transparently subversive and revolutionary. Ibn Fūdī started an insurrection that culminated in a complete change in the social and political organization of society. As we have seen earlier, he denied the intellectual authority of scholars who lived under un-Islamic social and political order and condemned such scholars as political *kuffār*. Subsequently, this antiestablishment focus of Ibn Fūdī's movement functioned to create and alternative Islamic authority. Although very different from Ibn Fūdī's model, the idealist Sanūsī state also had an adversarial relationship with established authority. In order to establish his new social order, al-Sanūsī moved into physical spaces free from the hegemonic control of both the Ottoman state (and other local powers) and the official organs of Islam that functioned in the shadow of this state. In practice and in theory, both Ibn Fūdī and al-Sanūsī were radical dissenters who sought to remodel and restructure the world of Muslims on a regional level.

In contrast to the political subversiveness of Ibn Fūdī and al-Sanūsī, the interventions of other reformers of the eighteenth century were primarily in the intellectual realm. As chief judge under three successive imams, Muḥammad Ibn ʿAlī al-Shawkānī served the state as the head of the highest intellectual office in Yemen. Shāh Walī Allāh al-Dihlawī, upon failing to forge alliances with various political powers, attempted to affect social change through intellectual reform. In both cases, the lack of direct hostility between these reformers and the prevailing political authorities of the time was offset by grand intellectual agendas that, in effect, subverted the dominant power structures, both political and intellectual. To be sure, al-Shawkānī and Walī Allāh conceived of the role of intellectuals in society in diverse ways. Yet irrespective of the role they aspired to play, the cultural capital of eighteenth-century intellectuals, and by extension their recognized merits, social status, and authority, derived from their intellectual achievements and not from their connection to power. The question then is how such authority related to power. Put differently, if indeed eighteenth-century thinkers sought through a reinterpretation of *ijtihād* to empower Muslim societies, the first question that needs to be addressed is the nature of the connection of these reformers to political authorities. One obvious aspect of the renewed calls for *ijtihād*, and the meanings grafted upon it, is the role it plays in undermining *madhhab* affiliations. As such, these calls for *ijtihād* engender the construction of new intellectual identities. The thorny questions of intellectual identity not only vexed such great scholars as Walī Allāh and al-Shawkānī but were hotly debated among their less accomplished contemporaries, and they continue to inspire spirited debates in contemporary Muslim societies and among historians of these societies. Quite deliberately, eighteenth-century thinkers often crossed the recognized *madhhab* boundaries only to be classified back into one of these compartments by modern observers.[2]

At a basic level, eighteenth-century reformers criticized the rampant injustice and disorder in their societies, as expressed in such acts as the extraction of illegal taxes by corrupt rulers, or the state's inability to provide security and defend Muslim territory. Early in his career, Walī Allāh devoted much energy to the restoration of the power of the Muslim state, before he finally gave up on his attempts to reform the state. However, his later focus on intellectual reform represented not an abandonment of his earlier goals but simply an attempt to achieve these goals through intellectual means. Unlike Walī Allāh, Muḥammad Ibn Ismāʿīl al-Ṣanʿānī entertained little ambition of working with the state; instead, he conceived of himself as an oppositional voice relentlessly critical of all social and political ills. Even his most doctrinal criticisms of contemporary religious practices and beliefs were wedded to social and political criticisms. Such, for example, was his criticism of the practice of shrine worship. Rather than focusing exclusively on the beliefs of individuals, he attributed this innovation to blind imitation and the resulting sectarianism that follows from it. In a typical manner, al-Ṣanʿānī says,

> Know that these matters about whose censure we continue to argue, and whose structures we seek to undermine, come from the commoners whose religion is the imitation of their forefathers' [beliefs] without evidence, and they follow it without distinction between low and high. Thus as one of them [the commoners] is growing up, and while still a child . . . the people of his village or town instruct him to call upon the name of whomever they believe in, and he sees them making vows to him, glorifying him, and traveling to visit his tomb. They rub him [the growing child] with soil [from his shrine] and make him circumambulate his tomb; he thus grows up with a conviction settled in his heart that the most glorious thing to him is the one they believe in. The young and the old would thus grow up with such beliefs without being reproached by anyone. On

> the contrary, those who adopt the titles of knowledge and claim to have virtue and take on the responsibility of judging, the issuing of fatwas, and teaching; those who claim sainthood and gnosis; and those who assume governorship and state positions, also venerate what they [the commoners] venerate; in fact, they confiscate the monetary gifts, and eat the offerings sacrificed at the tombs. [A Muslim growing up under these conditions] would think this to be the true religion of Islam. . . . However, it is not a secret to anyone who is qualified to think, or who has the slightest knowledge of the sciences of the Book and the Sunna, that the silence of a scholar, or even the whole world, when a reprehensible act occurs is not a proof of its permissibility.[3]

In the same breath as his critique of the hold of shrine worship over commoners and officials, al-Ṣanʿānī shifts the discussion to taxation:

> Let me give you an example of such [reprehensible acts], namely, these taxes called *majābī*: it is common knowledge that the prohibition of these taxes is established in religion, and yet they are widespread. . . . In fact, the hands of tax collectors have extended to the noblest of all places, Mecca. . . . They extort [taxes] from those who go to Mecca to perform the religious obligation of Islam. . . . These [pilgrims] encounter in the sacred city all kinds of unlawfulness. . . . Scholars and rulers, in contrast, refrain from renouncing [these acts]. . . . Would their silence then justify the extraction of [these taxes]? Surely, anyone with the slightest discernment would not make such a claim. In fact, I will give you another example: this is the sanctuary of God that is the best location in the world. . . . Some of the ignorant and misguided Circassian rulers have established four sites [of worship for each of the four schools] . . . thereby treating Muslims as if they belonged to different religions. Indeed, this is an innovation that pleases the eyes of Satan and makes Muslims the laughingstock of devils. And yet, scholars have been silent in regard to it. . . . So is this silence evidence of the permissibility [of establishing the four sites of worship]? If you say the logical consequence of this [argument] is that, by neglecting to condemn this grave stupidity, the community would have had agreed [*ajmaʿat*] on a misdeed, I say, true consensus is the agreement of the *mujtahid*s [independent scholars] of the *umma* of Muhammad (peace be upon him) on a matter after his time; and the scholars of the four schools argue that *ijtihād* after the four [imams of the schools] is impossible. Now, although this argument is invalid, from this perspective [of the scholars of the four schools] there is no consensus [*ijmāʿ*] after the four imams. This means that the question [of *ijmāʿ* on an error] does not even arise, because these innovations and the tomb heresy did not exist at

> the time of the imams of the four schools. Our certain opinion, however, is that the occurrence of *ijmāʿ* is impossible, since the *umma* of Muhammad has filled the horizons, and is now in every territory and under every star; therefore, its [the community's] established scholars are innumerable, and it is not feasible that anyone would be able to know their whereabouts. So one who claims that there is consensus after the expansion of the religion [of Islam], and despite the profusion of the Muslim scholars, would be making a false claim. . . . Moreover, even if we assume that these [scholars] knew of the reprehensible act and did not condemn it, and instead remained silent, their silence does not prove its permissibility . . . [because the instrument of denunciation (*inkār*) could be either the hand, the tongue, or the heart]. . . . So if one notes that a scholar refrains from voicing his condemnation [of a reprehensible act], and at the same time notes what a tyrant is capable of doing, one ought to assume that this [scholar] was not able to denounce through actions or words, and that he denounced in his heart. Indeed, it is obligatory to think well of fellow Muslims.[4]

The above quotations clearly illustrate the correlation, in al-Ṣanʿānī's thought, between the cult of saint worship, political corruption, illegal taxes, and the blind partisanship that divides Muslims and undermines their unity. What is notably absent here is an individualized approach to these innovations, in which they are construed as abstract religious and doctrinal violations for which individual Muslims are to be blamed. In fact, in his *ʿUdda*, al-Ṣanʿānī argues, based on a sound hadith, that it is lawful to pray at tombs, since the Prophet did so once and did not state that this is an act which only he can perform, while other Muslims could not. Al-Ṣanʿānī then makes a similar connection between the widespread innovation of building high, ornate domes over mausoleums and political corruption, and says that these are the doings of the kings and despots who unlawfully devour the wealth of people (*mulūk al-dunyā wa asāṭīn al-ẓulm alladhīna yaʾkulūna amwāl al-nās bil-bāṭil*).[5] Doctrine and politics are thus closely intertwined in al-Ṣanʿānī's thought, and the political order, or lack thereof, bears the largest responsibility for the moral and social ills of Muslim societies.

The history of the hadith-oriented Yemeni scholars is full of other examples of opposition to rulers and of political and intellectual stands that undermine the authority of these rulers. For example, Ṣāliḥ Ibn Mahdī al-Maqbalī (d. 1108/1696) accused Imam al-Mahdī Muḥammad (Ṣāhib al-Mawāhib, r. 1686–1718) of imposing illegal taxes not sanctioned in Islamic law.[6] Al-Ṣanʿānī, in contrast, took sides in a struggle over the imamate and supported a rival (who was eventually defeated), al-Nāṣir Muḥammad Ibn Isḥāq Ibn al-

Mahdī Aḥmad Ibn al-Ḥasan (d. 1167/1754), against Imam al-Manṣūr bi-Allāh al-Ḥusayn Ibn al-Mutawakkil (r. 1727–48).[7] The father of this last imam offered al-Ṣanʿānī the governorship of Mocha as well as the office of chief judge, but al-Ṣanʿānī turned down both offers and supported al-Nāṣir, a more qualified candidate by Zaydi standards.[8] Most eighteenth-century reformers were formally disengaged from the state. However, of all the reformers considered in this book, al-Shawkānī, as chief judge under three consecutive imams, seems to offer the least definitive example of opposition to political authority. Yet, as it will become apparent, al-Shawkānī's reform project, and many of his actual practices and positions, in effect undermined the status quo and subverted the authority of the prevailing political order.

Al-Shawkānī's Multifaceted Relationship with the State

Formally, al-Shawkānī was part of the power structure of the imamic state in Yemen.[9] As chief judge, he was in charge of overseeing the implementation of the law; furthermore, he was closely connected to the imams: he was in charge of their official correspondence with internal and external political powers; represented them on many official occasions and missions; and played a key role in confirming and assuring their legitimacy and that of their state. For example, upon the death of Imam al-Mutawakkil, al-Shawkānī secured the transition of authority to Mutawakkil's son al-Mahdī and "received on his behalf the oath of all the commanders of Sanaa and its governors and all the members of the family of the imam."[10] In addition to his official functions, al-Shawkānī expressed his views on political matters in many of his writings and promoted them through multiple strategies and means. Moreover, he elaborated in great detail his views regarding the appropriate relationship between intellectuals and political authorities. A close reading of al-Shawkānī's views and his actual positions vis-à-vis political authority shows, above all, that al-Shawkānī's affiliation with the state did not translate into blind loyalty. While he was usually a pillar in the power of the state, he often undermined it and subverted its exclusive claims to authority through his many critiques of state practices, including taxation policies, unwarranted calls for jihad, and tribal alliances. What made his critiques meaningful was that al-Shawkānī's own claim to authority, and hence of power, depended not exclusively on the state but, above all, on his intellectual achievement and integrity, and his ability to use his official position to wield power independent of the state. Moreover, al-Shawkānī was conscious of the pitfalls of engaging with the state and therefore articulated a theory that favored both an active engagement in politics and a regulated relationship with the state based on codes that would fortify scholars and prevent their co-optation.

Many examples of al-Shawkānī's complex relationship with the state can be gleaned from his biographies of various contemporaries that he compiled in his *Al-Badr al-Ṭāliʿ*. One such biography is of a certain Sharaf al-Dīn, a descendant of the house of the Prophet, the head of a family that had autonomous control over Kawkabān, one of the major cities of Yemen, and a rival to the imamate of Sanaa. Al-Shawkānī refers to the virtues of this man as a governor but also indicates that he interferes in scholarly matters of which he knows nothing, resulting in personal tension between the two men. Despite this, however, when the imam of Sanaa, al-Mutawakkil, invaded Kawkabān in 1228 and brought al-Shawkānī with him in the campaign, al-Shawkānī tried to dissuade him from using force and to convince him that there was no legal cause that justified taking such action. Needless to say, al-Mutawakkil did not agree, so al-Shawkānī tried to convince him not to take the imam of Kawkabān, Sharaf al-Dīn, and his family back to Sanaa and place them under house arrest, as al-Mutawakkil had intended to do. Al-Shawkānī also tried to convince the imam not to appoint in Kawkabān a weak figurehead from the people of the city under the effective control of a governor from Sanaa; this too was to no avail. Sharaf al-Dīn was placed under house arrest in Sanaa for a little over a year, during which time al-Shawkānī kept urging al-Mutawakkil to set him free, until the imam finally agreed and restored Sharaf al-Dīn to the governorship of Kawkabān. Al-Shawkānī claims credit for this action and even justifies his position further by asserting that during his stay in Sanaa, he got to know Sharaf al-Dīn better and saw numerous virtues in him, including good character, justice, and piety. Another incident led al-Mutawakkil to lay another siege to Kawkabān, but this time al-Shawkānī brokered a treaty between the imam and Sharaf al-Dīn.[11]

This account, like many others, is significant because it captures al-Shawkānī's thinking and perceptions in the course of these practical political engagements. His official position notwithstanding, al-Shawkānī is neither co-opted by the state to the extent of blindly justifying its actions, nor does he resort to outright defiance or rebellion in response to actions of which he does not approve. Rather, al-Shawkānī advocates active involvement in state institutions but provides a corrective to state policies by advocating interests other than those of the state. Al-Shawkānī no doubt retains a real interest in the preservation of the state, but he remains considerably independent of it. Another significant implication of this episode is that al-Shawkānī advocates a form of decentralization that recognizes a multiplicity of legitimate, quasi-independent powers within the political sphere. Al-Shawkānī seems to have grown weary of in-fighting among Muslims, and he used his office to promote compromises among antagonistic factions. As a result, the imams of Sanaa often asked him to negotiate the peaceful resolution of conflicts with internal or external opponents. It is all the more interesting to note that al-Shawkānī had unfriendly relations with Sharaf al-Dīn and in particular did not approve of the latter's views on religious and legal matters; nonetheless, al-Shawkānī insisted on defending the Sharaf al-Dīn's political rights before his commander, the imam. Al-Shawkānī thus clearly distinguishes between political claims and claims to religious authority that were not at stake in this specific case. Moreover, in al-Shawkānī's assessment, the legitimacy of the political claims to authority by the imam are of the same order as those of the local contender; as such, the optimal solution to the conflict between the two does not entail a restoration of exclusive power to the imam for symbolic or ideological reasons; rather, al-Shawkānī gives priority to the prevention of bloodshed among Muslims, and to an arrangement that perpetuates optimal conditions of stability and order.

Al-Shawkānī was also involved in internal disputes at the highest level of state power. On one occasion, a dispute broke out between the highest-ranking *wazīr* (vizier), Ḥasan al-ʿAlfī, and Aḥmad, the eldest son of the imam and the leader of the army. The former, according to al-Shawkānī, was abusing his considerable power by slighting the relatives and friends of the imam, and in 1223 AH was antagonizing the army by failing to pay the salaries of the soldiers. This, of course, created a potentially dangerous situation, but more serious still was the failure to pay the tribute to the tribes of highland Yemen, in retaliation for which the tribes blocked the roads surrounding Sanaa, attacking travelers, stealing money, and shedding blood. This situation continued for an extended period of time and posed a serious threat to the livelihood of the people of Sanaa. Al-Shawkānī offered the *wazīr* his advice, but the latter, because of his closeness to the imam, did not heed it. Finally, Aḥmad, the imam's son, summoned the *wazīr*, and when the *wazīr* refused to answer had him arrested along with his family members. This enraged the imam, who demanded that his *wazīr* be released; but instead of releasing him, Aḥmad laid siege to his father's palace, which had in it another son of the imam with some of his own followers. Fighting broke out between the two parties. At this point, Aḥmad, whom al-Shawkānī refers to as the caliph, asked al-Shawkānī to mediate between him and his father, and al-Shawkānī managed to convince the imam to accept an arrangement by which his son Aḥmad became the administrator of the country and the *wazīr* to his father, while the old *wazīr* remained in custody. In effect, therefore, al-Shawkānī was involved in brokering a mini coup d'état that transferred effective power to the son while retaining the father as a figurehead. A year later the father died, and al-Shawkānī was the first to pledge his allegiance to Aḥmad. He then hastened to secure for Aḥmad the allegiance of key officials and members of the ruling family.[12]

Rather than being a passive employee of the state, al-Shawkānī managed to alter the course of internal events in significant ways at the levels of regional politics, the central bureaucratic apparatus of the state, and the office of the imam. Moreover, al-Shawkānī left his imprint on the state's foreign policy. As chief judge, he was in charge of diplomatic correspondence between the imam and foreign powers. His most notable exchanges were with Ottoman officials and their local representatives in the Hejaz, as well as the representatives of the Wahhabi movement that, for a period of time, posed a threat to the imams' northern realm. His political interventions largely centered on two events: the French invasion of Egypt and the possible threat and response to this invasion, and the Wahhabi threat and the regional reorganization in the aftermath of the Ottoman recapture of the Hejaz. In both cases, al-Shawkānī composed the texts of the letters on behalf of the imams and also authored the foreign policies advocated in these exchanges. Again, the contexts of these exchanges, and the extent of al-Shawkānī's involvement in authoring the policies articulated in them, are often explained in various accounts that appear sporadically in al-Shawkānī's historical writings. One such account is provided in the biography of the leader of the Turkish army who recaptured the border area between the Hejaz and Yemen.[13] This area, known as al-Bilād al-ʿArīshiyya, which includes the regions of al-Laḥya, al-Ḥudayda, Zabīd, Bayt al-Faqīh, and al-Zaydiyya, had previously fallen under the control of the Wahhabis and their local agent, Sharif Ḥammūd. Al-Shawkānī reports that before they were captured by the Turks, the Ottoman governor of Egypt, Muḥammad ʿAlī Pāsha, sent a letter to the imam of Sanaa promising to return these lands to him. Al-Shawkānī then describes how indeed these lands were returned after some negotiations conducted in accordance with a policy that al-Shawkānī himself engineered. The Turks, according to al-Shawkānī, had no reason, aside from goodwill, to return these lands, and could have easily annexed them. Quite naturally, al-Shawkānī maintains, Yemeni officials were convinced that the Ottomans were bluffing, and that they intended to keep the Yemeni lands in their possession, especially since they were militarily superior and could overwhelm the Yemeni armies and the tribes of Yemen on whom the imam depended in times of war.[14] In fact, the Najdi (Wahhabi) forces were superior to the Yemeni forces and, according to al-Shawkānī, they were easily subdued by the Egyptian/Ottoman armies. From all over Yemen, people wrote to al-Shawkānī advising him that the arrangement he brokered with the Turks could not be trusted. In response, al-Shawkānī argued that the Turks "have initiated the offer of peace and truce, and we cannot turn down what they have been offering all along." Al-Shawkānī then contends that those tribes feigning to take up the struggle against the Turks would not raise a finger in the face of the Turkish armies should the Ottomans decide to march on Yemen; these tribes were "spiritless, indolent, and panicked, and all they cared about was their lives and families."[15] Al-Shawkānī thus dismisses those who opposed negotiations with the Turks and defends his strategy as one that is both realistic and effective in restoring imamic control over hitherto lost territory. But there is more than political expediency in al-Shawkānī's stand. To start with, al-Shawkānī's conception of who constitutes an enemy is tempered by his inclusive identification with Muslims of all ethnicities and confessional affiliations. Moreover, he seems more willing to trust the disciplined Turkish enemy than his unruly tribal allies. Above all, however, al-Shawkānī's stand is dictated by his strict interpretation of Islamic law, whereby peaceful relationships among Muslims are given priority, irrespective of their ideological inclinations or claims. In other words, given the offer of peace, al-Shawkānī had no legal justification to fight the Turks, whose political order was as legitimate as that of the state he served, or the satellite states on the borders of Yemen.

This principled stand, inspired by al-Shawkānī's reading of Islamic law and its dictates, permeates all of al-Shawkānī's attitudes toward political issues. One of al-Shawkānī's great heroes was the fifteenth-century scholar Muḥammad Ibn Ibrāhīm al-Wazīr, considered the father of the *ahl al-ḥadīth* school among the Zaydis of Yemen. Ibn al-Wazīr challenged many accepted Zaydi views and provided a model of the independent legal scholarship to which al-Shawkānī adhered. Among his many contributions, Ibn al-Wazīr articulated a systematic argument for using the standard compilations of Sunni hadith and for accepting the report of an innovator he would otherwise condemn as a heretic.[16] One of Ibn al-Wazīr's radical moves was to assert, much to the dislike of fellow Zaydis, that the traditions reported on the authority of Muʿāwiya should be accepted, since they are neutral and do not further his heretical cause.[17] Al-Shawkānī had great admiration for these foundational efforts by Ibn al-Wazīr, but he did not refrain from disagreeing with him on several important issues, some of which had immediate political import. For example, in his *Nayl al-Awṭār*, al-Shawkānī reports an opinion by Ibn al-Wazīr in which he maintains that the Banū Hāshim (the clan to which the Prophet Muhammad belonged) can be beneficiaries of certain kinds of alms taxes. In response, al-Shawkānī insists that the prohibition against paying any alms to Banū Hāshim is final and definitive: "In summary, the prohibition against paying alms tax [*zakat*] to the Hāshim clan is well known and there is no distinction in it between whether the one paying the *zakāt* is himself from the Hāshim clan or not. No exception for this known prohibition is accepted; only that which has truly been sanctioned by God [is accepted], and not the baseless and useless excuses fabricated by those who are caught in this fix; neither are the unsound traditions reported on the particularization [of this general injunction] acceptable."[18]

Al-Shawkānī then swiftly proceeds to discuss the prevalent situation in

Yemen; indeed, the fervor in al-Shawkānī's tone was a result not of his academic disagreement with Ibn al-Wazīr but mainly of the pertinence of the issue in question to the contemporary situation in Yemen. Thus, al-Shawkānī asserts that many members of the Banū Hāshim who are in positions of political authority illegally appropriate tax money and find scholars who justify their acts for them. "Because of the abundance of usurpers of *zakāt* among the clan of Hāshim in the country of Yemen in particular, especially those among them who are in positions of power, some scholars have attempted to defend them and to make lawful what God has forbidden them." Al-Shawkānī notes that some have gone as far as asserting that the land of Yemen is a *kharāj* land.[19] He vehemently attacks these assertions as "lies" used to perpetuate injustice against Muslims.[20] Of all the Yemeni independent thinkers since the fifteenth century, al-Shawkānī, as chief judge, had the closest affiliation to the official political establishment and was most closely identified with the interests of the regime he served. Since he wielded considerable power in this official position, al-Shawkānī's stand on the illegality of allocating this tax to the extended ruling family could not have been a random legal opinion of little practical ramifications. It is also significant that he would be more critical than his predecessors of this common Zaydi practice.

The independence of al-Shawkānī's political stands was not accidental or unintentional. Rather, al-Shawkānī addressed in many of his writings the question of dealing with presumably corrupt political authorities, and he offered numerous theoretical reflections on this sensitive issue. One of al-Shawkānī's books fully devoted to the treatment of this subject is *Al-Ittiṣāl bil-Ṣalāṭīn* (On dealing with sultans/authorities). Following the model of the Companions of the Prophet, al-Shawkānī argues that it is legitimate to make a living by occupying public office and offering services to rulers.[21] It is in fact necessary, he adds, to have a group of people cooperate with the political authorities in the execution of divine laws by occupying positions of judges, muftis, governors, commanders of armies, and so on; otherwise, sharia would be rendered inoperative, Islamic rules would be replaced by *jāhilī* rules, and the emblems of Islam would be eradicated.[22] This is all the more needed, al-Shawkānī insists, because without the participation of such knowledgeable and committed scholars in the public arena, rulers, their servants, and their officials would have free rein, disregard religion completely, and violate the wealth, honor, and sanctity of all; they would do all of this and absolve themselves of responsibility under the pretext that they do not know the law and have no one willing to teach it to them, having been abandoned by "those who know the religion."[23] Al-Shawkānī thus argues that the traditional advocacy, in the writings of many Muslim scholars, of the withdrawal of scholars from the public sphere and their avoidance of any form of contact with political authorities[24] actually serves the interests of these authorities by creating a scholarly vacuum, which is detrimental to Islam. In contrast, if scholars are part of the power base of the regime, then it is likely that the political authorities will accommodate at least some of the demands of these scholars. Furthermore, al-Shawkānī distinguishes between those scholars who work in the service of rulers and simply aid them in their oppression, and those who engage in legitimate contact with rulers to take advantage of their might and esteem for the purposes of putting the law into practice, enjoining the good, and forbidding the evil. Al-Shawkānī thus believes that a scholar's legitimate contact with rulers is not just to reprimand and warn them but especially to harness their power to the cause of the public interest.

Al-Shawkānī also maintains that assuming the office of a judge in particular is an unavoidable "affliction" that inevitably brings some harm to the person who accepts it. This, however, is less risky than the greater harm of not accepting such a position. He illustrates his point by recounting the story of a public official who was able to convince the ruler he served to mitigate the penalty imposed against an innocent person; the ruler agreed to reduce the penalty from a death sentence to a number of lashes with a cane on the condition that the official himself would execute the punishment. An uninformed observer might think that the official was an accomplice in the perpetuation of injustice while, in fact, he saved the life of an innocent person.[25] Despite this official's general responsibility in denouncing injustice, his participation in this case does not constitute a reprehensible act. Al-Shawkānī therefore concludes that "actions which at times may seem to contradict the law, as well as circumstances which appear to be contradictory, may in fact be contrary to what they appear to be, and may be among the greatest possible acts of worship and best acts of kindness."[26] Scholars who choose to withdraw from the public sphere, in contrast, may have good intentions and may appear morally superior because of their withdrawal; in reality, however, most of those who choose to withdraw either do so because they have no other options, in which case their attacks on public scholars are merely out of jealousy, or because they are incompetent scholars and, more important, inept in the advocacy of scholarship.[27]

Unlike many of his Yemeni predecessors, whose social and moral critiques were seldom applied or adhered to, al-Shawkānī was not forced to withdraw into a utopian dream of meaningless radicalism. It was indeed his ability to shape reality that led him to elaborate this pragmatic view of active engagement in the public sphere. However, al-Shawkānī clearly conceived of two realms of authority, the political and the intellectual, and recognized that the very nature of their relationship involves a compromise, or what he called an unavoidable "affliction," that should be judged finally on the basis of its outcome. Such a compromise should be assessed based on the extent to which it helps a scholar morally deter rulers' abuse of power, serve the interests of Muslims and defend them against injustice, and oversee the execution of Islamic law. Al-Shawkānī, therefore, was not simply justifying collaboration with rulers because he was one such collaborator. Rather, he was keenly aware of the risky nature of such contact, and he set strict standards for regulating it. Al-Shawkānī admits that some scholars are accomplices in the crimes of corrupt rulers but adds that he is talking only about those who do not fall into this category.[28] In any event, a scholar dealing with an oppressive ruler should do his utmost to alleviate injustice and in no way help perpetuate and legitimate it or reassure the ruler in his injustice.

> If you say that among kings there may exist those who are unjust and tyrannical, I say yes, but the one who deals with them does not do it to help them in their injustice and tyranny but to enforce God's law among people, issue a ruling on the basis of this law, collect from the subjects what has been obligated by God, or fight against one whom it is lawful to fight and to be the enemy of one who deserves enmity. If this is the case, then if the ruler has reached the highest degree of injustice, those who establish contacts with him [for the above reasons] bear nothing [of the responsibility] for his injustice. In fact, if one has a way of reducing this injustice, even by a very small amount, then he would be deserving of the highest reward on top of [what he gets from] his official office. . . . He should exert himself as much as he can to ward off [injustice], without aiding him [the ruler] in his injustice, or justifying or encouraging his state, or even suggesting that [his injustice] may be permissible. If he entangles himself in any of these things, then he would count among the unjust and in the camp of the tyrants, and among the traitors [of religion].[29]

Al-Shawkānī thus concedes to numerous risks stemming from engagement in the public sphere, not least of which is the corrupting temptation of power. And yet, the obligation of enjoining what is good and prohibiting what is reprehensible is a public act and, according to al-Shawkānī, one of the most fundamental duties of Islam. Therefore, the choice to withdraw, assuming good intentions, is a selfish choice through which a scholar protects himself but fails to fulfill his responsibility toward the larger Muslim community.[30] Despite all the real risks of associating with authorities, al-Shawkānī makes a plea against isolation and withdrawal in favor of the engagement of scholars and the fulfillment of their practical role in society:

> I do not advocate that those who are possessed of scholarship and know its secrets should refrain from taking up religious offices. How could I say

that, knowing that if these positions are not secured by them they are lost; if they are abandoned by good people they will be passed on to evil ones; if scholars do not attend to them, ignorant people will; if pious people turn away from them, oppressors will come along [and fill them]. How could I say this when scholars are religiously obliged to adjudicate among people with truth, justice, and equity, and in accordance with what God has revealed . . . [they are commanded] to deliver [God's] rules and remind people of His commands. . . . The people who deliver judgments and legal consultations . . . have the largest share of these responsibilities. . . . I do say, however, that the seeker of knowledge ought to seek it in the proper way, and to learn it as God wants him to, believing that it is the highest of religious and worldly matters, and hoping to benefit God's worshippers with it. . . . One such benefit obtains when kings and worldly authorities need him to assume a certain office and ask him to do this and insist that he accept, while recognizing the rights of scholarship and [the necessity of] abiding by the obligations of religion . . . assuming that he [the scholar] has achieved a level of knowledge that would qualify him for such a position . . . in this situation, it is not permissible for a scholar to refrain from responding or to refuse to accept, for should he, he would have abandoned what God has required . . . and the upholding of Islamic law would be impeded.[31]

Al-Shawkānī had little tolerance for the pious ideal of withdrawal and isolation.[32] On one occasion he quotes a dictum of the famous Sufi al-Qushayrī that one does not draw closer to God unless he moves away from humans. This, al-Shawkānī asserts, is true for someone who can be of no use to other human beings. However, for "one who can benefit them either by his knowledge, preaching, struggle, or by forbidding what is prohibited or enforcing what God has commanded his fellow [humans] to do, then such a person's closeness to humans draws him closer to the truth. This is the station of the prophets and the scholars to whom God has entrusted the guidance of people."[33]

Al-Shawkānī's detailed exposition is not limited to the scholar's end of the relationship; he also outlines the key aspects of a ruler's duties that merit the aid of scholars, as well as the main offenses that a ruler often commits. The duties of the ruler include providing security on highways and roads, protecting the weak from the transgressions of the powerful, waging holy war against unbelievers, enforcing the law, establishing the emblems of Islam, appointing judges, arbitrating disputes, appointing public supervisors, building and preparing armies, building schools, and standing up to villains and corrupters.[34] The list of offenses includes anger and lust, shedding blood, illegal appropriation of wealth, collective punishment, and so on.[35] In sum, therefore, it is permissible to maintain active contacts with rulers if this serves the public interest; and such a contact is, in fact, obligatory if this public interest is not achievable without it. However, this service may be forbidden if there is no religious benefit from it, or if it leads to corruption and the infliction of harm on the community.[36]

While *Al-Ittiṣāl bi-l-Salāṭīn* is largely an apologetic work, in that it justifies public engagement despite recognized moral risks, other works of al-Shawkānī focus more on the risks involved in taking a moral stand in the public sphere. In his *Adab al-Ṭalab*, al-Shawkānī talks about the vice of concealing the truth or intentionally opposing it, not only in the hope of worldly gain but also in deference to the mob and other people in power. Significantly, however, al-Shawkānī focuses more on the possibility of persecution that may result from the public exposure of scholars who tell the truth and stand for it.[37] Some may argue, he says, that a person who publicly advocates the truth in a land of innovation would only bring harm to himself. However, al-Shawkānī responds by invoking the history of scholars who did not shy away from political confrontation. Most such scholars, al-Shawkānī maintains, did not perish as a result of criticizing power and were ultimately protected from harm by God. Yet even to perish would be justified:

> Suppose what you have guessed is true . . . and that you will be afflicted and harm will befall you. Are you the same as the whole world and all the people [in it]? And do you think that you will last forever in this world? And what if you act in accordance with what you know is true and walk in the path that God commands you to follow? The most that can happen to you and inflict you is to be killed for the sake of truth and become a martyr in [the cause of] knowledge; you would thus win eternal happiness, become an exemplar for scholars to the end of time, a disgrace to innovators, and a burden that breaks their backs . . . and you will shame them [the innovators] as long as they embrace their transgression. . . . Many a worshipper of God have preceded you on this course and achieved this high status, and you have in them an example and a model.[38]

While describing the worst that could happen to a scholar who lives up to his public responsibilities, al-Shawkānī believes such worst-case scenarios are unlikely to occur. He insists that, unlike a warrior on the frontier who takes much more serious risks, the danger to a scholar on account of his preaching God's commands to fellow Muslims is minimal, and it usually does not go beyond some limited bodily harm or loss of wealth or, more often, some verbal abuse and defamation. In contrast, it is most likely that the steadfast struggle of scholars would eventually bear fruit. Thus, based on his reading of the historical record, al-Shawkānī outlines what he considers a more realistic view of the risks of public engagement and the possibilities of making a difference as a result of this engagement. Al-Shawkānī's historical ideal includes, among other things, the chain of Yemeni scholars in the school of *ahl al-ḥadīth*. All of these scholars were subjected to some kind of persecution and abuse including, in the most extreme cases, imprisonment and exile. They were nonetheless able to write and promote their views, and they managed to cultivate a strong following in Yemen. Moreover, the culmination of this tradition is al-Shawkānī himself, an illustration (at least in his own mind) of the claim that intellectual integrity will finally prevail.

Underlying his advocacy of public engagement is the need, in al-Shawkānī's view, for political order, a prerequisite for the performance of religious obligations, securing public interest, and protecting the community from harm.[39] Historically, al-Shawkānī maintains, there has been no consensus on the perfect justice of any Muslim ruler, with the exception of the Umayyad caliph ʿUmar Ibn ʿAbd al-ʿAzīz. Yet although all known Muslim rulers may have committed some sort of injustice, there can be no doubt that the presence of a ruler is an absolute necessity for the maintenance of law and order. It follows, then, that it is necessary to obey the ruler if this does not entail disobeying God. After giving evidence from the Qurʾān and the Sunna for this view, al-Shawkānī adds that it is also necessary to be patient in dealing with the injustice of rulers, since if a ruler is unjust, he will suffer the burden of the responsibility for it, and if he is just then the reward will belong to him and to his subjects. He points out also that the community has a collective duty to advise its rulers. Unlike Ibn ʿAbd al-Wahhāb, however, al-Shawkānī takes this notion of advice seriously and acts upon it. He also defines injustice and delineates the various kinds of violations to wealth and honor that constitute social and economic forms of injustice. He then reiterates that it is obligatory for Muslims to struggle against injustice through acts, words, or in their hearts, if the first two are beyond their capacity.

In these discussions, al-Shawkānī develops the idea that public order maintained through the state and its powers provides the medium that enables the law to function, but it is never in itself identical with the law. Politics, therefore, is clearly a mundane necessity not a religious one, and the realm of politics is not part of the sacred order of Muslims. Still, Muslims must get involved in politics and public life, since isolation and rejection can only contribute to social and moral decline and decadence. Unlike al-Ṣanʿānī, al-Shawkānī does not glorify isolation and withdrawal, nor does he promote formulas for individual salvation. In contrast to isolationists, as well as the many scholars who collaborated with authorities without addressing the pitfalls of such engagement, al-Shawkānī theorized a different mode of association with authority that is at once legitimate and subject to set rules that would regulate this association and preserve the integrity of the scholars involved in it.[40]

The theoretical model of an engaged but independent and critical intellectual outlined in *Al-Ittiṣāl biʾl-Salāṭīn* and *Adab al-Ṭalab* is illustrated and to a great extent balanced by the profiles of dissenting scholars assembled in *Al-Badr al-Ṭāliʿ*. While the two theoretical expositions encourage scholars to participate in the public sphere in a principled manner, the primary virtue celebrated in *Al-Badr al-Ṭāliʿ* is dissent. The book, al-Shawkānī's main historical work, was written with the professed purpose of celebrating the virtues of post-seventh-century Muslims.[41] These virtues include piety, literary talent, erudition, and so on. Some people are listed on account of the favors and status they received within the state.[42] The most celebrated virtues, however, are originality and independence, as well as intellectual integrity and political courage. Many of the scholars celebrated in al-Shawkānī's collection are listed because they did such things as shunning worldly positions, refusing to assume the position of judge, assuming a critical stand vis-à-vis the state, standing up to rulers and refusing to condone their injustice, and not hesitating to condemn unlawful actions.[43] One individual actually chided al-Shawkānī for his own seeming docility regarding matters of the state.[44] The merits of another person include his asking to assume several public offices but he accepted only what would not compromise his religion (*qabila minhā mā fīhi al-salāma li-dīnihī*).[45] Elsewhere, al-Shawkānī indicates that the decision of whether to accept public office is a function of specific historical factors: what may be acceptable under some conditions may not be acceptable under others. Thus an eighth-century scholar was offered the office of judge more than once but refused to accept it, arguing that for this position one would need not just wide-ranging knowledge but specific technical knowledge that he lacked.[46] In this case, the scholar's rejection was a function of not the nature of the position itself but his awareness of his own limitations, which would have prevented him from performing his duties properly.

To his credit, al-Shawkānī does not limit his ideal model to a description that fits his personal experience or his view of himself. For example, in the biography of one his teachers, al-Ḥasan Ibn Ismāʿīl Ibn al-Ḥasan Ibn Muḥammad al-Maghribī (after *Maghārib* Sanaa) (d. 1208), al-Shawkānī describes his teacher as a learned scholar who was also pious, modest, righteous, austere, did not refer to himself as a scholar, and had no sense of entitlement in relation to his students or others.[47] He did his domestic chores himself and had no other interests besides pursuing and spreading scholarship and attending to the bare necessities of making a living. While still young, he was offered the position of judge, but he turned it down and did so again on several occasions.[48] In short, al-Shawkānī maintains, the sight of this man who modeled everything in his life on the example of the early pious generations of Muslims made a person mindful of God. This man, al-Shawkānī reports, "is naturally modest, even though there are about ten *mujtahid*s among the students studying with him. . . . He remained in this beautiful state, only becoming more modest. . . . Let anyone who desires to reach the fruit of knowledge and to attain its rewards in the hereafter, follow his example." And yet, al-Shawkānī, who accepted appointment to the office of chief judge and was anything but modest, did not follow the model of his teacher.

Al-Shawkānī offers a positive assessment of intellectuals who have experiences similar to his; he even uses entries on such individuals as occasions to offer information on his own career and credentials, and to highlight what he considers to be his own virtues. In a biography of a contemporary and associate of his, Ismāʿīl Ibn ʿAlī . . . Ibn Ḥamīd al-Dīn Ibn Muṭahhar Ibn al-Imām Sharaf al-Dīn (d. 1215), al-Shawkānī describes the ideal intellectual. This scholar who studied under al-Ṣanʿānī, among others, was frequently invited, with al-Shawkānī, by Imam al-Manṣūr for consultation. "He has a way of nobility of purpose and pride which only one like him is capable of in such situations where the essence of true men becomes visible. For I have never heard from him, throughout the time when I encountered him there [in the audience of the imam], a word that implies submission to worldly desire, either explicitly or implicitly. Rather, he inserts in his speech stories and accounts which include exhortations that have great effect on the hearts [of listeners] aiming in that to gain reward in the hereafter."[49]

In a number of the biographies of his acquaintances, al-Shawkānī talks at length about his own experiences. Of particular interest are accounts in which al-Shawkānī situates himself in relation to his intellectual predecessors. In a biography of one Ismāʿīl Ibn Yaḥyā Ibn Ḥasan al-Ṣaʿdī then al-Dhamārī then al-Ṣanʿānī (d. 1209), al-Shawkānī tells of a private meeting between him and this caring older colleague six month before his death.[50] At the time, al-Shawkānī says, he had been slandered by a group of people who objected to his independent reasoning and determination to follow legal indicants rather than imitate. "Inferior minds," al-Shawkānī adds, are always hostile to those who follow proofs. Out of genuine concern, the older scholar advised al-Shawkānī that displaying this tendency to exercise independent judgment by following legal indicants would lead to strife. To illustrate, the older scholar mentioned the example of al-Ṣanʿānī, who was verbally and physically attacked despite the support he enjoyed from several powerful officials. In contrast, al-Shawkānī, according to this account, isolated himself from people in power and devoted himself solely to scholarship. Moreover, in contrast to al-Ṣanʿānī, who started on this confrontational path toward the end of his life, al-Shawkānī started on it at an early age, and was thus more likely to elicit the wrath and resentment of the authorities. Al-Shawkānī, of course, has the story reversed, for in reality it was he who enjoyed secure state support and protection, and al-Ṣanʿānī who did not; moreover, al-Ṣanʿānī was subjected to much harsher pressure than al-Shawkānī ever had to endure. This reversal of roles in al-Shawkānī's account provides a narrative of origins that serves to justify his ultimate choices. According to this narrative, al-Shawkānī started out as a radical intellectual, even more so than someone like al-Ṣanʿānī; later, he tempered his position on the advice of wise contemporaries following the example of earlier reformers. Moreover, the purpose of this moderation was not self-preservation but the desire to be more effective in championing his righteous cause.

In the various models he outlines, al-Shawkānī celebrates the intellectual integrity that compelled many of his predecessors to dissociate themselves from worldly power; at the same time, he strongly defends his choice of public engagement and association with power and provides a theoretical justification for this choice. Clearly, therefore, al-Shawkānī thought that it was possible for him to have a connection to power in which he would be strong enough to maintain a balanced and equal relationship with rulers without compromising the authority that his scholarly expertise had earned him. But was this self-confidence warranted? To answer this question we must examine both the sociopolitical context in which al-Shawkānī operated and the extent to which he was actually able to exercise power and influence the course of events.

Zaydi Yemen and al-Shawkānī's Rise to Power

Al-Shawkānī served as chief judge under three Zaydi imams. Zaydi Islam entered Yemen at an early date, with the first Zaydi political community in Yemen founded by al-Hādī ilā al-Ḥaqq Ibn al-Ḥusayn (d. 298/911). Zaydism quickly became a permanent feature of Yemen's political and religious landscape. The imamic dynasty under which al-Shawkānī served was founded toward the end of the sixteenth century by al-Manṣūr al-Qāsim Ibn Muḥammad (d. 1620). In 1636, al-Qāsim's son and successor, al-Muʿayyad Muḥammad (r. 1620–44), drove the Ottomans out of Yemen and extended the control of the imamate over all of Yemen. The highest point of this Qāsimī imamic dynasty was under the third ruler, al-Mutawakkil Ismāʿīl (r. 1644–76). In this period, the imamate also ruled over the Shāfiʿī population of lower Yemen, and Shāfiʿīs subsequently constituted a significant portion of the subjects of the imamate.[51] As is usually the case with dynastic powers, the Qāsimī imamate lost some of its rigor and strength with the passage of time, and its effective domain of influence gradually shrank. By the time of al-Shawkānī, the imamate's control over the southern parts of the state was reduced, and it lost many of its northern territories to the Wahhabis and other Hijazi powers. Yet despite these changes, the imamate retained its essential characteristics, namely, that it was decidedly a Zaydi state, in both its power base and official state ideology. I highlight the emphasis on the Zaydi character of the state here in order to avoid a possible misreading of al-Shawkānī and his context. At first glance, it is possible to assume that the incorporation of large numbers of Sunni subjects into the domain of the imamate had effectively changed the face of the state; consequently, it may also be argued, al-Shawkānī's appointment as chief judge, given his presumed affinity to Sunnism, is a reflection of this change in the overall population makeup of the Yemeni state. Additionally, one may also argue that the dilution of the Zaydi ideological hold over power was reflected in the makeup of the state and its institutions, and that al-Shawkānī's appointment provided ideological justification for the new structure of the imamic state.[52] In what follows I will argue that, despite the seeming logic of these assumptions, a close reading of both the historical record and al-Shawkānī's writings suggests otherwise. To start with, al-Shawkānī cannot be characterized as a Sunni and hence could not have provided a Sunni justification for the new Zaydi state. Moreover, the eighteenth-century imamic state was, above everything else, a Zaydi dynasty continuing the traditions set in place at the outset of the Qāsimī dynasty in the late sixteenth century.

The early imams of the Qāsimī dynasty were no doubt more charismatic than the later imams. As in other cases of newly instituted ideological regimes, the imamic state became more structured and routinized with the passage of time, and its authority subsequently more institutionalized. Still, from the beginning, rule passed through and within the Qāsimī lineage and, as such, was dynastic and patrimonial. This was equally true of early and late Zaydi successions in Yemen. In fact, an integral part of the Zaydi theory of the imamate is the principle of the authority of the *ʿitra*, the family or dynasty claiming descent from ʿAlī, the cousin of the Prophet. To be sure, in addition to descent, the classical Zaydi theory of the imamate stipulates other conditions that qualify a member of the *ʿitra* for the imamate, such as piety, justice, power, and the ability to exercise *ijtihād*. In theory, the rightful Zaydi imam is the member of the *ʿitra* who is best qualified based on these standards. In practice, however, there were always several contenders for the position of the imam, and the imamate effectively went to the one who was able to exercise the most power, even if he was not the most knowledgeable or just member of the family. This practical compromise was also incorporated into Zaydi legal theory, long before the establishment of the Qāsimī imamate. This was also true of the Hādawī branch of Zaydism, the interpretative school of legal thought that prevailed in the Qāsimī imamate. The Hādawī school was the official school of thought to which the state and a majority of its officials and bureaucrats adhered. In fact, even al-Shawkānī, the one state official who did not adhere to this school, continued to engage the Hādawī tradition in his writings and practices. And although the Hādawīs lost their exclusive hold on power with the appointment of al-Shawkānī to the office of chief judge, a majority of the state officials, and a large portion of the judiciary, came from their ranks. The imams, in contrast, aspired to the same status and authority as their predecessors; they were, however, considerably less resourceful than the early imams and often failed to consolidate their power effectively throughout their domains. As such, the erosion of the power of the Hādawī Zaydis was itself a symptom of the erosion of the imams' power, not a deliberate move by the latter to undermine the threatening ideological power of traditional Zaydism.[53]

In contrast to the personal and charismatic character of the early Qāsimī imams, the later imams were more predictable and in some sense more constrained by the structure of their state. And although al-Shawkānī promoted the arrogation of significant functions of the imamic power to jurists like himself, this was not inspired by Sunni inclinations; rather, despite a romantic characterization of Zaydi political theory by modern scholars,[54] the classical formulations of this theory had already allowed for such sharing of power and thus had departed from the ideal of the imam as the ultimate, unrivaled intellectual and political authority.[55] In any event, the survival of early as well as late Qāsimī states depended primarily on the ability of the imams to wield power, and not on their piety, charisma, or idealized qualifications. This power rested on a number of intertwined elements including a legitimizing state ideology, an army of bureaucrats and officials loyal to this ideology, a reliable and controllable source of revenue, and a strong military capable of ensuring the state's continuing hold on power. Zaydi Islam, irrespective of its mutations and compromises, was the source of the state ideology. Revenue was derived mainly from taxation of agricultural lands and trade. Occasionally, military campaigns would generate some income but, more often than not, they were a drain on the state resources. The ability to extract taxes was obviously tied to the ability to exercise coercive power through the actual or projected military might of the state. This might depended on a small army of slave soldiers and a large body of recruits. The latter, accounting for the real power of the army in large-scale battles against internal as well as external enemies, were drawn from the Zaydi tribes of highland Yemen, the primary power base of the Zaydi state.

As noted above, the Qāsimī imamate gradually expanded to include a significant portion of Shāfiʿī subjects from southern Yemen. Moreover, these Shāfiʿīs accounted for a large section of the tax base of the Zaydi state. It is thus likely that the status of Sunna-oriented scholars such as al-Shawkānī was enhanced as a result of the expansion and the resulting contacts between Zaydis and Shāfiʿīs. Still, it is important to note that the tendency among some Zaydi scholars to positively engage Sunni scholarship and to create hybrid intellectual identities that cut across traditional sectarian lines started long before al-Shawkānī or the expansion of the Qāsimī state into southern Yemen. The founding father of this tradition among the Zaydis was the fifteenth-century scholar Muḥammad Ibn Ibrāhīm al-Wazīr (d. 1436).[56] Ibn al-Wazīr was the first to systematically use the Sunni collections of hadith and provide a theoretical argument in support of this use. Earlier Zaydi scholars also drew upon Sunni hadith collections, but this earlier use was neither systematic nor theoretically grounded.[57] Therefore, the rise of this scholarly tradition to which al-Shawkānī belonged cannot be explained in terms of the state's need to accommodate its Shāfiʿī subjects. It is also noteworthy that al-Shawkānī does not accord a higher status to Shāfiʿī scholars than members of other schools. In fact, with the exception of the fifteenth-century Shāfiʿī polymath Jalāl al-Dīn al-Suyūṭī, al-Shawkānī's list of Sunni heroes includes mostly eccentric Ḥanbalīs and Ẓāhirīs; moreover, al-Shawkānī's views on *ijtihād* and other legal matters seems to have an affinity with the Ḥanbalī and Ẓāhirī schools. Thus, Shāfiʿī material or intellectual influence must be ruled out as a cogent explanation for the emergence of the Sunna-oriented scholars or al-Shawkānī's prominence and position in the state.

If al-Shawkānī's rise to power cannot be explained in terms of the need of the Zaydi state to accommodate its Sunni/Shāfiʿī subjects, it also cannot be explained as a result of the erosion of the imams' Zaydi credentials. It may be argued that the later imams of Sanaa themselves no longer fulfilled the rigorous requirements of traditional Zaydi political theory, and thus they may have turned to the less demanding and supposedly ruler-friendly Sunni political theories to legitimate their authority. Were this the case, however, the appointment of al-Shawkānī to the office of chief judge would have provided ideological underpinning for the dynastic claims of the later imamate, at a time when it could no longer rely on the Hādawīs to sustain claims to legitimacy based on the standards of traditional Zaydi political theory.[58] However, the actual historical record and the writings of al-Shawkānī rule out this possibility. To start with, this scenario idealizes Hādawī political theory that, as stated above, had long allowed for compromises both in practice and in theory. Moreover, al-Shawkānī and all the Sunna-inclined scholars of Zaydi Yemen were not politically subservient, and they were as spirited and exacting as any scholar could be, short of resorting to outright insurrection. Of course, none of al-Shawkānī's predecessors was appointed to office, and hence none could have served to legitimate the state directly or through association with it. All along, these Sunna-oriented scholars had their own agendas that in many instances undermined the state's authority rather than reinforced it. In contrast, many of al-Shawkānī's Hādawī contemporaries were affiliated with the state and were more than willing to legitimate its authority on Zaydi grounds. Al-Shawkānī relates that, in reaction to one of his works, *Irshād al-Ghabī*, in which he takes a balanced stand on the question of the status of the Companions and the family of the Prophet (*ahl al-bayt*), more than twenty responses were written, and all were unfailingly negative.[59] The real motive for these responses, al-Shawkānī contends, was to please the commoners (*ʿāmma*) and state officials in positions of power (*man lahu ṣawla wa dawla*). He adds that even those scholars who may have harbored support for al-Shawkānī would not reveal their views for fear of persecution. No doubt al-Shawkānī, like his predecessors, was promoting ideas deemed unacceptable by the Zaydi official establishment. As such, these are oppositional views advanced despite, and not in collusion with, the established power base of the imamic state.

Subverting the State

Both in his practices and in the views he promoted, al-Shawkānī proved to be independent and capable of assuming a critical stand toward the state. As mentioned earlier, al-Shawkānī became involved in a coup staged by al-Mutawakkil Aḥmad against his father, Imam al-Manṣūr ʿAlī. On a practical level, al-Shawkānī's role involved negotiating, apparently on behalf of the son, a deal with the father whereby effective power was passed to the son while the father retained the title. A year after this transfer, when the father died, al-Shawkānī rallied support for the son and rapidly secured his confirmation to the office of the imam in apparent anticipation of opposition from other quarters of the ruling dynasty, including al-Mutawakkil's brother. In his writings, al-Shawkānī provides theoretical justifications for both junctures of this episode: he presents the transfer of effective power during the father's lifetime as a natural transfer given al-Manṣūr's preoccupation and isolation, which impeded his ability to perform his duties properly and subsequently led to the loss of order, security, and justice.[60] Al-Shawkānī justifies al-Mutawakkil's takeover as a corrective to the corruption that prevailed when his father delegated authority to his dishonest *wazīr* al-Faqīh Ḥasan Bin Ḥasan ʿUthmān al-ʿAlfī.[61] It should be noted here that, in effect, al-Shawkānī justifies an act of rebellion against the current imam in the name of restoring justice and public order, even though he did not and would not use the term *rebellion* to describe these events.

On a more fundamental level, al-Shawkānī subverted the state by opposing the extraction of illegal taxes despite the long tradition of levying these taxes as a main source of state income. Al-Shawkānī used the occasion of the loss of Tihāma (the Red Sea coastal plain of Arabia) to compose a book, *Al-Dawāʾ al-ʿĀjil fī Dafʿ al-ʿAduw al-Ṣāʾil*, in which he offers his own diagnosis of the ills that weakened the hold of the imamic state over its territories. In this book, al-Shawkānī reports that after the loss of Tihāma, he convinced the imam to issue the Manṣūrī edict, which he considered a blueprint for restoring imamic power and authority. An important prerequisite for the restoration of imamic authority, according to al-Shawkānī, is the alleviation of injustice. The principal advice of the edict is to refrain from the collection of illegal taxes (*maks*, pl. *mukūs*) because these antagonize the population; as such, the edict was composed to check arbitrary power by introducing rules that even the *ijtihād* of the imam could not override. Indeed, al-Shawkānī argues, no *ijtihād* could justify the introduction of extralegal taxes not stipulated in Islamic law. In the Manṣūrī edict, al-Shawkānī envisions a network of judges that has final say in running the affairs of the state at the local level. By relegating the power to administer the state to this network of scholars, the edict effectively undermines the power of the imam and his officers. In a similar vein, al-Shawkānī also asserts that the most effective measures a ruler can take to fortify his rule are to alleviate injustice and end the extortion of illegal taxes.[62] Al-Shawkānī also advised that these measures be publicized and the population made aware of them, to dissuade them from welcoming the armies of rival polities. To be sure, the political establishment resisted al-Shawkānī's directive by rightly identifying it as something that weakens the state. Yet al-Shawkānī suggests that his critique was motivated by his desire to preserve the territorial integrity of the imamate, and this he proposed to do by limiting the arbitrariness of its power. This bid to limit and regulate the power of the state, in the name of justice, does not fit an assumed model of Sunni quietism and subservience to political authority, and therefore it cannot be explained in terms of al-Shawkānī's Sunni or Zaydi affiliations. Moreover, his ability to maintain a critical distance from the interests of the state that employed him must have owed much to his independence and intellectual integrity.[63]

Al-Shawkānī's theoretical stand on the subject of political authority reflects his intellectual independence. In his discussions of the conditions of the imamate, al-Shawkānī treads the middle ground that diverges from both the traditional Zaydi and Sunni models. It should be noted, however, that these theoretical views might have in fact been inspired by real historical paradigms in which the Zaydi and Sunni models of governance were not as divergent as a purely theoretical consideration suggests. In one clear departure from traditional Zaydi political theory, al-Shawkānī suggests that the imam need not be a *mujtahid*, and he gives priority to the ruler's power and ability to rule with justice.[64] In a description of the reign of al-Mutawakkil ʿalā Allāh Ismāʿīl Ibn al-Imām al-Qāsim Ibn Muḥammad (d. 1087), the son of the founder of the Qāsimī dynasty, al-Shawkānī provides a blueprint for what he considers an ideal rule. Al-Shawkānī reports that al-Mutawakkil was not intimidated by his brother's claim to the imamate, since the brother was not a *mujtahid*. Still, the traits that al-Shawkānī celebrates in al-Mutawakkil are his ability to provide security and prosperity for his subjects, his application of justice, which prevented him from the arbitrary use of his power, and the awe he inspired, which deterred people under his rule from committing illegal acts.[65]

In one of many examples, al-Shawkānī further delineates his notion of what legitimates political authority in the biography of Tankar (d. 741 AH), the governor of Syria under the Mamlūk Sultan al-Nāṣir.[66] Tankar's justice, according to al-Shawkānī, was evidenced by the fact that, rather than wasting his energy on food, drinking, clothing, and sex, he devoted himself to "guaranteeing the security of the subjects: the roads became safe during his days; prices went down; and, during his reign, no one was abused, not even the unbelievers."[67] In addition, Tankar did not accept bribes and never appointed anyone to public office, such as an *amir*, deputy, judge, *wazīr*, secretary, or any other major or minor official, in return for gifts or bribes; in fact, he would return such gifts and hold a grudge against those who offered them. People in his days felt safe in all respects; he upheld the law without compromise and treated scholars with great respect.[68] One of his achievements was reviewing the status of the *waqf* endowments dedicated to schools, mosques, *khāniqa*s, and *zāwiya*s. He also made the payment of salaries to the supervisors of these endowments conditional on their restoration and upkeep of the endowed properties. He reduced epidemics by cleaning the sewage systems; he also worked on water supply systems, and trade flourished under him.[69] Al-Shawkānī quotes the negative assessment of Tankar by the historian al-Dhahabī, who describes Tankar as a man who is "reckless, and lacks good sense and cunning."[70] The real reason for al-Dhahabī's negative opinion of Tankar, al-Shawkānī adds, is that Tankar used to criticize Ibn Taymiyya, while al-Dhahabī was biased toward the Ḥanbalīs, although he himself was appointed to teach in the schools of hadith under Tankar without paying a bribe or without differential treatment on account of his connections. This long entry for Tankar in *Al-Badr al-Ṭāliʿ*, dedicated to a Mamlūk governor from the distant Islamic past with whom al-Shawkānī had no political or religious affinity, explicates al-Shawkānī's views on the ideals of governorship. Tankar's mistreatment of Ibn Taymiyya,[71] one of al-Shawkānī's few heroes, suggests that a ruler's stand on religious matters is not of primary importance to al-Shawkānī, so long as these views do not translate into systematic religious persecution, and so long as the ruler provides security, upholds the law rather than abuses it, maintains social order, enhances public services, and recognizes and respects scholarly talent. This is a purely functional notion of political legitimacy that does not idealize the ruler on religious grounds. For al-Shawkānī, a clean sewage system, and not the treatment of Ibn Taymiyya, is the gauge for this legitimacy.

As suggested earlier, despite this departure from traditional Zaydi political theory, al-Shawkānī's emphasis on justice, as well as his opposition to the imam's extraction of illegal taxes, conforms with the image of the early Zaydi rulers, and as such reflects a Zaydi ideal. Al-Shawkānī's stand on the illegality of taxation could be seen as a denial of the imam's right to use his *ijtihād* to justify injustice. Yet in traditional Zaydi theory, the justice of the imam takes priority over his lineage and the sacredness and presumed infallibility of his knowledge. In a sense, therefore, al-Shawkānī plays one Zaydi principle against another.[72] What is important here is that the imam need not be a *mujtahid* because, in al-Shawkānī's view, *ijtihād* and the authority that derives from it are not restricted to the *ʿitra*, the descendants of the Prophet, but instead reside in a much larger sector of society. Hence al-Shawkānī's notion that the imam need not be a *mujtahid* did indeed diverge from traditional Zaydi legal theory in one main respect: his theory advocated significantly reducing the imam's power and provided for a wider diffusion of political and religious authority.[73] Elsewhere, al-Shawkānī opposes rebellion (*khurūj*) against the imam, but he qualifies his theoretical opposition to rebellion on several occasions and seems to condone it under certain conditions, as in his above-mentioned involvement in the small-scale rebellion against al-Manṣūr.[74]

Al-Shawkānī was always willing to assign the responsibility for corruption and Yemen's social and political crises to all levels of the state political hierarchy. Unlike other scholars who might blame state officials but refrain from implicating the head of the state, al-Shawkānī held the imam responsible for appointing corrupt individuals. Although assigning responsibility in this fashion is but a step away from legitimizing action against the state, al-Shawkānī tackled the question of rebellion head on in his writings. In *Nayl al-Awṭār*, he sides with the standard legal view that Muslim rebels should not be pursued if they are retreating, and that the permission to kill them is an exception contingent on their initiation of battle and may be granted only for the duration of the fighting. Whenever they stop fighting, the initial rule is restored, namely, their blood is sanctified and their persons are inviolable.[75] This relative lenience toward renegades and rebels is perhaps a remnant of traditional Zaydi sympathy with rebels who stand up to tyrannical rulers; in fact, standing up to tyranny is one of the conditions of the legitimate Zaydi imam. However, immediately after he expresses these sympathies al-Shawkānī espouses different traditions that counsel patience in dealing with unjust rulers (*aʾimmat al-jūr*).[76] Al-Shawkānī maintains that it is not lawful to rise against such rulers so long as there is any room for justifying their actions, and as long as they do not publicly exhibit clear and unambiguous unbelief and do not force Muslims to sin. Al-Shawkānī adds, however, that this should not be taken to mean that contemporary Muslims should feel free to criticize earlier generations of Muslims that rebelled against tyrannical regimes, whether they be members of the *ʿitra* or other Muslims; that is, whether Shiʿis or Sunnis. These rebels, he contends, resorted to rebellion on the basis of "their *ijtihād*, and they were more fearful of God and more obedient to the tradition of His Prophet than many of the scholars who came after them."[77] Elsewhere, al-Shawkānī lists the duties of rulers in return for which they can demand the tolerance and obedience of their subjects.[78] Clearly then, although he does not openly call for it, al-Shawkānī's stand allows for rebellion under extreme cases of injustice and in the name of *ijtihād*. This is, no doubt, a far cry from a docile view that idealizes obedience to rulers under all conditions. This is not to say that al-Shawkānī's views on rebellion are Zaydi or that they are at odds with Sunni views but rather to note that a linear and simplistic explanation of al-Shawkānī's stand on this matter fails to capture the historical context of his position as well as the nuances of his scholarship and practice.

There can be no doubt that the imamic state at the time of al-Shawkānī was weaker than in earlier periods, and that it was more accommodating of its Shāfiʿī subjects. Yet this imamate continued to be a Zaydi state in terms of both its power base and its official ideology. Although the Shāfiʿī population was not a small minority, it certainly remained in the minority as far as the real makeup of the power base of the Zaydi state was concerned. Equally important was the makeup of the imamate's armies. From its very inception, the imamic state's military might, its ability to project its power within Yemen, and its power to deter its outside enemies, depended, above all, on the alliance between the imamic dynasty and the Zaydi tribes of highland Yemen. These tribes, who made up the bulk of the army, cared little about the ideal qualifications of the imam, but they were decidedly committed to the Zaydi identity of the state and the prevalence of the Zaydi *madhhab* in Yemen.[79] The army was further supplemented by a core force of slave soldiers, most of whom, like the *wazīr*s and other bureaucrats, were also staunchly loyal to the Zaydi state. In contrast, the Shāfiʿī subjects were not recruited to this army and thus had no leverage over this aspect of power in the imamic state.

Therefore, to situate al-Shawkānī in the complex web of power relations that existed in Yemen, it is imperative to distinguish between his interests and those of the state he served. Al-Shawkānī was no longer a Zaydi in the traditional understanding of the word, neither in the way he was perceived by his contemporaries and rivals, nor in the way he thought of himself. However, al-Shawkānī did not become a Sunni, although some of his contemporaries accused him of that. But what was al-Shawkānī?

The Carving of a New Intellectual Identity

In the eighteenth century, ethnic and even protonational identities, no matter how strong an echo they had in the consciousness of individuals or collectivities, remained void of intellectual content and did not inspire the articulation of a collective consciousness or political and social norms that had a bearing on the regulation of social relations. In contrast, the newly defined intellectual identities had significant social implications. To a great extent, eighteenth-century reform ushered the emergence of new intellectual identities at the expense of older affiliations. By all accounts, al-Shawkānī represents the culmination of a trend among several generations of Zaydi reformers who were open to Sunni thought and were strong advocates of the discipline of hadith and its study. The attitude of these scholars toward different sects and schools of law has been a subject of frequent commentary. Contemporary scholarship often tries to determine whether these reformers were Zaydi or Sunni.[80] In particular, the attempt to resolve the question of the legal and sectarian affiliations of al-Shawkānī, and al-Ṣanʿānī before him, has generated much debate and speculation among contemporary historians of Yemen. This quest is not without justification, for it seems to have been an issue with which the Yemeni scholars themselves struggled. Moreover, the resolution of this question is no doubt important for understanding the political as well as intellectual connections of both al-Ṣanʿānī and al-Shawkānī. However, some of the current interest in this question is a by-product of contemporary political agendas and sheds little light on the political and intellectual careers of these reformers. In the case of al-Shawkānī, in particular, perhaps no other aspect of his career has received more attention than his relationship to the Zaydi and Sunni schools, and the impact of this relationship on his stand vis-à-vis the political authorities. Although al-Shawkānī's whole career defies narrow categorization, modern scholars and politicians alike consistently elevate the question of whether he was a Zaydi or a Sunni above all other aspects of his complex and rich career. This section will address the vexed question of intellectual identity. Again, the primary focus here will be on al-Shawkānī, since his case presents a more complex model than previous reformers of the same trend.

Al-Shawkānī was born to a Zaydi family in the little town of Shawkān, north of Sanaa.[81] While still young, al-Shawkānī's father moved to Sanaa, where he served for forty years as a local judge in the Zaydi tradition. Al-Shawkānī received all of his education in Sanaa, although some of his teachers had traveled in pursuit of knowledge. At a young age, al-Shawkānī was appointed as the imamate's chief judge, thus occupying both the highest position in the judiciary, and one of the highest positions under the imamate. Al-Shawkānī, therefore, was part of the power apparatus of the Zaydi state and, at least to some extent, furthered the interests of this state. Al-Shawkānī took pride in his ancestry, the fact that his ancestors were staunch supporters of the Qāsimī imams and played a prominent role in driving the Ottomans out of Yemen.[82] In a telling example, al-Shawkānī relates an anecdote about Ibn al-Wazīr, who went to Mecca to study hadith; at one point, his teacher entreated him to affiliate himself with the schools of either Imam Shāfiʿī or Abū Ḥanīfa, but this only angered Ibn al-Wazīr, who said, "If I were in need of such imitation and affiliation I would choose only Imam Qāsim Ibn Ibrāhīm or his grandson al-Hādī."[83] An almost identical story is reported about an encounter between al-Maqbalī, one of the Sunna-inclined Yemeni scholars, and a Shāfiʿī scholar in Mecca. Al-Maqbalī resided in Mecca for a long time in a kind of self-imposed exile, which he resorted to under pressure from Zaydi zealots who did not approve of his independent views. As a result of the great impression that al-Maqbalī left on the scholars of the Ḥaramayn, the Shāfiʿī mufti of Mecca intimated to him that he wished al-Maqbalī would become a Shāfiʿī. Al-Maqbalī's response, which al-Shawkānī reports with great approval, was that if he were to be affiliated with any single *madhhab*, he would certainly choose the great school of his Zaydi ancestors.[84] Such, then, was Ibn al-Wazīr's, al-Maqbalī's, and al-Shawkānī's pride in their background. On the one hand, they all had a basic loyalty to the Zaydi tradition but strove to stand outside it as well, and they did not view themselves as narrowly bound by it. On the other hand, they were not bound by any of the other Sunni schools, and they unequivocally refused to be partisans of any *madhhab*.

In a biography of Aḥmad Ibn Ṣāliḥ Ibn Abī al-Rijāl (d. 1092), the author of *Maṭlaʿ al-Budūr wa Majmaʿ al-Buḥūr*, al-Shawkānī praises him for compiling this book of biographies of Zaydi notables.[85] Such books, al-Shawkānī maintains, are especially needed because the Zaydis, who have numerous distinguished traits and can boast of individuals from all generations who are talented in all possible areas of excellence, are nonetheless experts at obscuring the excellence of their notables and hiding their achievements. They do not pay attention to what they compose either in prose or verse, although they are fond of tracing the achievements of other groups and learning all about the conditions of other sects. As a result, al-Shawkānī adds, Zaydi scholars, notables, and poets, among others, have been neglected by the compilers of histories as well as in the biographies of people from a particular century or generation. In the unlikely event that anything is mentioned about any of the distinguished Zaydis of Yemen, the biographical entry is usually without substance and "devoid of even a fraction of what the person deserves." This is so because knowledge about individuals derives primarily from their own contemporaries, acquaintances, and fellow countrymen. If these people neglect to report such knowledge, then other, more removed authors will do the same. Al-Shawkānī himself confesses that he too is often at a loss when it comes to the biographies of early Zaydis. Al-Shawkānī thus recognizes the regional character of accumulated biographical knowledge, and the role that each region plays in producing its own local historical knowledge. He further laments the tendency among Zaydi historians to efface the good deeds of their noteworthy scholars, including the most eminent among them.

Al-Shawkānī sets out to change this tradition and he states that one of the objectives of his own biographical collection is to highlight the achievements of fellow Zaydis, preserve their memory, celebrate and promote their scholarship and literary contributions, and give them their due recognition and praise. Furthermore, al-Shawkānī does not restrict the preservation of this legacy to his historical writings but also seeks to preserve the scholarship produced within this tradition. Thus, in his *Itḥāf al-Akābir bi Isnād al-Dafātir*, al-Shawkānī indicates that he collected in this treatise all the works he had studied and taught, as well as the continuous chains of transmission of these works from their source up until al-Shawkānī himself. These works, al-Shawkānī adds, cover all disciplines of learning and include the "books of the family of the Prophet, may God be pleased with them, and the books of other [scholars] who belong to various schools of law, may God have mercy on them."[86] Al-Shawkānī thus became engaged in the preservation of Zaydi scholarship and memory, and the abundance of the chains of transmission through Zaydi imams illustrates the seriousness with which he dealt with this tradition. Once again, al-Shawkānī was not just proud of his Zaydi background but played an active role in preserving the collective memory of the Zaydi tradition. In other words, one of al-Shawkānī's main objectives in his historical writings, and in other intellectual works, was to usher the Zaydis into mainstream Islamic history by highlighting their personal and intellectual merit, and their contribution to Islamic knowledge in general.[87]

To be sure, al-Shawkānī's motivation for constructing this kind of history derived, at least partly, from his desire to dispel the impression that Zaydis were zealous extremists who made no contribution to the larger world of Islamic knowledge. In reference to the ridiculously short entries for Ibn al-Wazīr in the classical biographical dictionaries of Ibn Ḥajar al-ʿAsqalānī al-Sakhāwī, al-Shawkānī maintains that there is no doubt that scholars belonging to various schools do not pay much attention to the people of Yemen, because they blindly repeat information generated by earlier writers who knew nothing of the conditions of Yemen and its people.[88] In contrast to the impression one gets from these classical biographical dictionaries and histories, al-Shawkānī asserts that the lands of the Zaydis have innumerable scholars of the Book and the Sunna; they adhere to the textual indicants [*adilla*] and depend on what has been established as sound in the classical compilations of hadith. . . . They do not resort to imitation in any way or form, and their religion is not tainted with the innovations from which the people of the different schools are never totally free. The Zaydis follow the example of the first generation of pious Muslims in acting in accordance with what is indicated in the Book of God and in the Sunna of the Messenger of God. . . . Suffice it for them to have this special characteristic of adherence to the texts of the Book and the Sunna, and abandoning imitation, since this is a characteristic with which God privileged the people of these [Yemeni] lands in these late times, and it is rarely found in anyone else. There is no doubt that in the Egyptian or Syrian lands there are great scholars whose status is hardly matched by most of the people of our lands; they, however, do not forsake imitation, which is the habit of those who do not understand the proofs of God and His Messenger; the scholarship of one who does not forsake imitation is not of great benefit. Those who act in accordance with indicants and who forsake imitation are a rare minority, such as Ibn Taymiyya and his like.[89]

Although al-Shawkānī does not strictly idealize Zaydis, he nonetheless argues that the ranks of the Zaydi school have provided more independent scholars than any other school of law, and, as such, there is much to be proud of in the regional Zaydi tradition. What is also clear is that al-Shawkānī equates the Yemeni regional tradition with the Zaydi one, and uses the two terms, *Yemeni* and *Zaydi*, interchangeably. It is also important to note at the outset that al-Shawkānī does not exonerate Yemen by arguing that it has Sunni scholars; rather, better than that, Yemen has independent scholars and *mujtahid*s who have abandoned imitation and recognized the superior authority of hadith.

Pride aside, al-Shawkānī's praise for Yemeni Zaydi contributions to Islam was in no way uncritical. In fact, aside from the Qurʾān and the Prophet Muhammad, one would be hard pressed to find a single person, work, or tradition that al-Shawkānī praised without some critical qualification. In the case of Zaydi legal thought, a subject close to al-Shawkānī's heart, the critique was often devastating. In one typical example, al-Shawkānī marvels at the "stupidity" of Yemeni imitators. He maintains that although he has prohibited imitation, most Yemenis persist in imitating al-Imām al-Hādī Yaḥyā Ibn al-Ḥusayn (end of the thirteenth century AD)—after whom the dominant Hādawiyya branch of Zaydi law is named. These Yemenis then contend that "they imitate him, even though he does not consider it lawful to do so, in agreement with the opinion of some later scholars that it is permissible to imitate al-Imām al-

Hādī even though he prohibits *taqlīd*."[90] Thus, according to al-Shawkānī, most Yemeni Zaydis imitate al-Hādī on all but his views on the question of imitation, which he prohibits. In all cases, these imitators do not make any logical inferences of their own but instead justify their opinions on the basis of someone else's opinion. Again, al-Shawkānī tries here to maintain a delicate balance between his criticism of extreme Hādawī Zaydis, as well as some errors in the legal formulations of the Hādawī school,[91] and his simultaneous claim to represent the correct understanding of this tradition.

Aside from imitation, a fault shared by Muslim masses and elites alike, irrespective of their schools, al-Shawkānī criticizes Zaydism harshly when it degenerates into *rafḍ* (extreme Shiism, rejectionism). Al-Shawkānī's references to Shiʿis and Shiism are distinct from his references to Zaydism. Of Twelver Shiism, al-Shawkānī displayed little knowledge. On the whole, he is indifferent to Twelver Shiʿis, although not without an occasional positive reference to an individual or even to a Twelver legal opinion.[92] For example, in one instance he adopts the Twelver view on the best sequence of rituals to be performed in the pilgrimage, which he also attributes to Mālik and Ibn Ḥanbal, but not to their followers.[93] However, this example notwithstanding, al-Shawkānī seems to have known little about Twelver Shiism, and he seldom quotes Twelver Shiʿi legal views. Rather, he tends to ignore them, and his references to Shiism are usually to the Ismāʿīlīs, whom he refers to as *Rāfiḍa* (rejectionists), and whom he cites as examples of abominable heresy. This, of course, owes much to his firsthand encounter with the large Ismāʿīlī communities in Yemen, whereas there was no such Twelver Shiʿi presence. On multiple occasions, al-Shawkānī expresses concern about the adoption of extreme Shiʿi dogmas by common Zaydis, especially the slandering of the Companions of the Prophet.[94]

There are, according to al-Shawkānī, exceptions to this general tendency, namely, the independent scholars who "act in accordance with the indicants [of the law], do not adhere to any one school, and do not zealously defend any one individual."[95] In fact, al-Shawkānī asserts, it is rare to find in any Muslim city as many independent scholars as one finds in Sanaa; the scholars of Sanaa do not rely on speculation and imitation of school doctrines; they accept only what is definitively attributable to the Lawgiver. With very rare exceptions in other Muslim cities, this is a virtue unique to Yemen. Elsewhere, even when such scholars exist, they often hide their knowledge and disagreement with the doctrines of the prevailing *madhhab* for fear of persecution by zealous followers of this *madhhab*.[96] Thus, while al-Shawkānī is very critical of the tendency toward imitation and rejection of the Sunna and argues that it is tantamount to *rafḍ*, he exonerates independent Yemeni scholarship and scholars who are free of sectarian zeal, and argues that in this respect Zaydi Yemen is no doubt superior to other Sunni lands.

A strong sense of regional identity and loyalty to the Zaydi tradition is thus evident in al-Shawkānī's work. Even his numerous critiques of Zaydi views are offered in the name of the original founders of the Zaydi *madhhab* and its leading imams. At one level, therefore, his critical stance of many trends in Zaydism can be read as an attempt to doctrinally disengage Zaydism from *rafḍ* and to limit the political sphere of influence of the Ismāʿīlī Shiʿis in the domain of the imamate.[97]

On account of its prevalence in Imami Yemen, al-Shawkānī was intensely engaged in a critical evaluation of the Hādawī Zaydi tradition. Like all the Sunna-oriented Zaydi scholars before him, al-Shawkānī wrote extensive commentaries on classical works of Zaydi law. On one level, his engagement reflects the seriousness with which al-Shawkānī treated this tradition. Although his writings on Zaydi law were full of criticisms, he did not write polemics against Zaydism, as an outsider to this tradition would have done. Thus, when al-Shawkānī writes commentaries on, and not polemics against, the Hādawī legal doctrine, no matter how critical he may be, he starts from a premise of recognition and not rejection. This is also true of al-Shawkānī's commentaries on Sunni legal doctrines in which the fundamental legitimacy of these doctrines is recognized, although he was just as critical of countless details in the Sunni works he commented on, as he was in his treatment of Zaydi works. In principle, therefore, for al-Shawkānī, the four Sunni schools of law were as legitimate as the Zaydi one, and none of them was immune to his sharp criticism.[98] Neither did one school hold a necessary edge over the others, although at times al-Shawkānī exhibits a desire to defend the Zaydi views, if at all possible, according to his rigorous and systematic criteria of legal reasoning.[99]

The critical views that al-Shawkānī expresses on Zaydi law appear perhaps more frequently in his writings than those on Sunni law. This is understandable given that he was educated in the Zaydi tradition; moreover, Zaydi law was the law of the land, and hence, in his capacity as the head of the judiciary, it was of a more immediate practical concern to al-Shawkānī. Still, he was no less critical of Sunni law, and more important, his critique of *madhhab* zeal was directed equally at Sunnis and Zaydis. In fact, since, according to al-Shawkānī, *madhhab* zeal is primarily a by-product of imitation and the suspension of *ijtihād*, and since the practice of *ijtihād* was commonly advocated in the Zaydi school, at least at the level of the elite, the Sunni schools seem to bear a larger share of the responsibility for the sectarian tendencies among Muslims. It is in Sunni scholarship that one encounters the argument that, after the death of the founding fathers of the four schools of law and after the elaboration of the doctrines of these schools, *ijtihād* was no longer possible. Al-Shawkānī maintains that this claim supposes that the nature of human understanding has changed since the establishment of these schools and serves to impose "the innovation of *taqlīd* upon all Muslims, as if the divine law . . . has been abrogated."[100] People who make this argument, al-Shawkānī contends, "recognize no divine law other than that which has been established in the schools." The implication of the alleged closure (*insidād*) of the gates of *ijtihād*, al-Shawkānī adds, is that there is no living Muslim who can understand the Book and the Sunna; if this were true, Muslims would no longer have the ability to access these texts and understand them. Making this argument is tantamount to fabricating lies about God by claiming that "He is incapable of creating humans who can understand what He legislated for them, and what He required them to observe, as if what He legislated for them is not an absolute Law but a limited, interim code that was to last until these schools were established." Al-Shawkānī thus concludes that even if they deny the charges, people who make this argument in effect "legislate a new law and create a new religion for this community [of Muslims]."[101]

In his characteristic style, al-Shawkānī invariably makes sure that his criticism of one group is not understood as advocacy of another. After criticizing the presumably Sunni adherence to *madhhab*s, he adds that the Zaydis of Yemen have a parallel "detestable" and "satanic" predilection, namely, accusing someone who applies and teaches the classical books of hadith of departing from the school of the family of the Prophet, simply because the compilers of these books were not Shiʿis. Thus, those Zaydis "use this damned contention to reject all of the purified Sunna, since one can find the Sunna that comes from the Messenger of God only in these compilations, and there is no Sunna aside from what one finds in them."[102] Unlike these Zaydis, the Sunni imitators and deniers of *ijtihād* still revere the books in which the Sunna is compiled and concede the excellence of these books. More important, they recognize that, taken together, these compilations are the "records of Islam and the sources and compendiums of hadith on which scholars of all times have relied." The essence of al-Shawkānī's advocacy of the Sunna is the centrality of the canonical collections of the Sunna of the Prophet both to Islam in general, and to the exercise of *ijtihād* in particular. The virtue of the Sunnis is not in their adherence to their respective *madhhab*s but in their use of hadith. In al-Shawkānī's view, the use of hadith, despite Zaydi beliefs to the contrary, does not amount to a rejection of the school of the family of the Prophet (*madhhab ahl al-bayt*). Al-Shawkānī thus makes a very conscious distinction between the use of Sunna and being a Sunni. And although his hadith methodology is closer to the traditional Sunni methodology, he also diverges from this methodology in significant, and at times radical, ways.[103] On the other hand, he treats the Zaydi legal tradition as a legitimate tradition just as worthy of examination and engagement as the other Sunni *madhhab*s, clearly a position that is not in agreement with traditional Sunni views.

Al-Shawkānī, therefore, was a traditionalist, but of an unconventional brand of traditionalism peculiar to Zaydi Yemen. In fact, al-Shawkānī consciously presents himself as continuing this peculiar Yemeni trend, which starts with Ibn al-Wazīr (d. 840/1436) and includes al-Ḥasan al-Jalāl (d. 1084/1673), al-Maqbalī (d. 1108/1696), and al-Ṣanʿānī (d. 1182/1769). In varying degrees, each of these five scholars placed hadith above school affiliation. Moreover, all of these scholars identified with eccentric, unconventional Sunnis, such as Ibn Taymiyya and Ibn Ḥazm al-Ẓāhirī, and not with mainstream Sunnism. It is, therefore, decidedly inaccurate to view al-Shawkānī, on account of his traditionalism, as a Zaydi turned Sunni, or to try to place him within either tradition. There are, no doubt, numerous influences that shaped al-Shawkānī's thought, but his intellectual profile is not reducible to its ancestries. His rejection of Zaydi zeal is part of his larger rejection of *madhhab* partisanship of all kinds. Furthermore, al-Shawkānī's highly complex and intricate system of thought cannot be exclusively understood in terms of his relationship with political authority. In fact, despite changing political conditions, the continuities in the Yemeni reformative intellectual tradition since the ninth/fifteenth century attest to the relative autonomy of this intellectual heritage and the need to examine its internal logic on its own merits.[104]

One example that illustrates the peculiarity of this Yemeni intellectual tradition is the attitude toward *kalām* (Islamic theology). In contrast to Sunnis who largely adopted Ashʿarī theology, the Zaydis of Yemen continued to advocate Muʿtazilī theology even after its general demise in the Muslim world. Starting with Ibn al-Wazīr, however, one of the hallmarks of the Yemeni reform tradition, in addition to the study and use of hadith, was the critique of Muʿtazilī theology. And yet, this ostensible Sunni influence had distinct characteristics that were peculiar to Yemen. To start with, the reformers of Yemen rejected Muʿtazilī and Ashʿarī theology, both of which, they argued, were not needed for the proper understanding and practice of Islam.[105] Moreover, al-Shawkānī in particular veered away from the traditional Ashʿarī notion that God's creation and law are not necessarily bound by any purpose; instead, he maintained, there is definite wisdom in God's creation and law. Unlike the Muʿtazilīs, however, he added that human understanding may not always perceive this wisdom, and human action is not conditional on understanding the wisdom behind God's commands. Al-Shawkānī also advocated the Muʿtazilī concept that, in theory, goodness and badness (*ḥusn* and *qubḥ*) are so on rational grounds (*ʿaqlī*), although, once again, human understanding may not always be able to identify in practice what can be identified in theory.[106]

Theology was more of an issue for the early reformers of Zaydi Yemen, and by the time of al-Shawkānī it was no longer one of the pressing intellectual issues, thus he dealt with it only in passing. However, for al-Shawkānī and his predecessors, just as urgent were other items on this reform agenda: the use of the canonical compilations of hadith and what that entailed with regard to the attitude toward the Companions of the Prophet and the history of the formative period of Islam. The problem that continued to engage all of the Yemeni reformers who advocated the use of the canonical works of hadith was that many of these traditions were transmitted on the authority of Companions and followers who were in the anti-Shiʿi camp. The question posed was how the use of hadith related to the relative evaluation of the Companions and the ideologically laden construction of an image for the history of the formative period of Islam.[107] Al-Shawkānī invoked the systematic argument articulated by Ibn al-Wazīr, and incrementally refined ever since by all the other Sunna-inclined Yemeni reformers, to justify the acceptance of traditions transmitted on the authority of sinners or even innovators who professed Islam but were considered apostates by other Muslims. One transmitter of hadith, Muʿāwiya, could not be easily reconciled with even the most moderate Zaydi groups. In fact, the justification for accepting the traditions transmitted by Muʿāwiya was all the more reason why al-Shawkānī and al-Ṣanʿānī before him were pressed to take a stand on the religious judgment regarding Muʿāwiya and the conflict between him and ʿAlī. A similar assessment was articulated regarding the civil wars of the formative period of Islamic history.

Not surprisingly, al-Shawkānī, often blunt in expressing his views on all kinds of religious and political issues, was very careful when it came to the thorny question of the relative merits of the Companions of the Prophet. His stand on this subject could easily undermine the very project of reconciliation that defined his intellectual career. To be sure, the Zaydi tradition produced diverse opinions regarding the attitude toward the first three caliphs and the other Companions of the Prophet who fought ʿAlī and undermined his authority. The range of Zaydi opinions spanned a wide spectrum, from accusing these Companions of apostasy, to the lesser accusation of sin, to charging them with error but not sin, to deferring judgment on them. Of course, distinctions were made among the various Companions, and whereas many Zaydis maintained a positive assessment of the first two caliphs, Abū Bakr and ʿUmar, it was unlikely that such a judgment could be passed on ʿUthmān or Muʿāwiya. An alternative debate among the Zaydis was on the symbolic value attached to acceptable formulas that could be used in reference to these individuals; thus it was debated whether one should use the formula of *taraḍḍī* (that is, saying *raḍiya Allāhu ʿanhu* [may God be pleased with him]) upon mentioning the names of the first two caliphs, for example, or whether one should curse them or simply refrain from saying anything.[108] The founder of the Qāsimī dynasty in Yemen, Al-Qāsim Ibn Muḥammad (d. 1620), advocated the position of *tawaqquf* (withholding the curses) with regards to the first two caliphs, but not Muʿāwiya who, al-Qāsim argued, ought to be cursed.[109] Another example of an even more moderate statement, attributed to a Zaydi group known as al-Batriyya, is the official view of Imam al-Muʿayyad Yaḥyā Ibn Ḥamza (d. 749/1348) in his *Al-Risāla al-Wāziʿa lil-Muʿtadīn ʿan Sabb Ṣaḥābat Sayyid al-Mursalīn*. In this work, Yaḥyā Ibn Ḥamza rejects *takfīr* (accusation of unbelief) or *tafsīq* (accusation of sin) of the Companions and advocates association with them (*muwālātuhum*) and using the formula of *taraḍḍī* upon invoking their names or memories. He also argues that they committed a simple error of judgment when they did not recognize ʿAlī's right to be the first caliph.[110] To varying degrees, the reformers of Zaydi Yemen went even further than this position, although, of course, they still differed from the standard Sunni views on this matter.

Al-Shawkānī shared these moderate sentiments, and in many of his works, he insisted on the collective exoneration of the Companions. Although the content of al-Shawkānī's arguments did not derive from traditional Zaydi thought, he still made an effort to situate his defense within the larger Zaydi tradition by invoking earlier Zaydi views in support of his own. Throughout his defense of the integrity of the Companions and the prohibition against cursing them, al-Shawkānī insists that this is in fact the position of the Hādawīs, who do not curse or condemn the Companions as the Rāfiḍīs do. In his *Irshād al-Ghabī ʿilā Madhhab Ahl al-Bayt fī Ṣaḥb al-Nabī* (Guiding the fool to the view of the family of the Prophet regarding the [question of cursing] the Companions of the Prophet), al-Shawkānī maintains that the prohibition against cursing the Companions, or accusing them of sin or unbelief, is in fact the position of *ahl al-bayt*, and that the only ones excepted from this prohibition are those who are famous for their opposition to religion.[111] Al-Shawkānī maintains that this prohibition is not on account of the infallibility of the Companions, but simply a consequence of the consensus of the *ahl al-bayt*. He also asserts that there is agreement among *ahl al-bayt* and other scholars that those who curse the Companions, for example the Rāfiḍa, are misguided and are innovators; some say that they are sinners whereas others say that they are unbelievers.[112] Al-Shawkānī adds, however, that the final stand on this matter should be determined on the basis of one's own *ijtihād*. In other words, imitation is not permissible in taking a stand on the question of cursing, and determination of whether the curser is an unbeliever or a sinner should be the result of the exercise of *ijtihād*.[113] Al-Shawkānī argues his case in a way that dispels the impression that his views were a total departure from Zaydism.[114] In fact, al-Shawkānī had good reason to worry about the reception of his views, since, as he reports, more than twenty works were written in response to his book *Irshād al-Ghabī*, simply because he defends the Companions and insists on the religious obligation to venerate them.[115]

In the interest of a unified Muslim community, which he championed throughout his career, al-Shawkānī argued that there is no benefit, much less need, to rank the Companions or dwell on their conflicts in an attempt to assign responsibility for these conflicts. Discussion of these matters, al-Shawkānī argued, leads only to further disagreement, and is thus detrimental to Muslims. Al-Shawkānī therefore says that he is in favor of refraining from discussion (*imsāk al-khawḍ*) of these historical questions, since these futile debates are no longer relevant to the current interests of Muslims.[116] He asserts that this discussion is tantamount to gossiping about fellow Muslims, while religion encourages the cultivation of good faith toward Muslims and prohibits *ghayba* against them (maligning them behind their back).[117]

To be sure, al-Shawkānī himself did not refrain from discussing these early events, but he opted for interpretations that would minimize the polarization of Muslims into opposing camps. Moreover, his reluctance to carry on long debates on the subject does not translate into withholding judgment, subtle as this judgment may have been. Thus, for example, after saying that there is no point in contemporary Muslims' discussing these early conflicts, he adds that it is sufficient to say that "those who rebelled against ʿAlī and persisted in fighting him without repenting are renegades [*bughāt*]; he was right and they were wrong."[118] Such, therefore, was al-Shawkānī's way of vindicating ʿAlī and asserting his superior stature, while at the same time allowing for the possibility that most of the Companions who fought him actually repented, and can thus be venerated as well. Elsewhere, after discussing and rejecting as unauthentic a version of a hadith anticipating the death of the Companion ʿAmmār Ibn Yāsir, who died fighting on ʿAlī's side, al-Shawkānī reminds his readers that "another hadith, 'The oppressive party kills ʿAmmār,' is sound and is (included) in *Ṣaḥīḥ Bukhārī*."[119] In other words, much as he wished to avoid divisive discussions, he still insisted that ʿAlī and those fighting on his side were right and that their enemies were wrong.

Of the reformers of Zaydi Yemen, al-Shawkānī was the most subtle in expressing his view on ʿAlī's stature. As late as al-Ṣanʿānī, this issue, more than any other, demarcates the ultimate identity and loyalty of these reformers. For example, in a treatise titled *Al-Rawḍa al-Nadiyya fī Sharḥ al-Tuḥfa al-ʿAlawiyya*, al-Ṣanʿānī asserts the authenticity of the hadith of Ghadīr Khumm, in which the Prophet Muhammad is said to have declared that whoever accepted his leadership should accept ʿAlī's leadership (*man kuntu mawlāhu fa hādhā ʿAlīyun mawlāhu*).[120] Al-Ṣanʿānī maintains that ʿAlī was the righteous party in the armed conflicts that broke out during his reign.[121] Al-Ṣanʿānī also argues that the reference in the Qurʾān (Al-Aḥzāb 33:33) to the purification of the family of the Prophet (*ahl al-bayt*) is to ʿAlī, Fāṭima, Ḥasan, and Ḥusayn, and not to the wives of the Prophet as is commonly assumed in Sunni interpretations of this verse.[122] In laying out the scheme of his manuscript, al-Ṣanʿānī indicates that he "relies on reports in the books of the Sunnis, so that the reader would know that they (the Sunnis) recognize the virtues of this imam (ʿAlī) and his family."[123] From these and other references it is clear that al-Ṣanʿānī treats the Sunnis as others, whose otherness is tempered by their recognition of ʿAlī's virtues. Al-Ṣanʿānī's book, therefore, identifies the common denominator shared with the Sunnis regarding the attitude toward ʿAlī; it also recognizes the authenticity of the Sunni sources and the legitimacy of using these sources. Nevertheless, Sunnis are treated in this work as rivals who recognize a truth that is best expressed in what al-Ṣanʿānī often calls the school of the family of the Prophet (*madhhab ahl al-bayt*).[124]

ʿAmmār's status comes up again in a discussion of a tradition attributed to the Prophet in relation to infighting between Muslims which states that "both the killer and the one who is killed are doomed to hell." In reference to the Muslims who died in the battle of Ṣiffīn, al-Shawkānī quotes the exegetical work of al-Qurṭubī, who maintains that "this tradition shows that if the fighting is due to ignorant worldly pursuit or following one's whims, then this is when both the killer and the killed are doomed to hell. . . . Consequently, those who withdrew from fighting in the [battles of] the Camel and Ṣiffīn are less in number than those who fought, and all of them are interpreters and, God willing, all will be rewarded. This is in contrast to those who came after them and fought in pursuit of worldly gain."[125]

After a long quote from al-Qurṭubī, al-Shawkānī comments that this judgment would be valid if the intentions of all of those who fought in the battles of Camel and Ṣiffīn were to defend religion and the well-being of Muslims, and not the pursuit of worldly gain and the desire to seize power for its own sake. This, al-Shawkānī adds, is very unlikely, especially in light of the sound tradition that anticipates the death of ʿAmmār at the hands of the renegade, oppressive party (*al-fiʾa al-bāghiya*).[126] Al-Shawkānī then adds that any fair person could see that fighting against the camp of ʿAmmār was an act of obstinacy and more than just a minor misdeed. According to al-Shawkānī, therefore, most of those who fought against ʿAlī are doomed to hell. Right after making this point, however, al-Shawkānī reverts to his conciliatory stance and reminds his readers that he has no desire to open the gates to slandering the Companions of the Prophet; that he has constantly preached against those who slander the Companions; and that he composed a treatise on this subject that brought him much abuse by the Rāfiḍīs.[127]

In comparison to those of his predecessors, al-Shawkānī's views on the early history of the conflict were the most elusive. And yet, as we have seen, despite all his tact and deliberate attempts at moderation, he retained his basic loyalty to the memory of *ahl al-bayt*. Al-Shawkānī sought to avoid positions that would undermine his claim to be an independent *mujtahid* who does not adhere to any one *madhhab*. As such, it is all the more significant that he repeatedly betrays his general preference for ʿAlī over his rivals.[128] Equally telling is his notion that those who curse the Companions on the basis of their interpretation of the historical facts are not total unbelievers.[129]

On several other occasions, al-Shawkānī expresses views on the early formative period of Islamic history that, although not typically Zaydi, are in no way Sunni. In his *Baḥth fī al-Kalām ʿalā Umnāʾ al-Sharīʿa*, al-Shawkānī expresses his disagreement with a view he attributes to Abū Bakr. The latter is said to have argued that since governors and officials need to have authority to maintain law and order, and since people by nature are inclined to hold grudges against anyone in power, he (Abū Bakr) would not limit the authority of his governors and would not question their decisions and subject them to scrutiny by the people under their jurisdiction. Al-Shawkānī adds that it was because of this attitude by Abū Bakr that the situation deteriorated and reached its unacceptable state under ʿUthmān.[130] The interesting thing about this account is that it conforms to the Zaydi view that the reign of ʿUthmān witnessed a considerable erosion of Islamic norms, but it also blames Abū Bakr's strategies for this erosion. However, the faults attributed to both Abū Bakr and ʿUthmān are seen as ones of judgment and not deliberate violations of Islamic norms and political values, and thus do not represent a sin or transgression by either man.

Elsewhere, al-Shawkānī provides a tactful but unconventional evaluation of Fāṭima, the daughter of the Prophet, in reference to the dispute between Fāṭima and Abū Bakr over the inheritance of the land of Fadak. Al-Shawkānī contends that Abū Bakr was simply telling the truth, which Fāṭima did not like; he further quotes Imam Yaḥyā Ibn Ḥamza in support of this view and then concludes that if Fāṭima "got angry, then it is the truth that made her angry."[131] As if to make sure that he leaves no side unoffended by his views, al-Shawkānī provides a similarly disapproving assessment of one of ʿAlī's legal judgments. In *ʿUqūd al-Zabarjad*, he responds to several questions solicited by a scholar from Ḍamad.[132] One of the questions is whether it is permissible to impose financial penalties in lieu of other legal penalties, or in instances when prohibition is specified but the penalty for violating the prohibition is not. The questioner gives the example of ʿAlī's burning of illegally hoarded food or his burning of the houses of people who were selling wine. In response to this question al-Shawkānī says, "The deeds of Companions are not sufficient to particularize the indicants of the Book and the Sunna, and do not constitute valid authoritative evidence in matters of dispute."[133] The first thing to note here is that al-Shawkānī refers to ʿAlī as one of the Companions and does not grant him a special stature as far as legal judgment is concerned. Moreover, this and other actions and judgments by ʿAlī are not necessarily binding on other Muslims. This sort of argument is no doubt unacceptable in a Zaydi environment, where the common view is that ʿAlī and some of his descendants are infallible. Al-Shawkānī admits that many (Shiʿis) argue that ʿAlī is infallible, whereas the majority of Muslims as well as some of the scholars of *ahl al-bayt* maintain that only the prophets are infallible, and they alone have unqualified authority.[134] Al-Shawkānī reports both sides of the argument but also notes that the traditions invoked to prove the infallibility of ʿAlī have parallels that apply to many or even all of the Companions, something no one else maintains.[135] It is clear, therefore, that al-Shawkānī does not believe in the infallibility of ʿAlī, although he does indicate that one need not assert such infallibility to prove that ʿAlī resides in paradise.

Al-Shawkānī's references to contested historical narratives are scattered throughout his huge corpus and can be misleading if read singly. In his many works on hadith he frequently rejects the authenticity of traditions that seem to support either a Sunni stand or a Zaydi one. However, his criteria for doing so are always formal (the strength of the *isnād*) and have nothing to do with his approval or rejection of the content of the traditions in question. For example, he examines the hadith "Abū Bakr is my minister. . . . ʿUmar is my beloved. . . . I am from ʿUthmān and he is from me . . . and ʿAlī is my brother and the carrier of my banner." This hadith vindicates the four caliphs, and conforms to the Sunni order of preference, which al-Shawkānī accepted as well. And yet, al-Shawkānī argues on purely formal grounds that this hadith is not authentic.[136] On the other side of the sectarian spectrum, al-Shawkānī questions the authenticity of the hadith *anā madinat al-ʿilm wa Alī bābuha* [I (Muhammad) am the city of knowledge and ʿAlī is its gate].[137] However, in his later work on fabricated traditions, he lists numerous fabricated traditions in praise of ʿAlī.[138] Al-Shawkānī concludes, after examining the various versions of the hadith that refers to ʿAlī as the gate to the city of knowledge, that this hadith is "good [*ḥasan*] and that neither of its versions reaches the rank of soundness [*ṣiḥḥa*)] or falls to the rank of falsehood [*kadhib*)]."[139] Later, al-Shawkānī undermines the authenticity of a similar hadith in which the Prophet allegedly commands that all open gates in a mosque be closed except that of ʿAlī, but al-Shawkānī proceeds to say that the general sense of the hadith "is established and it is not permissible for a Muslim to declare it invalid."[140] In a similar vein, he rejects a version of the tradition that says ʿAlī is to Muhammad like Aaron is to Moses, only to conclude that the original version of this tradition is authentic.[141] Therefore, his seeming rejection of many exaggerated traditions attributing special stature to ʿAlī does not stop him from accepting the general sense indicated by these traditions, namely, the uniqueness of ʿAlī's connection to the Prophet, and his numerous virtues and merits.

An even more telling example is al-Shawkānī's rejection as fabricated of the hadith "Cursing my Companions is an unforgivable sin," although he himself wrote extensively on the prohibition against cursing the Companions and the great sin of doing so.[142]

Al-Shawkānī on History: The Authority of the Present

Al-Shawkānī's reluctance to delve into the history of the old conflict, and his attempts to walk a thin line between the extreme Shiʿi and Sunni views of this history, are countered by his unrestrained emphasis on the authority of the present and his relentless efforts to construct and promote a coherent history of Islamic dissent. Al-Shawkānī's historical perspective was shaped, to a large extent, by his experience and conception of sectarianism and communal strife among Muslims. Furthermore, his drive for intellectual revitalization was itself intertwined with his perceptions regarding the crisis of partisanship (*tamadhhub*). For example, in *Adab al-Ṭalab*, a book on acquisition of knowledge, he asserts, "Know that just as partisanship results in the effacement of the blessings of knowledge, the dissipation of its splendor, and the loss of the reward that derives from it, so too does it cause strife that leads to the shedding of blood, violation of sanctities, vilification of honors, and making violable that which is protected by the Divine Law."[143] At some level, therefore, al-Shawkānī's whole intellectual output was his vision for a way out of the dual problem of intellectual sterility and divisive and destructive partisanship. This drive informed all of al-Shawkānī's writings, whether on law, hadith, *ijtihād*, or history. To be sure, these genres were often intertwined, and one finds, for example, many references to normative history in al-Shawkānī's legal writings. Still, al-Shawkānī wrote a separate work on history, which, like many of his other works, is quite original in form and content. In this book, *Al-Badr al-Ṭāliʿ fī Maḥāsin man baʿd al-Qarn al-Sābiʿ* (The rising/shining moon on the virtues of those [who lived] after the seventh century], al-Shawkānī makes no apologies for his intention to write a history whose primary concern was not to establish facts or to give full accounts of historical episodes, including, as was common in traditional historical accounts, dates of birth and death and the like. Rather, al-Shawkānī's *Al-Badr al-Ṭāliʿ* was deliberately structured to communicate meaning and to construct an image of history that illustrates this meaning. Moreover, this book was an optimistic statement on the possibility of carrying out al-Shawkānī's own scheme for revival. As such, this book can be viewed as yet another expression of al-Shawkānī's conception of the historical connection between intellectual and political authority, and as a rationale for intellectual intervention in lived political history. For this reason, we will now examine *Al-Badr al-Ṭāliʿ* in some detail.

Al-Badr al-Tāliʿ is a book of biographies. Al-Shawkānī started compiling it in the year 1213 AH, but he later revised and expanded it.[144] The book is arranged alphabetically, rather than according to generation, chronological time, region, or city. Al-Shawkānī also does not limit the biographies to any one professional group. His declared objective, as the title indicates, is to highlight the virtues of Muslims who lived after the seventh century AH/thirteenth century CE and to illustrate their intellectual achievements in various fields of knowledge. In his statement of purpose, al-Shawkānī says that his objective is to document the achievements of latter-day Muslims and enumerate their good deeds. Al-Shawkānī recognizes that his accounts may be provincial, and he leaves the door open for withdrawing his endorsement of certain individuals should the accounts he received of them turn out to be inaccurate.[145] Al-Shawkānī also states that he is not interested in documenting the bad traits of people. This is not to say that the people he writes about were perfect, but they need not be so to illustrate his point. In fact, for al-Shawkānī, virtue, whether collective or individual, could only be partial. Moreover, the record of such partial virtues, and hence partial histories, was all that al-Shawkānī needed to prove the vitality of post-seventh-century Islamic history and the possibility of progress, as opposed to dissolution and decline.

Al-Badr al-Ṭāliʿ served another important purpose: to construct an image of the ideal, dissenting intellectual and to argue for the centrality of the role of such intellectuals in Islamic history. In contrast to his relatively brief attempts to discern some normative unity in the early turbulent events of Islamic history, his biographical work is replete with examples of critical and eccentric scholars who dared to oppose the mainstream, did not compromise their intellectual integrity under pressure from political authority, and did not conform to the oppressive dictates of the established and entrenched schools and *madhhab*s. From *Al-Badr al-Ṭāliʿ*, we can discern what constitutes virtue to al-Shawkānī, as well as who his intellectual heroes were and how he viewed their impact on history.

The achievements al-Shawkānī celebrates in these biographies cover a wide variety of activities, practical as well as intellectual, in many spheres of action and fields of knowledge. In all of these fields, the present carries as much if not more authority than the past. Al-Shawkānī is even willing to recognize excellence in Sufi practice and mystical thought, despite his general dislike of Sufism.[146] His concept of intellectual virtue is remarkably open and is not limited to religious knowledge to the exclusion of other forms of literary achievement. One such field, dear to al-Shawkānī's heart, was poetry.[147] In his many entries on poets, both male and female,[148] al-Shawkānī discusses such matters as their writing styles, linguistic excellence, mastery of the language, poetic skill, artistic creativity, use of images and similes, the themes of their poetry as well as its emotional effect and sincerity of intent. Many of the celebrated poets have no claim to fame other than their poetry.[149] Sometimes, al-Shawkānī's biographies focus on the religious scholarship of individuals who also happen to be poets.[150] In both cases, however, the evaluation of poetry is not subjugated to other categories and is discussed at length and in its own right in what amounts to a celebration of poetic *ijtihād*.[151] Al-Shawkānī also provides occasional assessments of the literary pieces he quotes, as in the reference to a poem punctuated with sections of rhymed prose, which al-Shawkānī praises for its "harmony, simplicity, and lack of verbosity and artificiality," while the inserted prose includes allusions to basic instructions in the various linguistic and religious disciplines.[152] This poetic excellence, to al-Shawkānī, is no less an illustration of historical progress than any other field of knowledge. Thus, for example, in a biography of a contemporary with whom he exchanged poetry, al-Shawkānī quotes long parts of a poem; he then apologizes for drifting in his praise but adds that, by quoting this beautiful and expressive poetry, he wanted to provide "one of the most definitive proofs that these latter times are not devoid of people who attend to the preservation of the standards of literature."[153]

Al-Shawkānī also includes biographies of scientists who wrote on such fields as logic, mathematics, and inheritance computation (*farāʾiḍ*).[154] Again, some biographies are for individuals who excelled in a combination of fields such as jurisprudence, language, one of the exact scientific disciplines, and *zuhd* (asceticism) and *karāmāt* (saintly miracles).[155] Al-Shawkānī relates that he himself studied the exact sciences, composed a treatise on astronomy for beginners, and even taught metaphysics (*ʿilm al-ḥikma al-ilāhiyya*) to the physician and Ḥanafī jurist Muḥammad ʿĀbid al-Sindī al-Anṣārī.[156] Here too, al-Shawkānī often has some comments to make, as in the entry on the polymath Quṭb al-Dīn al-Shīrāzī (al-Shāfiʿī) (d. 710), whom al-Shawkānī praises for knowledge as well as piety and religion. Al-Shawkānī objects, however, to the exaggeration of al-Shirāzī's students and followers in reserving the title of *ʿallāma* (great, well-rounded scholar) exclusively for their master, thus implying that he alone has combined a mastery of religious and exact science. Al-Shawkānī explains that both among his contemporaries and in following generations, one will find many other scholars even more accomplished than al-Shīrāzī in their acquisition of encyclopedic knowledge.[157]

The celebration of such traits as poetic excellence, scientific exactitude, saintly devotion, and independence in legal scholarship is intricately intertwined in al-Shawkānī's historical narratives with intellectual integrity. There is hardly a page in his book where he does not write about scholars who shunned worldly power, turned down appointments as judges or other officials, and were not afraid of criticizing the state. Al-Shawkānī's exemplars also include many scholars of little note, scholars not considered exceptional but who nonetheless did not adhere to any one school or imitate in legal matters and who followed what is entailed by the indicants of the law (*al-ʿamal bimā yaqtaḍīh al-dalīl*) and practiced *ijtihād* without imitating anyone (*ʿāmilun bi-ijtihādi nafsihi lā uqallidu aḥadan*).[158] Al-Shawkānī also celebrates Zaydis involved in the study and teaching of the classics of hadith.[159] Yet it is in a few biographies of truly distinguished scholars that al-Shawkānī fully spells out his model of intellectual integrity and dissent.

In *Al-Badr al-Ṭāliʿ*, al-Shawkānī praises the deeds and achievements of individuals but never idealizes them. In a handful of cases, however, he comes close to such idealization. To be sure, in keeping with his independent thinking, al-Shawkānī inevitably expresses disagreement with each of his biographical subjects.[160] Without exception, however, his praise of these select individuals is inspired by their dissent and the price they paid for it. Despite all of the afflictions they suffer, al-Shawkānī maintains, "those who uphold the truth and who transmit it as God commands . . . attain more praise and far-reaching reputation than anyone else can ever achieve."[161] Such scholars who suffered during their lifetime but achieved renown and great reputation afterward include Mālik Ibn Anas, Ibn Ḥanbal, al-Bukhārī, Ibn Ḥazm, and Ibn Taymiyya. In Yemen, they include Ibn al-Wazīr, al-Jalāl, al-Maqbalī, and al-Ṣanʿānī.[162] Since he was primarily interested in latter-day Muslims, and since the likes of Mālik, Ibn Ḥanbal, and al-Bukhārī had already been idealized, al-Shawkānī devoted his attention to the remaining scholars on this list.

Prototypes of the Ideal Intellectual

"After Ibn Ḥazm, I do not know of any other person of the caliber of Ibn Taymiyya, and I do not think that the period between the generations of the two men allowed for someone like or even close to them."[163] In these words al-Shawkānī describes two "unrivaled" scholars of medieval Islam. The appeal of the first, Ibn Ḥazm, is that he belonged to the Ẓāhirī school, which no longer existed, and hence served as an example of scholarship that was not bound by *madhhab* affiliation. Moreover, the Ẓāhirīs were textual "fanatics" and adhered strictly to the letter of the law, which was also a trait that al-Shawkānī appreciated. Rather than a collective legal doctrine, this trait is what al-Shawkānī extracted from the model of Ibn Ḥazm.

> The literalist school [*madhhab al-ẓāhir*] is the source of thinking and the goal of action for anyone who is endowed with fairness, and whose basic nature has not been diverted from its original state by some accidental effect. It is not just the school of Dāwūd al-Ẓāhirī and his followers;

> rather, it is the school of the leading scholars who have adhered to the scripture from the time of the Companions till this day. Dāwūd is only one of them. He is reputed for being rigid in matters where he persisted in the literal meaning when he should not have done so, and where he neglected certain kinds of analogy that a fair person ought not neglect. In general, [to adhere to] the school of Ẓāhir is to abide, in all legal indicants, by the apparent meaning of the pure Book and the Sunna and to forsake reliance on mere opinions that cannot be used to provide any kind of evidence. . . . The appellation *Ẓāhirī* means one who adheres to the apparent meaning of the law, and this, not Dāwūd al-Ẓāhirī, is the origin of the attribution.[164]

In yet another reference, al-Shawkānī explicitly states that there is an affinity between the Ẓāhirīs and hadith. Thus, in a biography of a certain scholar who was raised as a Ḥanafī and then turned Shāfiʿī, al-Shawkānī relates that this scholar devoted himself to the study of hadith to the point that he was accused of belonging to the school of Ibn Ḥazm.[165] Therefore, according to al-Shawkānī, the main appeal of the Ẓāhirīs is that their methodologies undermined *madhhab* practices and gave priority to the authority of the scripture.

Ibn Taymiyya, in contrast, did belong to a living school, but even by these Ḥanbalī standards, his knowledge was so encompassing and his thought so original and independent that even his many enemies could not help but be impressed by his intellectual courage and depth. Perhaps more important to al-Shawkānī, however, was Ibn Taymiyya's political struggle. Al-Shawkānī reports that Ibn Taymiyya suffered from the intrigues of his contemporaries and was

> afflicted time and again during his life. There were several conflicts in which people were divided into two groups regarding him: some gave him less than he deserved, and even accused him of serious misdeeds, and others were zealous in defending him, just as the first group was zealous against him. A general rule regarding every scholar who becomes deeply versed in scholarly knowledge and surpasses his contemporaries, and who adheres to the Book and the Sunna, is that such a scholar is invariably denounced by inferior people. . . . Eventually, his reputation gains ascendency and his views prevail. Due to this turmoil he gains a reputation of truthfulness among other people. . . . This is exactly true of this imam, for after his death people recognized his value and tongues converged in praising him, except for a few who do not count, and his writings and views gained wide reputation.[166]

In a rare expression of outrage, al-Shawkānī writes about the zealous Mālikī jurist Ibn Makhlūf, whom he refers to as "one of their devils" for issuing death sentences against Muslims based on misinterpretation of their words.[167] As an example of the outrageous practices of Ibn Makhlūf, al-Shawkānī cites his claim to have established the unbelief of Ibn Taymiyya and to have determined that he deserved the death penalty; for al-Shawkānī, this is where Ibn Makhlūf demonstrates that he "is not even worth a single hair of his [Ibn Taymiyya], nay, he is not even fit to be the sole of his shoe." The Mālikī jurists of Cairo, in particular, seem to have earned al-Shawkānī's enmity: "God has afflicted the people of these lands with jurists of the Mālikī school who dare shed the blood [of Muslims] over matters where even the slightest castigation [*taʿdhīr*] is not lawful. They shed the blood of some scholars out of ignorance, misguidedness, and insolence toward God, and in contradiction of the law of the Messenger of God and distortion of his religion. All of this they do on the basis of mere juristic texts and inferences of applied law that do not have the slightest trace of knowledge in them."[168]

Such was the passion of al-Shawkānī for Ibn Taymiyya, and his anger at the Mālikī jurists who abused him. Of course, Ibn Taymiyya had enemies from other schools as well. Of particular significance is a biography of a Shāfiʿī jurist for whom al-Shawkānī has limited praise, but who had the misfortune of having been involved in the official campaign of abuse against Ibn Taymiyya. This jurist, al-Shawkānī reports, was delegated to lead a disputation against Ibn Taymiyya and would not have accepted to do so had he any idea of the scholar's true value. For Ibn Taymiyya was an imam deeply versed in all possible areas of knowledge, and the Shāfiʿī jurist could not be even remotely compared to him. This jurist was qualified only to discuss Shāfiʿī law with Ibn Taymiyya, and it was indeed a sign of ignorance on his part that he could contemplate a debate in any other branch of knowledge. And even in Shāfiʿī law, there is no way an imitator could match a *mujtahid*. The ultimate responsibility for this outrage, al-Shawkānī concludes, must fall on the shoulders of the political authorities who meddled in matters they had no business dealing with.[169] Al-Shawkānī, therefore, was resolutely biased in favor of Ibn Taymiyya; and yet al-Shawkānī did not celebrate his hero because he followed him or agreed with all or even most of his views. Rather, he celebrated Ibn Taymiyya's erudition, his courageous stand before the political and intellectual authorities, and the price he was willing to pay for his intellectual integrity and independence.

It is thus not just knowledge that al-Shawkānī idealized, but the way knowledge was deployed in practice. He measured scholars not only by what they knew but also by how they used their knowledge, and how they acted in the course of using it. Al-Shawkānī describes such aspects of Ibn Taymiyya's legacy in great detail. For example, he describes Ibn Taymiyya's conduct under interrogation: when his interrogators held him accountable for certain things he said, Ibn Taymiyya would invoke possible but improbable interpretations of his statements. Because of their own inadequacies, Ibn Taymiyya's interrogators would not accept the truth, so Ibn Taymiyya offered these alternative meanings to avoid strife. This, al-Shawkānī asserts, "is exactly what a consummate scholar should do: say the truth as he must, then avert discord to the extent he can."[170] The ideal scholar would thus say the truth for the record, and then, without compromising this basic truth, take note of practical issues and try to minimize the damage that may result from a blunt statement of this truth. Al-Shawkānī refers to this practice as warding off the harmful effects of strife (*dafʿ mafsadat al-fitna*), which should be one of the priorities of the scholar, but never at the expense of the truth.

Of similar integrity, but with some potentially problematic traits, was Ibn Qayyim al-Jawziyya (d. 751 AH): Ibn Taymiyya's student and ardent defender and follower. Al-Shawkānī quotes a negative account by the historian al-Dhahabī of Ibn al-Qayyim, and then responds to this account.[171] Al-Dhahabī maintains that at the beginning of his career, Ibn al-Qayyim persisted in attacking the practice of pilgrimage to the shrine of Ibrahim al-Khalīl (the friend of God), and that later he devoted himself to scholarship and the spreading of knowledge. Still, al-Dhahabī asserts, Ibn al-Qayyim was audacious in certain matters, conceited, and thought too highly of his own opinions. To be sure, al-Shawkānī had his own reservations regarding Ibn al-Qayyim, ones that he did not fail to express, although in gentler terms than usual. According to al-Shawkānī, Ibn al-Qayyim was "overtaken by his love for Ibn Taymiyya to the extent that he would not depart from any of his views, and would defend every single one of them."[172] This, of course, is a kind of imitation that al-Shawkānī disapproved of. However, he did not let this flaw obscure the main traits of Ibn al-Qayyim's scholarship and career, his intellectual integrity and unrelenting fighting spirit. Thus, in response to al-Dhahabī's criticism, al-Shawkānī asserts that Ibn al-Qayyim "adhered to sound indicants, prized acting in accordance to these indicants, and did not rely on opinion. He said the truth out loud without deference to anyone, and what a wonderful audacity this was."[173]

While his narratives regarding early, eccentric scholars like Ibn Ḥazm and Ibn Taymiyya provided the raw materials from which al-Shawkānī could then extract his norms for ideal scholarly excellence, his biographies of the reformers of Zaydi Yemen served the added purpose of constructing a regional genealogy of dissent. Needless to say, this narrative of origins augmented al-Shawkānī's own local claims to moral and intellectual authority. And yet again, as with all of his other writings, which were produced under local conditions but drew on transregional knowledge, the significance of al-Shawkānī's genealogy of dissent was not just as an ideological tool of legitimation but also as a heuristic tool through which intellectual history was understood and made to inform al-Shawkānī's own illustrious intellectual career. More than anything else, al-Shawkānī's reading of this particular history was the prism through which he viewed and constructed an image for the ideal intellectual, an image that he then strove to emulate.

Nonconformists always suffer, but their memories ultimately prevail. Such was the moral of the story of each of the Yemeni reformers al-Shawkānī celebrated in *Al-Badr al-Ṭāliʿ* and elsewhere. All of these scholars adhered to the textual indicants (*dalīl*, pl. *adilla/dalāʾil*) and rejected imitation and narrow *madhhab* partisanship; as a result, during their lifetime, they suffered various kinds of hardships and intrigues, and yet they all attained a glorious reputation, in addition to the promised rewards they no doubt attained in the hereafter.[174] The father of this Yemeni phenomenon, according to al-Shawkānī, was Ibn al-Wazīr, whose book *Al-ʿAwāṣim wal-Qawāṣim*, "the like of which has not been composed in these Yemeni lands," inaugurated the Yemeni tradition of reform.[175] In a clear indication of what he valued most in Ibn al-Wazīr, al-Shawkānī incorporated in his biography a mini-treatise on *ijtihād* and *taqlīd*.[176] Al-Shawkānī stresses the nonconformist character of Ibn al-Wazīr's thought; his views, al-Shawkānī maintains, "do not resemble those of his generation, nor of the following ones; rather, they are akin to the views of Ibn Ḥazm and Ibn Taymiyya. In many of his investigations, he often comes up with insights [*fawāʾid*] that never occurred to anyone else before him."[177] To be sure, Ibn al-Wazīr's originality is ultimately the deep erudition with which it is informed. "During his time, no one [scholar] could match up to him, because he belonged to a class [of his own], one that did not even include any of his own teachers, let alone opponents. In all likelihood, if all of his teachers were to be gathered in one person, their combined knowledge would not reach the level of his knowledge."[178]

The special honors reserved for Ibn al-Wazīr, in comparison to other similar Yemeni reformers, no doubt have much to do with his foundational role and his ability to initiate a compelling program for rethinking the received intellectual traditions. Owing to its intellectual rigor, this program would engage Yemen's best scholars in the centuries to come. In other words, Ibn al-Wazīr charted a new intellectual agenda that informed the scholarship of subsequent Yemeni reformers through the time of al-Shawkānī. Several other scholars in this tradition also left their marks on it. The next station in this tradition was represented by Al-Ḥasan Ibn Aḥmad al-Jalāl (1014–84). Al-Jalāl, according to al-Shawkānī, was a prolific writer who mastered all the rational and traditional disciplines.[179] Of his many writings, *Ḍawʾ al-Nahār*, a commentary on the classic Zaydi work on applied law, *Al-Azhār* by al-Mahdī,[180] was particularly worthy of mention by al-Shawkānī. According to al-Shawkānī, al-Jalāl wrote down his own "reasoning in accordance with legal indicants, without paying attention to scholars who agree or disagree with him. It is an unequaled commentary on *Al-Azhār*; in fact it has no equivalent in the written books of law. It has things that are acceptable and others that are not, as with all humans."[181] As is clear from this statement by al-Shawkānī, and from many critical remarks in his other works on law, he disagreed with many of al-Jalāl's individual legal judgments and conclusions. Nevertheless, he qualifies this work by al-Jalāl as an "unequaled commentary on *Al-Azhār*." What is "unequaled" in this work, therefore, is not the actual results but the spirit of the undertaking and al-Jalāl's manifest independence of thought. Thus, al-Shawkānī tries to explain away his disagreement with al-Jalāl's views on points of detail and to highlight the larger significance of the work as a laudable example of courageous dissent: "I think that the reason for the frequent oversights in this book is that this master [al-Jalāl] is like a resounding sea, and his mind is like a flame of fire; he thus rushes to prohibit what becomes visible to him trusting his manifold knowledge, the scope of his reach and the sharpness of his mind." In other words, al-Shawkānī's excuse for al-Jalāl is that he was ahead of himself, and thus he rushed into making some unwarranted legal conclusions without proper validation; this is excusable because, for the most part, al-Jalāl knew what he was talking about: "I have many objections to the [legal] preferences that he compiled in his writings; however, at the same time I continue to recognize his great prominence, the extent of his mastery, and his distinction in all areas of knowledge." Al-Shawkānī also adds, as a noteworthy trait of distinction, al-Jalāl's poetic talents.[182]

Al-Shawkānī's sympathy with al-Jalāl was governed by the same criteria that attracted him to Ibn Taymiyya: al-Jalāl was one of those scholars who "give preference to the statements of legal indicants over the opinions of men [*al-muʿthirīn li-nuṣūṣ al-adilla ʿalā aqwāl al-rijāl*]." Moreover, like the other Yemeni reformers, al-Jalāl was subjected to harassment and abuse by the people of Yemen. The next figure in the chain of Yemeni dissenters is Ṣāliḥ Ibn Mahdī al-Maqbalī (1047–1108) who, like al-Jalāl, warranted al-Shawkānī's praise not so much for his final conclusions and opinions but for the spirit of his approach to knowledge.[183] Again, despite several criticisms and disagreements on legal details, al-Shawkānī hails al-Maqbalī for his "insistence on acting in accordance with what is entailed by legal indicants, and paying no attention to imitation," and because "once he adheres to an indicant he pays no heed to any person, no matter who it may be."[184] Moreover, this attitude of al-Maqbalī antagonized many of the establishment Zaydi scholars of Sanaa, and the resulting mounting pressure on al-Maqbalī drove him to Mecca. In Mecca, the most distinguished scholar of the city at the time, al-Barzanjī, wrote a response to al-Maqbalī's major work against imitation titled *Al-ʿAlam al-Shāmikh fī al-Radd ʿalā al-Ābāʾ wal-Mashāyikh*;[185] Al-Maqbalī then wrote a rejoinder to al-Barzanjī, *Al-Arwāḥ al-Nawāfiḥ*.[186] Following this unwavering exchange, the scholars of Mecca teamed up against him and accused him of heresy because of his attacks on *taqlīd* and because he did not recognize their authority. They wrote to the Ottoman authorities, who sent one of their court scholars to interrogate al-Maqbalī; the official found nothing wrong in al-Maqbalī and exonerated him. In the meanwhile, several students who studied with al-Maqbalī, including some from Dagestan, went back to their countries and built a following for him. During al-Shawkānī's own time, some of these came all the way from Dagestan because they had a copy of al-Maqbalī's *Al-Manār*[187] but did not have al-Mahdī's *Al-Baḥr al-Zakhkhār*[188] and wanted to acquire a copy so they could better understand al-Maqbalī's commentary.[189]

Like the other Yemeni reformers, al-Maqbalī was abused by the established scholarly authorities. He held his ground despite this official intimidation and pressure, and thus he was qualified for inclusion in al-Shawkānī's genealogy of dissent. To be sure, personal characteristics distinguish al-Shawkānī's beloved reformers from each other. Al-Maqbalī's words, according to al-Shawkānī, have such power and charm that, upon reading them carefully, it is no longer possible to remain an imitator.[190] This captivating style enables al-Maqbalī to tear false opinions to pieces while using the sweetest expressions. Such were his criticisms of the theological arguments of the Muʿtazilīs as well as of the Ashʿarīs, most of the arguments of the Sufis, many views of jurists regarding applied law, and the extremism of traditionalists.

Yet al-Maqbalī also had flaws, including a hot temper (*ḥidda*).[191] Another was that, despite his wide-ranging knowledge, al-Maqbalī did not have a firm command of the terminology of hadith scholars, and as a result he sometimes could not recognize hidden defects in traditions reported in the classical compilations; he would thus adopt these defective traditions thinking they were sound. Therefore, al-Shawkānī adds, the reader of al-Maqbalī should approach his writings carefully, particularly in this area of hadith, his weak point.[192] Thus al-Shawkānī maintains that in *Al-Manār*[193] al-Maqbalī exhibits fairness but, like all humans, also makes mistakes of judgment.[194] In other words, al-Shawkānī acknowledges the critical approach exhibited throughout *Al-Manār*, but he does not endorse or reject all the legal views expressed in it. Despite these reservations on the style and content of his scholarship, it is al-Maqbalī's independent reasoning, his intellectual courage, and the fluidity of his prose, and not his actual detailed opinions on applied law, that won him al-Shawkānī's respect. The lesson that al-Shawkānī extracted from al-Maqbalī's example is that he was guided by his direct reading of the textual indicants, which is the trait of a *mujtahid* who may hit the mark or miss it but is rewarded nonetheless for his intellectual honesty and effort.

The last figure in al-Shawkānī's list is Muḥammad Ibn Ismāʿīl al-Amīr al-Ṣanʿānī[195] (1688–1769), "the great imam, the absolute *mujtahid*, author of numerous books . . . who became the exclusive head of scholarship in Sanaa, openly practiced *ijtihād*, acted in accordance with indicants, discouraged people from imitation, and refuted legal opinions which had no proof."[196] Al-Ṣanʿānī also suffered from the intrigues of zealous Zaydis, once during the reign of Imam al-Mutawakkil ʿalā Allāh al-Qāsim Ibn al-Ḥusayn, another time during the days of his son al-Manṣūr bi-Allāh al-Ḥusayn Ibn al-Qāsim, and yet again during the days of the latter's son al-Imām al-Mahdī al-ʿAbbās.[197] Imam al-Manṣūr appointed him to preach in the mosque of Sanaa, and he continued in this position until the days of his son al-Mahdī, when he was removed from this position. On one occasion a mob tried to kill al-Ṣanʿānī, but "God saved him from their intrigues and treachery, and shielded him from their evil."[198] Of particular significance is the context of the mob's attempt to kill al-Ṣanʿānī and his eventual prevention from preaching at the mosque of Sanaa.[199] This episode began when al-Ṣanʿānī failed to mention the names of the Zaydi imams in one of his Friday *khuṭba*s (sermons during the Friday congregational prayer).[200] Several members of the imam's family of the imam who, according to al-Shawkānī, had no learning, started to intrigue against al-Ṣanʿānī. Together with some members of the mob (*ʿawām*), they plotted to kill al-Ṣanʿānī the following Friday while he was delivering his *khuṭba* on the pulpit. Imam al-Mahdī heard of the plot and, to thwart it, he summoned a number of the notables of his family as well as al-Ṣanʿānī himself and imprisoned the whole lot. He also gave his instructions that a certain Sayyid Yūsuf, the main plotter in the planned murder, be driven out of the lands of Yemen. Two months later, after the sedition subsided, al-Ṣanʿānī was released from prison but was not allowed to resume preaching in the mosque of Sanaa. Still, al-Shawkānī maintains, al-Ṣanʿānī continued to spread his knowledge through writing, teaching, and issuing fatwas. He also continued to be the favorite target of the mob, which accused him of hating and of cursing the family of the Prophet (*naṣb*) on account of his study and adherence to the canonical compilations of hadith.

Al-Ṣanʿānī's enemies were not just the envious members of the imam's family and their supporters among the commoners but, perhaps more dangerously, members of the tribes of highland Yemen. Thus, rumors that al-Ṣanʿānī was undermining the Zaydi *madhhab* spread among the tribes of Mount Barṭ, including the Muḥammad and Ḥusayn clans (Dhawī Muḥammad and Dhawī Ḥusayn). At the time, these were among the most powerful tribes in Yemen, and their influence could not be ignored. The elders of these tribes met, and they decided to amass large armies to march on Sanaa against Imam al-Mahdi himself. They even sent letters to the imam informing him that they were rebelling to defend the Zaydi *madhhab* against the subversive acts of al-Ṣanʿānī and the support the latter had received from the imam. Scholars who knew the truth tried, to no avail, to dissuade the tribes, and only a sizeable increase in the yearly payment they received from the imam convinced them to return to their territories. Of course, to al-Shawkānī their acceptance of the payment was proof that the real motivation behind this rebellion was extortion and worldly gain.

The memory of al-Ṣanʿānī was still vivid during al-Shawkānī's time, and the dynamics of power that dominated Yemen's political landscape during al-Ṣanʿānī's life were, to some extent, still operative during that of al-Shawkānī. In particular, two pillars of the power of the imamic state—the family of the imam and the tribes, opposed al-Ṣanʿānī and later al-Shawkānī. Thus al-Shawkānī asserts that the commoners (*ʿawām*) have always accused people who study hadith of *naṣb* (hating and cursing *ahl al-bayt*), especially if a person happens to outwardly follow the example of the Prophet, as in raising the hands when saying "Allāhu Akbar" in prayer, or holding the hands together while standing. It is interesting that al-Shawkānī hastens to add that the Zaydi imams themselves never ceased to study and transmit the books of hadith, and some of them, like Zayd Ibn ʿAlī, believed that raising the hands in prayer and holding them together was lawful.[201] Quite understandably, the mob invoked these highly symbolic rituals and practices to prove that al-Ṣanʿānī and later al-Shawkānī were undermining the Zaydi school. Al-Shawkānī responded, however, by asserting the conformity of these acts and practices with the basic teachings of the Zaydi school.

Al-Shawkānī also points out with satisfaction that among the commoners and the elites, and even in the ranks of the army, the number of al-Ṣanʿānī's followers increased despite all the plots against him.[202] Many more people openly accepted his *ijtihād* and studied the books of hadith with him. In fact, even the imam was influenced by al-Ṣanʿānī's teachings, as was his grand *wazīr* the jurist Aḥmad Ibn ʿAlī al-Nihmī and his chief army commander al-Māsī al-Mahdī. In a way, therefore, al-Ṣanʿānī represents a transitional phase for the Yemeni reformers from a stage of pure intellectual struggle, which did not translate into any real political power, to a stage where they could actually infiltrate the power structure and begin to gain a following within the official institutions of the state.

Although he was better off than the earlier Yemeni reformers, al-Shawkānī projected an image of himself that was modeled after his rebellious predecessors, an image of a scholar who suffered as a result of his intellectual integrity. Thus, despite al-Shawkānī's favorable fortunes, he continued to claim descent from this line of nonconformist intellectuals, a lineage symbolically bestowed on him in a dream by none other than al-Ṣanʿānī himself. In this dream encounter, al-Ṣanʿānī instructed al-Shawkānī to "be precise in regard to the chains of transmission, and meticulous in the interpretation of the sayings of the Messenger of God," and he informed him that hadith scholars are destined for paradise. Al-Ṣanʿānī then hugged al-Shawkānī and wept, an act the latter interpreted as a sign that he would suffer tribulations similar to those suffered by al-Ṣanʿānī.[203]

Al-Shawkānī, the chief judge of Yemen, was no victim, and he wielded considerably more power than any of the earlier Yemeni reformers did. However, as he wrote the history of their dissenting tradition, he also wrote himself into it, and he shaped a good part of his intellectual career in conformity with it. Although al-Shawkānī did not write a separate biography for himself, he took every occasion to include aspects of his past in the larger history. Although he reports some of the basics of his life, he does not give the kind of autobiographical information that one finds in traditional historical narratives.[204] Rather, he selectively traces patterns of experience in his own life and in the lives of earlier reformers and combines the historical narratives of these experiences with legal commentary. In particular, al-Shawkānī is keen to present himself as a target of the hatred and plots of *madhhab* partisans, including some of his own students and friends.

In one of many similar accounts, al-Shawkānī speaks of a student of his who turned against him. This student, presumably Zaydi, had borrowed one of al-Shawkānī's books where he had jotted some views on the question of the redeemed group (*al-firqa al-nājiya*). Al-Shawkānī had written something to the effect that this group was not just one of the many subdivisions of the various Muslim schools and *madhhab*s but a reference to any of the followers of the various schools who adhered to the indicants of the law and the teachings of the Prophet. Of course, al-Shawkānī was refuting the claim by specific groups that they were the only ones to be redeemed on the Day of Judgment. Upon reading al-Shawkānī's views, his former student rightly understood them to undermine the exclusive claim of his own *madhhab* and started maligning al-Shawkānī. The incident was contained, but al-Shawkānī suggests that this student knew very well that his teacher was correct; furthermore, al-Shawkānī sadly notes that this student's zeal led him to violate the code of proper behavior by a student toward his teacher.[205]

Another story of similar import is included in the biography of al-Ḥusayn Ibn Yaḥyā Ibn Ibrāhīm al-Dhamārī (d. 1249 AH), a close friend and colleague of al-Shawkānī who studied hadith with him under a common teacher.[206] Al-Shawkānī reports that, in 1208, when he wrote his *Irshād al-Ghabī* on the prohibition against cursing the Companions of the Prophet according to the school of *ahl al-bayt*, his book fell in the hands of a zealous Rāfiḍī (that is, Ismāʿīlī). Upon reading the treatise, this man lost his intellectual bearings and, with the support of some state officials, started inciting others against al-Shawkānī, soliciting more than twenty responses to his treatise. Most of these responses were pure invective with no substance to them, and yet the campaign against al-Shawkānī gained momentum with many people taking sides and offering comments on the subject. The controversy spread all over Yemeni cities, although all the treatise purported to do was defend the honor of the Companions of the Prophet, and although it was exclusively based on the opinions of the imams of *ahl al-bayt* in order to disprove the claims of those who attributed lies to them and claimed to belong to their school. Al-Shawkānī contends that the silence of many moderate scholars and their fear of saying the truth allowed the extremists to occupy center stage and mobilize such campaigns. Out of fear of the mob, many scholars remained silent to avoid harm and disgrace, and some even said what the mob wanted to hear. It was this silence, al-Shawkānī maintains, that led to the persecution of the scholars of Yemen and to the tyranny of the mob over them. Moreover, concealing the truth obscured the reputation of these scholars and lowered their status. This complicity further emboldened the mobs in their abuse of scholars. In contrast, if the scholars who knew better had united in their defense of the truth, the mob and their accomplices among the ignorant jurists would have been deterred from instigating further strife. To al-Shawkānī's great surprise and disappointment, his friend al-Dhamārī was one of those good scholars who were drawn into the controversy. Knowing of their close connection, the mob pressured al-Shawkānī's friend to write a response, which he did. And although the response did not stray from the truth and actually reiterated some of al-Shawkānī's arguments, it gave the impression that its author disagreed with al-Shawkānī, which, in turn, gave additional impetus to the campaign against him. Al-Dhamārī's response, al-Shawkānī adds, was the only one that merited consideration. Al-Shawkānī therefore wrote a reply, which, he concedes, was at times harsh.

Al-Shawkānī was particularly careful in discussing his friend's involvement in this intrigue, as he eventually apologized to al-Shawkānī. In contrast, a former teacher of al-Shawkānī knowingly and deliberately participated in spreading accusations against al-Shawkānī and became the spokesman for the extremists who, in collaboration with a state official, orchestrated this campaign.[207] This and other narratives by al-Shawkānī serve to bolster his subversive credentials. This narrative underscores his assessment of a scholar's role during times of strife. Al-Shawkānī notes that, on the one hand, his previous teacher was driven by envy; this teacher, identified as ʿAbd Allāh Ibn Ismāʿīl Ibn Ḥasan Ibn Hādī al-Nihmī, was skilled in the grammatical and language sciences as well as logic; however, al-Shawkānī quickly learned all of what this teacher had to give and stopped taking his classes, moving on to other teachers.[208] Clearly, the teacher was offended and held a grudge against al-Shawkānī. On the other hand, the colleague of al-Shawkānī who wrote a modest, although hurtful response was driven by fear of the mob. In reality, this scholar was a righteous scholar who promoted the study of hadith, but he did so in secret.[209] Both examples illustrate the perils of intellectual authority. Lack of intellectual courage and integrity, like professional competition over authority and turf, can lead to polarization and aggravate sectarian strife. In these narratives, therefore, al-Shawkānī submits that although he did not suffer as much as the earlier reformers of Zaydi Yemen, he was no less a target of hatred campaigns by *madhhab* partisans. Moreover, his ability to weather these campaigns, al-Shawkānī suggests, was in no small measure a result of his steadfastness, courage, and refusal to compromise his principled beliefs under pressure from the mob or the entrenched institutional powers.

Optimistic Historiography and the Possibilities of the Present

To best appreciate the uniqueness of al-Shawkānī's history it is useful to compare it to the most studied and quoted history of this period, namely, that of the Egyptian historian ʿAbd al-Raḥmān al-Jabartī.[210] Much of the modern scholarship on eighteenth-century historical writings has been informed by al-Jabartī's accounts of the turbulent events preceding and following the French occupation of Egypt. Simply put, al-Jabartī's history is one of upheavals and disasters, of what seemed to him like a crumbling world, hence the pessimistic and anxious tone of his accounts. In contrast, al-Shawkānī's account was optimistic and confident of the possibilities of the present. Al-Shawkānī himself was an illustration of the propitious culmination of a history of intellectual dissent and resistance. As a result, al-Shawkānī's history projects an image of rise and vibrancy, in contrast to al-Jabartī's history of decline and stagnation. The writings of the other eighteenth-century reformers were full of assessments of historical experience and traditions, which informed every aspect of their reform projects. Some of these I have already discussed, and others we will examine later. For the sake of comparison, I will consider additional examples from the writings of Shāh Walī Allāh.

One of the instances in which Walī Allāh deploys a reading of history to inform and illustrate his reform views is in his attempt to provide a historicist explanation of difference (*ikhtilāf*) in Islam. As we have seen, Walī Allāh's project was primarily one of intellectual reconciliation between the various modes of knowledge and within each of these. His recourse to *ijtihād* was in part a way of mediating differences among jurists. The status of divergent rulings issued by these jurists was the next issue on his agenda of reconciliation. The *ijtihād* of Walī Allāh was not simply a prescription to include more opinions and hence dissent but a way of coming to terms with differences of opinion and creatively bypassing them in the interest of the community. He believed there were historical reasons for differences among scholars and their approaches to the study of law. Early traditionalists, he argued, did not derive rulings from the hadith, fearing that they may have misunderstood its meanings. Instead, they simply transmitted the traditions as they heard them.[211] Early jurists were afraid of attributing wrong traditions to the Prophet and thought it less risky to issue new rulings and opinions.[212] Later followers of both groups, the traditionalists and the jurists, attributed to their predecessors exclusive claims they did not make, and the zealotry of these followers is one of the causes of later differences.[213] The situation was aggravated when some scholars compromised their integrity, lured by the prospect of wealth and power.[214] Legal disputation was a favorite subject in the courts of rulers, and scholars seeking wealth focused their studies on it in order to gain the rulers' patronage, thus diverting their attention from the more scholarly pursuits of the first generations of Muslims.[215] Legal divergences (*ikhtilāfāt*) were also caused by structural factors, including conflicting transmitted hadiths and their varying linguistic interpretations. Added causes for *ikhtilāf* include differences in the methods of applying a general rule to a specific situation or deriving a general ruling from a specific one, and the interpretation of a general rule in a specific context in opposition to the requirement of common sense and simple reasoning.[216]

Walī Allāh charts the causes of legal divergences and then suggests ways of dealing with them. Difference, he asserts, is a natural and unavoidable outcome of *ijtihād*. It is sanctioned in the prophetic tradition, which assigns two rewards to a *mujtahid* who hits the mark and one reward to one who does not.[217] According to Walī Allāh, this does not mean that one of the two opinions in question is wrong, only that one is more correct than the other. The claim that only one of the two opinions corresponds to the ruling intended by God implies that the other is in opposition to God's ruling, which is a sin and cannot be deserving of God's reward.[218] Therefore, in differences resulting from most kinds of *ijtihād*, the truth is on both sides of the difference,[219] and the choice between different legal opinions, and by extension, different legal schools, is a choice between equally valid options. Based on this argument, Walī Allāh then asserts that it is prohibited to believe in and promote one school of law to the exclusion of others.[220] These schools have no exclusive claim to truth—there are only four of them because it so happened that their followers were more active than those of other, now extinct schools.[221] Clearly therefore, history and doctrine are intertwined in this analysis. As in the case of al-Shawkānī, the primary purpose of reading history is to inform a specific agenda of intellectual reform. Unlike al-Jabartī, Walī Allāh's digressions into history do not paint a hopeless picture of the present but draw on the past to optimistically chart ways its resources might be redeployed to revitalize Muslim tradition and society in the present.

Such, then, was the self-confidence of these reformers and their conceptions of history. But was their optimism a mere illusion? Put differently, was the grand sense of intellectual authority projected by scholars like Walī Allāh and al-Shawkānī warranted and, if so, what was the source of this authority? It is easier to answer these questions for reformers without political leverage than it is for al-Shawkānī, who had claims to both political and intellectual authority. In the case of al-Ṣanʿānī, for example, it is safe to conclude that his political leverage did not amount to much, and that his influence derived largely from his scholarly achievements and his ability to demonstrate his intellectual excellence. Similarly, we know that Walī Allāh tried to solicit political support from several political powers that, he hoped, would come to the rescue of Indian Muslims and restore a measure of social order to their ranks. We also know, however, that all such solicitations failed, at which point Walī Allāh gave up on rulers, turned to scholarship, and proposed his intellectual reforms as an alternative way of reviving Muslim societies. And although Walī Allāh's efforts may not have succeeded at the social and political levels, his views were so compelling that there is hardly any Muslim scholar in India after Walī Allāh who does not recognize him as the greatest Muslim scholar of the Indian subcontinent, and claim to be the true representative of his thought. In addition to the respect that these scholars cultivated as a result of their scholarly achievements, the distance they maintained vis-à-vis tainted political authorities raised their standing and added to their credibility in the eyes of posterity. In other words, their lack of political power provided these scholars with a moral authority, which in turn had significant social and political implications.

The cases of Ibn Fūdī and al-Sanūsī are slightly more complex since they both introduced new social and political formations. Still, in both cases, political and social reform were inspired and informed by comprehensive programs of intellectual reform. Moreover, both thinkers were prolific in their own right and promoted ideas that were original in their contexts. Al-Sanūsī advocated doctrines similar to those of al-Shawkānī, most notably regarding the use of hadith, the prohibition of *taqlīd*, and the universal obligation of *ijtihād*. Ibn Fūdī was perhaps the most notable Muslim scholar and reformer to ever emerge in sub-Saharan Africa; and while he did not attempt to reform the classical Islamic tradition, he systematically drew on it to construct an intellectual edifice that would underpin his program of social and political reform.

Unlike the other reformers of this period, al-Shawkānī held state office. A prolific scholar who wrote on intellectual integrity and advocated steadfastness in the face of political authority, he derived at least some of his influence from his appointment to the office of chief judge by that authority. We will therefore examine this aspect of al-Shawkānī's complex relationship to power as a way of probing the larger question of the relationship between intellectual and political authority.

The Intellectual and the State

Despite wide differences in their connections to various sites of institutional power, the foundation of authority of all the reformers in Zaydi Yemen was primarily intellectual. The various reformers of the eighteenth century had diverse relationships to power; yet, they seem to have thought of themselves as belonging to a general trend or tradition of reform, one that relied on indicants of the law and questioned, if not rejected, the exclusive authority of the schools of law (*madhhab*s). As we have seen, in the consciousness of al-Shawkānī there was in fact a particular tradition whose genealogy and intellectual traits he set out to construct and delineate. This tradition was to a great extent construed in terms of the role of the intellectual in society and in connection to power. In this way, al-Shawkānī provided a theoretical examination of the foundation on which the legitimacy of the intellectual could be based. And although he was part of the power structure, al-Shawkānī insisted on identifying himself with this oppositional tradition. Put differently, al-Shawkānī thought of himself as an intellectual with a mission, and this mission was defined primarily in the genealogies of dissent that he constructed for his intellectual forerunners as well as for himself. His connection to power was thus subordinate to this larger subjectivity. Again, the main elements of this subjectivity are not just one's depth of knowledge but also the independence of this knowledge, and the oppositional role it plays vis-à-vis the oppressive tendencies of states and of corporate schools alike. It is only natural, therefore, to question whether al-Shawkānī's real career corresponded to this projected image.

On the face of it, al-Shawkānī's relation to power appears complementary. Tracing his career path, however, reveals a competitive relationship with political authority, one in which the absolute authority of the Zaydi imam, an authority idealized in Zaydi doctrine, was undermined in multiple ways by the creation of competing sites of power and norms for the exercise of this power.

Al-Shawkānī's father was a professional jurist who, early in his life, moved south from the town of Shawkān to the city of Sanaa in search of better career opportunities. There he served as a modest judge and does not seem to have achieved much distinction or prominence. The image presented in al-Shawkānī's biography written of his father is of a minor and relatively uninfluential judge who did not have significant connections to powerful state officials, did not amass wealth, did not own the house he lived in, and, when he died after forty years of service, left nothing for his family by way of inheritance.[222] Al-Shawkānī does not mention any other family member who served, or had connections with, political authorities. Al-Shawkānī, therefore, did not inherit wealth, prominence, or social status from his father or family. What his father provided, however, was the opportunity for him to study in Sanaa with some of the leading scholars of the city and to obtain as diverse an education as the city at that time could provide.[223] Al-Shawkānī clearly availed himself of this education and, at a very young age, became a scholar in his own right. Such was his knowledge, al-Shawkānī reports, that he was able to abandon imitation and became a *mujtahid* before he was thirty years old.[224] Already at this early age, al-Shawkānī had transmitted over 500 works in all disciplines and had written many of his books.[225] Al-Shawkānī was also very active in teaching and issued fatwas without charging money. Many of these fatwas circulated among the leading judges of the imamate, who recognized the superiority of his scholarship,[226] although they did not know al-Shawkānī personally as he then avoided contact not only with state officials but also with scholars who had contacts with the state (*arbāb al-dawla kāʾinan man kān*).[227]

Al-Shawkānī was thus recognized as a leading scholar, and by some accounts the leading scholar, of his period already before the imam sought to appoint him chief judge of Zaydi Yemen.[228] There could be no doubt that al-Shawkānī's appointment to the office of chief judge reinforced his power and provided him with previously unavailable opportunities. Al-Shawkānī, however, did not become the unrivaled scholar of Yemen on account of this appointment, as is evident by the fact that he had already written some of his most important works. Moreover, based on all available information, there seems to have been no contemporary Zaydi Hādawī scholar of a comparable scholarly stature. Al-Shawkānī's reputation must have been enhanced by his appointment to office, but it had to be on account of his manifest scholarly superiority that the imam sought to appoint him in the first place.[229] It is important to note here that al-Shawkānī's intellectual legacy was recognized beyond his immediate temporal and geographical context: he had a following in India and North Africa and was celebrated as the reviver of his time (*mujaddid al-ʿaṣr* or *al-qarn*) in later Islamic historical writings.[230]

Given the evidence from all available biographical sources, the appointment of al-Shawkānī by the Zaydi imam cannot be attributed to al-Shawkānī's social status or connections. One possible explanation of al-Shawkānī's sudden rise to power could be the imam's desire to employ someone with the requisite erudition but with no social and political connections to draw on; this would have ensured al-Shawkānī's loyalty to the imamate, since he had none to rival powers within Yemen. This, no doubt, is a common practice even in modern states. Another factor that might have made the appointment of al-Shawkānī more appealing to the imam is the possibility of appeasing Shāfiʿī subjects by appointing a hybrid scholar with scholarly links to and knowledge of their own legal tradition. These explanations, however, are unlikely: with no prior knowledge of and connection to al-Shawkānī, the imam and his staff had no way of ensuring that he would legitimate their rule and serve them with unquestioned loyalty. In fact, al-Shawkānī had multiple loyalties and did not give his full and undivided loyalty to the imams he served. One telling indication of the lack of such subservient loyalty is that al-Shawkānī did not compose a "mirrors of princes" type of work; in this genre, the norms of proper behavior of the ruler are delineated, but the purpose of this advisory exercise is not to correct the ruler's behavior and undermine his power but to enhance this power and secure the stability of his regime. In contrast, al-Shawkānī composed works that advocate the regulation of the relationship between jurists and rulers, so that the jurist does not simply serve the interests of the regime that employs him but also uses this relationship to further his own practical authority.

The position of *al-Qāḍī al-Akbar* (grand judge), which later came to be known as *Qāḍī al-Quḍāt* (chief judge), was first created in the eighteenth century when the imam al-Mutawakkil al-Qāsim bestowed the title on Sayyid Aḥmad Bin ʿAbd al-Raḥmān al-Shāmī (d. 1759).[231] The next person appointed to this position was Yaḥyā Bin Ṣāliḥ al-Saḥūlī[232] (d. 1795), who served for part of Al-Mahdī ʿAbbās's reign and was removed from office and then reinstated under al-Manṣūr ʿAlī (r. 1775–1809). Al-Shawkānī, who was appointed next to this position, emphatically asserts that "there has never been any contact between me and him [al-Saḥūlī], nor did I ever meet him," as if to highlight the fact that his nomination was on account of his scholarly reputation and not personal contacts and connections.[233] Both scholars who occupied the position of *al-Qāḍī al-Akbar* before al-Shawkānī were Zaydi scholars with knowledge of Sunni hadith compendiums. Al-Saḥūlī, for example, had a Zaydi education, distinguished himself in Zaydi applied law (*furūʿ*) with partial knowledge of other disciplines, had a profound knowledge of the books of the Zaydi imams and the rest of the Zaydi scholars, and worked extensively in this area of scholarship. In addition, a group of Sanaa scholars used to study *Ṣaḥīḥ Muslim* with him.[234] Yet despite this knowledge and teaching of Sunni works on hadith, al-Saḥūlī's affiliation is decidedly different from that of the other reformers of Zaydi Yemen. One of his books was a critical response to a critique by al-Ḥasan al-Jalāl of a book on transmissions within the Zaydi school.[235] This suggests that al-Saḥūlī did not nominate al-Shawkānī to succeed him on account of their shared intellectual affiliations.

In the biography of Imam al-Manṣūr (r. 1189–1224), al-Shawkānī describes his own appointment as chief judge after the death of the previous judge, al-Saḥūlī, in 1209 AH.[236] At that time, al-Shawkānī maintains, he was busy teaching the sciences of *ijtihād*, as well as issuing fatwas and writing on various scholarly subjects. Al-Shawkānī also adds that beyond this sort of public engagement, he had isolated himself from the public, especially from officials with whom he had no contacts whatsoever, and had no desire to do anything aside from scholarship.[237] Of course, al-Shawkānī's public engagement before appointment to office was quite substantial; he himself reports that each day he gave about thirteen lessons in *tafsīr*, *uṣūl*, language, applied law, and hadith. No doubt, this teaching must have contributed to al-Shawkānī's reputation, despite his claim that he was surprised when the messengers of the caliph (Imam al-Manṣūr) approached him about a week after the death of al-Saḥūlī. The caliph informed al-Shawkānī that he was chosen to fill the vacant position of chief judge. His first reaction, al-Shawkānī tells us, was to apologize by explaining that he was overstretched and overburdened with teaching. In response, the caliph assured al-Shawkānī that it was possible to continue teaching while in this new position, and that all he needed to do was to arbitrate the disputes that were presented in court during the two days of the week in which the judges met. Al-Shawkānī then requested time for consultation on the matter. His initial hesitation, which lasted a week, was then overcome by the insistence of a majority of scholars in Sanaa that it was his obligation to accept this appointment since if he did not, the responsibility for the judgeship of all of Yemen could go to someone who was not qualified for it, either in knowledge or in piety. Al-Shawkānī quickly discovered, however, that the job could not be done in just two days per week and that he was left with very little time to read or finish his writing projects. Al-Shawkānī also tells of other anxieties during his first days on the job; he was especially concerned because he had no prior knowledge of the conventions of the profession of a judge and had never attended arbitration, not even his father's sessions. Al-Shawkānī adds, however, that, thanks to the respect and dignity with which the caliph treated the office of the chief judge and al-Shawkānī personally, as well as the caliph's willingness to apply the rulings of this office to himself and his family, al-Shawkānī was able to overcome the initial hurdles and develop the knowledge and expertise needed to run the office properly.[238]

Even if somewhat exaggerated, this account clearly illustrates the image that al-Shawkānī wished to project of his own relationship to power. Al-Shawkānī insists that he did not seek to gain favor with political authority and that he never desired to become a member of the official establishment or to be affiliated with the state. Over and over, he reminds us that he agreed to serve reluctantly in order to further his own project of promoting justice, a project that he had articulated, both in his writings and fatwas and in his teaching, before he took office. Al-Shawkānī also maintains that he was not preparing himself for such a position, which is why he did not bother to learn more about the conventions and procedures of the profession. Even though his position as a judge took over most other aspects of his own intellectual career, al-Shawkānī the jurist took pride in the knowledge and skills he had accumulated in the years before his appointment, knowledge and skills he acquired independent of the state and without any aspiration to join its ranks. This knowledge, according to al-Shawkānī, was not developed for the purpose of serving rulers and, by extension, was not cultivated in the hope of allowing him to partake in the power and privileges of the ruling elite.[239] Indeed, he did not rise through the ranks and was surprised that he was approached to fill this position in the first place. In his account, al-Shawkānī insists that his knowledge was independently cultivated, even though he eventually happened to serve in an official capacity. This independence is further amplified by his hesitation at the time of appointment and his ultimate decision to accept so as to serve his own objectives. Therefore, in contrast to his definite intellectual identification with the dissenting intellectuals of Yemen, al-Shawkānī portrays his service as a provisional compromise that did not imperil his professional independence. Above all, al-Shawkānī tells us that he derived his authority from his scholarly credentials and from the reputation he cultivated through this scholarship and intensive teaching.

Al-Shawkānī was able to create a large network of students and, after appointment to office, planted these students in various official positions. Al-Shawkānī's compelling intellectual credentials, therefore, were aided by this tangible networking, which gave him a power base of his own. Al-Shawkānī was also conscious of the power implications of such networking. For example, in reference to a certain Zaydi scholar, al-Shawkānī reports that because of the large number of his students, people would not give their oath of allegiance to the imams if this scholar were not present.[240] Al-Shawkānī's appointment of his students to the offices of local judges, preachers, and other administrative posts can be read as an effort to infiltrate and subvert the institutions of the Zaydi imamate. Yet again, as the above account suggests, the building of a network of students started as an intellectual act before al-Shawkānī became chief judge, and he had already won the intellectual loyalty of his students before he was able to cultivate and draw on their professional loyalties.[241] In fact, al-Shawkānī reports that even members of the family of the imams came under the sway of the reformative ideas he advocated. One such case is al-Qāsim, the son of Imam al-Mutawakkil, who studied hadith with Muḥammad ʿĀbid al-Sindī when he came to Yemen, and with al-Shawkānī himself later on.[242]

Despite his rejection of *taqlīd*, a stand that inhibited his ability to impose his views on fellow Muslims, both the power that was invested in his office by the state as well as the network of students and followers he was able to build throughout Yemen gave al-Shawkānī's normative, juristic discourse the power to coerce. Arguably, therefore, al-Shawkānī's authority was not just moral: the substantial powers at his disposal augmented the hegemonic sway of his ideas. Yet it is important to remember here that many of al-Shawkānī's ideas were not executionable and thus could not benefit from the coercive powers of his office. Even when he conceived of himself as a guardian of a particular, legitimate method of reasoning, al-Shawkānī was restrained by his conviction that Muslims have the right, indeed duty, to exercise *ijtihād* and make their own choices. Moreover, many of his views contradicted the official doctrines of the state and, at some level, undermined the prevailing paradigm of the hegemonic culture associated with it. To be sure, al-Shawkānī contributed to the production of this culture, but the domain of cultural production was not the exclusive, or even main, purview of the dominant political authority and its institutions. Numerous other sites of political and cultural authority existed, and al-Shawkānī partook in many of them. Above all, al-Shawkānī's authority was an intellectual authority derived from his intellectual abilities, achievements, and credentials, and not from the office that he occupied. Scholarly integrity thus comes before political leverage, important as the latter was in al-Shawkānī's actual career.

Al-Shawkānī's determined stand on authority does not rule out the possibility of serving the state and collaborating with it. As we have seen, al-Shawkānī suggested that scholars could realistically hope for a balanced relationship with political authorities in which they not only served the state but also promoted their own interests and views. And yet, al-Shawkānī's willingness to compromise and collaborate with political authorities is countered by his resolve to defend the independence of his scholarship and to fortify scholars against pressures as well as temptations that could undermine their intellectual integrity. The ideal intellectual who is engaged in public service, as conceived of by al-Shawkānī, is one who may compromise his style of interaction but not his basic principles. Moreover, styles of communication differ and are judged by their outcomes, whereas principles are fixed. As examples of such variations, al-Shawkānī cites the case of Nūr al-Dīn al-Maṣrī al-Shāfiʿī (d. 724), who had the courage to criticize the sultan in public. One scholar serving the sultan suggested to his master that al-Maṣrī was on the verge of competing with the sultan for power, at which point the sultan ordered that al-Maṣrī's tongue be cut out.[243] Luckily for the latter, however, another scholar (Ṣadr al-Dīn Ibn al-Wakīl) calmed the sultan's rage by persuading him to consider al-Maṣrī's piety, despite his crude manners, which were due to the "dryness of his brain." Al-Maṣrī was thus forgiven.[244] Both the courageous actions of the scholar who criticized the sultan publicly and the diplomatic scholar who rescued his colleague's tongue are models of commendable scholarly behavior that stand apart from subservient collaboration in which scholarly credentials become a tool for legitimating the oppression of rulers. Of course, al-Shawkānī, aware of the numerous compromises that scholars make in order to justify rulers' illegal acts, often hastens to condemn such compromises. Thus, for example, in reference to the prohibition against ornamenting mosques, al-Shawkānī maintains that earlier generations of Muslims did not denounce such ornamentation because it is a latter-day innovation that did not exist at their time. This innovation was introduced by tyrants who did not bother to consult scholars on the permissibility of their acts. Mosque ornamentation is not a commendable innovation, even though a majority of scholars may have failed to condemn it. The silence of these scholars, al-Shawkānī contends, can be read as a refusal to condone rather than an approval of this ornamentation. However, al-Shawkānī adds that some scholars' apologetic attempts to justify such innovations compel them to come up with arguments that even a "dumb beast" would not accept. Scholars, therefore, debase themselves by playing this subservient role.[245] Elsewhere, al-Shawkānī maintains that judges are prohibited from accepting presents of any kind, even from family members. Such presents function as bribes that might affect the judges' neutrality and bias their judgments. Al-Shawkānī points out that after he became a judge he refused to accept gifts of any sort, no matter where they came from.[246]

A judge, to al-Shawkānī, is the quintessential example of the intellectual who serves the community through public office. Al-Shawkānī's stipulated requirements for judges are distinguished by his intermingling of standard theoretical considerations with more practical ones, which are clearly informed by his own experience in public service. Of course, to qualify for this position, a scholar must be a *mujtahid*, fearful of God (*mutawarriʿ*) in regard to the wealth of people, and not actively seeking appointment with the state.[247] One of the central traits that al-Shawkānī continually refers to is fairness (*inṣāf*), which he invariably defines in practical terms. A fair person (*munṣif*) is one who consults with specialists over matters in which he lacks knowledge or expertise. Great scholars, al-Shawkānī notes, are always susceptible to making absurd mistakes in areas outside their specialty; thus, for example, Ḍiyāʾ al-Dīn al-Juwaynī and Abū Ḥāmid al-Ghazālī quote fabricated traditions in their work because they were not experts on hadith. Despite their great knowledge, they should have consulted the books of hadith to supplement their limited knowledge in this area. What applies to such great scholars, al-Shawkānī adds, no doubt applies to less accomplished ones. Of course, al-Shawkānī's example is also meant to illustrate the danger of relying uncritically on the legal works of even great scholars like al-Juwaynī and al-Ghazālī, thus underscoring the need to abandon imitation and rely instead on the compilations of hadith.[248] *Inṣāf* includes the meaning of modesty, that is, the modesty to recognize one's own limitations as well as the limitations of the doctrine of one's school. The lack of such modesty, in al-Shawkānī's view, amounts to recklessness: the rulings of irresponsible scholars are not forgivable within the limits of *ijtihād* but are transgressions against God and His law.

Having identified *inṣāf* as a central trait of the ideal intellectual, and taking into consideration that no scholar lives in an ideal world, al-Shawkānī proceeds to sketch out what it takes to maintain this ideal posture in a less than ideal reality.[249] In particular, al-Shawkānī addresses the problem of maintaining fairness in an intellectual world populated by partisans of different law schools, and especially in a world of scholarship that is produced by these partisans. The challenge is that this scholarship is produced mostly in a sectarian milieu, yet fairness requires the use of this scholarship irrespective of its sectarian origins, and without being prejudiced by its biases. One of the signs of fairness is the willingness to accept verifiable reports irrespective of their transmitter's doctrinal position. Yet to al-Shawkānī, fairness and transcendence of *madhhab* partisanship are no less a function of personal character than of knowledge and erudition. Al-Shawkānī's ideal intellectual thus has certain personal traits that predispose him to live up to the intellectual and practical challenges of his vocation.

The Complacent Intellectual and the Masses

Just as al-Shawkānī tried to distinguish himself from the political authorities he served, he also distanced himself from the masses (*ʿawām*). At a most obvious level, al-Shawkānī displayed opulence in his dress and standard of living. He deliberately exhibited his wealth as a sign of God's bounty toward him.[250] As with most everything else in his life, his attitudes toward class and social status found theoretical expression in his writings and overall system of thought. According to al-Shawkānī, appearance and social background count. But only virtuous people are truly capable of appreciating virtue, whereas ignorant people are deluded by appearances and wrongly consider them to be signs of scholarly distinction. Rather than focusing on substance and content, these ignorant people pay attention to such appearances as official positions and titles, proximity to rulers, class size, number of fatwas issued, special dress that goes with a position, and size of headgear. The "science of imitation [*ʿilm al-taqlīd*]" depends on these appearances to delude the ignorant masses, which is why rulers turn to scholars to derive a deceptive aura of legitimacy from their presence and service. This is also the reason why the courage of a *mujtahid* to deal with such deceptive scholars invariably leads those same scholars to lobby against the sincere *mujtahid* and either hurt him physically or slander him.[251]

Clearly then, aside from rulers, whom al-Shawkānī sees as prone by the nature of their vocation to corruption, there are two culprit groups that can undermine the advocacy of truth and ultimately justice. These are the collaborating scholars and the people who are impressed by their deceptive claims and appearances. In contrast, certain seemingly inherited social aptitudes predispose a person to becoming a *mujtahid*, not just for one's own purposes, but also for the purpose of issuing of fatwas in the interest of other people. These aptitudes, al-Shawkānī contends, make a person a suitable receiver of knowledge and learning.[252] The main factor accounting for such predisposition is what al-Shawkānī calls "nobility of descent [*sharaf al-maḥtad*]." Hailing from a noble lineage itself "attracts a person by nature to ulterior matters." Such nobility also deters a person from indulging in vices and inculcates in him the attraction to noble status and meritorious undertakings. Thus, a student with such character would neither be conceited nor exhibit haughtiness in acquiring knowledge. In contrast, however, the dispositions of people of inferior social backgrounds, including those with "such professional skills as tailoring, oil pressing, selling food for sheep, and other similar menial professions and lowly crafts" have no natural aversion to lowliness, humiliation, or injustice.[253] Thus, when a person of such ignoble background pursues a scholarly profession and attains a share in it, there is a risk that this person will become conceited and overtaken by vanity and pride. This is due to the sudden change in the social status of this person from the "lowest position and meanest rank . . . to the highest place and noblest status." And in the place of the company of tailors, bloodletters, butchers, or such lowly tradesmen, this person suddenly finds himself in the company of revered learned scholars. For this reason alone, such a person may exhibit conceit, insolence, and arrogance in his dealings with people, and by so doing bring harm both to the scholarly class and those below him. Al-Shawkānī adds that one rarely finds exceptions to this rule, and these are usually due to some distant noble background of the scholars in question.[254]

In contrast to ignoble scholars, al-Shawkānī asserts that a person who is worthy of knowledge, and who is already noble, "attains through knowledge additional nobility and acquires fine modesty, pure dignity, and superb manners that further elevate his scholarship and glorify his knowledge. . . . He thus recognizes the rights of knowledge and extols it . . . and does not muddy it with greed, degrade it by submission to other humans, or darken it by using it to obtain what is in the possession of rich people. Knowledge thus becomes his master not his servant, and his ultimate goal not his instrument."[255] Al-Shawkānī further explains the motives behind his unreserved criticism of the middle group of tradesmen turned scholars; these people are used to subservience and continue to act in this fashion even after they join the ranks of scholars. Their vanity is only matched by total obedience to the officials who employ them, and they blindly follow their masters' instructions without questioning the legality of what they are asked to do or defend. As a result, naïve observers associate this model of behavior with scholarship in general and think that all scholars are doomed to corruption the minute they are appointed to office.[256] Outside observers then develop an aversion to scholars and scholarship and pursue worldly careers in order to avoid the humiliation manifest in the behavior of these contemptible men, who bring disrepute and disgrace to themselves and scholars generally.[257]

Al-Shawkānī thus exhibits an aristocratic attitude based not so much on class division as on a kind of cultural determinism.[258] He justifies this haughtiness on the grounds that people of menial backgrounds become pompous as soon as they achieve the status of scholars, and he situates his essentialist discourse in the context of his attempt to rescue scholarship from the double curse of self-conceit and vanity, on the one hand, and abject humility and subservience, on the other. What is at stake, according to al-Shawkānī, is the independence of knowledge, as well as a scholar's ability to preserve his integrity in a world of corrupting temptations. Al-Shawkānī pleads that one not approach knowledge with the mentality of a merchant or a tradesman who seeks profit or power. In contrast to the sense of inferiority that haunts scholars of ignoble background, noble descent fortifies scholars against the temptations of power and provides them with a sense of pride and self-righteousness in the face of tyranny. Al-Shawkānī, the chief judge, knew too well that his coercive abilities were totally dependent on the state he served. In the absence of alternative sources of physical power, a scholar who serves in public office will perforce run the risk of co-optation and corruption. Thus the need, according to al-Shawkānī, for correctives that preserve the integrity and independence of publicly engaged intellectuals. Above all, this integrity rests on knowledge, and it is further fortified by a sense of moral authority and social dignity, all of which were reflected in al-Shawkānī's own example and in the examples of the predecessors he celebrated in his historical works.

The Intellectual and the Corporate Authority of *Madhhab*s

To be sure, knowledge, according to al-Shawkānī, should be innocent of the opportunist scholars who claim its authority. The real bearers of knowledge are those who adhere to the Sunna and endure all kinds of hardship on account of this adherence. In contrast, commoners are not to be blamed for their hostility toward such scholars, since it is not driven by any kind of scientific knowledge but by what they are told by school partisans who have partial and defective knowledge. Mediocrity, rather than simple loyalty to their particular schools, is responsible for the poisonous attitudes of this inferior class of scholars. Thus, although the authors of the books they quote and adhere to reliably emphasize the existence of other legitimate legal views, they consider the slightest deviation from the stated opinions in their legal manuals an unacceptable aberration and accuse a *mujtahid* who exercises independent legal reasoning of apostasy. This, according to al-Shawkānī, is not the fault of the consulted books but the inferior minds of the readers of these books. All of these claims, al-Shawkānī adds, are tied to worldly gain and are in no case based purely on intellectual concerns. The hope of worldly advancement is often tied to the defined interests of *madhhab*s. Thus a person who slanders a hadith scholar is considered a defender of the school of *ahl al-bayt* and claims merit on account of this presumed defense. Again, were the common people to know the truth, they would surely distance themselves from such extremist claims, especially since the real views of the school of the imams encourages *ijtihād* rather than prohibits it.[259] Imitation and the scholars who promote it are the ultimate sources of this great calamity. In addition to the inevitable opposition between political and intellectual authorities, the ultimate battle lines are drawn within the intellectual sphere, between imitators and *mujtahids*, between the ardent adherers to *madhhab*s and those who transcend *madhhab* affiliation and promote an open and independent attitude to the law.

Al-Shawkānī's critique of *madhhab* affiliation permeates his whole intellectual production. Given his own projected self-image as an independent *mujtahid* who does not belong to any *madhhab*, it is not surprising that his attitude toward all established schools of law, including the official Zaydi school of Yemen, amounts to neither complete adherence nor categorical rejection. Even as he rejects commonly accepted legal opinions of particular schools, al-Shawkānī often suggests that his rejection is not equivalent to a negation of the school doctrine in its totality, or an adherence to an opposing school of law. One way through which al-Shawkānī maintains his balanced approach to *madhhab*s is by tackling the main points of contention between schools in the area of applied law. The legal differences between Shiʿis and Sunnis in applied law are no more pronounced than differences among the various Sunni schools. And yet, historically, a handful of differences over matters of applied law have been overcharged with meaning and turned into symbolic embodiments of the larger doctrinal differences between the two groups. The list is short but the topics are immediately recognizable to Shiʿis and Sunnis alike. Rather than avoiding the potentially slippery discussion of these controversial issues, al-Shawkānī discusses almost all of these issues and provides an unconventional view on virtually every one of them.

For example, al-Shawkānī addresses the question of whether it is permissible to wipe off one's shoes without removing them during ritual ablution.[260] This is one of few highly charged symbolic rituals that have served, historically, to distinguish Sunni and Shiʿi legal practices.[261] In opposition to the common Twelver Shiʿi and Zaydi view, al-Shawkānī holds that wiping the shoes is permissible on the basis of a tradition reported by Jarīr, a Companion of the Prophet. This report, al-Shawkānī notes, is dismissed by some on the grounds that its transmitter, Jarīr, is not trustworthy since he broke away (*fāraqa*) from the camp of ʿAlī. Al-Shawkānī replies that Jarīr did not actually part company with ʿAlī but simply withdrew from the conflict for personal reasons after ʿAlī sent him to Muʿāwiya, presumably to negotiate on his behalf. Even if Jarīr were considered a sinner on account of this action, his report would still be acceptable. Al-Shawkānī invokes Ibn al-Wazīr's classic argument in support of accepting the reports of a sinner by interpretation (*fāsiq al-taʾwīl*). Moreover, al-Shawkānī goes beyond Ibn al-Wazīr's argument and adds that the dismissal of Jarīr's report could only be justified had there been consensus among the members of the family of the Prophet (*ʿitra*) on this dismissal; as these members spread all over the world, and since they followed the different schools that prevailed in the regions where they settled, it is impossible to verify that they agreed on anything.[262] In fact, according to al-Shawkānī, the members of the family of the Prophet were not necessarily Zaydis or even Shiʿis in general, and they belonged to diverse schools of law. The *ʿitra*, therefore, does not constitute an identifiable entity, and it is therefore not possible to claim an authoritative stand on the basis of such identity.

Other highly charged points of contention between Shiʿis and Zaydis, on the one hand, and Sunnis, on the other, include raising the hands at the beginning of the prayer when saying, "Allāhu Akbar," or holding the two hands together when standing in prayer. In reference to the first, al-Shawkānī quotes Zaydi authorities that attribute to the Zaydis in general the prohibition against raising the hands at the beginning or any other time during the prayer. This, he adds, "is a false attribution to the Zaydis, since their imam Zayd Ibn ʿAlī mentioned the tradition of raising [the hands] in his book known as *Al-Majmūʿ* and maintained that it is recommended. The same is true of their other distinguished imams, whether early or late, who stated that it is recommended. The only one who maintained that it should not be done is al-Hādī Yaḥyā Ibn al-Ḥusayn, and a similar view is reported on the authority of his grandfather al-Qāsim Ibn Ibrāhīm, although recommendation is also reported on the authority of the latter."[263]

It is significant that the last two figures are among the most important authorities for the Yemeni Zaydis, and they are credited with elaborating the doctrinal and legal principles of the school. By identifying credible Zaydi opinions in opposition to the dominant views of al-Hādī, al-Shawkānī manages to dilute this highly charged issue and allow for a multiplicity of legitimate Zaydi choices. In other words, by citing Zaydi authorities, al-Shawkānī undermines the claim that Zaydis unanimously prohibit this practice. On the question of holding the hands together in prayer, he even goes further, asserting that "the opinion that [holding the hands together] is obligatory is the one [I have] chosen, unless some consensus prevents from it. We, however, do not believe in the authoritativeness of consensus; rather, we deny its possibility and assert that it cannot occur."[264] Thus al-Shawkānī makes a choice that contradicts the Zaydi opinion on this question, but he clearly indicates that this is a juristic choice that does not polarize Muslims along school lines. More important, al-Shawkānī manages to venerate the scholars of the house of the Prophet without idealizing them collectively as an identifiable school. His meticulous attention to detail enables him to engage the opinions of individual Zaydi imams without committing himself to the standard collective views of the Zaydi school.

Another point of contention between Sunnis and Zaydis relates to the validity of prayer behind an imam who lacks probity (*ʿadāla*). The Zaydis in particular are keen to define the imam not just in terms of his descent but also in terms of his personal qualifications, first among which is rectitude and justice. This requirement is clear in the case of the imam as the political leader of the community, but it also extends, as al-Shawkānī indicates, to the leader of the congregational prayers. After a long exposition of the various views on the matter, al-Shawkānī affirms, "The result of all of this is that the basic rule is not to stipulate probity [as a condition for the imam, leader of prayer] and that if a person's prayer is valid for himself, it is equally valid for others. . . . Those who claim that probity is a condition, as has been attributed to the *ʿitra* and to Mālik . . . need [additional] indicants to depart from this basic principle."[265] After this radical challenge to a highly symbolic Zaydi view, al-Shawkānī tempers his position slightly by maintaining that "the issue being contested is whether the congregational prayer behind a person who lacks probity is valid; there is no disagreement, however, on its being reprehensible."[266]

On the subject of temporary marriage (more accurately, pleasure marriage [*mutʿa*]), al-Shawkānī provides evidence for the abrogation of the initial permission, and hence the subsequent prohibition of this kind of marriage.[267] Here, too, in what seems like an attempt to subvert the association of his opinion with Sunni Islam, al-Shawkānī maintains that the basis for prohibition of temporary marriage is a sound hadith, not just the prohibition by Caliph ʿUmar as some may think. He adds, "At any rate we worship according to what we have received from the lawgiver (the Prophet); eternal prohibition has been established for us on his authority. The disagreement of a group of the Companions does not undermine the authoritativeness [of this prohibition], and neither does it provide us with a valid excuse for not complying with it; how so, when the majority of the Companions have established this prohibition, acted according to it, and reported it to us."[268] Al-Shawkānī thus sides with the prevalent Sunni view on this highly symbolic question, but he makes sure to point out that he is not according a special authority to ʿUmar but simply acting in accordance with the established indicants of the law.

On other occasions, al-Shawkānī expresses willingness to disagree with ʿUmar, as well as mainstream Sunni and Zaydi views. Such is the case, for example, in al-Shawkānī's discussion on the validity of triple divorce.[269] All schools of law agreed that after three consecutive divorces a woman would have to marry and divorce a second husband before she could remarry the first one. Most schools of law also agreed that the man, who can initiate divorce at will, can in fact initiate all three divorces at once by repeating to his wife, "You are divorced," or its equivalent, three times. At various points in time, this issue also became a center of charged controversy. Ibn Taymiyya, as well as his student Ibn Qayyim al-Jawziyya, both argued that only one divorce is valid at any one point in time, since a man has to be married to a woman to be able to divorce her, and after the first utterance he would not be married to her. Therefore, according to this view, the second and third divorces are not effective unless the woman and the man remarry and then redivorce. The symbolic importance of this question was such that Ibn Taymiyya's and Ibn Qayyim's views on the matter were held against them and used to justify their subsequent persecution. On one occasion, the latter was placed backward on a donkey and driven through the streets of his hometown to humiliate and punish him for ruling that only one divorce can be effective at any particular time.[270] Like Ibn Taymiyya and Ibn al-Qayyim, al-Shawkānī bases his opinion on the matter on not just logical arguments but a tradition reported by Ibn ʿAbbās that nullifies triple divorce. Al-Shawkānī maintains that

> in summary, the ones who hold the opinion of [the validity of] sequential divorce [*tatābuʿ*, i.e., three divorces at once] have produced many responses to the tradition reported by Ibn ʿAbbās, yet none of these is free of arbitrariness. The truth is more worthy of being followed. If their defensive stance is in the interest of their schools, then it is too base and inferior to impinge on the purified Sunna. If it is because of ʿUmar Ibn al-Khaṭṭāb, then where does the poor man stand in comparison with the Prophet of God? Moreover, which Muslim prefers, on the basis of his reason and knowledge, to give more weight to the opinion of a Companion than to the statement of the chosen one [the Prophet]?[271]

Of course, al-Shawkānī does not condemn ʿUmar, but he also refuses to idealize him and has no qualms about disagreeing with him. It is also significant that in his most critical stand vis-à-vis ʿUmar, al-Shawkānī concurs not with Zaydi views but with unconventional Sunni ones.[272]

A similar, though perhaps even more significant equivocation is traceable in al-Shawkānī's discussion of the meaning of the verse *li yudhhiba ʿankum al-rijsa Ahla al-Bayti wa yuṭahhirakum taṭhīrā* (al-Aḥzāb 33:33, And God only wishes to remove all uncleanness from you, O you members of the family [of the Prophet], and to purify you to utmost purity].[273] Al-Shawkānī surveys the views on the meaning of *ahl al-bayt* in this verse and gives the arguments for and against various readings of this meaning, including the wives of the Prophet, his descendants, Banū Hāshim, the latter with Banū al-Muṭṭalib, Fāṭima and ʿAlī and their two sons, or the whole *umma*. Although he indicates what objections could and have been raised against each of these interpretations, he refrains from making a choice himself. Given that the specific restrictive interpretation of this verse is central to Shiʿi creed, the simple fact that al-Shawkānī does not clearly choose or at least express a preference is itself a significant divergence from traditional Zaydi views.

Perhaps the most sensitive issue that al-Shawkānī dealt with is the question of succession after Muhammad. The standard Shiʿi view that the Prophet designated ʿAlī as a successor is shared by the Zaydis, and al-Shawkānī is no exception. Yet al-Shawkānī is careful to articulate his view in a conciliatory manner that conforms to his other attitudes and beliefs. Al-Shawkānī composed a treatise titled *Al-ʿIqd al-Thamīn fī Ithbāt Waṣiyyat Amīr al-Muʾminīn* (The precious necklace on confirming the designation of the commander of the faithful [ʿAlī]).[274] In the introduction to this treatise, al-Shawkānī takes up the denial by ʿĀʾisha that any such designation was articulated by the Prophet. Unlike other Shiʿis, al-Shawkānī is not willing to dismiss ʿĀʾisha by slandering her or questioning her integrity, not the least because she is the authority in the transmission of a large number of traditions. Al-Shawkānī therefore approaches his response to ʿĀʾisha formally, treating her as a Companion and transmitter of hadith. At the outset, he provides a series of theoretical rules that have been established in the discipline of principles of jurisprudence including the principles that "the opinion of a Companion is not [in itself] authoritative evidence [*ḥujja*]; an affirmative statement has priority over a negative one; one who knows has authority over one who does not; and, even if its authority is granted, an interrupted tradition cannot contradict one [whose chain of transmission] is continuous all the way to the Prophet."[275] Like any other "Companion," ʿĀʾisha's opinion is not binding on other Muslims, and what counts is her reporting, not the actual opinion. This assessment does not discredit ʿĀʾisha in any way, since according to al-Shawkānī the same formal rules are applicable to each and every Companion, with no exception. Al-Shawkānī also maintains, in accordance with his stated legal principles, that ʿĀʾisha's negative assertion simply indicates that she was not aware of the Prophet's designation, and is not equivalent to a denial of the existence of such a tradition. Other Companions were aware of such a designation, and those who know have authority over those who don't. Barring outstanding impediments, the reports of Companions are all equally acceptable; as such, ʿĀʾisha's report of not hearing the Prophet designate a successor is accepted as truthful, but inconsequential because other, equally truthful Companions report that they did hear the Prophet designate ʿAlī. Finally, al-Shawkānī maintains that ʿĀʾisha's report is *maqṭūʿ*, meaning that she does not report hearing something from the Prophet; in other words her statement stops with her, whereas other statements confirming ʿAlī's designation are on the authority of the Prophet himself.[276]

Al-Shawkānī moves on to address some of ʿĀʾisha's practices. His discussion, however, does not amount to personal invective, as in traditional Shiʿi literature. Rather, al-Shawkānī applies the techniques of personal criticism of transmitters (*al-jarḥ wa al-taʿdīl*), which he uses systematically elsewhere, to determine ʿĀʾisha's style of transmission, so as to know how to situate and understand her reports. It is well known, he says, "that, as happens often with *mujtahid*s, the mother of the faithful, may God be pleased with her, was hasty to reject [traditions] that did not agree with her *ijtihād* [legal reasoning], and used to go to extremes in denouncing their reporters."[277] Significantly, al-Shawkānī treats ʿĀʾisha not just as a reporter but also as someone who exercises *ijtihād*, which reflects not just caution but respect in his approach to her. Al-Shawkānī illustrates his point by referring to opposed judgments by ʿĀʾisha and ʿUmar, in reference to an incident when the Prophet is said to have spoken to dead people in their grave. ʿUmar reported that he had questioned the Prophet's claim of talking to the dead, to which the latter responded by saying, "You are not more capable of hearing than they are." Al-Shawkānī next notes that ʿĀʾisha, rather abrasively, rejected this report by ʿUmar after he died and invoked instead God's statement in the Qurʾān, "You cannot make those who are [buried] in graves hear" (Fāṭir 35:22). Al-Shawkānī then argues that ʿĀʾisha's assertion does not justify the rejection of the report of a Companion of the caliber of ʿUmar; at most, after acknowledging its truthfulness, she could argue that the Qurʾānic statement is general and the hadith is specific to the people in question. Al-Shawkānī remarks, however, that the particular has priority over the general, and the particularization of the general statements of the Qurʾān by sound, singularly transmitted traditions is accepted by the majority of legal scholars. In contrast to the standard Shiʿi attitude, al-Shawkānī treats ʿĀʾisha with all the respect that is due to a mother of the faithful (*umm al-muʾminīn*); he does not question her status as one of the major authorities on hadith; he treats her as a legal scholar entitled to *ijtihād*; and, finally, his disagreement with her on a sensitive question of consequence to Sunni-Shiʿi relations is informed not by partisan views but by the view of ʿUmar, an idealized icon of Sunni Islam.

Al-Shawkānī gives other examples in which the differences between ʿĀʾisha and other Companions are assessed on the basis of legal theory, and then asserts that her denial of the tradition in which ʿAlī is named as a successor falls into the same category.[278] Al-Shawkānī thus manages to dismiss ʿĀʾisha's rejection of the hadith on succession without dismissing her personally. In a notable concession to non-Shiʿi views, al-Shawkānī maintains that one only has to believe in the designation of ʿAlī in general terms and is not obliged to believe in a specific set of details regarding this designation.[279] He also recognizes that some haters of the Shiʿis treat this tradition as yet another fabricated Shiʿi myth; al-Shawkānī, however, insists that this is not a simple Shiʿi slogan but a much larger legitimate stand supported by the reports of a number of credible Companions.[280]

The Perils of *Taqlīd*

These eclectic opinions illustrate al-Shawkānī's hybrid identity, and the fact that this identity cannot be reduced to either Zaydism or Sunnism. Implied in these views as well is a practical rejection of the authority of corporate *madhhab*s, whether Sunni or Zaydi. On these and many other less controversial legal issues, al-Shawkānī, like the earlier Yemeni reformers before him, translates into actual intellectual practice his theoretical condemnation of *taqlīd* and advocacy of *ijtihād*. In turn, this rejection of *taqlīd* is yet another expression of al-Shawkānī's subversive relation to established political and intellectual authorities. To be sure, the advocacy of *ijtihād* and the corollary rejection of *taqlīd* were staples of Yemeni reform. As we have seen earlier, the theories of *ijtihād* advocated by these reformers were not mirror images of Zaydi *ijtihād*, if only because the latter is primarily practiced by the imams whose *ijtihād* entails, rather than precludes, the *taqlīd* of other Muslims. The Yemeni reformers, in contrast, considered *ijtihād* the obligation of every Muslim and prohibited the imitation of any school of law or individual *mujtahid*, including the Zaydi imams. We have also seen that the theories of *ijtihād* and *taqlīd* of the Yemeni reformers were influenced by the views of both the Ẓāhirīs and Ibn Taymiyya and Ibn al-Qayyim. In addition to this intellectual indebtedness, however, the Yemeni reformers were also informed by a historical understanding of the social significance of their theories and the implications of these theories on hierarchies of power and authority.

In one of many similar instances in which the question of *taqlīd* is treated as one of power and authority, al-Ṣanʿānī maintains that "the crimes of the imitators against the hadith traditions of the Prophet of God, as well as the imams of their own schools who declared themselves innocent of any opinion that may oppose a prophetic text, have become so grave. Thus, if [a hadith] is reported contrary to what has been stated by the person they imitate, these [imitators] distort the hadith and give it a meaning other than the one intended by the Prophet."[281] The motive behind such distortions, al-Ṣanʿānī adds, is the "preservation of the *madhhab*." The discussion of this issue is often academic and involves meticulous examination of various traditions, their transmitters, and their contents. And yet, these discussions invariably conclude on a political note. Thus, after listing eleven arguments by supporters of *taqlīd* and responding to each of them, al-Ṣanʿānī concludes,

> In summary, one who believes in a particular *madhhab* becomes defensive of it, and as a result he diverts the [Qurʾānic] verses and the [prophetic] traditions away from the meanings that God and His Prophet intended for them. So, for example, one who argues that the food of the People of the Book and their slaughtered animals are forbidden would claim that the verse "And the food of scriptured people is lawful to you and your food is lawful to them" [Al-Māʾida 5:5] applies only to accepting grains like wheat and barley from them. So let the believer who favors truth over [the opinions of] humans be careful of such arguments and also of interpreting the hadith traditions and verses in a manner similar to the interpretation of the *bāṭiniyya* [extreme Shiʿi] sects.[282]

Al-Shawkānī is even clearer on the disastrous social and political ramifications of *taqlīd*. Al-Shawkānī argues that *taqlīd* is the greatest affliction that befell the Muslim community.[283] What started with a group of Muslims following the opinions of a single dead scholar, accompanied by their blanket rejection of any other opinion, quickly degenerated into slander and conspiracy against independent scholars who do not follow their school doctrine, and even accusing them of sin and unbelief. Worse still, the followers of each school act as if they were independent religions and treat the scholar they imitate as if he were the prophet of this religion. The followers of the four Sunni schools in particular claim that consensus is restricted to the views of only four scholars of the whole Muslim community, that there is no *ijtihād* other than theirs, and that all authority is invested in them. It would thus appear, al-Shawkānī adds, as if the whole purified sharia belongs to these four individuals, with no share for anyone else in it, as if God did not grant any of His servants what He has granted these four. Al-Shawkānī had no qualms about asserting that all four imams were erudite and virtuous Muslims with outstanding knowledge and strong belief. His objection was to the exclusive claims made by their followers on their behalf. Al-Shawkānī contends that if these claims were based on knowledge, then who could deny that many of the followers have had more knowledge than the imams they imitate. If these exclusivist claims were based on the priority of previous generations, then the Companions and their followers would be considered far more worthy of such distinguished ranking than the imams of the four schools.[284]

Such was al-Shawkānī's rejection of *taqlīd* and *madhhab* affiliation. He further insists that the view that *ijtihād* was not possible after the four schools were established and after the imams of these schools perished implies a "judgment that God . . . is incapable of granting his servants what He directed them to learn and teach."[285] Al-Shawkānī dismisses the suggestion inherent in the argument against *ijtihād* that there is no one left in the whole community of Muslims who is capable of understanding the Book of God and the Sunna of the Prophet, that the nature of human understanding has changed, and that humans are no longer capable of understanding sharia. According to al-Shawkānī, the ultimate purpose of this self-serving argument is to make sure that the authority of *taqlīd* prevails.[286] In fact, al-Shawkānī maintains, the argument in favor of *taqlīd* effectively implies that sharia was an interim code of law that has been abrogated by the legal doctrines of the various schools. Even if they deny it, these schools effectively created new religions for Muslims, and the ultimate explanation of such aberration is in the desire of corporate schools to assert their intellectual authority over society.

Conclusion

Both in theory and in practice, al-Shawkānī advocated new modes of relating to authority. These new modes were radically unconventional but rigorously justified and rather well received by Muslims in Yemen and beyond. Whether in his relationship with political and intellectual authorities, or in his own self-identification and the intellectual genealogy he constructed for himself, al-Shawkānī was a dissenter. Even when he was part of the state's power structure, al-Shawkānī was primarily inspired by his intellectual identity, his role within a tradition of dissent, and not his formal political or sectarian affiliation. His legacy engendered a new reality in which the political was subservient to the intellectual, so much so that al-Shawkānī's actions, and not only ideas, often *undermined* the state and subverted its hegemonic scripts. Al-Shawkānī's subversive tendencies are all the more notable since they undermined the institutionalized intellectual authority he headed.

The examples cited in this chapter are meant to illustrate the genuine hybridity of al-Shawkānī's intellectual identity, which exemplifies the hybridity of the reformers of the eighteenth century in general. In a move that has its own hegemonic undertones, contemporary historiography has often tended to circumscribe scholars like al-Shawkānī within specific and known doctrinal boundaries. This tendency usually translates into an attempt to determine al-Shawkānī's affiliation, that is, whether he was Zaydi or Sunni. Alternatively, in its more nuanced forms, this scholarly tendency attempts to break down al-Shawkānī's system of thought into its constitutive elements and then identifies each of these with their Zaydi or Sunni origins. All of these approaches fail to appreciate the genuineness of the hybridity of eighteenth-century thought. To be sure, as we have seen, the reformers of the eighteenth century anticipated such attempts to classify them into narrow categories and devoted much intellectual effort to defy such categorization. In this regard, al-Shawkānī was no exception. His thought was simply a culmination of a trend that started much earlier in Yemen and was evident elsewhere throughout the Muslim world. In fact, the fluidity of the intellectual world of eighteenth-century reformers is documented in the rich writings by the reformers of this and earlier periods. The official religious establishment's resistance to this fluidity indicates its substantial influence. Already the early example of al-Maqbalī's experience in Mecca illustrates this point—although al-Maqbalī did not get along with the religious establishment of the city, Mecca's intellectual plurality was such that there was room for this scholar of Zaydi origins to be affiliated with Ibrāhīm al-Kurdī, one of the city's leading scholars at the time. Moreover, as a sign of the buoyancy of this open intellectual atmosphere, we know that the official religious authorities tried but failed to crack down on al-Maqbalī.[287] Other examples of such fluidity are illustrated in the common phenomenon of having scholars from different schools exchange transmission licenses (*ijāzas*) in multiple subjects. Such, for example, were Walī Allāh's exchange of *ijāzas* with al-Kurdī and al-Shawkānī's exchange of *ijāzas* with Ḥanafī and Shāfiʿī scholars.[288] It is also a telling indication of the spirit of the times that none of these scholars tried to conceal their intellectual loyalties and identities but rather were quite bold in asserting them.[289]

Historians have struggled to identify the intellectual identities of such scholars. In the case of al-Shawkānī, for example, assessments have varied from considering him an open-minded Zaydi to a Sunni who is trying to undermine the Zaydi school from within. Attempts to explain al-Shawkānī's intellectual identity in terms of such affiliations miss what al-Shawkānī himself consciously devoted his whole intellectual career to, namely, the forging of a hybrid and truly independent intellectual identity that undermines strict adherence to *madhhabs* of all sorts.[290] Al-Shawkānī's emphasis on hadith in effect meant that the law of the land was to be derived from hadith works rather than from the old manuals of school law that were used in the courts of the imamic state.[291] Following the example of earlier Yemeni reformers, al-Shawkānī generated a large body of literature in which the primary authority is that of hadith and not the traditional legal manuals. Furthermore, al-Shawkānī trained a large number of students and appointed them to key administrative positions throughout the imamic realm. Indeed, almost everything in al-Shawkānī's intellectual career undermined the established authorities, whether scholars, schools, or the canonical books defining the discursive culture of these schools.

The attempt to force al-Shawkānī and his predecessors into the cast of particular *madhhab*s is a by-product of the view that before modern, twentieth-century nationalist politics there was "sharia politics grounded in *madhhab* affiliation."[292] Yet this is exactly the opposite of what the reformers of the eighteenth century set out to do, with varying degrees of success. Eighteenth-century reform was above all an attempt to undermine *madhhab* politics as manifested in the institutions of the state and in the cultural ideology that legitimated it. Eighteenth-century thinkers argued that the prevalent *madhhab*s were tools that reinforced the power of the central political authority rather than diluted this power and dispersed it. They also considered the subservience of scholars to rulers the main reason behind the disastrous divisions inflicting Muslim societies. Their earnest efforts, therefore, cannot be dismissed as mere attempts to distinguish themselves within the existing power hierarchies; instead, they were radical attempts to restructure these relations of power. A shared characteristic of eighteenth-century reformers was their emphasis on the study of hadith.[293] These reformers were all traditionalists, but they championed new varieties of traditionalism reflecting their radical critique of prevalent hierarchies of power and principles of authority. So we will now turn to the theories of hadith.

Chapter 5

Humanizing the Sacred

Under the common banner of *tawḥīd,* the eighteenth century generated a multitude of cultural identities bearing the imprints of particular regional traditions and echoing the intricate and relatively separate histories of diverse regions of the Muslim world. Some of the distinctive features of these identities I have already discussed in the previous chapters, as I have pointed out some of the shared concerns of the regional cultural traditions. The local character of eighteenth-century reform was always balanced by the strong tendency among the reformers of this period to draw on outside Islamic sources and intellectual trends. The modes through which these reformers invoked the intellectual legacies of the greater Muslim world were also diverse. So were the ways they related to institutional power. Although marked differences in the levels of political oppression caused some, though not all, to withdraw from the public sphere, or to seek spaces not yet claimed by the established authorities of the time, eighteenth-century reformers exhibited a remarkable optimism that reflected their confidence in the prospects for change. Moreover, despite the difficulties and challenges they faced, which they often described in their writings, they did not withdraw to the intellectual or political margins of society, and they always conceived of themselves as dynamic agents of social revival and reform. Underlying this optimism was a sense that the political institutions were weak and that intellectual reform could fill the resulting vacuum.

The persistent confidence of the eighteenth-century reformers is best reflected in their advocacy of *ijtihād*. As we have seen, different reformers held different views on this subject and, for the most part, the contents of their theoretical expositions were not original. The one shared and innovative trait that characterized all eighteenth-century theories was their advocacy of *ijtihād* in the public sphere. These reformers also personalized their *ijtihād*; Shāh Walī Allāh al-Dihlawī did this directly by proclaiming his divinely ordained mission as the reviver of the age (*mujaddid al-ʿaṣr*).[1] The Yemeni reformers were less direct, if only because such claims went against the grain of their struggle against exclusive claims to authority. Still, the unique scholarly credentials of these Yemeni reformers were celebrated by their contemporaries and followers; thus, for example, al-Shawkānī was considered the *mujaddid* of his age by many of his followers in Yemen and elsewhere in the Muslim world.[2] However, the originality of the eighteenth-century discourse on *ijtihād*, whether it emphasized *tajdīd* (renewal) or not, was in projecting *ijtihād* into the public sphere, where it was subsumed within the larger discussions of authority.

In the previous chapters we have examined several ways different eighteenth-century thinkers related to power, and how their relationships to all kinds of authority were informed by their experiences as well as the intellectual legacies of their respective regional traditions. We also noted examples of the reconstruction of historical narratives in light of new conceptualizations of authority. The negotiation of new concepts of authority, however, was not restricted to practical, political, or historical discourses. More interesting than the not-so-hidden critique of the dominant modes for the exercise of political power was an implicit critique from within through which traditional intellectual norms and dominant forms of knowledge were engaged and reformed. At its most fundamental level, this implicit critique found expression in changing notions of authority, systematically challenged in works on the theory of hadith and jurisprudence (*uṣūl al-ḥadīth* and *uṣūl al-fiqh*).

The critical eyes of the intellectuals of the eighteenth century scanned a wide array of intertwined religious, political, and social issues. When considered individually, many of the problems they dwelled on appear similar. Such problems included, for example, the cultic and creedal excesses of tomb worshippers, the corruption and injustice of rulers, and the division of Muslims. The thinkers of this century shared the view that sectarian zeal and blind imitation of bygone authorities were at the root of all socioreligious ills. Equally shared was the conviction that hadith scholarship offered an effective solution to these ills: hadith, it was argued, is the source of valid dogma; knowledge of it is an indispensable requisite for the exercise of *ijtihād*; and, as the only reliable criteria for arbitrating differences among the various Islamic schools, hadith provides the one genuine opportunity to overcome these differences and unite Muslims. Hadith, in short, was central to eighteenth-century definitions and delineations of Islamic priorities and identities.

These apparent similarities, however, obscure significant differences that distinguish eighteenth-century Islamic discourses. Once integrated into a composite whole, each of the individual problematics addressed by eighteenth-century thinkers acquires different, and often divergent meanings. By giving priority to specific sets of problems, and hence by proposing specific courses of action to address these problems, each thinker provided his unique account of the crisis of the age and of the optimal way to overcome it. The uniqueness and distinction of each of these accounts is best reflected in the specific role that each thinker assigns to hadith. Beyond the shared recognition of its centrality, hadith occupied different positions and served distinct purposes in the thought of various eighteenth-century thinkers. Moreover, the renewed eighteenth-century emphasis on the role of hadith is itself a product of specific regional traditions, each of which is cognizant of the larger Islamic tradition of hadith scholarship but is largely shaped by the historical peculiarities of its own regional origins.

In the following pages, I provide a comparative outline of various trends in the development of regional schools of hadith scholarship. In particular, I examine the Yemeni and the Indian traditions. Each of these emerged in the course of criticizing conventional theories of hadith study.[3] Differences in the choice of issues to be reexamined led to the production of distinctly divergent schools and approaches to the study of hadith. The one shared trait that characterized all of these revisionist approaches to hadith was erudition and a remarkable command of details. The thinkers of the eighteenth century proposed a thorough reformulation of the well-established discipline of hadith studies. They also redefined the position of the discipline in relation to other traditional disciplines of learning. These thinkers were firmly situated in the classical tradition itself, and their achievements are hardly conceivable without the groundwork done by their predecessors. Yet, even when both the traditional and innovative approaches to the study of hadith seemed to serve similar objectives, the way they arrived at these objectives was different. The focus of the following analysis, therefore, is not to speculate on the function of the discourse elaborated within each tradition but to account for its process of development, as well as its internal logical and structural coherence. Rather than identifying the interests these new ideas sought to preserve, legitimate, or reinforce, I try to recover the social as well as intellectual circumstances and sympathies driving them from within their respective traditions.

Hadith in Yemen

The fifteenth-century Zaydi scholar Muḥammad Ibn Ibrāhīm al-Wazīr (775–840/1376–1437) was instrumental in introducing hadith scholarship to Yemen. Although Yemen was not devoid of hadith scholars prior to the fifteenth century, Ibn al-Wazīr was the first to argue rigorously for establishing hadith as a principal discipline in Islamic scholarship. Ibn al-Wazīr's arguments were especially significant when viewed in the context of the then-prevalent Muʿtazilī tendencies of the Zaydi scholars of Yemen. One of the main stated objectives of Ibn al-Wazīr was to demote theology by arguing against its centrality in relation to other Islamic disciplines of learning and to introduce in its place the more traditional discipline of hadith. An immediate consequence of this and other reformulations by Ibn al-Wazīr (as well as by other scholars) was to bring the views of the Zaydi school closer to those of the Sunnis. For this reason, Ibn al-Wazīr is often called the initiator of a reform tradition that opened up Zaydism to Sunni Islam. Ibn al-Wazīr's work is characterized by an incessant emphasis on the principle of seeking evidence (*dalīl*) in the Qur'ān and hadith for any legal ruling, as opposed to imitating a dead or living imam.

At first glance, Ibn al-Wazīr's argument would not seem to diverge from traditional Zaydi views. His radical move, however, was to argue that since the Zaydis have no extant reference books on hadith, they have to rely on the Sunni works. Ibn al-Wazīr's reforms, therefore, served primarily to establish the authority of Sunni hadith collections as the basic sources for deriving Zaydi law.[4] Later Yemeni scholars working within the tradition initiated by Ibn al-Wazīr continued to adhere to the basic principle of the ultimate authority of the Qur'ān and hadith.[5] There was, however, a significant shift in the nature of the discourse on hadith after Ibn al-Wazīr, who, it should be remembered, was the first major Zaydi scholar to attempt such a thorough study of hadith. Ibn al-Wazīr imported Sunni hadith scholarship without critical reexamination of this scholarship. His efforts were devoted to gaining acceptance for the authority of hadith among Zaydis. In areas where a strong, well-established scholarly tradition existed among the Zaydis, Ibn al-Wazīr was more discriminate in accepting the Sunni position. This is notably the case in his critical works on theology (*kalām*), *Al-ʿAwāṣim wal-Qawāṣim fī al-Dhabb ʿan Sunnat Abī al-Qāṣim* and its abridgment *Al-Rawḍ al-Bāsim fī al-Dhabb ʿan Sunnat Abī al-Qāṣim*, arguably Ibn al-Wazīr's most famous and influential books. In both works, Ibn al-Wazīr repeatedly discusses the role of hadith and the methods of using it, but his discussions are directed against the Zaydi position, which seemingly rejects or at best fails to recognize this role. The main subjects tackled in the two books, however, are theological questions reminiscent of debates between the Ashʿarī and Muʿtazilī schools. Despite several criticisms of the Muʿtazilī views that were prevalent among Yemeni Zaydis, Ibn al-Wazīr is more critical of the Ashʿarī positions; he also argues that Ashʿarī *kalām* is no less an innovation than that of the Muʿtazilīs, since neither is sanctioned by clear textual statements in either the Qur'ān or in hadith.[6]

Ibn al-Wazīr's main work on the theory of hadith (*fiqh al-ḥadīth* or *uṣūl al-ḥadīth*) is *Tanqīḥ al-Anẓār fī ʿUlūm al-Āthār*, but he discusses hadith in most of his other works as well.[7] In an effort to question strict adherence to Zaydism, Ibn al-Wazīr defends the Sunna, by which he means the normative sayings and practices of Prophet Muhammad, and argues that it should serve as the ultimate arbiter in all instances of disagreement on legal or doctrinal matters. Ibn al-Wazīr also defends the Sunni imams and maintains that the methods of theologians and philosophers are of no use to the traditional disciplines.[8] Finally, Ibn al-Wazīr exhibits in his work a comprehensive command of the traditional disciplines of *tafsīr*, hadith, and jurisprudence, as well as the various linguistic sciences.[9] In sum, Ibn al-Wazīr did not make original contributions to the established Sunni discipline of hadith studies. Rather, his creative efforts were in the systematic introduction of this discipline to Zaydi scholarship.[10]

In the generations after Ibn al-Wazīr, the interest in theology gradually faded, and the critical efforts of Yemeni scholars shifted toward scrutinizing the accepted traditional Sunni theories of the discipline of hadith and reexamining in detail every principle of this discipline. A notable example of the crucial developments in the Yemeni tradition of hadith scholarship is *Tawḍīḥ al-Afkār li Maʿānī Tanqīḥ al-Anẓār* by Muḥammad Ibn Ismāʿīl al-Amīr al-Ṣanʿānī (1099–1182/1688–1769). This is a commentary on Ibn al-Wazīr's *Tanqīḥ al-Anẓār* in which al-Ṣanʿānī sets out to accomplish two aims: first, he attempts to popularize what he views as a foundational work in the Yemeni intellectual tradition, and second, he attempts to complement, explain, correct, and systematize Ibn al-Wazīr's argument. In the process, al-Ṣanʿānī provides methodological critiques and comments that reflect and explain the developments that took place within the contours of the particular regional tradition of Yemen. Al-Ṣanʿānī's comments address more than what would have been better organizational strategies, or what further explanations could be useful to clarify the arguments of Ibn al-Wazīr.[11] Al-Ṣanʿānī points out several disagreements with Ibn al-Wazīr, especially on the issues of *taqlīd* and on the theory of hadith. Al-Ṣanʿānī also discusses outstanding issues that come up in Ibn al-Wazīr's other important works, including *Al-ʿAwāṣim min al-Qawāṣim*, *Al-Rawḍ al-Bāsim*, *Al-Mukhtaṣar fī ʿUlūm al-Ḥadīth*, and *Īthār al-Ḥaqq ʿalā al-Khalq*.[12] In addition, al-Ṣanʿānī uses this commentary to provide a comprehensive overview of all the classical theories of hadith scholarship; he sifts through Ibn al-Wazīr's sources and adds numerous other opinions that Ibn al-Wazīr fails to report. Al-Ṣanʿānī then provides a thorough critical reevaluation of these sources and, in the process, systematically constructs his own alternative theory of hadith.

Before discussing al-Ṣanʿānī's ideas, it would be useful to list the main sources on which he relies. The list of sources quoted and almost always acknowledged by al-Ṣanʿānī is indeed humbling: it includes all the classical works in *ʿulūm muṣṭalaḥ al-ḥadīth* (hadith technical terminology). The sources quoted most are *Al-Nukat ʿalā Ibn al-Ṣalāḥ* by Ibn Ḥajar al-ʿAsqalānī (d. 852), perhaps the most famous commentary on the classical work on hadith scholarship, and *Muqaddima fī ʿUlūm al-Ḥadīth* by Ibn al-Ṣalaḥ (d. 643). Al-Ṣanʿānī also uses Ibn al-Ṣalāḥ's *Muqaddima* as well as other writings by Ibn Ḥajar; *Maʿrifat ʿUlūm al-Ḥadīth* by al-Ḥākim al-Nīshāburī (d. 405); *Sharḥ Alfiyyat al-Ḥadīth*, both (the *Alfiyya* and its *Sharḥ*) by Zayn al-Dīn al-ʿIrāqī (d. 806); and a commentary on this last *Sharḥ* titled *Fatḥ al-Mughīth Sharḥ Alfiyyat al-Ḥadīth* by Shams al-Dīn al-Sakhāwī (d. 902). In addition, al-Ṣanʿānī makes extensive use of works by Abū Nuʿaym al-Aṣfahānī (d. 430), al-Khaṭīb al-Baghdādī (d. 463), al-Qāḍī ʿIyāḍ (d. 544), al-Badr al-Zarkashī (d. 794), al-Ḥāfiẓ al-Balqīnī (d. 805), al-Nawawī (d. 676), Jalāl al-Dīn al-Suyūṭī (d. 911), al-Ḥalabī (d. 851), Badr al-Dīn Ibn Jamāʿa (d. 733), Abū al-Fidāʾ Ibn Kathīr (d. 774), Burhān al-Dīn al-Biqāʿī (d. 885), Zakariyya al-Anṣārī (d. 928), and many others.[13]

In the ancillary disciplines of *ʿilm al-rijāl* (the science of men, including biographies of many women), *al-jarḥ wal-taʿdil*, and *isnād* (authentication based on scrutinizing the probity of individual reporters and the chains of transmission), al-Ṣanʿānī's sources include such classical works as *Istīʿāb* by Ibn ʿAbd al-Barr (d. 463); *Iṣāba*, *Taqrīb al-Tahdhīb*, *Tahdhīb al-Tahdhīb*, and *Lisān al-Mizān* by Ibn Ḥajar (d. 852); *Ansāb* by al-Samʿānī (d. 562); *Tārīkh Baghdād* by Al-Khaṭīb al-Baghdādī (d. 463); *Al-Tārīkh al-Kabīr* by Muḥammad Ibn Ismāʿīl al-Bukhārī (d. 256); *Tadhkirat al-Ḥuffāẓ*, *Siyar Aʿlām al-Nubalāʾ*, *Al-Mughnī min al-Ḍuʿafāʾ*, and *Mīzān al-Iʿtidāl* by al-Dhahabī (d. 748); *Tahdhīb al-Asmāʾ* and *Tahdhīb al-Thiqāt* by al-Nawawī (d. 676); *Tahdhīb al-Kamāl* by al-Mizzī (d. 742); *Ṭabaqāt al-Shāfiʿiyya* by Tāj al-Dīn al-Subkī (d. 771); *Al-Ṭabaqāt al-Kabīr* by Ibn Saʿd (d. 230); *Wafiyyāt al-Aʿyān* by Ibn Khallikān (d. 681); *Al-Madkhal ilā al-Ṣaḥīḥ* by al-Ḥākim al-Nīshābūrī (d. 405); *Al-Musnad al-Kabīr ʿalā Asmāʾ al-Rijāl* by Muslim Ibn Ḥajjāj Ibn Muslim (d. 261); *Mashāʾikh al-Bukhārī* by Ibn ʿAdī (d. 361); and many others.[14]

These lists are significant because they situate al-Ṣanʿānī's scholarship in the mainstream tradition of hadith scholarship and because they are suggestive of the scope of his critical undertaking. However, a closer examination of the content of this work is needed for a more accurate evaluation of al-Ṣanʿānī's ideas. Although he agrees wholeheartedly with Ibn al-Wazīr's refreshing interest in and use of hadith, al-Ṣanʿānī includes many criticisms over the course of his commentary. These stem primarily from Ibn al-Wazīr's predictable lapses: Ibn al-Wazīr, it should be remembered, was practically the first major Zaydi scholar to attempt a serious study of hadith. In the three centuries between the two scholars, Yemeni scholars advanced considerably in their mastery of the discipline of hadith. One of the main issues with which al-Ṣanʿānī contends is the relative authority of the compilations of sound hadith traditions by al-Bukhārī and Muslim. These two works are often considered to be the most authentic collections of traditions. Al-Ṣanʿānī maintains, however, that sound (*ṣaḥīḥ*) hadiths are not found only in compilations that specialize exclusively in sound hadiths, and certainly not only in the works of al-Bukhārī and Muslim.[15] Sound traditions, he adds, can be found in compilations that include weak (*ḍaʿīf*), good/worthy (*ḥasan*), and sound (*ṣaḥīḥ*) traditions, such as the *Musnad* of Aḥmad Ibn Ḥanbal. Quoting Ibn al-Wazīr on the "standard classification [of sound traditions] that is found in the books of the science of hadith,"[16] Al-Ṣanʿānī lists the following seven ranks, starting with the soundest of all: (1) that on which al-Bukhārī and Muslim agree; (2) hadith reported by Bukhārī; (3) hadith reported by Muslim; (4) hadith that fulfills the conditions of both; (5) hadith that fulfills al-Bukhārī's conditions; (6) hadith that fulfills Muslim's conditions; and (7) hadith that is sound according to the standards of other imams of hadith but does not fulfill the conditions of either al-Bukhārī or Muslim.[17] Al-Ṣanʿānī then takes issue with those who are willing to concede his point that sound hadith can be found outside the compilations of al-Bukhārī and Muslim but stipulate that such additional traditions should satisfy their conditions (*ʿalā sharṭihimā*). In response to this stipulation by Ibn al-Wazīr, al-Ṣanʿānī says,

> One may respond by saying that we can determine that they [al-Bukhārī and Muslim] were satisfied with the transmitters of a tradition that they reported [*akhrajāh*] if they identified its transmitters. As for what meets their conditions, there is no conclusive evidence specifying these conditions. Rather, the [later] imams of hadith presumed certain conditions for the transmitters and claimed that they were the conditions of the two shaykhs. However, they [the scholars of hadith] did not agree on these [conditions], and they questioned each other. . . . Thus a hadith that allegedly meets their [al-Bukhārī's and Muslim's] conditions engenders only the weak presumption that it may meet these conditions, because they did not spell them out. In contrast, if they transmit [traditions] in their books on the authority [of someone], then we surmise that they are satisfied with that person, even if some of their transmitters are found objectionable—although this is unlikely; when in doubt we judge according to the general case. Yes, if a hadith is transmitted duplicating their same transmitters without any deficiency, then that hadith has the same standing as what we find in their [books].[18]

So far, al-Ṣanʿanī's argument is twofold: first, he maintains that sound hadith can be found outside al-Bukhārī and Muslim, and outside other hadith compilations devoted exclusively to sound traditions. Second, he categorically rejects the stipulation that a hadith can be accepted only if it meets the conditions of al-Bukhārī and Muslim, partly because these conditions are not stated, and because there is no sure way of determining them. Al-Ṣanʿānī further maintains that

> one should refrain from asserting that a hadith that is not given in either one of the two books fulfills their conditions. For their conditions are not known with any certainty; so how can we definitively describe a hadith which they did not give, and assert that it is sound, while we are in

> doubt about the conditions from which such an assertion derives? Indeed, certainty cannot be based on doubt. Neither are we impressed by the agreement of enumerable outstanding scholars that a hadith which they [al-Bukhārī and Muslim] did not report fulfills their conditions. The conclusive word [in this matter] is [one that derives from] tangible evidence, not from mere opinions.[19]

Al-Ṣanʿānī, then, is well aware that a majority of traditional hadith scholars believe it is possible to infer what the conditions of al-Bukhārī and Muslim are. Nevertheless, al-Ṣanʿānī is not impressed by the concurrence of these scholars. Instead, he deconstructs the notion that majority consent confers authority, and the related assertion of the favorable reception by the community of Muslims of the two *ṣaḥīḥ* works (*talaqqī al-umma lil-ṣaḥīḥayn bil-qabūl*):[20]

> Know that the meaning of the favorable reception by the community of a hadith is that the community either acts upon it or interprets it. . . . As for the reception of the hadith traditions of the two *Ṣaḥīḥ*s, the person who makes such a claim needs proof to substantiate it. I say that this claim requires further clarification regarding its two components. [First], does this [statement] refer to all of the community, both the masses and the elites, as is apparent from the generalization? Or is it just the *mujtahid*s of the community? It is well known that the first [interpretation] cannot be intended, so the second is—namely, the claim that every single individual among the *mujtahid*s of the community has received the two books with approval. Such a claim requires evidence, but it should not be hard to see that providing it is practically impossible, as it is impossible to provide evidence for the claim of consensus [*ijmāʿ*]. After all, the former [claim] is a special case of the latter. Aḥmad Ibn Ḥanbal and others have asserted that anyone who claims consensus is a liar. If this is true of his time, which is before the compilation of the two *ṣaḥīḥ*s, how [more true would it be] after that time? . . . Furthermore, it is very likely that among the scholars who are *mujtahid*s there are some who do not know the two *Ṣaḥīḥ*s, since knowing them in their particular form is certainly not a condition for *ijtihād*. In short, this claim is not acceptable.[21]

Al-Ṣanʿānī therefore rejects the claim that the whole community of Muslims, or the community of *mujtahid*s, could have favorably received the two *ṣaḥīḥ* works. This claim lacks evidence to substantiate it. It is also based on the erroneous assumption that consensus is possible, or that it is knowable. Moreover, this assertion makes knowledge of the two *ṣaḥīḥ* compilations a prerequisite of *ijtihād*, thereby formally conferring on them, rather than on the traditions they report, an authority to which they are not entitled.

All of these objections by al-Ṣanʿānī, however, are not aimed at questioning the reliability of the compilations of al-Bukhārī and Muslim. Al-Ṣanʿānī's position is clarified as he moves on to the second point in his analysis. Granting, for the sake of argument, that the community favorably received the two works, al-Ṣanʿānī wonders,

> Is the intended meaning of the community's reception of these two momentous works that the community knows that they were compiled by the two scrupulous [*ḥāfiẓayn*] imams? [If so, then] this would only imply the correctness of attributing these two works to their authors; obviously, this is not what is intended. Or is the intended meaning that the community has accepted the attribution of every single one of their [al-Bukhārī's and Muslim's] hadiths to the Messenger [of God]? This [reading] seems to correspond to the intended [meaning], since the [claim of] agreement over the authenticity of [all] their transmitters is based on it. "Favorable reception" is what the infallible [consensus of the community] has implicitly deemed to be sound, as the author [Ibn al-Wazīr] has stated in his books. This corresponds to what we have attributed earlier to the legal theorists, namely, that it [an accepted hadith] is what the community either interprets or acts upon, since this is true only of what the community deems to be sound. However, it is not difficult to see that a similar claim cannot be substantiated for every single hadith in the two *ṣaḥīḥ* books. . . . For that would mean that each individual *mujtahid* has examined every single hadith in the two books.[22]

It is clear from al-Ṣanʿānī's choice of adjectives that he has no misgivings over the value of the two compilations of *ṣaḥīḥ* traditions, nor does he question the superb credentials of their compilers. His real objection is to the arguments used to establish the reliability and authority of these two works. In particular, he rejects the assertion that there is a consensus on accepting the two works in their entirety. Al-Ṣanʿānī, therefore, recognizes the authority of these works, but he rejects the arguments often used in traditional studies of hadith to justify this authority.[23]

In the course of probing this question, al-Ṣanʿānī spells out his views on consensus (*ijmāʿ*):

> What we know with certainty is that the community has been granted infallibility from wrongdoing [*ḍalāla*], not from error. . . . Thus, the judgment by the community that a certain *āḥādī ḥadīth* [a tradition that is reported through a singular chain of transmission] is sound, when, in fact, it is not sound in itself [*laysa ṣaḥīḥ fī nafs al-amr*], is certainly not a wrongdoing. And even if we grant that all the *mujtahid*s of the community have

favorably received the traditions of the two *Ṣaḥīḥ*s, and either acted upon each of these traditions or interpreted them, this still does not prove the claim that [all the traditions] are sound [*ṣaḥīḥ*]. This is because favorable reception is not restricted to *ṣaḥīḥ*; rather, good/worthy [*ḥasan*] hadith is also interpreted and acted upon. Therefore, the statement by the author [Ibn al-Wazīr] that favorable reception [of a hadith] is an implicit judgment by the infallible [community] that it is sound, would only apply had this infallible [community] not acted on the basis of *ḥasan* or interpreted it; this, we know, is not the case. And even if we grant the claim of the author and those who came before him, their claim would only apply to the traditions of the two *Ṣaḥīḥ*s, and nothing else; it would not apply to the traditions that meet their conditions, since there are no conditions that we can attach to them with certainty.[24]

According to al-Ṣanʿānī, therefore, consensus protects from wrongdoing but not from error. Put differently, errors committed by the community do not implicate it morally. One outcome of such a position would be to alleviate some of the burdens of collective responsibility: the community is not expected to always identify the ultimate truth, and thus correctness is not a prerequisite for rectitude. The more obvious implication of al-Ṣanʿānī's assertions, however, is to dispute the alleged possibility, and hence authority, of *ijmāʿ*. Al-Ṣanʿānī, therefore, does not oppose the accepted conviction that al-Bukhārī and Muslim are the most reliable compilations of sound hadith, or that they contain the most authoritative texts after the Qurʾān. This he reiterates in numerous places in his writings. Rather, his purpose is to question the consequences, with regard to general questions of authority, of a particular argument used to assert the established superiority of these two works. Thus, the compilations of al-Bukhārī and Muslim, according to al-Ṣanʿānī, are authoritative, but their hypothetical "conditions" are not. Moreover, this authority cannot rest on a "favorable reception" or acceptance by the community. Both of these arguments that al-Ṣanʿānī challenges, it should be pointed out, were widely accepted in the traditional literature on hadith studies and were accepted without question by Ibn al-Wazīr.

The radical nature of Ibn al-Wazīr's adoption of hadith as the ultimate authority in creedal as well as legal matters can hardly be overstated. The fact remains, however, that he was not fully aware of the nuances of the tradition of hadith scholarship that he invoked. Al-Ṣanʿānī, in contrast, fully mastered the discipline of hadith studies; he carefully classified its various schools and delineated the fundamental assumptions underlying them; and he questioned many of these long-established assumptions. Another such assumption questioned and rejected by al-Ṣanʿānī is the widely accepted notion, also accepted by Ibn al-Wazīr, that the traditions reported in al-Bukhārī's *Ṣaḥīḥ* are superior to those in Muslim's *Ṣaḥīḥ*.

Al-Ṣanʿānī contends that the arguments provided by Ibn al-Wazīr in support of al-Bukhārī do not establish that the latter's reports are sounder than Muslim's collection; at best, these arguments simply establish the soundness of al-Bukhārī's reports.[25] In fact, if the superiority of either al-Bukhārī or Muslim is, as the traditional argument goes, "on account of the above-mentioned [favorable] reception [by the community], then they are both equal in correctness, and there is no point in making what they agree upon take precedence over what they each separately report. Nor do we consider those [traditions] that uniquely belong to al-Bukhārī superior in terms of reception, since they are all equal in this regard."[26] Moreover, al-Ṣanʿānī adds, the two shaykhs overlapped in most of their transmitters, while a few transmitters appear only in al-Bukhārī and another unique group appears only in Muslim.[27] As for the majority of transmitters upon which they agree, both stand on the same footing in terms of authenticity. This point, however, is not as obvious as one may think; for it can be argued that even though the chains of transmission are the same, what counts is the conditions that the compilers require in their transmitters. Thus, according to this argument, the identity of the two chains might be accidental. To this al-Ṣanʿānī responds by stating that al-Bukhārī requires that adjacent transmitters in a chain of transmission should have met for their reports to be accepted; Muslim, in contrast, requires that the transmitters be contemporaneous, which subsumes within it al-Bukhārī's conditions. As such, the argument that al-Bukhārī's transmission standards are sounder than Muslim's conditions in those traditions where they agree both on the texts and the chains of transmission is totally arbitrary. And since these equivalent reports comprise the majority of the reports of both works, then there is no basis for the blanket judgment that al-Bukhārī's book is superior to Muslim's.

As for the relatively small number of traditions that are not common to the two books, al-Ṣanʿānī suggests that an argument can be made that, on the whole, al-Bukhārī's traditions are sounder than Muslim's. More important, however, al-Ṣanʿānī maintains that this judgment should be limited to those traditions whose transmitters have not been discussed, since the soundness of hadith is determined by the transmitters quoted in their books, and not by reference to the persons of the two shaykhs themselves. So, if the transmitters are known, then the judgment of the hadith should be based on what is known about these transmitters.[28]

Al-Ṣanʿānī adds yet another objection. He argues that al-Bukhārī requires that his transmitters should have met at least once. Al-Ṣanʿānī finds this condition questionable, because a person may transmit numerous traditions on the authority of another although we may have information of only a brief encounter between the two. So, for the condition of meeting to be meaningful, we have to add to al-Bukhārī's conditions the requirement that the meeting be long enough to accommodate the transmitted traditions, a condition which, according to al-Ṣanʿānī, verges on being absurd. Alternatively, we revert back to the simple requirement that the transmitters be contemporaries, with the added stipulation that they should have resided in close locales for the contact between them to be possible.[29]

Al-Ṣanʿānī then maintains that after all of the above discussion, there remains only one real difference between the two shaykhs, namely, the *muʿanʿan ḥadīth*. This type of tradition uses the formula, "From X on the authority of Y, etc. (*ʿan* X *ʿan* Y)," rather than the more accurate formula, "X said, I heard from Y, or Y told me, and so on." In the introduction to his compilation, Muslim discusses this matter and indirectly criticizes al-Bukhārī without mentioning his name. Al-Ṣanʿānī points out that in this introduction, Muslim says that the *ʿanʿana* transmission is acceptable only if the two transmitters are trustworthy, contemporaries, and if the meeting between them was physically possible. In this case, even if we do not have a report of an actual meeting, the reported tradition is acceptable. Thus, according to al-Ṣanʿānī, Muslim did not just require that the transmitters be contemporaries, but he also required that the meeting between them be a real possibility. How then, al-Ṣanʿānī wonders, can one continue to overgeneralize regarding the superiority of al-Bukhārī over Muslim?[30]

Al-Ṣanʿānī's contentions about the relative soundness of al-Bukhārī versus Muslim are not merely academic. In a similar argument, al-Ṣanʿānī refuses to issue blanket judgments regarding the relative soundness of *musnad* compilations in relation to the standard *sunan* works.[31] In contrast to hadith collections that are classified by subject, the traditions of a *musnad* are grouped under the Companions who report them. Al-Ṣanʿānī mentions, among others, the *musnad*s of Tayālīsī (d. 203/818) and Ibn Ḥanbal (d. 241/855). In contrast, the standard *sunan* works are the two *ṣaḥīḥ* collections of al-Bukhārī (d. 256/870) and Muslim (d. 261/875), as well as those of Abū Dāwūd (d. 275/888), al-Tirmidhī (d. 279/892), al-Nasāʾī (d. 303/915), and Ibn Māja (d. 273/886).[32] Al-Ṣanʿānī reports that Ibn al-Wazīr, in agreement with the prevalent view in hadith scholarship, argues that the *musnads* are less rigorous and further from the rank of soundness than the *sunan*. Al-Ṣanʿānī then argues against this view: the *musnads,* he contends, include worthy (*ḥasan*) traditions as well as sound ones, some of which could be superior to those of the *sunan* collections.

> The correct position, then, is not to judge a whole collection of *sunan* superior to a whole collection of *musnad*s, such as the *musnad* of Ibn Ḥanbal. Rather, we can only give preference to individual traditions. . . .

> As such, their statement [that of Ibn al-Wazīr and other hadith scholars] should be taken to mean that most of the traditions of the *sunan* are of a higher rank than those of the *masānīd*. Yet even then, other drawbacks to this [judgment] remain; this is because, when it comes to application, there is little value in this comparison. So, for example, if a tradition from the *musnad* of Aḥmad [Ibn Ḥanbal], which is known to contain many worthy traditions, is in disagreement with a tradition from the *sunan* of Ibn Māja, which is known to contain many weak traditions, we do not give preference to Ibn Māja, since it could be one of his weak hadiths, and because it is conceivable that the hadith of the *musnad* is one of the worthy ones. Therefore, the application [in points of law] is contingent on [a case by case] investigation, thus making generalized preferences useless.... [After all,] this [kind of reasoning] is not sufficient when it comes to legal rulings.[33]

Granting that certain compilations carry more weight and are more reliable than others, al-Ṣanʿānī in the above arguments advocates a case-by-case examination of each individual hadith in these collections. Under no condition should Muslims posit the absolute truth of any single book aside from the Qurʾān. Moreover, al-Ṣanʿānī points out that not all of the transmitters of the two *ṣaḥīḥ* books are free of blemish.[34] He adds, however, that sometimes the dubiousness of these transmitters is not asserted in general terms; rather, the reasons for questioning their integrity are often specified. Thus, some transmitters are criticized for their *irjāʿ*, *naṣb*, *tashayyuʿ*, *qadr*, and the like.[35] Others are accused of innovation (*bidʿa*). Al-Ṣanʿānī then says that scholars of hadith usually "include safety from *bidʿa* in their definition of probity, since, according to them, *bidʿa* impairs probity. This is especially true because among these innovators are some who preach their innovation." Al-Ṣanʿānī goes on to say that Ibn al-Qaṭṭān went too far in his attack on some of the innovators among the transmitters in al-Bukhārī and Muslim, and that al-Maqbalī (d. 1696) approvingly quoted Ibn al-Qaṭṭān when he asserted that "among their men there are some whose Islam is not known." Al-Ṣanʿānī comments, however, that such an assertion "is only a result of extremism, since it is well known that the imams of hadith only transmit on the authority of Muslims."[36]

Elsewhere in his book al-Ṣanʿānī surveys the various opinions regarding the acceptance of the report of *fāsiq al-taʾwīl* and *kāfir al-taʾwīl*.[37] This is a person who is pronounced a sinner (*fāsiq*, innovator) or unbeliever (*kāfir*) not because he either professes to be an unbeliever, or on account of some outrageous act or utterance that puts him outside the pale of Islam; rather, he is condemned on the basis of the interpretation of his acts and beliefs by other Muslims. The prime example of this group is the Khārijites, who are unequivocally condemned by other Muslims, including the Yemenis, but who genuinely believe in their version of Islam.[38] Al-Ṣanʿānī discusses the status of sects that clearly violate the normative principles of the Sunna but whose violations are based on interpretations that, at least on the face of it, have some justification. Al-Ṣanʿānī maintains that there is disagreement among hadith scholars on whether to accept the reports of such people, assuming, of course, that they are free from dishonoring faults, known to be pious, and are not liars. Some argue that hadith transmitted by such people is always rejected, while others argue that it is always accepted. For Al-Ṣanʿānī, a more reasonable position is one that distinguishes between a polemicist innovator, that is, one who preaches his heretic dogma, and a nonpolemicist. The key criterion is that if the report contains reinforcement of the innovative dogma being preached and makes it more attractive, then it should not be accepted; otherwise, there is no reason to reject the hadith.

An innovator, therefore, can still be a pious and honest person, despite an innovation that threatens to bring him dire punishment in this world and very likely in the hereafter. Al-Ṣanʿānī's judgment is not a simple theoretical gesture but entails accepting the authority of such heretics as conveyers of one of the most important sources of Islamic law. This authority is not based on an inquisitive assessment of the transmitter's doctrinal views, as long as these views are not completely outside the flexible boundaries of normative Islam. Rather, it is based on the person's honesty and genuineness, no matter how wrong he or she may be, and on his or her technical qualifications (memory, regularity, etc.). Al-Ṣanʿānī also maintains that there is in fact agreement on two basic requirements to establish the probity (*ʿadāla*) of transmitters: (1) truthfulness and precision and (2) that the transmitter's virtues outweigh his or her vices in matters of religion. Beyond these requirements, al-Ṣanʿānī continues,

> Some add the conditions of safety from innovation and sustained dignity [*murūʾa*], thus making *ʿadāla* a name for something that can hardly be attained except by an infallible person. . . . Whoever requires these [additional] conditions would not be able to fulfill them. In fact, the report of an innovator . . . is acceptable if he is truthful. . . . Thus when someone says such and such a person is trustworthy [*ʿadl*], then the former's report informs us that this person is truthful, and that his virtues outweigh his vices. Such a person is acceptable to us . . . even if he is accused of innovation of *qadar* or the like, since this does not impair the transmission of a truthful person.[39]

Al-Ṣanʿānī manages to eliminate the unrealistic requirements of perfection and near infallibility in his transmitters, both rationally objectionable requirements that cannot be conditions for a meaningful authority. Because his authorities are real people, al-Ṣanʿānī's attempt to establish the authority of hadith does not entail an idealization of the past; rather, al-Ṣanʿānī simply makes the past usable by devising practical tools to facilitate this use. Individual transmitters of hadith, as well as its most reliable compilers, like al-Bukhārī and Muslim, need not be ideal or infallible. Nor is there any hypothetical power—like the consensus of the community—that endows a particular compilation with unmitigated truthfulness. In fact, one of the most striking features of al-Ṣanʿānī's work is his ability to make a consistent argument in favor of the practical authority of hadith while maintaining a critical, though usually respectful, attitude toward its transmitters and compilers. Thus, after dismissing the concurrence of many "great masters" on the notion that the two *ṣaḥīḥ* works derive their authority from their "favorable acceptance" by the community, al-Ṣanʿānī provides an alternative explanation for their distinction:

> Once you realize the weakness in the inference [that al-Bukhārī and Muslim are superior because of their favorable acceptance by the community], even when great masters are in conformity over it, then, in my view, the more appropriate proof for the advanced rank of the two *Ṣaḥīḥ*s is the reporting [*ikhbār*] by the two compilers that their traditions are sound. For we know without doubt that they [al-Bukhārī and Muslim] are upright [*ʿadlān*], and we are obligated to accept the report of the upright person [*khabar al-ʿadl wājib al-qabūl*]. So, al-Bukhārī's assertion, "These are sound traditions," is tantamount to his saying, "The transmitters of these traditions are trustworthy [*ʿudūl*], precise [*ḍābitūn*], and there are neither anomalies [*shudhūdh*] nor defects [*ʿilla*] in them." In such cases his report has to be accepted in the same way we accept his attestation to the probity of an unknown transmitter, that his reporting is accurate, and that the hadith is free of defect or irregularity. This is so because the word *ṣaḥīḥ* includes all of these meanings, as we elaborated in our treatise *Irshād al-Nuqqād ilā Taysīr al-Ijtihād*.[40]

Al-Ṣanʿānī, therefore, is arguing that the acceptance of a hadith reported in either al-Bukhārī or Muslim is not equivalent to a submission to their judgment regarding this or any other hadith. Rather, each respective receiver of a hadith accepts the testimony of the transmitter, not his judgment, and in turn decides on the basis of this testimony whether this hadith is authentic. The receiver, therefore, is exercising *ijtihād*, and is not a mere imitator.[41] Put differently, we do not trust the judgment of al-Bukhārī, Muslim, or any other transmitter, but we trust their reporting (*ikhbār*). An analogy given both by al-Ṣanʿānī and al-Shawkānī[42] to illustrate this point is the ruling of a judge in a court of law. The judge, both argue, may know with full certainty what the truth of the matter is in the case he is handling, yet, his certain knowledge (*yaqīnī* or *qaṭʿī*) does not constitute evidence that is acceptable in a court of law. The judge, therefore, is not allowed to base his ruling on his knowledge, certain as it may be. Rather, he is obliged to base his ruling on the presumptive knowledge (*dhann*) derived from the testimony of two trustworthy witnesses. In the same way, when we accept a statement by al-Bukhārī or Muslim that a hadith is sound, we are accepting their testimony that, as far as they know, the hadith was transmitted by a trustworthy person (*ʿadl*), who in turn testifies to the trustworthiness of his or her source, and so on until we reach the Prophet Muhammad. In fact, al-Ṣanʿānī unequivocally states that what is meant by sound hadith is that which, based on what we surmise from its chains of transmission, appears to be sound.[43] Judging a hadith to be sound does not mean that we can confirm its soundness with certainty, since only God knows the absolute truths of things. A hadith, as well as testimony on its authenticity by a reporter, provide only presumptive knowledge. Yet, for the purposes of action, such uncertain knowledge is sufficient and is the only kind of knowledge that is attainable by humans.[44]

There are, in al-Ṣanʿānī's view, many great Muslim thinkers. They are trustworthy, they deserve respectful treatment, and their opinions are to be consulted. However, they should not be idealized. Al-Ṣanʿānī's unwavering historicization and humanization of the authorities of hadith goes as far as recasting one of the most untouchable links in the chains of these authorities. Al-Ṣanʿānī comments on Ibn Ḥajar al-ʿAsqalānī's assertion that the highest rank in authentication is when the transmitter is a Companion of the Prophet. Al-Ṣanʿānī remarks that, according to Ibn Ḥajar, "the trait of companionship takes care of both conditions of probity and precision." Against this idealization of the authority of the Companions, al-Ṣanʿānī then adds that, as far as probity is concerned, Ibn Ḥajar's assertion conforms to the principles set by the scholars of hadith. However, when it comes to precision and memory, the assertion is problematic, "since memorization and lack thereof are human attributes that do not contradict [the attribute of] companionship; in fact, they do not even contradict prophethood, since it has been reported in sound traditions that he [the Prophet] forgot during his prayer and in other instances. So how is it possible that simply by being a Companion, a transmitter becomes more reliable than one [the Prophet] who is characterized by being the most reliable of all people?"[45]

Al-Ṣanʿānī carries this argument further when he questions not just the memories and other miscellaneous faculties of the Companions but also their understanding: "The understanding of the Companions is not an authority [*ḥujja*] over us, [though their report is], as is implied by the hadith 'Many a transmitter of *fiqh* has more understanding of it than the one who [originally] heard it'; the 'one who heard it' refers to the Companions. This demonstrates that those to whom they [the Companions] conveyed [the traditions] may be more cognizant of it than they were. This proves that we are held responsible [*mukhāṭabūn*] according to what we understand, not according to what they [the Companions] understood."[46]

The comparison of the "understandings" of earlier and later generations of Muslims is obviously tied in al-Ṣanʿānī's thought to the question of *ijtihād*. Al-Ṣanʿānī maintains that those who argue that *ijtihād* is impossible are ungrateful; they do not recognize God's grace manifested even in the arguments they make against *ijtihād*: after all, when they provide their proofs (*adilla*) for the alleged impossibility of *ijtihād* and for the validity of *taqlīd*, they are engaging in a kind of *ijtihād*.[47] In fact, al-Ṣanʿānī remarks, the arguments used by more recent generations against *ijtihād* are far more sophisticated than those used by earlier generations, and as such the more recent generations are not simply reproducing older arguments but are coming up with new ones. It would be much easier for them to reflect on the Book of God and the Sunna of His Prophet in the same way they reflect and speculate on the opinions of their imams. Once again, al-Ṣanʿānī argues that the intellects of the Companions are no different from our intellects; had they been different there would no longer be *taklīf* (legal responsibility) because we will not be able to understand God's commands.[48] Moreover, we can imitate only if we have proof in support of imitation; and we can come up with such proof only if we are capable of understanding the indicants (*dalīl*) from the Book and the hadith. And if we are capable of understanding evidence once, why not do it over and over again, hence why not exercise *ijtihād*?[49] Al-Ṣanʿānī recognizes the sacredness and immutability of a basic layer of scriptures. Intervening "understandings" produce legitimate but not sacred interpretations of this basic layer; the authority of these intermediate interpretations is strictly historical; that is, it provides grounds for action but is not binding on later generations. Even the superior understanding of the Companions, according to al-Ṣanʿānī, is not binding on more recent Muslims.

Whereas al-Ṣanʿānī concedes the superior probity of the Companions, al-Shawkānī is not willing to grant them even this superiority.[50] After an exhaustive analysis of all the traditions related to this subject, al-Shawkānī concludes that "the Companions are more virtuous on account of the virtue of companionship. As for their superiority when it comes to good deeds, they are like other Muslims, such that there may be after them those who are better than all or some of them in deeds, and whose reward on this account will be higher. Such a person would be better than the Companions in this particular respect."[51] Al-Shawkānī adds that some traditions give the impression that the Companions are superior in every way; this, maintains al-Shawkānī, is true only in reference to characteristics that no one else can share with them.

The Companions saw the Prophet and fought under his leadership; they had the privilege of executing his commands and serving him. In short, they were blessed by knowing the Prophet directly. More recent generations, however, have a unique characteristic that the earlier generation does not share with them: they believed in Muhammad's message in absentia and without the incentive deriving from Muhammad's charisma. Al-Shawkānī asserts that only a truly unfortunate person could have seen the Prophet and not believed in him. In a way, therefore, the Companions had the benefit of knowing Muhammad, while later generations of Muslims enjoy no such advantage. This view, according to al-Shawkānī, is further supported by the reports that indicate that during periods of strife, "the rewards of a Muslim who adheres to the dictates of Islam are fifty times as much as those of a Companion."[52] Moreover, the traditions that indicate that the Companions are better than later generations are "true only of the early ones," in comparison with later converts among them.[53] In other words, these traditions compare early and later converts among the Companions, and not the Companions as a group with later generations of Muslims. "As for the deeds of those who come after the Companions, nothing was reported that would indicate the general unqualified superiority [of the latter]. Rather, there are reports specific only to the days of strife and the estrangement of religion."[54] Furthermore, all of these references pertain only to rewards of good deeds; as for other considerations, each group or generation has a distinguishing trait, although, if all things were considered together, the Companions would still have an edge over later generations. Still, "this does not contradict the possibility of ascribing higher virtues to an individual or a group of a certain generation over an individual or a group of another generation [including the Companions]."[55]

The sensitive question of the Companions' authority often comes up in discussions of *ijtihād*. As advocates of hadith, the Yemeni reformers upheld the authority of the Companions in religious matters, a clear divergence from traditional Shiʿi and Zaydi positions. However, this authority is clearly different from the authority bestowed on these Companions in traditional Sunnism. Even when discussing traditions that are meaningful only within a Sunni context, al-Shawkānī manages to ingeniously read such traditions through the prism of his own theory of authority. According to al-Shawkānī, advocates of *taqlīd* argue that ʿUmar imitated Abū Bakr as illustrated by his statement "I am ashamed before God to disagree with Abū Bakr."[56] In response, al-Shawkānī first notes that the historical record provides ample evidence not just of ʿUmar's agreement, but also his disagreement with Abū Bakr on several issues. In both cases, al-Shawkānī adds, ʿUmar based his agreement or disagreement on his own independent reasoning and as such he was not an imitator. Moreover, even if one grants for the sake of argument that ʿUmar did imitate Abū Bakr, al-Shawkānī asserts that this example is not binding on Muslims because the sayings and actions of the Companions are not authoritative in themselves. According to al-Shawkānī, the most that one can derive from this example is that the scholars among the Companions imitated in specific questions where the truth was hidden to the *mujtahid*, while, on other occasions, they considered that disagreement was perfectly valid. This, al-Shawkānī adds, "is quite different from the desire of an imitator to imitate a particular scholar in all matters of religion and to accept his opinion rather than his report without asking him to provide the indicant. . . . This is comparable to treating rabbis and monks as lords." In summary, al-Shawkānī reiterates that the opinions of the Companions who are not infallible are not a binding authority on Muslims.[57]

Mindful of the Sunni arguments for the normative weight of the traditions of the four caliphs, al-Shawkānī maintains that "the reason for adhering to the traditions of the Rightly Guided Caliphs after the Prophet is nothing but the command of the Prophet to do so . . . and to follow the model of Abū Bakr and ʿUmar, may God be pleased with them."[58] As for the imams of the four Sunni schools of law, al-Shawkānī adds that the Prophet did not say, "Abide by the traditions of Abū Ḥanīfa, Mālik, Shāfiʿī, and Ibn Ḥanbal." Moreover, emulating the model of the Companions is nothing more than abiding by the example of the Prophet, as they did.[59] In fact, al-Shawkānī even asserts that, even though they are the best of generations, the majority of the early Companions and their successors were commoners in the sense that they were not full-fledged *mujtahid*s, and the "scholars in their ranks were no doubt a small minority."[60] Ultimately, therefore, their authoritative model is reduced to one of adherence to the hadith, and not to their own opinions or interpretations of it. Furthermore, al-Shawkānī adds, the Prophet instructed Muslims to follow the example of the Companions because they are the ones who report on his behalf and transmit his law to the Muslims who come after them. The exemplary practices of the Companions are to be emulated only because they are to be understood "in lieu of reporting the practices of the Prophet." In this way, the Companion's authority is one of transmission and not interpretation, much as their disagreement is "a disagreement in transmission, not opinion."[61]

It may be suggested that these radical views are dismissible because they come from Zaydis who were amenable to criticizing Sunni authorities or Sunni notions of authority. Moreover, this objection can still be raised even though most of these Yemeni scholars would consider themselves independent *mujtahid*s and not Zaydis; one can argue that, by virtue of their upbringing, the Yemeni scholars did not venerate Sunni authorities and were thus favorably predisposed to part ways with them. However, although the broader intellectual horizons of the Yemeni scholars account for much of their creativity and originality, their engagement with traditional Sunni Islam in general, and hadith in particular, cannot be easily dismissed. To start with, Yemeni scholars did not dispense with Sunni authorities but simply provided alternative theoretical justifications for establishing them. The *ṣaḥīḥ* collections of al-Bukhārī and Muslim, Yemeni scholars argued, remain the most authoritative books after the Qurʾān, and a meaningful Islam is not feasible without recourse to these and other standard Sunni works on hadith. In fact, most of the intellectual efforts of Yemeni reformers, starting with Ibn al-Wazīr and on to al-Ṣanʿānī and al-Shawkānī, were devoted to gaining a strong foothold for hadith in Yemen. A striking example of the tenacity of this effort is Ibn al-Wazīr's arguments (with which both al-Ṣanʿānī and al-Shawkānī agree) in favor of accepting the report of *fāsiq al-ta'wīl* and even *kāfir al-ta'wīl*.[62] Ibn al-Wazīr not only promotes the standard Sunni hadith collections (*al-ṣiḥāḥ al-sitta*) in general terms, but he also addresses their least acceptable features for Zaydis. Of all the possible objections to these compilations, Ibn al-Wazīr singles out the traditions reported on the authority of Muʿāwiya.[63] After indicating that there are thirty hadiths reported by Muʿāwiya in the six collections of sound traditions, Ibn al-Wazīr goes over each of these traditions, analyzing their chains of transmissions as well as their contents. He then concludes that

> there is nothing whatsoever in these traditions which is objectionable [from a non-Sunni point of view]. . . . This is proof of the truthfulness of the people of that generation, and that they did not descend to the level of liars. . . . In fact there is enough evidence of this [truthfulness] in the fact that Muʿāwiya did not report anything that would malign ʿAlī or detract from his sanctity; nor did he report anything on the virtues of ʿUthmān, or the vices of his opponents. This, despite the fact that his [Muʿāwiya's] soldiers would have believed him; in fact, they would have been encouraged by such [reports]. Muʿāwiya did not do any of this throughout the long period [of his rule], during the life of ʿAlī or after his death; neither did he singularly report something that contradicts Islam and undermines its principles. This is why several distinguished Companions and followers reported on the authority of Muʿāwiya.[64]

Of similar import is al-Shawkānī's reference to a hadith on the permissibility of wiping the shoes instead of washing the feet during ritual ablution.[65] Al-Shawkānī states that some dismiss the hadith legalizing this practice by questioning the transmitter of this hadith, the Companion Jarīr, who abandoned ʿAlī's camp during the Battle of Ṣiffīn. In response, al-Shawkānī maintains that Jarīr did not abandon ʿAlī but, for personal reasons, chose seclusion after he was sent on a delegation by ʿAlī to Muʿāwiya. Al-Shawkānī then invokes Ibn al-Wazīr's arguments in support of accepting the report of *fāsiq al-taʾwīl* and repeats Ibn al-Wazīr's assertions that some of the leading Zaydi imams agreed that the report of a Companion is acceptable, whether reported before or after the civil war. Al-Shawkānī thus concludes that dismissing a particular hadith by slandering the noble Companion who transmitted it is unacceptable by the standards of both the family of Muḥammad (*ʿitra*, *ahl al-bayt*) and the rest of the Muslim scholars.

On similar grounds, al-Shawkānī argues against dismissing a hadith transmitted by someone who committed grave acts against the family of the Prophet. For example, al-Shawkānī argues in favor of accepting a report of a zealous Khārijī who wrote a poem praising Ibn Muljam al-Murādī, the murderer of ʿAlī; such a report ought to be accepted as long as it does not serve the Khārijī cause and is not part of its propaganda.[66] The purpose of these arguments is neither to vindicate the Khārijīs nor to exonerate Muʿāwiya or other enemies of ʿAlī. Both Ibn al-Wazīr and al-Shawkānī hold the view that the Khārijīs are damned to hell, and that Muʿāwiya is part of the camp of corruption.[67] Thus, for example, al-Shawkānī maintains that reports on the actions and beliefs of the Khārijīs suggest that they are unbelievers, even though they profess to be Muslims and perform the rituals of Islam. Al-Shawkānī adds, however, that most Sunni scholars of principles law and hadith (*ahl al-uṣūl*) tend to consider the Khārijīs sinners because they rely in their heretical beliefs on erroneous interpretations; therefore, their food is lawful and their contracts are binding. Al-Shawkānī further quotes al-Ghazālī, who recommends that one should do everything possible to avoid accusing people of unbelief.[68] Clearly, therefore, al-Shawkānī argues that the Khārijīs are legitimate transmitters of hadith without absolving them of their transgressions against ʿAlī. In fact, al-Shawkānī does not hide his bias toward ʿAlī in other cases as well. In one such case, al-Shawkānī responds to the recurrent Sunni assertion that ascribes righteousness to ʿAlī, but withholds judgment on his opponents. Al-Shawkānī addresses this issue in his monumental work on hadith titled *Nayl al-Awṭār*. One of the traditions discussed in this book refers to Muslims who fight and kill each other, and states, "Both the killed and the killer are [doomed to] hell."[69] Al-Shawkānī, following his standard procedure throughout this book, lists the various interpretations of this tradition. One of these interpretations maintains that those who fought on either side in the Battles of the Camel and in Ṣiffīn did not fight for worldly gain or power; rather, they sought to gain favor in the hereafter and were driven by their desire to establish a just and righteous public order. In theory, therefore, all parties will be rewarded by God for fighting what each thought was a just war (*kulluhum mutaʾawwil maʾjūr*). In response, al-Shawkānī says that it is very unlikely that this description fits the actual parties to the conflict. Al-Shawkānī adds that those who were aware of the hadith indicating that the Companion ʿAmmār would be killed by the oppressive party and still persisted in fighting ʿAmmār's party (i.e., ʿAlī's camp), knew very well who was right and who was wrong. Any fair-minded person, al-Shawkānī argues, would grant that much. Al-Shawkānī then apologetically asserts that he is not about to slander any of the Companions, especially given his own record of struggling against division and trying to close all the gates of sedition and disagreement among Muslims. This, he adds, gained him only blame from his friends and led many people to accuse him of abandoning the schools of *ahl al-bayt*, counting him as one of their enemies.[70]

Despite his care for unity, and his desire to foster reverence for all of the Companions among his fellow Zaydis, al-Shawkānī asserts that most of ʿAlī's opponents did not commit an unintended error but deliberately committed a major offense. And yet, like Ibn al-Wazīr and al-Ṣanʿānī before him, al-Shawkānī accepts the authority of someone like Muʿāwiya as a conveyor of a most important source of the law. The ultimate purpose of this position, however, is to make a solid argument for the authority of the Sunni hadith corpus without having to submit to the authority of specific individuals affiliated with this textual corpus. Thus the central distinction in Yemeni thought is among three kinds of authority: first, the authority of the hadith corpus; second, the interpretive authority of various Muslim individuals or schools of law; and finally, the testimonial authority of individual Muslims.

To be sure, the question of the authority of hadith is not only contingent on its chain of transmission but also depends on its content. Commentators often invoke the doctrinal content of a hadith as a criterion for assessing its reliability. However, consistent with Sunni hadith scholarship, the Yemeni scholars paid more attention to formal syntactical considerations, which, in turn are tied up with the authority of transmitters. Al-Ṣanʿānī, for example, provides a detailed discussion of syntax requirements when he takes up a question that Ibn al-Wazīr raises but does not pursue.[71] In reference to a Companion who prefaces a report with the formula "The Messenger of God commanded us," Ibn al-Wazīr says that some hadith scholars and theologians consider such a report unacceptable, unless the transmitter actually conveys the exact words that the Prophet uttered. The justification for such a requirement is that the Companion may have misunderstood what he heard and took it to be a command or a prohibition when in fact it is not. To this al-Ṣanʿānī responds by saying that if we are to allow for all such possibilities, then we can only accept reports where the exact words of the Prophet are given, and we will not be able to accept reports that convey the general meaning of what he said. Al-Ṣanʿānī contends that this latter kind comprises the majority of traditions; in fact, he adds, some scholars maintain that only two hadiths have been reported through numerous channels with the exact same wording. The more important issue to al-Ṣanʿānī, however, is that unless there is evidence to the contrary, a Companion who has probity, and who knows his language, would not have made a general statement unless he had tangible evidence that the Prophet is in fact the source of the particular command or prohibition included in that statement; this is true in spite of the theoretical possibility that the listener misunderstood the statement by the Prophet, which may not be in itself a command or a prohibition.[72]

In other words, according to al-Ṣanʿānī, we do not have immediate and direct access to Muhammad that would enable us to figure out the "essential" meaning of every single statement he made. Everything we have is mediated through language, but that should not deter us from acting upon these language-mediated statements. Significantly, al-Ṣanʿānī juxtaposes the two levels of mediation: mediation through language and through the transmission of a tradition by a series of transmitters. The rules devised to regulate the second level of mediation also suffice for regulating the first. The most important of these rules is that a transmitter functions as a witness who is supposed to report what he or she hears or sees with minimal exercise of judgment on her part. On the receiving end, a tradition is accepted in the same way a judge accepts the evidence presented to him by two witnesses. In other words, a transmitter conveys raw information without processing it; a receiver only needs to confirm that this information is handed down by a person who fulfills the formal requirements of probity and accuracy, and that there are no outstanding hidden reasons that might call the transmitted tradition into question. Al-Ṣanʿānī thus conflates syntax and transmission. He also draws parallels between the process of establishing the trustworthiness of a witness, the probity of a transmitter, and the soundness of a tradition.[73] He further adds that when we accept a statement regarding any of these matters, we are not imitating; rather, we are acting on the basis of the only kind of evidence that we can have in such situations. For example, when we accept a statement by al-Bukhārī that a certain hadith is sound, we are exercising *ijtihād*, much as he did when he accepted the reports of his predecessors regarding the trustworthiness of the transmitters of his hadiths. Thus when a transmitter reports that a hadith is sound, he is in effect reporting that the transmitters of this hadith are trustworthy, that they have good memories, and that there is no hidden irregularity or weakness in it. In short, all that we accept is the report, the passing down of unprocessed information about other people (*ikhbār ʿan al-ghayr*); this is not a judgment based on the opinion of the transmitter that he in turn predicates on evidence known only to him. As such, what we accept is the unit of *khabar* after verifying its authenticity as best as humanly possible.

Al-Ṣanʿānī manages to distinguish between the aura of divinity or sacredness that surrounds hadith and the unquestionable humanity of its transmitters. His concern, all along, is to facilitate the ability to use hadith and to make a convincing argument for its applicability, in spite of the fact that it is mediated by fallible humans. It is not surprising, therefore, that in the context of his discussion of hadith, al-Ṣanʿānī takes up the question of the presumed original status of the Muslim *umma*.[74] This question is related to hadith scholarship, since, among other things, it affects the appraisal of an unknown transmitter about whose probity there is no available testimony (*majhūl al-ʿadāla*). Al-Ṣanʿānī quotes several authorities who argue that the community is in an original state of sin (*al-aṣl fī al-umma al-fisq*) and assume that probity is accidental and acquired (*al-ʿadāla ṭāriʾa*). According to this view, probity is an exception, and therefore one needs positive evidence to affirm it. One of the scholars who argue this view is al-Ḥasan Ibn Aḥmad al-Jalāl (d. 1084/1673), one of the major figures in the Yemeni reform tradition. Al-Jalāl interprets the Qurʾānic verses "Only a few of my servants are thankful" (Sabaʾ 34:13) and "The greatest part of mankind will not be believers, however much you strive for it" (Yūsuf 12:103). These verses, al-Jalāl maintains, demonstrate that the *umma* at large is presumed guilty until proven innocent. Of course, al-Jalāl's notion of sin is only relevant to the determination of the probity of a specific person. In other words, al-Jalāl and others with whom he agrees are not arguing that Muslims should be penalized or treated in practice as sinners until they prove their true belief. Rather, this argument simply means that the testimony of a Muslim, either in a court of law or in the transmission of hadith, should not be accepted until we have hard evidence of his or her probity and righteousness. Al-Ṣanʿānī does not agree: he argues that the quoted verses mean that Muslims are a minority when compared to non-Muslims, not that the "true believers" are a minority compared to Muslims who lack probity. The original status of all people, according to al-Ṣanʿānī, is that of *fiṭra* (natural innocence). Thus, if a person is born to Muslim parents, he or she will turn into a legally responsible Muslim while still in this state, unless something specific happens that compromises his or her original guiltlessness. Only if this person persists in taking up sinful acts after reaching the age of *taklīf* (legal responsibility) would he or she be judged a sinner. Al-Ṣanʿānī adds that even if he grants al-Jalāl's argument that the majority of Muslims are in an original state of sin, this does not justify the conclusion that an unknown individual should be lumped with this majority. This is so because "it is not up to us to ascribe sin to a Muslim of unknown probity simply because sin is prevalent. This would be a charge with no evidence either from texts or by analogy; they [al-Jalāl and other scholars] concede that such a charge is not valid without conclusive evidence." As for those who insist that the original state is sin, al-Ṣanʿānī concludes, the least they should do is to refrain from judging a Muslim of unknown probity either way (*yabqā . . . ʿalā al-iḥtimāl*), that is, "Do not reject his report by presuming him to be a sinner, or accept it by confirming his probity. Rather, admit both possibilities pending further investigation regarding him."[75] To be sure, this last suggestion does not reflect al-Ṣanʿānī's preference, for he remains committed to the principle that the original state is that of innocence, and therefore the probity of a Muslim is assumed unless we have evidence to the contrary.

Al-Ṣanʿānī devotes a special treatise to a hadith dealing with the status of the community,[76] *Ḥadīth Iftirāq al-Umma ilā Nayyif wa Sabʿīn Firqa*. As the title indicates, the treatise deals with the tradition that predicts the division or separation of the community into some seventy groups or sects (hereafter, the tradition of separation). Al-Ṣanʿānī, in his usual manner, provides an exhaustive survey of the different variants of this tradition and, more important, its different interpretations. Al-Ṣanʿānī maintains that, in all its forms, this tradition is problematic for two reasons: first, it implies that a majority of the Muslims are doomed to eternal torment in hell, which is contrary to the numerous traditions that assert that God will be merciful and that the Muslim *umma* is blessed with God's mercy (hereafter, the tradition of mercy).[77] Some tried to avoid this problem by asserting that "what is meant by the *umma* is *ummat al-daʿwa* not *ummat al-ijāba* [the community which is summoned to Islam, not the one which already accepted Islam]; this would mean that the community which the Prophet called to believe in God and to profess His unity is the community which will be divided into these groups, and the one which accepts is the redeemed one."[78] This explanation, al-Ṣanʿānī adds, is a clever answer, but it is incorrect because the term *umma* in the Prophet's usage has in most cases referred to those who actually became Muslims: "Thus when the term *umma* is used without qualification it can only be taken to mean what it conventionally means . . . and it cannot be assigned another arbitrary meaning, even if other meanings are, on rare occasions, possible."[79] Al-Ṣanʿānī gives other reasons that make this interpretation unlikely; he then gives his preferred interpretations, ones that would eliminate the apparent contradiction between the "tradition of separation" and the "tradition of mercy."

Al-Ṣanʿānī argues that the way out of this contradiction is to entertain the possibility that "these groups which are doomed to suffering are small in number, and that the sum total of all of these groups is still smaller than the redeemed one. . . . As such, the reference to the number [some seventy] does not imply that those who will perish are more numerous; rather, it simply implies that the ways of going astray are extensive and manifold, while there is only one way to truth."[80] Another interpretation that resolves the apparent contradiction between the two sets of traditions is to assume that "the judgment that these groups are doomed to perish and reside in hell is a judgment on the basis of their outside actions and dereliction. This judgment is equivalent to saying, 'Considering their apparent actions, these groups are doomed.' . . . This does not negate the possibility that they may be pardoned [by God] on some other grounds, such as God's mercy, the intercession of the Prophet, or the intercession of its [the community's] pious members on behalf of its delinquent ones."[81] Alternatively, the general threat to condemn the various deviant groups may be qualified by adding the conditional phrase "unless they were punished in this world." Thus, if these groups receive their punishment in this world, they are not subject to further retribution in the hereafter.[82]

Finally, al-Ṣanʿānī argues that a problem in the interpretation of the tradition of separation arises only if we assume that the particular contexts in which a group is condemned exist in perpetuity.[83] Under this assumption, the division of the community as well as the ensuing torment is continuous and permanent, from the time the Prophet uttered his words until the Day of Judgment. However, al-Ṣanʿānī adds, "the judgment of separation and perishing only pertains to a specific situation and a specific time," and therefore, "those who perish are not necessarily the majority, neither are those who are redeemed the minority."[84] Moreover, the time in which the community will be divided and perish could very well be the end of time.[85] Having presented all of these alternative interpretations, al-Ṣanʿānī insists that one of them must be correct. He maintains that, since we are dealing with two attested sets of sound traditions, they should both be accepted. Furthermore, since a real contradiction in the sayings of the Prophet is not an option, "we must harmonize those things that give the impression of contradiction [*lā budda min al-jamʿ bayn mā yūhim al-tanāquḍ*]." In other words, al-Ṣanʿānī's interpretation has to be accepted because it eliminates the apparent contradiction between two sound traditions.

Al-Ṣanʿānī's basic reason for finding the tradition of separation problematic becomes clear when he discusses a second set of objections to standard interpretations of this tradition.[86] Al-Ṣanʿānī complains that "each group now claims that it is the redeemed one, and then sets up arguments in support of this claim that are flimsier than a spiderweb. Some even waste their time counting the various groups that disagree with them, go after those with unorthodox views, and list these views to try to prove that adopting them is a cause for damnation while shunning them leads to redemption. If one were to dig up the opinions of any one of these groups, one would usually find that they hold worse views than the ones held by their opponents."[87] Al-Ṣanʿānī then adds that instead of taking the negative approach in order to identify the redeemed group, one should take a positive approach by invoking the Prophet's definition of this group.[88] The Prophet, al-Ṣanʿānī argues, has identified the *al-firqa al-nājiya* as the one that adheres to his example and to the example of his Companions. Moreover, the redeemed group is not one sect or school, such as, for example, the Ashʿarīs or the Muʿtazilīs; rather, redemption is equally attainable by the virtuous of each group, by "the followers of the Prophet in words and deeds, irrespective of their school."[89]

Al-Ṣanʿānī's insistence that Muslims who commit grave sins will not reside eternally in hell is clearly incompatible with standard Muʿtazilī views on this matter. Though radical by the standards of Ibn al-Wazīr's time, in the eighteenth century al-Ṣanʿānī's anti-Muʿtazilī stance is neither unusual nor especially nonconformist. The significance of the above elaborate discussions, which are typical of eighteenth-century thought, lies elsewhere: in the exhaustive and systematic examination of the form as well as the content of hadith, of its transmitters as well as its legal applications, and of its relevance to the definitions of textual as well as societal authorities. This interlacing of the textual and the contextual is best exemplified in the manifold textual arguments provided in support of the integrity of the majority of Muslims. The purpose of this exhaustive textual elaboration is to redeem the living Muslim community and to confer upon it an authority similar to that of earlier generations. In the process of reconciling contradictory traditions, an ideological rationale for the unity of the community is constructed.

Eighteenth-century thinkers were cognizant of the unconventional nature of their theories of hadith. They were also aware and respectful of a long tradition of scholarship in this field, of canonical views within this tradition of scholarship, and of what it takes for noncanonical views to be recognized and legitimized. Legitimacy, before the coming of the nation-state, was not bestowed by state institutions but was an achievement secured on grounds of merit and erudition. To expand, even redefine, the canon of hadith scholarship, eighteenth-century thinkers displayed an erudition surpassing that of many of the classical icons of this same canon.[90] They did not simply theorize about hadith; rather, they plunged into every possible aspect of its study. The fruit of their extraordinary intellectual endeavor was as canonical as any of the classics of hadith.[91] The emergence of hadith scholarship in India, as in Yemen, had its peculiar history and involved a radical revisiting of structures of authority.

Hadith in India

The name of the seventeenth-century scholar ʿAbd al-Ḥaqq al-Dihlawī (d. 1052/1642) is closely associated with the introduction of hadith studies to India. Prior to ʿAbd al-Ḥaqq, Indian Ḥanafī scholars did not expend much energy in the study of hadith and related disciplines. Indian scholars were so occupied in jurisprudence that they opposed any attempt to judge their derived laws on the basis of their conformity with the Sunna.[92] These scholars seldom studied hadith, and even when they did, their purpose was to "gain God's blessings" rather than to derive laws from it.[93] In addition to basic illiteracy in hadith and great interest in the rational sciences, the primary reason for this neglect was a perception, common among Indian Ḥanafīs, that the compilations of *ṣaḥīḥ* traditions[94] are, for the most part, opposed to the rulings of Ḥanafī law.[95] This perception was reinforced by the unease that characterized the historical relationships between jurists (*fuqahā'*) and traditionalists (*muḥaddithūn*). Shortly before the time of ʿAbd al-Ḥaqq al-Dihlawī, several Indian scholars traveled to the Hejaz, where they studied hadith with the local scholars of Mecca and Medina, and brought the discipline of hadith studies back with them upon their return to India. The efforts of these scholars, however, were particularly concentrated in the region of Gujarat, while elsewhere in India the earlier patterns of education persisted.[96] In contrast to these Gujarati scholars, ʿAbd al-Ḥaqq al-Dihlawī managed to popularize hadith throughout India and to train several students who continued his efforts after him. His influence was such that he is often mistakenly considered to be the person who introduced hadith to India.[97] ʿAbd al-Ḥaqq popularized the study of hadith in India through devoting his whole career to the teaching of hadith and to serious scholarly work on the subject. Moreover, in an effort to make this study accessible to a larger sector of the scholarly population, he used Arabic as well as Persian for both teaching and writing about hadith. He also overcame various obstacles facing the newly emerging discipline by devising a series of creative techniques that enabled him to recast the relationship between Ḥanafī law and hadith. A crucial factor that contributed to his success was his ability to use hadith to corroborate Ḥanafī law, as well as to authenticate the teachings of the Qādiriyya and Naqshbandiyya Sufi orders—two of the most popular orders in India at the time. ʿAbd al-Ḥaqq's credibility was enhanced by his deliberate avoidance of contact and conflict with political authorities.[98] His nonconfrontational attitude, however, was most effective in his approach to the study and application of hadith.

ʿAbd al-Ḥaqq al-Dihlawī often came across traditions that contradicted Ḥanafī legal practices. Although this contradiction did not prevent him from reporting the hadith, he tended to refrain from drawing the logical conclusions from it. As a rule, ʿAbd al-Ḥaqq did not criticize the Ḥanafī legal tradition, nor did he present himself as a reformer of the Ḥanafī school.[99] In addition to the long duration of his teaching career (about fifty years), it is perhaps because of this ostensible conformity that his reforms were so effective. After all, within a century after ʿAbd al-Ḥaqq's pioneering efforts, India became one of the strongholds of hadith scholarship in the Muslim world.[100] ʿAbd al-Ḥaqq's posture was crucial for easing the resistance to hadith among adamant Ḥanafī jurists. This passive attitude alone, however, would have hardly sufficed to do the job. It was ʿAbd al-Ḥaqq's positive contributions to scholarship that secured the status of hadith in India. One of the main challenges for ʿAbd al-Ḥaqq was to open up the hadith corpus and to come up with a substantial number of traditions that were in harmony with Ḥanafī law. Toward this end, he consistently built up the case for accepting any tradition that fulfilled the conditions of soundness of the six *ṣaḥīḥ* collections, rather than using only these six sources to the exclusion of all other sources. ʿAbd al-Ḥaqq thus used later hadith compilations by al-Suyūṭī and others to verify and thereby sanction Ḥanafī laws.[101] Drawing on a much larger body of hadith literature, he amassed enough traditions to serve this purpose. Subsequently, he was able to convince the mass of Ḥanafī jurists that hadith scholarship would not undermine their school. ʿAbd al-Ḥaqq's main achievement, therefore, was to eliminate a situation where one had to choose between hadith and *fiqh*; under the new terms, it became feasible to combine the two with flexibility and ease.

ʿAbd al-Ḥaqq's reflections on hadith were not confined to the question of its authoritative sources. In addition to his discussion of the relative authority of various books of hadith, ʿAbd al-Ḥaqq also proposed new rules and standards for hadith criticism. Against accepted views, he tried to salvage some of the weak traditions commonly used by the Ḥanafīs. ʿAbd al-Ḥaqq argued that a particular hadith may have been excluded from the *ṣaḥīḥ* compilations due to a weakness in one of the links in its chain of transmission, while the same hadith may have been used by Abū Ḥanīfa and his companions. The reason for this discrepancy, according to ʿAbd al-Ḥaqq, may be that a weak link occurred between the time of Abū Ḥanīfa and a later compiler like al-Bukhārī. Thus, although one may apply the same standards for assessing hadith, what was sound to Abū Ḥanīfa may have become weak by the time of al-Bukharī because of the intervention of a weak transmitter between the two.[102] Admittedly, this argument may itself be weak, but it served its intended purpose of reconciling Ḥanafī law and hadith. Although his methodology for hadith criticism was not rigorous, ʿAbd al-Ḥaqq al-Dihlawī did recognize hadith as the ultimate criterion for judging applied Ḥanafī law. This recognition, together with the full-fledged study of hadith, ushered in an era of systematic study and use of hadith in India. Perhaps because the initiators of the study of hadith did not challenge the traditional authorities of Ḥanafī India, they were instrumental in introducing a decisive modification of the accepted canons of knowledge. Hadith, initially introduced to corroborate Ḥanafī law, was soon used as the principle instrument to scrutinize this law and to redefine the Ḥanafī school.

The next generation after ʿAbd al-Ḥaqq al-Dihlawī was more methodical in negotiating the relationship between hadith and Ḥanafī law. The new interest in hadith led scholars to travel in pursuit of mastering the techniques of the discipline. Aḥmad Sirhindī (twelfth century AH) was a notable example.[103] Having grown up in an environment that recognized the authority of hadith, he traveled to the Ḥaramayn (Mecca and Medina) to pursue its study. Although he derived his interest in the study of hadith from a conducive Indian environment, Sirhindī's uses of hadith did not conform with the outlines set by the Indian school of hadith established by ʿAbd al-Ḥaqq al-Dihlawī. Rather than deploying it in the service of the Ḥanafī law, Sirhindī used hadith as the criterion against which this law is judged, and as a basis for criticizing a number of Ḥanafī practices. Moreover, as an authority on hadith, Sirhindī could legitimately claim to be a qualified *mujtahid*. He thus opposed *taqlīd*, was an advocate of *ijtihād*, and claimed to be a *mujtahid* not just in Ḥanafī but also in Shāfiʿī law. He is best known, however, for his criticism of Ibn al-ʿArabī's idea of "unity of being [*waḥdat al-wujūd*]." Against this school, which was very popular among Indian Sufis, Sirhindī introduced the concept of *waḥdat al-shuhūd* (the unity of witnessing), which was intended to salvage the principle of a unified Sufi experience of being while maintaining the absolute oneness and transcendence of God. In contrast to ʿAbd al-Ḥaqq al-Dihlawī, whose efforts gained wide approval among contemporary Indian scholars, Sirhindī's critical stand gained him many opponents. In the eighteenth century, the legacies of both scholars, with all of their conflicting trends, were inherited by Shāh Walī Allāh and were instrumental in shaping his thought and career.

The predicaments of Shāh Walī Allāh and his son Muḥammad Ismāʿīl (the martyr) bear some resemblance to those of ʿAbd al-Ḥaqq al-Dihlawī and Aḥmad Sirhindī. Like Sirhindī, Muḥammad Ismāʿīl had many opponents and was accused by many Indian scholars of being anti-Ḥanafī. One reason that may account for this opposition is the confrontational attitude that both scholars displayed in their reform efforts. Walī Allāh, in contrast, was more like ʿAbd al-Ḥaqq: he managed to introduce new ideas without antagonizing his audience. Unlike those of ʿAbd al-Ḥaqq, however, Walī Allāh's reforms were far-reaching, multifaceted, and rigorous. He did not avoid charged issues, but he managed to resolve them in a way that was acceptable to most parties involved. He is thus widely recognized as the leading scholar of Islamic India, and he continues to be revered by various schools across the intellectual spectrum of Indian Muslims.

While Walī Allāh's reforms relied on and were shaped by those of his Indian predecessors, his were far more radical than theirs, both in scope and depth. As with his Yemeni contemporaries, hadith was central to his project. He used hadith to question and propose alternative structures of authority within the Ḥanafī school. Inspired by the particular Indian intellectual background, Walī Allāh also developed a unique theory of hadith and argued for specific ways of using hadith to define both textual and social authorities. The most characteristic feature of Walī Allāh's intellectual career was his attempt to reconcile seemingly disparate Islamic intellectual traditions of scholarship. His thought is fundamentally unsectarian, as it aimed to iron out differences within each discipline and among different disciplines. Hadith was a central weapon in Walī Allāh's war against all kinds of sectarian zeal.

Unlike ʿAbd al-Ḥaqq, Walī Allāh did not accept the notion that all hadith collections are equally authoritative. Instead, he reverted to a definite ranking of sources, with a notable diversion from the traditional ranking system recognized by hadith scholars: he asserted that the highest rank in hadith collections goes not to al-Bukhārī and Muslim but to the *Muwaṭṭaʾ* of Mālik Ibn Anas (d. 179/796), which serves as the cornerstone of Walī Allāh's new theory of hadith.[104]

Walī Allāh wrote a two-volume Arabic commentary on the *Muwaṭṭaʾ*, as well as a Persian version of the same work.[105] In the introductions to both, Walī Allāh spells out his views on the role and status of the *Muwaṭṭaʾ* in relation to other works of hadith.[106] He first provides a dramatic account of his confusion as he tried to sort out differences between various legal schools and parties of scholars.[107] The reason for his anxiety, he adds, is that with endless differences among scholars, he was having great difficulty deciding which of their views was valid. After failing to find anyone to help him resolve this problem, Walī Allāh turned to God and received an inspiration that directed him toward the *Muwaṭṭaʾ*. Other factors, aside from divine inspiration, may have helped turn Walī Allāh to the *Muwaṭṭaʾ*; foremost among these is his earlier training during his stay in the Ḥaramayn under Wafd Allāh al-Makkī Ibn Muḥammad Sulaymān al-Maghribī and Tāj al-Dīn al-Qalaʿī al-Makkī al-Ḥanafī.[108] Irrespective of the motivation, however, Walī Allāh contends that he "became certain that, in *jurisprudence*, there is no other book today which is stronger than the *Muwaṭṭaʾ* of Mālik."[109]

Fortunately, Walī Allāh provides his own justification for his views on the superiority of the *Muwaṭṭaʾ*. Books, he argues, are given preference over each other for a number of different reasons: the credibility of their authors; the reputation of their hadiths; their criteria for the inclusion of hadiths; their favorable acceptance by the majority of Muslims; and their organization and scope. Walī Allāh then asserts that "in comparison to all books currently available throughout the world, all of these criteria are found in their most perfect way in the *Muwaṭṭaʾ*."[110] Thus, the *Muwaṭṭaʾ* is the only extant book that is written by a member of the second generation of successors. No other author of any book is as praised by scholars of hadith as Mālik is. Moreover, there is no book by any of the imams of the "successors of the successors" of the Companions, that is, of the third generation of Muslims, other than the *Muwaṭṭaʾ*.[111] In addition to his precedence, Mālik is also praised by some of the leading scholars of his period: "al-Shāfiʿī said, 'If scholars are mentioned, Mālik is their star.' . . . He also said, 'I am not indebted to any other scholar in matters of religion as I am to Mālik.'"[112] In fact, according to Walī Allāh the Shāfiʿī school of law is an elaboration on the *Muwaṭṭaʾ*; the source for the *Mabsūṭ*, the main legal work of the Ḥanafī scholar Muḥammad Ibn al-Ḥasan al-Shaybānī (d. 805), is the *Muwaṭṭaʾ*. Of the four imams of the Sunni legal schools, only Abū Ḥanīfa and Mālik belong to the second generation of successors; of the two, only Mālik transmitted hadith, whereas, according to Walī Allāh, not a single hadith has been transmitted in any of the six *ṣaḥīḥ* books on the authority of Abū Ḥanīfa. In contrast, scholars of hadith have agreed that if a hadith can be authenticated through Mālik's report, then it is of the highest possible rank of soundness.[113]

Walī Allāh also provides testimonies by distinguished Muslims of the early generations in which Mālik is portrayed as a strict traditionalist who requires the highest standards of his transmitters and who reports only sound traditions.[114] Shāfiʿī asserts, Walī Allāh adds, that next to the book of God, there is no book on the surface of the Earth that is sounder than the book of Mālik.[115] The soundness of the traditions of the *Muwaṭṭaʾ*, however, is not as self-evident as these assertions may suggest. Aware of this problem, Walī Allāh quotes Ibn Ḥajar, who states that the *Muwaṭṭaʾ* is considered sound by Mālik and his followers on the basis of a criterion they adopted: to accept the authority of *mursal* traditions (attributed directly to the Prophet without a continuous chain of transmission) as well as of *munqaṭiʿ* ones (with an interrupted chain of transmission).[116] Walī Allāh understands this to mean that scholars have differed over the implementation of interrupted traditions, with Mālik, Abū Ḥanīfa, and a majority of scholars among the second generation of successors arguing in favor of this implementation. These scholars also derived juristic inferences from the sayings of Companions like ʿUmar, from the practice of Ibn ʿUmar, and from the agreement of a group of successors among the people of Medina. So, according to Walī Allāh, Mālik acted in accordance with what is entailed by his principle, since the defect of interruption does not, in Mālik's view, detract from the soundness of a hadith. Because of this, Mālik did not feel a need to provide "connected chains of transmission for traditions lacking them, nor to identify the scriptural sources for the interrupted traditions of ʿUmar or the practices of ʿAbd Allāh Ibn ʿUmar."[117] Following this reasoning, "therefore, all of the *Muwaṭṭaʾ* would be sound to Mālik, Abū Ḥanīfa, and the rest of the second generation of successors."[118]

Simply put, this circular argument for the soundness of the traditions of the *Muwaṭṭaʾ* is based on a redefinition of soundness that is modeled after these same traditions. This reasoning is remnant of ʿAbd al-Ḥaqq's attempts to define sound hadith in relative terms. However, Walī Allāh's actual approach to the study of the traditions of the *Muwaṭṭa'* is more rigorous and critical than that of his predecessor. For example, Walī Allāh indicates that Mālik often says, "According to us the Sunna is such and such."[119] Walī Allāh maintains that this particular formulation does not necessarily imply the consensus of the people of Medina or their general practice; rather, it could refer to either the opinions of the seven jurists of Medina,[120] a group of the teachers of Imam Mālik, or even Mālik's own personal preference. For this reason, Walī Allāh states that he will include in his commentary on these kinds of traditions in the *Muwaṭṭa'* only those traditions agreed upon by a majority of scholars, and that he will "exclude whatever Imam Mālik was the only one to report."[121] Walī Allāh also specifies which of Mālik's interrupted traditions he would include in his commentary: "Since our purpose is to go along with the vast majority of the traditionalists who maintain that there is a difference between a connected and an interrupted tradition, it is necessary that we explain how interrupted traditions can be connected through the art of considering follow-up and corroborative hadiths. Similarly, it is necessary to identify the sources on which the sayings of the Companions are based, whether these are the allusions of the Book and the Sunna or analogy to what is stated in them. These matters are contingent on skillfulness in the legal arts."[122] In other words, Walī Allāh does not include in his commentary on the *Muwaṭṭa'* all of the traditions given by Mālik, only those that are of attested soundness. So, in practice, Walī Allāh does not consider all the traditions of the *Muwaṭṭa'* to be sound. This tension between the real and the idealized Mālik results from Walī Allāh's attempt to elevate the *Muwaṭṭa'* to the highest rank of authority. Walī Allāh is willing to drop traditions from the *Muwaṭṭa'* that do not conform to the standards of soundness accepted by the majority of scholars of hadith. However, he wishes to maintain his general assessment regarding the relative superiority of the *Muwaṭṭa'*, specifically because of the powerful implications of this assertion for his own intellectual program.

Walī Allāh then goes further in trying to vindicate the whole of the *Muwaṭṭa'*. He argues that the compilers of the six (sound) books, as well as al-Ḥākim in his *Mustadrak*, made great efforts to provide connected chains of transmission for the interrupted traditions of Mālik (*waṣl al-mursal* and *rafʿ al-mawqūf*).[123] Therefore, the compilations of sound traditions are in certain respects commentaries on the *Muwaṭṭa'*. Walī Allāh even asserts that the *Muwaṭṭa'* does not have a single tradition that goes back to a Companion (*mawqūf*) or a saying of a successor, which does not also have a counterpart in the Book (that is, the Qur'ān) and the Sunna. The authenticity of the *Muwaṭṭa'*, according to Walī Allāh, is further confirmed by the continuous interest of Muslim scholars in reporting and commenting on its traditions, from the time of the compilation of the six *ṣaḥīḥ* collections to the days of Walī Allāh.[124] In fact, according to Walī

Allāh, this interest started already during Mālik's lifetime, when many works were written with the aim of sorting out the lines of transmission of Mālik's hadiths and connecting their interrupted chains back to the Prophet.[125] Walī Allāh asserts that more than 1,000 men directly transmitted Mālik's book, and that, just as the Prophet had foretold in a hadith, people traveled from distant places to study it with Mālik. With the passage of time, the *Muwaṭṭaʾ* only became more famous and interest in it grew stronger. The learned scholars of Muslim cities, including even some of the Ḥanafī scholars of Iraq, based their law schools on the *Muwaṭṭaʾ*. Scholars continue to verify the authenticity of its traditions and to provide corroborating hadith in their support. This persistent interest not only illustrates the status of the *Muwaṭṭaʾ* but also ensures that it will be kept alive through the renewed energies of generations of scholars.

Walī Allāh also argues that in addition to this interest in the transmission of the *Muwaṭṭaʾ*, it was favorably received by the leading Muslim traditionalists as well as jurists.[126] For example, whenever al-Bukhārī found a hadith reported by Mālik and with a continuous transmission back to the Prophet, he gave it precedence over any other hadith unless it did not fulfill his conditions; in this latter case, al-Bukhārī provided other supporting hadiths to substantiate Mālik's report.[127] Moreover, on several occasions al-Bukhārī substantiated even the nonprophetic traditions of the *Muwaṭṭaʾ* by reference to the allusions and implications of hadith. Like jurists, the Mālikīs base their legal practice on the *Muwaṭṭaʾ*; it is the origin of the school of Shāfiʿī and the substance for his independent reasoning; and it is the source of the legal works of Muḥammad Ibn al-Ḥasan.[128] In sum, all four "schools of law are, in relation to the *Muwaṭṭaʾ*, like commentaries, and it is to them like a tree is to its branches."[129]

While one purpose of Walī Allāh's *Musawwā* is to establish the authority of the *Muwaṭṭaʾ* by demonstrating that its interrupted traditions have corroborating counterparts, and by arguing that it continued to be the basis for all other schools of law, another purpose was to elaborate the superior stature of Mālik. According to Walī Allāh, Mālik's authority stemmed from the fact that Medina, where Mālik lived and worked, was the center for the leading scholars of Islam. Mālik inherited the legacies of all of these scholars and "received knowledge from them just as one of us receives a tangible object in his hand over which there could be no doubt. . . . He wrote down everything he learned from them, thus becoming an authority for all groups of scholars, including traditionalists and jurists."[130]

The portrayal of Mālik as an authority for jurists as well as traditionalists is central to understanding the place of the *Muwaṭṭaʾ* in Walī Allāh's general thought. Mālik is made into a symbol of the conciliation that Walī Allāh himself hopes to achieve:

> With regard to inferring the juristic significance [from] and the issuing of rulings [based on hadith], earlier generations were of two kinds: the first collected the Qurʾān, hadith, and the sayings of the Companions and derived [meanings] from them. This method is the origin of the practice of the traditionalists. The other one referred to the general rules that had been cultivated and refined by a group of earlier imams, without paying much attention to the way they are derived. Whenever they were faced with a question, they sought its answer following these rules; this method is the origin of the practice of the jurists. . . . As for Mālik, he is an authority in both methods.[131]

By asserting that Mālik's *Muwaṭṭaʾ* is the most authoritative book after the Qurʾān, Walī Allāh forced his fellow Ḥanafīs to recognize an authority outside their own legal tradition. What gave his claim added significance was that he was not simply promoting the general authority of hadith but the particular traditions that were reported by Mālik. In contrast to Mālik, no legal schools crystallized around the teachings of al-Bukhārī, Muslim, or any of the compilers of the remaining *ṣaḥīḥ* books. A Ḥanafī, therefore, may be able to reconcile his intensive loyalty to his school while also using hadith as a source of the law. Already ʿAbd al-Ḥaqq had succeeded in introducing hadith into the unfriendly environment of Ḥanafī India. However, to accept the authority of Mālik, even if the acceptance were restricted to hadith and not jurisprudence, would require a considerable concession by members of the Ḥanafī school of law. Walī Allāh's prescription, therefore, seems to have been carefully calculated to unsettle narrow-minded Ḥanafīs and to undermine the partisan tendency to define authority within one school to the exclusion of all others. Walī Allāh even compares the *Muwaṭṭaʾ* to two of the earliest canonical works for the Ḥanafī school: the *Kitāb al-Āthār* of Muḥammad al-Shaybanī (d. 189/813) and the *Amālī* of Abū Yūsuf (d. 182/799).[132] Walī Allāh asserts that the difference between the *Muwaṭṭaʾ* and the two Ḥanafī texts is greater than the distance between east and west. According to Walī Allāh the "plain truth" is that it is almost impossible to find a jurist or a hadith scholar who took an interest in the works of either al-Shaybānī or Abū Yūsuf. As such, the foundational works of the Ḥanafī school do not come close to the *Muwaṭṭaʾ* in their value and authoritativeness.

Walī Allāh's fight against sectarian zeal (*tamadhhub*) also impelled him to search for convincing criteria, which would not fall into the trap of partisanship, for comparing various legal opinions and giving preference to one of them (*tarjīḥ*). While hadith in general supplied a standard background against which all juristic opinions could be judged, the special choice of Mālik's

Muwaṭṭaʾ provided added protection against the appropriation of hadith by narrowly defined sectarian interests. Still, Walī Allāh did not dispense with the Ḥanafī school, nor did he seek to abolish legal schools in general. It is already significant that Walī Allāh diluted his message by treating the *Muwaṭṭaʾ* not just as a legal work but also as a book of hadith. Presumably, it would be easier for a Ḥanafī jurist to accept Mālik's authority as a hadith scholar than as an icon of a competing legal school. Furthermore, in Walī Allāh's formulation, the Mālikī school does not partake in this newly asserted authority of its founder. In fact, explaining his methodology in the introduction, Walī Allāh indicates that he mentions under each section the opinions of "the Shāfiʿīs and the Ḥanafīs, because they are the two major groups of the day, they are the majority of the community [of Muslims], they are the main composers [of books] in most religious disciplines, and they are the leading imams."[133] In other words, Walī Allāh's use of Mālik is not to cite the supremacy of the Mālikī school—which is in a different league from the two schools that merit primary consideration, the Shāfiʿī and the Ḥanafī. Walī Allāh therefore transforms Mālik into a symbol: on the one hand, his *Muwaṭṭaʾ* epitomizes the reconciliation of hadith and *fiqh*; and, on the other hand, as articulated by Walī Allāh, the scope of the intended influence of the *Muwaṭṭaʾ* extends well beyond the boundaries of any particular school.

> My heart brightened and I became certain that the *Muwaṭṭaʾ* is the soundest book on Earth after the Book of God. I also became certain that the road to exercising independent reasoning and acquiring jurisprudence is blocked in these days except through one approach: to make the *Muwaṭṭaʾ* the focus of one's attention, and to exert oneself in connecting its interrupted traditions and identifying the [scriptural] sources for the opinions of the Companions and followers [reported in it]. Next, one should follow the example of independent jurists by specifying the conventional meanings of utterances; . . . deriving the general and exhaustive rules; recognizing the rationale for legal rulings; and determining whether [the legal rulings] are general or specific depending on the nature of the reason.[134]

According to Walī Allāh, then, the use of the *Muwaṭṭaʾ* is the only way through which it is possible to exercise *ijtihād*, which is a collective obligation for every generation of Muslims. Walī Allāh adds, however, that *ijtihād* does not have to be absolute. Rather, to fulfill this obligation it is sufficient to derive legal rulings from their specific indicants, even if this is done under the guidance of the founder of a school. *Ijtihād*, therefore, does not undermine adherence to legal schools; it simply modifies the structure of authority within each school by stipulating that their laws must conform to outside canons and standards.[135]

After stating that all thorough scholars agree that *ijtihād* is an obligation, Walī Allāh explains that the reason for this obligation is that outstanding problems continue to arise endlessly, and it is necessary to know the legal rulings regarding such new problems. However, "what is written and documented is not sufficient; differences are numerous and cannot be resolved without reference to indicants; chains of transmission for the opinions attributed to the independent imams are for the most part interrupted; and the heart does not feel satisfied by relying on these [reports]. Therefore, the matter cannot be settled without considering these [juristic views] in light of the fundamentals of *ijtihād*."[136] By the fundamentals of *ijtihād* Walī Allāh means hadith. However, he also maintains that the connected traditions alone are not sufficient to derive all the needed laws; rather, they need to be complemented with the traditions of the Companions and the sayings of the successors. In conclusion, Walī Allāh asserts that "there is no book which encompasses both kinds of reports, and which is at the same time maintained by scholars and examined by consecutive generations of *mujtahid*s, other than the *Muwaṭṭaʾ*."[137]

For Walī Allāh, then, the *Muwaṭṭaʾ* and the scholarly tradition of studying it provide the fundamentals of *ijtihād*. Moreover, Walī Allāh intimates that what he does in his own work is, in fact, what constitutes *ijtihād*: he clarifies the terminology of the traditions of *Muwaṭṭaʾ*; organizes its traditions in a way that facilitates their use; adds related sections from the Qurʾān and exegesis the jurist should know in connection with these traditions; gives for each hadith of the *Muwaṭṭaʾ* the rulings derived by jurists; points out differences in the views of jurists regarding each of these traditions; explains how the reasons behind a ruling can be identified; and deduces general and exhaustive rules.[138] Thus both the text of the *Muwaṭṭaʾ* as well as Walī Allāh's commentary on it are prototypes of *ijtihād* that are grounded in but go beyond the simple transmission of hadith.

Walī Allāh draws a clear distinction between the career of a traditionalist and that of a jurist. The task of the traditionalist, Walī Allāh maintains, is to report hadiths, single out distorted ones, explain unfamiliar ones, clarify their meaning according to the requirements of the Arabic language, identify reporters and provide critical information on them (*jarḥ wa taʿdīl*), decide whether a hadith is sound or weak, consider follow-up and corroborative traditions, and so on.[139] According to Walī Allāh, a traditionalist who is competent to perform all of these tasks would have attained the highest level of "memory, exactness, and command." He then defines the duties of the jurist, whom he now calls a *mujtahid*. The task of the *mujtahid*, he argues, is to determine the principles, conditions, and procedures in all matters; to specify whether imperative formulations imply recommendation or obligation and whether negative formulations imply reprehension or prohibition; to identify the rationales for legislation together with their indicants; and to decide, based on the indicants, whether the application of a certain ruling is general or specific to a particular situation.[140] According to Walī Allāh, a scholar who commands these matters, and is capable of explaining all rulings through the reflection of *ijtihād*, becomes an absolute *mujtahid*. Such a person, Walī Allāh adds, exercises independent legal reasoning even if he cultivates his practical skills by studying under another scholar or analyzing (*tatabbuʿ*) his book.[141]

According to Walī Allāh, therefore, *ijtihād* is the domain of jurisprudence, not hadith. While hadith is necessary, it is not a sufficient requirement for *ijtihād*, and it takes a jurist to finish the job. Yet, what hadith does to the juristic undertaking of a *mujtahid* is ensure that this juristic exercise is not exclusive or divisive. *Ijtihād*, though it may be exercised within the general norms of a particular school, is by definition open to other schools. Thus, when Walī Allāh says that he himself has acquired the art of *ijtihād*, he adds that he was first inspired to it by tracing the book *Al-Umm* of Imam Shāfiʿī, and that he benefited greatly from the *Sharḥ al-Sunna* of al-Baghawī, and from other books by Shāfiʿī scholars.[142]

In the introduction to the Arabic *Musawwā*, Walī Allāh states that jurisprudence is the "noblest, most beneficial, and most extensive of all religious sciences," and that "the *Muwaṭṭaʾ* is the soundest, most celebrated, oldest, and most comprehensive of all the books of jurisprudence."[143] In a way, therefore, Walī Allāh treats the *Muwaṭṭaʾ* as a book on legal traditions (*aḥādīth al-aḥkām*); this explains his assertion that it combines hadith and *fiqh*, and his later insistence that it is superior to all other books of jurisprudence. These equivocal references to the *Muwaṭṭaʾ* are carefully employed by Walī Allāh to delineate the role of the *Muwaṭṭaʾ* in relation to other schools of law. Walī Allāh maintains that even though members of the various legal schools may have accepted or rejected the rulings of Mālik, commented on them, and rectified some of them, they would not have been able to develop their schools without Mālik's efforts in organizing and refining his own book.[144] The debt of later scholars is not to the juristic merits of the *Muwaṭṭaʾ* but to the manner of its formal organization. Walī Allāh also maintains that *sunan* compilations like Muslim's and those of Abū Dāʾūd and Nasāʾī, as well as the parts dealing with jurisprudence in al-Bukhārī and the *Jāmiʿ* of Tirmidhī are all, in some sense, elaborations on (*mustakhrajāt ʿalā*) the *Muwaṭṭaʾ*. The most any such elaboration can hope to achieve is to connect the interrupted traditions of the *Muwaṭṭaʾ*, add what is missing, provide corroborative traditions for those already mentioned in it, and mention reports that differ from it.[145] In short, even for one who disagrees with the juristic deductions of Mālik, the bedrock of the science of jurisprudence is the *Muwaṭṭaʾ*.

In his commentary on the traditions of the *Muwaṭṭaʾ*, Walī Allāh conforms to the general blueprint outlined in his introduction. He frequently favors the concurrence of Mālik and al-Shāfiʿī over the accepted opinion of the Ḥanafīs. In cases where he opposes the Ḥanafī school, Walī Allāh often tries to absolve Abū Ḥanīfa and to blame errors of interpretation on later Ḥanafīs. In most cases, however, Walī Allāh simply notes his opinion without putting much emphasis on the differences among the various schools. For example, Walī Allāh approvingly reports the views of Mālik and al-Shāfiʿī that ritual ablution is required after a man and a woman kiss or touch each other, even if there is no sexual intercourse between them. The Ḥanafīs, Walī Allāh adds, do not consider this to be a requirement, and they use a tradition transmitted by ʿĀʾisha to justify their view. According to this tradition, the Prophet did not repeat his ablution every time he kissed one of his wives. Suggesting that this tradition is itself questionable, Walī Allāh adds that later Ḥanafīs who wanted to corroborate Abū Ḥanīfa's opinion invoked this tradition by ʿĀʾisha.[146] The problem then is not in the actual opinion of Abū Ḥanīfa, who is simply exercising *ijtihād*, but in the use by later Ḥanafīs of the problematic hadith of ʿĀʾisha.

In another example, Walī Allāh agrees with the majority opinion that a pot from which a dog drinks should be washed seven times, against Abū Ḥanīfa's view that, as in the case with any other impurity, one washing is sufficient.[147] It is significant that in both examples, as well as in many others, Walī Allāh manages to clearly express his preference for the majority opinion while downplaying the differences that occur over the issues in question. Such differences, often encountered among the established legal scholars, are presumably within the limits of legitimate *ijtihād*. Walī Allāh even maintains that the Companions did not disagree in reporting what they saw of the actions of the Prophet; rather, they differed only in articulating descriptions of these actions.[148] Therefore, the way to handle divergent reports by the Companions is similar to the way one deals with the differences on issues derived by independent reasoning (*ijtihādiyyāt*).

In his *Musawwā*, Walī Allāh excludes the opinions of Mālik that are based on mere inference.[149] This is possible because ultimately Walī Allāh is not trying to idealize Mālik himself but to extract from the *Muwaṭṭaʾ* a substratum that serves the cause of unity he championed. Once again, the purpose of this exercise is not to eliminate all kinds of disagreement among the legal schools but to mitigate their contentious feuds and to foster constructive relationships among them. An equally important objective is to promote hadith as a discipline through which the gaps between the various schools can be bridged.[150]

Walī Allāh addresses the problem of contradictory hadiths in a number of his works. In a book titled *Sharḥ Tarājim Abwāb Ṣaḥīḥ Bukhārī*, Walī Allāh surveys and compares the opinions of the leading jurists on each of the chapters of *Ṣaḥīḥ Bukhārī*.[151] Often in this book Walī Allāh compares a hadith in al-Bukhārī with Mālik's statement on the same subject. For example, Walī Allāh reports the traditions in al-Bukhārī on whether the thigh should be covered during prayer. Walī Allāh adds that according to Abū Ḥanīfa and Shāfiʿī it should be, while Mālik argues that it does not have to be covered for the prayer to be valid. According to Walī Allāh, however, "the traditions of this section are contradictory, yet, from the point of view of transmission, Mālik's opinion is stronger."[152] Walī Allāh then offers a way for reconciling the disparate traditions and concludes with a general rule: "The Prophet has illustrated to us two manners of prayer: the prayer of the righteous [*muḥsin*] and that of the common believer. There are many things that he made permissible in the second case and prohibited in the first. So, if you learn this rule, many of the contradictory instances in the section on prayer will be clarified for you."[153] Presumably, the righteous would cover his thigh; yet this argument is more about techniques for reconciling seemingly incompatible traditions than it is about the extent to which thighs may be uncovered.

Walī Allāh's commentary on *Ṣaḥīḥ Bukhārī* illustrates that his work on hadith was not exclusively devoted to Mālik's *Muwaṭṭa'*. One of the objectives of Walī Allāh's commentary on al-Bukhārī is to try to identify the strategies underlying al-Bukhārī's organization and presentation of his work. For example, Walī Allāh remarks that al-Bukhārī may dedicate a section in his book to a specific instantiation of a more general case, although his purpose is to determine that general case.[154] He does this in order to identify one of the various possible forms of the case in question. To be able to use al-Bukhārī properly, Walī Allāh continues, one has to examine the work carefully to discern the implicit assumptions and intentions of the compiler.[155] Thus al-Bukhārī, according to Walī Allāh, may report a hadith that is not related at all to the section in which it is reported, but which has other versions of which one is related to this section.[156] Such tendencies in al-Bukhārī are often a source of confusion, and Walī Allāh offers his commentary as a way of filling in the gaps and eliminating possible obscurities in al-Bukhārī.[157] Significantly, Walī Allāh asserts that in matters where there is disagreement among the imams of the schools of law, al-Bukhārī often words his report in a way that lends itself to more than one interpretation without making a choice or suggesting a preference.[158] In short, Walī Allāh contends that a deliberate strategy underlies the structure of al-Bukhārī. His *Ṣaḥīḥ*, therefore, is not just a compilation of raw and unprocessed hadiths. Rather, its organization is informed by juristic considerations; to make proper use of it, these considerations need to be inferred and elaborated. Once again, even a most canonical work of hadith cannot dispense with the need for juristic explication.

One of the most obvious results of Walī Allāh's approach to the sources is to narrow the gap between them. He treats al-Bukhārī as an ordered book of hadith that can only be understood in light of jurisprudence. Alternatively, he treats the *Muwaṭṭaʾ* of Mālik as an authentic compilation of hadiths. All great authoritative works, according to Walī Allāh, partake of both hadith and jurisprudence. Moreover, if hadith collections like al-Bukhārī's are in fact based on hadith as well as *fiqh*, then it is possible to argue that the *Muwaṭṭaʾ*, which is also based on hadith and *fiqh*, stands above any particular school of law and has an authority similar to those of the canonical works of hadith. Ascribing such a status to the *Muwaṭṭaʾ* is essential to Walī Allāh, who considers this work to be the centerpiece of his whole intellectual career. On several occasions, Walī Allāh expresses his full awareness of the significance of his undertaking: in a moment of inspiration he declares that God made him realize that his work on the *Muwaṭṭaʾ* leads to "an opening of the gates of goodness; a reunification of the community blessed with God's mercy [*jamʿ al-umma al-marḥūma*]; a shaking off of the ossified natures that have been stagnant for a long time; and a guidance to long-abandoned kinds of knowledge."[159]

To achieve this objective of "a reunification of the community blessed with God's mercy," Walī Allāh clearly tries to maintain a delicate balance among prevalent and often conflicting intellectual tendencies. Rather than eliminating or simply ignoring potentially divisive disciplinary practices, he proposes alternative readings of these practices that would bring them in line with his ideals of inclusion. Thus Walī Allāh argues that identifying the reasons for the rulings of jurists (*takhrīj al-aḥādīth*) and tracing the wording of the hadith have deep roots in religion. Therefore, a scholar should not neglect either one, as the general adherents of the two groups, traditionalists and jurists, often do. The plain truth, according to Walī Allāh, is that each should be synchronized (*yuṭābaq*) with the other, and the shortcomings of one discipline should be rectified by reference to the other. "An expert on hadith should scrutinize [*yaʿruḍ*] what he chooses and selects against the opinion of the *mujtahid*s of the successors; one who belongs to the people who identify the reasons for the rulings ought to uphold enough traditions to guard against opposing the clear and sound [hadiths], and avoid, as best as he can, relying on his opinion in places where there is a hadith or a tradition."[160]

What distinguishes Walī Allāh from al-Ṣanʿānī and al-Shawkānī is that as Walī Allāh carefully reconfigures relationships among various accepted authoritative figures and works, he does not reject or even question these authorities. Once again, Walī Allāh's purpose is not to establish one final criterion against which all Islamic disciplines can be judged but to reconcile and harmonize these disciplines by identifying the various relative aspects of truth in each of them.

The general theoretical formulations that are indirectly implied in the *Musawwā* are clearly stated in Walī Allāh's celebrated work *Ḥujjat Allāh al-Bāligha*.[161] In this book, as in the introductory remarks of the *Musawwā*, Walī Allāh argues that "the principle of all certain sciences and their fountainhead, and the basis and foundation of the religious disciplines is the science of hadith."[162] Walī Allāh, however, divides this discipline of hadith into several branches that include what is traditionally known as hadith as well as jurisprudence. He delineates a hierarchy of subdisciplines under the general rubric of hadith: the closest layer to the surface is the art of identifying whether traditions are sound or weak, multiply transmitted or unfamiliar, and so on.[163] Walī Allāh adds that among the early generations of Muslims, many brilliant traditionalists endowed with excellent memories undertook this kind of study. The next level of depth is the art of determining the meanings of unfamiliar hadiths and controlling problematic ones. This kind of study, according to Walī Allāh, is the domain of the leading literary scholars and Arabic language experts. An even deeper layer is the art of inferring the juristic significance of hadiths and deriving applied laws from them. This level of study also includes the use of legal analogies, deduction from indirect allusions (*īmāʾāt*, sing. *īmāʾ*) and indications (*ishārāt*, sing. *ishāra*) of the scriptural texts, and the recognition of "the abrogated, the unequivocal, the preferred, and the conclusive."[164] Walī Allāh adds that, according to the majority of scholars, this last kind of study is at the core of the general discipline of hadith and is the gem of the various subfields of this discipline; it is undertaken by the most erudite scholars of Islam.

As far as the traditional disciplines are concerned, Walī Allāh posits a definite hierarchy of knowledge within what he calls *al-funūn al-ḥadīthiyya*, that is, all the sciences whose raw material is hadith. These include the proper discipline of hadith, in addition to language and jurisprudence. The last of these, according to Walī Allāh, is the most nuanced of the three. Walī Allāh's point, therefore, is not to make hadith more important than *fiqh* but to establish that the latter, in spite of its higher status, is and should be founded on the former. In fact, according to Walī Allāh, the highest science is neither of the above; rather, "the most subtle of all of the arts of hadith, . . . the primary among the entirety of all of the religious sciences, in my opinion, the highest in rank, and the greatest in value, is the science of the inner meanings [*asrār*] of religion. This science investigates the wisdom and rationale [*lammiyya/limmiyya*] behind the rulings and the secrets of the properties and fine points of actions. Of all the branches of knowledge, this, by God, is worthiest of the precious time of qualified scholars, . . . since only through it can a human being gain a true insight into what was sanctioned by the divine law."[165] According to Walī Allāh, then, there is yet another layer of hadith study, a secret science that is the deepest of all.[166] Still, this assertion does not affect the relative hierarchy that he establishes among the more traditional disciplines: hadith proper, language, and jurisprudence. This is especially true since the "inner dimension" of the science of the inner meanings of religion can only be discerned by one who has strong command of the entirety of the religious disciplines.[167] However, despite Walī Allāh's disclaimers, the notion of a secret science poses a serious challenge to his theory of hadith and its prescribed reformative role within Islamic intellectual traditions in general. Indeed, Walī Allāh was well aware of this tension and devoted a considerable portion of his work to negotiating a consonant relationship between the various layers of knowledge that he outlined in his work.

In discussions echoing age-old traditions of theological controversies, Walī Allāh maintains that there is a correlation between human actions and God's rewards or punishments for these actions.[168] Walī Allāh adds that many people believe God rewards and punishes on account of humans' obedience or disobedience, and not because of the nature of the action committed. According to this last opinion, obligations and prohibitions have no intrinsic value in themselves; rather, they are simply devised to test people's obedience to God. In response, Walī Allāh asserts that this is a false supposition disproved both by the Sunna (the practice of the Prophet) and the consensus of the pious generations of Muslims. To illustrate this point, Walī Allāh goes over the main religious obligations and indicates their purposes as illustrated in the scripture. Prayer, he says, is legislated to remember God; alms taxes to ward off the vice of miserliness and to provide for the needs of the poor; fasting to subdue the soul; pilgrimage to honor the emblems of God; retaliation (*qiṣāṣ*) as a deterrent to killing; jihad to uphold the word of God and to eliminate sedition; the rules of economic transactions and marriages to establish justice; and so on.[169] Walī Allāh adds that the Prophet not only prescribed religious obligations and acts of worship but also, on several occasions, explained the rationale behind designating particular times for performing them. The Prophet, according to Walī Allāh, also explained the reasons behind the imposition of some rules; such reasons include the wish to ward off harm, or to deliberately differentiate Muslims from nonbelievers. On other occasions, according to Walī Allāh, the Prophet also explained the inner meanings of deterrence from sin and encouragement to goodness.[170] The successors and after them the *mujtahid*s continued to explain the rationale of various pieces of legislation on the basis of the beneficial purposes they serve (*maṣlaḥa*) and to attribute to every textually based ruling an inherent significance such as preventing a harm or bringing about a benefit.

So far, Walī Allāh sounds like the Muʿtazila who, among other things, believed that actions are either good (*ḥasan*) or repugnant (*qabīḥ*) for internal rational reasons that have to do with the nature of the acts and not simply the fact they are prescribed by God. This view clearly endows human reason with an authority comparable to that of scripture, including hadith. It is significant, however, that Walī Allāh invokes the traditional authorities of the Sunna and the consensus of Muslims to support his untraditional views. This is not just a maneuver by Walī Allāh to promote rationalistic views disguised in traditionalist language. Rather, he qualifies his advocacy of rationalism in a way that allows him to pursue his search for the inner meanings of religion without undermining the ultimate authority of scripture. Walī Allāh argues that in the same way the Sunna and the consensus entail recognition of the existence of a rationale behind legal rulings, this same Sunna requires that

> the revelation of a decree making something compulsory or forbidden is itself a great cause for rewarding the obedient and punishing the disobedient, irrespective of the beneficial purposes of the act. This is contrary to the view that the goodness and repugnance of acts, in the sense of the doer's meriting reward or punishment, are completely [derivable] by reason. Nor is it the task of the law to report on the characteristics of actions as they are in themselves, without establishing what is compulsory or forbidden. . . . This is a spurious contention that the Sunna rejects. . . . How could this be so when the Prophet says that the Muslim who commits the greatest crime is one who asks about something that had not been forbidden to the people, so that it becomes forbidden because of his inquiry?[171]

Therefore, an action may have inherent goodness or repugnance, but it only becomes obligatory or prohibited based on clear textual commands to this effect. However, according to Walī Allāh, the contrary is not correct; for designating an act as compulsory or prohibited is not random but rooted in the intrinsic nature of the act. Furthermore, Walī Allāh maintains that we cannot make compliance with the rules of the divine law contingent on our recognition of their beneficial purposes.[172] This is because we are often unable to independently recognize many of these beneficial purposes, and because the Prophet is more dependable, for us, than our own reasoning. Therefore, knowledge of the inner meanings of religion (*ʿilm asrār al-dīn*) continues to be withheld from people who are not qualified for it (*maḍnūnan bihi ʿalā ghayri ahlihi*). The conditions that are laid down for acquiring this knowledge are the same conditions that are required in interpreting the Book of God: in both cases, it is forbidden to resort to speculation on the basis of pure personal opinion not founded on the traditions of the Prophet and the reports of the Companions.

Fully aware of the suspicion with which orthodoxy has looked on the idea of secret knowledge, Walī Allāh offers to alleviate some of these suspicions by giving precedence in his "science of the inner meanings" to textual commandments; by stipulating formal requirements for this science that are similar to those of Qur'ānic exegesis; by recognizing that some intrinsically good or bad acts may not be compulsory or forbidden; and by making hadith the basis for deriving this secret knowledge. Therefore, to sanction the science of the inner meanings of religion, Walī Allāh formally ties it to hadith, the most orthodox of all disciplines. He even calls his potentially controversial science the science of the secrets of hadith (*ʿilm asrār al-ḥadīth*) to highlight the formal connection between the two.

Walī Allāh also responds to those who concede that legal rulings have their rationale in beneficial purposes but argue that the codification of this science (*asrār al-dīn*) is either rationally impossible, due to the obscurity and vagueness of its subject matter, or that it is prohibited, because the first generations of Muslims did not record it despite their proximity to the era of the Prophet.[173] This neglect, it is argued, is tantamount to an agreement among the early generations to disregard this subject. Alternatively, Walī Allāh adds, some may say that there is no benefit in writing this science down, since compliance with the divine law does not depend on recognizing the beneficial purposes behind it. Walī Allāh rejects all of these arguments. The difficulty of codification, he argues, does not mean that it is impossible; other disciplines, such as the knowledge of God's unity and attributes, deal with more obscure matters, but God makes them possible for whomever He wills. In fact, the comprehension of any branch of knowledge at first appears almost impossible to attain; yet, with constant training, and upon acquiring the required skills, the most difficult of disciplines becomes easy. Walī Allāh concedes that this science is particularly difficult but adds that this is a challenge through which "the superiority of certain scholars becomes apparent."[174]

As for the fact that earlier generations did not commit the science of the secrets of religion to writing, Walī Allāh maintains that there is no harm in this fact when the Prophet himself laid down its basic principles and outlined its branches, and when Companions like ʿUmar and ʿAlī followed the example of the Prophet. Walī Allāh adds that the early generations did not need to write on this subject because they were blessed by their closeness to the Prophet and did not need to authenticate reports attributed to him. They hardly disagreed and were not concerned with the challenge of accommodating tradition to reason. Having direct access to reliable authorities, they did not record this or any of the other hadith disciplines. None of these disciplines was recorded or delineated until much later when such documentation became needed, and when the welfare of Muslims became dependent on it.[175]

Walī Allāh, therefore, defines the intellectual needs of the Muslim community historically. Potentially, this means that each generation of Muslims may have needs for specific kinds of knowledge, which may in turn be reflected in trends among the intellectuals of that particular period. As such, none of these trends can be dismissed by reference to one timeless view of Islam. Unlike Ibn ʿAbd al-Wahhāb, for example, Walī Allāh responds in his work to what he perceives as a particular historical situation in which new disciplines of learning or even kinds of knowledge come into existence. Rather than passing judgment on them by recourse to reductive formulas and definitions of Islam, Walī Allāh attempts to reformulate these disciplines so they can be integrated into the larger edifice of Islamic learning. Since one of the needs of his time was the accommodation of tradition and reason, and since this theme informed much of the contemporary debates of his intellectual environment, Walī Allāh found this to be not just a legitimate subject but one he had to attend to.[176] Accounting for the origins of the science of the inner meanings of religion and the purposes it serves, Walī Allāh maintains that

> differences increased among legal scholars following their disagreement over the reasons for legislation. This led them to deliberate over the reasons for legislation from the perspective of the beneficial purposes that are established in the law. Next, this gave rise to adherence to reason [*maʿqūl*] in many religious questions and to the casting of doubt over doctrinal and practical principles. All of this evolved to the point that striving to establish rational proofs in accordance with transmitted texts, and to correlate [*taṭbīq*] tradition with reason, as well as what is heard with what is understood came to constitute a strong support for religion, and a good effort to reunite [*jamʿ shaml*] Muslims. This was also counted as one of the greatest means of drawing nearer to God, and one of the leading acts of piety.[177]

Walī Allāh adds that innovators questioned basic Islamic principles on the ground that they contradict reason, and they therefore rejected and interpreted traditions accordingly. The only way to disprove these allegations, according to Walī Allāh, is to resort to the principle of beneficiary purposes (*maṣāliḥ*, sing. *maṣlaḥa*) as a textually hinged rational criterion.[178] Walī Allāh thus legitimizes reason by using it in defense of the textually established tradition. His aim is to amalgamate the reasoned with the transmitted, an objective that, if achieved, would reaffirm the authority of tradition as the ultimate legitimizing principle even for the rational. At the same time, Walī Allāh carves a niche for the rational not just by basing it on hadith but by portraying his undertaking as an attempt to rein in the wild tendencies of unanchored rationalism and to defend—and in a way redeem—the foundational authority of hadith. As a result, Walī Allāh draws a distinction between independent and unanchored rationalism in religious matters, which is heretical, and the blending of hadith and reason, which is yet another facet of the project of restoring the intellectual unity of Muslims.

Along the same lines, Walī Allāh argues that the Prophet brought forth the most complete divine law, containing beneficial purposes the like of which humans are incapable of articulating. During the lifetime of the Prophet, people recognized the nobility of what they received. However, after that generation had passed, it became necessary to have among Muslims people who could identify the traditions that proved that the Prophet's legal code is the most perfect one, and who could illustrate the inimitability of this code. Walī Allāh thus suggests that in the rationalistic part of his project he simply comes to the praise and defense of the texts and traditions of the Prophet and attempts to prove by rational arguments their superiority and miraculous nature.[179]

Walī Allāh admits that he may sometimes be forced to introduce views that the majority of theologians did not hold before him. Such is, for example, the idea that there is a nonelemental world in which meanings and actions are embodied by forms of corresponding characteristics, and in which accidents are created before they are created on Earth. Walī Allāh assures his reader, however, that "I did not venture to do this [introduce unconventional views] until after I saw the Qur'ānic verses, the hadiths, and the reports of the Companions and the successors openly displaying them. I also saw that among the elite of the people of the Sunna, some who were distinguished by intuitive knowledge, professed them [the unconventional views], and based their principles on them."[180] Walī Allāh, therefore, provides all kinds of traditional justifications for his use of nontraditional views. He introduces most of these ideas when discussing such theologically controversial articles of belief as the questioning of the dead in the grave by angels, the weighing of acts, passing over the bridge (*ṣirāṭ*), seeing God in the hereafter, and the miracles of the saints.[181] Walī Allāh argues that Muslims have dealt with these questions in radically different ways, which reflect varying conceptions for the relationship between reason and the outer meaning of the scripture. The people of the Sunna, he maintains, opted for the literal meaning of the scripture and held fast to the beliefs of the ancestors. They did not try to twist their beliefs so these agree with the principles of reason, and they invoked reason only to impose their proofs on their adversaries, to respond to them, or to reassure themselves. They did not use reason to derive the basic articles of belief. At the other extreme, some people resorted to interpretation and dismissed the literal meaning of the scriptural texts whenever they opposed their rational principles, or when, as in the case of the above list, these literal meanings were outside the confines of human rationality. This use of reason, therefore, overrides the use of texts and is the basis through which this group identifies the fundamental creeds of Islam.

Walī Allāh seems to identify himself with yet another group that asserts its belief in whatever the scriptural texts clearly state, even if it fails to identify the true meaning of these statements, and even if reason does not provide a satisfactory explanation of what this meaning may be. However, Walī Allāh maintains, "we believe in all of this based on proof from our Lord, and reason attests to it for us."[182] Walī Allāh thus upholds the authority of the outer meanings of scriptural texts while confidently asserting that reason must and will conform to these meanings. Rather than suspend reason, he offers an alternative reading in which he insists that reason is in harmony and fully reconcilable with tradition.

In further elaboration on his theory of reasoned scriptural authority, Walī Allāh distinguishes between the divine law, whose rulings cannot be known except through the traditions of the Prophet, and the beneficial purposes for which these rulings are intended. The latter can be discerned through "experience, honest reflection, intuition [*ḥads*], and so on." Walī Allāh remarks that the traditions of the Prophet would not have reached us were it not for the reporting through continuous chains of transmission or through the *muʿanʿan ḥadīth*s. He then adds that in more recent times, knowledge of the various reports and their chains of transmission all the way back to the Prophet would not be possible without the use of the books written on the science of hadith; this is particularly true since, according to Walī Allāh, one can no longer find a reliable report that has not been written down in one of these books.[183]

Having made the transition between the genre of hadith as a source of authority and the actual physical books where this authority is canonized, Walī Allāh then considers the relative authority of the various books of hadith. As far as soundness and reputation is concerned, he maintains that each collection of hadith falls into one of four ranks.[184] The highest rank is that of multiply transmitted hadith (*mutawātir*), which the community agreed to accept and to act upon. The second level is that of abundantly transmitted hadiths (*mashhūr*) that are transmitted through enough lines that there remains no significant doubt regarding their authenticity. According to Walī Allāh, the majority of legal scholars working in the main cities of Islam, and in particular the scholars of the two sacred cities, Mecca and Medina, are also in agreement regarding the soundness of this second kind.[185] This group of hadith books includes the four *sunan*, the *Musnad* of Ibn Ḥanbal, and other similar works. Most of the religious sciences, according to Walī Allāh, are based upon the hadiths of these books. The third category is of sound or good hadiths that have been sanctioned by hadith scholars and that are not discarded from the legal practices of the community. Although books of this rank did not receive the same attention as those of the first two groups, Walī Allāh asserts that they include sound as well as weak hadiths in them, and may, therefore, contain useful legal information.[186] Walī Allāh cautions, however, that, in contrast to the traditions of the first two groups: "Only the rare brilliant [scholars] who have memorized the names of the transmitters and the defects of the hadiths should undertake to implement and endorse [the hadiths of] the third group, even though supporting evidence for the texts or meanings of other hadiths can well be taken from them."[187]

Unlike ʿAbd al-Ḥaqq, therefore, Walī Allāh limits the utility of noncanonical hadith compilations, although he recognizes that, at least in theory, they still have some usefulness. The difference between the two scholars is itself a function of the role each of them assigns to hadith. For ʿAbd al-Ḥaqq, hadith is simply a tool that complements and reinforces Ḥanafī law. For Walī Allāh, however, hadith mitigates the exclusive claims to authority made by Ḥanafī jurists; it also represents an autonomous bedrock upon which all schools of law converge.

The remaining kinds of hadith books include, among others, weak, invented, transposed, or fabricated hadiths. These books, according to Walī Allāh cannot be accepted, nor can action be based on them. Walī Allāh adds that "preoccupation with collecting them or deriving [laws] from them is a kind of hairsplitting [*taʿammuq*] exhibited by latter-day writers" and that serious scholars do not invoke these traditions.[188]

Walī Allāh also explains what soundness and reputation mean when it comes to a compilation of hadith as opposed to one particular report or chain of transmission. For a hadith compilation to be sound, the compiler of the book must stipulate that he includes in his compilation only what is sound or good, and that he has not included traditions that are transposed, anomalous, or weak unless he provides an explanation of their status. Walī Allāh adds that if a weak tradition is included in a compilation together with a clarification of its status, then this would not detract from the general soundness of the compilation.[189]

For a book of hadith to be reputable, according to Walī Allāh, the traditions reported in it must be current among hadith scholars both before and after its compilation.[190] The book must thus include hadiths reported through various chains by the leading scholars of hadith who lived before the time of the compiler. Moreover, hadith scholars after the time of the compiler should have transmitted the book, memorized it, clarified its obscurities, explained its uncommon words, inferred the legal significance of its hadiths, and investigated all possible questions related to them. According to Walī Allāh, therefore, the reputation of a book implies that hadith critics both before and after the compiler have cited the traditions reported in the book and have judged them to be sound. In particular, this reflects a kind of consensus to accept the compiler's assessment of the traditions he reports and to receive his book with praise and commendation. Walī Allāh also adds that the trait of reputation also means that leading jurists continue to derive rulings from the hadiths of the compilation and that the general public continues to believe in and honor them.

The significance of this intricate argument becomes clear when contrasted with the rationale of the Yemeni arguments in favor of the authority of hadith. According to both al-Ṣanʿānī and al-Shawkānī, a sound hadith is authoritative but its text is not absolute in itself. As we have seen above, both scholars systematically rejected the illusive and idealized notion of consensus and proposed instead a historicized concept of authority that is at once binding and practical. For both, it is neither possible nor necessary to establish the veracity of hadith with absolute certainty. In contrast to the Yemenis, Walī Allāh asserts that the consensus of scholars and the community in general endows the specific hadiths in their formal expressions, and even in the physical books in which they are compiled, with inherent and absolute authority. Therefore, Walī Allāh's recognition of the authority of consensus enables him to hold that a hadith enjoying such consensus becomes in itself a source of certain knowledge and, by extension, of absolute authority. In reference to the compilations of al-Bukhārī and Muslim, for example, Walī Allāh maintains that "hadith scholars have agreed that all of the uninterrupted traditions going back to the Prophet in these books are *certainly* sound; that they reached their compilers in multiple transmitted chains; and that whoever slights them is an innovator who is not following the path of the believers."[191] In other words, recognition of the absolute certainty of these traditions becomes part of defining what it means to be a Muslim. This also allows Walī Allāh to extend his assessment of hadith from a theoretical discussion that would be applied on a case-by-case basis to a blanket ranking of the various books of hadith.

Walī Allāh's views regarding the relative authority and merits of various generations of Muslims are also less radical than those of al-Shawkānī and al-Ṣanʿānī. Walī Allāh maintains that the superiority of the first community is a functional concept, but not necessarily an exclusive one, and that the said superiority of earlier generations over later ones is a general statement that is not pertinent to all possible virtues. Moreover, it is not possible that each individual from the preferred generation be better than each individual from later generations; after all, Walī Allāh observes, the earlier generations of Companions and successors had their own hypocrites, sinners, and numerous others whose wretched status is no secret to anyone. So far, Walī Allāh, like al-Shawkānī and al-Ṣanʿānī, is arguing that individual scholars belonging to all generations of Muslims may acquire various degrees of authority on the basis of intellectual achievements that may equal or even surpass those of the scholars of earlier generations. Walī Allāh, however, parts company with the Yemeni scholars when he insists that it is vital to recognize that the majority of the first generation was better than the majority of the second one, and so on. This recognition, he argues, is of paramount importance because religion can only be established through transmission and bequest. These, in turn, require that we venerate those who witnessed the occasions of the revelations, learned their interpretations, and observed the practice of the Prophet. Unlike the Yemeni scholars, for whom transmission is tantamount to a simple testimony by a trustworthy reporter, and can very well be accepted from a condemned sinner, Walī Allāh requires an idealization of the first generation of Muslims as a necessary condition for the perpetuation of Islam.[192]

In the hierarchy of authority posited by the Yemeni scholars, the renewed vitality of Islamic thought is secured by the systematic development and application of the discipline of hadith. For Walī Allāh, however, this vitality requires, in addition to the procedural safeguards, a formal recognition of the authority of the first generations of Muslims. In fact, Walī Allāh argues that, just as jurists are capable of developing partisan tendencies, traditionalists (*muḥaddithūn*) are also susceptible to narrow-mindedness.[193] A traditionalist, Walī Allāh adds, who is totally engaged in the intricacies of his craft, can easily miss or even dismiss illuminating perspectives that derive from other disciplines. To illustrate this tendency, Walī Allāh gives the example of Ibn Ḥazm, who rejected a hadith prohibiting the use of stringed instruments because al-Bukhārī's report of this hadith is interrupted. Although Walī Allāh is careful not to attack Ibn Ḥazm personally, he clearly rejects his academic assessment. The hadith in question, according to Walī Allāh, does not contradict any other hadith and can be corroborated through several other connected reports; therefore, an interruption in the chain of transmission of one of these reports does not undermine its soundness.

For Walī Allāh, strict adherence to the procedures and techniques of the discipline of hadith studies does not, on its own, provide sufficient guard against rigid formalism and hairsplitting (*taʿammuq*). On the contrary, pedantic profundity in jurisprudence, hadith studies, or any other individual discipline can easily lead to zeal and division. Specialists of each discipline should allow themselves to be informed by the other ones, and the ideal education should provide familiarity with the methods of the jurists as well as the traditionalists.[194]

Walī Allāh's stance is consistent with his larger objectives: to foster openness at the expense of bigoted partisanship and professional isolationism and to empower larger sectors of the community and enable them to contribute to the intellectual regeneration of Islamic thought. Unlike the Yemeni scholars,

Walī Allāh's theory of hadith does not issue a radical challenge to the accepted structures of authority. Throughout his work, he reasserts the authority of an idealized first generation of Muslim transmitters of hadith. He also conforms to the traditional Sunni arguments for establishing a formal hierarchy of the canonical books of hadith. In a way, therefore, Walī Allāh uses hadith to serve unconventional ends: to undermine the rigid sectarian tendencies among Indian Ḥanafīs. In the course of this undertaking, Walī Allāh also creatively negotiates new relationships among various canonical hadith works. He does not, however, propose a new understanding for the internal dynamics of the discipline of hadith. Walī Allāh's work on hadith, therefore, had momentous consequences for Islamic thought in India but not for the internal working of the theory of hadith per se. In contrast, hadith scholarship in Yemen was traditional in its formal application but revolutionary in its underlying theory.

Unlike the Yemeni authors who plunged into the heart of the problem of authority, Walī Allāh's primary concerns were relational. He did not question the rationale for accepting the authority of the compilers of the canonical works of hadith; instead, he rearranged the power relationships among various authors and texts. In other words, he did not examine the nature of the authority of particular texts and authors but mapped out ways these related to each other. While the Yemeni scholars used hadith to make a sustained and persuasive argument for eliminating legal schools altogether, Walī Allāh used hadith to demonstrate and reinforce the interdependence of these schools.

For al-Shawkānī and al-Ṣanʿānī, the criterion for judging all legal rulings, and by extension legal schools, is hadith. For them, although it does not provide certain knowledge, hadith serves as the absolute standard that stands above all other forms of religious knowledge. As we have seen, Walī Allāh does not ascribe the same kind of authority to hadith. Moreover, for him, the primacy of hadith is simply because it comes first, and because it is a prerequisite for other forms of religious knowledge. This is why the *Muwaṭṭaʾ* of Mālik is superior to the compilations of al-Bukhārī and Muslim, although the latter two works are clearly sounder than the former. The Yemeni scholars, in contrast, had no such use for Mālik's *Muwaṭṭaʾ*. Al-Ṣanʿānī, for example, mentions in passing those who argue that Mālik's *Muwaṭṭaʾ* is the first collection of *ṣaḥīḥ* traditions but moves on to assert, without even bothering to respond to this view, that the first collections of real sound traditions are al-Bukhārī and Muslim.[195] Elsewhere, he maintains that the consensus of the people of Medina is not a proof (*ḥujja*) (and therefore authority) over Muslims; this is because the people of Medina constitute only a portion of the Muslim *umma*, and there is no textual evidence that their consensus, on which the *Muwaṭṭaʾ* is based, is an authority.[196]

Hadith serves yet another purpose in the program of Walī Allāh. Rather than asking his fellow Ḥanafīs to submit to the standards of other schools of law, he proposes hadith as a potentially neutral mediator between the various schools. However, this last solution also has its shortcomings, and Walī Allāh was fully aware of these. Historically, the traditionalists have functioned as a professional group that competes with the jurists of the legal schools for authority and social power. To resolve this difficulty, Walī Allāh proposed an abstract standard in which all other standards converge. He called this new hypothetical construct *al-jādda al-qawīma*, the upright road, a name that echoes but is different from the Qur'ānic *al-ṣirāṭ al-mustaqīm*, the straight path.

Walī Allāh argues that, as in the general case of the divine law (sharia), each school of law has irregular (*shādh*) as well as standard or apparent elements.[197] Walī Allāh's use here of the term *shādh* has no negative connotations; it simply refers to that part of the law that is not readily perceivable to the common person. The apparent part of sharia comprises the Qur'ān, as well as the recurrent hadiths reported in al-Bukhārī, Muslim, and the *Muwaṭṭa'* of Mālik, on the condition that there is neither contradiction in the reporting of these traditions nor glaring differences in their wordings. This apparent part, according to Walī Allāh, is *al-jādda al-qawīma*. Walī Allāh advises his readers to treat this *al-jādda al-qawīma* as one supraschool that belongs to all schools, to forgive differences in opinion, and not to exclude anyone from this "upright path" because of such differences.[198] In answer to a questioner who asks how to identify this path, Walī Allāh asserts that this is an easy matter that only requires knowledge of the *Muwaṭṭa'*, the two *Ṣaḥīḥ*s, the *Sunan* of Abī Dāwūd, and the *Jāmi'* of Tirmidhī. Walī Allāh adds that "these books are famous and known and it is possible to master them in the shortest time."[199]

So far, Walī Allāh's definition of his alternative hypothetical standard does not override sectarian tensions but simply adds another school based primarily on hadith. As we have seen above, however, Walī Allāh's peculiar method of using the above works of hadith does not assign exclusive authority to professional traditionalists. Elsewhere, Walī Allāh provides additional clarification of what is entailed in his new supraschool. In a series of revelatory experiences (*kashf*, *fayḍ*) documented in his *Fuyūḍ al-Ḥaramayn*, Walī Allāh relates how he became aware of the true meaning of what God has destined him to do; in one of his visions, the Prophet Muhammad tells him that God wishes to "bring about a kind of unity of the blessed community of Muslims through you. So beware the allegation that a truthful person does not become truthful unless a thousand friends accuse him of heresy. Beware also not to contend with people over the applied law, for then you would be contradicting the intention of the Truth [*al-Ḥaqq*, that is, God]."[200]

Clearly then, hadith occupies a privileged position in Walī Allāh's *al-jādda al-qawīma*, but the professional group of hadith scholars does not. Walī Allāh reconciles these two seemingly irreconcilable concepts as he describes the revelatory experience where he is made aware of an ideal method (*kushifa lī inmūdhajan*) through which the Sunna and Ḥanafī law can be fused together. This, Walī Allāh says, can be done by choosing from the views of one of the three main authorities of the Ḥanafī school (Abū Ḥanīfa, Abū Yūsuf, or Muhammad) the opinion that would allow him to stay within the bounds of the wording of the Sunna. Walī Allāh adds that this method enables him to avoid having to resort to far-fetched interpretations, assert that various traditions are in opposition, or reject a sound hadith on the basis of the opinion of an imam of the Ḥanafī school.[201]

Lest he be misunderstood, Walī Allāh stresses that the other Sunni schools of law enjoy equal theoretical status in his prescribed system. In one of his visions he observes the Prophet "to see to which legal school he is inclined so that I could follow it and adhere to it. It turned out that all schools are the same to him. The science of applied law in its current state does not constitute part of the habits of his noble spirit. Rather, what is subsumed in the essence of his spirit is the principle underlying the science of applied law: the concern of the Truth for the souls of humans and their welfare from the perspective of their actions and manners."[202]

The observation that the Prophet is equally disinterested in all four schools of law does not lead Walī Allāh to ignore these schools. On the contrary, he asserts that, although by nature he is "repulsed by imitation and is utterly offended by it," he was instructed (in one of his visions) to adhere to the four schools and to the extent possible not diverge from them, and to worship by following one of the schools of law although imitation was against his natural disposition.[203] In fact, despite his sustained promotion of *ijtihād*, Walī Allāh suggests that it is obligatory to recognize the authority of the four schools. He argues that

> the law [sharia] cannot be known except through transmission and inference. Transmission is not regulated unless each generation receives [traditions] from the preceding one through direct contact. Inference requires knowledge of the schools of the early generations to avoid opposing all of them and violating their consensus. Thus one builds on them [the schools] and is aided in this process by all of those who came before one. This is because all technical skills—such as morphology, grammar, medicine, poetry, smithery, carpentry, and goldsmithery—can only be acquired through the apprenticeship under the masters of these professions. Any other arrangement is rare and does not usually occur, even though it is logically possible.[204]

Walī Allāh goes on to assert that the four schools of law serve as reservoirs of the earlier historical experience of Muslims, and that reliance on them is indispensable for obtaining religious knowledge. Walī Allāh considers himself to be functioning within the bounds of the schools of law rather than delineating the criteria that ought to be used for judging these schools.[205] He maintains that the primary principle he uses to gauge his own contributions is that under no condition should his new ideas cause disagreement or strife.[206] In fact, as one who "follows the path of the prophets and carries their burdens," he envisions his own mission not in terms of creating a new system of thought but as a social reformer who "sympathizes with people by teaching and guiding them; who seeks their contentment, and brings about their welfare."[207]

The code of conduct of the ideal religious leader, whom Walī Allāh calls *ʿālim rabbānī*, a divine (spiritual) scholar, sums up his own intellectual as well as practical program.[208] Such a scholar, with whom Walī Allāh obviously identifies, must refrain from making preferences between the opinions of the various legal schools. Instead, he should consider all of them to be equally legitimate and should follow only opinions that are in harmony with the explicit and known Sunna. He should exhibit a similar attitude toward the various Sufi orders. He should avoid the company of ignorant Sufis, ascetic and austere jurists, literalist traditionalists, and eccentric theologians. Instead, he should be a scholar and Sufi who upholds the traditions of the Prophet and his Companions. The list goes on but always reaffirms the authority of the Sunna and hadith, not in opposition to the other fields of Islamic knowledge but in harmony with them.

Given the difficulties facing the Muslims of India during his lifetime, one would expect a more pessimistic tone in the work of Walī Allāh. On the contrary, however, he was fundamentally optimistic, rejecting notions of the estrangement of truth and the isolation of the virtuous. The political crisis of Walī Allāh's time did not lead him to view contemporary Muslims as enemies who fail to see the truth, and he never lost sight of his main objectives: to bring about the well-being of his fellow Muslims and to iron out intellectual differences that impede this well-being. Sectarian tendencies among followers of the schools of law (*tamadhhub*), and not the schools themselves (*madhāhib*), were the targets of Walī Allāh's sustained attacks. A combination of his actual sympathy with fellow Indian Ḥanafīs and intense aversion toward sectarian zeal led Walī Allāh to elaborate "an elegant method within the Ḥanafī school, which is the most appropriate of the known Sunni approaches."[209] This method involves subjecting the various Ḥanafī opinions to the criteria of hadith and choosing those that conform with it, while still remaining within the boundaries of the school. Walī Allāh asserts, much to the satisfaction of his fellow Ḥanafīs, that "each and every one of these choices remains a Ḥanafī school [*wal-kull madhhab Ḥanafī*]." Thus, if an uncommon Ḥanafī opinion is corroborated by hadith, Walī Allāh chooses it over a standard Ḥanafī opinion lacking such corroboration. This way he remains within the boundaries of both the school and the Sunna. It should be noted here that this is a systematic and deliberate strategy that balances two tendencies in the thought of Walī Allāh: on the one hand, his appeal to the intellectual power of hadith as a means for narrowing the gap among schools of law, as a mutually recognized medium of communication between these schools, and as the prerequisite for the continuing exercise of *ijtihād*; and, on the other hand, his concern for the interests of the people who, in the case of India, are followers of the Ḥanafī school.

To sum up, Walī Allāh identifies a supraschool that he calls *al-jādda al-qawīma*, the upright path or road. He articulates its principles in the various idioms of jurists, traditionalists, theologians, Sufis, politicians, and the general populace. In a sense, his purpose all along is to give credibility to this new principle and to provide fresh outlines of the various schools (especially the Ḥanafī) in its light. He steers away from any attempt to undermine the Ḥanafī school among Indians. In the interest of unity, however, he makes sure to re-present the school in a nonexclusive way, which he achieves by asserting the authority of hadith—canonized in the *Muwaṭṭaʾ* and the five *ṣaḥīḥ* compilations—and by promoting Ḥanafī opinions that conform with these canonical works of hadith. To be sure, Walī Allāh posed significant challenges to the intellectual autonomy of Ḥanafī authorities. At the same time, however, his arguments provided stronger and more flexible justifications for the continued upholding of these authorities.

The role of hadith in mitigating differences among Muslims is extensively discussed in the work of Muḥammad Bin ʿAlī al-Sanūsī. Reproducing many of the arguments of al-Shawkānī, al-Sanūsī also argues against *taqlīd* without questioning the scholarly excellence of the imams of the imitated schools, or the authoritative texts of Islam. Al-Sanūsī explicitly states that the ultimate authority is vested in the texts of the Qurʾān and the hadith, and it is the obligation of every Muslim to try to extract the scriptural commands from these sources.[210] Hadith hence becomes the best of all disciplines and the real basis of jurisprudence:[211] in the event that a tradition opposes the ruling of a school, one should always side with the tradition,[212] and neither *ijtihād* nor legal analogy are valid when there is a text.[213] In fact, al-Sanūsī argues, every generation should revisit the rulings of earlier legal schools and evaluate these rulings against the known bodies of hadith literature.[214] The imams of the four schools (Abū Ḥanīfa, Mālik, Shāfiʿī, and Ibn Ḥanbal) are also redeemed in al-Sanūsī's analysis. It is prohibited to claim that one of the recognized imams would intentionally contradict a sound tradition, or that he would make lawful what God prohibited and prohibit what God made lawful.[215] According to al-Sanūsī, it is impossible for anyone to know the whole of the hadith corpus;[216] when contradicting a hadith the imam must have the excuse of not knowing it, rejecting it on the basis of its weakness, or the like.[217] Whatever the reason, however, an error that results from an imam's *ijtihād* is not a sin and is deserving of God's reward.[218] Al-Sanūsī goes as far as to state that imams are not infallible, and it is not unthinkable that they may sin,[219] but even if they do, we should wish them well on account of all the good work they have done.[220] It is clear, therefore, that al-Sanūsī had no argument with the ranking of the great masters of the law; his objection was to anyone who defers to their authority when there is a contradiction between their legal opinions and hadith.

The questions of the relationship between different fields of knowledge and their relative authority were at the heart of the scholarship of eighteenth-century reformers. Ultimately, Walī Allāh's main objective was to open up the canon by asserting that it is far larger than what is traditionally recognized among Indian Ḥanafīs. The *Muwaṭṭa'* of Mālik, a veritable outsider text, was the symbolic key through which Walī Allāh flung open the doors of Islamic learning in India. In contrast, the primary focus of al-Ṣanʿānī, al-Shawkānī, and al-Sanūsī was on procedures rather than antecedent texts. Yet all of these scholars, each in his peculiar way, undermined received notions of authority and clearly argued that all feasible jurisprudential activities are by necessity exercises that pertain to history not to eternal truth. For the Yemenis, the transfer of the subject of examination from the unit of *khabar* (the content of a report) to the process of *ikhbār* (the process of reporting) deemphasized established doctrine, as contained in the actual contents of the transmitted hadiths, and defined authoritativeness in reference to tools and mechanism of transmission.[221] And since the process of transmission is fluid and human, this focus on procedure meant that, within the realm of logical possibility, the only way to discriminate between traditions is through *isnād* (chains of transmission). This, in turn, meant that the knowledge derivable from hadith is never certain, though it is binding as a basis of action.

A stark example of the primacy of formal considerations over those of content is al-Shawkānī's *Al-Fawā'id al-Majmūʿa fī al-Aḥādīth al-Mawḍūʿa*.[222] This book provides an exhaustive list of fabricated traditions, 1,279 in total, that appear in various standard and commonly used books of hadith. The purpose of this exercise, al-Shawkānī maintains, is to "alert those who have insufficient knowledge of the science of Sunna to what has been falsely attributed to the Prophet so that they can avoid it."[223] He adds that many jurists and authors in other specialized fields of study such as *zuhd* (asceticism) use fabricated traditions without being aware of it. He further explains that the fact a hadith is *bāṭil* (invalid) or *mawḍū'* (fabricated) does not mean that its reporter intentionally lied, nor does it rule out the possibility that the fabricated tradition is in agreement with other authentic and sound traditions. In fact, throughout his book, al-Shawkānī asserts that the contents of various sound traditions do not need to be supported with the "hadiths of liars." Moreover, "the hadiths of fabricators, even if they are extremely numerous, do not corroborate each other, and do not deserve the title of worthy [*ḥasan*]."[224] Conversely, "if it is not possible to reconcile [seemingly contradictory traditions], it does not become lawful for anyone to assert that one of these is fabricated. The most one can do is to prefer the stronger one, which in itself does not make [the less preferred one] fabricated."[225] Authenticity, therefore, is determined mainly on the basis of the chains of transmission (*isnād*s) of the traditions in question, and not on the basis of the contents of these traditions.

In the writings of eighteenth-century reformers, *isnād* acquired multiple meanings and implications. In its original understanding, *isnād* meant providing chains of transmission for various hadiths attributed to the Prophet Muhammad, in order to verify their soundness and authenticity of attribution. Long before the eighteenth century, however, a number of books, of varying degrees of authenticity, were recognized as a canon of hadith and were used by scholars of all fields and periods, including the reformers of the eighteenth century, as undisputed and authoritative reference books. In other words, the *isnād*s provided up until the compilations of these books were now canonized and thus were in no further need of authentication.[226] In a sense, authority traditionally invested in individuals was now transferred to books. Such, for example, is the import of al-Ṣanʿānī's argument:

> God made reading, copying, studying and transmitting hadith the sustenance and pleasure of the imams of hadith, and endowed them with amazing memories. . . . God the Exalted preserved the Sunna by means of them. . . . They memorized the words of hadith as they would the Qurʾān, and they learned every single word of it with accuracy and certainty. They also composed useful compendiums, and encyclopedic authenticated collections. They then labored over the conditions of the transmitters, their traits, journeys, birth, places of residence, and deaths, to the point that one who knows their biographies and conditions would be similar to one who has seen them and mingled with them. In fact, he would be more knowledgeable of their conditions than a contemporary of theirs who had come across and seen them, because some of their conditions could have remained hidden to him. As for one who reads their biographies and who receives their accounts from trustworthy authorities, he will find that these authorities have compiled their whereabouts, and written about the specifics of their traditions (that is, the traditions they transmitted), their

> journeys, and their wakefulness and sleep. They track down their conditions from anyone who knew them, whether or not they agree with them. Thus, one who reads their biographies would have at his disposal information that is not at the disposal of one who sees them, and only an unfair person would deny this fact.[227]

The actual, physical books of hadith no longer need verification through oral testimony, and their authority is no longer called into question.[228] These books, according to al-Ṣanʿānī's argument, can provide more reliable and more accessible information than direct transmission. In fact, all eighteenth-century reformers state that, with the widespread availability of authoritative books, memorization is no longer a requirement for *ijtihād*.[229] Al-Shawkānī, for example, outlines the amount of learning, in the various fields of linguistic and religious studies, that is sufficient for a person who seeks to practice *ijtihād*. He then maintains that

> if one finds differences in the interpretations of the earlier generations which one becomes aware of through reading, then [recall that] the Qur'ān is in Arabic, and the reference is the language of the Arabs, such that what is closer to it is more correct than what is far from it. . . . As for what [knowledge] is required to determine whether a hadith is sound or not . . . we say: if a leading scholar among the scholars of hadith who is renowned for his memorization, probity, and sound knowledge states that he only included in his book sound [traditions], and in the absence of [a living scholar] who has practiced this matter thoroughly—as in the case of the authors of the two *Ṣaḥīḥ*s, and after them the *Ṣaḥīḥ*s of Ibn Ḥibbān, Ibn Khuzayma, and the like—then this statement [by the compiler of the book of hadith] authorizes [the reader of this book] to act in accordance with what is in it, and makes it obligatory to give priority to it over imitation. This is not considered imitation because it is action on the basis of the report of a trustworthy person, whereas imitation is action in accordance to his opinion. This distinction [between *taqlīd* and *ittibāʿ*, *ʿamal bil-riwāya* and *ʿamal bil-dalīl*] is more obvious than the sun, even if it may be confusing to many people.[230]

Al-Shawkānī thus clearly refers to the use of books and to critical knowledge acquired through reading and not through oral transmission. In a way, according to al-Shawkānī, users of books are more equipped to know the truth, to the extent the truth is knowable, than those who rely on memory[231] and orality.[232] And yet, whereas it was no longer practiced in most other fields of traditional Islamic scholarship,[233] *isnād* continued to dominate the field of hadith both in the way it was practiced and in the theoretical writings about it.

Isnād was also transformed into a genre in its own right wherein various scholars documented their own educational pedigrees; in practice, this amounted to a listing of the chains of people who studied and taught books in various disciplines, sometimes starting with the authors of these books and all the way to the scholar who lists the study and teaching of these books among his own scholarly credentials.[234] Al-Shawkānī wrote one such book, *Itḥāf al-Akābir bi-Isnād al-Dafātir*, where he lists over 500 books and the various chains through which the teaching of these books reached him. The largest number of these books is in the field of hadith, but they also include numerous books in various other disciplines such as law, Qur'ānic exegesis, the language sciences, and Sufism. In the particular field of hadith, al-Shawkānī reports his transmission of almost all the classical works of hadith through multiple channels. These channels often go through al-Shawkānī's teacher, Shaykh ʿAbd al-Qādir Ibn Aḥmad, and the main scholars who, in the generation before al-Shawkānī, taught hadith in Mecca and Medina, including Muḥammad Ḥayāt al-Sindī, al-Baṣrī, al-Bābulī, and Ibrāhīm al-Kurdī.[235]

Despite its similarity to traditional biographical works on *isnād*, al-Shawkānī's *Itḥāf* is not reducible to a simple attempt to invoke the authority of some original texts in order to authenticate their current transmissions. Al-Shawkānī's extensive writings and critical commentaries indicate that he does not recognize the unquestioned authority of most of the texts he comments on. Rather than clarify the "crowded" meanings of basic authoritative texts, the declared purpose of most of al-Shawkānī's commentaries is to criticize these texts and delineate their errors and weaknesses.[236] In fact, in al-Shawkānī's scheme of things, aside from the Qur'ān and the Sunna, the only authority is that of interpretation, and no original text enjoys such authority. And this authority that al-Shawkānī invests in current interpretations is not predicated on the recovery of the "author's voice, and thus his presence and his truth . . . through the technique of recitation" or through *isnād*.[237] Rather, recitation and *isnād* are simply pedagogical and instructional tools that illustrate the scholarly credentials of the scholar and ensure his adherence to proper procedures.

This function of *isnād* can be inferred not only from al-Shawkānī's elaborate discussion of his notions of authority but also from his discussions of the meaning of *isnād*. In the introduction to his *Itḥāf al-Akābir*, al-Shawkānī articulates his conception of the term's meaning and significance.[238] God, al-Shawkānī maintains, has preserved sharia through the instrument of the great imams, who have pulled together its scattered details (*qayyadū shawāridahā*). Al-Shawkānī adds that the imams "pinned down" the details of sharia by means of the chains of transmission; "thus guidance was attained by means of continuous reporting [*ittiṣāl al-riwāya*]," and the uninterrupted *isnād*s fortified the various sciences and served as emblems of knowledge.[239] Therefore, according to al-Shawkānī, *isnād* guarantees the authentic delineation and transmission of knowledge that, otherwise, would be too scattered and random. *Isnād* provides a reliable method to circumscribe a body of knowledge that, on the grounds of content alone, admits no finality or certitude. Procedures, in contrast, establish the authority of the never-ending end of the chain, rather than specific texts of origin. *Isnād* also enables Muslims of all times to act as if they "lived in the time of the Prophet and listened directly to his discourse," just as the Companions did.[240] Again, rather than idealizing the Companions or the knowledge attributed to them, al-Shawkānī aims to undermine both. Thus the gist of this enterprise is to allow a Muslim to bypass all intermediary authorities and exercise *ijtihād* "as if no scholar has preceded him and no *mujtahid* takes precedence over him."[241] In short, *isnād* eliminates the advantage that the Companions had over the living community of Muslims on account of their temporal proximity to the Prophet. It underscores the authority of the present and recasts the role of the living community of Muslims not just as receiver of perennial knowledge inscribed in fixed, sacred texts but as processor and producer of this very knowledge.

The discourse of the regional schools of hadith scholarship was not simply a practical tool for ordering society and enforcing moral conformity among Muslims. Rather, the discussions of hadith were primarily theoretical and aimed, above all, at questioning and restructuring inherited standards of intellectual authority. A similar questioning of past authority and assertion of the authority of the present was carried out in the field of the principles of jurisprudence, to which we now turn.

Conclusion

The Limits of the Sacred

As we have seen throughout this book, eighteenth-century discussions of the theory of *ijtihād* relied on the standard taxonomies elaborated in classical Islamic writings on this subject. The novelty in these discussions, however, was in the widening of the scope of *ijtihād*, and in the deliberate and systematic effort to make its tools accessible to wider segments or even a majority of Muslims. In effect, therefore, the significance of eighteenth-century *ijtihād* is in deploying it to loosen the disciplinary hold of authoritative intellectual and cultural traditions and institutions. The not-so-hidden agenda of this deployment was to subvert traditional structures of intellectual authority by opening up ordered traditions to multiplicity.[1] One of the main tools for reviving *ijtihād* was hadith, and the primary discipline for this novel deployment of hadith was the discipline of *uṣūl al-ḥadīth* or *ʿilm muṣṭalaḥ al-ḥadīth* (the theory of hadith, or the science of the conventions of hadith). The other primary field in which notions of intellectual authority were revisited and radically challenged was *uṣūl al-fiqh* (the principles of jurisprudence or legal theory).

In the eighteenth century, the critical interventions of the law were not primarily in the form of fatwas directed against the excesses of the political establishment or the religious elites connected to it. Such interventions existed, but contrary to what might be expected, protesting extralegal transgressions by authorities did not lead to a proliferation of fatwa writings either to justify or criticize the rulers. Rather, the primary sites for questioning authority were the disciplines of *uṣūl*. Contrary to common assertions in traditional Orientalist scholarship, the disciplines of *uṣūl* were sites of original and critical reflection and not merely mechanisms to retroactively justify and codify existing practices. *Uṣūl*, the disciplines in which knowledge was classified and categorized, and in which definitive interpretive practices were outlined and standardized, were themselves the subjects of scrutiny, and were also used to subvert traditional orders of intellectual authority. As such, *uṣūl* were not just means of the institutional dispersion of intellectual authority, or for prescribing rules and procedures for disciplining fields of knowledge, but were also subversive disciplines through which normative disciplinary authority was questioned and radically undermined.

The ability to use legal theory as a platform for dissent was facilitated by the consistent historicization of legal thought. Whether through a deliberate and conscious reconfiguring of choice juristic symbols and idioms, or through an academic attempt to order and classify the cumulative outcomes of a gradually evolving legal tradition, the legal writings of eighteenth-century reformers were also historical writings that reflected on the historical contexts in which the law was articulated[2] and commented on the social and political crises of their times. As such, the legal writings of eighteenth-century reformers were sites in which traditional notions of authority were assessed, contested, and restructured. And while in normal times, legal texts, and especially legal theory, reflect normalized practices, at times of perceived crisis, legal discourse echoes broader social and juristic concerns that are addressed through processes of correction, interpretation, or reconfirmation.[3]

As we have seen, the technicalities of *ijtihād* were exhaustively discussed, but this technical discussion was neither new nor the ultimate purpose of the treatment of this topic. Rather, it was the very idea or theory of *ijtihād*, and the new conceptualization of notions of authority based on it, that was the objective of the extensive writings on *ijtihād*.

The Dubious Authority of Texts and *Mujtahid*s

One of the salient characteristics of Islamic historiography, and perhaps one of its main contributions to the science of history writing, is chains of transmission. The reporters of texts are not just assumed but foregrounded in recognition that all accounts are mediated and that there is no such thing as an autonomous unmediated text. The practice of listing the chain of reporters originally derived from the reporting of hadith, the sayings of the Prophet Muhammad. This scrutiny means that the authoritative power of a text is not granted unless the mediating agency of this text is scrutinized. Eighteenth-century scholars confronted the question of what social agencies are qualified to endow texts with authority.

In contrast to age-old reliance on *madhhab* manuals (*mutūn*),[4] a dominant trend in the eighteenth century was to compose long, multivolume compendiums[5] that provided exhaustive histories of diverse legal opinions. More important, despite occasional use and composition of abridged works, eighteenth-century writers underscored the inadequacy of *madhhab* manuals, rejected the reliance on texts that documented the final unjustified opinions of canonical scholars, and focused instead on writing exhaustive compilations and commentaries that presented the indicants (*ʿilal*, singular *ʿilla*) and the evidence on which such opinions are based. As such, these long works did not offer final judgments that must be imitated but outlined arguments or reasoning that would help every Muslim make an informed choice, and thereby exercise his or her own *ijtihād*.

A legal text, therefore, has no authority in itself or through the status attributed to it by adherents of *madhhabs*, and it only assumes authority through the agency of *ijtihād*.[6] For example, in *Adab al-Ṭalab* Muḥammad Ibn ʿAlī al-Shawkānī lists abridged and comprehensive texts that are useful for the exercise of *ijtihād*, but he insists that none of these texts carries exclusive authority, and that different regions have their own canons of useful texts. Clearly, al-Shawkānī does not endow any single, spiritless text in any field with ultimate authority,[7] and thinks of these texts as aids in the process of *ijtihād*, whether the *ijtihād* of the scholar or the commoner,[8] thereby investing authority in the understandings of Muslims (not as muftis but as responsible individuals endowed with rational faculties). To be sure, a mufti is by necessity a *mujtahid*,[9] and it is acceptable for someone who is not a *mujtahid* or *faqīh* to solicit fatwas and ask such a scholar about the indicants for a particular ruling. However, al-Shawkānī adds, accepting the opinion of the Prophet is a far cry from *taqlīd*, which is accepting an opinion without asking for its evidence.[10]

And just as texts have no ultimate authority in themselves, neither does the opinion that derives from the process of *ijtihād*, as opposed to the process itself. Al-Shawkānī maintains that *ijtihād* "has been defined as a jurist's exhaustion of his efforts to arrive at a presumptive ruling of Islamic law." Throughout his work, al-Shawkānī encourages this kind of undertaking and even considers it obligatory for many, though not all Muslims. However, al-Shawkānī asserts that this *ijtihād* is not an authority for any Muslim "who does not himself or herself arrive at the same presumptive ruling, or has not already exhausted his or her own efforts to do so." "An authoritative ruling," al-Shawkānī adds, "is not the speculation of some individuals for whom adherence to the law is obligatory."[11] According to this view, it is even forbidden to ascribe an unqualified authority to a *mujtahid* over fellow Muslims.[12] In other words, *ijtihād* does not confer authority on the *mujtahid* but imposes a responsibility to teach and guide. In fact, the insistence on the moral stature of the *mujtahid* is perhaps intended to compensate for depriving him or her of institutionalized religious authority.[13]

Having denied the authority of living *mujtahids* and the legal manuals they produce, the only authority left, according to al-Shawkānī, is that of the Qurʾān and the authentic hadith books compiled by scholars of proven rectitude and probity. The authority of these hadith compilers rests on their reliability as witnesses to the correctness of the reports they transmit, and the reliability of the transmitters of these reports, and does not rely on their legal judgments or opinions. Their only task is to provide generations of Muslims with the raw building blocks of the law, and it is up to every Muslim to decide how these building blocks come together in the formulation of a legal position. In contrast, according to al-Shawkānī, bestowing authority on the legal opinions of jurists may result in accepting views based on "fabricated traditions falsely attributed to the Messenger of God, peace be upon him, and then deriving from them [legal] positions that are not part of the Divine Law, thereby attributing to God things He did not say, and imposing on His worshippers duties He did not require." A person who argues that legal scholars should be imitated, al-Shawkānī adds, bears responsibility for himself and for other Muslims who adhere to invalid legal positions, and such a person cannot excuse himself by claiming to exercise *ijtihād* for which he would be doubly rewarded if he hits the mark, and singly rewarded if he does not.[14] Rather, he is a "reckless transgressor and forger of the Divine Law because he relies on those who do not know the purified Divine Law, transmit it on their own authority, and ignore its recognized transmitters."[15]

The Politics of *Ijtihād*

In addition to its implications for the authority of texts and legal scholars, al-Shawkānī's theory of *ijtihād*, or rather his corollary rejection of *taqlīd*, directly impinges on political authority. Al-Shawkānī responds to one more argument in support of the *taqlīd* of *mujtahid*s, namely, the Qur'ānic injunction to obey the people in charge (*ūlī al-amr*). He maintains that even if this reference includes scholars, obeying them entails forsaking *taqlīd* because they commanded people not to imitate them. Alternatively, if such scholars demand that Muslims imitate them, then they would be asking them to obey humans and disobey God. However, al-Shawkānī adds, this injunction is applicable to the obligation of obeying political leaders in worldly matters connected to the maintenance of communal order in times of war, and the preservation of public order that society needs for its survival. "It is not unlikely," al-Shawkānī adds, "that what is intended by the command to obey is simply obedience in such *matters that are not part of the Divine Law* . . . as long as the commands of these [worldly authorities] do not entail disobeying God, and as long as the one commanded does not observe an outward disbelief by these [worldly authorities]. . . . *The Book of God and the Sunna of His Messenger suffice for the matters that are part of the pure religious law.*"[16] Al-Shawkānī thus suggests that, at its roots, political jurisprudence is a public matter relegated to human discretion (whether in jurisdiction or the execution of policies and regulations), and the "human" law that derives from it is outside the realm of the sacred.[17]

Like al-Shawkānī, Muḥammad Bin ʿAlī al-Sanūsī refers to the opinion that makes it obligatory for a knowledgeable non*mujtahid* to imitate, because one who has partial or defective knowledge should give it up and submit to the higher judgment of the *mujtahid*. He maintains that there are three false assumptions behind this erroneous view, namely that: *ijtihād* is not divisible, that the legal signification of a text is a matter that is subject to *ijtihād*, and that one has to search for and rule out contradictory indicants before deriving a ruling from a text.[18] To be sure, al-Sanūsī adds, there are various reasons that explain the failure of individuals to act in conformity with the directives of hadith (*tark al-ʿamal bi-l-ḥadīth*). One such reason is ignorance of its existence, which is a legitimate excuse. However, someone who knows the existence of a valid hadith and chooses to act on the basis of an opposing legal ruling would be mistaken and possibly a sinner.[19] A third category of neglect is due to the desire to postpone acting in conformity with hadith until there is conclusive evidence that there is no other abrogating hadith or opposing consensus. Al-Sanūsī concedes that there is disagreement over this matter, although his own preference is to act on the basis of hadith unless there is valid contradictory evidence for vacating it.[20] In all cases, however, al-Sanūsī maintains that the real motivation behind the denial of the continuing possibility of *ijtihād* is to monopolize professional appointments and to exclude people who do not adhere to the corporate authority of one of the four law schools from issuing rulings and fatwas.[21] *Taqlīd*, al-Sanūsī adds, renders void the benefit of the intellect, and "it is abhorrent for one who is given a candle to light up his way to put it off and walk in the dark."[22]

Eighteenth-century thinkers used every opportunity to reflect on theoretical questions regarding the derivation of the law, the authoritativeness or validity of various mechanisms used for this derivation, the historical roots of different views, and their social and political implications. Compilations of hadith and compendiums of applied law are full of unrelenting discussions of such theoretical questions. And at the heart of all of these discussions is the insistence on the primacy of the authority of textual sources, and the connected argument that these sources are in fact enablers of individual *ijtihād*, whether for all Muslims (as per Muḥammad Ibn Ismāʿīl al-Ṣanʿānī, al-Shawkānī, and al-Sanūsī) or for larger segments of the educated classes (as per Shāh Walī Allāh al-Dihlawī).

Uṣūl as an Interpretive Genre

In the eighteenth century, scholarly activity was pervasive and vigorously encouraged and enabled. But while extolling intellectual reflection and engagement, eighteenth-century scholars also insisted on the academic nature of all intellectual production: that there is no certainty in the law and no absolute certainty in knowledge generated through the rational faculties of human beings. Perhaps the most comprehensive articulation of this position is al-Shawkānī's argument that not only are the disciplines of *furūʿ* (branches of the law or applied jurisprudence) uncertain, but so is the discipline of *uṣūl al-fiqh* (principles of jurisprudence or legal theory).

Uṣūl al-fiqh is a discipline that does not set out to justify the rulings and practices of a particular school of law but simply elaborates rules and techniques for the law's derivation and sets norms for proper juristic practices. At least in theory, the discipline is not bound to particular legal schools or methodologies and is supposed to regulate the process of derivation of applied law in conformity with the discipline's generalized linguistic and hermeneutical rules.[23]

In fact, even in Twelver Imami Shiism, works on *uṣūl al-fiqh* bore great resemblance to the works produced by Sunni scholars, so much so that Akhbārīs accused the Uṣūlīs[24] of basing their work on Sunni *uṣūl* sources.[25] This is not because Shiʿi scholars of *uṣūl* were somehow less Shiʿi, or because they were any less or more sectarian than their Sunni counterparts,[26] but simply because the discipline of *uṣūl* was not organized along *madhhab* lines or based on *madhhab* principles. Its articulated rules and principles were mostly hermeneutical and could therefore be used by any qualified *mujtahid* without the need to obtain the approval or sanction of the *madhhab*.

This nonsectarian character of *uṣūl* led many traditional as well as modern scholars of Islamic law to argue that, unlike applied law, which admits multiple interpretations, the rules of *uṣūl al-fiqh* are certain and not subject to interpretation. However, the eighteenth century's persistent tendency to historicize knowledge culminated in a historical understanding of the discipline of *uṣūl*. It argued that the field of *uṣūl al-fiqh* is presumptive, that there is no certainty in the *uṣūl* principles, just as there is no certainty in the branches of the law (*furūʿ*), and that it is an *ijtihādī* discipline that admits multiple interpretations.

Al-Shawkānī expresses this view in the opening of his work on *uṣūl al fiqh*, *Irshād al-Fuḥūl ilā Taḥqīq al-Ḥaqq min ʿIlm al-Uṣūl*. The rules of this discipline, al-Shawkānī maintains, "are accepted on face value, such that if someone cites so much as a word from the writings on *uṣūl*, his rivals, no matter how erudite, would submit to him thinking that the questions of this discipline are rules founded on indisputable truths and based on rational and transmitted evidence that cannot not be refuted by even the most learned scholars." As a result, al-Shawkānī adds, many who think they are following conclusive transmitted evidence by applying the principles of *uṣūl* are in fact following mere opinion. Hence the purpose of composing this book is "to distinguish between its strong and weak arguments and to outline the parts of it that are reliable and those parts which are not fit for use as reference." This is especially needed because many who resort to it slip into *taqlīd* without knowing it, and "a majority of those who adhere to [textual] indicants inadvertently end up following mere opinion because of it."[27]

Al-Shawkānī accounts in great detail for the standard views of the discipline of *uṣūl al-fiqh*, and as in many of his other works, he provides a thorough survey of these manifold views and their historical contexts. All the subjects of this art, al-Shawkānī maintains, boil down to "the verification of indicants for rulings [*ithbāt al-adilla lil-aḥkām*] and the confirmation of rulings by indicants [*thubūt al-aḥkām bil-adilla*]."[28] *Uṣūl*, he adds, are derived from three fields: speculative theology (*ʿilm al-kalām*), because legal indicants are contingent on knowledge of the Creator, and the truth of the Messenger; the Arabic language, because understanding of the Book and the Sunna are dependent on it; and the conceptualization of legal rulings (*al-aḥkām al-sharʿiyya min ḥayth taṣawwurihā*), because the aim is to confirm or deny them.[29] Al-Shawkānī argues against the common view among Uṣūlīs that language is created by God, noting that the Qurʾānic reference "And He taught Adam all the names" (Baqara 2:31) could very well be, as in all crafts, to God's inspiring humans, who then invent languages. As such, Arabic is invented by humans (*min waḍʿ al-nās*); however, Arabic is transmitted through *tawātur*,[30] and as such it is conventional (man-made) but known through transmission, which means that it cannot be independently understood through reason (*lā yastaqill al-ʿaql bi-idrākiha*), nor can it be confirmed through such mechanisms as analogy (*manʿ ithbāt al-lugha bil-qiyās*).[31]

As in all works on *uṣūl al-fiqh*, al-Shawkānī dedicates significant space to linguistic discussions, including of general and particular modes of speech (*khāṣ* and *ʿām*) and their legal implications. From a linguistic point of view, al-Shawkānī notes, discourse addressing one individual does not extend to others; however, external indicants provide evidence that the totality of Muslims are subject to the rulings of such discourse. Therefore, the general rule regarding speech is to generalize the import of a command (*taʿmīm*) unless there is valid evidence for its specification (*takhṣīṣ*).[32] Al-Shawkānī discusses over thirty topics related to specification and argues that, in contrast to abrogation (*naskh*), where a ruling is retracted, specification restricts the applicability of a ruling but does not cancel it altogether.[33] Al-Shawkānī also maintains that in some particular cases specification based on rational evidence is valid, although this does not imply that rational evidence is superior to religious indicants (*dalīl al-sharʿī*).[34] Furthermore, because the applicability of a general speech to its individual instances (*dalālat al-ʿām ʿalā afrādihi*) is not certain, specification on the basis of singularly transmitted reports (*āḥād*) is valid.[35]

Al-Shawkānī notes that some jurists argue that the choice of a Companion of the Prophet is a valid basis for specification, because an upright Companion (*ʿadl*) would not turn away from what he heard from the Prophet without evidence available to him that justifies such specification. Al-Shawkānī rejects this view because a Companion might base his specification of a general address on what he thinks is a valid indicant. However, the Companion's opinion of what constitutes valid evidence in a particular case is not binding for other Muslims. As such, specification based on the choice of a Companion or group of Companions is not valid unless all Companions agree to this specification, in which case *takhṣīṣ* would be based on consensus and not on unqualified opinion or choice.[36]

Despite his substantive discussions of the signification of language in *Irshād al-Fuḥūl*, al-Shawkānī seems to dedicate less space to this subject than do other writers on *uṣūl*. Al-Shawkānī's primary focus, both in his *uṣūl* work and almost in every other work in his extensive oeuvre, is on the larger question of what constitutes legal evidence (*dalīl sharʿī*), the authority of different types of indicants, and the principles that can effectively guide their use.[37] The invention of technical terms by scholars of *uṣūl* does not endow these terms with any special authority, and such terms simply refer to the meanings intended by their authors.[38] In fact, al-Shawkānī maintains, "some of what the scholars of principles [of jurisprudence] have written down in their books has nothing to do with any principles; rather, it is part of the science of speculation, which is far removed from the Divine Law or the other sciences that lead to it."[39] Such is "the claim of the scholars of principles [of jurisprudence] that only definitive evidence is acceptable in establishing the subject matter [*masāʾil*] of the discipline." This, according to al-Shawkānī, is disproved by practice and refuted by the very *masāʾil* of the discipline of *uṣūl*, which they themselves have written down.[40] Furthermore, to those who "disregard the clear Sunna on the allegation that it contradicts *uṣūl*," al-Shawkānī says, "These *uṣūl* have no [real] existence and are mere precepts that have not been validated by reports or corroborated by reason."[41]

The Sources of Sharia

Traditional Islamic sources, including works on legal theory, usually identify four sources for the derivation of law, in this order of authority: the Qurʾān, Sunna (traditions of the Prophet), *ijmāʿ* (consensus), and *qiyās* (analogy).[42] Al-Shawkānī recognizes only the first two, the Qurʾān and Sunna, as authoritative sources, and devotes much effort to questioning the authority of *ijmāʿ* and *qiyās*. The Qurʾān, al-Shawkānī says, has parts that are unequivocal (*muḥkam*), and others that are ambiguous (*mutashābih*). Al-Shawkānī adds that it is obligatory to act in accordance with the former, but while there is disagreement over the obligation to act in accordance with ambiguous verses, al-Shawkānī argues that it is not permissible to do so. This is not because ambiguous verses have no meaning but simply because the human understanding is limited and incapable of knowing God's intention. Exerting oneself to extract this meaning can only be interpretation based on pure opinion (*tafsīr kalām Allāh bi maḥḍ al-ra'y*), and inevitably attributing to God things that He did not say (*al-taqawwul ʿalā Allāh bimā lam yaqul*).[43]

While there is agreement that most references to the branches of religion admit interpretation (*ta'wīl*), there are three views regarding the admissibility of interpretation in *uṣūl* fields, such as religious doctrine (*ʿaqīda*), principles of religion (*uṣūl al-dīn*), and the attributes of the Creator (*ṣifāt al-Bārī*). The first view suspends all interpretation and, according to al-Shawkānī, leads to anthropomorphism. The second, which is al-Shawkānī's preference, admits the principle that certain verses are subject to *ta'wīl*, but steers a middle ground between literalist anthropomorphism and outright denial of God's attributes (*taʿṭīl*). The third allows unchecked *ta'wīl*. Al-Shawkānī blames three scholars for expanding the circle of *ta'wīl*: al-Ḍiyā' al-Dīn al-Juwaynī (d. 1085), Abū Ḥāmid al-Ghazālī (d. 1111), and Fakhr al-Dīn al-Rāzī (d. 1209), but he contends that all three eventually returned to the correct school of the *salaf*.[44]

Although al-Shawkānī's reflections on the Qur'ān were many,[45] the subject that occupied him most was hadith. Sunna, according to al-Shawkānī, is a second source of legislation and is similar to the Qur'ān in providing evidence for determining obligations and prohibition (*kal-Qur'ān fī taḥlīl al-ḥalāl wa taḥrīm al-ḥarām*). Al-Shawkānī insists, however, that hadith is an independent source in its own right, and that the alleged instruction by the Prophet that his sayings be accepted only if in agreement with the Qur'ān is fabricated by *zanādiqa* (atheists) and Khawārij. In other words, al-Shawkānī suggests that the scrutiny and validation of hadith is based on formal criteria and not on simple comparison with the Qur'ān.[46] An authentic "sound hadith," he contends, "is one whose chain of transmission is connected [all the way to the Prophet] through trustworthy [*ʿadl*] and accurate [*ḍābiṭ*] reporters, and which does not have an anomaly or discrediting defect [*shudhūdh, ʿilla qādiḥa*]." As such, an interrupted hadith, such as the *mursal ḥadīth*, is not sound and not authoritative.[47] Foremost among the criteria for authenticating reports are the qualities of the reporter; these are legal charge (*taklīf*);[48] Islam; probity (*ʿadāla*); accuracy (*ḍabṭ*);[49] and that the reporter is not known to forge either texts or chains of transmission (*allā yakūn al-rāwī mudallisan fī al-matn aw al-isnād*).[50] Al-Shawkānī defines *ʿadāla* as the adherence to the ethical conventions (or manners) of religious law (*ādāb al-sharʿ*); violating these *ādāb* in a way that casts doubt on a person's religion (*qadaḥ fī dīn*) implies that this person is not *ʿadl*. However, conventional habits of people (etiquette, *ʿādāt jāriya*), are not related to religious *ʿadāla* on which "the two great pillars . . . are based, namely, reporting and testimony [*al-riwāya wal-shahāda*]." So, if someone commits acts that contradict conventional dignity (*murūʿa ʿurfiyya*), that person would have relinquished his conventional *murūʿa*, but this does not necessitate relinquishing his religious dignity [*murūʾa sharʿiyya*].[51]

According to al-Shawkānī, the authentication of reports requires knowledge of the reporter's identity and conditions (*ḥāl*). This is because establishing the authenticity of a report requires knowledge of the reporter's *ʿadāla*.[52] Al-Shawkānī rejects the authority of an interrupted report (*mursal*) whose reporter is anonymous and of unknown probity, "even if the transmitter of this report says: 'I was told by a person of probity whom I consider trustworthy,'" but fails to mention the name of this source.[53] The rejection of *taʿdīl al-mubham*—the attribution of probity to an unknown person—as in saying "a trustworthy person told me [*ḥaddathanī al-ʿadl*]," is because what counts in hadith is the report of the reporter and not his judgment. In the case of an interrupted hadith (*mursal*), Muslims are asked to blindly accept a judgment about an unknown reporter in the chain of transmission of the hadith. Should this reporter be named, perhaps evidence would emerge for considering him unworthy of trust (*majrūḥ*). And, in all cases, each individual recipient of the report should accept or reject it only after weighing all available evidence, which, according to al-Shawkānī's logic, is nonexistent in the case of *mursal* traditions.[54] In effect, therefore, al-Shawkānī's reasoning reduces the legal burden on Muslims (whether obligations or prohibitions), whenever there is no compelling reason to add to this burden. Furthermore, al-Shawkānī reiterates his fundamental principle of investing the ultimate authority to accept traditions in each and every receiver of these traditions.

As for reporters of known identity, a sinner (*fāsiq*), according to al-Shawkānī, is not *ʿadl*, and therefore a sinner's report is not accepted. However, if this state of sin is not known with certainly, then "the likelihood of truthfulness is more probable [*dhann ṣidqihi rājaḥ*], and acting on the basis of such likelihood is obligatory [*al-ʿamal bi-hadha al-dhann wājib*]."[55] Put differently, when in doubt, one has to assume the best about Muslims, even if this relates to the critical responsibility of transmitting authoritative hadith. In fact, as we saw in chapter 5, al-Shawkānī argues in support of accepting the report of someone who, based on an interpretive judgment, is considered to be a sinner, or even an unbeliever (*fāsiq* or *kāfir al-taʾwīl*), except in cases where the report would promote and strengthen the reporter's deviant doctrine (*bidʿa*).[56]

Al-Shawkānī then clearly accepts the report of *fāsiq* and *kāfir al-taʾwīl* but does not accept the report of an unknown person. The rationale for the former is the obligation to assume the probity (*ʿadāla*) of Muslims unless there is a definite reason to deny it. In the latter case, the rationale is to refrain from imposing obligations and prohibitions on Muslims based on the reporting of anonymous individuals who do not satisfy the minimum requirement of *ʿadāla*; and despite the likelihood of truthfulness, a positive trait cannot be attributed to a person of unknown identity. In both cases, there is an assumption of an original (almost natural) state of integrity (truthfulness of individuals unless there is positive evidence to the contrary) and freedom from legal liability (unless there is positive evidence for imposing legal responsibilities).

Al-Shawkānī further expounds the criteria for assessing the credibility of reporters. The attribution of defect or of probity (*al-jāriḥ wal-muʿaddil*) is not necessarily self-evident, and what is considered to be evidence for either by some hadith critics may not be recognized by others, "especially in light of the differences of schools and sects." So, for example, an unsubstantiated assertion of lack of probity might be based on the fact that a reporter belongs to a different school or doctrine, and vice versa. To al-Shawkānī, however, the operational definition of *jarḥ* (*al-jarḥ al-maʿmūl bihi*) "is to describe [a reporter] of weakness of memory, carelessness [*tasāhul*] in narration, or recklessness in doing things that reflect disregard of religion." In contrast, the operational definition of *taʿdīl* (*al-taʿdīl al-maʿmūl bihi*) "is to describe [a reporter] of probing deep to verify the report [*al-taḥarrī fī al-riwāya*], preserving [through strong memory] [*ḥifẓ*] that which he narrates, and refraining from doing things that reflect disregard of religion."[57] Al-Shawkānī's point is that *jarḥ* and *taʿdīl* are subjects of *ijtihād* and should be based on formal evidence and not doctrinal affinity. Moreover, *jarḥ* overrides *taʿdīl* because the former cannot be based on exterior appearance (*dhāhir al-ḥāl*), whereas *taʿdīl* can be.[58]

To be sure, the reports of Companions are accepted without further probing into their conditions, but this is based on general textual evidence from the Qurʾān and Sunna and not an unqualified rational acceptance of their judgments or opinions. Perhaps, al-Shawkānī adds, the reasons for this acceptance is that the Companions are the transmitters of sharia (articulated by the Prophet), and if their reporting were to be questioned, then sharia would not have been passed beyond the time of the Prophet. As for the wars among them, "these are matters based on [their] *ijtihād*, and each *mujtahid* is correct, or rather, one is correct while the mistaken one is excused and rewarded [for exercising *ijtihād*] [*mukhṭiʾ maʾjūr*]." In fact, al-Shawkānī suggests that the only unqualified virtue that the Companions share is the virtue of companionship (*ṣuḥba*), which does not make them immune to faults, but neither does it deprive them "of the trait of companionship."[59]

What applies to the Companions in general also holds for the Companions who fought Imam ʿAlī. On several occasions, al-Shawkānī leaves no doubt that he thinks these Companions were in the wrong. However, he maintains that their persistence in adhering to their erroneous acts suggests that they did not engage in the wrongful fight against ʿAlī out of defiance of God's commands, or because they took His religion lightly (*jarāʾatan ʿalā Allāh wa tahāwunan bi dīnihi*). The honor of companionship is a grave matter, al-Shawkānī adds, and one would run a great risk in violating this honor. Despite their shortcomings, some of the people of Shām (Syria) are good Companions who wouldn't have fought ʿAlī had they not been afflicted by an ambiguity (*ʿaraḍat lahum shubuha*). And even so, they are still subsumed under the general heading of Companions, to whom the Qurʾān and Sunna attribute trustworthiness. Therefore, should a reporter say, "on the authority of one of the Companions" without naming him, the report is considered authoritative.[60]

Al-Shawkānī does not restrict the criterion of authenticity to the conditions of the reporters; he also includes assessment of the texts of the reports. Thus, he argues, a report (*khabar*) is rejected if (1) it is logically impossible (*in aḥālahu al-ʿaql rudda*); (2) it contradicts a definitive text (*naṣṣ maqṭūʿ bihi*) and it is impossible to reconcile the two texts; and (3) it opposes consensus according to those who are of the opinion that consensus constitutes valid evidence. As for definitive analogy (*qiyās qaṭʿī*), al-Shawkānī maintains that, if the two cannot be reconciled, a sound or good (*ṣaḥīḥ* or *ḥasan*) report supersedes any kind of *qiyās*.[61]

Of equal importance to al-Shawkānī is the delineation and rebuttal of arguments often used to undermine the authority of hadith reports. "Know that the actions of the majority of the community in contradiction to a report do not diminish the report's authority, because the opinion of the majority does not constitute valid evidence." Furthermore, in disagreement with most Ḥanafīs and some Mālikīs, al-Shawkānī argues, "The action of a reporter in contradiction of a report [he or she transmits] does not diminish the report's authority, because we are held accountable based on the reports that reach us and not based on the transmitter's understanding of or adherence to that report."[62] In fact, in contrast to standard works on *uṣūl al-fiqh*, al-Shawkānī frequently interrogates various juristic (*uṣūlī*) and legal (*fiqhī*) rules that, he argues, cannot and should not diminish or undermine the authority of *akhbār*, and his *Irshād al-Fuḥūl* often functions as a defense of hadith against *uṣūl*.

Authority resides not only in orally transmitted reports but also in the authentic compilations of hadith, which al-Shawkānī refers to as the registers of Islam (*dawāwīn al-Islām*).[63] In a chapter on recommended prayers,[64] al-Shawkānī notes that there is no fixed prescription for these prayers, but that the people of Yemen (meaning Zaydis) settled on a couple of specific formulas and treated them as if they were obligatory. The only explanation of this mistake, according to al-Shawkānī, is a lack of familiarity with the books of the Sunna; in fact, they are almost totally disregarded and treated as if they were the books of the enemies, although in reality their compilers are not rivals of any group but members of the Muslim community and compilers of the authoritative Sunna of the Prophet.[65]

As I noted in chapter 5, al-Shawkānī's views on the authority of hadith are tied to his advocacy of *ijtihād* for all Muslims and his adamant rejection of *taqlīd*. He defines *taqlīd* as acting on the basis of someone else's uncorroborated opinion (*al-ʿamal bi-qawl al-ghayr min ghayr ḥujja*). According to al-Shawkānī, this definition excludes acting based on the sayings of the Prophet; the action of a commoner based on the fatwa of a mufti; the action of a judge based on the testimony of trustworthy witnesses; or accepting the reports of reporters, which is different from accepting their opinions, and is nothing other than accepting the command of the one on whose authority the reports are transmitted, that is, the Messenger of God.[66]

Despite his recognition of the prominence of the Yemeni reformer al-Ḥasan Ibn Aḥmad al-Jalāl (d. 1673), al-Shawkānī cites, and harshly responds to, a view al-Jalāl expresses in his commentary on *Kitāb al-Azhār*.[67] With regard to probable rulings (*ẓanniyyāt*), al-Jalāl maintains that a commoner is only expected to observe "what he understands, which is nothing other than the necessities of the law [*ḍarūriyyāt al-sharʿ*]. Acting on the basis of necessities is not *taqlīd*, because necessity is the greatest indicant. This is why there is agreement that the actions of a commoner are sanctioned and only censured when they violate consensus." This statement, al-Shawkānī asserts, "is corrupt and invalid [*kalām sāqiṭ wa fāsid*]." This is because al-Jalāl's notion of understanding suggests an understanding of the benefit that derives from a ruling, which would imply that all unbelievers are absolved of any legal accountability because they do not concede or comprehend the benefits of sharia. In contrast, understanding to al-Shawkānī is simply the understanding of the word composition of God's discourse, which is accessible to every rational individual and is only impossible for an insane person or a small child.[68] Furthermore, al-Shawkānī adds, "necessities" are only a small fraction of the legal obligations delineated in the Book and the Sunna. As such, sinners and violators of God's law among the commoners would be thrilled to know of al-Jalāl's view and would use it to justify their violations. This is because most *sharʿī* obligations and prohibitions are established based on general injunctions, which are probable (*ẓannī*) and not definitive (*qaṭʿī*) or necessary. And since according to al-Jalāl, the commoners, who are the vast majority of Muslims, are not bound by these injunctions, this would lead to the suspension of sharia.[69]

Al-Shawkānī also criticizes al-Jalāl's opinion that *ʿadāla* and *ijtihād* are innate aptitudes, and that there is no way to know them except indirectly through their attendant signs. Al-Jalāl argues that the identification of these signs can only be known through *taqlīd*, thereby basing the confirmation of *ʿadāla* and *ijtihād* on *taqlīd*. Al-Shawkānī maintains that what al-Jalāl describes is not *taqlīd* but simply the acceptance of a report from someone who is in a position to identify this *ijtihādī* aptitude. As for the aptitude of probity, it is known to the perfect and imperfect alike, and what is considered in this regard are those actions and sayings that suggest it (or refraining from actions that contradict it); this too, al-Shawkānī adds, is based on accepting validated reports, not mere opinions.[70] Furthermore, presumably speaking of *ijtihād* in the sense of issuing fatwas for others, al-Shawkānī argues that *ijtihād* cannot be apportioned (*yatabaʿaḍ*), and one either has the aptitude (*malaka*) for *ijtihād* and is able to use it in all matters, or one lacks it and is not able to perform *ijtihād* in any matter; a person of the latter type would not trust himself because of his deficiencies, and others would not trust him for the same reason.[71] And by the same argument, a *mujtahid* within a *madhhab* is actually an imitator.[72]

Al-Shawkānī directs an equally harsh critique at Muḥammad Ibn Ismāʿīl al-Amīr al-Ṣanʿānī, who suggests that *taqlīd* is permissible for an unperceptive person with dull understanding (*balīd al-fahm*) and a thick mind (*jāmid al-fikra*) but not for someone who has the capacity for reflection and discernment. This distinction, al-Shawkānī affirms, is bleak and based on shabby evidence. The reason is that if a *muqallid* has enough brain to understand the speech of the person he is imitating, then by this same faculty he is able to understand the words of someone who is reporting to him the indicants and explaining their meaning. As such, this person has no need for *taqlīd*, since the opinion of a scholar is no more evident than the meanings of the *sharʿ*, and nothing justifies seeking the mere opinion of an individual when others can report the indicants of God's law.[73]

Al-Shawkānī spares no one in his quest to assert the authority of hadith and its function as the basis for *ijtihād*. For example, he notes that many followers of Abū Ḥanīfa, Mālik, Shāfiʿī, and Ibn Ḥanbal, the eponyms of the four Sunni schools of law (*madhhab*s), believe that *taqlīd* is obligatory for commoners. Moreover, these same followers admit that they themselves are imitators of the four eponyms of the *madhhab*s. However, since in matters of legal difference only the views of *mujtahid*s count, it follows that the views of these followers carry no authority. As such, the only remaining views that count are those of the majority of the remaining *mujtahid*s who prohibit *taqlīd*.[74]

A corollary of the above argument is that, in the absence of a valid stated indicant, a *mujtahid* has a license to follow his own opinion. However, al-Shawkānī adds, it is not permissible under any condition for anyone else to follow this opinion.[75] Al-Shawkānī makes a similar argument in the conclusion of a chapter listing different views on ritual purity and ablution. He maintains that all these digressions (*tafrīʿāt*) are based on mere opinion, and it is not lawful to base religious law on them. "A special license is given to a *mujtahid* to use these opinions for himself in the absence of indicants from the Book and the Sunna, but it is not permissible for others to act on the basis of his opinion."[76]

It follows, therefore, that al-Shawkānī does not adhere to or advocate any specific *madhhab*. He strongly rejects arguments to this effect by, among others, the Shāfiʿī al-Kiyā al-Harāsī (d. 1110) and the Mālikī Ibn al-Munīr (d. 1284).[77] He is equally critical of the argument in al-Mahdī's *Al-Azhār* that a *muqallid* is bound to a particular *madhhab* once he sets his mind to imitate and is forbidden from then on from changing *madhhab*s. Al-Shawkānī passionately responds saying that "altogether, these views are heretical blunders that dare to attribute to pure sharia what does not belong to it, or even what opposes it and contradicts what is in it."[78] As he often does in his writings, after stating his position and dismissing his opponents, al-Shawkānī elaborates by citing different views and perspectives. For example, the Shāfiʿī scholar al-Juwaynī (d. 1085) says that once someone acts based on a legal opinion, he cannot abandon it (for a more convenient one). The Ḥanafī scholar al-Qadūrī (d. 1037) says that a *muqallid* can switch *madhhab*s if he is convinced that the view of another scholar is stronger than that of his imam. The Shāfiʿī Ibn ʿAbd al-Salām (d. 1261) says that once the ruling is implemented, a *muqallid* cannot switch. The Shāfiʿī Ibn Daqīq al-ʿĪd (d. 1302) says that a *muqallid* can switch if his heart opens up to another *madhhab*, as long as he is not being manipulative (*lā lil-talāʿub*). The Ḥanafī then Shāfiʿī al-Āmidī (d. 1233) and Ibn al-Ḥājib (d. 1249) "claimed that there is agreement that [switching] is allowed before implementation but not after."[79] Assuming, for the sake of argument, that *taqlīd* is permissible, al-Shawkānī rejects all of these views for which there is no evidence, but he notes that "they are less corrupt and less removed from the truth than asserting the obligation of *taqlīd* and prohibiting the change of *madhhab* because of mere intention."[80]

One way of reading this seemingly gratuitous criticism of scholars from all schools is as al-Shawkānī's way of brandishing his independence from all schools, especially on this most central issue of *ijtihād*. The disproportionate criticism he levels at Zaydi scholars in *Al-Azhār* does not suggest that he is a Sunni, as many students of al-Shawkānī assert. In fact, he clarifies that the purpose of composing *Al-Sayl al-Jarrār* is not just to criticize and correct *Al-Azhār* but also to defend it against unfair critics.[81] In one instance, he offers a strong retroactive criticism of Imam Mālik in defense of a view in *Al-Azhār*.[82] His writings are also full of criticism of various consensus views of the four Sunni *madhhab*s based on his prioritization of the Sunna. Moreover, he argues, the imams of hadith did not adhere to a particular *madhhab*.[83] Clearly then, al-Shawkānī draws a sharp distinction between Sunnism and *Ahl al-Sunna*. And by divorcing it from the four *madhhab*s, he reclaims the Sunna as an autonomous source of the law, a source that is identifiable, verifiable, and publicly accessible to all Muslims irrespective of their school affiliation.

The Impossible Consensus

In traditional Islamic legal theory, *qiyās* (legal analogy) and *ijmāʿ* (consensus) are considered to be the main sources for the derivation of law after the Qurʾān and hadith. A pervasive tendency in eighteenth-century scholarship is the questioning and often outright rejection of these two principles of traditional Islamic legal theory.

Al-Shawkānī notes that the verse "You are the best community sent out to people, commanding what is known, and forbidding what is reprehensible" (Āl Imrān 3:110) is often invoked to make a case for the authority of the consensus of the Muslim community (or its *mujtahid*s). In response, he says that this verse "does not entail that their [the community's] opinion is a legal proof [*ḥujja sharʿiyya*] that becomes a binding religion for the whole community. Rather, what is meant is that they command what is known in this sharia and forbid what is reprehensible in it, but the indicant for something being known or reprehensible is the Book and the Sunna, not their consensus."[84]

Al-Shawkānī also argues that the consensus of a subgroup within the community, namely, the Companions of the Prophet, does not constitute valid evidence,[85] and the same is true of the consensus of the first four caliphs. The two hadiths, "Abide by my Sunna and the Sunna of the rightly guided caliphs" and "Follow those who come after me, Abū Bakr and ʿUmar," simply prove that these caliphs "are worthy of being followed, not that their opinions are binding evidence for other Muslims." Likewise, the consensus of the family of the Prophet (*ʿitra*) is not a *ḥujja* (binding proof), as the Imamis and Zaydis argue. The verse, "God only intends to remove impurity from you, O people of the house [of the Prophet], and cleanse you with intense purification" (33:33), refers either to the wives of the Prophet or to ʿAlī, Fāṭima, and Ḥusayn; and in all cases this is a reference to their copious honor and great virtue but not to the authority of their opinions.[86]

Al-Shawkānī systematically undermines the possibility and authority of *ijmāʿ* as he examines the conventional definition of the term. *Ijmāʿ* is defined as "the agreement of the *mujtahid*s of the community of Muhammad from a particular era [*ʿasr min al-aʿṣār*] after his death, on a specific matter." Agreement means concurrence expressed through "belief, utterance, or action." Limiting consensus to the *mujtahid*s excludes the agreement of commoners, because neither their agreement nor their disagreement is authoritative. The definition also rules out a consensus produced by the agreement of a subgroup of *mujtahid*s. Moreover, putting agreement in construct with the community of

Muhammad excludes previous communities. And specifying it to a particular era also rules out the stipulation of consensus of all Muslim *mujtahid*s of all eras until the Day of Judgment, which would mean that there is no consensus before the Day of Judgment, which makes consensus obsolete because it is not needed after that day. The reference to a particular era (*ʿaṣr*) is to the living scholars who have already attained the status of *mujtahid* at the time a particular question comes up. Those who are yet to become *mujtahid*s do not count, even if they were alive at the time of the question. And finally, the expression "on a specific matter" encompasses religious, rational, conventional, and linguistic matters. Some stipulate for the authoritativeness of consensus the passing away of the era of *mujtahid*s who have agreed on a particular matter, thereby adding the constraint of extinction to the definition of *ijmāʿ*. Others add the further constraint that it should not be preceded by strong disagreement. And others still stipulate the probity of those who agree, or that their numbers reach the level of *tawātur*.[87]

The above serves to illustrate the complexity inherent in a seemingly simple definition. After setting the tone for the following discussion, al-Shawkānī proceeds to question the conceptual possibility of consensus (*fī nafsihi*), presenting various arguments and counterarguments before he concludes, "Assuming that it is possible in itself, it would still be impossible to know it . . . for if by knowledge we mean the agreement of the community, then this does not obtain without knowing each member [of this community], which is certainly impossible. . . . Besides, some of those who count in consensus may be compelled to feign agreement and avoid revealing disagreement out of dissimulation or fear for oneself."[88] Al-Shawkānī rejects the argument that certain kinds of agreement are known by necessity, such as the agreement over the prophethood of Muhammad. Al-Shawkānī maintains that if by this is meant implicit as well as explicit agreement, then there is no way to ascertain this kind of knowledge, and in fact we know by necessity that it is impossible. If, however, what is meant is explicit agreement that is deduced from general reputation and abundant reporting (*shuhra* and *istifāḍa*), then this does not satisfy the above definition of consensus. For each particular question, one needs to know what each individual *mujtahid* believes, openly and privately, and verify that he or she has no reason to hide his or her true belief or to pretend to agree; in turn, this kind of knowledge must come from each individual *mujtahid*, and therefore requires familiarity with their whereabouts and conditions. Needless to say, al-Shawkānī contends, it is absurd to assume that a reporter of consensus is capable of knowing all the scholars of the world and their views, since this type of knowledge is unquestionably impossible; indeed, this is why Aḥmad Ibn Ḥanbal said, "One who claims that consensus is obligatory is a liar."[89]

Al-Shawkānī further argues that, even if consensus is logically possible, "it does not constitute a valid indicant (for the derivation of the law). This is because there is no textual indicant that proves its authoritativeness. . . . Moreover, it is not logically possible because of the expanse of the Muslim countries and the abundance of scholars . . . and the impossibility of exhaustively inferring the knowledge possessed by each of them." Again, al-Shawkānī notes that another impediment to knowing the opinions of all the scholars of the Muslim world is that many of them conceal their true views out of fear of the zealotry of imitators and partisans of schools.[90] Elsewhere al-Shawkānī argues against the concept of tacit consensus and asserts that "the silence of scholars who are truly worthy of the title is not significant, because most of them are intimidated by the might [literally, hit by the whip] of the common people to whom rulers and soldiers belong."[91]

Even in his discussion of a theoretical issue such as the authority or even logical possibility of consensus, al-Shawkānī invokes social issues, once again highlighting the intimate link between the theoretical and the mundane in his thought. Al-Shawkānī illustrates the problematic practices that are justified in the name of consensus by citing the example of laws promoted under the pretext of precedence, which is claimed to be a form of tacit consensus because it was not openly opposed by scholars. Al-Shawkānī reports that he had advised the imam (al-Manṣūr) to eliminate unjust practices that are in opposition to the definitive injunctions of the law, such as the customary tax (*maks*) levied by the rulers of Yemen and elsewhere. Initially, al-Manṣūr accepted al-Shawkānī's advice and sent instructions to this effect to his governors. Al-Shawkānī adds, however, that many scholars opposed his fatwa, claiming that the dominion cannot be maintained without such taxes, but also claiming that this is an age-old practice that is therefore sanctioned by tacit consensus. Under the influence of these counterviews, the imam thought that al-Shawkānī's fatwa is not in accordance with the divine law; he thus wavered and, as a result, the practice resumed.[92]

Al-Shawkānī delves further into the refutation of consensus using *uṣūlī* arguments. He maintains, along with many scholars of *uṣul*, that "the universals of religion [*kulliyāt al-dīn*] are known through definitive indicants of the Book and the Sunna," and not through consensus.[93] He then marvels at jurists who confirm consensus on the basis of the general inferences (*ʿumūmāt*) from Qurāʾnic verses and reports, and yet also agree that someone who denies what is evidenced by such general inferences is not an unbeliever or a sinner if this denial is based on interpretation. They also claim, however, that a particular ruling whose evidence is consensus is definitive, and that one who diverges from it is an unbeliever or a sinner. In so doing, al-Shawkānī notes, "they seem to have made the branch stronger than the root, and this is a great lapse on their part."[94]

In *Irshād al-Fuḥūl*, after his systematic refutation of consensus, al-Shawkānī presents various views related to its technical use by Uṣūlīs[95] and states that he would not refute these views since his earlier criticism is sufficient.[96] Nevertheless, on occasion, he takes on some of these views when they touch on principles he considers essential. For example, he cites the argument by al-Juwaynī that "established scholars give no weight to the difference of the Ẓāhirīs [over consensus], because most of sharia derives from *ijtihād*, and the available texts only suffice for a tenth of a tenth of it." In response, al-Shawkānī asserts, "One who truly knows of the textual sources of sharia, reflects on the verses of the glorious Book, and carefully explores the purified Sunna, would know that the texts of sharia are a legion. The only fault of the Ẓāhirīs is to abandon acting on the basis of invalid opinions that are not backed by evidence from either the Book or the Sunna or suitable analogy. . . . Yes they were inflexible in matters over which they ought to have forsaken rigidity, but this [flaw] is insignificant compared to what has happened in other schools in terms of acting based on no evidence whatsoever."[97] In all cases, according to al-Shawkānī, the claim of authoritativeness of consensus, despite opposition by credible scholars like the Ẓāhirīs, is the cause of irresolvable disputes and endless problems.[98]

Although al-Shawkānī's rejection of *ijmāʿ* is not unprecedented in Islamic intellectual history,[99] it certainly is not in conformity with the classical standards of *uṣūl al-fiqh*. Moreover, al-Shawkānī's rejection of *ijmāʿ* was eccentric even by the standards of the eighteenth century. And yet, his views are all the more remarkable because, in their very peculiarity, they embodied the main issues that eighteenth-century reforms struggled with and, through their tenacious exhaustiveness, managed to bring to the mainstream.

The Illegible *Qiyās*

Al-Shawkānī's rejection of *qiyās* is even stronger than his refutation of *ijmāʿ*. In the context of distancing the conveyers of religious doctrine—the Companions of the Prophet, their successors, the imams of schools, and even Prophets—from the practice of *qiyās*, al-Shawkānī maintains, "If a person claims that one of those would introduce into God's law things that do not belong to it, or charge the worshippers of God with obligations that did not come from Him, then this person would have fabricated a big lie about God, and attributed to Him what He has not said." The introduction of legal responsibilities, adds al-Shawkānī, "is a privilege that belongs exclusively to God, and a status which no one else may rightly attain or claim."[100] As such, according to al-Shawkānī, attributing the use of *qiyās* to these venerated individuals is an affront not just to them but to God Himself. Al-Shawkānī in fact posits a link between partisanship and bias to particular scholars, and turning scholars from interpreters of the law to lawgivers, from worshippers to objects of worship. This amounts to a betrayal of sharia that was entrusted by God to humans because "there is no authority other than God, no ruling but from Him, and no divine law other than what He sent forth. The opinions of *mujtahid*s hold no binding authority over anyone, and are in no way an integral part of the Divine Law. Rather, they are relevant only to the specific person who issues them, and they do not extend beyond him to any other person. Neither is it lawful for him to make them binding to any of God's worshippers. It is also not lawful for someone else to accept them from him and make them an authority over himself through which he would worship God."[101]

Al-Shawkānī therefore argues that a person who claims that any pious Muslim, including the Prophet or credible scholars, uses *qiyās* or other means to introduce new laws would be slandering these Muslims, because this is equivalent to accusing them of fabricating laws and claiming for themselves what they know is the exclusive right of God. Through this argument, al-Shawkānī invests the authority to legislate exclusively in God. In effect, this seemingly theocratic notion serves to limit the purview of divine law and restrict the range of human behavior and actions that are regulated by this law.

To be sure, not all kinds of *qiyās* are rejected by al-Shawkānī. In a discussion of the conditions of valid interpretation (*taʾwīl*), al-Shawkānī lists three conditions. First, the interpretation must conform with the conventions of language and customary linguistic usage, as well as the repeated usage by the Lawgiver; anything that contradicts this usage is not valid. Second, when positing an allegorical interpretation that is not attested by common usage of the language, there must be stated evidence that what is meant by a certain utterance is this claimed allegoric meaning. Third, if the interpretation is based on analogy (*qiyās*), then this must be manifest analogy (*qiyās jalī*), where the underlying cause is evident.[102] Yet this kind of authoritative *qiyās*, according to al-Shawkānī, can only be used as a basis of action on account of the strength of its indicants that are on par with textual evidence. Specifically, the evidence must either be stated (*ʿilla manṣūṣa*) or be the object of consensus (*ʿilla mujmaʿ ʿalayhā*), which in turn is only possible if there is stated textual evidence over which such consensus is based. In effect, therefore, the two or three types of *qiyās* recognized by al-Shawkānī must be based on the stated evidence or "the indicant behind consensus and not consensus itself."[103] One other example of uncontested *qiyās* is derived from the Qurʾānic verse, "Do not say to them [your parents] as much as *uff* and do not rebuff them" (Isrāʾ 17: 23). If one is not to say as much as *uff* to one's parents, then it is evident that, by analogy, one should not hurt them. This, according to al-Shawkānī, "is a case of strong *qiyās*, which is referred to as the analogy of the superior [*qiyās al-awlā*] or as the meaning of the content of discourse [*faḥwā al-khiṭāb*]." Yet at the same time al-Shawkānī uses this exceptional example to illustrate a type of valid *qiyās*, he also argues that it is very different from most other types of *qiyās* that he does not recognize.[104]

Beyond these general guidelines, al-Shawkānī mentions a couple of definitions of *qiyās*. One definition is the "extraction of the equivalent of a stated ruling for that which has not been stated, based on an association between the two [*istikhrāj mithl ḥukm al-madhkūr limā lam yudhkar bi-jāmiʿin baynahumā*]."[105] Another definition is "including a branch under a principle because of a joining indicant [*idrāj farʿ taḥt aṣl li ʿilla jāmiʿa*]."[106] Yet before he dwells further on these definitions he argues that "there is agreement that analogy is an authority in worldly matters [*ḥujja fī al-ʿumūr al-dunyawiyya*] . . . but the disagreement is over [the authority of] analogy in religious law [*al-qiyās al-sharʿī*], and a majority of companions, followers, jurists, and theologians [*mutakallimūn*] are of the view that it is one of the principles [*aṣl*] of sharia which is used as an indicant for rulings that reach us through narration [*samaʿ*]."[107] Then, after making this distinction between worldly legislation and *sharʿī* legislation, al-Shawkānī elaborates further on the subject of *qiyās*, leaving no ambiguity over his own position.

Al-Shawkānī notes that those who deny the validity of the *qiyās sharʿī* use all sorts of rational and textual proofs (*adilla ʿaqliyya wa naqliyya*) to make their point, but they do not need these proofs, since the presumption that *qiyās* is disallowed is the natural thing to assume, and the burden of proof is on those who posit it. In fact, al-Shawkānī adds, those trying to prove the authoritativeness of *qiyās* as a basis for the derivation of religious law have offered flawed rational and textual proofs. They collected textual proofs and claimed that evidence for worshipping on the basis of religious analogy (*al-taʿabbud bil-qiyās al-sharʿī*) can be found in the Book, Sunna, and consensus.[108] It is to this alleged evidence that al-Shawkānī now turns.

Evidence for the authoritativeness of *qiyās* is often drawn from the verse of the Qurʾān, "So learn a lesson, O you who have vision [*fa iʿtabirū yā ulī al-abṣār*]" (59:2). Some argue that *iʿtibār* implies going beyond (*mujāwaza*), just as *qiyās* involves the crossing from the principle ruling to the branch ruling (*min ḥukm al-aṣl ilā ḥukm al-farʿ*). Al-Shawkānī does not concede that *iʿtibār* and *mujāwaza* have parallel meanings, but he adds that even if this similarity is granted for the sake of argument, "we don't submit that the command to 'go beyond' is the same as a command to exercise *sharʿī* analogy." This is because anyone who uses an indicant (*dalīl*) moves beyond it to that which is indicated (*madlūl*), so the term *iʿtibār* is "common to inference [*istidlāl*] through definitive rational indicants, through texts, through the principle of legal nonliability,[109] and through *sharʿī* analogy."[110]

Another argument frequently used by advocates of *qiyās* is the hadith of

Muʿādh, who was sent by the Prophet to become the governor of Yemen. Regarding matters not covered in the Qurʾān and the Sunna that he would face as governor, Muʿādh is reported to have said he would exercise his judgment. Al-Shawkānī maintains that the *ijtihād bil-raʾy* invoked by Muʿādh excludes *qiyās*, and just as it includes such things as "the extraction of indicants from the Book and the Sunna, it can be through adherence to the principle of original innocence, or the principle that things are originally permissible . . . or by upholding of public benefits [*maṣāliḥ*]."[111] Moreover, the *qiyās* that falls under *ijtihād al-raʾy*, which can be used as a basis for action, includes the analogy whose indicant is stated (in textual sources, *ʿillatuhu manṣūṣa*), or the analogy in which there is definite negation of the difference in the indicants between the two sides of the analogy (*mā quṭiʿa fīhi bi-nafy al-fāriq fī al-dalīl*). This kind of analogy is evidenced by the indicant of the principle ruling (*madlūl ʿalayhi bi dalīl al-aṣl*) and falls under it. And all the pointless efforts to prove otherwise "lead nowhere and simply assert things which are not in any way related to *sharʿ*, nor are they part of the easy and munificent sharia."[112] Al-Shawkānī adds that the most compelling argument in support of *qiyās* is that "texts do not cover all [needed] rulings, because they are finite, whereas events are infinite." In response, al-Shawkānī repeats his earlier contention that God informed Muslims that He has completed their religion, and that His Prophet informed them that he left them with a clear sharia, "its night as clear as its day." Put differently, al-Shawkānī contends that the injunctions of sharia are sufficient, and the unwarranted addition of more injunctions through *qiyās* attributes to God things He did not say or command.[113]

A classic example of *qiyās* that al-Shawkānī rejects is the expansion of the laws of usury (*ribā*) beyond the specific types of exchange explicitly prohibited in the texts, namely, the hand-to-hand exchange of gold, silver, dates, raisins, salt, wheat, and barley. Using analogy, the majority of *madhhab*s expand this rule to include all cases of exchange of like for like, whereas al-Shawkānī (and before him the Ẓāhirīs) argues that there is no valid evidence that requires the extension of this rule to other kinds of exchange.[114]

Finally, al-Shawkānī argues that the consensus that Uṣūlīs claim is the basis for *qiyās* is not an evidence that is binding on Muslims, and that there is no valid indicant that confirms its alleged authoritativeness, that is, there is no textual evidence in the Qurʾān or hadith stating that analogy is a legal indicant. The analogy against which al-Shawkānī argues is one in which the effective cause (*ʿilla, ratio legis*) of a certain ruling is deduced by jurists and then applied to other cases for which the same *ʿilla* applies. Al-Shawkānī argues that as long as there is no explicit text from the Qurʾān or the Sunna stating what the effective cause for the ruling is, we cannot posit that the law was sent by the Lawgiver on account of that cause, let alone apply it to other cases based on apparent resemblance to the first one. If the effective cause is identified in a text, then the application of this cause to another case is on the basis of the textual indicant and not analogy; because in this case it is as if the Lawgiver is telling us that this particular effective cause has a general applicability and is to be applied whenever it is found.[115]

Al-Shawkānī's rejection of *qiyās* is admittedly extreme, yet the logic of his analysis captures some of the key characteristics of Islamic reform in the eighteenth century. To be sure, other eighteenth-century thinkers do not hold the same radical views on *qiyās*, but despite this difference, the rationale and ultimate objectives for rejecting or accepting *qiyās* converge. Walī Allāh, for example, differs from al-Shawkānī on the definition of analogy and underscores the importance of finding and applying the *ʿilla* of a legal ruling.[116] In explaining what is entailed in the art of *ijtihād* (*al-ṣināʿa al-ijtihādiyya*), Walī Allāh treats *ijtihād* as a professional skill that is acquirable by mastering its techniques. One of the things entailed in *ijtihād* is identifying the rationale for a legal ruling (*maʿrifat ʿillat al-ḥukm*). On the necessity of identifying the rationale for a legal ruling, Walī Allāh maintains that "God wants to inform His worshippers of what pleases and displeases Him. It is not possible in legal codes to explicitly cover all the actions of legally responsible individuals; therefore there has to be a general designation around which the ruling revolves. This designation can either be a specific description of those who are legally responsible . . . , or a description of the action [regulated by the ruling]; sometimes the description is composite. . . . This description is called the indicant [or rationale] of the ruling [*ʿillat al-ḥukm*]; the ruling revolves around it, whether it is permissibility, reprehension, or prohibition. Nothing more is meant by rationale [*ʿilliya*]."[117] Walī Allāh adds that the distinction between the confirmed obligation and the unconfirmed recommendation, as well as the confirmed wrath (of God) called prohibition and the unconfirmed wrath called reprehension, is determined by tracing legal indicants. The most apparent indicant is in cases where the predicament of one who violates a ruling is specified. Next are the cases where injunctions like "it is necessary" or "it is not permissible" are used. Next are the cases where something is identified as the cornerstone of Islam or of unbelief; or where extreme threats are used for those who commit or neglect a certain action. Figuring out the status of an act also requires reflecting on whether it complements an act of obedience, removes pretexts for sin, or is subsumed under dignity and good manners, although in these cases the ruling is not definitive.[118] All of these technicalities, adds Walī Allāh, "are introductions to the exercise of independent reasoning and to juristic inference, which help in deciding on legal matters; they are not part of the craft of disputation and argumentation, which does not belong to the sanctioned religious sciences but was invented by the scholars who care about this world to market their commodities."[119]

It is clear, therefore, that, unlike al-Shawkānī, Walī Allāh relates *ijtihād* to some sort of analogical reasoning, but he also dissociates both from disputation and discord. As we have seen, the genealogy and architecture of the intellectual projects of al-Shawkānī and Walī Allāh were different, and both were different from the projects of other eighteenth-century reformers. Yet despite their distinctiveness, parallel objectives pertaining to the scope of the sharia animated these projects. But before turning to these common threads, we will continue the exploration of al-Shawkānī's views on the other sources of the law.

Other Sources for the Expansion of the Law

At a most fundamental level, according to al-Shawkānī, the purpose of sharia is not only to bring benefits (*maṣāliḥ*) and prevent harm (*mafāsid*) but also to develop mechanisms to balance and prioritize these benefits and harms, which must always be based on valid indicants and not mere speculation.[120] Al-Shawkānī contends that analogical investigations are typically mere speculation, and no definitive evidence can be derived from them. Additionally, "among the objectives [*maqāṣid*] that are mentioned in the books of *uṣūl*, and which amount to no more than pure speculation, are discretionary opinion *istiḥsān*,[121] *istiṣḥāb* [juristic preference], and *talāzum* [correlation]."[122] According to al-Shawkānī, all of these theoretical instruments of *uṣūl* are mediated through human agency, cannot claim divine certitude, and lack authoritativeness in the derivation of sharia. "God does not require that His servants worship Him [*taʿabbada ʿibadahu*] on the basis of the mere deductions of a scholar. . . . This is true even if there is nothing in the Book or the Sunna that contradicts these deductions . . . and all the more so in cases where there are clear and famous indicants that opposes these deductions."[123] Al-Shawkānī develops this argument beyond *ijmāʿ* and *qiyās* and interrogates other forms of unhinged legislation. *Istiḥsān*, he argues, "has been defined as a [concealed] indicant that dawns on the soul [*yanqadiḥu fī al-nafs*] of the *mujtahid* without being able to clearly articulate it." Sarcastically, al-Shawkānī remarks that God does not require people to abide by indicants that scholars can express unless they can provide the textual proof that these are authoritative indicants; so how could it be that an inexpressible indicant could carry any authority when "we do not even know what or how it has dawned on him." Al-Shawkānī marvels at "these hallucinations, and the manner by which holders of such views consider it permissible to determine that such things constitute legal indicants; they falsely ascribe to the law things that do not belong to it, and attribute to God things that He does not say."[124]

Another kind of unwarranted expansion of the realm of *sharʿ* is through *istiṣḥāb al-ḥāl*, which is based on the assumption that a ruling confirmed for a particular past time remains operative in the future, unless something happens to change from it. As in all similar cases, al-Shawkānī goes over several views on this matter and sides with the view that no valid evidence can be derived through this type of inference.[125] Quoting al-Zarkashī (d. 1391), al-Shawkānī maintains that the only valid *istiṣḥāb* is *istiṣḥāb al-ʿadam al-aṣlī*, that is, assuming the continuation of a state in which there is no legal burden or obligation, until a valid indicant suggests a change from this original state and justifies the imposition of rules (*ḥattā yadul dalīl sharʿī ʿalā taghyīrihi*). This, al-Shawkānī adds, is the principle of freedom from legal obligation (*barāʾat al-dhimma min al-taklīf*).[126] In fact, a person who claims that "evidence in God's religion is established through means other than the Book of God and the Sunna of His Prophet, in addition to what is based on these two sources, would be asserting with regard to God's religion things that cannot be proven, and would be establishing in this religious law legislation that is not decreed by God."[127] "It is indeed a grave matter to contend that the opinions of an individual or groups of individuals constitute binding legal proof [*ḥujja sharʿiyya*] that Muslims must act upon, thereby becoming established and determined legislation that affects all Muslims." This, al-Shawkānī continues, "is the exclusive prerogative of messengers whom God sent with legal codes to His worshippers, and applies to no one else no matter the elevation of their knowledge or status."[128]

This last rearticulation of what constitutes authority for the derivation of sharia comes in the context of arguing that the *ijtihād* of the Companions is not authoritative evidence (*ḥujja*). But as we have seen, it can just as well appear in a discussion of principles of jurisprudence or a specific legal injunction. The authority of individuals, however, is a nuanced matter that al-Shawkānī discusses in great detail. In his thought a key distinction can be traced between the authority of bygone figures and the authority of living political and religious figures. As we have already seen, the former is important because it affects the way the authority of textual sources is established, and it also impinges on questions of *ijtihād* and *taqlīd*. In contrast, discussions of the authority of living individuals affect the present and future unfolding of Islamic social and political orders, and as such cannot be mechanically subsumed under the former. For example, in the context of discussing various categories of legal and illegal taxes,[129] al-Shawkānī argues that an imam who has received an oath of allegiance is authorized to lead in religious and worldly matters (*umūr al-dunyā wal-dīn*), even if he is not always just, and obedience is due to him as long as it does not entail disobedience of God.[130]

Al-Shawkānī thus may seem willing to accord an imperfect, and likely unjust, living imam a mundane authority he will not accord to the upright *mujtahid* Companions of the Prophet, including the four rightly guided caliphs. But this is not the case. For example, al-Shawkānī is adamant that the taxes imposed on Muslims are not subject to interpretation and must not deviate from the clearly stated stipulations of the law. In contrast, *kharāj* land, that is, land captured in war from non-Muslims, is public land under the control of the imam, who is not bound by arrangements made by former imams and has the discretion to change these arrangements as he considers to be in the interest of Muslims. As such, the imam can impose more or less taxes on tenants of *kharāj* land, or even reclaim the land altogether.[131] Al-Shawkānī, therefore, concedes the right of political authorities to act, and even legislate, on the basis of their assessment of the public interest (*maṣlaḥa*) of Muslims, and this legislation must be obeyed as long as it does not entail disobedience of God. However, this *maṣlaḥa* is a valid principle for the derivation of human law outside the realm of sharia and does not presume to expand the realm of the sacred. "An insightful imam," al-Shawkānī maintains, "who is mindful of the springs and sources of sharia will not fail to discern what entails benefit or harm, and he is entitled to have his correct judgment [*lahu naẓarahu al-muṭābiq lil-ṣawāb*] on what would affect Muslims by bringing benefit and warding off harm." Therefore, the *maṣlaḥa* recognized by al-Shawkānī is one that is connected to the opinion (*naẓar*) of the imam, and it serves as a valid basis for worldly legislation. But although this type of legislation is sanctioned by sharia, it remains decidedly distinct from it.[132] In fact, the imam is neither infallible nor a legislator,[133] but his ability to preserve the interests of the Muslim community is more important than his knowledge or piety, the latter being essential ingredients of the authoritativeness of the sources of the divine law.[134]

Another sphere in which the political and the legal appear to intersect is the implementation of the law. Al-Shawkānī uses the same principles for establishing probity in hadith as he does for ascertaining the authority of witness testimony in a court of law.[135] The kernel of the notion of *ʿadāla* is to verify the truthfulness and accuracy of a person, and once these two are established, there is no need for further scrutiny and questioning of this apparent *ʿadāla*. Furthermore, although sin (*fisq*) undermines *ʿadāla*, there is no need to probe deep in order to prove the absence of sin. Rather, one should assume the lack of sin as the original state of a person, unless something arises to prove otherwise.[136] Of course, conflict of interest is a reason for not accepting a testimony, as in the prospect of personal gain from a specific testimony, personal bias and grudge, or testifying against rivals.[137] Again, these qualifiers parallel the technical flaws that disqualify reporters of hadith.

A judge, in contrast, is invested with executive authority and, even more than the imam, treads the thin line between the interpretation and the execution of the law. Highlighting this distinction, al-Shawkānī argues that a judge should not be dismissed from his office when the imam who appoints him dies; this is because the appointment of the judge is based on his probity and knowledge, and not on the fact that he was placed in his position by the imam.[138] Additionally, the presence of an imam is not a condition for upholding the law and imposing legal penalties (*iqāmat al-ḥudūd*), because *ḥudūd al-sharʿ* do not belong to the imams and should not be neglected simply because one Muslim is missing, when the Book and the Sunna are available, along with good and knowledgeable people qualified to use them.[139] Moreover, whereas a measure of injustice is tolerated, in fact even expected, in the case of the imam, a judge should be dismissed from his position for such failures as, for example, injustice or accepting a bribe.[140] Yet, unlike in the case of the imam, the functional authority of the judge, and the obligation to implement his sentences, is contingent on his correctness. So the indicants requiring the litigants' submission to the judge's ruling can be suspended if the person sentenced knows that the ruling is incorrect. In such a case, after exhausting other options to explain the truth of the matter under judgment, the sentenced person should escape if he can.[141] The ruling of a judge, al-Shawkānī argues, "is only formally executed [*ḥukmuhu yanfudh ẓāhiran faqṭ*], so that the one who receives a ruling in his favor is not entitled to it unless the ruling is congruent with the reality [*faman quḍiya lahu bi-shay' fa lā yaḥillu lahu illā idhā kāna al-ḥukm muṭābiqan al-wāqiʿ*]." However, one who receives a ruling that he knows is illegal, as far as the truth is concerned, is prohibited from executing this ruling. In other words, the ruling of a judge does not make the forbidden lawful.[142]

Beyond these technical considerations related to the functions of the judge, perhaps the most important issue that pertains to the Uṣūlī focus on the normativity and authoritativeness of legal judgments is the question of the status of the knowledge that informs these judgments. Consistent with his views elsewhere, al-Shawkānī argues that a judge is commanded to discharge God's rule, and this can only be reached through confession, testimony, or oath.[143] Moreover, a judge is supposed to rule based not on his own conviction but on external evidence.[144] External evidence includes a judge's direct observation (*mushāhada*), because the testimony of witnesses produces probable, uncertain knowledge (*ẓann*), whereas direct observation is stronger than the knowledge that derives from testimony or confession.[145] Put differently, a judge can rely on his own material knowledge (*mushāhada*) that qualifies him to testify, but in this case he acts in his capacity as an external trustworthy *ʿadl* bearing witness to an event. However, his conviction, no matter how strong, is an opinion and cannot serve as a valid basis for a legal ruling.

We have seen so far how, for al-Shawkānī, the authoritativeness of the sources of sharia is not contingent on the opinions of men, including the first four caliphs, the Companions of the Prophet, recognized religious scholars (individually or collectively), imams, or judges. The same rule applies to the family of the Prophet, the *ʿitra* or *ahl al-bayt*, whose consensus does not constitute valid evidence, because it cannot be confirmed and, for those who believe in its possibility, because it is permissible to exercise *ijtihād* against their assumed consensus.[146] Neither does al-Shawkānī concede the authority of rulings collectively ascribed to the *madhhab* of *ahl al-bayt*, just as he rejects such corporate authority for all *madhhab*s. For example, in reference to the common Zaydi view that it is recommended (*mustaḥabb*) to fast on the day of Ghadīr Khumm, the day on which the Prophet designated ʿAlī as his representative (*mawlā*), al-Shawkānī maintains that claiming that something is *mustaḥabb* is a legal ruling, which needs a valid indicant to prove it, and the assertion by a group of people is not sufficient to attribute such a ruling to God. And without denying the virtue of ʿAlī, or of the day of his designation, al-Shawkānī argues that there are more deserving days of the year that have collective significance to all Muslims, such as the battle of Badr, the conquest of Mecca, the birth of the Prophet, and the day he started receiving revelations.[147]

In all the above positions, al-Shawkānī knowingly and willfully contradicts majority opinions without hesitation, and in so doing appears to maintain equal distance from, or perhaps equally offend, all schools. One telling illustration of this attitude is al-Shawkānī's view on divorce. Against the position of almost all schools that divorce is effective once the word "divorced" is uttered, al-Shawkānī argues that if the man who utters the word says he did not mean it, then the divorce is not enforceable, although, al-Shawkānī concedes, uttering the word and then denying its meaning is not the sort of thing rational people usually do. Al-Shawkānī's choice of opposing the view of the majority on this matter is because intention can only be determined based on the profession of the speaker under oath.[148]

An even more controversial departure from the majority opinion is al-Shawkānī's opposition of the validity of triple divorce. Al-Shawkānī recognizes that the four *madhhab*s concur on this validity, but then refers to the hadith reported by Ibn ʿAbbās indicating that during the life of the Prophet, and until the Caliph ʿUmar changed the ruling, the practice was to consider a triple divorce as one divorce. The change occurred under ʿUmar, but no indicant is provided to justify this switch. Al-Shawkānī insists that, in this case, the consensus of the schools is arbitrary (*taʿassuf*).[149] Additionally, he exclaims, if abandoning the Sunna of the Prophet is for the sake of ʿUmar, "how does this poor man compare to the Messenger of God, and what Muslim gives preference to the opinion of a Companion over the injunction of the chosen one [the Prophet]."[150]

The Limitedness of Sharia

The arguments that legal principles are presumptive, and that *qiyās* and *ijmā'* are not legitimate tools for the extraction of the law, are subsumed under a larger argument shared by the reformers of the eighteenth century: that Islamic law is limited and does not cover all aspects of life. In addition to advocating strict adherence to the letter of the law, eighteenth-century thinkers argued that the scope of the sacred law is limited. As noted earlier, there are significant differences among the various eighteenth-century reformers over principles of jurisprudence, but their formulations invariably point toward a shared layer of fundamental guidelines and principles.

Al-Shawkānī directs Muslims to these basic principles when he offers the following guidance: "Know this and hold on to it: the only messenger God sent to you and to the rest of this community is Muhammad; He only commanded you to follow him; He did not legislate for you a single letter through any member of his community other than him; and he did not make the opinions of anyone but him binding on you [*ḥujja ʿalayk*]." In the same breath al-Shawkānī adds, "If people disagree over a specific matter and have different opinions, accept as little of these as you can [*al-akhdh bi aqall mā qīl*], as long as there is no outstanding evidence for accepting the addition to this bare minimum." According to al-Shawkānī, therefore, a most fundamental principle of jurisprudence is to hold back on the addition of legal obligations or prohibitions until valid evidence necessitates this addition; and the burden of proof is on those who propose it.[151] This view is not only expressed in theoretical works by al-Shawkānī, but it is frequently repeated in many of his other works, including his commentaries on applied law, where he takes every opportunity to reiterate or illustrate this principle. For example, in the opening statement of a long chapter on ritual purity in *Al-Sayl al-Jarrār*, he offers the following juristic principle: "The right to give juristic preference to the original state of legal nonliability [*ḥaqq istiṣḥāb al-barāʾa al-aṣliyya*] and the originality of purity [*aṣālat al-ṭahāra*] entail that someone who claims the impurity of a particular object must provide the evidence. If he can [provide the evidence], as in the impurity of human urine and feces and of manure, then the ruling is confirmed. But if he cannot provide evidence or can only provide defective proofs, then we are obliged to stop at what is entailed by the origin [*al-aṣl*] and by nonliability [*barāʾa*]."[152] Al-Shawkānī then gives specific examples that follow from and illustrate this general rule, although these examples seem to defy a simple, commonsense expansion of the categories of impurity.[153] Al-Shawkānī contends that there is no necessary correlation between prohibition and impurity.[154] Thus, there is no evidence that intoxicants are impure;[155] that anything of dogs other than their saliva is impure;[156] or that pigs are impure.[157]

In fact, al-Shawkānī distinguishes between two concepts of impurity: legal impurity (*najāsa ḥukmiyya*) and essential physical impurity (*najāsa ḥissiya*); the first does not automatically imply the second unless there is further evidence to this effect.[158] "The Lawgiver," al-Shawkānī contends, "who taught us how to cleanse impurities, also taught us which specific object is impure in itself [*najis*] or becomes impure [*mutanajjis*] because of an external factor, and our obligation is to follow His instructions and obey His commands, and to let go of satanic doubts and corrupt delusions. In addition to contradicting *the magnanimous, easy sharia*, this [obsession] is also an exaggeration [*ghulū*] in religion, which has been explicitly forbidden."[159]

As always, al-Shawkānī fluctuates between theoretical reflection and detailed illustration with specific examples. This stands to reason, since al-Shawkānī was fully aware of the weight of the legal traditions (both *uṣūl* and *furūʿ*) he was challenging. A few examples suffice to illustrate this. In reference to the view in *Al-Azhār* that it is recommended to perform ritual washing of the whole body (*ghusl*) before entering Mecca, Jerusalem, or the tombs of prophets, al-Shawkānī says that not only obligations and prohibitions but also recommended acts (*mandūb*) are *sharʿī* rulings whose introduction requires valid indicants; legislating without such indicants would be "expanding the circle of the purified sharia based on shaky illusions and feeble opinions." Al-Shawkānī adds that this sort of speculation does not count as incorrect *ijtihād*, which would be the case if there were seeming contradiction between multiple valid indicants. Nor is it alleged *qiyās*, which, according to those who believe in it, requires the existence of an original case (*aṣl*) and a new case (*farʿ*), and a link between the two (*amr jāmiʿ baynahumā*).[160] Al-Shawkānī applies similar reasoning to the question of performing *ghusl* for a *mustaḥāḍa* (washing the whole body by a woman who undergoes bleeding or discharge that is not menstrual or postpartum). "This type of onerous obligation," al-Shawkānī maintains, "cannot be asserted without a valid proof that is clearer than the sun." In this case, he argues, not only is evidence lacking, but also there is strong counterevidence of the highest rank. Above all, however, one should not impose an unwarranted legal burden in accordance with the principles on which sharia is founded: namely, facility and the elimination of hardship (*al-taysīr wa ʿadam al taʿsīr*), and bringing good tidings and the absence of repulsion (*al-tabshīr wa ʿadam al-tanfīr*).[161]

Another example is al-Shawkānī's prohibition against indefinite fasting (*ṣawm al-dahr*), which, in addition to the severe hardship it imposes, is not in agreement with the Sunna of the Prophet.[162] Other "minority" views that al-Shawkānī adamantly defends are the argument that there is no evidence that seminal discharge invalidates fasting;[163] or his rejection of *Al-Azhār*'s contention that sexual intercourse invalidates the pilgrimage. While al-Shawkānī agrees that intercourse during the hajj is forbidden, he argues that *Al-Azhār*'s view that it annuls the whole act of worship and necessitates its repetition is unfounded and imposes unattested legal burdens on Muslims on the basis of "the delusions of opinion and false *ijtihād*."[164] Elsewhere, at several junctures during his discussion of sale transactions, al-Shawkānī argues that the primary operative cause of rulings of sales (*manāṭ aḥkām al-bayʿ al-sharʿiyya*) is mutual consent (*tarāḍī*). Rather than apply this straightforward, minimalist principle, jurists have resorted to linguistic acrobatics and devised complex conventions on which they based sales rulings. Again, al-Shawkānī argues, this unwarranted exercise only leads to "the expansion of the circle of *sharʿ* rulings based on mere invalid opinion and false *ijtihād*."[165]

To be sure, al-Shawkānī makes the reverse argument, that the original principle of *barāʾa* cannot be invoked where there is a clear definitive indicant that demands legislation (*lā barāʾa baʿd wujūd al-dalīl*).[166] Similarly, if on a particular matter there is a valid indicant that explicitly permits action based on probable knowledge (*tajwīz al-ʿamal bil-ẓann*), then a definitive indicant is not a prerequisite for legislation.[167] Al-Shawkānī, therefore, displays no epistemological flexibility when he dismisses the notion that all *mujtahid*s are correct, insisting instead that there is only intended truth in God's ruling on any one case, although this truth might not be always retrievable by *mujtahid*s. Likewise, he exhibits no willingness to dilute the law and is quite strict when it comes to definitive rulings. For example, he launches a severe attack on the art of *ḥiyal*, through which jurists come up with legal tricks to circumvent the law. The use of *ḥiyal*, al-Shawkānī argues, is prohibited, and he deplores the great efforts exerted by jurists to circumvent the law and release God's servants from their religious obligations. Furthermore, he urges his readers not to be fooled by the seemingly legal veneer that is projected on non-Islamic practices by jurists who manipulate the law to their own ends; in so doing, these people deceive themselves and others who lack the ability or interest to pursue the truth.[168] However, al-Shawkānī maintains that these tricks, which have no basis in the valid indicants of the law, are different from *taysīr*, which is directly sanctioned by the Lawgiver.[169] The rush to legislate rulings and to impose them on Muslims is tantamount to attributing to God things He did not say.[170] In fact, one should not provoke an expansion of the law on matters over which the Lawgiver is silent because, "as the law states, this silence is in fact a license [*ʿafū*]" from God.[171]

But how representative was al-Shawkānī of reformative trends in the eighteenth century? Or, to ask this question differently, are al-Shawkānī's views dismissible as eccentric ideas on the margins of the mainstream of Islamic intellectual tradition? In this book I have argued that the intellectuals I discuss were extremely influential, at least within their regional contexts, both during their own lifetimes and beyond. Al-Shawkānī in particular had followers farther east and west, far beyond the borders of Yemen. Nonetheless, it is also accurate to say that al-Shawkānī's views on *ijmāʿ* and *qiyās* were not shared by Shāh Walī Allāh, the other towering figure of this era. Yet despite the unstated as well as professed regional genealogy of Walī Allāh, rooted as he was in the Indian Ḥanafī tradition, a genealogy that explains some of the differences between his reconciliatory views and al-Shawkānī's radical departures, there are fundamental parallels between the two. So we will now briefly examine some of these parallels in the realm of *uṣūl*.

With his primary focus on reconciling differences between various Islamic intellectual currents, Walī Allāh charts the causes of legal divergences and then suggests ways of dealing with them. Difference, he asserts, is a natural and unavoidable outcome of *ijtihād*. It is sanctioned in the prophetic tradition, which assigns two rewards to a *mujtahid* who hits the mark, and one reward for one who does not.[172] Unlike for al-Shawkānī, however, to Walī Allāh this does not mean that one of the two opinions in question is wrong, only that one is more correct than the other. The claim that only one of the two opinions corresponds to the ruling intended by God would pitch the other one in opposition to God's ruling, which is a sin and cannot be deserving of God's reward.[173] Therefore, in differences resulting from most kinds of *ijtihād*, the truth is on both sides of the difference,[174] and the choice between different legal opinions, and by extension different legal schools, is a choice between equally valid options. So far, the difference between Walī Allāh and al-Shawkānī is deep. However, based on the above argument, Walī Allāh asserts that it is prohibited to believe in and promote one school of law to the exclusion of other schools.[175] To be sure, al-Shawkānī, at least nominally, invests no authority in the views of *madhhabs* as corporate entities, but in practice he continually engages these schools and inhabits their intellectual spaces. And, more important to both Walī Allāh and al-Shawkānī, these schools have no exclusive claim to truth. In fact, Walī Allāh maintains, there are only four Sunni *madhhabs* because it so happened that their followers were more active than those of other extinct schools.[176] Moreover, to both Walī Allāh and al-Shawkānī, a measure of *ijtihād* should be exercised by any discerning Muslim in opting for one of different opinions. And while al-Shawkānī maintains that it is an obligation for every legally accountable Muslim (*mukallaf*) to choose the evidence to follow, Walī Allāh argues that this choice must be based on the strength of the evidence behind each opinion, the soundness of its reasoning, and how easily it can be followed.[177] Since the choice is made between equally valid opinions, and on the basis of the principle of *taysīr*, Walī Allāh sees no reason why people should not adopt the easier and least demanding of the options.[178]

Walī Allāh envisions revival through intellectual synthesis, and the inclusion of the community in this process has broad social ramifications. Knowledge, according to Walī Allāh, is of two kinds: the first pertains to a core of specific and well-defined rules that guarantee humanity's natural and logical interests.[179] Observance of these rules, which are subsumed under God's revealed injunctions and prohibitions, is mandatory whether one recognizes the wisdom in them or not.[180] It follows that this first kind of knowledge is transmitted rather than acquired through speculation, and that its authority derives from the letter of the law.[181] The second kind of knowledge is general, unspecified, and flexible. It is based on human interest and seeks the amelioration of society and individual lives.[182] God's instructions regarding this second kind of knowledge are general, and intention rather than strict observance determines the validity of related judgments and actions.[183] Central to Walī Allāh's scheme is the effort to limit the applicability and prevent the undue extension of knowledge derived from divine law.[184] For Walī Allāh, a proper legal analogy (*qiyās*), for instance, is the derivation of a legal ruling on the basis of a common legal cause (*ʿilla mushtaraka*) rather than on the basis of a common interest (*maṣlaḥa mushtaraka*).[185] This would restrict the imposition of opinions derived from the application of general knowledge under the limited and binding *sharʿ* of God. To be sure, this view is not identical with al-Shawkānī's, but yet again both scholars circumscribe the scope of the law and argue that this is the real meaning of the ease and facility (*taysīr*) intended by God for his worshippers.

For Walī Allāh Islam is the religion of nature (*fiṭra*).[186] He introduces a theory of human development in stages, which he calls *irtifāqāt*[187] (sing. *irtifāq*). An *irtifāq* is characterized as the art of searching for ease (*taysīr*) and beneficial acts, and ease obtains specifically because God commands acts for which people have a natural inclination and which are required by both nature and reason. The first and most basic *irtifāq* includes those aspects of knowledge and conduct that are specific to the human species and essential to its survival, such as language, cultivation, and family relations. The second includes experiential and acquired faculties and customs that are utilized in the home and marketplace. The third relates to the administration of life in the city, and the fourth and final one regulates the relations between all cities within a universal order. Aside from the specific core of commands that God unequivocally communicated to humans, Walī Allāh maintains that most laws are guiding principles, and their precise determination is left to the reasoning of people and to what they think is best for their well-being, and to what is in harmony with and in the interest of their natural dispositions.[188]

Nature, in the language of Walī Allāh, refers not only to human nature but to the physical world as well. The laws of an expanded nature govern all phenomena that humans may observe or experience in life, including miracles.

Miracles, he maintains, are simply the result of uncommon or less frequent natural causes.[189] God interferes in nature through nature itself, by suppressing (*qabḍ*) certain aspects of nature and expanding (*basṭ*) others.[190] In his account of Muhammad's night journey to Jerusalem and his ascension to heaven, Walī Allāh contends that the laws of the spirit became operative while the laws of physical bodies were suspended.[191] The actual occurrence of this incident is not denied, nor is it metaphorically interpreted; rather, a different and unfamiliar set of laws produced this "natural" miracle.

It does not follow, however, that God's agency in the life of men is mediated through, and thus limited by, nature. While he asserts the principle of causation, Walī Allāh attributes it to the intention or will of an agent he calls *al-shakhṣ al-akbar* (the greater being or "metaphysical man").[192] This greater being is God's first creation; God then creates the things that are ingrained in its universal nature, and its existence is sustained through continuous emanation from the First.[193] According to this theory, natural causation is the intention of an agent, which is itself, together with its soul, created and sustained by God. Causation is thus recovered without compromising the power of God. The reconciliation between natural laws and causation, on the one hand, and transmitted knowledge, on the other, is sanctioned by scripture, and specifically by the Qurʾānic principle of *taysīr*.[194] It is important to note that the ultimate authority that enables this mediation is the transmitted tradition.[195] According to Walī Allāh, the classification of scholars into those who pursue independent legal opinion (*ahl al-raʾī*) and literalists (*ahl al-ẓāhir*) is based on an invalid delineation. The real difference between these two groups is not over the exclusive use of either tradition or reason; rather, it lies in their supreme source of authority, and Walī Allāh exhibits no willingness to compromise the authority of tradition in the interest of any reconciliation.[196]

It is doubtful that al-Shawkānī would have condoned some of Walī Allāh's spiritual and philosophical excursions, but in the end they both underscore the authority of stated, definitive indicants and the primacy of *taysīr*, both of which, when properly applied, result in limiting the scope of the law. In one instance Walī Allāh observes that Muḥammad (al-Shaybānī, d. 805) and Abū Ḥanīfa (d. 767) noted that Ibn ʿUmar (d. 693) dismounted when he wanted to perform the *witr* prayer, and that al-Shaybānī and Abū Ḥanīfa deduced from this that it is obligatory to dismount to pray. Walī Allāh says that this inference is neither valid according to the principles of jurisprudence nor common convention, since Ibn ʿUmar may have chosen to dismount because of a personal preference and not because of his knowledge that praying while mounted is prohibited. Importantly, Walī Allāh argues here that the law should not be expanded on the basis of such invalid evidence.[197]

Al-Shawkānī goes one step further: in addition to his forceful argument that God's law is limited and should not be expanded without explicit valid textual evidence, he also embarks on what may be described as an attempt to compile this limited definitive law in his *Al-Darārī al-Muḍiyya Sharḥ al-Durra al-Bahiyya*. This is a commentary (*Al-Darārī al-Muḍiyya*) on an abridged *fiqh* handbook (*Mukhtaṣar*: *Al-Durra al-Bahiyya*) also by al-Shawkānī. The laws discussed in both books are those for which there are direct definitive indicants, the establishment of which does not require the exercise of *ijtihād* (*aḥkām manṣūṣa ghayr ijtihādiyya*)—also called prophetic rulings (*aḥkām nabawiyya*)—over which presumably there is consensus. Al-Shawkānī provides evidence for the soundness of hadiths on which these rulings are based (*taṣḥīḥ*), determines the proof texts governing each particular ruling (*tanqīḥ*), and isolates and extracts the grounds of a divine ruling and its rationale (*takhrīj*). What is noteworthy about al-Shawkānī's unconventional separation of these specific rulings from other rulings that rely on the input of *mujtahid*s is that (1) presumably this collection of rulings can serve as a common denominator shared by all *madhhab*s on account of its compelling indicants; (2) the collection distinguishes prophetic *fiqh*, which is incontestable from *fiqh ijtihādī* over which there could be *ijmāʿ*. In other words, this group does not require recognition of the authority of *ijtihādī ijmāʿ* and is based on more compelling, irrefutable evidence; and (3) this compilation provides a concise, accessible, and definitive reference to a jurist, who can use it to assess the rulings handed over to him by his imam in order to figure out the parts that derived through *qiyās* and those based on definitive indicants. In short, the purpose of this exercise for al-Shawkānī is "to compile all the rulings whose evidence is sound, and whose derivation is impeccable, and leave aside all that is based on opinion." Once again, in theory and in practice, al-Shawkānī's project revolves around the identification of the definitive yet contained core of the law.[198]

Sharia, Human Law, and the Meaning of *Taysīr*

As hinted above, both Walī Allāh and to a greater extent al-Shawkānī distinguish between the sacred law, sharia, and a human law that is not subsumed within the realm of the sacred. Al-Shawkānī clearly recognizes laws of human provenance, derived by Muslims to regulate various aspects of their lives. These laws are necessary for orderly life, and therefore Muslims are obliged to abide by them, but they are not part of the divine law and lack divine sanctity. The divine law commands Muslims to abide by this worldly law and the human temporal authorities that generate and implement it, as long as this obedience does not entail disobedience of God.

In a telling discussion of the prohibition against selling a free person, al-

Shawkānī argues that this is a straightforward definitive rule that needs no further evidence. He adds, however, regarding the penalties that should be imposed on someone who sells a free person, that this matter falls outside the scope of sharia, which does not regulate the penalty, because the penalty is part of *aḥkām al-waḍʿ* (declaratory law, or the positive laws that fall outside the scope of *uṣūl al-fiqh*) and not *aḥkām al-taklīf* (rules of obligation that define sharia). Without questioning the legitimacy or validity of declaratory law, al-Shawkānī maintains that it is outside the realm of the divine law (*ʿalā ghayr qānūn al-sharʿ*).[199] On numerous other occasions, al-Shawkānī draws a distinction between the rights of humans and the rights of God. In one example, he maintains that there is no point in discussing various possibilities of retribution (*qiṣāṣ*) that involve the rights of humans. These are regulated by the imam, whose duty it is to do justice to someone who has been wronged.[200] In another example he argues that if a group of people steals an amount punishable by amputation, this penalty is not enforced unless each individual in this group steals this amount, "because the Lawgiver made the unqualified minimum amount a condition for the unqualified amputation penalty; and since blood is inviolable it should not be spilled unjustly." Al-Shawkānī then argues that it is not valid to draw an analogy between this case and the case of enforcing the execution penalty on a group that murders one person, because the latter is the right of a human (*ḥaqq li-ādamī*), whereas the former is the right of God.[201]

Of course it can be argued that the rights of humans and the rights of God can both be part of sharia, but al-Shawkānī leaves no doubt that he conceives of a human law outside the realm of the divine sharia. *Al-Sayl al-Jarrār* is only one of several works by al-Shawkānī that is full of arguments against the imposition, in the name of divine law, of prohibitions or obligations for which there are no valid explicit indicants. Such, for example, are his rejection of stipulating requirements for the lawful slaughter of animals other than those spelled out in valid indicants;[202] his argument that while circumcision is permissible, and that there is no evidence to corroborate the widely held belief that it is a religious obligation;[203] and his contention that foods that have not been expressly prohibited are permissible.[204] And in another example still, in reference to the reports that prohibit Muslims from eating from gold or silver plates, and prohibit men from wearing gold or silk, al-Shawkānī argues that this *sharʿī* ruling applies only to these specific prohibited uses and cannot be extended beyond them.[205] In the absence of valid evidence for "moving from the principle [*aṣl*] of permissibility to prohibition, one should hold to the principle that is corroborated by the original state of innocence [*barāʾa aṣliyya*]; this is the duty of every fair-minded person [*munṣif*] who has not been struck by the scourge of fear of the majority."[206] The key reasoning in all of the above is that these are permissible acts, but their permissibility is not regulated in sharia law. Rather, al-Shawkānī refers to this permissibility as *ḥalāl ṭaliq*, that is, unbounded permissibility that is *outside the jurisdiction of sharia.*

In all of the above, al-Shawkānī puts the law in the service of the community and its well-being. Against the pious tendency to choose the safer, more restrictive interpretations of the law when the indicants are ambiguous, he frequently argues in favor of choosing the easiest and less onerous options (*rukhaṣ*).[207] And, like Walī Allāh, he repeatedly argues that it is the intent of the Lawgiver to provide facility and ease (*taysīr*) to His worshippers. In fact, a legal license that mitigates a certain obligation, or provides a leeway that spares a Muslim the risk of failing to comply with a difficult legal injunction, is as constitutive of "pure and unblemished sharia" as any valid obligation or prohibition.[208] In the same spirit of *taysīr*, al-Shawkānī discusses at length the actions and sayings of the Prophet and their applicability to the rest of Muslims. He notes the varying views on this subject and suggests that, in general, whatever laws have been revealed regarding the Prophet apply equally to his community, unless there is an indicant (*dalīl*) that shows that a certain action is exclusively applicable to him.[209] However, al-Shawkānī adds, if the Prophet says that something is forbidden to him and permissible to his community, then it is not lawful for Muslims to emulate the Prophet in his abstention (*lā yusharraʿ al-tanazzuh*), since "there is no piety in abandoning that which is lawful [*laysa fī tark al-ḥalāl waraʿ*]."[210] To al-Shawkānī, the purified, magnanimous law is founded on the principle of bringing about benefit and warding off harm (*jalb al-maṣāliḥ* and *dafʿ al-mafāsid*); this is the purpose of every injunction, abrogation, or particularization in the law. Muhammad's religion is a "guide to ease [*yusr*] and not suffering [*ʿusr*]"; it brings about good tidings not repugnance, and "it facilitates harmony and unity and prevents division and discord."[211]

Barāʾa: The Natural State of Innocence

Underlying this general concept of *taysīr*, and in fact underlying all the other valid principles of jurisprudence, is the grand principle of *barāʾa* that, according to al-Shawkānī, applies to everything in sharia. Of course, the concept of *barāʾa* was not invented by Walī Allāh or al-Shawkānī, but the centrality of its deployment in their respective projects is remarkable. And for al-Shawkānī in particular, the only principle (*aṣl*) that he seems to add to the two textual *uṣūl*, the Qurʾān and the Sunna, is *barāʾa*. In the usage of contemporary radicals, as in the usage of Ibn ʿAbd al-Wahhāb, *barāʾa* means dissociation: dissociation from unbelievers, sinners, political and doctrinal opponents, and so on. However, for most of the reformers of the long eighteenth century, *barāʾa* had several connotations, but almost all are diametrically opposed to this restrictive and adversarial understanding of the term.

Al-Shawkānī deploys the principle of *barā'a* in various contexts, but he frequently uses the concept in conjunction with, and to corroborate the general concept of, *taysīr*. In his major works on law or hadith, al-Shawkānī frequently reflects on legal *uṣūl* and derives legal precepts that he deploys in his derivation and authentication of legal injunctions. One of many such examples is his *Nayl al-Awṭār min Aḥādīth Sayyid al-Akhyār*.[212] The book is a commentary on *Muntaqā al-Akhbār* by Abū al-Barakāt Majd al-Dīn Ibn Taymiyya (d. 1255),[213] and focuses on hadiths that have legal import. In this book, al-Shawkānī traces different transmissions and versions of hadith and investigates their soundness or weakness;[214] examines the language usages and terminology in various hadith and explains their conventional *sharʿī* meanings; infers the legal rulings from these hadiths, commenting on the ways these rulings are derived, and on the relative strength of the evidence behind varying derivations; and deduces general juristic precepts and principles that are then assessed against the views of jurists and reapplied to the branches of the law. In numerous instances, this last step of theorizing concepts and principles that become *uṣūl* in their own right culminates in reiterating the principles of *taysīr* and *barā'a*.

Barā'a is used to refer to the state of persons, objects, and legal categories. One of the areas where the principle is most invoked is ritual purity: "The origin [*aṣl*] in everything," al-Shawkānī argues, "is purity, because positing impurity would require people to observe certain religious rulings, while the principle is the absence of such requirement. [The principle of] *barā'a* requires that there be no obligation in something that is possible unless this obligation is determined in a way that overrides this probability in favor of more certainty. Someone who asserts rulings and attributes them to the *sharʿ* without evidence is no less of a transgressor than one who nullifies rulings that have been established by textual evidence. Both result either from attributing to God things He does not say, or from nullifying, without evidence, what He legislates for His worshippers."[215] That the principle state of things is purity is known from both the general (*kulliyāt*) and particular rulings of sharia; without a positive definitive evidence one should not depart from this original assessment of innocence (*barā'a*) from impurity and impose rulings that have broad implications for people (*taʿummu bihi al-balwā*). The Messenger of God, says al-Shawkānī, "instructed us to remain silent on matters over which God is silent, and informed us that this silence is tantamount to pardon."[216] Thus, in the absence of textual evidence that justifies the departure from the original assessment of purity (based on *barā'a*), no worshipper of God should claim the impurity of something based on mere opinion. A possible reason for this arbitrary assertion of impurity is the erroneous assumption that impurity and prohibition are adjoined. According to al-Shawkānī, "the prohibition of something does not prove its impurity, neither through congruency, nor implication, nor concomitance. Thus the prohibition of wine, carrion, and blood do not imply their impurity." In fact, the Prophet told his community that "it is only the eating of carrion that is forbidden," suggesting that carrion is not impure in itself. If the simple prohibition of something indicates its impurity, then God's saying, "Your mothers are forbidden to you" would be evidence of the impurity of mothers! A Muslim, adds al-Shawkānī, never becomes impure, in life or in death.[217]

In the above example, *barā'a* refers to a person's original state of purity. "Ritual impurity is a legal ruling that transfers from the judgment entailed by the original state and by innocence [*nāqil 'an al-ḥukm alladhī yaqtaḍihi al-aṣl wal-barā'a*]. So the opinion of one who claims it [impurity] is not accepted unless there is an indicant that is appropriate to affect this transfer."[218] *Barā'a* also refers to the original freedom from legal liability, which means that, in the absence of a stated textual evidence for an obligation, or in the absence of an indicant that justifies departure from a state of legal nonobligation, one should not add obligations (or prohibitions) where there are none. In sum, the rules of obligation cannot be confirmed without evidence (*al-aḥkām al-taklīfiyya lā tathbut bidūn dalīl*), and refraining from the addition of legal obligations conforms with the principle of *barā'at al-dhimma* (freedom from legal obligation) because of the presumption of the continuation of the original state of freedom from legal obligation (*al-barā'a al-aṣliyya mustaṣḥaba*).[219]

As noted earlier, al-Shawkānī rejects the addition of unattested obligations even if they are meritorious. In a section in a book on forged hadiths, al-Shawkānī examines various reports asserting that "it is permissible to act on the basis of what has been attributed to the Prophet without examining the soundness of these reports, as long as their content is benevolent." Al-Shawkānī scrutinizes the chains of transmission of these reports and dismisses some of them for their faulty *isnād*s. However, he also notes that some of these traditions are reported in the compilations of Ibn Ḥanbal and Ibn Māja and have *isnād*s in which there is no one who can be accused of fabrication. And yet, al-Shawkānī quickly adds, with the support of yet another sound hadith, "even if the [absence of fabricators] attests to this tradition, I still say, my heart and mind reject it, and I suspect it is unlikely [to have come] from the Prophet." Al-Shawkānī adds that scholars in general are lenient in regard to traditions encouraging virtuous acts; they report them on the authority of a group, without a clear chain of transmission, and they are only careful about the traditions that have legal import. Al-Shawkānī maintains, however, that all legal rulings are on equal footing, and there should be no distinction between them when it comes to methods for establishing their authority. This, he explains, is a grave matter because it entails attributing to God things He did not say.[220]

Walī Allāh invokes similar principles in his writings. When acts of obedience (*ṭāʿāt*) are prescribed, some principles ought to be observed, such as "obligating only what is within capacity [*muyassar*]" and incorporating among religious obligations only things that are based on clear, precise, and unambiguous evidence. For this reason, Walī Allāh maintains, virtuous actions such as modesty are not considered among the pillars of Islam for lack of evidence ascribing them as such, although there is no doubt about their merit.[221] In another context, Walī Allāh argues against excessive eagerness in the application of the law, because it can be counterproductive. So, the fulfillment of a *farḍ kifāya*, the collective obligation for Muslims that is fulfilled once a sufficient number perform it, would have detrimental effects on their livelihoods if all Muslims performed it at once. Such, for example, are the obligations to teach the religious sciences, or to perform the duties of the office of the caliph, both of which are legislated in the interest of order and would be fulfilled if a small number of people (one in the case of the caliph) undertake them. The reason that these duties are issued collectively to Muslims is that it is not possible in advance to designate the individuals to whom these duties can be assigned. Moreover, failure by some individuals to perform these obligations would not result in the corruption of the soul or the prevalence of savagery.[222]

One of the purposes of legislation, according to Walī Allāh, "is to block the gates of profundity in religious matters; so as not to have people holding firmly (to pious practices) who are followed by others who doubt that these are obligatory divine acts of worship, to be followed by yet another generation for whom the doubt becomes certainty. . . . As such, religion would continue to be distorted, as in His saying, may He be exalted: 'And a monasticism they invented which We have not prescribed for them' (Qurʾān, Ḥadīd 57:27). . . . Because of all of these meanings the Prophet asserted to his community that they should be provident in actions, and not to be excessive to the point that would lead to apathy and confusion in religion, or to the neglect of means for civilizational development."[223] Therefore, according to Walī Allāh, ease and lack of profundity are both intentional aspects of legislation, needed for the maintenance of a sustainable social order. This is why the Prophet frequently specified the valid licenses and exceptional permissions and did not relegate the identification of these to people's judgment.[224]

Despite their significantly different styles, it is clear that both Walī Allāh and al-Shawkānī, along with other eighteenth-century reformers, were concerned with ease and facility and argued against the expansion of the law without valid evidence. In its most far-reaching articulation, the principle of *barā'a* is nothing less than a proclamation of the limitedness of the sphere of divine law, a law that coexists with a parallel legal system that falls outside the realm of the sacred and is regulated by humans. Moreover, al-Shawkānī's categorical dismissal of *qiyās* amounts to a total rejection of what some have termed an analogical discursive mind (*'aql fiqhī*), one that posits an idealized past and attempts to extend it through analogical thinking into the future. The intellectual consequences of these departures were momentous, as were the fruits of the attempt to combine various modes of thinking and knowing, including legal reasoning, Sufi gnosticism, and rational demonstration. Equally radical was the renewed emphasis on *ijtihād* that was reinvigorated and "democratized" in varying degrees across the Muslim world, thereby unsettling the traditional hierarchies of authority in the interest of an empowered populace, a populace of participants not spectators, and a restrained and accountable intellectual elite.

In the literature of reformers we consider today as the custodians of the modern Islamic reform traditions, tradition is present but largely symbolic, and often articulated in response to the needs of a threatened identity seeking refuge in an idealized past. In contrast to this idealism, a most distinctive feature of eighteenth-century reformative discourse is its historicity, the awareness that forms of authority are historically produced, and that history, human history, is the essential dimension for understanding authority. Eighteenth-century reformers professed the temporal and logical priority of the divine in the universe, as well as the centrality of revelation as the focal point of all thought, but they also acknowledged that the ultimate truth about the sacred is a potential that can only be recovered through the mediation of the human, and that all such attempts at recovery are historical.

The religious discourse of eighteenth-century thinkers had multiple degrees of engagement with sites of power and authority: political authority, intellectual authority, the authority of ordinary Muslims, and the authority of the present. The binding intermediary authority of mediating knowledge, of jurists as well as textual traditions that had become normative and authoritative, was rejected. And nothing escaped the rigorous systematic scrutiny of the age. The authority of individual reason was upheld by underscoring the right of ordinary Muslims to think and choose, as well as the responsibility of intellectual elites to relinquish demands for obedience and to exchange with the public the tools that make individual choice possible. Aware of their presentness, eighteenth-century reformers re-created tradition in the present and demanded recognition of its excellence and singularity.

The reform tradition of the eighteenth century questioned classical knowledge and self-consciously set out to remake it. It sought to rehabilitate its present by renegotiating its relationship with the past. This creative feat challenges the hegemony of the scheme of decline that permeates the current imagination of most inquiries—academic as well as popular—into eighteenth-century history. What this book has sought to capture is a glimpse of the remarkable spirit—at once original and radical—of this century as defined by intellectual giants of Islamic thought from diverse regions of the Muslim world. It is only to the extent that we can recapture their vision in their own words, and within their own epistemic paradigms, that we can begin to imagine the relevance of their reform projects to today's Muslim communities.

Notes

Introduction

1. See, for example, H. Islamoglu, ed., *The Ottoman Empire and the World-Economy* (Cambridge: Cambridge University Press, 1987); R. Kasaba, *The Ottoman Empire and the World Economy: The Nineteenth Century* (Albany: SUNY Press, 1988). Both Islamoglu and Kasaba are proponents of the world systems theory developed by Immanuel Wallerstein, and they examine ways in which the Ottoman Empire was integrated into capitalist markets. More recent studies have shifted the focus to local social and economic histories and have underscored the existence of vibrant economies in the Ottoman period. These studies undermine the Orientalist paradigm of eighteenth-century decline. See, for example, Beshara Doumani, *Rediscovering Palestine: Merchants and Peasants in Jebal Nablus, 1700–1900* (Berkeley: University of California Press, 1995); Hala Fattah, *The Politics of Regional Trade in Iraq, Arabia, and the Gulf, 1745–1900* (Albany: SUNY Press, 1997); and Dina Rizk Khoury, *State and Provincial Society in the Ottoman Empire: Mosul, 1540–1834* (Cambridge: Cambridge University Press, 1997). For an overview of this historiography, see the introduction to Joel Beinin, *Workers and Peasants in the Modern Middle East* (Cambridge: Cambridge University Press, 2001).

2. For a recent work that questions the notion of decline in the seventeenth century in the Ottoman Empire and the Maghreb, see Khaled El-Rouayheb, *Islamic Intellectual History in the Seventeenth Century: Scholarly Currents in the Ottoman Empire and the Maghreb* (New York: Cambridge University Press, 2015). El-Rouayheb provides compelling evidence to question the notions of intellectual decline in the seventeenth century and argues for the "need to look elsewhere for more reliable indicators of what was going on at the time" (26). El-Rouayheb contends that there was a lively tradition of studying philosophy and the rational sciences in the seventeenth-century Ottoman Empire, reflected in, among other things, the "dramatic increase in the number and length of Ottoman writings on ādāb al-baḥth" (discussions of dialectics and logic) (70), and the emergence of "a newly articulated ideal of the acquisition of knowledge through deep reading" (98). In the Maghreb, the doctrinal treatise of Muḥammad b. Yūsuf al-Sanūsī (d. 1490) was rediscovered and transmitted to Egypt and the Hejaz, and with it an emphasis on the rejection of imitation (*taqlīd*) in matters of faith, and the insistence on the importance of logic and theology. El-Rouayheb also adduces intellectual vibrancy in the philosophical discussions of mysticism, as reflected in the defenses of the concept of *waḥdat al-wujūd* of Ibn al-ʿArabī by such thinkers as al-Kurānī (d. 1690) and ʿAbd al-Ghanī al-Nābulsī (d. 1731). As I show in this book, the direct and compelling deployment of *ijtihād* by eighteenth-century thinkers was far more deliberate, pervasive, and systematic, and had radical transformative effects. Moreover, a key feature of eighteenth-century discussions of *ijtihād* is the attempt to extend its scope and purview to include larger segments of the educated population or, in the case of Yemeni scholars, to include all ordinary Muslims.

3. For an overview of the rise of autonomous provincial powers, their local social and economic contexts, and their links to interregional as well as world capitalist markets, see Beinin, *Workers and Peasants in the Modern Middle East*, chap. 2.

4. This book's primary focus is cultural, not political or social. The main reason for the relative lack of social and political analysis is that it would take several book-length studies to exhaust the multiple regional contexts of the diverse intellectual traditions considered in the book. However, throughout the chapters, I offer insights into such social and political contexts, and I outline for each of the key scholars under examination the sense of crisis that drives their respective reform initiatives. Additionally, chapter 4 offers a case study that contextualizes the intellectual activities of the Yemeni scholar Muḥammad b. ʿAlī al-Shawkānī and attempts to provide a fuller understanding of his reform activities in their larger social and political contexts. This explains not only my longer discussion of al-Shawkānī but also the difficulty of providing similar full treatments in one book. I hope that this study of the intellectual vitality and transformative originality of eighteenth-century thought will invite future studies that provide fuller analysis of each of the traditions under examination.

5. Albert Hourani, *Arabic Thought in the Liberal Age, 1798–1939* (Cambridge: Cambridge University Press, 1983), introduction.

6. On the difference between al-Jabartī's experience of Europe and those of the reformers examined in this book, see chapter 4.

7. See Hourani, *Arabic Thought*, 69–83.

8. For a recent articulation of the revisionist views as represented mainly in the works of Ibrahim Abu al-Lughud, Roger Owen, Peter Gran, and John Voll, see Reinhard Schulze, "Was ist die islamische Aufklarung?," *Die Welt des Islams* 36, no. 3 (1996): 276–325.

9. I discuss the second viewpoint in chapter 2.

10. For example, in a long introduction to a work by al-Shawkānī, one of the leading intellectuals of the eighteenth century, the editor asserts that al-Shawkānī was an "intellectual summit in an age void of summits," and that he laid the foundation for Afghānī and ʿAbdu. Muḥammad b. ʿAlī al-Shawkānī, *Rafʿ al-Aṣāṭīn fī Ḥukm al-Ittiṣāl bil-Salāṭīn*, ed. Ḥ. M. Muḥammad (Beirut: Dār Ibn Ḥazm; Sanaa: Maktabat al-Jīl al-Jadīd, 1992), 22–23. Thus, although the editor recognizes the richness of al-Shawkānī's thought, he reiterates the two main misconceptions about the eighteenth century: that it was an age of decline and that there was continuity between exceptional figures like al-Shawkānī and the later Muslim thinkers who deserve to be called reformers, namely, Afghānī and ʿAbdu.

11. Thus Fazlur Rahman argues that as a result of the "belief that the *Sunna* of the Prophet and the Qur'anic rulings on social behavior have to be more or less literally implemented in all ages," the ideas of eighteenth-century thinkers did not contribute to the "rethinking of the social content of Islam" or to its reformulation; see Rahman, "Revival and Reform in Islam," in *The Cambridge History of Islam*, vol. 2, ed. P. M. Holt, Ann K. S. Lambton, and B. Lewis (London: Cambridge University Press, 1970), 632–56, esp. 640. Also see John Obert Voll, *Islam: Continuity and Change in the Modern World* (Boulder, Colo.: Westview, 1982). Voll speaks of a "widespread spirit of socio-moral reconstruction based on a more strict adherence to the Quran and the Sunnah of the Prophet" (38). He highlights the intense interest in hadith scholarship in Cairo, Medina, and other regions (54, 58), and connects this scholarship to the desire, among the reformers of the eighteenth century, to bridge the "gap between the ideal community that was described by the traditions" and the actual practices in contemporary Muslim societies (60).

12. See Rahman, "Revival and Reform in Islam"; Roger Owen, "The Middle East in the Eighteenth Century: An 'Islamic Society in Decline'? A Critique of Gibb and Bowen's *Islamic Society and the West*," *Review of Middle East Studies* 1 (1975): 101–12; Peter Gran, *Islamic Roots of Capitalism: Egypt, 1760–1840* (Syracuse, N.Y.: Syracuse University Press, 1998); and Voll, *Islam*. I offer a detailed analysis and critique of these revisionist accounts in the chapters that follow.

13. For the traditional Orientalist views, see H. A. R. Gibb and H. Bowen, *Islamic Society and the West: A Study of the Impact of Western Civilization on Moslem Culture in the Near East*, vol. 1, *Islamic Society in the Eighteenth Century*, part 1 (London, 1950), part 2 (London, 1957). Other examples of the historiography of decline include Uriel Heyd, "The Later Ottoman Empire in Rumelia and Anatolia," in *The Cambridge History of Islam*, vol. 1A, *The Central Islamic Lands from Pre-Islamic Times to the First World War*, ed. P. M. Holt, Ann K. S. Lambton, and Bernard Lewis (Cambridge: Cambridge University Press, 1995), 354–73. Heyd chronicles a process of steady decline from the end of the seventeenth century onward. For the argument that decline accelerated in the eighteenth century, see P. M. Holt, "The Later Ottoman Empire in Egypt and the Fertile Crescent," in *The Cambridge History of Islam*, vol. 1A, 374–93. Ann K. S. Lambton makes a similar argument for Iran in her "Persia: The Breakdown of Society," in *The Cambridge History of Islam*, vol. 1A, 430–67. Another standard example of the decline thesis is Ali Merad, "Reformism in Modern Islam," *Cultures* 4, no. 1 (1977): 108–27. Merad argues that decline was due to the "triumph of legalistic Islam" and the closure of the gates of *ijtihād*; he also argues that revival began toward the end of the eighteenth century as a result of the "awakening of Muslim consciousness" due to the efforts of Wahhābīya movement and the cultural contacts with the European Enlightenment.

For a political economy approach, see Roger Owen, "The Middle East in the Eighteenth Century: An 'Islamic Society in Decline?' A Critique of Gibb and Bowen's *Islamic Society and the West*," *Review of Middle East Studies* 1 (1975): 101–12; and Thomas Naff and Roger Owen, eds., *Studies in Eighteenth-Century Islamic History* (Carbondale: Southern Illinois University Press, 1977).

14. Owen, "The Middle East in the Eighteenth Century," 109.

15. Naff and Owen's *Studies in Eighteenth-Century Islamic History* also confirms this general notion of intellectual decline. The book is divided into three sections dealing with politics, economics/society, and culture. Introductory essays by Naff, Owen, and Albert Hourani provide the general synthesis for each of these sections. The book as a whole does not reject the general thesis of decline, but it argues that there are some exceptions to this thesis, in terms of both regions and social groups. So while the studies in this book provide a more nuanced understanding of the eighteenth century, for the most part they also confirm the notion of relative decline of the Middle East, both internally and vis-à-vis Europe. In contrast to the more optimistic note in his review of Gibb and Bowen, Owen also draws a dim picture in his introduction to a set of studies that see nothing but decline in the economic sphere (trade, population, urban wealth). Rather than providing an argument in favor of revising accepted views about eighteenth-century economic history, Owen focuses on the difficulties of finding data and deciding on the appropriate theoretical basis for studying eighteenth-century economy; such difficulties, according to Owen, highlight the relative nature of any judgment on the eighteenth century.

In the sphere of culture, the picture is even more bleak; faced with a lack of evidence of traditional cultural vitality, Hourani adduces such evidence from increased contact with the West and the increased European influence in the Middle East (although he points out that the effect of this contact is not necessarily positive as far as traditional Islamic institutions were concerned). The only exception to the overall tone of the book is a study by Hamid Algar that illustrates the intellectual vigor of Persian Shiism. Yet even this excellent study is undermined by the grim portrayals by Ann Lambton and Charles Issawi of the political paralysis and economic disintegration of eighteenth-century Iran.

Therefore, despite many contrary assertions, this book neither provides a revisionist view of the eighteenth century nor illustrates the utility of the paradigm of political economy in providing such revisions. For further discussion in support of political economy, see, for example, Peter Gran, "Political Economy as a Paradigm for the Study of Islamic History," *International Journal of Middle East Studies* 11, no. 4 (1980): 511–26.

More recent studies of the premodern period have been much more successful in undermining the paradigm of decline (see, e.g., Doumani, *Rediscovering Palestine*; and Khoury, *State and Provincial Society in the Ottoman Empire*). Through the prism of political economy, these studies look at specific developments in specific regions and demonstrate the vibrancy of various societies and economies. For example, in *Rediscovering Palestine*, Doumani examines the regional commerce and peasant economy of Nablus and its hinterland; by focusing on underlying economic and cultural processes, he underscores the local character of change and provides a compelling counter to the tendency to limit political history to groups with direct contact with the West.

Closer to the realm of culture, Julia A. Clancy-Smith maintains that, at the beginning of European colonial expansion, "for many saints and Sufis, had politics not come to find them the preferred mode of coping would have surely been to ignore the presence of the infidels"; these ignorers of the West, Clancy-Smith argues, were historically and numerically important. Thus, for local communities, even as their awareness of larger regional and international forces around them increased, the world did not stop turning. Clancy-Smith, *Rebel and Saint: Muslim Notables, Populist Protest, Colonial Encounters (Algeria and Tunisia, 1800–1904)* (Berkeley: University of California Press, 1994), 5. See also references to the Sufi Ibn Idrīs as belonging to a group of "ignorers of the West" who, though aware of it, were not concerned with the encroachment of the West on Muslim lands. R. S. O'Fahey, *Enigmatic Saint: Aḥmad Ibn Idris and the Idrisi Tradition* (Evanston, Ill.: Northwestern University Press, 1990), 5, 18.

16. See, for example, Owen's "The Middle East in the Eighteenth Century," his much-quoted critique of Gibb and Bowen's *Islamic Society in the Eighteenth Century*. Rudolph Peters, a critic of Schulze, suggests that the perception of an eighteenth-century enlightenment may be valid if based on cultural activities, but doubts that it would hold if one examines economic and political developments. Peters, "*Idjtihād* and *Taqlīd* in 18th and 19th Century Islam," *Die Welt des Islams* 20, nos. 3–4 (1980): 131–45.

17. The thesis of the closure of the gates of *ijtihād* has been thoroughly undermined in the work of Wael Hallaq, but it continues to be invoked uncritically by historians of the modern period. See, for example, Wael Hallaq, "Was the Gate of *Ijtihād* Closed?," *International Journal of Middle East Studies* 16 (1987): 42–67.

18. Abū al-Ṭayyib al-Sayyid Ḥasan al-Qanūjī, *Al-Ḥiṭṭa fī Dhikr al-Ṣiḥāḥ al-Sitta* (Lahore: Islāmī Akadimī, 1977), 171.

19. As far as I can tell, these last two scholars were not as important in terms of either their intellectual productivity or their social significance.

20. Zaydism is one of the branches of Shiʿi Islam.

21. Muḥammad b. ʿAlī al-Shawkānī, *Al-Badr al-Ṭāliʿ bi Maḥāsin man baʿd al-Qarn al-Sābiʿ*, 2 vols. (Beirut: Dār al-Maʿrifa, n.d.), 2:133–39.

22. For general information on Shāh Walī Allāh and his time, see the introductory sections of G. N. Jalbani, *Teachings of Shāh Walīyullāh of Delhi* (Lahore: Sh. Muhammad Ashraf, 1967). See also J. M. S. Baljon, *Religion and Thought of Shah Walī Allah Dihlawi* (Leiden, the Netherlands: E. J. Brill, 1986); Sayyid Athar Abbas Rizvi, *Shāh Walī-Allāh and His Times* (Canberra: Maʿrifat, 1980); and the chapter on the eighteenth century in Barbara Daly Metcalf, *Islamic Revival in British India: Deoband, 1860–1900* (Princeton, N.J.: Princeton University Press, 1982). On Walī Allāh's momentous influence on Islamic thought in India, and on the scholarly views about him, see Marcia K. Hermansen, introduction to *The Conclusive Argument from God:*

Shāh Walī Allāh of Delhi's "Ḥujjat Allāh al-Bāligha," trans. Marcia K. Hermansen (Leiden, the Netherlands: E. J. Brill, 1996), xxxiii–xxxvi. On the works of Walī Allāh, see Hermansen, *The Conclusive Argument from God*, xxxvi–xxxvii. I have used Hermansen's translation with occasional adjustments; none of these differences has to do with quality of translation but are a matter of emphasis and to conform to my own translations of other texts. Also see Mawlawi H. Hidayat Husain, "The Persian Autobiography of Shāh Walīullah Bin ʿAbd al-Raḥmān al-Dihlavī: Its English Translation and a List of His Works," *Journal and Proceedings of the Asiatic Society of Bengal*, n.s., 8 (1912): 161–75.

23. On the notion of crisis, see Fazlur Rahman, "The Thinker of Crisis: Shah Waliy-Ullah," *Pakistan Quarterly* 6, no. 2 (1956): 44–48; Jalbani, *Teachings of Shāh Walīyullāh*, 112–13; and Aziz Ahmad, "Political and Religious Ideas of Shāh Walī-Ullāh of Delhi," *Muslim World* 52, no. 1 (1962): 22.

24. Marcia K. Hermansen aptly describes Walī Allāh's project as follows: "He understood his mission to be the integration of the increasingly fragmented and disparate articulations of the Islamic intellectual tradition in his own time." See Hermansen, *The Conclusive Argument from God*, xv–xvi.

25. On the life of Muḥammad Ibn ʿAbd al-Wahhāb, see Amīn Saʿīd, *Sīrat al-Imām al-Shaykh Muḥammad Ibn ʿAbd al-Wahhāb* (Beirut: Sharikat al-Tawzīʿ al-ʿArabīya, 1384 AH),; and A. M. Naṣīr, *Al-Shaykh al-Imām Muḥammad Ibn ʿAbd al-Wahhāb wa Manhjuhu fī Mabāḥith al-ʿAqīda* (Beirut: Dār al-Shurūq, 1983); there is also some useful information in the otherwise dated article by "Phoenix," "A Brief Outline of the Wahabi Movement," *Journal of the Central Asian Society* 17 (1930): 401–16.

26. There are several good studies on the life and writings of Ibn Fūdī and on the Fulani jihad movements. See, for example, Marilyn Robinson Waldman, "The Fulani Jihād: A Reassessment," *Journal of African History* 6, no. 3 (1965): 333–55; J. O. Hunwick, "Religion and State in the Songhay Empire, 1464–1591," in *Islam in Tropical Africa*, ed. I. M. Lewis (Oxford: Oxford University Press, 1966); Murray Last, "Reform in West Africa: The Jihād Movements of the Nineteenth Century," in *The History of West Africa*, vol. 2, ed. J. F. A. Ajayi and Michael Crowder (Essex, UK: Longman, 1974); Peter B. Clarke, *West Africa and Islam* (London: Edward Arnold, 1982); Mervyn Hiskett, *The Development of Islam in West Africa* (London: Longman, 1984); and B. G. Martin, *Muslim Brotherhoods in Nineteenth-Century Africa* (Cambridge: Cambridge University Press, 1976).

27. An excellent study of the development of the thought of Ibn Fūdī is Louis Brenner, "Muslim Thought in Eighteenth-Century West Africa: The Case of Shaykh Uthman b. Fudi," in *Eighteenth-Century Renewal and Reform in Islam*, ed. Nehemia Levtzion and John Obert Voll (Syracuse, N.Y.: Syracuse University Press, 1987). For the purposes of this study, the thought of Ibn Fūdī will be examined in its final shape, although it is interesting to note how his early ideological predications conditioned his later work. For material relating to the status and role of education before and during the jihad, see Louis Brenner and Murray Last, "The Role of Language in West African Islam," *Africa* 55, no. 4 (1985): 432–46; A. D. Bivar and M. Hiskett, "The Arabic Literature of Nigeria to 1804: A Provisional Account," *Bulletin of the School of Oriental and African Studies* 25 (1962): 104–49; and Mervyn Hiskett, "Material Relating to the State of Learning among the Fulani before Their Jihād," *Bulletin of the School of Oriental and African Studies* 19 (1957): 550–78.

28. On other West African movements, see Last, "Reform in West Africa"; Martin, *Muslim Brotherhoods*; Clarke, *West Africa and Islam*; and Hiskett, *The Development of Islam*.

29. For reference to some of the writings of these scholars, see Saiyid ʿAbdallāh Muḥammad al-Ḥabshī, *Muʾallafāt Ḥukkām al-Yaman* (Wiesbaden, Germany, 1979).

30. I am aware of only one book on Yemen in the eighteenth and nineteenth centuries that has a section on al-Shawkānī: Ḥusayn b. ʿAbdullāh al-ʿAmrī, *The Yemen in the 18th and 19th Centuries: A Political and Intellectual History* (London: Ithaca, 1985). There is also an Arabic book on al-Shawkānī by the same author, and another one by ʿAbd al-Ghanī Qāsim Ghālib al-Sharjī, *al-Imām al-Shawkānī, Ḥayātuhu wa Fikruhu* (Beirut and Sanaa, 1988). Also see works by Ibrāhīm Hilāl. All of these works are descriptive and do not address the questions raised in this research project. Al-Sharjī's book contains a particularly useful list of al-Shawkānī's unpublished manuscripts. The only other studies of al-Shawkānī are those by Bernard Haykel, who focuses on the Yemeni context of al-Shawkānī's career rather than the larger intellectual implications of his thought and how it relates to other eighteenth-century intellectual developments. See, for example, Bernard Haykel, "Al-Shawkānī and the Jurisprudential Unity of Yemen," *Revue du Monde Musulman et de la Méditerranée* 67 (1993): 53–65; and Haykel, *Revival and Reform in Islam: The Legacy of Muhammad al-Shawkani* (Cambridge: Cambridge University Press, 2003).

There is no complete list of al-Shawkānī's works, and the number of books attributed to him currently stands at least at 150. Al-Sharjī, *al-Imām al-Shawkānī, Ḥayātuhu wa Fikruhu* (192–229) lists 278 works. ʿAbdullāh al-Ḥabshī attributes 250 works to him; see his "Thabt bi Muʾallafāt al-ʿAllāma Muḥammad Ibn ʿAlī al-Shawkānī," in *Dirāsāt Yamaniyya*, no. 3 (1979): 65–86. While many of his works have been published, a large number remain in manuscript form. For this research project I analyze most of al-Shawkānī's published works, some of the most important of which are (1) *Nayl al-Awṭār fī Sharḥ Muntaqā al-Aḥkām* (on hadith); (2) *Fatḥ al-Qadīr al-Jāmiʿ bayn Fannay al-Riwāya wal-Tafsīr* (on Qurʾānic exegesis); (3) *Irshād al-Fuḥūl ilā Taḥqīq al-Ḥaqq min ʿIlm al-Uṣūl* (on legal theory); (4) *Al-Sayl al-Jarrār al-Mutadaffiq ʿalā Ḥadāʾiq al-Azhār* (on applied Zaydi law); (5) *Durr al-Saḥāba fī Manāqib al-Qarāba wal-Ṣaḥāba* (on the virtues of the companions of Muḥammad); (6) *Al-Badr al-Ṭāliʿ fī Maḥāsin man baʿd al-Qarn al-Sābiʿ* (biographies of post-seventh-century Muslim intellectuals); (7) *Al-Qawl al-Mufīd fī Aḥkām al-Ijtihād wal-Taqlīd* (on independent legal reasoning); (8) *Qaṭr al-Walī ʿalā Ḥadīth al-Walī* (on the Sufi concept of sainthood); (9) *Al-Dawāʾ al-ʿĀjil fī Dafʿ al-ʿAdū al-Ṣāʾil* (on the origins of the social problems of Yemen); (10) *Sharḥ al-Ṣudūr fī Taḥrīm Rafʿ al-Qubūr* (on the prohibition against worshipping at tombs); (11) *Kashf al-Astār ʿan Ḥukm al-Shafāʿa bil-Jiwār* (on the validity of the Sufi principle of intercession); (12) *Al-Fawāʾid al-Majmūʿa fī al-Aḥādīth al-Mawḍūʿa* (on fabricated hadith); and (13) *Adab al-Ṭalab* (on knowledge and the proper ways of acquiring it).

31. On the life of al-Sanūsī, see Nicola A. Ziadeh, *Sanūsīyah: A Study of a Revivalist Movement in Islam* (Leiden, the Netherlands: E. J. Brill, 1958); E. E. Evans-Pritchard, *The Sanusi of Cyrenaica* (Oxford: Oxford University Press, 1954); and Martin, *Muslim Brotherhoods*, 99–124. These works deal more with the history of the Sanūsī order than with the thought of the Grand Sanūsī. For some discussion of al-Sanūsī's opinions on *ijtihād*, see Peters, "*Idjtihād* and *Taqlīd*." For a study that covers both the life and works of al-Sanūsī, see Knut S. Vikor, *Sufi and Scholar on the Desert Edge: Muḥammad b. ʿAlī al-Sanūsī and His Brotherhood* (Evanston, Ill.: Northwestern University Press, 1995).

32. Almost all the non-Sanūsīya lodges mentioned by Evans-Pritchard were urban; see Evans-Prichard, *The Sanusi of Cyrenaica*, 84–97.

33. On al-Shawkānī, for example, see Brinkley Messick, *The Calligraphic State: Textual Domination and History in a Muslim Society* (Berkeley: University of California Press, 1996), 49 ("counted as an intellectual ancestor by virtually all Yemeni shariʿa scholars").

34. Schulze argues that this tendency, in effect, brings God closer to man and makes religion "more human"; this, according to Schulze, serves to replace the theocentric worldview

with an anthropocentric one, "founded on the assumption of man's capability to create his own order." See Bernd Radtke, "Sufism in the Eighteenth Century: An Attempt at a Provisional Appraisal," *Die Welt des Islams* 36, no. 3 (1996): 326–64, esp. 360–61; and Radtke, "Erheuchtung und Aufklarung: Islamische Mystik und europaischer Rationalismus," *Die Welt des Islams* 34, no. 1 (1994): 48–66.

35. First by Rahman, then Gibb and others (see following references).

36. Fazlur Rahman, *Islam* (Chicago: University of Chicago Press, 1968), 205.

37. For example, Nikki Keddie, ed., *Scholars, Saints, and Sufis: Muslim Religious Institutions in the Middle East since 1500* (Berkeley: University of California Press, 1972).

38. So far, not a single monograph has been written to substantiate the use of the term as applied to Sufi movements from this period.

39. O'Fahey, *Enigmatic Saint*; and more fully in R. S. O'Fahey and Bernd Radtke, "Neo-Sufism Reconsidered," *Der Islam* 70, no. 1 (1993): 52–87; and Radtke, "Sufism in the Eighteenth Century." Also see Ahmad Dallal, "Origins and Objectives of Islamic Revivalist Thought, 1750–1850," *JAOS* (1993): 341–59. Interestingly, the concept of neo-Sufism has currency among historians but is squarely rejected by scholars who specialize in Sufism and study its content.

40. This is the theme of Michel Chodkiewicz's book on this subject. See Michel Chodkiewicz, *Seal of the Saints: Prophethood and Sainthood in the Doctrine of Ibn 'Arabī* (Cambridge: Islamic Text Society, 1993), 60–88.

41. See O'Fahey and Radtke, "Neo-Sufism Reconsidered"; and Radtke, "Sufism in the Eighteenth Century." This point is a valid criticism of Schulze but also has its problems. Schulze uses the wrong evidence to illustrate the anthropocentric tendencies of the eighteenth century, but there is much evidence elsewhere, as I will argue later.

42. See Voll, *Islam*; Schulze, "Was ist die islamische Aufklarung?"; and many others who take after them, and even their critics.

43. The term *socio-moral* was used extensively by Fazlur Rahman and has since been adopted by many scholars of modern Islam, especially John Voll. See, for example, Rahman, "Revival and Reform in Islam," 632–56, esp. 637; and Rahman, *Islam and Modernity: Transformation of an Intellectual Tradition* (Chicago: University of Chicago Press, 1982). The term appears in many of Voll's studies of eighteenth-century movements. See, for example, Voll, *Islam*, esp. 38.

44. Voll makes this point in his "The Sudanese Mahdī: Frontier Fundamentalist," *International Journal of Middle East Studies* 10 (1979), 145–66.

45. The main advocate of this view is John Voll. See, for example, Voll, *Islam*; Voll, "Fundamentalism in the Sunni Arab World: Egypt and the Sudan," in *Fundamentalisms Observed*, ed. Martin E. Marty and R. Scott Appleby (Chicago: University of Chicago Press, 1991), 345 and 347–352 on the "Eighteenth-Century Antecedents." Also see Voll, "Scholarly Interrelations between South Asia and the Middle East in the Eighteenth Century," in *The Countries of South Asia: Boundaries, Extensions, and Interrelations*, ed. Peter Gaeffke and David A. Utz (Philadelphia: Department of South Asian Regional Studies, 1988), 49–59; Voll, "Muḥammad Ḥayyā al-Sindī and Muḥammad Ibn 'Abd al-Wahhab: An Analysis of an Intellectual Group in Eighteenth-Century Madīna," *Bulletin of the School of Oriental and African Studies* 38, no. 1 (1974), 32–39; Voll, "The Sudanese Mahdī"; and Voll, "Hadith Scholars and Tariqahs: An Ulama Group in the 18th Century Haramayn and Their Impact in the Islamic World," *Journal of Asian and African Studies* 15, nos. 3–4 (1980), 264–73. See also Nehemia Levtzion and John Obert Voll, eds., *Eighteenth-Century Renewal and Reform in Islam* (Syracuse, N.Y.: Syracuse University Press, 1987); and Peter Gran, *Islamic Roots of Capitalism: Egypt, 1760–1840* (Syracuse, N.Y.: Syracuse University Press, 1998).

To my knowledge, the first articulations of many of these same ideas were by Fazlur Rahman. See in particular his "Revival and Reform in Islam," where he traces the premodern origins of modern reform and argues for a continuity between the two. Rahman also used the term *socio-moral reconstruction* to refer to the focus of eighteenth-century reform and coined and used the term *neo-Sufism* to refer to a Sufism that is subservient to legalistic Islam. Rahman also noted that eighteenth-century reforms were indigenous and "owed nothing whatsoever to any foreign influence in their genesis." For the "pre-modernist reform movements," Rahman maintains, "the consciousness of degeneration, and of the corresponding need to remedy social evils and raise moral standards, was generated from the heart of Muslim society itself"; this, Rahman posits, is in contrast to a "common error" that "regards these as being primarily the result of the impact of the West." Rahman contends that modernist thinking differs from the eighteenth-century legacy in its "positive content," and that it "had to go far beyond anything achieved by the pre-Modernist reform." He asserts, however, that "the purificationist reform-legacy of pre-Modernist days . . . could only have prepared the ground for this modernist thinking." Rahman, "Revival and Reform in Islam," 641–42.

46. It is certainly the case that the eighteenth century witnessed vibrant reform activity, yet it would be wrong to characterize the intellectual legacy of this century as a bridge between classical Islam and modernity. In fact, rather than basing itself on the legacy of the eighteenth century, the so-called modern reform movement was predicated on the abortion of eighteenth-century reform activities due to the encounter with Europe.

47. See, for example, Voll, *Islam*, esp. 38.

48. Perhaps one of the reasons why this thesis is appealing is because it gives the impression, illusive in my view, that because one is examining social activities, the movement of scholars, and tangible human contacts, and not just the circulation of abstract ideas, this makes for good social history and not just old-fashioned intellectual history. This is especially problematic considering that this examination, at least in the studies that have appeared so far, pays little if any attention to ideas.

49. For a useful example of the study of the construction of local knowledge and its social organization, see Messick's discussion of the concept of *ʿadāla* (probity) as a form of social organization of tradition in *The Calligraphic State*. In contrast, my primary interest is in the theoretical formulations of this concept by various eighteenth-century thinkers. See chapter 5 on hadith.

50. For example, al-Shawkānī's connection to the Imamic state that he served does not explain his influence in North Africa or India; for more on this subject, see my chapters that follow.

51. Thus the Yemeni reform tradition to which al-Shawkānī belonged can be traced back to the fifteenth-century writings of Ibn al-Wazīr; this tradition includes such figures as al-Maqbalī and al-Jalāl; needless to say, these individuals' connections to structures of political authority were very different, as can be determined from a study of the evolution of the Zaydi state and its attitude toward each of them. Zaydism came to Yemen through Ṣaʿda at the end of the ninth century, when the Zaydi imam was invited by the tribes of the northern highlands. Zaydism gradually spread its control to the southern highlands. In 1635, the Qāsimī imamate was established after driving out the Ottomans and ending Ottoman rule in Yemen, and it lasted until approximately the middle of the nineteenth century. In 1872, the Ottomans returned to Yemen and remained until the end of the empire. After the end of Ottoman rule, the Ḥamīd al-Dīn imams controlled Yemen until the 1962 revolution. For a concise but excellent general historical overview, see R. B. Serjeant, "The Post-medieval and Modern History of Ṣanʿāʾ and the Yemen," in *Ṣanʿāʾ: An Arabian Islamic City*, ed. R. B. Serjeant and R. Lewcock (London: World of Islam Festival Trust, 1983), 68–107.

52. For an excellent corrective to the common historical narratives that portray the reign of Muḥammad ʿAlī Pāsha as the beginning of Egyptian nationalism, see Khalid Fahmy, *All the Pasha's Men: Mehmed Ali, His Army and the Making of Modern Egypt* (Cambridge: Cambridge University Press, 1997). For portrayals of various eighteenth-century reformers as nationalist heroes struggling to pull their nations out of the darkness of the eighteenth century, see my chapters that follow.

53. Such interest in the "primitive" explains, for example, much anthropological interest in the study of Yemen.

54. For example, Walī Allāh's discussion of *asbāb al-ikhtilāf*—the causes for legal differences—or of *shurūṭ al-Bukhārī*—al-Bukhārī's conditions for including a hadith in his collection.

Chapter 1

1. See W. Bjorkman, "Kafir," in *Encyclopedia of Islam*, CD-ROM ed. (Leiden, the Netherlands: E. J. Brill, 1999), 4:407; D. Gimaret, "Shirk," in *Encyclopedia of Islam*, 9:484; J. O. Hunwick, "Takfir," in *Encyclopedia of Islam*, 10:122; and Elizabeth Sirriyeh, "Wahhabis, Unbelievers and the Problem of Exclusivism," *British Society for Middle Eastern Studies* 16 (1989): 123–32.

2. The main primary sources on Ibn ʿAbd al-Wahhāb are ʿUthmān Ibn Bishr, *ʿUnwān al-Majd fī Tārīkh Najd*, 2 vols. (Riyadh, 1999); and Ḥusayn Ibn Ghannām, *Tārīkh Najd* (Cairo, 1961). Some useful studies of Wahhabism include David Commins, *The Wahhabi Mission and Saudi Arabia* (London, 2006); Michael Cook, "On the Origins of Wahhābism," *Journal of the Royal Asiatic Society of Great Britain and Ireland* 2, no. 2 (1992): 191–202; Natana DeLong-Bas, *Wahhābi Islam: From Revival and Reform to Global Jihād* (New York, 2004); Samira Haj, "Reordering Islamic Orthodoxy: Muḥammad Ibn ʿAbd al-Wahhāb," *Muslim World* 92 (2002): 333–68; Christine Moss Helms, *The Cohesion of Saudi Arabia: Evolution of Political Identity* (Baltimore: Johns Hopkins University Press, 1981); Alexei Vassiliev, *The History of Saudi Arabia* (New York: New York University Press, 2000); John O. Voll, "Wahhābīyah," in *Encyclopedia of Religion*, vol. 15 (New York, 1987), 313–16; H. Laoust, "Ibn ʿAbd al-Wahhāb," in *Encyclopedia of Islam*, 2nd ed., vol. 3 (Leiden, the Netherlands: E. J. Brill, 1971), 677–79; Henry Laoust, *Essai sur les doctrines sociales et politiques de Taki-D-Din Ahmad b. Taimiya* (Cairo: Imprimerie de L'Institut Français d'Archéologie Orientale, 1939); and Abdulaziz H. al-Fahad, "Commentary: From Exclusion to Accommodation: Doctrinal and Legal Evolution of Wahhabism," *New York University Law Review* 79 (2004): 485–519.

3. Incidentally, this is the main argument used to vindicate colonialism as a way of reviving creative thinking in the colonized Muslim world.

4. For example, H. A. R. Gibb and H. Bowen, *Islamic Society and the West: A Study of the Impact of Western Civilization on Moslem Culture in the Near East*, vol. 1, *Islamic Society in the Eighteenth Century*, part 1 (London, 1950), part 2 (London, 1957), 1:161: "Islamic intellectual culture in the eighteenth century . . . had fallen so far below even its own medieval standards, and appeared to be quite unconscious of the decline."

5. Albert Hourani, *Arabic Thought in the Liberal Age, 1798–1939* (Cambridge: Cambridge University Press, 1983), iv–vii.

6. The emphasis on reforming or modernizing elites who responded to European influence is reflected in most of the studies on this period. The literature is vast, and it includes, in addition to Hourani's *Arabic Thought*, such classics as Niyazi Berkes, *The Development of Secularism in Turkey* (Montreal: McGill University Press, 1964); and Sherif Mardin, *The Genesis of Young Ottoman Thought: A Study in the Modernization of Turkish Political Ideas* (Princeton,

N.J.: Princeton University Press, 1962). Later works include Nikki R. Keddie, ed., *Scholars, Saints, and Sufis: Muslim Religious Institutions in the Middle East since 1500* (Berkeley: University of California Press, 1972); Hamid Enayat, *Modern Islamic Political Thought* (Austin: University of Texas Press, 1982); and Leonard Binder, *Islamic Liberalism* (Chicago: University of Chicago Press, 1988).

7. Nikki Keddie notes that there is little analysis of traditional, "majoritarian" Muslim thinkers, especially Sunni thinkers, and that early modern traditional movements are treated as a "trend[s] with no future." She also suggests that the "door of *ijtihād* was less firmly closed than was thought," as evidenced by the continuing interest in Aristotelian "rationalist Islamic philosophy" in Iran and to a lesser extent in Egypt. Despite her attention to traditionalist thought, therefore, Keddie concedes the general decline of the Islamic world in the eighteenth century and only suggests the existence of exceptions to this general trend, especially in Iran. My point, however, is that the vibrancy of the eighteenth century is not an exception and not restricted to Iran. Moreover, I do not measure the quality of eighteenth-century thought through the narrow prism of Aristotelianism. See Keddie, "Iran: Change in Islam, Islam and Change," *International Journal of Middle East Studies* 11, no. 4 (1980): 527–42, esp. 527–28, 531.

8. I discuss the second viewpoint in chapter 2.

9. This view is reflected in any number of studies on modern Islamic thought, including H. A. R. Gibb, *Modern Trends in Islam* (Chicago: University of Chicago Press, 1947); Wilfred Cantwell Smith, *Islam in Modern History* (Princeton, N.J.: Princeton University Press, 1977); Annemarie Schimmel, *Islam in the Indian Subcontinent* (Leiden, the Netherlands: E. J. Brill, 1980); and Fazlur Rahman, *Islam and Modernity: Transformation of an Intellectual Tradition* (Chicago: University of Chicago Press, 1982).

10. Contrast, for example, with Voll, "Wahhābiyah," *Encyclopedia of Religion* (New York, 1987), 15:313–16. Voll maintains that, after *tawḥīd*, *ijtihād* is the second basic concept in the teachings of Ibn ʿAbd al-Wahhāb (315). On the notion that the call for *ijtihād* characterizes eighteenth- and nineteenth-century Islamic reformist thought, see Rudolph Peters, "*Idjtihād* and *Taqlīd* in 18th and 19th Century Islam," *Die Welt des Islams* 20, nos. 3–4 (1980): 131–45. I shall return to retrospective reconstructions of eighteenth-century thought, but first I will illustrate the fundamental opposition between Ibn ʿAbd al-Wahhāb's thought and that of other eighteenth-century thinkers by examining the evidence preserved in the writings of these thinkers. As I will illustrate, any assertion of an affinity between the thought of Ibn ʿAbd al-Wahhāb and his contemporaries can only be made if their writings, the obvious evidence relevant to such an assertion, are totally neglected.

11. Almost every work by Ibn ʿAbd al-Wahhāb discusses this issue.

12. Muḥammad Ibn ʿAbd al-Wahhāb, "Rasāʾil al-Daʿwa," in Amīn Saʿīd, *Sīrat al-Imām al-Shaykh Muḥammad Ibn ʿAbd al-Wahhāb* (Beirut: Sharikat al-Tawzīʿ al-ʿArabīya, 1384 AH), 43.

13. Ibn ʿAbd al-Wahhāb, "Rasāʾil," 139–40; and "Masāʾil al-jāhilīya," in Muḥammad Ibn ʿAbd al-Wahhāb, *Majmūʿat al-Fatāwā wal-Rasāʾil wal-Ajwiba* (Cairo: Dār al-Waḥī, 1400 AH), 105, 128.

14. Ibn ʿAbd al-Wahhāb, "Rasāʾil," 139.

15. Ibn ʿAbd al-Wahhāb, "Rasāʾil," 116.

16. Ibn ʿAbd al-Wahhāb refers to *ṭāghūt*, which, in its modern usage, translates as "tyrant" or "tyranny" and may imply a concern for social justice. Ibn ʿAbd al-Wahhāb steers away from this possible political meaning, however, and uses the word in a specific creedal sense in conjunction with worshipping God through intermediaries or worshipping idols. See, for example, Muḥammad Ibn ʿAbd al-Wahhāb, "Risāla fī Maʿnā al-Ṭāghūt," in *Majmūʿat al-Tawḥīd*,

ed. Rashīd Riḍā (Cairo: Al-Maṭbaʿa al-Salafiyya), 122–24; also see "Rasāʾil," 142; and *Majmūʿat al-Fatāwā*, 119–21.

17. Ibn ʿAbd al-Wahhāb, "Rasāʾil," 57, 168; Muḥammad Ibn ʿAbd al-Wahhāb, "Kitāb al-Tawḥīd," in Amīn Saʿīd, *Sīrat al-Imām al-Shaykh Muḥammad Ibn ʿAbd al-Wahhāb* (Beirut: Sharikat al-Tawzīʿ al-ʿArabīya, 1384 AH), 227; Muḥammad Ibn ʿAbd al-Wahhāb, *Al-Kalimāt al-Nāfiʿa fī al-Mukaffirāt al-Wāqiʿa* (Cairo: Al-Maṭbaʿa al-Salafiyya, 1393 AH), 2–3.

18. As Ibn ʿAbd al-Wahhāb maintains was actually the case at the time of Ibn Ḥanbal; see Ibn ʿAbd al-Wahhāb, "Rasāʾil," 112.

19. Ibn ʿAbd al-Wahhāb, "Rasāʾil," 113.

20. Ibn ʿAbd al-Wahhāb, "Kitāb al-Tawḥīd," 223.

21. Ibn ʿAbd al-Wahhāb, "Rasāʾil," 49, 58.

22. Ibn ʿAbd al-Wahhāb, "Rasāʾil," 55.

23. Ibn ʿAbd al-Wahhāb, "Rasāʾil," 58–62; Muḥammad Ibn ʿAbd al-Wahhāb, "Kitāb Kashf al-Shubuhāt," in Amīn Saʿīd, *Sīrat al-Imām al-Shaykh Muḥammad Ibn ʿAbd al-Wahhāb* (Beirut: Sharikat al-Tawzīʿ al-ʿArabīya, 1384 AH), 302–3.

24. Ibn ʿAbd al-Wahhāb, *Majmūʿat al-Fatāwā*, 105–7. He also rejects the *taqlīd* of the scholar when it is in opposition to a text; Ibn ʿAbd al-Wahhāb, *Majmūʿat al-Fatāwā*, 137.

25. Ibn ʿAbd al-Wahhāb, "Kitāb Kashf," 302.

26. Ibn ʿAbd al-Wahhāb, "Rasāʾil," 46–47, 64–65; "Kitāb al-Tawḥīd," 233; and "Kitāb Kashf," 300.

27. Ibn ʿAbd al-Wahhāb, "Rasāʾil," 46–47, 64–65, 155; *Majmūʿat al-Fatāwā*, 34, 37, 40–44; and *Kalimāt*, 45.

28. Ibn ʿAbd al-Wahhāb, "Rasāʾil," 64–65, 108; and *Al-Kalimāt*, 6.

29. Ibn ʿAbd al-Wahhāb, "Rasāʾil," 64–65; "Kitāb al-Tawḥīd," 237–38, 239; and *Al-Kalimāt*, 4.

30. Ibn ʿAbd al-Wahhāb, "Rasāʾil," 46–47, 84; and "Kitāb Kashf," 312.

31. Ibn ʿAbd al-Wahhāb, "Rasāʾil," 64–65, 83.

32. Ibn ʿAbd al-Wahhāb, "Rasāʾil," 105; and "Kitāb al-Tawḥīd," 232–33, 257–58.

33. Ibn ʿAbd al-Wahhāb, "Kitāb al-Tawḥīd," 238; and *Majmūʿat al-Fatāwā*, 109.

34. Ibn ʿAbd al-Wahhāb, "Rasāʾil," 145. He then extends this concept to include similar attitudes toward much of what is often referred to as jurisprudence.

35. Ibn ʿAbd al-Wahhāb, "Rasāʾil," 82, 108.

36. Ibn ʿAbd al-Wahhāb, "Rasāʾil," 136.

37. Ibn ʿAbd al-Wahhāb, "Rasāʾil," 93.

38. Ibn ʿAbd al-Wahhāb, "Rasāʾil," 46; "Kitāb al-Tawḥīd," 231–32; "Kitāb Kashf," 299; *Majmūʿat al-Fatāwā*, 104; and *Majmūʿat al-Tawḥīd*, 122.

39. Ibn ʿAbd al-Wahhāb, "Rasāʾil," 73–74.

40. Ibn ʿAbd al-Wahhāb, "Rasāʾil," 96.

41. Ibn ʿAbd al-Wahhāb, "Kitāb al-Tawḥīd," 265–67; and *Majmūʿat al-Fatāwā*, 32.

42. Ibn ʿAbd al-Wahhāb, "Kitāb al-Tawḥīd," 266.

43. Ibn ʿAbd al-Wahhāb, "Rasāʾil," 79; "Fī Tafsīr Kalimat al-Tawḥīd," in *Majmūʿat al-Tawḥīd*, 122–24; and *Majmūʿat al-Fatāwā*, 56–57.

44. Ibn ʿAbd al-Wahhāb, "Rasāʾil," 46–47, 79; "Kitāb Kashf," 307; and *Al-Kalimāt*, 25.

45. Ibn ʿAbd al-Wahhāb, "Rasāʾil," 46–47; "Kitāb Kashf," 299; *Majmūʿat al-Tawḥīd*, 110–14; and *Majmūʿat al-Fatāwā*, 37–44.

46. Ibn ʿAbd al-Wahhāb, *Majmūʿat al-Tawḥīd*, 106–8.

47. Ibn ʿAbd al-Wahhāb, "Rasāʾil," 79, 96; and *Majmūʿat al-Fatāwā*, 56–57.

48. Ibn ʿAbd al-Wahhāb, "Kitāb al-Tawḥīd," 222, 226, 231–32; *Majmūʿat al-Tawḥīd*, 110–14; and *Majmūʿat al-Fatāwā*, 32.

49. Ibn ʿAbd al-Wahhāb, "Rasāʾil," 93; and *Majmūʿat al-Fatāwā*, 32.

50. Ibn ʿAbd al-Wahhāb, "Kitāb al-Tawḥīd," 222, 231–32; *Majmūʿat al-Tawḥīd*, 122–24; and *Majmūʿat al-Fatāwā*, 32, 106–8.

51. Ibn ʿAbd al-Wahhāb, "Rasāʾil," 159.

52. Ibn ʿAbd al-Wahhāb, "Rasāʾil," 76.

53. Ibn ʿAbd al-Wahhāb, "Rasāʾil," 47; and "Kitāb Kashf," 307.

54. On this movement, see Christine Dobbin, *Islamic Revivalism in a Changing Peasant Economy: Central Sumatra, 1784–1847* (London: Curzon, 1983).

55. See Muin-ud-Din Ahmad Khan, *History of the Faraʾidi Movement in Bengal (1818–1906)* (Karachi: Pakistan Historical Society, 1965).

56. William R. Roff, ed., *Islam and the Political Economy of Meaning: Comparative Studies of Muslim Discourse* (London: Croom Helm, 1987), 31–52.

57. Roff, *Islam and the Political Economy of Meaning*, 32.

58. Roff, *Islam and the Political Economy of Meaning*, 33.

59. Roff, *Islam and the Political Economy of Meaning*, 34.

60. The main work on intellectual networks of scholars is by John Voll and will be discussed, together with other notions of the eighteenth century, in chapter 2.

61. Roff, *Islam and the Political Economy of Meaning*, 34–35.

62. Although numerous other studies, and Roff himself in several places in his article, note the inadequacy of using Wahhabism as a paradigm of analysis, Roff continues to use this paradigm; this is perhaps a result of the unrelenting assertions of a Wahhabi influence in most of the scholarly literature dealing with this period.

63. Moreover, Ibn ʿAbd al-Wahhāb's writings are very repetitive. Misconceptions about Wahhabi thought are particularly surprising given that a significant and fully representative portion of Ibn ʿAbd al-Wahhāb's work has been translated into English and other European languages and is readily accessible to researchers. The Arabic originals are also published in multiple modern editions.

64. Roff, *Islam and the Political Economy of Meaning*, 38.

65. Roff, *Islam and the Political Economy of Meaning*, 39.

66. Roff, *Islam and the Political Economy of Meaning*, 40.

67. Roff, *Islam and the Political Economy of Meaning*, 41.

68. The focus of Roff's book is expressed in its title and in the theoretical contribution to Roff's collection by Dale F. Eickelman, "Changing Interpretations of Islamic Movements" (13–30); see also Eickelman's article "The Political Economy of Meaning," *American Ethnologists* 6 (1979): 386–93. It is remarkable that there is hardly any consideration of meaning in these essays, only theorization of how the relationship between the prescriptive and social/real is important and needs to be examined; that "meaning" or content is not examined is clear from the continued use of the adjective *Wahhabi* to describe many unrelated movements. See also David Dean Commins, *Islamic Reform: Politics and Social Change in Late Ottoman Syria* (New York: Oxford University Press, 1990). In this excellent sociointellectual history of nineteenth-century Syria, Commins documents criticisms of Wahhabis by Syrian Ḥanbalīs but nonetheless repeats the idea that the Wahhabis influenced Islamic reform movements from West Africa to India. See Commins, *Islamic Reform*, 21.

69. ʿAbd al-Ghanī al-Nābulsī, *Dhakhāʾir al-Mawārīth fī al-Dalāla ʿalā Mawāḍiʿ al-Ḥadīth*, 4 parts in 2 vols. (Cairo: Jamʿiyyat al-Nashr wal-Taʾlīf al-Azhariyya, 1934).

70. For example, al-Kūrānī and al-Singkeli; on these scholars and their focus on reconciliation and opposition to *takfīr*, see H. Johns, "Friends in Grace: Ibrāhīm al-Kūrānī and ʿAbd

al-Ghanī al-Ra'uf al-Singkeli," in *Spectrum: Essays Presented to Sutan Takdir Alisjahbana on His Seventieth Birthday*, ed. S. Udin (Jakarta: Dian Rakyat, 1978); and H. Johns, "Al-Kūrānī, Ibrāhīm," in *Encyclopedia of Islam*, 2nd ed., vol. 5 (Leiden, the Netherlands: E. J. Brill, 1979), 432–33. Also see Alexander Knysh, *Ibn ʿArabī in the Later Islamic Tradition: The Making of a Polemical Image in Medieval Islam* (Albany: SUNY Press, 1999); and Knysh, "'Orthodoxy' and 'Heresy' in Medieval Islam: An Essay in Reassessment," *Muslim World* 83, no. 1 (1993): 48–67.

71. ʿAbd al-Ghanī al-Nābulsī, *Al-Fatḥ al-Rabbānī wal-Fayḍ al-Raḥmānī*, ed. Father A. Shiblī (Beirut: Catholic, 1960), 47.

72. ʿAbd al-Ghanī al-Nābulsī, *Ahl al-Janna wa Ahl al-Nār* (Cairo: Maktabat al-Turāth al-Islāmī, 1983), 11.

73. Al-Nābulsī, *Ahl al-Janna wa Ahl al-Nār*, 57–60.

74. ʿAbd al-Ghanī al-Nābulsī, *Īḍāḥ al-Dalālāt fī Samāʿ al-Ālāt*, ed. M. U. Al-Khasht (Cairo: Maktabat al-Maʿārif al-Islāmiyya, n.d.), 22–23.

75. Al-Nābulsī, *Īḍāḥ al-Dalālāt*, 24.

76. Al-Nābulsī, *Īḍāḥ al-Dalālāt*, 8.

77. Note the similarity to the Sufi notion of *al-insān al-kāmil*, the perfect human.

78. Al-Nābulsī, *Īḍāḥ al-Dalālāt*, 10.

79. Al-Nābulsī, *Īḍāḥ al-Dalālāt*, 13–14.

80. Al-Nābulsī, *Īḍāḥ al-Dalālāt*, 15.

81. Al-Nābulsī, *Īḍāḥ al-Dalālāt*, 14. On the bias between city and village, see Gabriel Baer, "Fellah and Townsman in Ottoman Egypt: A Study of Shirbīnī's Hazz al-Quḥūf," *Asian and African Studies: Journal of the Israel Oriental Society* 8, no. 3 (1972): 221–56, especially on the notion of *fuqahāʾ al-rīf* (rural scholars).

82. Al-Nābulsī, *Īḍāḥ al-Dalālāt*, 73–74.

83. Al-Nābulsī, *Īḍāḥ al-Dalālāt*, 74.

84. Al-Nābulsī, *Īḍāḥ al-Dalālāt*, 120.

85. Al-Nābulsī, *Īḍāḥ al-Dalālāt*, 122.

86. ʿAbd al-Ghanī al-Nābulsī, *Dīwān al-Ḥaqāʾiq wa Majmūʿ al-Raqāʾiq* (Damascus: ʿAbd al-Wakīl al-Darūbī, 1968), 8.

87. Al-Nābulsī, *Īḍāḥ al-Dalālāt*, 123.

88. Al-Nābulsī, *Dīwān*, 3.

89. Al-Nābulsī, *Dīwān*, 4.

90. *Takdir Alisjahbana* al-Ghanī al-Nābulsī, "Khamrat al-Ḥān wa Rannat al-Alḥān," in *Shurūḥ Risālat al-Shaykh Arsalān*, ed. ʿIzza Ḥuṣriyya (Damascus: Maṭbaʿat al-ʿIlm, 1969), 74.

91. Al-Nābulsī, *Dīwān*, 6. This last formulation is in contrast to the standard Sunni theological formula *kullu mā yakhṭuru fī bālika fa huwa bi-khilāfi dhālika* (God is different from anything that can be imagined by the mind).

92. Al-Nābulsī, *Dīwān*, 6.

93. Ahmad Muḥammad al-ʿUlaymī, *Al-Ṣanʿānī wa Kitābuhu Tawḍīḥ al-Afkār* (Beirut: Dār al-Kutub al-ʿIlmiyya, 1987), 43–46; and Muḥammad b. ʿAlī al-Shawkānī, *Al-Badr al-Ṭāliʿ bi Maḥāsin man baʿd al-Qarn al-Sābiʿ*, 2 vols. (Beirut: Dār al-Maʿrifa, n.d.), 2:133–36.

94. Muḥammad b. Ismāʿīl al-Amīr al-Ṣanʿānī, *Dīwān al-Amīr al-Ṣanʿānī* (Beirut: Sahrikat al-Tanwīr lil-Ṭibāʿa, 1986), 166–71.

95. Al-Ṣanʿānī, *Dīwān*, 244–45.

96. *Mukūs* (sing. *Maks*) is the term used for extralegal taxes that are not sanctioned by Islamic tax law.

97. Al-Ṣanʿānī, *Dīwān*, 244–45.

98. On the essentially apolitical nature of Wahhabi thought, see Christine Moss Helms, *The Cohesion of Saudi Arabia: Evolution of Political Identity* (Baltimore: Johns Hopkins University Press, 1981).

99. Al-Ṣanʿānī, *Dīwān*, 166–71.

100. Al-Ṣanʿānī, *Dīwān*, 171.

101. Al-Ṣanʿānī, *Dīwān*, 172. Also see al-Qāḍī Ismāʿīl b. ʿAlī al-Akwaʿ, *Hijar al-ʿIlm wa Maʿāqiluhu fī al-Yaman*, 5 vols. (Beirut: Dār al-Fikr al-Muʿāṣir, 1995), 5:1815.

102. Al-Ṣanʿānī, *Dīwān*, 171–75.

103. Al-Ṣanʿānī, *Dīwān*, 174.

104. Al-Ṣanʿānī, *Dīwān*, 175.

105. Sayyid Murtaḍā al-Riḍawī, *Ṣafḥā ʿan Āl Saʿūd al-Wahhābiyyīn wa Ārāʾ ʿUlamāʾ al-Sunna fī al-Wahhābiyya* (n.p., n.d.), quotes the negative reactions to the praise poem written by al-Ṣanʿānī, and the subsequent retraction of the poem (117). Al-Riḍawī's book is polemical, but it cites useful material; for example, it includes a list of scholars who reportedly responded to Ibn ʿAbd al-Wahhāb (113); the first of these is a response by "his own teacher, Muḥammad b. Sulaymān al-Kurdī al-Shāfiʿī which is [found] in the acclamation of a treatise by his brother Aḥmad b. ʿAbd al-Wahhāb, as well as a letter which is about three folios [in length]; this teacher of his discerned in him that he was misguided and misguiding, just as his other shaykh Muḥammad Ḥayāt al-Sindī and his father ʿAbd al-Wahhāb did" (13–14). The author also includes the following quote from al-Kurdī's letter: "I advise you to hold back your tongue from [slandering] Muslims; so if you hear from a person that he believes in the influence of a person whose help is invoked, independent of God [*min dūn Allāh*], the Exalted, then inform him of the truth and clarify to him the evidence [in this regard]. If then he [this person] persists [in his error] then you can pronounce him in particular [*bi-khuṣūṣihi*] an unbeliever. Still, you have no way of pronouncing the majority of Muslims to be of unbelief when you are the one who has deviated from this majority. In fact, attributing unbelief to a person who deviates from the majority is more likely since this person would have followed a path other than that of believers" (113).

The clear and concisely stated views in al-Ṣanʿānī's poem are elaborated at length in several other works by him. In the introduction to *Minhat al-Ghaffār*, al-Ṣanʿānī blames sectarian zeal and *takfīr* for all other aberrations: "*Tamadhhub* [blind partisanship to schools] is the origin of the division among Muslims, and the gate to all sedition in worldly matters and religion. What else would divide prayers at the sacred House of God, which we are commanded to perform collectively, except for the division of schools/sects that grows out from the planted tree of strict subservience [*iltizām*, a type of imitation, *taqlīd*]? And would the blood of Muslims be shed, and would Muslims accuse each other of unbelief were it not for *tamadhhub*? God, may He be exalted, commanded people to obey Him and His prophet, peace be upon him, and He did not obligate the community to obey one particular person in everything he commands and prohibits except for the prophet of God, peace be upon him. This is why more than one imam has said, 'The opinions of all but the prophet have parts which are accepted and others which are discarded.' Moreover, the four imams have forbidden people from imitating them" (qtd. in al-ʿUlaymī, *Al-Ṣanʿānī wa Kitābuhu Tawḍīḥ al-Afkār*, 89).

106. When they attempted to discredit Walī Allāh's grandson Shāh Ismāʿīl, his rivals accused him of being a Wahhabi and an innovator; his followers, however, denied these accusations and asserted that they are "futile since he neither knows Najd nor its ruler, and he has no taste or liking for their beliefs or actions." See Abū al-Ṭayyib al-Sayyid Ṣiddīq Khān Ḥasan al-Qanūjī, *Al-Ḥiṭṭa fī Dhikr al-Ṣiḥāḥ al-Sitta* (Lahore: Islāmī Acādimī, 1977), 162–63.

107. For example, John O. Voll, "Muḥammad Ḥayyā al-Sindī and Muḥammad Ibn ʿAbd al-

Wahhāb: An Analysis of an Intellectual Group in Eighteenth-Century Madīna," *Bulletin of the School of Oriental and African Studies* 38, no. 1 (1974): 32–39; and Voll, "Hadith Scholars and Tariqahs: An Ulama Group in the 18th Century Ḥaramayn and Their Impact in the Islamic World," *Journal of Asian and African Studies* 15, nos. 3–4 (1980), 264–73.

108. These visionary dreams serve to legitimate Walī Allāh's undertakings by asserting that he is only doing what God destined him to do. Typically, Walī Allāh has a vision of the Prophet Muhammad, who informs him of what God wants him to do. See Shāh Walī Allāh, *Fuyūḍ al-Ḥaramayn* (Delhi: Mālik Maṭbaʿ-e-Aḥmadī, n.d.).

109. See, for example, Walī Allāh, *Fuyūḍ al-Ḥaramayn*, 62–63. Also qtd. in ʿUbayd Allāh al-Sindī, *Al-Tamhīd li-Taʿrīf Aʾimmat al-Tajdīd* (Haidarabad: Maṭbaʿat Jamiʿat al-Sind, 1976), 440.

110. Shāh Walī Allāh al-Dehlawī (d. 1176 AH), *Ḥujjat Allāh al-Bāligha*, ed. M. S. Hāshim, 2 vols. (Beirut: Dār al-Kutub al-ʿIlmiyya, 1995), 1:162–63.

111. Walī Allāh, *Ḥujjat Allāh*, 1:163.

112. Walī Allāh indicates that prostration could be seen as either an act of worship or simply greeting; Walī Allāh, *Ḥujjat Allāh*, 1:60.

113. Walī Allāh, *Ḥujjat Allāh*, 2:38; and Shāh Walī Allāh, *Al-Tafhīmāt al-Ilāhiyya*, ed. G. M. Qāsimī, 2 vols. (Haidarabad: Ākādimyyat al-Shāh Walī Allāh al-Dihlawī, 1967), 2:49.

114. Walī Allāh, *Ḥujjat Allāh*, 1:61–62.

115. Shāh Walī Allāh, *Al-Budūr al-Bāzigha*, ed. Ṣaghīr Ḥasan al-Maʾṣūmī (Hyderabad: Shah Wali Allah al-Dihlawi Academy, n.d.), 252.

116. Walī Allāh, *Ḥujjat Allāh*, 1:117.

117. Walī Allāh, *Ḥujjat Allāh*, 1:118.

118. Walī Allāh, *Ḥujjat Allāh*, 1:118–19.

119. Walī Allāh, *Ḥujjat Allāh*, 1:119.

120. Walī Allāh, *Ḥujjat Allāh*, 1:119–21.

121. See, for example, Mervyn Hiskett, *The Development of Islam in West Africa* (London: Longman, 1984), 289–91; and William R. Roff, "Islamic Movements: One or Many?" 31–52.

122. See, for example, Mervyn Hiskett, "An Islamic Tradition of Reform in the Western Sudan from the Sixteenth to the Eighteenth Century," *Bulletin of the School of Oriental and African Studies* 25, no. 3 (1962): 577–96.

123. Roff admits that there are problems with the use of the name *Wahhabi* to refer to the Fulani jihad, but he then proceeds to assert that "the jihadists too had significant links with the Sufi and Hijazi intellectual circles of the time" and repeats without questioning John Voll's assertion of teacher-student networking through "Muhammad Hayya al-Sindi who had taught ʿAbd al-Wahhab." Roff, "Islamic Movements," 43.

124. Not only is this material available, but it has been the subject of first-rate studies by a number of scholars who work on Islam in sub-Saharan Africa, and it has been compared to other examples and cases elsewhere in Africa. It should be noted, however, that Roff, for example, recognizes the "extraordinary quantity of Muslim discourse on which to base understanding of the imperatives claimed by the [Fulani] movement" (46), but he does not examine this discourse to determine whether there are in fact grounds for positing parallels between Ibn Fūdī and Ibn ʿAbd al-Wahhāb.

125. On the standard Islamic education in West Africa prior to the jihad, see Mervyn Hiskett, "Material Relating to the State of Learning among the Fulani before Their Jihād," *Bulletin of the School of Oriental and African Studies* 19 (1957): 550–78.

126. ʿUthmān Ibn Fūdī, "The Wathīqat Ahl al-Sūdān: A Manifesto of the Fulani Jihād," Arabic text and translation with introduction by A. D. H. Bivar, *Journal of African History* 2, no. 2 (1961): 240; ʿUthmān Ibn Fūdī, "The Translation of the *Nūr-al-Albāb*," Arabic text and transla-

tion with introduction by Yusuf Wali, *Kano Studies* 2, no. 1 (1980): 18; and ʿUthmān Ibn Fūdī, "Sirāj al-Ikhwān," in "An Islamic Tradition of Reform in the Western Sudan from the Sixteenth to the Eighteenth Century," translation of selections from Sirāj al-Ikhwān, Bayān al-Bidaʿ al-Shayṭānīya, and Naṣāʾiḥ al-Umma al-Muḥammadīya by M. Hiskett, *Bulletin of the School of Oriental and African Studies* 25, no. 3 (1962): 579.

127. Ibn Fūdī, "The Translation of the *Nūr-al-Albāb*," 19; and ʿUthmān Ibn Fūdī, "Unbelief in the Western Sudan: ʿUthmān dan Fodio's *Taʿlīm al-Ikhwān*," ed. and trans. with an introduction by B. G. Martin, *Middle Eastern Studies* 4 (1976): 63.

128. Ibn Fūdī, "Sirāj," 579; "The Translation of the *Nūr-al-Albāb*," 20, 27–28; and ʿUthmān Ibn Fūdī, "Bayān al-bidaʿ al-Shayṭānīya," in "An Islamic Tradition of Reform in the Western Sudan from the Sixteenth to the Eighteenth Century," by M. Hiskett, *Bulletin of the School of Oriental and African Studies* 25, no. 3 (1962): 594.

129. Ibn Fūdī, "The Translation of the *Nūr-al-Albāb*," 28–30; ʿUthmān Ibn Fūdī, *Bayān wujūb al-Hijrā ʿalā al-ʿIbād*, ed. and trans. F. H. El-Masri (Khartoum: Khartoum University Press; and Oxford: Oxford University Press, 1978), 29.

130. Ibn Fūdī, "The Translation of the *Nūr-al-Albāb*," 25; and ʿUthmān Ibn Fūdī, "*Kitāb al-Farq*: A Work on the Habe Kingdoms Attributed to ʿUthmān Dan Fodio," ed. and trans. with introduction by M. Hiskett, *Bulletin of the School of Oriental and African Studies* 23, no. 2 (1960): 561.

131. Ibn Fūdī, "The Translation of the *Nūr-al-Albāb*," 34; and ʿUthmān Ibn Fūdī, "Naṣāʾiḥ al-Umma al-Muḥammadīya," in "An Islamic Tradition of Reform in the Western Sudan from the Sixteenth to the Eighteenth Century," by M. Hiskett, *Bulletin of the School of Oriental and African Studies* 25, no. 3 (1962): 587.

132. Ibn Fūdī, "The Translation of the *Nūr-al-Albāb*," 33–34.

133. Ibn Fūdī, "The Translation of the *Nūr-al-Albāb*," 30; "*Kitāb al-Farq*," 560–61; and "Naṣāʾiḥ," 587.

134. Ibn Fūdī, "*Kitāb al-Farq*," 560, 563; and "Naṣāʾiḥ," 586.

135. Ibn Fūdī, "The Translation of the *Nūr-al-Albāb*," 21.

136. Ibn Fūdī, "Naṣāʾiḥ," 588; "Sirāj," 585; and "Unbelief in the Western Sudan," 54–55, 60. He adds that this was the way of the Khārijites and Muʿtazilītes, and that it was forbidden by consensus; "Naṣāʾiḥ," 588. He also criticizes his teacher Jibrīl Ibn ʿUmar for his excessive zeal; "Naṣāʾiḥ," 589.

137. Ibn Fūdī, "Unbelief in the Western Sudan," 60.

138. Ibn Fūdī, "Unbelief in the Western Sudan," 61.

139. Ibn Fūdī, "Unbelief in the Western Sudan," 60. Compare this strong anti-Wahhabi position to Gibb, *Modern Trends in Islam*, 30, who speaks of strong Wahhabi influences on Ibn Fūdī.

140. Ibn Fūdī, "Bayān al-bidaʿ," 594. Note that Ibn ʿAbd al-Wahhāb counts these as either prohibited sins or *shirk*.

141. Ibn Fūdī, "Bayān al-bidaʿ," 594.

142. Ibn Fūdī, "The Translation of the *Nūr-al-Albāb*," 28.

143. Ibn Fūdī, "Unbelief in the Western Sudan," 69.

144. See, for example, Murray Last, "Reform in West Africa: The Jihād Movements of the Nineteenth Century," in *The History of West Africa*, vol. 2, ed. J. F. A. Ajayi and Michael Crowder (Essex, UK: Longman, 1974), 5; and Marilyn Robinson Waldman, "The Fulani Jihād: A Reassessment," *Journal of African History* 6, no. 3 (1965): 349.

145. On the development of Ibn Fūdī's thought, see Louis Brenner, "Muslim Thought in Eighteenth-Century West Africa: The Case of Shaykh Uthman b. Fudi," in *Eighteenth-Century*

Renewal and Reform in Islam, ed. Nehemia Levtzion and John Obert Voll (Syracuse, N.Y.: Syracuse University Press, 1987); a similar analysis of this development can be found in Waldman, "The Fulani Jihād," 349–50.

146. ʿUthmān Ibn Fūdī, "An Early Fulani Conception of Islam," 2 parts, trans. of *Tanbīh al-Ikhwān* with introduction by H. R. Palmer, *Journal of the African Society* 13 (1913–14) and 14 (1914–15): part 1, 414.

147. Customs characterizing un-Islamic rule include hereditary succession by force and without consultation; unlawfully violating the person, sanctity, and property of people; extorting unlawful taxes such as a cattle tax, prayer tax, townspeople tax, merchant and traveler tax, and meat and cotton sales tax; taking women without marriage, and seizing their wealth; perpetuation of corruption by the ruler's concubines; bribery in courts and of officials in order to withhold the application of the law or to suspend the conclusion of contracts, and to circumvent the laws of God; enlisting Muslims by force to fight in the armies of non-Muslims; and prohibiting Muslims from observing the requirements of their religion, as in prohibiting men from wearing turbans and women from wearing veils; Ibn Fūdī, "*Kitāb al-Farq*," 560–63.

148. Ibn Fūdī, "The Wathīqat," 240; "An Early Fulani Conception of Islam," 2, 53–54; and *Bayān wujūb*, 12–17.

149. Ibn Fūdī, "The Wathīqat," 239–40; "An Early Fulani Conception of Islam," 2, 54; and *Bayān wujūb*, 12–17.

150. Ibn Fūdī, "An Early Fulani Conception of Islam," 1, 414; and *Bayān wujūb*, 12–17.

151. Ibn Fūdī, "Unbelief in the Western Sudan," 53, 70, 73; and *Bayān wujūb*, 21–24.

152. Ibn Fūdī, "The Wathīqat," 239; "Sirāj," 584–85; and *Bayān wujūb*, 46–49.

153. Ibn Fūdī, "The Wathīqat," 240; "An Early Fulani Conception of Islam," 1, 414; "Unbelief in the Western Sudan," 65; and *Bayān wujūb*, 18–20.

154. In contrast to the creedal *takfīr* of Ibn ʿAbd al-Wahhāb.

155. Ibn Fūdī, "The Wathīqat," 242; "The Translation of the *Nūr-al-Albāb*," 22; "Unbelief in the Western Sudan," 61, 72; and *Bayān wujūb*, 107–12.

156. For example, while the person, children, wives, and wealth of an unbeliever can be taken, these measures can only be applied to the wealth but not the person or family of a Muslim captured in enemy territory; Ibn Fūdī, *Bayān wujūb*, 107–8.

157. Ibn Fūdī's justification of the jihad against the Bornu rulers is a clear illustration of this point; after he initially accused them of unbelief, a Bornu scholar initiated a correspondence with Sokoto and challenged Ibn Fūdī's accusations; Ibn Fūdī then withdrew his general characterization of Bornu as a land of unbelief and restricted it to individuals known to commit *kufr*; he also added that the war against Bornu was in self-defense; after this correspondence the war between the two states stopped, although the political conflicts between them were not yet resolved; see Ibn Fūdī, "Unbelief in the Western Sudan," 53.

158. Although he does not engage in theoretical discussion of Sufism, he does quote Ibn ʿArabī approvingly (Ibn Fūdī, "Unbelief in the Western Sudan," 65–66), in contrast to Ibn ʿAbd al-Wahhāb, who considers him an unbeliever.

Roff, among others, has noted the spiritual significance of Sufism to Ibn Fūdī, but he fails to draw the obvious conclusion from this observation. Roff reports that Ibn Fūdī's account of the beginning of his struggle was based on a series of "visions, in which first the Prophet Muhammad appeared before him, and then, in 1794, ʿAbd al-Qadir al-Jilani, founder of the Qadiriya order, who gave him a green robe" (Roff, "Islamic Movements," 45). Roff fails to note, however, that this sort of assertion is tantamount to unbelief in the eyes of Ibn ʿAbd al-Wahhāb; it is unthinkable that a Wahhabi-like thinker would invoke a "dead" Sufi of all of the Muslim authorities of the past. If, as Roff maintains, "the imperatives claimed by the movement, and how they spoke to those who became its adherents" (Roff, "Islamic Movements," 46) are of paramount importance for understanding them, then we can dismiss neither Ibn Fūdī's presentation of himself nor the fact that a Wahhabi would most certainly characterize such a presentation as unbelief.

159. For his poems, see Muḥammad b. ʿAlī al-Shawkānī, *Dīwān al-Shawkānī, Aslāk al-Jawhar wal-Ḥayāt al-Fikriyya wal-Siyāsiyya fī ʿAṣrihi*, ed. Ḥusayn b. ʿAbd Allāh al-ʿAmrī (Damascus: Dār al-Fikr, 1986), 160–64. Also see Muḥammad b. al-Ḥasan b. ʿAlī b. Aḥmad b. Nāṣir al-Shijanī (al-Shijnī) al-Ḥimyarī al-Dhamārī, *Ḥayāt al-Imām al-Shawkānī al-Musammā Kitāb al-Tiqṣār fī Jīd Zamān ʿAllāmat al-Aqālīm wal-Amṣār* (Sanaa: Maktabat al-Jīl al-Jadīd, 1990) (hereafter cited as al-Shijnī, *Kitāb al-Tiqṣār*), 180–82.

160. Muḥammad b. ʿAlī al-Shawkānī, *Dhikrayāt al-Shawkānī: Rasāʾil lil-Muʾarrikh al-Yamanī Muḥammad b. ʿAlī al-Shawkānī*, ed. Ṣāliḥ R. Maḥmūd (Beirut: Dār al-ʿAwda, 1983), 136–38.

161. Al-Shawkānī, *Dhikrayāt al-Shawkānī*. 165. In *Wabl al-Ghamām*, al-Shawkānī says, "If accusing one man of unbelief without a valid reason that necessitates this *takfīr* makes the accuser an unbeliever, what then do you think of someone who aims at a group of Muslims that includes countless numbers of versed scholars and elevated worshippers, and then accuses them all of unbelief? . . . If you say this is based on *ijtihād* after exhausting one's means, I say, throw this *ijtihād* of yours behind the wall, and leave the umma of Muḥammad in this general attribution, for your damned *ijtihād* has inflicted you with a crime that all of your [good deeds] will not pay a portion of its indemnity." Muḥammad b. ʿAlī al-Shawkānī, *Wabl al-Ghamām ʿalā Shifāʾ al-Uwām*, ed. M. Ḥallāq, 2 vols. (Cairo: Maktabat Ibn Taymiyya, 1995), 1:195–96.

162. See Muḥammad b. ʿAlī al-Shawkānī, *Al-Durr al-Naḍīd fī Ikhlāṣ Kalimat al-Tawḥīd*, ed. A. al-Ḥalabī (Saudi Arabia: Dār Ibn Khuzayma, 1414 AH), where al-Shawkānī responds to al-Ṣanʿānī's poem in which he criticizes Wahhabi notions of *takfīr*. Al-Shawkānī takes issue with al-Ṣanʿānī's distinction between doctrinal *kufr* (*kufr iʿtiqād*) and practical *kufr* (*kufr ʿamal*), and the assertion that only the former entails exclusion from the fold of religion (*khurūj ʿan al-Dīn*); al-Shawkānī argues that uttering the words of *tawḥīd* does not suffice when coupled with actions that contradict it (*Al-Durr al-Naḍīd*, 102–13). Still, al-Shawkānī maintains that there is no question that it is permissible for a person to visit a shrine and pray for God's favors by invoking the good deeds of the pious Muslim buried in the shrine (*Al-Durr al-Naḍīd*, 132–38). Once again, such a practice would be utterly unacceptable to Ibn ʿAbd al-Wahhāb and would qualify as *kufr*. It is also noteworthy that al-Shawkānī is closer to the position of Aḥmad Ibn Taymiyya than that of Ibn ʿAbd al-Wahhāb. On Ibn Taymiyya's position on the legality of tomb visitation as long as it is not for the purpose of worshipping the dead saints, see Laoust, *Essai sur les doctrines sociales et politiques*, 334–35, 353. For examples of the difference between Ibn ʿAbd al-Wahhāb's criticism of Sufism and those of Ibn Taymiyya and al-Shawkānī, see Laoust, *Essai sur les doctrines sociales et politiques*, 529; Aḥmad Ibn Taymiyya, *Majmūʿ Fatāwā Shaykh al-Islām Aḥmad Ibn Taymiyya*, ed. A. Ibn Qāsim al-ʿĀṣimī, 37 vols. (Beirut: Maṭābiʿ Dār al-ʿArabiyya, 1977), 1:91; Ibn ʿAbd al-Wahhāb, *Kitāb al-Tawḥīd*, 80–81; and al-Shawkānī, *Al-Durr al-Naḍīd*, 14.

163. Muḥammad b. ʿAlī al-Shawkānī, *Al-Sayl al-Jarrār al-Mutadaffiq ʿalā Ḥadāʾiq al-Azhār*, ed. Maḥmūd Ibrāhīm Zāyid (Beirut: Dār al-Kutub al-ʿIlmiyya, n.d.), 4:578, 580.

164. See, for example, al-Shawkānī, *Al-Sayl al-Jarrār*, 1:105, 4:578, 580, 584; and Muḥammad b. ʿAlī al-Shawkānī, *Irshād al-Ghabī ilā Madhab Ahl al-Bayt fī Ṣaḥb al-Nabī*, ed. A. Mashhūr b. Salmān (Riyadh: Dar al-Manār, 1992), 93.

165. Al-Shawkānī, *Al-Badr al-Ṭāliʿ*, 2:4–24.

166. Al-Shawkānī, *Al-Badr al-Ṭāliʿ*, 2:4.

167. Al-Shawkānī, *Al-Badr al-Ṭāliʿ*, 2:5. Indeed, Ghālib eventually gave in and joined the Wahhabis, although he kept oscillating between the Wahhabis and the Ottomans.

168. Al-Shawkānī, *Al-Badr al-Ṭāliʿ*, 2:5.

169. Al-Shawkānī, *Al-Badr al-Ṭāliʿ*, 2:6.

170. Al-Shawkānī, *Al-Badr al-Ṭāliʿ*, 2:6.

171. Abū Nuqṭa and Sharīf Ḥammūd ruled in the name of the Wahhabi ʿAbd al-ʿAzīz Āl Saʿūd as of 1803; see al-Shawkānī, *Al-Badr al-Ṭāliʿ*, 1:240, 262, on Sharīf Ḥammūd and his wars, and on Abū Nuqṭa and his joining the ranks of Ṣāḥib Najd; also see Ḥusayn b. ʿAbdullāh al-ʿAmrī, *The Yemen in the 18th and 19th Centuries: A Political and Intellectual History* (London: Ithaca, 1985), 49–53. Wahhabis took Mecca in 1805 and Medina in 1806; Abū Nuqṭa of northern ʿAsīr joined them in 1803. The ruler of Southern or Lower ʿAsīr was Sharīf Ḥammūd, who ruled in the name of Imam Manṣūr; in 1802 he declared independence and fought Abū Nuqṭa, but when he was defeated in 1803 he declared loyalty to the Wahhabis and subsequently much of Tihāma was lost between 1803 and 1818, when the Wahhabis were defeated by the armies of Muḥammad ʿAlī. Sahrīf Ḥammūd expanded into Tihāma and took Luḥayya, Hodeida, Zabid, and Bayt al-Faqīh. Only Mocha remained under Qāsimī control. Thus al-Shawkānī's positive tone in his correspondence with the Wahhabis is mainly motivated by the desire to ward off this threat, and not by any ideological affinity. Using similar skills, al-Shawkānī later successfully negotiated with the Egyptian troops.

172. Al-Shawkānī, *Al-Badr al-Ṭāliʿ*, 2:7.

173. Al-Shawkānī, *Al-Badr al-Ṭāliʿ*, 2:7–8.

174. Al-Shawkānī, *Al-Badr al-Ṭāliʿ*, 2:7.

175. Al-Shawkānī, *Al-Badr al-Ṭāliʿ*, 2:7–8.

176. Al-Shawkānī, *Al-Badr al-Ṭāliʿ*, 2:136.

177. The two professions of faith are that there is no god but God, and that Muhammad is His Prophet.

178. Al-Shawkānī, *Al-Badr al-Ṭāliʿ*, 2:136.

179. This negative attitude toward nonurban Muslims is not peculiar to al-Shawkānī. Compare, for example, with al-Nābulsī's negative reference to the lack of urban sophistication on the part of villagers and artisans (*ahl al-qurā wal-ḥiraf*) (*Īḍāḥ al-Dalālāt*, 14). The point I am making here is not that the urban elite culture is more representative of true Islam but simply that this view was held by the source under examination. For more on the lack of political and economic integration of city and village in the eighteenth century, and on the distinctions in cultural norms between towns and the countryside, see Baer, "Fellah and Townsman in Ottoman Egypt." For counterexamples, see Beshara Doumani, *Rediscovering Palestine: Merchants and Peasants in Jabal Nablus, 1700–1900* (Berkeley: University of California Press, 1995).

180. Muḥammad b. ʿAlī al-Shawkānī, *Irshād al-Ghabī ilā Madhab Ahl al-Bayt fī Ṣaḥb al-Nabī*, ed. A. Mashhūr b. Salmān (Riyadh: Dār al-Manār, 1992), 93; my emphasis.

181. *Dīwān al-Shawkānī*, 160–64. Also qtd. in Muḥammad b. ʿAlī al-Shawkānī, *Qaṭr al-Walī ʿalā Ḥadīth al-Walī*; published as *Wilāyat Allāh wal-Ṭarīq Ilayhā*, ed. Ibrāhīm Hilāl (Cairo: Dār al-Kutub al-Ḥadītha, 1969), 26. Also see al-Shawkānī, *Wabl al-Ghamām*, 2:341, where al-Shawkānī says in reference to extreme Shiʿis, "The truth regarding the *Bāṭiniyya*, although they conceal their unbelief, is that it is not permissible to kill any of them unless they commit or say what is plain unbelief without need for any interpretation; this is especially because it is known that they exhibit Islam and rectitude to their commoners, and delude them into thinking they are rightful; if this is true of them, then all of their commoners do not know they are unbelievers; rather, they think they are rightful; thus, rather than kill them, they need to be

familiarized with the truth. Therefore, it is not lawful to kill a member of the *Bāṭiniyya* unless he displays unequivocal unbelief, because their word is Islamic, and their call is Prophetic [*kalimatahum islāmiyya wa daʿwatahum nabawiyya*]."

182. Muḥammad b. ʿAlī al-Shawkānī, *Nayl al-Awṭār min Aḥādīth Sayyid al-Akhyār Sharḥ Muntaqā al-Akhbār*, ed. M. S. Hāshim, 8 vols. in 4 parts (Beirut: Dār al-Kutub al-ʿIlmiyya, 1995), part 1, 1:316, and 313–19.

183. Al-Shawkānī, *Nayl al-Awṭār*, 1:1:319.

184. Al-Shawkānī, *Nayl al-Awṭār*, 1:1:319.

185. Al-Shawkānī, *Nayl al-Awṭār*, 4:7:206.

186. Muḥammad b. ʿAlī al-Shawkānī, *Fāʾiq al-Kisā fī Jawāb ʿĀlim al-Ḥasā*, ed. M. Āl Ismāʿīl (Amman: Dār ʿAmmār, 1994), 43–49.

187. Al-Shawkānī, *Fāʾiq al-Kisā*, 50.

188. Al-Shawkānī, *Nayl al-Awṭār*, 2.4:118.

189. Muḥammad b. ʿAlī al-Shawkānī, *Tuḥfat al-Dhākirīn bi-ʿUddat al-Ḥiṣn al-Ḥaṣīn min Kalām Sayyid al-Mursalīn* (Beirut: Dār al-Qalam, 1984), 347–48.

190. Al-Shawkānī, *Tuḥfat al-Dhākirīn*, 353–54.

191. Al-Shawkānī, *Nayl al-Awṭār*, 2.4:52–54.

192. In Islamic law, *ḥadd* (pl. *ḥudūd*) refers to penal laws in which there are set punishments.

193. Al-Shawkānī, *Nayl al-Awṭār*, 4.7:158. See also al-Shawkānī, *Wabl al-Ghamām*, 1:193.

194. Literally, those who left the community. The Khawārij (Khārijites) are the earliest sect of Islam. In the civil wars that broke out under the fourth Caliph ʿAlī over succession, they first were in ʿAlī's camp and then left it and opposed all parties to this conflict.

195. Al-Shawkānī, *Nayl al-Awṭār*, 4.7:177, 166.

196. Al-Shawkānī, *Nayl al-Awṭār*, 4.7:178. Elsewhere, al-Shawkānī argues against *kufr al-taʾwīl*, accusing Muslims of unbelief based on an interpretation of their views: "What I say is that accusing a bunch of Muslims of unbelief because of an opinion they advocate in relation to an ambiguity that occurred to them is an unlawful act that one who believes in God and the hereafter should not fall into. This is especially so now that the circle of *takfīr* based on interpretation has grown wider, because of the whims that have taken hold of Muslims due to the differences between them, so much so that you see that in the case of a question on which there are two opinions among scholars, each group accuses the other of unbelief. . . . The danger of *takfīr* is no doubt great, and the *takfīr* which is based on interpretation is something that neither God allowed nor his Prophet explained to us; rather, we have been generally forbidden from doing it." Al-Shawkānī, *Wabl al-Ghamām*, 1:193.

197. See Khaled Abou El Fadl, *Rebellion and Violence in Islamic Law* (Cambridge: Cambridge University Press, 2001).

198. Al-Shawkānī, *Nayl al-Awṭār*, 4.7:180. Also see Muḥammad b. ʿAlī al-Shawkānī, *Al-Darārī al-Muḍiyya Sharḥ al-Durar al-Bahiyya* (Cairo: Maktabat al-Turāth al-Islāmī, 1986), 503–4.

199. Al-Shawkānī, *Nayl al-Awṭār*, 1.2:205.

200. Al-Shawkānī, *Nayl al-Awṭār*, 4.7:206.

201. The authors of *The Exoteric Aḥmad Ibn Idrīs* present him as being somewhat close to the Wahhabis but less extreme and opposed to *takfīr*. See Bernd Radtke, John O'Kane, Knut S. Vikor, and R. S. O'Fahey, *The Exoteric Aḥmad Ibn Idrīs: A Sufi Critique of the Madhāhib and the Wahhābīs* (Leiden, the Netherlands: E. J. Brill, 2000), 1–43. However, considering that Ibn Idrīs was living under Wahhabi authority and susceptible to Wahhabi pressure, the guarded language he uses in his criticism of Wahhabi ideas should not obscure the radical nature of his

critique. In defiance of some of the fundamental stands of the Wahhabis, Ibn Idrīs holds to his principled positions. For example, he defends Ibn al-ʿArabī and maintains that he is worthy of veneration because he is a "mediator of Divine knowledge." In his *Risālat al-Radd* (in Radtke et al., *The Exoteric Aḥmad Ibn Idrīs*) he justifies, under obvious constraints, why he would not become a Wahhabi. His position is clearest in *Munāẓarat Aḥmad Ibn Idrīs maʿa Fuqahāʾ ʿAsīr*, where Ibn Idrīs directs his attacks at the extreme positions of a Wahhabi novice and claims that Ibn ʿAbd al-Wahhāb would not approve of his follower's views. Ibn Idrīs also derides the vulgar Bedouinity of his interlocutor (*badāwa, jafāwa*); Radtke et al., *The Exoteric Aḥmad Ibn Idrīs*, 159). Moreover, Ibn Idrīs does not shy from criticizing Ibn ʿAbd al-Wahhāb, maintaining that his commendable desire to undermine wrong innovations was marred by his extremism and the *takfīr* of Muslims who believe in nothing but God. Ibn Idrīs then asserts that, in all cases, it is not permissible to imitate Ibn ʿAbd al-Wahhāb in his errors (Radtke et al., *The Exoteric Aḥmad Ibn Idrīs*, 156–57). Also see R. S. O'Fahey, *Enigmatic Saint: Ahmad Ibn Idris and the Idrisi Tradition* (Evanston, Ill.: Northwestern University Press, 1990), 66–69, 96–105.

202. Muḥammad Bin ʿAlī al-Sanūsī, "Al-Masāʾil al-ʿAshr al-Musammā Bughyat al-Maqāṣid fī Khulāṣat al-Marāṣid," in *Al-Majmūʿa al-Mukhtāra*, ed. Muhammad ʿAbdū Ibn Ghalbūn (Manchester, 1990), 8.

203. Al-Sanūsī, "Al-Masāʾil," 9.

204. Al-Sanūsī, "Al-Masāʾil," 9–10; and Muḥammad Bin ʿAlī al-Sanūsī, "Iqāẓ al-Wasnān fī al-ʿAmal bi al-Ḥadīth wal-Qurʾān," in *Al-Majmūʿa al-Mukhtāra*, ed. Muhammad ʿAbdū Ibn Ghalbūn (Manchester, 1990), 84, 124.

205. Al-Sanūsī, "Iqāẓ," 36.

206. Al-Sanūsī, "Iqāẓ," 37.

207. In a work on prophetic tradition, al-Sanūsī starts with the tradition of mercy, and he justifies his commencing with this hadith on the ground that this is the essence of God's creation; Muḥammad ʿAlī al-Sanūsī, "Al-Musalsalāt al-ʿAshra fī al-Aḥādīth al-Nabawīya," in *Al-Majmūʿa al-Mukhtāra*, ed. Muhammad ʿAbdū Ibn Ghalbūn (Manchester, 1990), 8–10. Also in arguing that legal analogy is not valid when there is a textual statement in which the issue in question is mentioned, he maintains that such a text either contradicts the result of the analogy or makes no ruling on the specific issue under consideration. In the latter case the silence must be interpreted as a license, and a ruling on the basis of analogy would be a denial of God's license; see al-Sanūsī, "Iqāẓ," 89–90. This interpretation is comparable to Walī Allāh's notion of *taysīr*.

208. The desire to avoid leveling accusations against fellow Muslims is captured in a response by Aḥmad Ibn Idrīs to certain Wahhabis who questioned his teaching of works by Ibn al-ʿArabī. Ibn Idrīs says, "Call the passages (by Ibn al-ʿArabī) unbelief—if you are unable to explain or interpret them, but don't call Ibn al-ʿArabī an unbeliever, because there is no way you can be positive he was an unbeliever." O'Fahey, *Enigmatic Saint*, 102.

Chapter 2

1. See chapter 5 and the conclusion.

2. Muḥammad b. ʿAlī al-Shawkānī, *Adab al-Ṭalab wa Muntahā al-Irab* (Cairo: Dār al-Arqam, 1981), 68.

3. Qeyamuddin Ahmad, *The Wahabi Movement in India* (Calcutta: Firma K. L. Mukhopadhyay, 1966).

4. Lansine Kaba, *The Wahhabiyya: Islamic Reform and Politics in French West Africa* (Evanston, Ill.: Northwestern University Press, 1974).

5. Bari argues convincingly that the name "Indian Wahhabis" given to the nineteenth-century militant reform movement led by Sayyid Aḥmad Barelvī (d. 1831) was an afterthought, "perhaps given by co-religionist opponents to discredit them." M. A. Bari, "The Politics of Sayyid Ahmad Barelwi," *Islamic Culture* 31, no. 1 (1957): 158. He also argues that the name was adopted by British administrators for the same purposes; M. A. Bari, "A Nineteenth-Century Muslim Reform Movement in India," in *Arabic and Islamic Studies in Honor of Hamilton A. R. Gibb*, ed. George Makdisi (Cambridge, Mass.: Harvard University Press, 1965), 84. Ahmad adds, however, that "the title became unavoidable on account of its wide prevalence"; Ahmad, *The Wahabi Movement*, v. In his *Al-Tamhīd li Ta'rīf A'immat al-Tajdīd*, 'Ubayd Allāh al-Sindī (d. 1944) maintains that the enemies of Muḥammad Ismā'īl al-Shahīd, the grandson of Shāh Walī Allāh, "claimed that his way is that of the Najdi Shaykh [Ibn 'Abd al-Wahhāb], and called him [Ismā'īl] and his followers Wahhābīyya"; this, al-Sindī adds, is a bogus and untenable claim because Ismā'īl knew neither Najd nor its ruler, and he had no taste or affinity for Wahhabi individuals, doctrines, or practices; 'Ubayd Allāh al-Sindī, *Al-Tamhīd li Ta'rīf A'immat al-Tajdīd* (Hyderabad: Maṭba'at Jāmi'at al-Sind, 1976), 406. The name was given to the mid-twentieth-century movement of West Africa by the French head of the Bureau of Muslim Affairs in Bamako in the 1950s. Kaba, *The Wahhabiyya*, 8.

6. Rudolph Peters, "*Idjtihād* and *Taqlīd* in 18th and 19th Century Islam," *Die Welt des Islams* 20, nos. 3–4 (1980): 145.

7. John O. Voll, "The Sudanese Mahdī: Frontier Fundamentalist," *International Journal of Middle East Studies* 10 (1979): 160.

8. There are abundant studies of eighteenth- and nineteenth-century Islamic thought and movements in which these themes are said to define the common intellectual trend of fundamentalist or revivalist Islam; see, for example, Wilfred Cantwell Smith, *Islam in Modern History* (Princeton, N.J.: Princeton University Press, 1977), 42, 52; Fazlur Rahman, *Islam* (Chicago: University of Chicago Press, 1968), 242–50; John Esposito, "Tradition and Modernization in Islam," in *Movements and Issues in World Religions*, ed. Charles Wei-hsun Fu and Gerhard E. Spiegler (New York: Greenwood, 1987), 92; Mervyn Hiskett, *The Development of Islam in West Africa* (London: Longman, 1984), 157; John O. Voll, "Muḥammad Ḥayyā al-Sindī and Muḥammad Ibn 'Abd al-Wahhāb: An Analysis of an Intellectual Group in Eighteenth-Century Madīna," *Bulletin of the School of Oriental and African Studies* 38, no. 1 (1974); John O. Voll, "Hadith Scholars and Tariqahs: An Ulama Group in the 18th Century Ḥaramayn and Their Impact in the Islamic World," *Journal of Asian and African Studies* 15, nos. 3–4 (1980), 264–73; Louis Brenner, "Muslim Thought in Eighteenth-Century West Africa: The Case of Shaykh Uthman b. Fudi," in *Eighteenth-Century Renewal and Reform in Islam*, ed. Nehemia Levtzion and John Obert Voll (Syracuse, N.Y.: Syracuse University Press, 1987), 61; Muin ud-Din Ahmad Khan, "Farā'idī Movement," *Islamic Studies* 9 (1970): 123; and B. G. Martin, *Muslim Brotherhoods in Nineteenth-Century Africa* (Cambridge: Cambridge University Press, 1976), 107–8.

9. Voll, "The Sudanese Mahdī"; H. A. R. Gibb, *Modern Trends in Islam* (Chicago: University of Chicago Press, 1947), 32; and Peters, "*Idjtihād* and *Taqlīd*," 132.

10. Smith, *Islam in Modern History*, 52; Voll, "Muḥammad Ḥayyā al-Sindī and Muḥammad Ibn 'Abd al-Wahhāb," 39; Rahman, *Islam*, 242–50; Aziz Ahmad, "Political and Religious Ideas of Shāh Walī-Ullāh of Delhi," *Muslim World* 52, no. 1 (1962): 22; and Esposito, "Tradition and Modernization in Islam," 92.

11. Gibb, *Modern Trends in Islam*, 27, 30; Hiskett, *The Development of Islam*, 289–91.

12. Gibb, *Modern Trends in Islam*, 27; Hiskett, *The Development of Islam*, 256, 259; Martin, *Muslim Brotherhoods*, 99, 103. In fact, this intellectual genealogy is often stretched back in

time to include, in addition to the Sanūsī and Wahhabi movements, the Murābiṭūn and the Muwaḥḥidūn of North Africa. See Gibb, *Modern Trends in Islam*, 26; and Nehemia Levtzion, introduction to *Rural and Urban Islam in West Africa*, ed. Nehemia Levtzion and Humphrey J. Fisher (Boulder, Colo.: Lynne Rienner, 1987), 12.

13. Voll, "Muḥammad Ḥayyā al-Sindī and Muḥammad Ibn ʿAbd al-Wahhāb," 39. Most of the research on the theory of a common network of scholars was done by Voll; for references to several writings by Voll, see introduction above, n45. This theory has also gained wide currency among scholars of modern Islam; for a reference to the common background of Shāh Walī Allāh and Ibn ʿAbd al-Wahhāb, see Annemarie Schimmel, *Islam in the Indian Subcontinent* (Leiden, the Netherlands: E. J. Brill, 1980), 153. On the link between West African education and the Arabian network of scholars, see Nehemia Levtzion, "The Eighteenth Century: Background to the Islamic Revolutions in West Africa," in *Eighteenth-Century Renewal and Reform in Islam*, ed. Nehemia Levtzion and John Obert Voll (Syracuse, N.Y.: Syracuse University Press, 1987), 32–33. Also on ʿUthmān Ibn Fūdī, see Brenner, "Muslim Thought in Eighteenth-Century West Africa," 61. On the teachers of al-Sanūsī, see Peters, "*Idjtihād* and *Taqlīd*," 145. See also Peter Gran, *Islamic Roots of Capitalism: Egypt, 1760–1840* (Syracuse, N.Y.: Syracuse University Press, 1998).

14. Compare, for example, with Rahman, *Islam*, 253–54; and Voll, "Hadith Scholars and Tariqahs."

15. Compare with Voll, "Muḥammad Ḥayyā al-Sindī and Muḥammad Ibn ʿAbd al-Wahhāb." Quoting Voll's "Hadith Scholars and Tariqahs," Hermansen also adopts the view that, through the teachers of Mecca, Walī Allāh was exposed to a "trend of increased cosmopolitanism in hadith scholarship which began to emerge there in the eighteenth century due to a blending of the North African, Hijazi, and Indian traditions of study and evaluation." She also notes the critique of the neo-Sufism thesis by Radtke and O'Fahey but then maintains that the "South Asian context" of Walī Allāh may provide a better example of neo-Sufism than the North African examples considered by Radtke and O'Fahey. See the introduction to Shāh Walī Allāh, *The Conclusive Argument from God: Shāh Walī Allāh of Delhi's "Ḥujjat Allāh al-Bāligha,"* trans. Marcia K. Hermansen (Leiden, the Netherlands: E. J. Brill, 1996), xxvi–xxvii. As I illustrate in chapter 5, Walī Allāh's views on hadith have an Indian pedigree and were formed before his contact with the teachers of Mecca. For an estimate of Walī Allāh's age when he traveled to Mecca, and his exchange with, rather than study under, Meccan scholars, see Mawlawi H. Hidayat Husain, "The Persian Autobiography of Shāh Walīullah Bin ʿAbd al-Raḥīm al-Dihlavī: Its English Translation and a List of His Works," *Journal and Proceedings of the Asiatic Society of Bengal*, n.s., 8 (1912): 161–75, esp. 166, 173. Furthermore, as I will argue in the chapter on Sufism, in addition to the fact that the South Asian reform of Sufism does not fit the model of neo-Sufism, Walī Allāh's views on Sufism are further removed from this model and are more in conformity with the philosophical Sufism of Ibn al-ʿArabī.

16. ʿAbd al-Qādir Ibn al-Sayyd Muḥammad Salīm al-Kīlānī al-Iskandarānī, *Al-Nafḥa al-Zakīya fī al Radd ʿAlā al Firqa al Wahhābīya* (Damascus: Maṭbaʿat al-Fayḥāʾ, 1340 AH), 4. Early Wahhabi and non-Wahhabi sources on Ibn ʿAbd al-Wahhāb are incomplete and often unreliable. For example, it is hard to determine with any certainty the places to which Ibn ʿAbd al-Wahhāb traveled. In his meticulous survey of the historical records, Michael Cook concludes that Ibn ʿAbd al-Wahhāb traveled to Basra, possibly Mosul and Iran, but less likely to Baghdad and almost certainly not to Damascus. Cook also illustrates the "lack of proximate inspiration" by contemporary scholars on Ibn ʿAbd al-Wahhāb, despite attempts by later Wahhabi sources to associate him with distinguished teachers in order to lend legitimacy to his views. See Michael Cook, "On the Origins of Wahhābism," *Journal of the Royal Asiatic Society*

of Great Britain and Ireland 2, no. 2 (1992): 191–202. Also see Ḥusayn Ibn Ghannām (d. 1810), *Tārīkh Najd*, ed. Nāsir al-Dīn al-Asad (Beirut: Dār al-Shurūq, 1994); ʿUthmān b. ʿAbd Allāh Ibn Bishr (d. 1873), *ʿUnwān al-Majd fī Tārīkh Najd* (Beirut, n.d.); Amīn Saʿīd, *Sīrat al-Imām al-Shaykh Muḥammad Ibn ʿAbd al-Wahhāb* (Beirut: Sharikat al-Tawzīʿ al-ʿArabīya, 1384 AH); and A. M. Naṣīr, *Al-Shaykh al-Imām Muḥammad Ibn ʿAbd al-Wahhāb wa Manhjuhu fī Mabāḥith al-ʿAqīda* (Beirut: Dār al-Shurūq, 1983). Ibn Ghannām is the earliest Wahhabi account on the life of Ibn ʿAbd al-Wahhāb, but he provides only two pages (82–83) on Ibn ʿAbd al-Wahhāb's life, travels, and education before he started preaching.

17. Al-Shawkānī's main teachers included his father and Sayyid ʿAbd al-Qādir b. Aḥmad al-Kawkabānī (d. 1207/1792). Muḥammad b. ʿAlī al-Shawkānī, *Al-Badr al-Ṭāliʿ bi Maḥāsin man baʿd al-Qarn al-Sābiʿ*, 2 vols. (Beirut: Dār al-Maʿrifa, n.d.), 1:360–69. Al-Shawkānī never left Yemen to study and did not even perform the pilgrimage.

18. In his autobiography, Walī Allāh describes his rounded education before his "longing for visiting the two respectable places," although he also states that he reported hadith on the authority of, and received Sufi initiation from, Abū Ṭāhir al-Kūrānī al-Kurdī, the son of the famous scholar/teacher of the Ḥaramayn, Ibrāhīm al-Kurdī. See Husain, "The Persian Autobiography of Shāh Walīullah Ibn ʿAbd al-Raḥīm al-Dihlavī," 166, 173. Rather than apprenticeship to al-Kūrānī, this indicates an exchange whereby Walī Allāh reports on the authority of yet another chain of transmission in addition to the ones he already commands; likewise, he can claim an added ritual of initiation into Sufism. Neither of these affects the content of Walī Allāh's views on hadith or Sufism. This is further confirmed by Abū Ṭāhir himself, who writes in the license he issued to Walī Allāh that the latter requested authorization to report parts of *Ṣaḥīḥ Bukhārī* and other classics, although he had no need for it since he had already achieved mastery over the content of these works from what he learned from his father and teachers in his homeland. Qtd. in ʿUbayd Allāh al-Sindī, *Al-Tamhīd li-Taʿrīf Aʾimmat al-Tajdīd* (Hyderabad: Maṭbaʿat Jāmiʿat al-Sind, 1976), 443.

19. Walī Allāh's main teacher was his father.

20. Once again, even Ibn ʿAbd al-Wahhāb's thought was formulated before the presumed trip to the Ḥaramayn, which lasted no more than two months. According to his biographers, he harbored his radical ideas while his father was alive but did not dare air them until his father died. Ibn Ghannām, *Tārīkh Najd* (1994), 82–83. The first reaction to these ideas was rejection, and this is why he traveled in the first place; so he had developed these ideas before his alleged meeting with al-Sindī or al-Kurānī, who are invoked by Ibn ʿAbd al-Wahhāb's biographers to add credibility to his thin intellectual profile.

21. One of the main wandering scholars (and Sufis) of the eighteenth century is Murtaḍā al-Zabīdī (d. 1791), who is often considered an exemplar of eighteenth-century scholarship and, more important, of the universal educational system of this period. For this view, see Gran, *Islamic Roots of Capitalism*, 51–52, 54–55, 60–65, 123; and Stefan Reichmuth, "Murtaḍā al-Zabīdī (d. 1791) in Biographical and Autobiographical Accounts: Glimpses of Islamic Scholarship in the 18th Century," *Die Welt des Islams* 39, no. 1 (1999): 64–102. Gran notes al-Zabīdī's approval of commercial activities; he also points out al-Zabīdī's achievements in the fields of lexicography and hadith studies, and the role he and his students played in the revival and spread of the discipline of hadith. There is no doubt that al-Zabīdī was a distinguished lexicographer and teacher with a wide network of connections. Yet even his primary work, the dictionary *Tāj al-ʿArūs*, remains true to traditional ways of compiling Arabic dictionaries. Similarly, in the field of hadith, on which he wrote several works, al-Zabīdī makes no original contributions: his works focus mostly on chains of transmission and are generally derivative. For a typical work on hadith by al-Zabīdī, see *Laqṭ al-Laʾālīʾ al-Mutanāthira fī al-Aḥādīth al-*

Mutawātira (Beirut: Dār al-Kutub al-ʿIlmiyya, 1985). In *ʿUqūd al-Jawāhir al-Munīfa fī Adillat Madhhab al-Imām Abī Ḥanīfa* (Beirut, 1985), al-Zabīdī defends the Ḥanafī school against accusations that its rulings often contradict the evidence of sound hadith; al-Zabīdī argues that sound hadith can be found outside the six canonical compilations, and that Ḥanafī law will be found to be in conformity with hadith once other compilations are considered. As we will see in chapter 5, this was a standard and well-established argument in India, al-Zabīdī's birthplace, and there is nothing original in it.

22. In some cases, this regional character of education was consciously advocated in pedagogy; for example, in *Adab al-Ṭalab*, al-Shawkānī speaks of books and intellectual traditions that are specific to each region and ought to be consulted by the students of these regions. In a kind of social and economic regionalism, al-Shawkānī recognizes and suggests solutions for the particular problems of Yemen; Muḥammad b. ʿAlī al-Shawkānī, "Al-Dawāʾ al-ʿĀjil fī Dafʿ al-ʿAduw al-Ṣāʾil," in *Al-Rasāʾil al-Salafiyya fī Iḥyāʾ Sunnat Khayr al-Bariyya* (Beirut: Dār al-Kutub al-ʿIlmiyya, reprint of the 1930 edition), 27–38. He also argues that "the imam ought to spend [*yarudd*] the alms [*ṣadaqāt*] [paid] by the rich [inhabitants] of a [certain] region on the poor [inhabitants of this same region]" (Muḥammad b. ʿAlī al-Shawkānī, *Al-Darārī al-Muḍiyya Sharḥ al-Durar al-Bahiyya* [Cairo: Maktabat al-Turāth al-Islāmī, 1986], 214–16). Thus al-Shawkānī recognizes, in theory and not just in practice, the existence of regional knowledge, regional politics, and regional economic interests.

23. In the sense that they realized they were working against strong local opposition from established scholarly circles as well as other forces; still, of course, they would not refer to themselves as innovators (*mubtadiʿ*) and always claimed to better represent the true original message of Islam.

24. See notes in Mervyn Hiskett, "An Islamic Tradition of Reform in the Western Sudan from the Sixteenth to the Eighteenth Century, Translation of Selections from *Sirāj al-Ikhwān, Bayān al-Bidaʿ al-Shayṭānīya*, and *Naṣāʾiḥ al-Umma al-Muḥammadīya*," *Bulletin of the School of Oriental and African Studies* 25, no. 3 (1962): 592–93.

25. On the organization of the Sokoto state, see, for example, Murray Last, *The Sokoto Caliphate* (London: Longmans, 1967), 149, 178, 185, 226, 330–32; and Hiskett's conclusions in his edition of ʿUthmān Ibn Fūdī, "*Kitāb al-Farq*: A Work on the Habe Kingdoms Attributed to ʿUthmān Dan Fodio," ed. and trans. with introduction by M. Hiskett, *Bulletin of the School of Oriental and African Studies* 23, no. 2 (1960): 579. On the role of the state in introducing social change, see Last, "Reform in West Africa: The Jihād Movements of the Nineteenth Century," in *The History of West Africa*, ed. J. F. A. Ajayi and Michael Crowder (Essex, UK: Longman, 1974), 2:25–29. The Islamic ethos of the city, characterized by puritanism, literacy, and egalitarianism, was instrumental in affecting a change in the rural hinterland, and in producing a central state in which the urban and the rural were integrated; in contrast, see Ernest Gellner, "A Pendulum Swing Theory of Islam," *Philosophical Forum* 2, no. 2 (1970–71): 234–44; and Gellner, "The Moslem Reformation," *New Republic*, November 22, 1982, 25–30. Gellner's "pendulum swing theory of Islam" seems to locate the rural and the urban on two opposite poles and allows for no possible synthesis between them.

26. On the roles of scholars in the pre- and postjihad periods, see Last, *The Sokoto Caliphate*, 57–60, 227–29, 232; and Last, "Reform in West Africa," 29; also see Humphrey J. Fisher, "Conversion Reconsidered: Some Historical Aspects of Religious Conversion in Black Africa," *Africa* 43 (1973): 36–37.

27. This radical transformation in terms of the reorganization of political order and social structure illustrates the revolutionary effects that literacy had in West Africa; it is thus hard to figure out what Jack Goody is referring to when he speaks of the "restricted" consequences of

literacy in Western Sudan (as well as elsewhere in black Africa and the Islamic world in general!) due to the "association of the Book with magic and religion." See Goody, "Restricted Literacy in Northern Ghana," in *Literacy in Traditional Societies*, ed. Jack Goody (Cambridge: Cambridge University Press, 1968), 237, 241.

28. He quotes such names as al-Maghīlī, al-Tinbuktī, al-Suyūṭī, al-Maḥallī, al-Kuntī, al-Qasṭalānī, al-Sanūsī, al-Shabrakhtī, al-Barmūnī, al-Ajhūrī, al-Zarqānī, and Ibn Khaldūn; see, for example, ʿUthmān Ibn Fūdī, "An Early Fulani Conception of Islam," translation of *Tanbīh al-Ikhwān* with introduction by H. R. Palmer, *Journal of the African Society* 13 (1913–14): 407–14, and 14 (1914–15): 53–59, esp. 57; "Unbelief in the Western Sudan: ʿUthmān dan Fodio's *ʿTaʿlīm al-Ikhwān*,'" ed. and trans. with an introduction by B. G. Martin, *Middle Eastern Studies* 4 (1976): 50–97, esp. 65–66; and *Bayān wujūb al-Hijra ʿalā al-ʿIbād*, ed. and trans. F. H. El-Masri (Khartoum: Khartoum University Press; and Oxford: Oxford University Press, 1978). For a study of the Arabic classics taught in West Africa, see Mervyn Hiskett, "Material Relating to the State of Learning among the Fulani before Their Jihād," *Bulletin of the School of Oriental and African Studies* 19 (1957): 550–78; and A. D. Bivar and M. Hiskett, "The Arabic Literature of Nigeria to 1804: A Provisional Account," *Bulletin of the School of Oriental and African Studies* 25 (1962): 104–49.

29. He does indicate that *ijtihād* is one of the conditions of the legitimate imam; however, he adds, this requirement can be overlooked if a qualified person is not found. See Ibn Fūdī, *Bayān wujūb*, 30–31; contrast with Martin, *Muslim Brotherhoods*, 32–34, who suggests a much greater emphasis on *ijtihād* in the work of Ibn Fūdī.

30. On sources for the study of al-Sanūsī, see Knut S. Vikor, *Sufi and Scholar on the Desert Edge: Muḥammad b. ʿAlī al-Sanūsī and His Brotherhood* (Evanston, Ill.: Northwestern University Press, 1995), 4–19.

31. On al-Sanūsī's organizational activities in Cyrenaica, see Vikor, *Sufi and Scholar*, 132–60, 181–217.

32. Vikor, *Sufi and Scholar*, 189.

33. Vikor, *Sufi and Scholar*, 190–94; R. S. O'Fahey and Bernd Radtke, "Neo-Sufism Reconsidered," *Der Islam* 70, no. 1 (1993): 52–87, esp. 74.

34. Qtd. in Vikor, *Sufi and Scholar*, 205.

35. Vikor notes reservations by Peters, O'Fahey, and Radtke about qualifying al-Sanūsī (and others) as a reformer, since there was little new in his so-called reform, and he "mainly continued trends that already existed in previous centuries." Vikor adds, however, that al-Sanūsī "was indeed a proponent of reform, but reform within a tradition," and that his "reform was the combination of ideas and organization" (Vikor, *Sufi and Scholar*, 2–3). While Vikor is right in underscoring the organizational dimension of al-Sanūsī's reforms, he seems to contrast reform within a tradition to some other kind of reform, when in fact all kinds of reform are within and in relation to traditions.

36. O'Fahey and Radtke, "Neo-Sufism Reconsidered," 74.

37. Vikor rightly notes that there was no "trace of a concern about any Western Christian encroachment on the lands of Islam in his [al-Sanūsī's] writings," but he wrongly takes this as an indication that al-Sanūsī "was not a political thinker or leader," as if the only way to be political is to engage the West (Vikor, *Sufi and Scholar*, 1). Vikor also dismisses the idea that al-Sanūsī moved south to escape from the Ottomans (265–66). Although al-Sanūsī avoided confrontation with both the French and the Ottomans, and deliberately moved into spaces where there was no opposition from political and religious authorities associated with either, he was nonetheless political in his attempt to build a political order with distinct structures of authority. Moreover, his ambiguous relationship with the Ottomans, which evolved over time,

was mainly guided by a desire to remain independent. See Michel Le Gall, "The Ottoman Government and the Sanusiyya: A Reappraisal," *International Journal of Middle East Studies* 21, no. 1 (1989): 91–106.

38. Contrast to J. Spencer Trimingham, *The Sufi Orders in Islam* (Oxford: Oxford University Press, 1971), 119–20. Trimingham asserts that al-Sanūsī's ambition to "achieve a simple Islamic theocratic organization of society," was only achievable in "a country without a history," hence his choice of sub-Saharan Africa. Trimingham also asserts that "history was in fact to catch up with and overrun his [al-Sanūsī's] order." However, Trimingham does not recognize the fact that the Sanūsiyya order, as it were, spread not only through the efforts of Sanūsī missionaries but also through those of local agents. Trimingham's assertion notwithstanding, the Africa into which the Sanūsī order spread was not a void without history. Of course, Trimingham's "history" is none other than the French colonial armies, hardly a universal principle of social organization. There is also a pervasive contradiction in Trimingham's presentation of the Sanūsiyya as at once a pan-Islamist movement and an isolated fringe phenomenon of the Muslim world (132).

39. On the influence of Ibn Idrīs, see Vikor, *Sufi and Scholar*, 100–131. For his later education in the East, see Vikor, *Sufi and Scholar*, 81–90.

40. Contrast with Vikor, who contends that there is no significant intellectual difference between al-Sanūsī and his teacher Ibn Idrīs, and that the only distinction is that the student was "perhaps soft on Wahhābism" (Vikor, *Sufi and Scholar*, 131). I would take issue with Vikor's assessment on two counts: first, al-Sanūsī's views on *takfīr* were as opposed to Wahhabism as those of Ibn Idrīs were. If the latter's articulation of a critique of Wahhabism was more direct, it was because the Wahhabis publicly challenged him and questioned the integrity of his beliefs. Second, and more important, al-Sanūsī differed significantly from his teacher, mainly in that while Ibn Idrīs's *ijtihād* was grounded in revelatory knowledge (*kashf*), al-Sanūsī's *ijtihād*, like that of al-Shawkānī, was based on structured legal reasoning. For more on this point, see below.

41. For more on the life and education of al-Sanūsī, see Vikor, *Sufi and Scholar*, 22–90. Also see Aḥmad Ṣidqī al-Dajānī, *Al-Ḥaraka al-Sanūsiyya: Nash'atuha wa Numuwwuha fī al-Qarn al-Tasiʿ ʿAshar* (Beirut: Dār Lubnan, 1967).

42. I. M. Lewis, *A Pastoral Democracy: A Study of Pastoralism and Politics among the Northern Somali of the Horn of Africa* (Oxford: Oxford University Press, 1961), 100, 223.

43. On the teachings of the Tījāniyya, see Jamil M. Abun-Nasr, *The Tijaniyya: A Sufi Order in the Modern World* (New York: Oxford University Press, 1965), 27–57.

44. Abun-Nasr, *The Tijaniyya*, 10–14. On the cooperation of Tījānī chiefs with French colonial authorities and their conflict with ʿAbd al-Qādir al-Jazāʾrī, the leader of the anticolonial resistance, see Abun-Nasr, *The Tijaniyya*, 62. On the influences of the Sokoto tradition of jihad on Ḥāj ʿUmar, see Abun-Nasr, *The Tijaniyya*, 101. On the teachings of Ḥāj ʿUmar, see ʿUmar b. Saʿīd al-Fūtī, "Rimāḥ Ḥizb al-Raḥīm ʿalā Nuḥūr Ḥizb al-Rajīm," printed in margins of Abū al-ʿAbbās al-Tījānī, *Jawāhir al-Maʿānī wa Bulūgh al-Amānī fī Fayḍ Sīdī Abī al-ʿAbbās al-Tījānī*, ed. ʿAlī Ḥarāzim Bin Barāda, 2 vols. (Cairo, 1927). For another example of Sufi organization under direct state control, see F. de Jong, *Ṭuruq and Ṭuruq-Linked Institutions in Nineteenth-Century Egypt: A Historical Study in Organizational Dimensions of Islamic Mysticism* (Leiden, the Netherlands: E. J. Brill, 1978). The Ottomans legalized and patronized the Bakriyya order in Egypt and used it to undermine the authority of the *ʿulamāʾ*. However, this state-sponsored Sufism was far less learned and intellectually vibrant than the independent Sufism of al-Sanūsī.

45. Muḥammad b. Ismāʿīl al-Amīr al-Ṣanʿānī, *Irshād al-Nuqqād ilā Taysīr al-Ijtihād*, ed.

M. Hallāq (Beirut: Mu'assasat al-Rayyān, 1992), 11–12, qtd. in Aḥmad Muḥammad al-ʿUlaymī, *Al-Ṣanʿānī wa Kitābuhu Tawḍīḥ al-Afkār* (Beirut: Dār al-Kutub al-ʿIlmiyya, 1987), 91–92.

46. Al-Ṣanʿānī, *Irshād al-Nuqqād*, 22–24.

47. For a concise list of these disciplines, see Bernard Haykel, *Revival and Reform in Islam: The Legacy of Muhammad al-Shawkani* (Cambridge: Cambridge University Press, 2003), 105–6.

48. Al-Shawkānī, *Adab al-Ṭalab*, 107–8. Contrast with Haykel, who, after noting al-Shawkānī's remark, concludes that "his claims are not national or regional but universal" (*Revival and Reform*, 103). It is not clear how by deferring to other regional canons al-Shawkānī would be making universal claims on behalf of the curriculum he is proposing for his Yemeni readers when he refers other readers to their respective regional canons.

49. Al-Shawkānī, *Adab al-Ṭalab*, 113–24.

50. See, for example, al-Shawkānī, *Adab al-Ṭalab*, 108. Contrast to Haykel, *Revival and Reform in Islam*, 102. Haykel suggests that the seemingly universal content of al-Shawkānī's proposed curriculum does not translate into universal applicability; in contrast, I am arguing that al-Shawkānī's curriculum was regional in content but universal in applicability.

51. See, for example, Muḥammad b. ʿAlī al-Shawkānī, *Itḥāf al-Akābir bi Isnād al-Dafātir* (Haydar Abad al-Dakkan: Maṭbaʿat Majlis Dā'irat al-Maʿārif al-Niẓāmiyya, 1328 AH), 3, 7, 8, 18, 24, 25, 30, 31, 42–69, 89, 94, 96, 100, 101.

52. See, for example, al-Shawkānī, *Itḥāf al-Akābir*, 5, 6, 19. For the transmission of the works of Ibn al-Wazīr through Yemeni Sunni scholars, such as the Ahdal and ʿUjaymī families, see, for example, al-Shawkānī, *Itḥāf al-Akābir*, 18–19.

53. Al-Shawkānī, *Itḥāf al-Akābir*, 17.

54. See Louis Brenner and Murray Last, "The Role of Language in West African Islam," *Africa* 55, no. 4 (1985): 432–46.

55. For reference to 500 poems in Fulfulde that were composed in nineteenth-century West Africa, see Brenner and Last, "The Role of Language," 444.

56. The content of Walī Allāh's thought was largely shaped by the local Islamic tradition of India. Although he purported to articulate a universal Islamic vision, the perceived crises that he attempted to resolve were products of the experience of Muslims in India and the specific history of the Islamic tradition in India. See more on this in the chapters that follow.

57. This is especially true of his Sufi writings.

58. In addition to numerous works in Persian, Walī Allāh produced a translation of the Qur'ān (*Fatḥ al-Raḥmān fī Trjamat al-Qurʿān*), a Persian introduction to the science of Tafsīr (*Al-Fawz al-Kabīr fī Uṣūl al-Tafsīr*), a commentary on Mālik's *Muwaṭṭa'* (*Al-Muṣaffā*), and a translation of al-Bukhārī's *Ṣaḥīḥ*.

59. After Walī Allāh, translations and composition in Urdu became common.

60. Contrast to Trimingham, *The Sufi Orders*, 245. Oblivious to the rich and diverse reformative tradition of the period, Trimingham asserts that in the eighteenth and nineteenth centuries, only three kinds of Islamic religious movements existed; these advocated "salvation through return to Origins (the law): Wahhabism. Salvation through the Divinely-Sent Leader: Mahdism. Salvation through Ecstasy and Loss of Self-Volition in the Sufi Shaikh (charismatic leader): Ṭarīqah Revival." In addition to his erroneous understanding of Wahhabi creedal puritanism as a return to the law and his reductive and stereotypical misrepresentation of Sufi movements, Trimingham leaves out the rigorous legacy of eighteenth-century intellectual reform.

61. Studies of the modern Muslim world abound with references to the centrality of the concept of *ijtihād* to the nineteenth-century Muslim reformers. Like the reformers they

quote, these studies provide no substantive discussion of the theory of *ijtihād* and simply note the reference to it. See, for example, Albert Hourani, *Arabic Thought in the Liberal Age, 1798–1939* (Cambridge: Cambridge University Press, 1983), 127, 147, 148, 235, 240, 243, 244, 272; Nikki R. Keddie, *Sayyid Jamal ad-Dīn "al-Afghānī": A Political Biography* (Berkeley: University of California Press, 1972), 178–79, 396; Joseph Schacht, *An Introduction to Islamic Law* (Oxford, UK: Clarendon, 1969), 69–71; and N. J. Coulson, *A History of Islamic Law* (Edinburgh: Edinburgh University Press, 1964), 81.

62. Rudolph Peters considers *ijtihād* one of the themes of eighteenth-century revival, but he does not specify what was new about it. Peters, "*Idjtihād* and *Taqlīd*."

63. See chapter 5 and the conclusion for details.

64. Following Schacht's theories on Islamic law, Malcolm Kerr argues that the doctrines and principles of the field of *uṣūl al-fiqh* "were evolved as justifications for the borrowings by Islamic law from pre-Islamic practices in Syria and Iraq." See Malcolm Kerr, "Rashīd Riḍā and Islamic Legal Reform: An Ideological Analysis," part 1, "Methodology," and part 2. "Application," *Muslim World* 50, no. 2 (1960): 99–108, and no. 3 (1960): 170–81, 99. Similarly, Kerr cites Emile Tyan, *Institutions du droit musulman public*, vol. 1, *Le Califat* (Paris, 1954), and argues that Islamic political discourse "grew historically from the need to justify the record of the Umayyad and Abbasid dynasties." Kerr, "Rashīd Riḍā and Islamic Legal Reform," 99. For more on this subject, see the chapters that follow.

65. The first to use the term *socio-moral reconstruction* was Fazlur Rahman, and it has since been repeated by many, including John Obert Voll, William Roff, and others. See, for example, Fazlur Rahman, "Revival and Reform in Islam," in *The Cambridge History of Islam*, ed. P. M. Holt, Ann K. S. Lambton, and B. Lewis (London: Cambridge University Press, 1970), 632–56, 637. For more on the subject, see chapter 5.

66. This is also the implication of the revisionist focus on political economy as a paradigm for the study of eighteenth-century Islam. See Roger Owen, "The Middle East in the Eighteenth Century: An Islamic Society in Decline? A Critique of Gibb and Bowen's *Islamic Society and the West*," *Review of Middle East Studies* 1 (1975): 101–12. For a more nuanced use of the paradigm of political economy, see Gran, *Islamic Roots of Capitalism*. Gran argues that a surge in intellectual activity in eighteenth-century Egypt resulted from new economic activities and the creation of a new class of entrepreneurs. However, Gran does not offer much analysis of the content of the new intellectual activity, nor does he identify what is original in this activity.

67. Numerous works throughout Islamic history have discussed *ijtihād*, the religious need to practice it at all times, its ranks and types, and its conditions. See, for example, Jalāl al-Dīn al-Suyūṭī (d. 911 AH), *Al-Radd ʿalā man Akhlada ilā al-Arḍ wa Jahila anna al-Ijtihād fī Kull ʿAṣr Farḍ*, ed. F. A. M. Aḥmad (Alexandria: Muʾassasat Shabāb al-Jāmiʿa, 1985). The most exhaustive studies of this subject to date are by Wael Hallaq, who provides a thorough account of classical Islamic views on *ijtihād* as well as an account and compelling critique of modern scholarship on the subject. See, for example, Hallaq, "Was the Gate of *Ijtihad* Closed?," *International Journal of Middle East Studies* 16, no. 1 (1984): 3–41; and "On the Origins of the Controversy about the Existence of *Mujtahids* and the Gate of *Ijtihād*," *Studia Islamica* 63 (1986): 129–41.

68. Neither Ibn Fūdī nor Ibn ʿAbd al-Wahhab wrote on *ijtihad*. The main works on the subject are those of al-Ṣanʿānī, Walī Allāh, and al-Shawkānī. In contrast, al-Sanūsī's views are largely indebted to al-Shawkānī, while other works have little to add to the works of the three main figures. Other works of similar import include Muḥammad Ḥayāt al-Sindī (d. 1163 AH), *Tuḥfat al-Anām fī-l ʿAmal bi-Ḥadīth al-Nabī ʿalayh al-Salām*, ed. Bū Surayḥ (Beirut: Dār Ibn

Ḥazm, 1993); and Ṣāliḥ Bin Muḥammad al-ʿUmarī al-Fulānī (d. 1218 AH), *Iqāẓ Himam Ulī al-Abṣār li-l-Iqtidāʾ bi-Sayyid al-Muhājirīn wa-l-Anṣār, wa Taḥdhīrihim ʿan al-Ibtidāʿ al-Shāʾiʿ fī al-Qurā wa-l-Amṣār min Taqlīd al-Madhāhib maʿ al-Hamiyya wa-l-ʿAṣabiyya Bayn Fuqahāʾ al-Aʿṣār* (Lahore: Dār Nashr al-Kutub al-Islāmiyya, 1975).

69. Al-Ṣanʿānī, *Irshād al-Nuqqād*.

70. Muḥammad b. Ismāʿīl al-Amīr al-Ṣanʿānī, *Irshād al-Nuqqād ilā Taysīr al-Ijtihād*, ed. M. Hallāq (Beirut: Muʾassasat al-Rayyān, 1992), 36; al-ʿUlaymī, *Al-Ṣanʿānī wa Kitābuhu Tawḍīḥ al-Afkār*, 91–92; also qtd. in Ibrāhīm Hilāl, *Al-Wijha al-Salafiyya ʿind al-Amīr al-Ṣanʿānī* (Cairo: Dār al-Nahḍa al-ʿArabiyya, 1984), 11–12.

71. Al-Ṣanʿānī, *Irshād al-Nuqqād*, 37.

72. Al-Ṣanʿānī, *Irshād al-Nuqqād*, 106.

73. Muḥammad Ibn Ismāʿīl al-Amīr al-Ṣanʿānī, *Subul al-Salām Sharḥ Bulūg al-Marām min Jamʿ Adillat al-Aḥkām*, ed. F. A. Zamarlī and I. M. Jamal, 5 vols. (Beirut: Dār al-Kitāb al-ʿArabī, 1990), 4:227–30.

74. Al-Ṣanʿānī, *Subul al-Salām*, 4:229.

75. Al-Ṣanʿānī, *Irshād al-Nuqqād*, 69–72. Al-Ṣanʿānī quotes Muḥammad Ḥayāt al-Sindī, *Tuḥfat al-Anām fī al-ʿAmal bi-Ḥadīth al-Nabī ʿAlayhi al-Ṣalāt wal-Salām*, ed. A. Bū Surayḥ (Beirut: Dār Ibn Ḥazm, 1993); however, he rejects al-Sindī's view that once a person commits or adheres to a school, he is forbidden from switching to any other one. This, al-Ṣanʿānī adds, is because commitment or affiliation (*iltizām*) is itself forbidden. Al-Ṣanʿānī, *Irshād al-Nuqqād*, 73.

76. Al-Ṣanʿānī, *Irshād al-Nuqqād*, 72.

77. Muḥammad b. ʿAlī al-Shawkānī, *Al-Qawl al-Mufīd fī Adillat al-Ijtihād wal-Taqlīd*, ed. I. I. Hilāl (Cairo: Dār al-Nahḍa al-ʿArabiyya, 1979), 167.

78. Al-Shawkānī, *Adab al-Ṭalab*, 85.

79. Al-Shawkānī, *Al-Qawl al-Mufīd*, 125.

80. Al-Shawkānī, *Al-Qawl al-Mufīd*, 125.

81. Al-Ṣanʿānī, *Irshād al-Nuqqād*, 60–62.

82. Shāh Walī Allāh, *Iqd al-Jīd fī Aḥkām al-Ijtihād wal-Taqlīd* (Cairo: Al-Maṭbaʿa al-Salafiyya, 1385 AH), 3.

83. Walī Allāh, *ʿIqd*, 3; and Shāh Walī Allāh, *Al-Inṣāf fī Bayān Sabab al-Ikhtilāf* (Lahore: Maṭbaʿat al-Maktaba al-ʿIlmiyya, 1971), 46.

84. Walī Allāh, *ʿIqd*, 4.

85. Walī Allāh, *ʿIqd*, 3–4, 32–35. Following Ibn al-Wazīr, al-Ṣanʿānī also maintains that knowledge of *kalām* is not a requirement for *ijtihād*; see al-Ṣanʿānī, *Irshād al-Nuqqād*, 60.

86. Walī Allāh, *ʿIqd*, 3; *Inṣāf*, 36, 50; and Shāh Walī Allāh al-Dehlawī (d. 1176 AH), *Ḥujjat Allāh al-Bāligha*, ed. M. S. Hāshim, 2 vols. (Beirut: Dār al-Kutub al-ʿIlmiyya, 1995), 1:156.

87. On the kinds of *mujtahids*, see Walī Allāh, *ʿIqd*, 5, 17–19; and *Inṣāf*, 46–50.

88. For example, al-Shawkānī, *Al-Badr al-Ṭāliʿ*, 2:84.

89. Al-Shawkānī, *Al-Badr al-Ṭāliʿ*, 2:85–86.

90. Al-Shawkānī, *Al-Qawl al-Mufīd*, 166.

91. Al-Shawkānī, *Al-Badr al-Ṭāliʿ*, esp. 2:86–88.

92. See, for example, al-Shawkānī, *Al-Badr al-Ṭāliʿ*, 2:89.

93. Al-Shawkānī, *Al-Badr al-Ṭāliʿ*, 2:89.

94. In *Al-Sayl al-Jarrār* (1:15–17), al-Shawkānī harshly criticizes a view by al-Jalāl, which was partially supported by al-Ṣanʿānī. Al-Jalāl maintains that *taqlīd* is permissible in *ijtihādī* matters on the grounds that the difference between the commoner (*ʿāmmī*) and the *mujtahid* is like the difference between night and day, and because *ijtihād* is a faculty of which dull

minds are not capable. In opposition to al-Jalāl's contention, al-Shawkānī asserts that soliciting the help of a *mujtahid* by a commoner is not *taqlīd* in disguise, and that it simply falls under the category of accepting the report of someone who has the developed faculty of *ijtihād*. Contrast to Haykel, who argues that, because of his lack of knowledge of the law and inability to make comparative judgments, "the commoner effectively would still be practicing *taqlīd*, albeit under a new guise." Haykel, *Revival and Reform in Islam*, 102.

95. Contrast to Peters, who argues that, unlike traditional writings on the subject, al-Shawkānī does not differentiate among the different ranks of *ijtihād*. Peters, "*Idjtihād* and *Taqlīd*," 143.

96. Al-Shawkānī, *Adab al-Ṭalab*, 97.

97. Al-Shawkānī, *Adab al-Ṭalab*, 98.

98. Al-Shawkānī, *Adab al-Ṭalab*, 117.

99. Al-Shawkānī, *Adab al-Ṭalab*, 109.

100. Al-Shawkānī, *Adab al-Ṭalab*, 118. For recommendations of books that need to be studied, see 97–98.

101. Al-Shawkānī, *Adab al-Ṭalab*, 99–101, 136–37.

102. Al-Shawkānī, *Al-Qawl al-Mufīd*, 172.

103. Al-Shawkānī, *Adab al-Ṭalab*, 138–39. See also Muḥammad b. ʿAlī al-Shawkānī, *Qaṭr al-Walī ʿalā Ḥadīth al-Walī*; published as *Wilāyat Allāh wal-Ṭarīq Ilayhā*, ed. Ibrāhīm Hilāl (Cairo: Dār al-Kutub al-Ḥadītha, 1969), 323.

104. Contrast to Bernd Radtke, "*Ijtihād* and Neo-Sufism," *Asiatische Studien/Études Asiatiques* 48, no. 3 (1994): 909–21. Radtke examines and lumps together the positions of Ḥajj ʿUmar al-Tall of Futa Jalon, Senegambia (d. 1864); Ṣāliḥ al-Fulānī; and al-Sanūsī, and concludes that their views are mostly traditional, often invoking Aḥmad Ibn Taymiyya's views on the subject (917). Radtke also maintains that this eighteenth-century *ijtihād* was not absolute, was advocated within the context of existing schools, and amounted to the extension of these schools (918). Radtke fails to recognize the equally important approach to *ijtihād* that did not result in extending the purview of schools but undermined them altogether. As we will see below, al-Sanūsī was an advocate of this approach.

105. Al-Ṣanʿānī, *Irshād al-Nuqqād*, 73, quoting al-Sindī's *Tuḥfat al-Anām*.

106. Al-Ṣanʿānī, *Irshād al-Nuqqād*, 75–84, 92–107.

107. Qurʾān (Naḥl 16:43; and Anbiyāʾ 21:7).

108. Al-Ṣanʿānī, *Irshād al-Nuqqād*, 83–84.

109. Qurʾān (Tawba 9:100).

110. Al-Ṣanʿānī, *Irshād al-Nuqqād*, 93, 96.

111. Al-Shawkānī, *Al-Qawl al-Mufīd*, 109.

112. Al-Shawkānī, *Al-Qawl al-Mufīd*, 110.

113. Al-Shawkānī, *Al-Qawl al-Mufīd*, 110.

114. Al-Shawkānī, *Al-Qawl al-Mufīd*, 111–12.

115. Al-Shawkānī, *Al-Qawl al-Mufīd*, 126–27.

116. Al-Shawkānī, *Al-Qawl al-Mufīd*, 130.

117. Contrast to Vikor, who argues that al-Sanūsī was influenced by his teacher Ibn Idrīs. Vikor also lumps together the renewed claims of *ijtihād* in the eighteenth and nineteenth centuries, including those of al-Sanusı, Ibn Idrıs, and al-Mırghanı, as well as the Yemenı and Indian scholars, and refers to them as "the reform or novelty of the periphery" (Vikor, *Sufi and Scholar*, 20, 263). Of course a notion of a periphery that extends over such a wide area, even if it does not include Cairo or Istanbul, is quite problematic. Moreover, these notions of *ijtihād* were informed by and open to transregional intellectual influences, and there was

nothing peripheral about the intellectual universe of scholars like Walī Allāh, al-Shawkānī, or al-Sanūsī.

More important for the present argument is that al-Sanūsī's *ijtihād* was radically different from that of his teacher, despite significant parallels in their writings on the subject. For parallels between al-Sanūsī's *Iqāẓ al-Wasnān* and Ibn Idrīs's *Risālat al-Radd*, see Bernd Radtke, John O'Kane, Knut S. Vikor, and R. S. O'Fahey, *The Exoteric Aḥmad Ibn Idrīs: A Sufi's Critique of the Madhāhib and the Wahhābis* (Leiden, the Netherlands: E. J. Brill, 2000), 2–3, 23. Ibn Idrīs rejected schools by calling for an "inward orientation towards God, . . . rejecting, in effect, the weight of the whole preceding tradition." Radtke et al., *The Exoteric Aḥmad Ibn Idrīs*, x. The apparent similarity between al-Sanūsī and Ibn Idrīs conceals fundamental differences in their respective concepts of *ijtihād*. Ibn Idrīs forbids following schools but allows following individual scholars. Moreover, he argues that legal rulings can be attained through personal piety, and that mystical piety provides its owner with a discriminating ability and spares him the need for transmitted knowledge. Ibn Idrīs also asserts that basing knowledge on instruments, linguistic and otherwise, is inferior to knowing in the mystical sense, and that revelatory knowledge is the way the first generation of Muslims acquired their knowledge (Radtke et al., *The Exoteric Aḥmad Ibn Idrīs*, 13, 50–55, 70. Ibn Idrīs's views on *ijtihād* are elaborated in *Risālat al-Radd ʿalā Ahl al-Raʾī bi-l-Ṣawāb li-Muwāfaqat al-Sunna wa-l-Kitāb*). Ibn Idrīs's *ijtihād*, therefore, can be termed revelational *ijtihād* and is the exact opposite of al-Sanūsī's, which, like the *ijtihād* of al-Shawkānī, is based on formal legal reasoning. In contrast to his teacher, al-Sanūsī gives precedence to transmitted knowledge and, in the absence of such knowledge, *ijtihād* involves the exhaustion of the appropriate procedures of legal reasoning, in "matters over which there is no transmission from the prophet or where this (transmission) is not explicit." Muḥammad Bin ʿAlī al-Sanūsī, "Kitāb al-Masāʾil al-ʿAshr al-Musammā Bughyat al-Maqāṣid fī Khulāṣat al-Marāṣid," in *Al-Majmūʿa al-Mukhtāra*, ed. Muḥammad ʿabu Ibn Ghalbūn (Manchester, 1990), 83.

Another difference between Ibn Idrīs and al-Sanūsī is in their levels of political activism. In contrast to Trimingham's unfounded portrayal of Ibn Idrīs as an activist with a "pan-Islamic vision" whose emphasis was more on formal/ethical practicalities than on mysticism (Trimingham, *The Sufi Orders*, 106–7), O'Fahey rightly argues that, although Ibn Idrīs was a preacher and a teacher unafraid to speak his mind, there is no evidence of his alleged pan-Islamic activism (O'Fahey, *Enigmatic Saint*, 18). In addition, unlike for al-Sanūsī, there is no evidence that Ibn Idrīs was an activist in the organizational sense of the word.

118. Muḥammad Bin ʿAlī al-Sanūsī, "Iqāẓ al-Wasnān fī al-ʿAmal bil-Ḥadīth wal-Qurʾān," in *Al-Majmūʿa al-Mukhtāra*, 19.

119. Al-Sanūsī, "Shifāʾ al-Ṣadr bi Arī al-Masāʾil al-ʿAshr," in *Al-Majmūʿa al-Mukhtāra*, 21.

120. Al-Sanūsī, "Iqāẓ," 11–139, esp. 12, 19–20. To be sure, a scholar may commit a sin by issuing a ruling without proper investigation and reflection. Such sins, which undermine the intellectual integrity of a scholar, may be forgiven, however, as long as they are not deliberate falsehoods meant to uphold something the scholar knows to be wrong, and as long as he does not assert the correctness or falsehood of a legal opinion without knowledge. Al-Sanūsī adds that, since the imams are not infallible, committing errors (or even sins) does not diminish their elevated status. Al-Sanūsī, "Iqāẓ," 22.

121. Muḥammad Bin ʿAlī al-Sanūsī, "Al-Masāʾil al-ʿAshr al-Musammā Bughyat al-Maqāṣid fī Khulāṣat al-Marāṣid," in *Al-Majmūʿa al-Mukhtāra*, ed. Muhammad ʿAbdū Ibn Ghalbūn (Manchester, 1990), 53–61; and "Iqāẓ," 54, 84, 98.

122. Al-Sanūsī, "Iqāẓ," 96.

123. Al-Sanūsī, "Al-Masā'il," 65–77, 93–112; and "Iqāẓ," 96–97, 119.

124. Al-Sanūsī, "Al-Masā'il," 101–2.

125. Al-Sanūsī, "Al-Masā'il," 61–65.

126. Al-Sanūsī, "Iqāẓ," 101, 124.

127. Al-Sanūsī, "Al-Masā'il," 96–97.

128. Al-Sanūsī, "Al-Masā'il," 100.

129. Al-Sanūsī, "Iqāẓ," 94–96.

130. Al-Sanūsī, "Iqāẓ," 118–20.

131. Al-Sanūsī, "Iqāẓ," 98, 124.

132. See al-Sanūsī, "Iqāẓ," 99, 101, where al-Sanūsī argues that a common person (*ʿāmmī*) who claims to belong to a school is similar to one who has no knowledge of grammar and still claims to be a grammarian.

133. Al-Sanūsī, "Kitāb al-Masā'il al-ʿAshr," 40–41.

134. Al-Sanūsī, "Iqāẓ," 98.

135. Al-Sanūsī, "Al-Masā'il," 37–49; and "Iqāẓ," 85–97, 98, 116.

136. Al-Sanūsī, "Iqāẓ," 55, 116.

137. Al-Sanūsī, "Iqāẓ," 19, 117.

138. Al-Sanūsī, "Al-Masā'il," 119–20; al-Sanūsī, "Iqāẓ," 51–54. For a compelling interpretation of al-Qarāfī's views on *taqlīd*, see Sherman Jackson, *Islamic Law and the State: The Constitutional Jurisprudence of Shihab al-Din al-Qarafi* (Leiden, the Netherlands: E. J. Brill, 1996); and Jackson, "*Taqlīd*, Legal Scaffolding and the Scope of Legal Injunctions: Mutlaq and ʿāmm in the Jurisprudence of Shihāb al-Dīn al-Qarāfī," *Islamic Law and Society* 3, no. 2 (1996): 165–92.

139. Significantly, in response to al-Qarāfī, al-Sanūsī quotes such works as Ibn Qayyim al-Jawziyya's *Iʿlām al-Muwaqqiʿīn* (al-Sanūsī, "Al-Masā'il," 124–25), Ibn al-Wazīr's *Al-Rawḍ al-Bāsim* (al-Sanūsī, "Al-Masā'il," 114–15; "Iqāẓ," 47), and al-Maqbalī's *Al-ʿAlam al-Shāmikh* (al-Sanūsī, "Al-Masā'il," 117–18).

140. Al-Sanūsī, "Iqāẓ," 51.

141. In "Al-Masā'il," al-Sanūsī takes a somewhat less radical position; he argues that if a person has sufficient linguistic skills to comprehend the implications of common speech (*maqāṣid al-kalām*) and is capable of consulting books of language or commentaries on hadith, then this person is obligated to act on the basis of hadith. Al-Sanūsī adds that if a person lacks these basic skills, then it is permissible for him to join the ranks of utter commoners and not act on the basis of hadith. Al-Sanūsī, "Al-Masā'il," 127–28.

142. Al-Sanūsī, "Iqāẓ," 116. In a subtle difference from al-Shawkānī, al-Sanūsī states: "We do not say that *taqlīd* is forbidden to every individual; we simply require that one inquire about the indicants"; "Iqāẓ," 98–99. Still, this inquiry is what al-Sanūsī calls the *ijtihād* of the commoner or *ittibāʿ*.

143. Walī Allāh, *Inṣāf*, 50–51, qtd. in ʿUbayd Allāh al-Sindī, *Tamhīd*, 362.

144. Walī Allāh's stand on *ijtihād* and *taqlīd* is perhaps best understood in light of his attempt to reconcile the various intellectual legacies of Islam. A committed Ḥanafī, he studied and taught the *Muwaṭṭa'* of Imam Mālik and reassessed Ḥanafī legal opinions in its light, arguing that it is the most reliable book after the Qur'ān (Walī Allāh, *Ḥujjat Allāh*, 1:133; *ʿIqd al-Jīd*, 20; Walī Allāh also wrote a separate work in Persian titled *Sharḥ-i-Muwaṭṭa'*). He applied the principles of jurisprudence developed by al-Shāfiʿī to his theory of *ijtihād*, convinced that no *ijtihād* in any of the four schools could have been possible without these principles (Walī Allāh, *Ḥujjat Allāh*, 1:146–47; and *Inṣāf*, 19–22, 55–57). He also recognized the primacy of the authority of hadith, which is the central contribution of Aḥmad Ibn Ḥanbal, and adopted the

theory of *ijtihād* that was largely advocated by several generations of Ḥanbalī scholars (Walī Allāh, *Ḥujjat Allāh*, 1:2, 161; and *Inṣāf*, 62). In other words, despite his assertions that he was the *mujaddid* of his time, Walī Allāh did not shy from admitting that he was a follower of sorts.

145. Walī Allāh, *ʿIqd*, 14.

146. Walī Allāh, *Ḥujjat Allāh*, 1:154–55; and *ʿIqd*, 15–16, 27–28.

147. Walī Allāh, *Ḥujjat Allāh*, 1:121.

148. Walī Allāh, *ʿIqd*, 27.

149. Walī Allāh, *ʿIqd*, 23.

150. Walī Allāh, *ʿIqd*, 24–25.

151. Walī Allāh, *ʿIqd*, 30.

152. See, for example, al-Sanūsī, "Al-Masāʾil," 83–93; and "Iqāẓ," 61–75.

153. Al-Sanūsī, "Al-Masāʾil," 88–93; and "Iqāẓ," 72. Note also al-Sanūsī's indication that stipulating the memorization of all traditions as a prerequisite for *ijtihād* makes it impossible, and thus cannot be a condition; "Iqāẓ," 15.

154. Al-Sanūsī, "Iqāẓ," 62, 93.

155. Al-Sanūsī, "Iqāẓ," 74.

156. Al-Sanūsī, "Al-Masāʾil," 94. In a similar vein, al-Sanūsī refers to a tendency among Mālikī muftis to issue legal rulings simply by memorizing and regurgitating the legal opinions of Mālik and his companions, without exercising any scrutiny in the process. Al-Sanūsī adds that such muftis base their rulings on imitation without knowledge, and thus their rulings are not valid, even if they happen to be correct. He adds, however, that a scholar may issue rulings on the basis of Mālik's views if he can discern the validity of the opinions he is issuing ("Al-Masāʾil," 78).

157. Al-Sanūsī, "Iqāẓ," 44–46, 54. Also see "Al-Masāʾil," 77–83, on the different kinds and ranks of muftis, the scholars who exercise *ijtihād*. A *mujtahid* could be independent or affiliated with a school; in the latter case, he could be an absolute *mujtahid*, exercising *ijtihād* in all areas of the law, or a partial one whose *ijtihād* is restricted to specific topics. Moreover, an absolute, independent *mujtahid* has his own legal precepts (*qawāʿid*) and does not follow the established rules of the different schools ("Al-Masāʾil," 83; "Iqāẓ," 61); however, al-Sanūsī adds, some independent *mujtahid*s follow the method of al-Shāfiʿī not out of *taqlīd* but because they find it most conducive for the exercise of *ijtihād* ("Iqāẓ," 62–63).

158. Al-Sanūsī, "Iqāẓ," 54.

159. This is the kind of *ijtihād* required in a judge or a mufti; see al-Sanūsī, "Iqāẓ," 115; and "Al-Masāʾil," 49–52.

160. Al-Sanūsī, "Iqāẓ," 46.

161. Al-Sanūsī, "Iqāẓ," 62.

162. Al-Sanūsī, "Al-Masāʾil," 88–93.

163. Al-Sanūsī, "Al-Masāʾil," 115.

164. Al-Sanūsī, "Iqāẓ," 67, 72.

165. Al-Sanūsī, "Iqāẓ," 103.

166. Al-Sanūsī, "Al-Masāʾil," 45.

167. Al-Sanūsī quotes Imam Mālik's dictum that "a scholar does not issue a fatwa until people see him as qualified to do so"; Al-Sanūsī, "Iqāẓ," 105. Also in his definition of this kind of *ijtihād*, he indicates that he is referring to the technical and conventional usage of the term. Compare this distinction between the *ijtihād* of Walī Allāh and al-Sanūsī with Peters, who not only equates their notions of *ijtihād* with Wahhabi notions but also ignores the substantive differences between them on such questions as the validity of *taqlīd* for the *ʿāmmī*. Peters, "*Idjtihād* and *Taqlīd*."

168. Al-Sanūsī, "Iqāẓ," 105.

169. Al-Sanūsī, "Al-Masā'il," 79.

170. Al-Shawkānī, *Al-Darārī al-Muḍiyya*.

171. Walī Allāh, *Ḥujjat Allāh*, 1:256.

172. Walī Allāh, *Ḥujjat Allāh*, 1:286.

173. Walī Allāh, *Ḥujjat Allāh*, 1:292–99. A *mujtahid*, in contrast, is not allowed to imitate but may affiliate himself with another *mujtahid* by adopting his method of *ijtihād*. Walī Allāh, *'Iqd*, 34–35.

174. For a typical enumeration of *mujtahid*s across the ages that repeats many similar accounts by modern scholars and Muslim thinkers, see 'Abl al-Muta'āl al-Ṣa'īdī, *Al-Mujaddidūn fī al-Islām min al-Qarn al-Awwal ilā al-Rābi' 'Ashar* (Cairo: Maktabat al-Ādāb wa Maṭba'atihā, n.d.). For classic references to *ijtihād* in modern Islamic thought, see Hourani, *Arabic Thought*; and Rahman, "Revival and Reform in Islam." For references to the views of Jamāl ad-Dīn al-Afghānī and Muḥammad 'Abdu on *ijtihād*, see Malcolm H. Kerr, *Islamic Reform: The Political and Legal Theories of Muḥammād 'Abduh and Rashīd Riḍā* (Berkeley: University of California Press, 1966); and Keddie, *Sayyid Jamāl ad-Dīn*. For an account and critique of the thesis of the closure of the gates of *ijtihād*, see the studies by Wael Hallaq quoted above. Although Hallaq thoroughly undermines this thesis, it continues to be invoked in many studies of modern Islam.

175. Brinkley Messick, *The Calligraphic State: Textual Domination and History in a Muslim Society* (Berkeley: University of California Press, 1996), 56. In his brief remarks (and the footnotes that follow), Messick also provides a useful critique of ways in which this aspect of Islamic law has been studied, including a critique of Schacht and Coulson.

176. For additional discussions of the difference between the legal thought of modernists and eighteenth-century scholars, see Ahmad Dallal, "Appropriating the Past: Twentieth-Century Reconstruction of Pre-modern Islamic Thought," *Islamic Law and Society* 7, no. 1 (2000): 325–58.

177. See, for example, Messick, *The Calligraphic State*, 151: "Al-Shawkani acts as the scholar's scholar, the mufti's mufti."

178. Hermansen rightly compares Walī Allāh's project to that of Abū Ḥāmid al-Ghazālī, not just on account of the wide range of knowledge but, "more significantly, in the way in which he used his wide knowledge in an attempt to reconcile the tensions which he felt were tearing Islam and India apart." See Marcia K. Hermansen, "Shāh Walī Allāh of Delhi's *Ḥujjat Allāh al-Bāligha*: Tension between the Universal and the Particular in an Eighteenth-Century Islamic Theory of Religious Revelation," *Studia Islamica* 63 (1986): 143–57, esp. 143.

179. In addition to numerous other references throughout his writings, Walī Allāh's *Fuyūḍ al-Ḥaramayn* (Delhi: Mālik Maṭba'e Aḥmadī, n.d.) documents visions he received from the Prophet. In one of these visions, for example, Walī Allāh states that he saw the spirit of the Prophet not only in the world of spirits but also in the liminal world close to the senses (*Fuyūḍ al-Ḥaramayn*, 27). For examples of other grandiose self-visions, see 28–29, 32, 34. For additional discussions of Walī Allāh's self-visions, see Hermansen, "Shāh Walī Allāh of Delhi's *Ḥujjat Allāh al-Bāligha*," 143–57; and Hermansen, "Citing the Sights of the Holy Sites: Visionary Pilgrimage Narratives of Pre-modern South Asian Sufis," in *The Shaping of an American Islamic Discourse: A Memorial to Fazlur Rahman*, ed. Earle H. Waugh and Frederick M. Denny (Atlanta: Scholars, 1998).

180. Walī Allāh, *Al-Tafhīmāt al-Ilāhiyya*, 54.

181. Walī Allāh, *Al-Tafhīmāt al-Ilāhiyya*, 110–12.

182. Walī Allāh, *Al-Tafhīmāt al-Ilāhiyya*, 169.

183. Al-Shawkānī clearly considered himself a reformer in theory and practice; for example, in reference to corrupt judges (*quḍāt al-sū'*) who accept bribes, and their use of various false justifications for this harmful practice as a "bridge" through which they cross to the "unlawful confiscation of people's wealth," al-Shawkānī says that he was "aided by God to destroy this bridge . . . both in words and in deeds: in words, through what I have included in my writings; and in deeds, by getting rid of such corrupt judges." Muḥammad b. ʿAlī al-Shawkānī, *Wabl al-Ghamām ʿalā Shifā' al-Uwām*, ed. M. Ḥallāq, 2 vols. (Cairo: Maktabat Ibn Taymiyya, 1995), 2:161–62. Also see Haykel, *Revival and Reform*, 81–82.

184. Al-Shawkānī, *Adab al-Ṭalab*, 122.

185. Al-Shawkānī, *Adab al-Ṭalab*, 122.

186. As illustrated in this and numerous other examples, the rigorous and systematically critical thrust of al-Shawkānī's extensive intellectual output cannot be so reductively dismissed as a "vision of an Islamic order centered on himself"; Haykel, *Revival and Reform*, 108.

187. See, for example, Muḥammad b. ʿAlī al-Shawkānī, *Irshād al-Fuḥūl ilā Taḥqīq al-Ḥaqq min ʿIlm al-Uṣūl* (n.p.: Dār al-Fikr, n.d.), 254.

188. Contrast with Haykel, who suggests larger Shāfiʿī influence on al-Shawkānī; Haykel, *Revival and Reform*, 86–87, 99. Haykel argues that the list of Shāfʿī *mujtahid*s provided by al-Shawkānī confirms "his identification with this tradition." While there is no question that al-Shawkānī identifies with the *ijtihād* tradition, he does privilege one school's *ijtihād* over other schools. See also Ella Landau-Tasseron, "The Cyclical Reform: A Study of the *Mujaddid* Tradition," *Studia Islamica* 70 (1989): 79–117; and "Zaydī Imāms as Restorers of Religion: Iḥyā' and Tajdīd in Zaydī Literature," *Journal of Near Eastern Studies* 49 (1990): 247–63. In the latter essay, Landau-Tasseron argues, based in part on a work by Muḥammad Zabāra, who was himself influenced by al-Shawkānī, that the Zaydi conception of *tajdīd* is different from the Sunni one.

189. Contrast to Haykel, who argues that al-Shawkānī thought of himself as the "ultimate arbiter of the correctness of a given opinion"; Haykel, *Revival and Reform in Islam*, 100.

190. For a critique of *kalām*, see Muḥammad Ibn Ibrāhīm al-Wazīr al-Ḥasanī al-Yamanī al-Ṣanʿanī (775–840 AH), *Tarjīḥ Asālīb al-Qur'ān ʿalā Asālīb al-Yūnān* (Beirut: Dār al-Kutub al-ʿIlmiyya, 1984). Ibn al-Wazīr also includes partial critiques of *kalām* in *Al-Burhān al-Qāṭiʿ fī Ithbāt al-Ṣāniʿ wa Jamīʿ mā Jā'at bihi al-Sharā'iʿ* (Beirut: Dār al-Ma'mūn li-l-Turāth, 1988); *Al-ʿAwāṣim wa-l-Qawāṣim fī al-Dhabb ʿan Sunnat Abī al-Qāsim* (Amman: Dār al-Bashīr, 1985); its abridgement, *Al-Rawḍ al-Bāsim fī al-Dhabb ʿan Sunnat Abī al-Qāsim* (Cairo: Al-Maṭbaʿa al-Salafiyya, 1385 AH); and *Īthār al-Ḥaqq ʿalā al-Khalq fī Radd al-Khilāfāt ilā al-Madhhab al-Ḥaqq min Uṣūl al-Tawḥīd* (Sanaa: Al-Dār al-Yamaniyya li-l-Nashr wa-l-Tawzīʿ, 1985). See also Ṣāliḥ Ibn Mahdī al-Maqbalī (d. 1108 AH), *Al-ʿAlam al-Shāmikh fī Tafḍīl al-Ḥaqq ʿalā al-Ābā' wa-l-Mashāyikh* (Beirut: Dār al-Ḥadīth, 1985); al-Maqbalī provides systematic critiques of various schools of *kalām*, including both the Muʿtazilī and the Ashʿarī schools; he also notes that the Zaydis and the Muʿtazilīs have become almost identical (12–14). Note, however, that these and other critiques of *kalām* are not directed exclusively against the Muʿtazilī school and are leveled equally against the Ashʿarīs; see the chapters that follow for more on this point.

191. Al-Shawkānī, *Adab al-Ṭalab*, 124.

192. For example, al-Shawkānī, *Adab al-Ṭalab*, 115–16; and *Wabl al-Ghamām*, 2:90–92.

193. Al-Shawkānī, *Al-Qawl al-Mufīd*, 172.

194. For al-Shawkānī's changing assessment of Sufis, see chapter 3; for his criticism of imitating scholars, see *Al-Qawl al-Mufīd*, 172–79.

195. Al-Shawkānī, *Al-Qawl al-Mufīd*, 175–77.

196. Al-Shawkānī, *Al-Qawl al-Mufīd*, 178–79.

197. Al-Shawkānī, *Wilāyat Allāh*, 324; see also al-Shawkānī, *Irshād al-Fuḥūl*, 262.

198. Al-Shawkānī, *Wilāyat Allāh*, 325; and *Irshād al-Fuḥūl*, 259.

199. Al-Shawkānī, *Wilāyat Allāh*, 325; and *Al-Qawl al-Mufīd*, 164.

200. Al-Shawkānī, *Al-Qawl al-Mufīd*, 163.

201. See, for example, al-Shawkānī, *Wabl al-Ghamām*, 1:313–17.

202. Contrast to Haykel, who, despite al-Shawkānī's extensive discussion of this issue, argues that al-Shawkānī does not answer the important question, namely, how a commoner, who is ignorant of the workings of sharia, is to "make sense of the textual proof the *mujtahid* gives him." Haykel further contends that this commoner would be practicing *taqlīd* "under a new guise"; Haykel, *Revival and Reform*, 102.

203. Al-Shawkānī, *Al-Qawl al-Mufīd*, 131–33.

204. Al-Shawkānī, *Al-Qawl al-Mufīd*, 132.

205. See Haykel, *Revival and Reform*, 58–60.

206. Compare, for example, with al-Ghazālī's standard view that "the common person (*ʿāmmī*) is obligated to follow the mufti and to confirm his truthfulness, even though he (the mufti) may relate his uncertain opinion." Abū Ḥāmid al-Ghazālī, *Al-Mustaṣfā min ʿIlm al-Uṣūl*, ed. Muḥammad Sulaymān al-Ashqar, 2 vols. (Beirut: Muʾassasat al-Risāla, 1997), 1:410; 2:462, 466–47.

207. See further discussion in the ensuing chapters.

208. See, for example, al-Shawkānī, *Adab al-Ṭalab*, 45.

209. Al-Shawkānī, *Adab al-Ṭalab*, 45.

210. Al-Shawkānī's negative assessment of the "mob" is only matched by his hostility toward Bedouins and tribes. See, for example, Muḥammad b. ʿAlī al-Shawkānī, "Irshād al-Sāʾil ilā Dalāʾil al-Masāʾil," in *Al-Rasāʾil al-Salafiyya fī Iḥyāʾ Sunnat Khayr al-Bariyya* (Beirut: Dār al-Kutub al-ʿIlmiyya, reprint of 1930 edition), 39–51, esp. 43–44.

211. Compare with al-Sanūsī, who argues that the only reason to argue that *ijtihād* is not possible is to monopolize the professions and official appointments and to exclude people who do not abide by authority of one of the four schools from issuing fatwas. Al-Sanūsī, "Iqāẓ," 72.

212. Al-Shawkānī, *Adab al-Ṭalab*, 46.

213. Al-Shawkānī, *Adab al-Ṭalab*, 46–47.

214. Al-Shawkānī, *Adab al-Ṭalab*, 47–48, 132.

215. Compare with al-Sanūsī, who maintains that *taqlīd* renders void the benefit of the intellect, and that "it is abhorrent for one who is given a candle to light up his way to put it off and walk in the dark"; al-Sanūsī, "Al-Masāʾil," 111.

216. Al-Shawkānī, *Adab al-Ṭalab*, 129.

217. Al-Shawkānī, *Adab al-Ṭalab*, 132.

Chapter 3

1. For example, Walī Allāh criticizes the austere practices of Sufis who promote hardship and suffering while God intended religion to be a source of ease and facility for Muslims. See, for example, Shāh Walī Allāh, *Al-Tafhīmāt al-Ilāhiyya*, ed. G. M. Qāsimī, 2 vols. (Hyderabad: Ākādimyyat al-Shāh Walī Allāh al-Dihlawī, 1967), 1:284. Likewise, al-Shawkānī's optimism and self-confidence are reflected in his writings as well as in his career. In this, al-Shawkānī has certainly moved away from the more defensive attitude of one of his heroes, the founder of the prohadith school in Yemen, Muḥammad Ibn Ibrāhīm al-Wazīr. Ibn al-Wazīr wrote a

book on the virtues of withdrawal and isolation, arguing that this is the worship of the weak and the oppressed. See Muḥammad Ibn Ibrāhīm al-Wazīr, *Al-Amr bil-ʿUzla fī Ākhir al-Zamān* (Amman: Al-Maktaba al-Islāmiyya, 1412 AH).

2. Note that reform was not prevalent in Sufism, and that when it existed it was usually directed at reforming Sufi practices and not the content of mystical thought. In most writings on Sufism, older ideas were repeated or simply taken for granted. Significantly, many reformers who happened to be Sufis did not write much on traditional Sufism. For example, among the disciples of Ibn Idrīs, neither al-Sanūsī nor al-Mīrghānī "seems to have written much on specifically Sufi topics," and their scholarly credentials comprised expertise in several traditional fields of study; in contrast, Ibn Idrīs's third main disciple, al-Rashīd, the founder of the Rashīdiyya order (and later al-Ṣāliḥiyya), wrote much more on Sufism but was far less of a scholar than the first two, and not a reformer in any sense of the term. See R. S. O'Fahey, *Enigmatic Saint: Ahmad Ibn Idris and the Idrisi Tradition* (Evanston, Ill.: Northwestern University Press, 1990), 154.

3. So, for example, although many believed in it, none of the Sufi reformers advocated the belief in the *karāmāt* of saints as a viable option for social reform, nor did any call for withdrawal from society in the interest of otherworldly redemption. Quite the contrary, they focused on collective, structural solutions for social problems, led active social movements, or were engaged in an active, reconstructive dialogue with other Islamic intellectual traditions.

4. For a very useful discussion of historical trends in Sufism, see ʿAbd al-Majīd al-Ṣaghīr, *Ishkāliyyat Iṣlāḥ al-Fikr al-Ṣūfī fī al-Qarnayn 18/19: Aḥmad Ibn ʿAjība wa Muḥammad al-Ḥarrāq*, 2nd ed. (Al-Muhammadiya, Morocco: Dār al-Āfāq al-Jadīda, 1994), 25. Al-Saghir provides a tripartite division of attitudes within Sufism. For the purposes of my discussion here, I do not follow the exact taxonomy of al-Saghir, although I agree with his analysis and characterizations.

5. There are many examples of this tradition; the most famous and also most controversial is Ibn al-ʾArabī. The literature on Ibn ʿArabī is extensive. For a brief and useful sketch of his life and work, his image in biographical literature, and a substantial bibliography of scholarship on him and the main trends in this scholarship, see the introductory sections of Alexander D. Knysh, *Ibn al-ʿArabī in the Later Islamic Tradition: The Making of a Polemical Image in Medieval Islam* (Albany: SUNY Press, 1999). On the pervasive influence of Ibn al-ʾArabī at the popular and elitist levels of Sufism, see the introduction to Michel Chodkiewicz, *An Ocean without Shore: Ibn ʿArabī, the Book, and the Law* (Albany: SUNY Press, 1993).

6. There are many such groups throughout the history of Sufism; one of the most notable examples from the eighteenth century is the Tījāniyya movement, which was famous for its extreme practices. On the Tījāniyya, see Jamil M. Abun-Nasr, *The Tijaniyya: A Sufi Order in the Modern World* (Oxford: Oxford University Press, 1965), 27–57.

7. The main example from the classical period is Aḥmad Ibn Taymiyya. On Ibn Taymiyya's rejection of and complex attitude toward Sufism, see Knysh, *Ibn al-ʿArabī in the Later Islamic Tradition*, 87–111. Ibn Taymiyya's censure of Sufism became a blueprint for later critiques of extreme and philosophical Sufism. See below for eighteenth-century attitudes toward Sufism.

8. One of the main examples of this kind of Sufism is the seventh-/thirteenth-century Abu al-Ḥasan al-Shādhilī (d. 656). Al-Shādhilī left Morocco for Egypt to call for a new kind of Sufism consciously distinct from the philosophical Sufism of Ibn al-ʿArabī and Ibn Sabʿīn, and advocated a popular, "orthodox" kind of Sufism. Indeed, al-Shādhilī was able to establish his mainstream credentials: leading traditional scholars and jurists who attended his classes included the Sultan of Scholars ʿIzz al-Dīn Bin ʿAbd al-Salām and the great Shafiʿī scholar Ibn Daqīq al-ʿĪd. See ʿAbd al-Majīd al-Ṣaghīr, *Ishkāliyyat Iṣlāḥ al-Fikr al-Ṣūfī*, 25–36. Although he

was popular among traditional legal scholars, it would be absurd to argue that al-Shādhilī's Sufism was void of its spiritual dimensions or that it was subservient to dry legalistic interpretations of Islam. Rather, al-Shādhilī aimed to undermine the strict hierarchical and formalistic tendencies within Sufism and reinstitute what he considered to be its true esoteric dimensions.

9. For example, in addition to his work on hadith and legal differences, some of al-Sanūsī's main works on Sufism belonged to these genres. See, for example, *Al-Salsabīl al-Maʿīn fī al-Ṭarāʾiq al-Arbaʿīn*, where al-Sanūsī surveys the chains and prayers of forty orders; see also al-Sanūsī's *Al-Manhal al-Rāwī al-Rāʾiq fī Asānīd al-ʿUlūm wa Uṣūl al-Ṭarāʾiq* as well as parts of *Al-Masāʾil al-ʿAshr*. Of a similar nature are Ibn Idrīs's *Nubdha fī Ṣifat Dukhūl al-Khulwa* and *Kunūz al-Jawhar*, where various chains of transmission, procedures of initiation, kinds of prayer, as well as subtle differences between them are surveyed. Bernd Radtke, R. S. O'Fahey, and John O'Kane, "Two Sufi Treatises of Aḥmad Ibn Idrīs," *Oriens* 35 (1996): 143–78.

10. The one major exception to this rule is Ibn Idrīs, who, in my view, is not a proper representative of eighteenth-century reform, despite some novelties in his thought. Ibn Idrīs calls for a kind of *ijtihād* that is grounded in mystical knowledge; he rejects *qiyās* (legal analogy) not in the interest of other formal legal procedures but in the name of individualistic authority. Moreover, Ibn Idrīs's rejection of schools is replaced not by personal judgment but by personal access to God, and reason plays no role in this process. However, as we will see below, Ibn Idrīs's model certainly does not apply to other Sufi reformers such as al-Sanūsī or Walī Allāh. As such, Radtke's contention that in their rejection of *madhāhib*, Sufis "wished to base legal judgments on other foundations than textual or rational proofs" is inaccurate and is a result of his use of Ibn Idrīs as a reference for eighteenth-century Sufi thought. See Bernd Radtke, "Sufism in the Eighteenth Century: An Attempt at a Provisional Appraisal," *Die Welt des Islams* 36, no. 3 (1996): 326–64, esp. 338, 360. Also see Bernd Radtke, John O'Kane, Knut S. Vikor, and R. S. O'Fahey, *The Exoteric Aḥmad Ibn Idrīs: A Sufi's Critique of the Madhāhib and the Wahhābis* (Leiden, the Netherlands: E. J. Brill, 2000).

11. Michael Winter, "A Polemical Treatise by ʿAbd al-Ġanī al-Nābulsī against a Turkish Scholar on the Religious Status of the Dimmīs," *Arabica* 35 (1988): 92–103.

12. For a contrast between his traditional Sufism and radical politics, see, for example, ʿAbd al-Qādir al-Jazāʾirī, *Al-Mawāqif*, 3 parts in 2 vols. (Damascus: Dār al-Yaqdha, 1966); *Ḥusām al-Dīn li-Qaṭʿ Shubuh al-Murtaddīn*, Manuscript Landberg MSS 405, Beineke Library, Yale University, and *Ḥukm al-Hijra min Khilāl Thalāth Rasāʾil Jazāʾiriyya*, ed. Muḥammad Ibn ʿAbd al-Karīm (Algeria: Al-Sharika al-Waṭaniyya lil-Nashr wal-Tawzīʿ, 1981).

13. Contrast with Rahman, who argues that Sufism was the "focal point of all those trends of varying degrees of intensity which sought either to reform orthodox Islam, or to dissipate it completely." However, Rahman posits an opposition between Sufism and reform and asserts that eighteenth-century reform movements "bring into the center of attention the socio-moral reconstruction of Muslim society, as against Sufism, which had stressed primarily the individual and not the society." See Fazlur Rahman, "Revival and Reform in Islam," in *The Cambridge History of Islam*, ed. M. Holt, Ann K. S. Lambton, and B. Lewis (London: Cambridge University Press, 1970), 632–56, esp. 635, 637. In other words, Rahman subsumes all eighteenth-century Islamic movements under one of two rubrics: either the Sufi attempts to subvert orthodoxy or vice versa. Rahman's assertions notwithstanding, reform Sufism sustained a vibrant and lively mystical tradition while at the same time reinforcing its orthodox credentials. Moreover, Sufism was not the primary concern of most non-Sufi reform movements. Underlying Rahman's assertions is the assumption that Sufism is primarily individualistic, while reform has a social character. As such, he dismisses the mystical dimensions of

Sufi movements that are engaged in reform and argues that they are essentially the same as other reform movements of this period. He also collapses the practices of various movements over long periods of time into one pattern that fits his definition of reform. For example, in reference to the Sanūsī order he argues that "although it had the organized form of a Ṣūfī *ṭarīqa* and included some Ṣūfī practices as well, its objectives were radically different. It was basically a social reform movement, aiming at the purification of society from degenerate beliefs, and particularly from corrupting malpractices. Above all, it sought to promote a sense of moral solidarity based on honesty, egalitarianism and economic justice. . . . Subsequently it waged a bitter struggle against the expansionist policies of European colonial powers. On more or less similar, but basically more militant lines, were laid the foundations of the Fulānī Jihād movement of ʿUthmān dan Fodio and the Mahdist movement in Sudan." All of these movements, Rahman adds, "developed a much more positive Sufism, endeavored to eradicate the socio-moral evils that came in the wake of the spread of Sufism and, on the whole, gave it a more dynamic outlook"; the primary concern of all of these movements was with the "socio-moral reconstruction and reform of society." Rahman, "Revival and Reform," 639–40; see also Fazlur Rahman, *Islam* (Chicago: University of Chicago Press, 1968), 205–7, 153–202, 220, 237–39, where Rahman speaks of a Sufism stripped of its ecstatic and metaphysical character, and considers reform Sufism to be "nothing else but the postulates of the orthodox religion." Likewise, Trimingham argues that after the rigid organization of Sufism in orders "the mystical content of the orders had been weakened," thus leading to the submission and subservience of Sufism to legal standards, and "in the process many orders were emptied of their essential elements and left with the empty husks of mystical terminology, disciplines, and exercises." J. Spencer Trimingham, *The Sufi Orders in Islam* (Oxford: Oxford University Press, 1971), 103–4. Trimingham also recognizes only two possible forms of revival in the eighteenth and nineteenth centuries: Wahhabism and revived Sufi orders (105). See also H. A. R. Gibb's discussion of modern Islam in *Mohammedanism: An Historical Survey* (Oxford: Oxford University Press, 1970), where he argues that in the eighteenth-century movements, orthodox ideas were organized on the lines of Sufi orders. Also see John Obert Voll, *Islam: Continuity and Change in the Modern World* (Boulder, Colo.: Westview, 1982), 55.

An extreme expression of this reductive view of both Sufism and reform movements in the eighteenth century that lumps different individuals in one undifferentiated whole is in B. G. Martin, *Muslim Brotherhoods in Nineteenth-Century Africa* (Cambridge: Cambridge University Press, 1976). Martin argues that the "neosufi brotherhoods or Muhammadiya tariqas" were "founded only about the end of the eighteenth century or just after" and shared the goal of "the defense of Islam" (1–2). Furthermore, Martin speaks of several strains within one broad trend of neo-Sufism that includes Sirhindī, Walī Allāh, al-Zabīdī, Muṣṭafā al-Bakrī, Khālid Shahrzur, Ibn Idrīs, Muḥammad ʿAbd Allāh Ḥasan (of Somalia, whom Martin characterizes as a Sufi revivalist influenced by Ibn ʿAbd al-Wahhāb through the mediation of Ibn Idrīs), al-Ḥifnāwī (Shaykh al-Azhar, d. 1768), Maḥmūd al-Kurdī, Jibrīl Ibn ʿUmar, Ibn Fūdī, Ḥāj ʿUmar (1794–1864), and ʿAbd al-Qādir al-Jazāʾirī (202)!

14. The term *neo-Sufism* is usually used to refer to a kind of Sufism characterized by (1) the rejection of popular practices; (2) the rejection of Ibn al-ʿArabī's concept of unity of being (*waḥdat al-wujūd*) and the adoption in its place of the concept of unity of witnessing (*waḥdat al-shuhūd*); (3) the rejection of the master/disciple hierarchy and the emphasis instead on moral teachings; (4) replacing traditional devotional traditions and rites of initiation with modes of social organization revolving around the founder of the order and his family; (5) emphasis on the study of hadith; (6) rejection of imitation and emphasis on *ijtihād*; and (7) an intensified militancy reflected in the calls for jihad. For examples of the frequent uses of the

concept of neo-Sufism, in addition to Rahman's original uses, see the introduction to Nehemia Levtzion and John Obert Voll, eds., *Eighteenth-Century Renewal and Reform in Islam* (Syracuse, N.Y.: Syracuse University Press, 1987), 3–20. Levtzion and Voll argue that the use of hadith in conformity with orthodoxy by neo-Sufi activists implies a human agency of change. See also Edmund Burke and Ira M. Lapidus, eds., *Islam, Politics, and Social Movements* (Berkeley: University of California Press, 1988), 20; Ira Lapidus, *A History of Islamic Societies* (Cambridge: Cambridge University Press, 1988), 757–58. Also see Michael Gilsenen, *Recognizing Islam: An Anthropologist's Introduction* (London: Croom Helm, 1982), which refers to "austere and militant Sufism" (157–63).

In his *Enigmatic Saint*, O'Fahey uses the term *neo-Sufism* to refer to a new organizational phenomenon "without prejudging its intellectual content"; as examples of this newness, O'Fahey cites "more centralized" orders and "new forms of social organization, often based on autonomous agricultural communities" (*Enigmatic Saint*, 4); in his later assessment, however, O'Fahey notes that even if the organizational styles that Sufism brought were new to sub-Saharan Africa, they were not new within the Sufi tradition itself. While agreeing with this general assessment, I would argue that there is some newness in both content and organization. Also, O'Fahey maintains that the field of activity of neo-Sufi orders was the frontiers (*Enigmatic Saint*, 6). I would take issue with the use of *frontiers* to refer to areas where Islam had existed for centuries; the term invokes inaccurate parallels with expansionist movements imposed from the outside, whereas the Sufi movements were allied to and integrated within local groups through lineage, agriculture, and organization. Moreover, the newly forged patterns of loyalty transcended and reconfigured, but did not erase, older tribal and social boundaries.

15. It should be noted that no monograph has been written to illustrate this matter-of-fact use of the term *neo-Sufism*. Rather, several studies by scholars who work on Sufism have been written to undermine the use of this concept. For a convenient overview and a compelling critique of the neo-Sufism thesis, see R. S. O'Fahey and Bernd Radtke, "Neo-Sufism Reconsidered," *Der Islam* 70, no. 1 (1993): 52–87; and Radtke, "Sufism in the Eighteenth Century." See also Radtke, "Lehrer-Schuler-Enkel: Aḥmad b. Idrīs, Muḥammad ʿUthmān al-Mīrganī, Ismāʿīl al-Walī," *Oriens* 33 (1992); and Radtke, "Warum ist der Sufi orthodox?," *Der Islam* 71, no. 2 (1994): 302–7. These studies demonstrate the traditional nature of eighteenth-century Sufism, including the debates about purifying Sufism. It might be that the study of Sufism escaped the distortion of "decline" theories because of the implicit assumption that it is backward and irrational, and does not even warrant being addressed and undermined. Notions of neo-Sufism, however, are also entertained by historians who sympathize with Sufism and seem to want to restore Sufism to the historical narrative but express regret about the dilution of spirituality in eighteenth-century manifestations of Sufism. I do not wish to take sides in this debate that sometimes takes on existential dimensions, but I think that in this particular case, the personal preferences of some scholars may have obscured some of the diversity and complexity in eighteenth-century Sufism.

16. ʿAbd al-Ghanī al-Nābulsī (1050–1143/1641–1731) was one of the greatest Sufis since the end of the seventeenth century, and one of the leading Muslim thinkers of his time. No attempt to provide a comprehensive study of al-Nābulsī will be made here; his massive writings, many of which are not published, require separate analysis that is beyond the scope of this book. For biographies of al-Nābulsī, see Muḥammad Khalīl al-Murādī, *Silk al-Durar fī Aʿyān al-Qarn al-Thānī ʿAshar* (Baghdad: Maktabat al-Muthanna, 1301 AH), 3:33–37; and Muḥammad Amīn al-Muḥibbī, *Khulāṣat al-Athar fī Aʿyān al-Qarn al-Ḥādī ʿAshar* (Cairo: Al-Maṭbaʿa al-Wahhābiya, 1284 AH), 433. Also see W. A. S. Khālidī, "ʿAbd al-Ghanī Ibn Ismāʿīl al-Nābulsī," in

Encyclopedia of Islam, 2nd ed., vol. 1 (Leiden, the Netherlands: E. J. Brill), 60. Al-Murādī lists 188 titles by al-Nābulsī and maintains that of all the individuals listed in his biographical work, al-Nābulsī is the "most distinguished in scholarship, sainthood, asceticism, reputation and rational comprehension." Al-Nābulsī's accounts of travel to Jerusalem, Tripoli, and the Hejaz provide detailed descriptions of the vibrant institutions of Muslim cities, including mosques, madrasas, and Sufi lodges; they also offer accounts of intellectual interests that were common in al-Nābulsī's time. See, for example, *Al-Tuḥfa al-Nābulsiyya fī al-Riḥla al-Ṭarābulsiyya*, ed. Heribert Busse, Beiruter Texte und Studien 4, Orient-Institut der deutschen morgenlädischen Gesellschaft (Beirut: Imprimerie Catholique, 1971). Also see *Al-Ḥadra al-Unsiyya fī al-Riḥla al-Qudsiyya* (Cairo: Maktabat al-Qāhira, 1971). In his *al-Tuḥfa al-Nābulsiyya*, for example, al-Nābulsī reports a legal exchange over the permissibility of smoking tobacco; he takes issue with those who argue that smoking is prohibited under all conditions and argues that only when it is manifestly harmful to the smoker would it be prohibited (79–81). Al-Nābulsī also names the people he met during his travels, many of whom were his students, as well as the distinguished scholars, Sufis, and officials of the cities he visited. The warmth and respect with which al-Nābulsī was invariably received corroborates the accounts one finds in biographical sources regarding his scholarly distinction and reputation throughout the Muslim world. See also Elizabeth Sirriya, "Ziyārāt of Syria in a Riḥla of ʿAbd al-Ghanī al-Nābulsī (1050/1641–1143/1731)," *Journal of the Royal Asiatic Society* 2 (1979): 109–22. For a comprehensive study of al-Nābulsī, see Barbara Von Schlegell, "Sufism in the Ottoman-Arab World: ʿAbd al-Ghanī al-Nābulsī (d. 1731)," PhD diss., University of California, Berkeley, 1997.

17. ʿAbd al-Ghanī al-Nābulsī, *Taʿṭīr al-Anām fī Taʿbīr al-Manām*, 2 parts in 1 vol. (Cairo: Dār Iḥyāʾ al-Kutub al-ʾArabiyya, 1972).

18. Al-Nābulsī, *Taʿṭīr al-Anām*, 2–3.

19. Al-Nābulsī, *Taʿṭīr al-Anām*, 234.

20. ʿAbd al-Ghanī al-Nābulsī, *Al-Fatḥ al-Rabbānī wa-l-Fayḍ al-Raḥmānī*, ed. Antonious Shiblī al-Lubnānī (Beirut: Catholic Press, 1960), 169–70.

21. ʿAbd al-Ghanī al-Nābulsī, *Īḍāḥ al-Dalālāt fī Samāʿ al-Ālāt*, or *Al-Mūsīqā wa-l-Ghināʾ fī Mīzān al-Islām*, ed. Muḥammad ʿUthmān al-Khasht (Cairo: Maktabat al-Maʾārif al-Islāmiyya, n.d.), 78, 90.

22. Al-Nābulsī, *Īḍāḥ al-Dalālāt*, 93, 105–6.

23. Al-Nābulsī, *Īḍāḥ al-Dalālāt*, 118.

24. Al-Nābulsī, *Īḍāḥ al-Dalālāt*, 126–27.

25. Al-Nābulsī, *Īḍāḥ al-Dalālāt*, 130.

26. Al-Nābulsī, *Īḍāḥ al-Dalālāt*, 136–37.

27. ʿAbd al-Ghanī al-Nābulsī, *Īḍāḥ al-Maqṣūd min Waḥdat al-Wujūd*, ed. ʿIzza Ḥuṣariyya (Damascus: Maṭbaʿat alʾIlm, 1969), 7, 8.

28. Al-Nābulsī, *Īḍāḥ al-Maqṣūd*, 6.

29. Al-Nābulsī, *Īḍāḥ al-Maqṣūd*, 8.

30. Al-Nābulsī, *Al-Fatḥ*, 86–87.

31. Al-Nābulsī, *Īḍāḥ al-Dalālāt*, 72, 75.

32. ʿAbd al-Ghanī al-Nābulsī, "Khamrat al-Ḥān wa Rannat al-Alḥān," in *Shurūḥ Risālat al-Shaykh Arsalān*, ed. ʿIzza Ḥuṣriyya (Damascus: Maṭbaʾat alʾIlm, 1969), 103.

33. Al-Nābulsī, "Khamrat," 106.

34. Al-Nābulsī, "Khamrat," 100, 103.

35. Al-Nābulsī, "Khamrat," 104.

36. ʿAbd al-Ghanī al-Nābulsī, *Aḥkām al-Tawba*, published with Al-Ḥārith Ibn Asad al-Muḥāsibī, *Al-Tawba*, ed. ʿAbd al-Qādir Aḥmad ʿAṭṭa (Cairo: Dār al-Naṣr, n.d.), 101.

37. Al-Nābulsī, "Khamrat," 76.

38. Al-Nābulsī, *Īḍāḥ al-Maqṣūd*, 14.

39. Al-Nābulsī, *Īḍāḥ al-Maqṣūd*, 17.

40. Al-Nābulsī, *Al-Fatḥ*, 93–116.

41. Al-Nābulsī, *Al-Fatḥ*, 106.

42. See Marcia K. Hermansen, "Shāh Walī Allāh of Delhi's *Ḥujjat Allāh al-Bāligha*: Tension between the Universal and the Particular in an Eighteenth-Century Islamic Theory of Religious Revelation," *Studia Islamica* 63 (1986): 143–57, esp. 143.

43. Shāh Walī Allāh, *The Sacred Knowledge of the Higher Functions of the Mind: Translation of "Alṭāf al-Quds,"* trans. G. N. Jalbani, rev. David Pendlebury (London: Octagon, 1982), 82; and Shāh Walī Allāh, *Al-Tafhīmāt al-Ilāhīya*, ed. G. M. Qāsimī, 2 vols. (Hyderabad: Ākādimyyat al-Shāh Walī Allāh al-Dihlawī, 1967), 1:282–85.

44. Shāh Walī Allāh al-Dehlawī (d. 1176 AH), *Ḥujjat Allāh al-Bāligha*, ed. M. S. Hāshim, 2 vols. (Beirut: Dār al-Kutub al-ʿIlmiyya, 1995), 1:18.

45. Walī Allāh, *Al-Tafhīmāt al-Ilāhīya*, 1:266–67.

46. Walī Allāh, *Al-Tafhīmāt al-Ilāhīya*, 1:266–67. Also in Walī Allāh, *Al-Maktūb al-Madanī fī Taḥqīq Waḥdat al-Wujūd wa Waḥdat al-Shuhūd wa-l-Jamʿ bayn al-Qawlayn*, qtd. in Shāh Rafīʿ Al-Dīn al-Dihlawī, *Kitāb al-Fayḍ bi-l-Ḥaqq al-Mulaqqab bi Damgh al-Bāṭil* (Lahore, 1976), 76–94, esp. 80.

47. Walī Allāh, *The Sacred Knowledge of the Higher Functions of the Mind*, 80.

48. Walī Allāh, *Al-Tafhīmāt al-Ilāhīya*, 1:110–12.

49. Walī Allāh, *Al-Tafhīmāt al-Ilāhīya*, 1:275.

50. Walī Allāh, *Alṭāf*, 39; and *Al-Tafhīmāt al-Ilāhīya*, 2:263.

51. Walī Allāh, *Alṭāf*, 47, 52.

52. Walī Allāh thus maintains, "If you ask me about all of these opinions, I would not take issue with any except on account of expression or the use of words where they do not belong. Otherwise, it is rare for a person of illumination [*kashf*] to point to something that has no basis in truth." *Al-Tafhīmāt al-Ilāhīya*, 2:283.

53. Here, too, Walī Allāh's attempt to defend the concept parallels that of al-Nābulsī, although it is far more elaborate and complex, at least as far as I can tell from my incomplete reading of the latter.

54. Shāh Walī Allāh, *Sufism and the Islamic Tradition: The Lamahat and Sataʿat of Shah Waliullah*, trans. G. N. Jalbani, ed. D. B. Fry (London: Octagon, 1980), 81–82.

55. *Waḥdat al-wujūd* is often translated as ontological or existential monism, while *waḥdat al-shuhūd* translates as phenomonological monism; see, for example, Aziz Ahmad, "Political and Religious Ideas of Shāh Walī-Ullāh of Delhi," *Muslim World* 52, no. 1 (1962): 23.

56. Barbara Daly Metcalf, *Islamic Revival in British India: Deoband, 1860–1900* (Princeton, N.J.: Princeton University Press, 1982), 39. This is the common portrayal of Sirhindī in modern scholarship on Islam in India. However, closer analysis of Sirhindī's thought reveals a complex attitude toward Ibn al-ʿArabī and mysticism in general. In contrast to the common scholarly view, Yohanan Friedmann demonstrates that Sirhindī was primarily a Sufi interested in mystical thought and not just political matters or the "purification" of Islam, and that he did not evolve from an "intoxicated" Sufi to a "sober" one. Friedmann, *Shaykh Aḥmad Sirhindī: An Outline of His Thought and a Study of His Image in the Eyes of Posterity* (Montreal: McGill-Queen's University Press, 1971), 7, 20, 23–31. Moreover, Friedmann shows that Sirhindī's understanding of traditional Islamic disciplines was influenced by his mystical outlook (41), and that he attempted to interpret and vindicate "heretical" Sufis such as Ḥallāj (59). The traditionalist contemporary of Sirhindī ʿAbd al-Ḥaqq al-Dihlawī (d. 1642) wrote a

treatise criticizing him on account of such views, and several scholars from the Hejaz wrote polemical works against him for the same reason (Friedmann, *Shaykh Aḥmad Sirhindī*, 7–9, 87). Furthermore, despite the obvious difference between the two, Sirhindī maintains that the "utterances [of Ibn al-ʿArabī,] . . . if properly understood and interpreted, constitute a legitimate expression of Muslim religious experience." Sirhindī also speaks of the greatness and profound wisdom of Ibn al-ʿArabī, recommends studying his works, and considers this study indispensable (Friedmann, *Shaykh Aḥmad Sirhindī*, 62–65).

Also note that Sirhindī was the disciple of Khwāja Bāqī biʿ Llāh (d. 1012/1603), the leading Indian Naqshbandī master of his time and a staunch advocate of Ibn al-ʿArabī's doctrine of oneness of being. Although Sirhindī reoriented the doctrine, most Sufis before and even after him continued to believe in it. See K. A. Nizami, "The Naqshbandiyyah Order," in *Islamic Spirituality*, ed. Seyyed Hossein Nasr (New York: Crossroad, 1991), 162–93, esp. 175–76. Nizami points out that Sirhindī's insistence on strict adherence to the law and opposition to innovation were more a reaction to Sultan Akbar's religious experimentation and claims of prophethood and do not imply in any way that his Sufism was less mystical or spiritual (Nizami, "The Naqshbandiyyah Order," 180). Also see Saiyid Athar Abbas Rizvi, *A History of Sufism in India*, 2 vols. (New Delhi: Munshiram Manoharlal, 1983), who attributes some of Sirhindī's views to his hostility toward the Hindus, whom he considered a threat to Indian Muslims. Thus, Rizvi argues, Sirhindī's criticism of the concept of oneness of being was partly due to the affinity between this concept and some of the ideas of the yogis. Rizvi, *A History of Sufism in India*, 2:192–93, and, for ample evidence of Sirhindī's high level of mysticism, 2:201–2, 2:209–10.

It is possible that the some of Sirhindī's followers outside India gave his ideas a more radical tilt. On the followers of Sirhindī in the Ottoman Empire, see Hamid Algar, "Some Notes on the Naqshbandī *Ṭarīqat* in Bosnia," *Die Welt des Islams* 13, no. 3 (1971): 168–203, 173. For other influences of Sirhindī in the Ottoman world, see Albert Hourani, "Sufism and Modern Islam: Mawlana Khalid and the Naqshbandi Order," in *The Emergence of the Modern Middle East* (Berkeley: University of California Press, 1981), 75–89; and Butrus Abu-Manneh, "The Naqshbandiyya in the Ottoman Lands in the Early 19th Century," *Die Welt des Islams* 22, no. 1 (1982): 1–36. However, spirituality was not compromised in these orders; rather, as the masterly studies of Hamid Algar on the Naqshbandī order clearly demonstrate, the major Sufi orders acted as "guardians of an integral vision and practice of Islam, concerned both with asserting the supremacy of Sharīʿa in society, and with the cultivation of the spiritual life." See Hamid Algar, "The Naqshbanī Order: A Preliminary Survey of Its History and Significance," *Studia Islamica* 44 (1976): 123–52. See also Algar, "Bibliographical Notes on the Naqshbandi Tariqat," in *Essays on Islamic Philosophy and Science*, ed. George Hourani (Albany: SUNY Press, 1975), 254–59. See also Frederick de Jong and Bernd Radtke, eds., *Islamic Mysticism Contested: Thirteen Centuries of Controversies and Polemics* (Leiden, the Netherlands: E. J. Brill, 1999). In this collection of essays, several studies on the eighteenth- and nineteenth-century regional attitudes toward Sufism also demonstrate that, with the exception of the consistent Wahhabi condemnation and rejection of Sufism, all other critiques were partial, came mostly from Sufis, and were aimed at conforming Sufism to sharia rather than rejecting it altogether.

57. Walī Allāh, *Al-Tafhīmāt al-Ilāhiyya*, 1:114, 166, 252.

58. Walī Allāh, *Al-Tafhīmāt al-Ilāhiyya*, 2:262.

59. Walī Allāh, *Al-Tafhīmāt al-Ilāhiyya*, 2:263.

60. Thus he refers to Ibn al-ʿArabī as the Great Master (*al-shaykh al-akbar*) in a treatise written to reconcile the two schools; see Walī Allāh, *Al-Maktūb al-Madanī*, qtd. in Shāh Rafīʿ Al-Dīn al-Dihlawī, *Kitāb al-Fayḍ*, 76.

61. Walī Allāh, *Al-Tafhīmāt al-Ilāhiyya*, 2:282–83.

62. Walī Allāh, *Al-Maktūb al-Madanī*, 78. On the notion that the theoretical foundation for Muhammad-centered Sufism is found in Ibn al-ʿArabī's concepts of *al-ḥaqīqa al-Muḥammadiyya* and *khātam al-wilāya al-Muḥammadiyya*, see Michel Chodkiewicz, *Seal of the Saints: Prophethood and Sainthood in the Doctrine of Ibn ʿArabī* (Cambridge: Islamic Text Society, 1993), 60–88.

63. Walī Allāh, *Al-Maktūb al-Madanī*, 94. Elsewhere, Walī Allāh maintains that this kind of error is not restricted to the proponents of *waḥdat al-shuhūd* but that the proponents of *waḥdat al-wujūd* also are capable of it; the latter are correct in their view but err in the way they reach it. See Shāh Walī Allāh, *Fuyūḍ al-Ḥaramayn* (Delhi: Mālik Maṭbaʿ-e-Aḥmadī, n.d.), 4.

64. Walī Allāh, *Al-Maktūb al-Madanī*, 76–77.

65. Walī Allāh, *Al-Maktūb al-Madanī*, 93.

66. Walī Allāh, *Al-Maktūb al-Madanī*, 93.

67. Walī Allāh, *Ḥujjat Allāh*, 2:32–38.

68. Walī Allāh, *Ḥujjat Allāh*, 1:61.

69. Walī Allāh, *Ḥujjat Allāh*, 2:202.

70. Walī Allāh, *Ḥujjat Allāh*, 1:38; see also 38–40, where Walī Allāh quotes textual references that in fact provide information about the spirit. Also see Shāh Walī Allāh, *Fuyūḍ al-Ḥaramayn*, handwritten manuscript with a Persian translation by ʿAbd al-Ghanī Jaʿfarī (Delhi: Mālik Maṭbaʿ-e-Aḥmadī Mutaʿalliq Madras-e-Azīzī Dehlī Kulān Maḥall, n.d.), 4.

71. Walī Allāh describes his divinely inspired designation as the reviver of his own cycle, such that all "the rational, transmitted, and gnostic sciences" of the scholars of the Muslim community are combined within him (literally in his chest) and "applied to each other so that the differences between them are dissolved and each settles in its proper place." See, for example, *Al-Maktūb al-Madanī*, 76; the same theme is repeated in many of Walī Allāh's works, especially in *Fuyūḍ al-Ḥaramayn*, *Al-Tafhīmāt al-Ilāhiyya*, and *Hujjat Allāh*.

72. Walī Allāh, *Fuyūḍ al-Ḥaramayn*, 30–31.

73. Walī Allāh, *Fuyūḍ al-Ḥaramayn*, 32.

74. Walī Allāh, *Fuyūḍ al-Ḥaramayn*, 49.

75. Walī Allāh, *Fuyūḍ al-Ḥaramayn*, 50.

76. Walī Allāh, *Fuyūḍ al-Ḥaramayn*, 51, 65; and *Al-Tafhīmāt al-Ilāhiyya*, 323.

77. Walī Allāh, *Al-Tafhīmāt al-Ilāhiyya*, 7–8.

78. Muḥammad Bin ʿAlī al-Sanūsī, "Kitāb al-Masāʾil al-ʿAshr," in *Al-Majmuʿa al-Mukhtāra*, ed. Muhammad ʿAbdū Ibn Ghalbūn (Manchester, 1990), 274; and "Iqāẓ al-Wasnān fī al-ʿAmal bil-Ḥadīth wal-Qurʾān," in Ghalbūn, *Al-Majmūʿa al-Mukhtāra*, 129–35. In "Kitāb al-Masāʾil al-ʿAshr," written primarily to answer questions on the formalities of prayer and other similar legal issues, al-Sanūsī digresses twice to deal with subjects unrelated to the main topic of the book. The first digression is a long introduction on the subject of *ijtihād* ("Al-Masāʾil," 1–129). The second digression, tellingly titled "Aḥwāl al-Qawm al-Fākhira [The lofty conditions of the [Sufi] folks]," is a long discussion of Sufism, its definition, concepts, conventions, and terminology ("Al-Masāʾil," 272–93).

79. Muḥammad ʿAlī al-Sanūsī, "Al-Salsabīl al-Muʿīn fī al-Ṭarāʾiq al-Arbaʿīn," in *Al-Majmūʿa al-Mukhtāra*, ed. Muhammad ʿAbdū Ibn Ghalbūn (Manchester, 1990).

80. To be sure, al-Sanūsī recognizes that Sufis can commit grave errors, which he attributes to their faulty understanding of certain Sufi concepts and not the concepts themselves. Thus, for example, those who believe in the oneness of being err when they think that the highest stages of mystical perfection are achieved simply by believing in this concept. This knowledge, he adds, is not too helpful to the person who acquires it; rather, the true benefit for the seeker in his quest is to "witness the unity of being, since witnessing is a necessary state which

is achieved through self-exertion, consuming exercise, and humility." Simply by merging the two concepts of *waḥdat al-wujūd* and *waḥdat al-shuhūd* into one expression, "the witnessing of the unity of being" (*shuhūd waḥdat al-wujūd*), al-Sanūsī in effect reconciles the two concepts and suggests that one does not rule out the other ("Al-Masā'il," 279). This linguistic ploy, however, is far less elaborate than Walī Allāh's intellectual discussion of this subject.

81. Contrast to Trimingham, who asserts that "more closely than any other of Aḥmad's [Ibn Idrīs's] successors Muḥammad Ibn ʿAlī [al-Sanūsī] followed his aims in urging the elimination of the causes of disunity among Muslims. Like Aḥmad he advocated a return to the primitive sources of the Qur'ān and Sunna. Since this implied the rejection of ijmāʿ and qiyās and consequently the whole edifice of legalistic Islam, a result probably not envisaged by either Aḥmad or Muḥammad Ibn ʿAlī, the enmity of the ʿulamā' was ensured." Trimingham, *The Sufi Orders*, 119. Trimingham fails to note two very important differences between al-Sanūsī and his teacher Ibn Idrīs: despite the desire to undermine zealous adherence to schools, al-Sanūsī aimed to uphold the edifice of formal, legalistic Islam. Moreover, unlike Ibn Idrīs's thoroughly mystical and individualistic *ijtihād*, the exercise of *ijtihād* to al-Sanūsī was governed by formal procedures and squarely rooted in textual sources. Trimingham's misreading is part of a larger scholarly tendency to deploy the Weberian idea of charismatic leader to explain change in "nonrational" societies. This accounts for the general anthropological obsession with saints and cults and, in the case of al-Sanūsī, the readiness to dismiss his complex and manifold intellectual legacy and focus instead on his mysticism and the organization he built. For a general statement of this problem, see Peter Gran, "Political Economy as a Paradigm for the Study of Islamic History," *International Journal of Middle East Studies* 11, no. 4 (1980): 511–26, esp. 516.

82. Al-Sanūsī, "Iqāẓ," 129.

83. Al-Sanūsī, "Al-Masā'il," 272.

84. Al-Sanūsī, "Al-Masā'il," 274–75. Al-Sanūsī's matter-of-fact assumption of harmony between Sufism and the legal tradition is not surprising or unique. In Egypt, for example, many well-known legal scholars were practicing mystics and members of Sufi *ṭarīqa*s. See, for example, F. de Jong, *Ṭuruq and Ṭuruq-Linked Institutions in Nineteenth-Century Egypt: A Historical Study in Organizational Dynamics of Islamic Mysticism* (Leiden, the Netherlands: E. J. Brill, 1978), 21. Also, for the argument that the Sufi/scholar dichotomy does not work in practice, see Julian Johansen, *Sufism and Islamic Reform in Egypt: The Battle for Islamic Tradition* (Oxford: Clarendon Press, 1996), 10. There is substantial literature on eighteenth-century Sufism in Egypt, and especially on the Bakriyya branch of the Khalwatiyya order that was invested by the Ottomans with supreme authority over all other orders; de Jong, *Ṭuruq and Ṭuruq-Linked Institutions*, 20–24. Afaf Marsot maintains that in the eighteenth century most men in Cairo were members of Sufi *ṭarīqa*s; Afaf Lutfi al-Sayyid Marsot, "The Ulama of Cairo in the Eighteenth and Nineteenth Centuries," in *Scholars, Saints, and Sufis: Muslim Religious Institutions in the Middle East since 1500*, ed. Nikki R. Keddie (Berkeley: University of California Press, 1972), 151. The assessment of the Bakriyya varies. One view argues that it had wide popular appeal; B. G. Martin, "A Short History of the Khalwati Order of Dervishes," in Keddie, *Scholars, Saints, and Sufis*, 290. Another view notes that the order was popular among scholars and "propertied classes"; Voll, *Islam*, 47. Yet another contends that it was associated with the Turks and thus had no popular support; Michael Winter, *Society and Religion in Early Ottoman Egypt: Studies in the Writings of ʿAbd al-Wahhāb al-Shaʿrānī* (New Brunswick, N.J.: Transaction, 1982), 111. In any event, Frederick de Jong, who has done the most systematic work on this order, argues that there is no evidence of organizational or intellectual revival of Khalwatiyya Sufism under the Bakriyya branch. De Jong, "Mustafa Kamal al-Din al-Bakri (1688–1749): Revival and Reform of the Khalwatiyya Tradition?," in *Eighteenth-Century Re-*

newal and Reform in Islam, ed. Nehemia Levtzion and John Obert Voll (Syracuse, N.Y.: Syracuse University Press, 1987), 123. The main Egyptian Sufi movement, therefore, does not seem to fit the model of reform.

A similar absence of reform ideas seems to characterize the works of some of the main Muslim scholars of eighteenth-century Egypt. For example, Ḥasan al-ʿAṭṭār (d. 1263/1846), often cited as one of Egypt's leading intellectuals, wrote a treatise on *ijtihād* in which he argues that the conditions of *ijtihād* were only available in the early centuries of Islam, that later-day *ijtihād* can only be within the *madhhabs*, and that it is not allowed to combine elements from different schools. ʿAṭṭār, therefore, seems to have been an authoritarian partisan of *madhhabs* and effectively opposed to the exercise of *ijtihād*. For a positive assessment of ʿAṭṭār, see Peter Gran, *Islamic Roots of Capitalism: Egypt, 1760–1840* (Syracuse, N.Y.: Syracuse University Press, 1998), 75. On ʿAṭṭār's conservative views on *ijtihād*, as well as other views by Egyptian scholars, see Knut S. Vikor, *Sufi and Scholar on the Desert Edge: Muḥammad b. ʿAlī al-Sanūsī and His Brotherhood* (Evanston, Ill.: Northwestern University Press, 1995), 242–49.

85. Al-Sanūsī, "Iqāẓ," 130–31.

86. Al-Sanūsī, "Iqāẓ," 134–35. Generalizing from the model of Ibn Idrīs, and echoing Trimingham's assertions cited above, Radtke argues that in their rejection of schools, and their emphasis on direct access to God through the Prophet (*Ṭarīqā Muḥammadiyya*), the Sufis "wished to base legal judgments on other foundations than textual or rational proofs." Radtke, "Sufism in the Eighteenth Century," 360–61. While this applies to Ibn Idrīs, it does not apply to al-Nābulsī or Walī Allāh, and is certainly not true of al-Sanūsī. The latter upholds the textual sources as the alternative to *madhhab* zealotry and underscores hadith, not mystical knowledge, as the basis of *ijtihād*.

87. Al-Sanūsī, "Al-Masāʾil," 274.

88. Al-Sanūsī, "Al-Masāʾil," 273.

89. Al-Sanūsī, "Al-Masāʾil," 273; "Iqāẓ," 20, 129; and "Salsabīl," 18.

90. Al-Sanūsī, "Iqāẓ," 129–30.

91. Statements on al-Sanūsī's affinity with, or at least normalized feelings toward, Wahhabism completely ignore the clear opposition between them on issues of *takfīr* and Sufism; compare with Martin, *Muslim Brotherhoods*, 99, 103.

92. On the highly regimented social order in the Sanūsīya network of lodges, see E. E. Evans-Pritchard, *The Sanusi of Cyrenaica* (Oxford: Oxford University Press, 1954), 79; and Nicola A. Ziadeh, *Sanūsīyah: A Study of a Revivalist Movement in Islam* (Leiden, the Netherlands: E. J. Brill, 1958), 106–23.

93. Note that the Weberian characterization of mystic knowledge as uncommunicable does not apply to this kind of knowledge.

94. Al-Sanūsī, "Iqāẓ," 133.

95. In the generation before the eighteenth-century scholars, many of the leading Ḥaramayn teachers were active Sufis who taught Sufi classics including the works of Ibn al-ʿArabī and other "controversial" Sufis. Among these was the most famous teacher of the seventeenth century, Ibrāhīm al-Kūrānī (d. 1102/1690), who was initiated into several Sufi orders and taught many Sufi works. On al-Kurānī, see A. H. Johns, "Al-Kūrānī, Ibrāhīm," in *Encyclopedia of Islam*, 2nd ed., vol. 5 (Leiden, the Netherlands: E. J. Brill, 1979), 432–33; and A. H. Johns, "Friends in Grace: Ibrāhīm al-Kūrānī and ʿAbd al-Ghanī al-Raʾuf al-Singkeli," in *Spectrum: Essays Presented to Sutan Takdir Alisjahbana on His Seventieth Birthday*, ed. S. Udin (Jakarta: Dian Rakyat, 1978). Johns describes a treatise by al-Kūrānī as "a moving appeal for the recognition of Kashf as a valid guide to the understanding of the inner meaning of the Qurʾān and Tradition, for a total obedience to the prescriptions of the law, and for the acceptance of the

monistic philosophy of the Unity of Being (*Waḥda al-Wujūd*) as not simply a viable 'other way' to al-Ashʿarī's occasionalism, but as the conceptual structure most appropriate to the religious and moral truths, the symbolism and cosmology of the Qur'ān" ("Friends in Grace," 481). Al-Kūrānī was born in Kurdistan and studied in Turkey, Iran, Iraq, Syria, Egypt (at the Azhar University), and finally in Medina, where he studied with the leading scholars of the city, including al-Qashāshī. Al-Kūrānī was initiated into several Sufi orders, including the Naqshbandiyya, and he was an exponent of the school of Ibn al-ʿArabī. One of his books stirred a wide controversy and was criticized by Moroccan scholars because it argued the historicity of the Satanic Verses. On the work and the controversy surrounding it, see Alfred Guillaume, "*Al-Lumʿat al-Sanīya fī Taḥqīq al-Ilqā' fi-l-Umnīya* by Ibrāhīm al-Kūrānī," *Bulletin of the School of Oriental and African Studies* 20 (1957): 291–303. This work seems to underscore al-Kūrānī's unorthodox attitudes, since it argues the reality of the satanic interpolation in divine revelation, at a time when such a notion was readily dismissed by most if not all Muslim scholars on doctrinal grounds. For numerous references to his study and teaching of Sufi works, and for his defense of Ibn al-ʿArabī, as well as his initiation into various Sufi orders, see Ibrāhīm Bin Ḥasan Bin Shihāb al-Dīn al-Kurdī al-Kūrānī al-Shahrzūrī al-Madanī, "Amam li-Iqāẓ al-Himām," in *Majmūʿat Ḥaydar Ābād* (Hyderabad: Maṭbūʿāt Dā'irat al-Maʿārif, 1328/1910), 59, 112–18, 125–27.

96. Under the influence of Muʿtazilī doctrines, official Zaydis opposed Sufi practices and often banned them, and they totally rejected the teachings of Ibn al-ʿArabī. This official stand ranged from persecution of Sufis to tolerance of asceticism (*zuhd*) coupled with criticism of Sufi rituals involving music and singing as well as philosophical Sufism. See Wilferd Madelung, "Zaydī Attitudes to Sufism," in *Islamic Mysticism Contested: Thirteen Centuries of Controversies and Polemics*, ed. Frederick de Jong and Bernd Radtke (Leiden, the Netherlands: E. J. Brill, 1999), 124–44.

97. This is a general characterization; not all the Zaydis were antagonistic to Sufism and, as Brinkley Messick notes in *The Calligraphic State: Textual Domination and History in a Muslim Society* (Berkeley: University of California Press, 1996), not all Shāfiʿīs supported it. On the historical hostility of Zaydi jurists toward Sufis in Yemen, see ʿAbd Allāh Ḥibshī, *Al-Ṣūfiyya wa'l Fuqahā' fī al-Yaman* (Sanaa: Maktabat al-Jīl al-Jadīd, 1976), 52–53. On opposition to Sufism in Yemen as well as a general overview of Yemeni attitudes toward Ibn al-ʿArabī, see Knysh, *Ibn al-ʿArabī in the Later Islamic Tradition*, 225–69. Knysh shows that the divide in Yemen (and elsewhere) was not between Sufis and jurists but between different views within the orthodox scholarly community. See also Messick, *The Calligraphic State*, 49, 274–75.

98. In the introduction to a book titled *Taṭhīr al-Iʿtiqād ʿan Daran al-Ilḥād* (Purifying the creed from the tumors of disbelief), al-Ṣanʿānī says that he felt obliged to write this book after becoming aware of practices in all of Yemen and throughout the lands of Islam that amount to treating humans as rivals to God. These practices, he adds, include the belief in shrines and in degenerate and corrupt humans who observe none of the religious obligations and have no trace of knowledge, and yet claim to know the unknown. Muḥammad Ibn Ismāʿīl al-Amīr al-Ṣanʿānī, *Taṭhīr al-Iʿtiqād ʿan Daran al-Ilḥād* (Cairo: Maktabat al-Salām al-ʿĀlamiyya, 1980), 6. See also Muḥammad b. ʿAlī al-Shawkānī, *Al-Durr al-Naḍīd fī Ikhlāṣ Kalimat al-Tawḥīd*, ed. A. al-Ḥalabī (Saudi Arabia: Dār Ibn Khuzayma, 1414 AH). For additional references to the saints of lower Yemen, their saintly miracles, and visits to the shrines of saints, see Messick, *The Calligraphic State*, 49 and notes, 274–75.

99. See references from his *Al-Inṣāf fī Ḥaqīqat al-Awliyā' wa mā Lahum min al-Alṭāf wa-l-Karāmāt*, qtd. in Ibrāhīm Hilāl, *Al-Wijha al-Salafiyya ʿind al-Amīr al-Ṣanʿānī* (Cairo: Dār al-Nahḍa al-ʿArabiyya), 60–62, 69–73, 75–76, 78–79, 85–86.

100. Ibn Taymiyya, for example, was one of the most outspoken critics of Sufi excesses, and yet he did believe in the possibility of saintly miracles with the understanding that these are in essence miracles of prophets that are extended to saints.

101. Hilāl, *Al-Wijha al-Salafiyya*, 85–86. Note that al-Suyūṭī was highly respected among the scholars of Yemen.

102. Muḥammad b. Ismāʿīl al-Amīr al-Ṣanʿānī, *Risāla Sharīfa fīmā Yataʿallaq bi-l-Aʿdād li-l-Ḥurūf wa-l-Awfāq wa kam Bāqī min ʿUmr al-Dunyā* (Sanaa: Dār al-Quds, 1992), 21–23.

103. Al-Ṣanʿānī, *Risāla Sharīfa*, 30, 50–53.

104. Muḥammad b. Ismāʿīl al-Amīr al-Ṣanʿānī, *Subul al-Salām Sharḥ Bulūgh al-Marām min Jamʿ Adillat al-Aḥkām*, ed. Fawwāz Aḥmad Zamrlī and Ibrāhīm Muḥammad al-Jamal, 5 vols. (Beirut: Dār al-Kitāb al-ʿArabī, 1990), 2:286.

105. Al-Ṣanʿānī, *Taṭhīr al-Iʿtiqād ʿan Daran al-Ilḥād*, 6. Al-Ṣanʿānī also expresses his outrage at the fact that many of these revered so-called saints are in fact sinners "engrossed in their vices," who perform none of the religious obligations, make a living through unlawful means, and wrongfully claim to have knowledge of the unknown (21).

106. Al-Ṣanʿānī, *Taṭhīr*, 7.

107. Al-Ṣanʿānī, *Taṭhīr*, 7–8.

108. Al-Ṣanʿānī, *Taṭhīr*, 9.

109. Al-Ṣanʿānī, *Taṭhīr*, 12.

110. Al-Ṣanʿānī, *Taṭhīr*, 13.

111. Al-Ṣanʿānī, *Taṭhīr*, 11–12.

112. Al-Ṣanʿānī, *Taṭhīr*, 17–18.

113. Al-Ṣanʿānī, *Taṭhīr*, 19–20.

114. Al-Ṣanʿānī, *Taṭhīr*, 20–21.

115. Al-Ṣanʿānī, *Taṭhīr*, 21–22.

116. Al-Ṣanʿānī, *Taṭhīr*, 23.

117. For this and the following arguments, see al-Ṣanʿānī, *Taṭhīr*, 23.

118. Al-Ṣanʿānī, *Taṭhīr*, 28. Note that although his criticism is directed against standard Sufi practices, al-Ṣanʿānī identifies his target of attack as the *qubūriyyūn* and not Sufis in general, as if to single out particular practices and not Sufism as a whole.

119. Al-Ṣanʿānī, *Taṭhīr*, 29.

120. Al-Ṣanʿānī, *Taṭhīr*, 30.

121. Al-Ṣanʿānī, *Taṭhīr*, 24–26.

122. Muḥammad b. Ismāʿīl al-Amīr al-Ṣanʿānī, *Al-ʿUdda ʿalā Iḥkām al-Aḥkām Sharḥ ʿUmdat al-Aḥkām li-l-ʿAllāma Ibn Daqīq al-ʿĪd*, ed. ʿAlī Bin Muḥammad al-Hindī, 4 vols. (Cairo: Al-Maṭbaʿa al-Salafiyya, 1379), 1:273–74.

123. Al-Ṣanʿānī, *Subul al-Salām*, 2:422. The black stone is a sacred stone embedded in a wall of the Kaaba.

124. Thus he maintains that it is forbidden to perform pilgrimage to any mosque or shrine other than the three sacred mosques in Mecca, Medina, and Jerusalem. See Al-Ṣanʿānī, *Subul al-Salām*, 2:363–64.

125. Al-Ṣanʿānī, *Subul al-Salām*, 4:212–13.

126. Al-Ṣanʿānī, *Taṭhīr*, 35.

127. Muḥammad b. ʿAlī al-Shawkānī, *Al-Badr al-Ṭāliʿ bi Maḥāsin man baʿd al-Qarn al-Sābiʿ*. 2 vols. (Beirut: Dār al-Maʿrifa, n.d.), 2:37–39.

128. Al-Shawkānī, *Al-Durr al-Naḍīd*, 102–9.

129. Al-Shawkānī, *Al-Durr al-Naḍīd*, 102.

130. Al-Shawkānī, *Al-Durr al-Naḍīd*, 104.

131. Al-Shawkānī, *Al-Durr al-Naḍīd*, 105.

132. Al-Shawkānī, *Al-Durr al-Naḍīd*, 106.

133. Al-Shawkānī, *Al-Durr al-Naḍīd*, 108–9.

134. Al-Shawkānī, *Al-Durr al-Naḍīd*, 110.

135. Al-Shawkānī, *Al-Durr al-Naḍīd*, 113.

136. Al-Shawkānī, *Al-Durr al-Naḍīd*, 113–18.

137. Al-Shawkānī, *Al-Durr al-Naḍīd*, 132–38.

138. Other acts include the use of legal tricks (*hiyal*) to subvert the law.

139. Muḥammad b. ʿAlī al-Shawkānī, *Adab al-Ṭalab wa Muntahā al-Irab* (Cairo: Dār al-Arqam, 1981), 159; also see al-Shawkānī, *Wilāyat Allāh wal-Ṭarīq Ilayhā: Dirāsa wa Taḥqīq li Kitāb Qaṭr al-Walī ʿalā Ḥadīth al-Walī*, ed. Ibrāhīm Hilāl (Cairo: Dār al-kutub al-Ḥadītha, 1969), 353.

140. Al-Shawkānī, *Al-Badr al-Ṭāliʿ*, 2:31–39.

141. Al-Shawkānī, *Al-Badr al-Ṭāliʿ*, 2:37.

142. Al-Shawkānī, *Al-Badr al-Ṭāliʿ*, 2:37–39.

143. Muḥammad b. ʿAlī al-Shawkānī, *Itḥāf al-Akābir bi Isnād al-Dafātir* (Hyderabad Deccan: Maṭbaʿat Majlis Dāʾirat al-Maʿārif al-Nidhāmiyya, 1328 AH), 5.

144. Al-Shawkānī, *Itḥāf al-Akābir*, 75.

145. Al-Shawkānī, *Itḥāf al-Akābir*, 105. Other Sufi works studied and transmitted by al-Shawkānī include the famous *Risāla* of al-Qushayrī and *ʿAwārif al-Maʿārif* of al-Suhrūwardī; see al-Shawkānī, *Itḥāf al-Akābir*, 39, 73.

146. These subjects are forms of divination and deal with the magical powers of letters and numbers.

147. Al-Shawkānī, *Al-Badr al-Ṭāliʿ*, 1:313–14.

148. Al-Shawkānī, *Al-Badr al-Ṭāliʿ*, 1:406–8.

149. Al-Shawkānī also expresses his respect for Sufis and Sufism in numerous entries in his biographical work *Al-Badr al-Ṭāliʿ bi-Maḥāsin man baʿd al-Qarn al-Sābiʿ*, which is dedicated to exposing the virtues of Muslims after the seventh century of Hijra. Many of the people covered are Sufis and are included for their distinguished contributions in the areas of Sufi practice or thought; in fact, the very first biography in this book is of a Sufi, Ibrāhīm Ibn Aḥmad Ibn ʿAlī Ibn Aḥmad al-Kaynaʿī (d. 793 AH), whose supplications, according to al-Shawkānī, were fulfilled by God; see al-Shawkānī, *Al-Badr al-Ṭāliʿ*, 1:6.

150. In *Al-Marham al-Shāfī li-l-Dāʾ al-Khafī*, al-Shawkānī appropriates the language of the tradition of asceticism (*zuhd*) and talks about the inner matters of the soul (*umūr bāṭina*), including *niyya* (intention), *ikhlāṣ* (devotion), abandoning *riyāʾ* (hypocrisy), *taqwā* (piety), *yaqīn* (certainty), *ṣabr* (patience), *riḍā* (contentment), *tawakkul* (reliance on God), *tafwīḍ* (entrustment), *tawāḍuʿ* (modesty), and so on. See *Al-Marham al-Shāfī li-l-Dāʾ al-Khafī*, in *Al-Sulūk al-Islāmī al-Qawīm*, ed. Ḥusayn Bin ʿAbd Allāh al-ʿAmrī (Damascus: Dār al-Fikr, 1986).

151. *Karāmāt* are miracles granted by God as favors to reward the person's piety or on behalf of the Prophet, while *mukāshafāt* are revelations of certain kinds of hidden knowledge. See, for example, al-Shawkānī, *Al-Badr al-Ṭāliʿ*, 1:11, 36, 49–52.

152. See, for example, Muḥammad b. ʿAlī al-Shawkānī, *Tuḥfat al-Dhākirīn bi-ʿUddat al-Ḥiṣn al-Ḥaṣīn min Kalām Sayyid al-Mursalīn* (Beirut: Dār al-Qalam, 1984), 212, in reference to the permission to seek the intercession of the Prophet, and *Al-Durr al-Naḍīd*, 16, on the consensus that the Prophet Muhammad is the intercessor and mediator who will intercede before God on behalf of humans on the day of resurrection. See *Al-Durr al-Naḍīd*, 9, 10, on the permissibility of appealing for the help of human beings as long as they are actually capable of

providing such help, and as long as they are not asked to do things that only God is capable of doing, such as forgiving sins, making rain fall, and providing sustenance.

153. Published along with twelve other treatises by al-Shawkānī as *Umanāʾ al-Sharīʿa lil-Imām al-Shawkānī*, ed. Ibrāhīm Hilāl (Cairo: Dār al-Nahḍa al-ʿArabiyya, n.d.), 85–91.

154. Published in the same collection, al-Shawkānī, *Umanāʾ al-Sharīʿa*, 93–98.

155. Al-Shawkānī, *Umanāʾ al-Sharīʿa*, 95.

156. Al-Shawkānī, *Umanāʾ al-Sharīʿa*, 96. Another treatise that al-Shawkānī composed in the same spirit of moderate and guarded attitude to Sufism is *Ibṭāl Daʿwā al-Ijmāʿ ʿalā Taḥrīm Muṭlaq al-Samāʿ* (Refuting the claim of consensus on the prohibition of all kinds of *samāʿ*). I have not been able to read this treatise, which, to the best of my knowledge, is not published, but both its title and references to it suggest that it advocates a view similar to al-Nābulsī's argument that *samāʿ* is prohibited only in conjunction with certain kinds of corrupt behavior. For reference to this treatise, see, for example, Hilāl's introduction to Al-Shawkānī, *Al-Qawl al-Mufīd*, 29.

157. *Al-Durr al-Naḍīd*, 13; Busṭāmī says that one who appeals to mortal humans is no different from a drowning person who seeks the help of another drowning person.

158. Al-Shawkānī, *Wilāyat Allāh wal-Ṭarīq Ilayhā: Dirāsa wa Taḥqīq li Kitāb Qaṭr al-Walī ʿalā Ḥadīth al-Walī*, ed. Ibrāhīm Hilāl (Cairo: Dār al-Kutub al-Ḥadītha, 1969).

159. See, for example, George Makdisi, "Ibn Taymīya: A Sufi of the Qādirīya Order," *American Journal of Arab Studies* 1 (1974): 118–29.

160. Al-Shawkānī, *Wilāyat Allāh*, 219.

161. Al-Shawkānī, *Wilāyat Allāh*, 233. See also al-Shawkānī, *Nayl al-Awṭār*, where he argues that it is supererogatory to greet (*taslīm*) the people of the tombs and to pray for their well-being. Muḥammad b. ʿAlī al-Shawkānī, *Nayl al-Awṭār min Aḥādīth Sayyid al-Akhyār Sharḥ Muntaqā al-Akhbār*, ed. M. S. Hāshim, 8 vols. in 4 parts (Beirut: Dār al-Kutub al-ʿIlmiyya, 1995), 2.4:121.

162. Al-Shawkānī, *Wilāyat Allāh*, 236.

163. Al-Shawkānī, *Wilāyat Allāh*, 234.

164. Al-Shawkānī, *Wilāyat Allāh*, 245.

165. Al-Shawkānī, *Wilāyat Allāh*, 276.

166. Al-Shawkānī, *Wilāyat Allāh*, 290–343.

167. Al-Shawkānī, *Al-Badr al-Ṭāliʿ*, 1:139–40.

168. Al-Shawkānī, *Adab al-Ṭalab*, 172.

169. Al-Shawkānī, *Adab al-Ṭalab*, 175.

170. Al-Shawkānī, *Adab al-Ṭalab*, 173.

171. Al-Shawkānī, *Adab al-Ṭalab*, 174.

172. Al-Shawkānī, *Adab al-Ṭalab*, 172. Although he was little interested in the content of Sufi thought per se, it is interesting that al-Shawkānī uses the term used by some Sufis and thus approves of a branch of Sufism rather than opposing all Sufis as Ibn ʿAbd al-Wahhāb did.

173. Al-Shawkānī, *Adab al-Ṭalab*, 172.

174. Al-Shawkānī, *Adab al-Ṭalab*, 167.

175. Al-Shawkānī, *Adab al-Ṭalab*, 168.

176. Al-Shawkānī, *Adab al-Ṭalab*, 168–71.

177. Al-Shawkānī, *Nayl al-Awṭār*, 1:2:154–55.

178. Al-Shawkānī, *Nayl al-Awṭār*, 2:4:119. He also argues that an early hadith that prohibits visits to tombs had been abrogated.

179. Al-Shawkānī, *Nayl al-Awṭār*, 2:4:91. Also see *Sharḥ al-Ṣudūr fī Taḥrīm Rafʿ al-Qubūr*,

in *Al-Rasā'il al-Salafiyya fī Iḥyā' Sunnat Khayr al-Bariyya* (Beirut: Dār al-Kutub al-ʿIlmiyya, reprint of the 1930 edition), 9, 11; and Muḥammad b. ʿAlī al-Shawkānī, *Wabl al-Ghamām ʿalā Shifā' al-Uwām*, ed. M. Ḥallāq, 2 vols. (Cairo: Maktabat Ibn Taymiyya, 1995), 1:408–11.

180. Al-Shawkānī, *Nayl al-Awṭār*, 2.4:91.

181. Al-Shawkānī, *Nayl al-Awṭār*, 2.4:91. In *Sharḥ al-Ṣudūr fī Taḥrīm Rafʿ al-Qubūr*, al-Shawkānī maintains that the only Zaydi to allow the building of domes and shrines over the tombs of virtuous people is Imam Yaḥyā b. Ḥamza; this opinion, al-Shawkānī asserts, is in disagreement with other scholars from the *ahl al-bayt*, the Companions, their Followers, and the main scholars of the four schools. It is interesting, however, that rather than reproving Yaḥyā for his opinion, al-Shawkānī tries to explain it as the kind of mistake that scholars and *mujtahids* make, and goes on to say that Imam Yaḥyā was one of the most honest and painstaking imams in his search for truth. Al-Shawkānī, *Sharḥ al-Ṣudūr*, 4, 11–12.

182. Al-Shawkānī, *Al-Durr al-Naḍīd*, 20–21.

183. Al-Shawkānī, *Al-Durr al-Naḍīd*, 22–23. The verses in question are "Laysa laka min al-amr shay'an" (Āl ʿImrān 3:128, "The matter is not for you to decide, whether He shall accept their repentance or chastise them"), and "Qul lā amliku li nafsī nafʿan walā ḍarran" (Al-Aʿrāf 7:188, and Yūnus 10:49 ("Say it is not within my power to bring benefit to, or avert harm from myself").

184. Al-Shawkānī, *Al-Durr al-Naḍīd*, 28.

185. Al-Shawkānī, *Al-Durr al-Naḍīd*, 33.

186. Al-Shawkānī, *Al-Durr al-Naḍīd*, 39–40.

187. Al-Shawkānī, *Al-Durr al-Naḍīd*, 42.

188. Al-Shawkānī, *Al-Durr al-Naḍīd*, 44–49.

189. Al-Shawkānī, *Al-Durr al-Naḍīd*, 50–53. Al-Shawkānī says that belief in magicians may be, although in most case is not, accompanied by the belief that these magicians partake in God's knowledge of the unknown. The fact that he says that this is not usually the case clearly illustrates the distinction he draws between unbelief and acts that may lead to it.

190. Al-Shawkānī, *Al-Durr al-Naḍīd*, 57.

191. Al-Shawkānī, *Al-Durr al-Naḍīd*, 56–60.

192. Al-Shawkānī, *Al-Durr al-Naḍīd*, 65.

193. For additional examples of the subtle distinctions in al-Shawkānī's discourse, see *Al-Durr al-Naḍīd*, 86–87.

194. The later sections of *Al-Durr al-Naḍīd* use language that seems, on the face of it, similar to Wahhabi language; see al-Shawkānī, *Al-Durr al-Naḍīd*, 65. For example, al-Shawkānī maintains that the meaning of the idol worship of unbelievers before Islam is simply that they glorified these idols, believed that they could harm and benefit, sought their help at times of need, and made offerings to them. All of these acts, al-Shawkānī adds, have parallels in the practice of Muslims who believe in tombs and their powers; *Al-Durr al-Naḍīd*, 70. Yet his theoretical discussions in the long introductory sections of the treatise and the arguments he provides in defense of intercession indicate that al-Shawkānī's tough language is deliberately calculated to discourage what he considers to be illegal acts and not to irreversibly condemn Muslims who commit them.

195. Al-Shawkānī, *Al-Durr al-Naḍīd*, 72–76. Interestingly, al-Shawkānī responds to those who claim that an offering at a tomb is an act of charity by saying that one needs not go to a shrine to perform an act of charity to alleviate poverty, which is spread all over society.

196. Al-Shawkānī, *Al-Durr al-Naḍīd*, 77–83.

197. Al-Shawkānī, *Al-Durr al-Naḍīd*, 83.

198. Al-Shawkānī, *Al-Durr al-Naḍīd*, 91–92.

199. Al-Shawkānī, *Al-Durr al-Naḍīd*, 95–97.

200. On religious currents in Yemen, see Wilferd Madelung, "Islam in Yemen," in *Yemen: 3000 Years of Art and Civilization*, ed. Werner Daum (Innsbruck: Pinguin; Frankfurt am Main: Umschau, 1988), 174–76. Also see relevant references in Wilferd Madelung, *Der Imām al-Qāsim Ibn Ibrāhīm und die Glaubenslehre der Zayditen* (Berlin: Walter de Gruyter, 1965). Étienne Renaud, "Histoire de la pensée religieuse au Yémen," in *L'Arabie du sud: Histoire et civilisation*, ed. Joseph Chelhod (Paris: Maisonneuve et Larose, 1984). Also see the substantial discussions in Aḥmad Maḥmūd Ṣubḥī, *Al-Zaydiyya* (Alexandria: Munsha'at al-Ma'ārif, 1980).

201. See, for example, Muḥammad Ibn Ibrāhīm al-Wazīr, *Tarjīḥ Asālīb al-Qur'ān 'alā Asālīb al-Yūnān* (Beirut: Dār al-Kutub al-'Ilmiyya, 1984); *Al-'Awāṣim wa-l-Qawāṣim fī al-Dhabb 'an Sunnat Abī al-Qāsim*, ed. Shu'ayb al-Arna'ūṭ, 3 vols. (Amman: Dār al-Bashīr, 1985); and *Īthār al-Ḥaqq 'alā al-Khalq fī Radd al-Khilāfāt ilā al-Madhhab al-Ḥaqq min Uṣūl al-Tawḥīd*, ed. A. M. Ḥ. Ṣāliḥ (Sanaa: Al-Dār al-Yamaniyya lil-Nashr wal-Tawzī', 1985). See also Ṣāliḥ Ibn Mahdī al-Maqbalī, *Al-'Alam al-Shāmikh fī Tafḍīl al-Ḥaqq 'alā al-Ābā' wa-l-Mashāyikh* (Beirut: Dār al-Ḥadīth, 1985). For more on this subject, see chapter 5 on hadith.

202. Al-Shawkānī, *Adab al-Ṭalab*, 114–15.

203. Al-Shawkānī, *Adab al-Ṭalab*, 114.

204. Al-Shawkānī, *Adab al-Ṭalab*, 123.

205. Al-Shawkānī, *Adab al-Ṭalab*, 123–24.

206. Al-Shawkānī, *Adab al-Ṭalab*, 142.

207. Al-Shawkānī, *Adab al-Ṭalab*, 125.

208. The care for the self is the hallmark of the notion of the intellectual in classical philosophy and among the philosophers of the Enlightenment.

209. Shāh Walī Allāh, *Al-Inṣāf fī Bayān Sabab al-Ikhtilāf* (Lahore: Maṭba'at al-Maktaba al-'Ilmīya, 1971), 57–58.

210. To Walī Allāh, renewal is mainly in response to the problem of social division and is achieved through the intellectual reform of thought; see Walī Allāh, *Ḥujjat Allāh*, 1:8; and *Al-Tafhīmāt al-Ilāhiyya*, 1:37, 111–12, and 2:54.

211. Shāh Walī Allāh, *Al-Budūr al-Bāzigha*, ed. Ṣaghīr Ḥasan al-Ma'ṣūmī (Haidarabad: Shah Wali Allah al-Dihlawi Academy, n.d.), 91.

212. From Walī Allāh, *Fuyūḍ al-Ḥaramayn*, qtd. in J. M. S. Baljon, *Religion and Thought of Shah Walī Allah Dihlawi* (Leiden, the Netherlands: E. J. Brill, 1986), 162.

213. He states that his mission in life is to interpret sharia in a way that will allow differences within it to vanish; see Walī Allāh, *Al-Tafhīmāt al-Ilāhiyya*, 1:111–12, 2:54.

214. See Walī Allāh, *'Iqd al-Jīd fī Aḥkām al-Ijtihād wal-Taqlīd* (Cairo: Al-Maṭba'a al-Salafiyya, 1385 AH); and *Inṣāf*.

215. The works where Sufi differences are most discussed are Walī Allāh, *The Sacred Knowledge of the Higher Functions of the Mind*; and Walī Allāh, *Al-Tafhīmāt al-Ilāhiyya*.

216. Walī Allāh, *'Iqd*; *Inṣāf*; and Shāh Walī Allāh, *Ḥujjat Allah al-Bāligha*, 2 parts (Cairo: Dār al-Turāth, 1936).

217. See especially Walī Allāh, *Al-Tafhīmāt al-Ilāhiyya*, 1:54.

218. Walī Allāh, *Al-Tafhīmāt al-Ilāhiyya*, 1:8.

219. Walī Allāh, *Al-Tafhīmāt al-Ilāhiyya*, 1:8; and *Ḥujjat Allāh*, 2:215.

220. Walī Allāh, *Ḥujjat Allāh*, 1:120, 2:150.

221. Walī Allāh, *Ḥujjat Allāh*, 1:120, 2:21–22, 215.

222. Walī Allāh, *Ḥujjat Allāh*, 1:120.

223. Walī Allāh, *Ḥujjat Allāh*, 1:121.

224. Walī Allāh, *Inṣāf*, 57–58; and *Ḥujjat Allāh*, 1:152–53.

225. From Walī Allāh, *Fuyūḍ al-Ḥaramayn*, qtd. in Baljon, *Religion and Thought of Shah Walī Allah Dihlawi*, 162.

226. Walī Allāh, *Ḥujjat Allāh*, 2:21–22.

227. Walī Allāh, *Ḥujjat Allāh*, 1:120.

228. Walī Allāh, *Ḥujjat Allāh*, 1:179.

229. Walī Allāh, *Ḥujjat Allāh*, 1:252.

230. Walī Allāh, *Ḥujjat Allāh*, 1:253.

231. Walī Allāh, *Ḥujjat Allāh*, 2:38.

232. ʿUthmān Ibn Fūdī, "The Translation of the *Nūr-al-Albāb*," Arabic text and translation with introduction by Yusuf Wali, *Kano Studies* 2, no. 1 (1980): 10–36, esp. 23–24.

233. ʿUthmān Ibn Fūdī, "Sirāj al-Ikhwān," in Mervyn Hiskett, "An Islamic Tradition of Reform in the Western Sudan from the Sixteenth to the Eighteenth Century: Translation of Selections from *Sirāj al-Ikhwān, Bayān al-Bidaʿ al-Shayṭānīya*, and *Naṣāʾiḥ al-Umma al-Muḥammadīya*," *Bulletin of the School of Oriental and African Studies* 25, no. 3 (1962): 577–96, esp. 581.

234. Louis Brenner and Murray Last, "The Role of Language in West African Islam," *Africa* 55, no. 4 (1985), 432–46, esp. 436.

235. This has notably been the case after the recent and largely unanticipated revival in modern Islamic activism. In an attempt to provide a better understanding of modern Islamic thought, previously seen as a thing of the past, some historians put forth the hypothesis that nineteenth-century Islamic reforms were rooted in the intellectual legacy of eighteenth-century Muslim reformers, who developed their innovative ideas within the Islamic tradition and independent of European influence. For references, see the notes in the introduction.

236. Rudolph Peters, "*Idjtihād* and *Taqlīd* in 18th and 19th Century Islam," *Die Welt des Islams* 20, nos. 3–4 (1980): 145. An extreme form of continuity theory is expressed in Richard Martin and Mark Woodward, with Dwi Atmaja, *Defenders of Reason in Islam; Muʿtazilism from Medieval School to Modern Symbol* (Oxford, UK: Oneworld, 1997). The authors argue that fundamentalism is not just a reaction to modernism but a modern expression of a "historically rooted traditionalist reaction to rationalist tendencies in Islamic thought that goes back at least to the circle around Hasan al-Basri" and can be traced today in the thought of Fazlur Rahman, Muhammad Arkoun, Fatima Mernissi, and Hasan Hanafi!

237. John O. Voll, "The Sudanese Mahdī: Frontier Fundamentalist," *International Journal of Middle East Studies* 10 (1979): 160.

238. There is abundant reference in writings on eighteenth- and nineteenth-century Islamic thought and movements in which these themes are said to define the common intellectual trend of fundamentalist or revivalist Islam; see, for example, Wilfred Cantwell Smith, *Islam in Modern History* (Princeton, N.J.: Princeton University Press, 1977), 42, 52; Fazlur Rahman, *Islam* (Chicago: University of Chicago Press, 1968), 242–50; John Esposito, "Tradition and Modernization in Islam," in *Movements and Issues in World Religions*, ed. Charles Wei-hsun Fu and Gerhard E. Spiegler (New York: Greenwood, 1987), 92; Mervyn Hiskett, *The Development of Islam in West Africa* (London: Longman, 1984), 157; John O. Voll, "Muḥammad Ḥayyā al-Sindī and Muḥammad Ibn ʿAbd al-Wahhāb: An Analysis of an Intellectual Group in Eighteenth-Century Madīna," *Bulletin of the School of Oriental and African Studies* 38, no. 1 (1974); John O. Voll, "Hadith Scholars and Tariqahs: An Ulama Group in the 18th Century Haramayn and Their Impact in the Islamic World," *Journal of Asian and African Studies* 15, nos. 3–4 (1980): 264–73; Louis Brenner, "Muslim Thought in Eighteenth-Century West Africa: The Case of Shaykh Uthman b. Fudi," in *Eighteenth-Century Renewal and Reform in Islam*, ed. Nehemia Levtzion and John Obert Voll (Syracuse, N.Y.: Syracuse University Press, 1987), 61;

Muin ud-Din Ahmad Khan, "Farā'idī Movement," *Islamic Studies* 9 (1970): 123; and Martin, *Muslim Brotherhoods*, 107–8.

239. Voll, "The Sudanese Mahdī"; H. A. R. Gibb, *Modern Trends in Islam* (Chicago: University of Chicago Press, 1947), 32; Peters, "*Idjtihād* and *Taqlīd*," 132.

240. Smith, *Islam in Modern History*, 42. For a similar notion of the gradual spread of Wahhabism in the Muslim world, see Gibb, *Modern Trends in Islam*, 27–28.

241. See, for example, Ali Merad, "Reformism in Modern Islam," *Cultures* 4, no. 1 (1977): 108–27. Merad argues that "Islam's meeting with Western cultural models became the central theme of a vast debate, which dominated Moslem intellectual life throughout the nineteenth century" (114) and that "within Islamic cultural circles . . . the enlightened classes became more and more familiar with the fundamental values governing the social and cultural life of the developed European countries" (115). In contrast, I argue that the influence of cultural contact did not become apparent till the second half of the nineteenth century and, more important, that this contact radically compromised the quality of Islamic thought rather than stimulated it.

242. Contrast with a common scholarly view that treats neo-Sufism as a form of reactionary resistance to the expanding progressive Europeans. See, for example, Trimingham, *The Sufi Orders*, who attributes a pan-Islamic vision to Aḥmad Bin Idrīs (106, 114–16); also see Annemarie Schimmel, *The Mystical Dimensions of Islam* (Chapel Hill: University of North Carolina Press, 1974), who attributes the formation of the Sanūsiyya order and the adoption of the *ṭarīqa Muḥammadiyya* to a politically motivated desire to emulate the Prophet Muhammad in the fight against colonial powers (227–28). Of course Sirhindī, one of the main advocates of this new *ṭarīqa*, predates colonialism, and Walī Allāh does not deal with it. The transformation of the Sanūsiyya order into a resistance movement against Italian colonialism was a later development that was clearly not envisioned by the founder of the movement. Moreover, as O'Fahey and Radtke note in their critique of the concept of neo-Sufism, Ibn Idrīs was "born in a seaport with substantial European commercial presence, was in Cairo when the French marched in, and must have observed Muḥammad ʿAlī's 'New Model' army in Upper Egypt and Arabia, but there is not a line on the Franks in his writings." R. S. O'Fahey and Bernd Radtke, "Neo-Sufism Reconsidered," *Der Islam* 70, no. 1 (1993): 52–87; quotation on 66.

The view of Sufi orders as pan-Islamic, inherently fanatic, rebellious, violent, and opposed by their very nature to European power and state orders of any kind is a legacy of the French and British colonial views, which were shaped by concerns of colonial control. See, for example, Gabriel Warburg, *The Sudan under Wingate: Administration in the Anglo-Egyptian Sudan, 1899–1916* (London: Frank Cass, 1971); and Christopher Harrison, *France and Islam in West Africa, 1860–1960* (Cambridge: Cambridge University Press, 1988), 20–21, 42. Also see Marwan R. Buheiry, "Colonial Scholarship and Muslim Revivalism in 1900," *Arab Studies Quarterly* 4 (1982): 1–16. For a concise overview of French scholarship on Sufism and parallels with Russian scholarship, see Alexander Knysh, "Sufism as an Explanatory Paradigm: The Issue of the Motivations of Sufi Resistance Movements in Western and Russian Scholarship," *Die Welt des Islams* 42, no. 2 (2002): 139–73. Knysh argues that "the 'Neo-Sufism' thesis can be traced back to the 19th century European fears of 'secret societies' plotting to undermine imperial projects" (144). For a critique of the modernists' conceptions of Sufism, which is shared with colonial officers and pays little attention to the beliefs of Sufi groups, see Dale F. Eickelman, *Moroccan Islam: Tradition and Society in a Pilgrimage Center* (Austin: University of Texas Press, 1976), 17–29. However, despite this critique, Eickelman goes on to repeat the same notions that these Sufi groups were activist, Pan-Islamic, and anti-European. For the argument that anticolonial jihad was a later development not anticipated by the founders of the movements, see Knut S. Vikor, "Jihād, 'Ilm and Taṣawwuf—Two Justifications of Action from the Idrīsī Tradition," *Studia Islamica* (2000): 153–76. Also see Jean-Louis Triaud, *La légende noire de la Sanūsiyya: Une confrérie musulmane saharienne sous le regard français (1840–1930)* (Paris, 1995).

243. See chap. 2, "Boundaries of Faith."

244. Al-Shawkānī, *Al-Badr al-Ṭāliʿ*, 2:8–22.

245. Al-Shawkānī, *Al-Badr al-Ṭāliʿ*, 2:8–9.

246. Al-Shawkānī, *Al-Badr al-Ṭāliʿ*, 2:9.

247. Al-Shawkānī, *Al-Badr al-Ṭāliʿ*, 2:9–15.

248. Al-Shawkānī, *Al-Badr al-Ṭāliʿ*, 2:15–18.

249. Al-Shawkānī, *Al-Badr al-Ṭāliʿ*, 2:15–16.

250. Al-Shawkānī's official exchanges and correspondence are conveniently collected in *Dhikrayāt al-Shawkānī, Rasāʾil li-l-Muʾarrikh al-Yamanī Muḥammad Bin ʿAlī al-Shawkānī*, ed. Ṣalāḥ Ramaḍān Maḥmūd (Beirut: Dār al-ʿAwda, 1983). In addition to the exchange with Ottoman officials and the sharifs of Mecca regarding the French occupation of Egypt (37–101), al-Shawkānī also discussed issues related to the Wahhabi wars (113–90) and corresponded with the British governor of India. The Ottomans asked the imams of Sanaa to fortify their ports in anticipation of possible French attacks and to allow British and Russian vessels to use these ports if needed (61–62). It is interesting that after the withdrawal of the French from Egypt, the British tried to conclude trade agreements with Yemen, but the imam declined (67–75). The imam's reason, as articulated by al-Shawkānī, was that, on religious grounds, he could not conclude a trade treaty with the British at the expense of other Muslims (74–75). In other exchanges it is also clear that al-Shawkānī was aware of British schemes to monopolize Red Sea navigation (84–85).

251. Al-Shawkānī, *Dhikrayāt al-Shawkānī*, 92–93.

252. The quote appears on the dust jacket of Hilāl's edition of al-Shawkānī, *Wilāyat Allāh wal-Ṭarīq Ilayhā*. The first part of the book is a long study of al-Shawkānī's thought. Exaggerated as this statement may sound, it does reflect most views that posit a continuity of reform from the eighteenth century and up to the modern period. Like a majority of other studies of the eighteenth century, Hilāl also views all activism in this period through the Wahhabi prism, although he cites al-Shawkānī's criticisms of the Wahhabis. Hilāl edited several other works of al-Shawkānī; in the introduction to al-Shawkānī's *Al-Qawl al-Mufīd*, he asserts that al-Shawkānī focused on the call to purify the belief in the Oneness of God (*ikhlāṣ al-tawḥīd*) and thus became one of the imams of this cause like Ibn ʿAbd al-Wahhāb and Ibn Taymiyya before him. Hilāl adds that al-Shawkānī was not directly influenced by these thinkers but used their same sources and thus arrived at the same results in regard to the purification of creed; see al-Shawkānī, *Al-Qawl al-Mufīd*, 20–21. In one instance (*Wilāyat Allāh*, 120, 123), Hilāl projects his own views of what a reformer ought to believe and proceeds to respond to the respect that both al-Shawkānī and Ibn Taymiyya show toward a number of the leading Sufis by arguing that their true thought would rule out any such respect and recognition; he then proposes to undermine their professed respect by quoting their other ideas. Other modern references to al-Shawkānī highlight his call for *ijtihād*, his "tolerance," and his struggle against sectarian difference in the interest of achieving "national unity." These assertions reflect the hopes of their authors more than al-Shawkānī's own understanding and views. See, for example, Qāsim Muḥammad Ghālib, *Min Maʿālim al-Yaman: Shaykh al-Islām al-Mujtahid Muḥammad b. ʿAlī al-Shawkānī* (Cairo: Maṭābiʾ al-Ahrām al-Tijāriyya, 1969). In the genre of nationalist history, see also Qāsim Ghālib Aḥmad et al., *Ibn al-Amīr wa ʿAṣruhu: Ṣūra min Kifāḥ Shaʿb al-Yaman* (Ibn al-Amīr and his era: a portrayal of the struggle of the people of Yemen) (Sanaa: Wizārat al-

I'lām wal-Thaqāfa, 1983). Also see Ḥusayn b. 'Abdullāh al-'Amrī, *The Yemen in the 18th and 19th Centuries: A Political and Intellectual History* (London: Ithaca, 1985), 115–16, which celebrates al-Shawkānī as a leader of the "free Zaydīs." Haykel provides an account of the official narrative of Republican Yemen that rejected the Ḥamīd al-Dīn Imamate and its Hādawī legacy and appropriated al-Shawkānī's anti-Hādawī views to lend credibility to the Republican rhetoric. See Bernard Haykel, "Al-Shawkānī and the Jurisprudential Unity of Yemen," *Revue du Monde Musulman et de la Méditerranée* 67 (1993): 53–65. This, as well as the attempts by the Ḥamīd al-Dīn imams to combat nationalism by recasting some of the traditionalist ideas into a modern idiom (see Messick, *The Calligraphic State*, 123–31), explains some of the modern misrepresentations of al-Shawkānī.

253. H. A. R. Gibb and Harold Bowen, *Islamic Society and the West: A Study of the Impact of Western Civilization on Moslem Culture in the Near East*, vol. 1, *Islamic Society in the Eighteenth Century*, part 1 (London, 1950), part 2 (London, 1957), vol. 1, part 2, 1:161.

Chapter 4

1. It would be impossible to adequately address the political contexts of all the examined intellectuals in just one book. Instead, I will focus on the career of al-Shawkānī as a test case that suggests ways in which the intellectual and the political were intertwined.

2. Thus, for example, is the recurrent desire to classify al-Shawkānī as either a Zaydi or a Sunni, despite his unrelenting criticism of all kinds of *madhhab* affiliation.

3. Muḥammad Ibn Ismā'īl al-Amīr al-Ṣan'ānī, *Taṭhīr al-I'tiqād 'an Daran al-Ilḥād* (Cairo: Maktabat al-Salām al-'Ālamiyya, 1980), 35–36.

4. Al-Ṣan'ānī, *Taṭhīr*, 36–39.

5. Muḥammad Ibn Ismā'īl al-Amīr al-Ṣan'ānī, *Al-'Udda 'alā Iḥkām al-Aḥkām Sharḥ 'Umdat al-Aḥkām lil-'Allāma Ibn Daqīq al-'Īd*, ed. A. al-Hindī, 4 vols. (Cairo: Al-Maṭba'a al-Salafiyya, 1379 AH), 3:258–59.

6. See, for example, Ṣāliḥ b. Mahdī al-Maqbalī, *Al 'Alam al-Shāmikh fī Tafḍīl al-Ḥaqq 'alā al-Ābā' wal-Mashā'ikh* (Beirut: Dār al-Ḥadīth, 1985), 218, 220.

7. Muḥammad b. 'Alī al-Shawkānī, *Al-Badr al-Ṭāli' bi Maḥāsin man ba'd al-Qarn al-Sābi'*, 2 vols. (Beirut: Dār al-Ma'rifa, n.d.), 2:127–29.

8. Al-Qāḍī Ismā'īl b. 'Alī al-Akwa', *Hijar al-'Ilm wa Ma'āqiluhu fī al-Yaman*, 5 vols. (Beirut: Dār al-Fikr al-Mu'āṣir, 1995), 4:1830–32.

9. On al-Shawkānī's intimate involvement in all government affairs, see Muḥammad b. al-Ḥasan b. 'Alī b. Aḥmad b. Nāṣir al-Shijanī (al-Shijnī) al-Ḥimyarī al-Dhamārī, *Ḥayāt al-Imām al-Shawkānī al-Musammā Kitāb al-Tiqṣār fī Jīd Zamān 'Allāmat al-Aqālīm wal-Amṣār* (Sanaa: Maktabat al-Jīl al-Jadīd, 1990) (hereafter cited as al-Shijnī, *Kitāb al-Tiqṣār*), esp. 424. The book provides ample evidence of the power wielded by al-Shawkānī.

10. Al-Shawkānī, *Al-Badr al-Ṭāli'*, 1:376–77.

11. Al-Shawkānī, *Al-Badr al-Ṭāli'*, 1:274–76.

12. Al-Shawkānī, *Al-Badr al-Ṭāli'*, 1:466–49.

13. Al-Shawkānī, *Al-Badr al-Ṭāli'*, 2:368–72.

14. Al-Shawkānī, *Al-Badr al-Ṭāli'*, 2:370.

15. Al-Shawkānī, *Al-Badr al-Ṭāli'*, 2:370–71.

16. For more on this subject, see chapter 5 on hadith.

17. This argument occupies a large part of Ibn al-Wazīr's seminal work, *Al-'Awāṣim wa-l-Qawāṣim fī al-Dhabb 'an Sunnat Abī al-Qāsim*, ed. Shu'ayb al-Arna'ūṭ, 3 vols. (Amman: Dār al-Bashīr, 1985); the argument about Mu'āwiya is part of a larger argument on accepting the

report of *fāsiq al-taʾwīl*. See al-Wazīr, *Al-ʿAwāṣim*, 2:128, 3:159. Also see Muḥammad b. Ibrāhīm al-Wazīr, *Al-Rawḍ al-Bāsim fī al-Dhabb ʿan Sunnat Abī al-Qāsim*, 2 parts in 1 vol. (Cairo: Al-Maṭbaʿa al-Salafiyya, 1385 AH), 237, 260.

18. Muḥammad b. ʿAlī al-Shawkānī, *Nayl al-Awṭār min Aḥādīth Sayyid al-Akhyār Sharḥ Muntaqā al-Akhbār*, ed. M. S. Hāshim, 8 vols. in 4 parts (Beirut: Dār al-Kutub al-ʿIlmiyya, 1995), 2.4:186.

19. *Kharāj* is a tax levied on publicly owned lands that are forcibly conquered by Muslims and is considerably higher than the *ʿushr* tax levied on land privately owned by Muslims; for more on the subject, see Hossein Modarressi, *Kharāj in Islamic Law* (London: H. M. Tabātabāʾī, 1983).

20. Al-Shawkānī, *Nayl al-Awṭār*, 2.4:186.

21. Muḥammad b. ʿAlī al-Shawkānī, *Rafʿ al-Aṣāṭīn fī Ḥukm al-Ittiṣāl bil-Ṣalāṭīn*, ed. Ḥ. M. Muḥammad (Beirut: Dār Ibn Ḥazm; Sanaa: Maktabat al-Jīl al-Jadīd, 1992), 65–69. See also the somewhat parallel argument by al-Ṣanʿānī on the permissibility of receiving a payment for performing the religious duty of reciting the Qurʾān in Muḥammad b. Ismāʿīl al-Amīr al-Ṣanʿānī, *Iqāmat al-Ḥujja wal-Burhān ʿalā Akhdh al-Ujra ʿalā Tilāwat al-Qurʾān*, ed. A. al-Ruqayḥī (Sanaa: Manshurāt Dār al-Awqāf, 1984).

22. Al-Shawkānī, *Rafʿ al-Aṣāṭīn fī Ḥukm al-Ittiṣāl bil-Salāṭīn*, 69–74.

23. Al-Shawkānī, *Rafʿ al-Aṣāṭīn fī Ḥukm al-Ittiṣāl bil-Salāṭīn*, 74–75.

24. Such was, for example, the view of al-Ghazālī (d. 1111).

25. Al-Shawkānī, *Rafʿ al-Aṣāṭīn fī Ḥukm al-Ittiṣāl bil-Salāṭīn*, 86–87. Even if fictional, this story reflects al-Shawkānī's stand on the relationship to power.

26. Al-Shawkānī, *Rafʿ al-Aṣāṭīn fī Ḥukm al-Ittiṣāl bil-Salāṭīn*, 88.

27. Al-Shawkānī, *Rafʿ al-Aṣāṭīn fī Ḥukm al-Ittiṣāl bil-Salāṭīn*, 75–76.

28. Al-Shawkānī, *Rafʿ al-Aṣāṭīn fī Ḥukm al-Ittiṣāl bil-Salāṭīn*, 77.

29. Al-Shawkānī, *Rafʿ al-Aṣāṭīn fī Ḥukm al-Ittiṣāl bil-Salāṭīn*, 69–70.

30. Al-Shawkānī, *Rafʿ al-Aṣāṭīn fī Ḥukm al-Ittiṣāl bil-Salāṭīn*, 90–94.

31. Al-Shawkānī, *Adab al-Ṭalab*, 134–35.

32. Contrast to Muḥammad b. Ibrāhīm al-Wazīr, *Al-Amr bil-ʿUzla fī Ākhir al-Zamān*, ed. I. ʿAbd al-Majīd (Amman: Al-Maktaba al-Islāmiyya, 1412 AH); and Muḥammad b. al-Amīr al-Ṣanʿānī, *Ḥadīth Iftirāq al-Umma ilā Nayyf wa Sabʿīn Firqa*, ed. S. al-Saʿdān (Riyadh: Dār al-ʿĀṣima, 1415 AH).

33. Al-Shawkānī, *Wilāyat Allāh*, 399.

34. Al-Shawkānī, *Rafʿ al-Aṣāṭīn fī Ḥukm al-Ittiṣāl bil-Salāṭīn*, 78–79.

35. Al-Shawkānī, *Rafʿ al-Aṣāṭīn fī Ḥukm al-Ittiṣāl bil-Salāṭīn*, 79–80.

36. Al-Shawkānī, *Rafʿ al-Aṣāṭīn fī Ḥukm al-Ittiṣāl bil-Salāṭīn*, 81–83.

37. Al-Shawkānī, *Adab al-Ṭalab*, 44.

38. Al-Shawkānī, *Adab al-Ṭalab*, 44–45.

39. Al-Shawkānī, *Rafʿ al-Aṣāṭīn fī Ḥukm al-Ittiṣāl bil-Salāṭīn*, 84–85.

40. For classical works that deal with aspects of this subject, see Ibn Abī al-Rabīʿ (2nd–3rd century AH), *Sulūk al-Mālik fī Tadbīr al-Mamālik*, ed. Najī al-Takrītī (Beirut: Dār al-Andalus, 1980); ʿAlī b. Muḥammad al-Māwardī, *Al-Aḥkām al-Ṣulṭāniyya wal-Wilāyāt al-Dīniyya* (Cairo: Al-Maktaba al-Tawfīqiyya, 1975); Abū Ḥāmid al-Ghazālī, *Al-Iqtiṣād fī al-Iʿtiqād*, ed. M. M. Abū al-ʿUlā (Cairo: Maktabat al-Jundī, 1972); Aḥmad Ibn Taymiyya, *Al-Siyāsa al-Sharʿiyya fī Iṣlāḥ al-Rāʿī wal-Raʿiyya* (Cairo: Al-Maṭbaʿa al-Salafiyya, n.d.). Al-Shawkānī discusses these matters in a number of his books, including *Al-Sayl al-Jarrār al-Mutadaffiq ʿalā Ḥadāʾiq al-Azhār*, ed. Maḥmūd Ibrāhīm Zāyid (Beirut: Dār al-Kutub al-ʿIlmiyya, n.d.), esp. 4:503–28,

586–90; *Nayl al-Awṭār min Aḥādīth Sayyid al-Akhyār Sharḥ Muntaqā al-Akhbār*, ed. M. S. Hāshim, 8 vols. in 4 parts (Beirut: Dār al-Kutub al-ʿIlmiyya, 1995); *Fatḥ al-Qadīr al-Jāmiʿ bayn Fannay al-Riwāya wal-Dirāya min ʿIlm al-Tafsīr*, 5 vols. (Beirut: Dār al-Maʿrifa, n.d.); and *Al-Darārī al-Muḍiyya Sharḥ al-Durar al-Bahiyya* (Cairo: Maktabat al-Turāth al-Islāmī, 1986).

41. I will discuss this book in greater depth below. Al-Shawkānī's other works on law and hadith have a historical dimension and can be read, at some level, as histories of the respective disciplines.

42. For example, al-Shawkānī would say of a celebrated individual: "His rank before the Imam was elevated [*irtafaʿat darajatuhu ʿinda al-Imām*]" or "He mounted him on horses and conferred distinction on him [*arkabahu al-khayl wa ikhtaṣṣahu*]." *Al-Badr al-Ṭāliʿ*, 1:62.

43. For example, al-Shawkānī, *Al-Badr al-Ṭāliʿ*, 1:27, 29, 35.

44. Al-Shawkānī, *Al-Badr al-Ṭāliʿ*, 1:24.

45. Al-Shawkānī, *Al-Badr al-Ṭāliʿ*, 1:96.

46. Al-Shawkānī, *Al-Badr al-Ṭāliʿ*, 1:186.

47. Al-Shawkānī, *Al-Badr al-Ṭāliʿ*, 1:195–97.

48. Al-Shawkānī, *Al-Badr al-Ṭāliʿ*, 1:196.

49. Al-Shawkānī, *Al-Badr al-Ṭāliʿ*, 1:150.

50. For the following account, see al-Shawkānī, *Al-Badr al-Ṭāliʿ*, 1:157–58.

51. For an excellent overview of the history of this period, see R. B. Serjeant, "The Post-medieval and Modern History of Ṣanʿāʾ and the Yemen," in *Ṣanʿāʾ: An Arabian Islamic City*, ed. R. B. Serjeant and R. Lewcock (London: World of Islam Festival Trust, 1983), 391–431.

52. Bernard Haykel generally adopts these assumptions in his work on al-Shawkānī; see, for example, Haykel, "Reforming Islam by Dissolving the *Madhhab*s: Shawkānī and His Zaydī Detractors in Yemen," in *Studies in Islamic Legal Theory*, ed. Bernard Weiss (Leiden, the Netherlands: E. J. Brill, 2002), 339; and Haykel, *Revival and Reform in Islam: The Legacy of Muhammad al-Shawkānī* (Cambridge: Cambridge University Press, 2003).

53. On the history of Yemen under Zaydi imams, see A. S. Tritton, "Yemen in the Seventeenth Century," *Proceedings and Transactions of the Oriental Conference* (1922): 579–82; A. S. Tritton, "The Rise of the Imams of Sanaa (1006 to 1050, AH)," *Journal of Indian History* 1 (1921–22): 373–96; and William Robertson, "Sanʿa, Past and Present," *Moslem World* 33, no. 1 (1942): 52–57. One of the best studies of the establishment and development of Zaydi Islam in Yemen is Wilferd Madelung, *Der Imam al-Qāsim Ibn Ibrāhīm und die Glaubenslehre der Zayditen* (Berlin: Walter de Gruyter, 1965). See also Wilferd Madelung, "Islam in Yemen," in *Yemen: 3000 Years of Art and Civilization*, ed. Werner Daum (Innsbruck, Pinguin; and Frankfurt am Main: Umschau, 1988), 174–76; Wilferd Madelung, "Imāma," in *Encyclopedia of Islam*, 2nd ed., vol. 3 (Leiden, the Netherlands: E. J. Brill), 1163–69; and Étienne Renaud, "Histoire de la pensee religieuse au Yémen," in *L'Arabie du sud: Histoire et civilisation*, ed. Joseph Chelhod (Paris: Maisonneuve et Larose, 1984). On various aspects of Zaydi beliefs, see Wilferd Madelung, "Zaydiyya," in *Encyclopedia of Islam*, 2nd ed., vol. 11 (Leiden, the Netherlands: E. J. Brill), 479; Aḥmad Maḥmūd Ṣubḥī, *Al-Zaydiyya* (Alexandria: Munshaʾat al Maʿārif, 1980); R. B. Serjeant, "The Zaydīs," in *Religion in the Middle East*, ed. A. J. Arberry, 2 vols. (Cambridge: Cambridge University Press, 1969); Etan Kohlberg, "Some Zaydī Views on the Companions of the Prophet," *Bulletin of the School of Oriental and African Studies* 39, no. 1 (1976): 91–98; Ella Landau-Tasseron, "Zaydī Imāms as Restorers of Religion: Iḥyāʾ and Tajdīd in Zaydī Literature," *Journal of Near Eastern Studies* 49 (1990): 247–63; Wilferd Madelung, "Zaydī Attitudes to Sufism," in *Islamic Mysticism Contested: Thirteen Centuries of Controversies and Polemics*, ed. Frederick de Jong and Bernd Radtke (Leiden, the Netherlands: E. J. Brill, 1999), 124–44;

ʿAbd Allāh b. Muḥammad al-Ḥibshī, *Al-Ṣūfiyya wal-Fuqahāʾ fī al-Yaman* (Sanaa: Maktabat al-Jīl al-Jadīd, 1976); and ʿAbd Allāh al-Ḥibshī, *Maṣādir al-Fikr al-Islāmī fī al-Yaman* (Beirut: Al-Maktaba al-ʿAṣriyya, 1988).

54. See, for example, Haykel, "Reforming Islam by Dissolving the *Madhhabs*," 339.

55. See, for example, Aḥmad b. Yaḥyā al-Murtaḍā, *Kitāb al-Azhār fī fiqh al-Aʾimma al-Aṭhār* (Beirut: Maktabat al-Ḥayāt, 1973), 313–28. In this book, arguably the most important Zaydi legal text (*matn*), al-Murtaḍā argues that, in the absence of a qualified imam, the maintenance of order goes to the *muḥtasib* (market supervisor), clearly a recognition of multiple sites of authority. For more on this subject, see Madelung, "Imāma."

56. See the detailed biography of Ibn al-Wazīr in al-Shawkānī, *Al-Badr al-Ṭāliʿ*, 2:81–93.

57. See more on hadith in chapter 5.

58. For a detailed articulation of this view, see Haykel, *Revival and Reform*, 25–75.

59. Al-Shawkānī, *Al-Badr al-Ṭāliʿ*, 1:233–35; *Adab al-Ṭalab*, 29–35.

60. See the biographies of al-Manṣūr ʿAlī (al-Shawkānī, *Al-Badr al-Ṭāliʿ*, 1:459–67) and Mutawakkil Aḥmad (*Al-Badr al-Ṭāliʿ*, 1:77–79).

61. Al-Shawkānī, *Al-Badr al-Ṭāliʿ*, 1:78–79, 466–67.

62. Al-Shawkānī, *Adab al-Ṭalab*, 37. That this issue of taxation was not incidental in al-Shawkānī's thought is clear from the numerous occasions on which he addressed it. Al-Shawkānī returned to the problem of unlawful taxation in several of his works. For example, in *Al-Darārī al-Muḍiyya* he maintains that *zakāt* is one of the obligations of religion and one of its foundations and necessities; however, it is only obligatory to pay this tax on the kinds of wealth and property that the Lawgiver has clearly specified and spelled out. Al-Shawkānī adds that many scholars have extrapolated the payment of *zakāt* on items not spelled out in the law. In response to those who claim that the textual stipulation of *zakāt* is general, and who use the argument of generality to extend *zakāt* to items not specified by the law, al-Shawkānī argues that by this same logic, *zakāt* would have to be applied to people who are not commanded to pay it; and since the latter is rejected by consensus, so should the former. Al-Shawkānī maintains that, based on the clear statements of the Qurʾān and Sunna, the general rule is the inviolability of the wealth of people, and that nothing makes the taking of this wealth legal except mutual agreement and consent, or the specific statement by the law, as in the case of *zakāt*, blood money, and so on. Muḥammad b. ʿAlī al-Shawkānī, *Al-Darārī al-Muḍiyya*, 205–6.

63. Muḥammad b. ʿAlī al-Shawkānī, "Al-Dawāʾ al-ʿĀjil fī Dafʿ al-ʿAduw al-Ṣāʾil," in *Al-Rasāʾil al-Salafiyya fī Iḥyāʾ Sunnat Khayr al-Bariyya* (Beirut: Dār al-Kutub al-ʿIlmiyya, reprint of the 1930 edition), 27–38; *Adab al-Ṭalab*, 162–63. See also al-Shijnī, *Kitāb al-Tiqṣār*, 173–78.

64. See, for example, al-Shawkānī, *Al-Sayl al-Jarrār*, 4:505–15; and Muḥammad b. ʿAlī al-Shawkānī, *Wabl al-Ghamām ʿalā Shifāʾ al-Uwām*, ed. M. Ḥallāq, 2 vols. (Cairo: Maktabat Ibn Taymiyya, 1995), 2:418, 428.

65. Al-Shawkānī, *Al-Badr al-Ṭāliʿ*, 1:146–49.

66. Al-Shawkānī, *Al-Badr al-Ṭāliʿ*, 1:169–73.

67. Al-Shawkānī, *Al-Badr al-Ṭāliʿ*, 1:170.

68. Al-Shawkānī, *Al-Badr al-Ṭāliʿ*, 1:171.

69. Al-Shawkānī, *Al-Badr al-Ṭāliʿ*, 1:172.

70. Al-Shawkānī, *Al-Badr al-Ṭāliʿ*, 1:173.

71. See below on al-Shawkānī's celebration of Ibn Taymiyya.

72. On Zaydi requisites for the imam, especially *daʿwa* (summons to allegiance) and *khurūj* (taking up arms or rising), piety and righteousness, learning and scholarship (*ijtihād*), probity and justice, see Madelung, "Imāma." Later Zaydis compromised some of these requirements;

in much of Zaydi political history, including that of the Qāsimī imamate, the person who became imam was not necessarily the most qualified but the most powerful. Therefore, what al-Shawkānī argued suits both a doctrinal compromise and a historical model of Zaydism.

73. Also, as we saw in chapter 3, al-Shawkānī's *ijtihād* is very different from the Zaydi *ijtihād* of the imam in that the latter entails the obligation to imitate the imam, whereas al-Shawkānī is opposed to all forms of *taqlīd*.

74. See, for example, Al-Shawkānī, *Wabl al-Ghamām*, 2:398–402, and al-Shawkānī, *Al-Sayl al-Jarrār*, 4:505–15.

75. Al-Shawkānī, *Nayl al-Awṭār*, 4.7:180. For the standard treatment of the subject of renegades and rebels in Islamic law, see Khaled Abou El Fadl, *Rebellion and Violence in Islamic Law* (Cambridge: Cambridge University Press, 2001).

76. Al-Shawkānī, *Nayl al-Awṭār*, 4.7:181.

77. Al-Shawkānī, *Nayl al-Awṭār*, 4.7:185–86.

78. Al-Shawkānī, *Al-Darārī al-Muḍiyya*, 505–7.

79. On the dependence of the imamate on tribes for military support, see Paul Dersch, *Tribes, Government, and History in Yemen* (Oxford: Oxford University Press, 1994), 200.

80. Thus, for example, Brinkley Messick argues that in terms of his political commitments and his theory of *ijtihād*, al-Shawkānī was a Zaydi who "strove for an intellectual posture transcending conventional *madhhabs*"; Messick, *The Calligraphic State: Textual Domination and History in a Muslim Society* (Berkeley: University of California Press, 1996), 42–43. In other words, al-Shawkānī was a Zaydi with some Sunni credentials. This identification of al-Shawkānī is premised on Messick's argument that prior to twentieth-century nationalist politics, there was only "shariʿa politics grounded in *madhhab* affiliation" (53). Like Messick, Haykel, in *Revival and Reform*, argues that al-Shawkānī's theory of *ijtihād* is rooted in the Zaydi legacy. However, despite the difficulty of entirely situating al-Shawkānī (86), Haykel still contends that al-Shawkānī paid lip service to the Zaydis but in reality "fits into a tradition that is purely Sunni" (84), and that he was largely influenced by Shāfiʿī legal thought (86–87) and Ḥanbalī theological views (106). More generally, al-Shawkānī "defined his legal methodology and epistemology in Sunni terms and to the exclusion of Zaydi textual sources." Bernard Haykel, "Rebellion, Migration or Consultative Democracy? The Zaydis and Their Detractors in Yemen," in *Le Yémen contemporain*, ed. Rémy Leveau, Franck Mermier, and Udo Steinbach (Paris: Karthala, 1999), 193–201, esp. 195.

81. For a concise biography of al-Shawkānī and reference to the main sources for this biography, see Haykel, *Revival and Reform*, 18–23.

82. See, for example, al-Shawkānī's biography of his father, ʿAlī b. Muḥammad, *Al-Badr al Ṭāliʿ*, 1:478–85.

83. Al-Shawkānī, *Al-Badr al-Ṭāliʿ*, 2:90.

84. Al-Shawkānī, *Al-Badr al-Ṭāliʿ*, 1:288–92.

85. Al-Shawkānī, *Al-Badr al-Ṭāliʿ*, 1:59–61.

86. Muḥammad b. ʿAlī al-Shawkānī, *Itḥāf al-Akābir bi Isnād al Dafātir* (Hyderabad Deccan: Maṭbaʿat Majlis Dāʾirat al-Maʿārif al-Nidhāmiyya, 1328 AH), 3.

87. Note that somewhat similar attempts were made in the same period in Iran to have the Jaʿfarī School recognized as the fifth school of law, and hence to have Shiism recognized as part of mainstream Islam.

88. Al-Shawkānī, *Al-Badr al-Ṭāliʿ*, 2:83.

89. Al-Shawkānī, *Al-Badr al-Ṭāliʿ*, 2:83–84.

90. Muḥammad b. ʿAlī al-Shawkānī, *Al-Qawl al-Mufīd fī Adillat al-Ijtihād wal-Taqlīd*, ed. I. I. Hilāl (Cairo: Dār al-Nahḍa al-ʿArabiyya, 1979), 143.

91. For example, al-Shawkānī's main legal work, *Al-Sayl al-Jarrār*, is a running critique of traditional Zaydi law, especially as articulated in Aḥmad b. Yaḥyā al-Murtaḍā's *Kitāb al-Azhār*.

92. His indifference to Twelver Shiism is mostly the result of a lack of exposure. On one occasion, however, after getting to know an Imami scholar from Bahrain, he makes sure to note the scholar's "fairness and understanding," both of which, of course, are high on al-Shawkānī's list of credentials; see *Al-Badr al-Ṭāliʿ*, 1:269–70.

93. Al-Shawkānī, *Al-Darārī al-Muḍiyya*, 236–37.

94. Al-Shawkānī, *Adab al-Ṭalab*, 68, 72, 75, 128. One of the recurrent themes in al-Shawkānī's writings is the exoneration of the Companions and their centrality in Islamic doctrine. For example, in a book on the virtues of the companions and relatives of the Prophet, *Durr al-Saḥāba fī Manāqib al-Qarāba wal-Ṣaḥāba*, ed. Ḥusayn b. ʿAbd Allāh al-ʿAmrī (Damascus: Dār al-Fikr, 1984), he lists traditions relating to their praise drawn from sixty different sources.

95. Al-Shawkānī, *Adab al-Ṭalab*, 75.

96. Al-Shawkānī, *Adab al-Ṭalab*, 78–79.

97. Al-Shawkānī, *Adab al-Ṭalab*, 125–29.

98. A common intellectual tradition among the Zaydis in Yemen was manifested in dialogues between Shāfiʿī and Zaydi scholars. For example, the Shāfiʿī scholar ʿAbd al-Raḥmān al-Ḥaddād (1876–1922) wrote a commentary on the *ikhtiyārāt* (personal sharia interpretations, literally "choices") of the Zaydi imam Yaḥyā. As Messick explains (*The Calligraphic State*, 48), such a dialogue was not exceptional in Yemen. However, al-Shawkānī's writings do not belong to this genre, which is unidirectional, in that the affiliation of the commentator is clearly identified. Rather, al-Shawkānī did not comment on either Sunni or Zaydi legal works from the secure standpoint of the opposite *madhhab* but was cognizant of the positions of all schools and at the same time not bound by any one of them.

99. See, for example, al-Shawkānī, *Al-Darārī al-Muḍiyya*, 89, on the legitimacy of adding the formula *ḥayya ʿalā khayr al-ʿamal* (Thrive in the best of deeds) to the *adhān* (call to prayer). Note that this book was finished in 1220 AH and hence cannot be dismissed as an early view that al-Shawkānī later changed. Also see al-Shawkānī, *Nayl al-Awṭār*, 1.2:39–40.

100. Al-Shawkānī, *Al-Qawl al-Mufīd*, 144–46.

101. Al-Shawkānī, *Al-Qawl al-Mufīd*, 146.

102. Al-Shawkānī, *Adab al-Ṭalab*, 50.

103. For details, see chapter 5 on hadith.

104. So, for example, none of the earlier reformers wielded power comparable to that of al-Shawkānī, a chief judge; instead, they were mostly on the defensive. Also, the numbers and practical influence of Sunna-inclined Zaydi scholars increased significantly under al-Shawkānī's patronage, while there had been a much smaller minority until his time. The ideas of these reformers also underwent significant evolution over time, however, and they cannot be treated as one undifferentiated whole.

105. On the uselessness of *kalām*, see, for example, Muḥammad Ibn Ibrāhīm al-Wazīr, *Tarjīḥ Asālīb al-Qurʾān ʿalā Asālīb al-Yūnān* (Beirut: Dār al-Kutub al-ʿIlmiyya, 1984). See also al-Shawkānī, *Wabl al-Ghamām*, 1:374–75.

106. See, for example, Muḥammad b. ʿAlī al-Shawkānī, *Irshād al-Fuḥūl ilā Taḥqīq al-Ḥaqq min ʿIlm al-Uṣūl* (n.p.: Dār al-Fikr, n.d.), 8–9.

107. The other question that arose in this connection was the theoretical justification of the acceptance of the authority of transmitters of hadith who were condemned on religious and political grounds. This question, as well as the peculiar theory of hadith articulated by eighteenth-century Yemeni reformers, is discussed in chapter 5.

108. For Zaydi views on this subject, see Kohlberg, "Some Zaydī Views on the Companions of the Prophet"; and Madelung, "Imāma."

109. Al-Qāsim b. Muḥammad, *Kitāb al-Asās li ʿAqāʾid al-Akyās*, ed. Albert Nadir (Beirut: Dār al-Ṭalīʿa, 1980).

110. Al-Imām al-Muʾayyad bi-Allāh Yaḥyā b. Ḥamza (d. 749), *Al-Risāla al-Wāziʿa lil-Muʿtadīn ʿan Sabb Ṣaḥābat Sayyid al-Mursalīn*, in *Majmūʿat al-Rasāʾil al-Yamaniyya* (Cairo: Idārat al-Ṭibāʿa al-Munīriyya, 1348 AH), 13–14, 24–25.

111. Muḥammad b. ʿAlī al-Shawkānī, *Irshād al-Ghabī ilā Madhab Ahl al-Bayt fī Ṣaḥb al-Nabī*, ed. A. Mashhūr b. Salmān (Riyadh: Dār al-Manār, 1992), 50–51.

112. Al-Shawkānī, *Irshād al-Ghabī*, 70.

113. Al-Shawkānī, *Irshād al-Ghabī*, 92–93.

114. Al-Shawkānī provides thirteen different reports on the consensus of *ahl al-bayt* on prohibiting the cursing of the Companions. For references to Hādawī and other early Zaydi defenders of the Companions invoked by al-Shawkānī, and of his insistence on the veneration of the Companions, see al-Shawkānī, *Irshād al-Ghabī*. Also see *Al-Badr al-Ṭāliʿ*, 1:233–35. In *Al-Badr al-Ṭāliʿ*, 1:296–97, al-Shawkānī cites a *Risāla fī Tanzīh al-Ṣaḥāba* [A treatise on the veneration of the Companions] by al-Sayyid Ṣalāḥ b. Ḥusayn al-Akhfash (d. 1730?); and in *Al-Badr al-Ṭāliʿ*, 2:328, he cites two treatises regarding the veneration of the Companions by al-Sayyid Yaḥyā b. al-Ḥusayn b. al-Imām al-Qāsim b. Muḥammad (d. 1689) and describes the hardship (*fitan*) that he went through as a result of composing these two treatises.

115. Al-Shawkānī, *Al-Badr al-Ṭāliʿ*, 1:233–35; *Adab al-Ṭalab*, 29–35. Al-Shawkānī says that these responses were mere cursing and identifies the extreme responses as a mere rehashing of the views of the Imamis and extreme Jārūdiyya Zaydis; he also says that the real cause for responding to him was to please the commoners and the people in power in the state "man lahu ṣawla wa dawla."

116. Muḥammad b. ʿAlī al-Shawkānī, "Irshād al-Sāʾil ilā Dalāʾil al-Masāʾil," in *Al-Rasāʾil al-Salafiyya fī Iḥyāʾ Sunnat Khayr al-Bariyya* (Beirut: Dār al-Kutub al-ʿIlmiyya, reprint of 1930 edition), 39–51, esp. 45.

117. Al-Shawkānī, *Al-Sayl al-Jarrār*, 4:584–85.

118. Al-Shawkānī, "Irshād al-Sāʾil," 45.

119. Al-Shawkānī, *Al-Fawāʾid al-Majmūʿa fī al-Aḥādīth al-Mawḍūʿa*, ed. ʿAbd al-Raḥmān b. Yaḥyā al-Maʿlamī al-Yamānī and ʿAbd al-Wahhāb ʿAbd al-Laṭīf (Cairo: Maktabat al-Sunna al-Nabawiyya, 1960), 400.

120. Al-Ṣanʿānī, *Al-Rawḍa al-Nadiyya fī Sharḥ al-Tuḥfa al-ʿAlawiyya*, ed. Aḥmad Shāmī (Sanaa: Al-Dār al-Yamaniyya lil-Nashr wal-Tawzīʿ, 1985), 146.

121. Al-Ṣanʿānī, *Al-Rawḍa al-Nadiyya*, 185.

122. Al-Ṣanʿānī, *Al-Rawḍa al-Nadiyya*, 202.

123. Al-Ṣanʿānī, *Al-Rawḍa al-Nadiyya*, 26.

124. If al-Ṣanʿānī was not a Sunni, he also did not think of himself as a Zaydi in any traditional sense of the word. Like other great *mujtahids* of Yemen, al-Ṣanʿānī had many enemies in the established religious institutions of the imamic state. In Yemen, he was accused several times of attempting to undermine the Zaydi School, the official school of the Imamate of Sanaa and, as a result, was targeted by the mob and punished by the rulers. Eventually he left Yemen to the Hejaz, where he came into conflict with the local Sunni religious authorities and endured additional hardships as a result. Al-Shawkānī, *Al-Badr al-Ṭāliʿ*, 2:133–39.

125. Al-Shawkānī, *Nayl al-Awṭār*, 4.7:50.

126. Al-Shawkānī, *Nayl al-Awṭār*, 4.7:50.

127. The reference here is to *Irshād al-Ghabī ilā Madhab Ahl al-Bayt fī Ṣaḥb al-Nabī*, in

which al-Shawkānī enumerates through thirteen different channels of transmission instances in which leading imams of the family of the Prophet condemn the cursing and slandering of the Companions.

128. For example, al-Shawkānī, *Nayl al-Awṭār*, 4:7, 348.

129. Compare to *Wabl al-Ghamām*, 2:341, where al-Shawkānī maintains that most of the commoners among the Bāṭiniyya (extreme Shiʿis) are misled and not subject to the penalties that apply to apostates.

130. Al-Shawkānī, "Baḥth fī al-Kalām ʿalā Umnāʾ al-Sharīʿa," in *Umanāʾ al-Sharīʿa, Thalath ʿAsharata Risāla Ukhrā fī al-Fiqh wal-Tafsīr wal-ʿAqāʾid wal-Qaḍāʾ*, ed. I. I. Hilāl (Cairo: Dār al-Nahḍa al-ʿArabiyya, 1976), 197–208, esp. 206.

131. Al-Shawkānī, *Irshād al-Ghabī*, 82.

132. Al-Shawkānī, "ʿUqūd al-Zabarjad fī Jīd Masāʾil ʿAllāmat Ḍamad," in *Umanāʾ al-Sharīʿa, Thalath ʿAsharata Risāla*, 215–48.

133. Al-Shawkānī, *ʿUqūd al-Zabarjad*, 237.

134. Al-Shawkānī, *ʿUqūd al-Zabarjad*, 245.

135. Al-Shawkānī, *ʿUqūd al-Zabarjad*, 245–48.

136. Al-Shawkānī, *Durr al-Saḥāba fī Manāqib al-Qarāba wal Ṣaḥāba*, ed. Ḥusayn b. ʿAbd Allāh al-ʿAmrī (Damascus: Dār al-Fikr, 1984), 386.

137. Al-Shawkānī, *Durr al-Saḥāba*, 203.

138. Muḥammad b. ʿAlī al-Shawkānī, *Al-Fawāʾid al-Majmūʿa fī al-Aḥādīth al-Mawḍūʿa*, ed. ʿAbd al-Raḥmān b. Yaḥyā al-Maʿlamī al-Yamānī and ʿAbd al-Wahhāb ʿAbd al-Laṭīf (Cairo: Maktabat al-Sunna al-Nabawiyya, 1960), 342–84.

139. Al-Shawkānī, *Al-Fawāʾid al-Majmūʿa*, 348–49.

140. Al-Shawkānī, *Al-Fawāʾid al-Majmūʿa*, 361–66.

141. Al-Shawkānī, *Al-Fawāʾid al-Majmūʿa*, 356–59.

142. Al-Shawkānī, *Al-Fawāʾid al-Majmūʿa*, 386.

143. Al-Shawkānī, *Adab al-Ṭalab*, 68.

144. Al-Shawkānī, *Al-Badr al-Ṭāliʿ*, 1:274, 299. Many biographies indicate that certain contemporaries of al-Shawkānī were alive at the time their entries were first written but end by specifying the date of death of these individuals. This information was clearly added later.

145. Thus, for example, he gives an ideal portrayal of a Sufi of the Shādhiliyya order but then refers to some reports on his alleged extreme opposition to Ibn Taymiyya, one of al-Shawkānī's greatest heroes. Should these reports be true, al-Shawkānī adds, then the subject of the biography "would be a charlatan, and not one of those worthy of distinction." Al-Shawkānī, *Al-Badr al-Ṭāliʿ*, 1:107–8.

146. Thus, al-Shawkānī often uses such formulas as "He devoted himself to the matters of the soul" or "He was the ascetic and austere man of the age," and he is especially keen to laud the ability of some mystics to practice Sufism while at the same time "fulfilling the requirements of the Divine law and following the example of the messenger of God." See, for example, al-Shawkānī, *Al-Badr al-Ṭāliʿ*, 1:11.

147. Al-Shawkānī also celebrates achievement in such fields as grammar and other language sciences. See, for example, al-Shawkānī, *Al-Badr al-Ṭāliʿ*, 1:16–17, 18, 36–37, 48, 52–53, 54–56, 104.

148. On a female poet, who also was versed in the rational sciences and in language sciences, see al-Shawkānī, *Al-Badr al-Ṭāliʿ*, 1:258–59.

149. The second entry in *Al-Badr al-Ṭāliʿ* is for one such poet (1:7).

150. For example, ten pages of the biography of a *wazīr* (vizier) of Imam al-Mahdī al-ʿAbbās consist of nothing but quotes from his prose and poetry, although he was also an accom-

plished scholar and governor (al-Shawkānī, *Al-Badr al-Ṭāliʿ*, 1:446–56). Alternatively, some of the poets cited by al-Shawkānī for their poetic excellence may also have other virtues, such as adherence to legal indicants in religious matters, and enduring the attacks of *madhhab* partisans, as in the case of a twelfth-century poet who was accused in Sanaa of *naṣb* (cursing the family of the Prophet) and in Mecca of *rafḍ* (*Al-Badr al-Ṭāliʿ*, 1:384–85). In another case, for example, al-Shawkānī writes of a student of al-Ṣanʿānī who was "an eloquent poet and a famous judge, who has studied with a distinguished group of his contemporaries." The remainder of the biography, however, says nothing of this person's function as a judge and talks only of his poetry (*Al-Badr al-Ṭāliʿ*, 1:475–76).

151. Some people are mentioned on more than one count; thus, for example, al-Shawkānī writes about Ibrāhīm Ibn Aḥmad Ibn Nāṣir (d. 870), a Sufi, scholar, and poet who refused appointment as judge and preferred instead to be the shaykh of a Sufi shrine (*khāniqa*) (*Al-Badr al-Ṭāliʿ*, 1:9–10).

152. Al-Shawkānī, *Al-Badr al-Ṭāliʿ*, 1:455.

153. Al-Shawkānī, *Al-Badr al-Ṭāliʿ*, 1:340–51.

154. See, for example, the biographies of the mathematician Ibn al-Hāʾim (al-Shawkānī, *Al-Badr al-Ṭāliʿ*, 1:117–18) and the astronomer al-Qūshjī (1:495–96); see also *Al-Badr al-Ṭāliʿ*, 2:171–73, 173, 174–76, 242, 247–49.

155. Al-Shawkānī, *Al-Badr al-Ṭāliʿ*, 1:38.

156. Al-Shawkānī, *Al-Badr al-Ṭāliʿ*, 2:219–21.

157. Al-Shawkānī, *Al-Badr al-Ṭāliʿ*, 2:299–300.

158. See, for example, al-Shawkānī, *Al-Badr al-Ṭāliʿ*, esp. 1:18, 19, 113–14, 135–37, and 2:299–300.

159. For example, al-Shawkānī, *Al-Badr al-Ṭāliʿ*, 1:362.

160. For example, in reference to the question of performing a missed religious obligation (*qaḍāʾ*), al-Shawkānī cites the views of the Ẓāhirīs, Ibn Taymiyya, and some Zaydi imams who say that one who neglects to perform an obligation in its allotted time without a legal excuse is bound by his sin but does not need to make up the missed obligation. Although these are among al-Shawkānī's most respected scholars, he still disagrees with them and asserts that they have no evidence for their ruling either from the Qurʾān or from the Sunna (*Al-Darārī al-Muḍiyya*, 146). See below for more examples.

161. Al-Shawkānī, *Adab al-Ṭalab*, 25–26.

162. Al-Shawkānī, *Adab al-Ṭalab*, 27–28. Al-Shawkānī notes that not even a minor composition by the rivals of these Yemeni scholars became famous, while their reputation spread around the world. In the case of these Yemeni scholars in particular, al-Shawkānī reports that he studied and transmitted all of their works (*Itḥāf al-Akābir*, 18–19, 35, 35–36).

163. See al-Shawkānī, *Al-Badr al-Ṭāliʿ*, 1:63–72, 661–738; quotation on page 64.

164. Al-Shawkānī, *Al-Badr al-Ṭāliʿ*, 2:290. Elsewhere (*Nayl al-Awṭār*, 1.1:116), al-Shawkānī takes issue with al-Nawawī's claim that Dāwūd's disagreement does not affect *ijmāʿ*, because his opinion does not count. He says, "Paying no heed to the disagreement of Dāwūd despite his knowledge and piety, and despite the fact that many of the great imams follow his school, is a kind of zeal which has no excuse other than whim and partisanship. This behavior is abundant among the members of the schools of law; I do not know what evidence these people have to justify excluding Dāwūd from the circle of Muslim scholars. If this is because of some of his far-fetched views, then compared to the opinions of other scholars, which are based on sheer opinion and are opposed to explicit transmission, these are quite minimal. Indeed, relying on opinion and not paying attention to the science of indicants [*ʿilm al-adilla*] had led people to become partisans of schools in which only a rare minority agree with sharia." Here,

too, the issue for al-Shawkānī is not that the legal doctrine of the Ẓāhirīs is to be accepted in its totality but that their views are not to be discarded for lack of *madhhab* status.

165. Al-Shawkānī, *Al-Badr al-Ṭāliʿ*, 1:79.

166. Al-Shawkānī, *Al-Badr al-Ṭāliʿ*, 1:65. Al-Shawkānī provides a similar assessment in his biography of Jalāl al-Dīn al-Suyūṭī (d. 911) (*Al-Badr al-Ṭāliʿ*, 1:334), who was criticized for his claim of *ijtihād*. Al-Shawkānī maintains that, as in the case of Ibn Taymiyya and as one deduces from going over the historical record, if a scholar suffers because of his scholarship during his lifetime, eventually his reputation spreads after he dies and God elevates his status and privileges him with a kind of praise and esteem that none of his contemporaries enjoys.

167. Al-Shawkānī, *Al-Badr al-Ṭāliʿ*, 1:6.

168. Al-Shawkānī, *Al-Badr al-Ṭāliʿ*, 1:21. Al-Shawkānī refers to another outrage by the Mālikīs, who were behind the execution of the eighth-century belle-lettrist and *wazīr* Lisān al-Dīn Ibn al-Khaṭīb as one of many plunders committed by Mālikī judges, through which they shed the blood of Muslims without any justification (*Al-Badr al-Ṭāliʿ*, 2:191–94).

169. Al-Shawkānī, *Al-Badr al-Ṭāliʿ*, 1:115–16.

170. Al-Shawkānī, *Al-Badr al-Ṭāliʿ*, 1:71.

171. Al-Shawkānī, *Al-Badr al-Ṭāliʿ*, 2:143–44.

172. Al-Shawkānī, *Al-Badr al-Ṭāliʿ*, 2:143–46.

173. Al-Shawkānī, *Al-Badr al-Ṭāliʿ*, 2:143–44.

174. See, for example, al-Shawkānī, *Al-Badr al-Ṭāliʿ*, 1:395.

175. Al-Shawkānī, *Al-Badr al-Ṭāliʿ*, 1:485. According to al-Shawkānī, "had this book [*Al-ʿAwāṣim*] reached non-Yemeni lands, it would have been a pride of Yemen and its people. They (the Yemenis), however, were deprived of that (honor) because of their inherent habit of belittling their own virtues and obscuring the excellence of their own notables." *Al-Badr al-Ṭāliʿ*, 2:91.

176. Al-Shawkānī, *Al-Badr al-Ṭāliʿ*, 2:83. This section of Ibn al-Wazīr's biography is essentially a summary of al-Shawkānī's separate work on the subject, *Al-Qawl al-Mufīd fī Adillat al-Ijtihād wal-Taqlīd*.

177. Al-Shawkānī, *Al-Badr al-Ṭāliʿ*, 2:91.

178. Al-Shawkānī, *Al-Badr al-Ṭāliʿ*, 2:92.

179. Al-Shawkānī, *Al-Badr al-Ṭāliʿ*, 1:191–95.

180. Al-Ḥasan b. Aḥmad al-Jalāl, *Ḍawʾal-Nahār al-Mushriq ʿalā Ṣafaḥāt al-Azhār*, 4 vols. (Sanaa: Majlis al-Qaḍāʾ al-Aʿlā, n.d.).

181. Al-Shawkānī, *Al-Badr al-Ṭāliʿ*, 1:192.

182. Al-Shawkānī, *Al-Badr al-Ṭāliʿ*, 1:193.

183. Al-Shawkānī, *Al-Badr al-Ṭāliʿ*, 1:288–92.

184. Al-Shawkānī, *Al-Badr al-Ṭāliʿ*, 1:289.

185. Al-Shawkānī, *Al-Badr al-Ṭāliʿ*, 1:289–90. Al-Maqbalī, *Al-ʿAlam al-Shāmikh*.

186. Ṣāliḥ b. Mahdī al-Maqbalī, *Kitāb al-Arwāḥ al-Nawāfikh li-Āthār Īthār al-Ābāʾ wal-Mashāʾikh* (Sanaa: Al-Maktaba al-Yamaniyya lil-Nashr wal-Tawzīʿ, 1985).

187. Ṣāliḥ b. Mahdī al-Maqbalī, *Kitāb al-Manār fī al-Mukhtār min Jawāhir al-Baḥr al-Zakhkhār*, 2 vols. (Beirut: Muʾassasat al-Risāla, 1988).

188. Al-Imām al-Mahdī li-Dīn Allāh Aḥmad b. Yaḥyā al-Murtaḍā, *Kitāb al-Baḥr al-Zakhkhār al-Jāmiʿ li-Madhāhib ʿUlamāʾ al-Amṣār*, corrected by al-Qāḍī ʿAbd Allāh b. ʿAbd al-Karīm al-Jarāfī al-Yamanī al-Ṣanʿānī, A M. Ṣiddīq, and A. H, S. ʿAṭiyya, 5 vols. (Cairo: Maktabat al-Khānjī, 1947).

189. Al-Shawkānī, *Al-Badr al-Ṭāliʿ*, 1:288–90.

190. Al-Shawkānī, *Al-Badr al-Ṭāliʿ*, 1:288–89.

191. Al-Shawkānī, *Al-Badr al-Ṭāliʿ*, 1:288.

192. Al-Shawkānī, *Al-Badr al-Ṭāliʿ*, 1:291.

193. This was a famous glossary on al-Mahdī's *Al-Baḥr al-Zakhkhār*, which is itself a commentary by al-Mahdī on his own *Al-Azhār.*

194. Al-Shawkānī, *Al-Badr al-Ṭāliʿ*, 1:289.

195. Al-Shawkānī, *Al-Badr al-Ṭāliʿ*, 2:133–39.

196. Al-Shawkānī, *Al-Badr al-Ṭāliʿ*, 2:133.

197. Al-Shawkānī, *Al-Badr al-Ṭāliʿ*, 2:133–34.

198. Al-Shawkānī, *Al-Badr al-Ṭāliʿ*, 2:134.

199. Irrespective of the accuracy of this account, what is especially relevant here is in the way al-Shawkānī reports this event and makes sense of it.

200. Al-Shawkānī, *Al-Badr al-Ṭāliʿ*, 2:134.

201. Al-Shawkānī, *Al-Badr al-Ṭāliʿ*, 2:134.

202. Al-Shawkānī, *Al-Badr al-Ṭāliʿ*, 2:137.

203. Al-Shawkānī, *Al-Badr al-Ṭāliʿ*, 2:138.

204. For example, in *Al-Badr al-Ṭāliʿ*, 2:214–25, al-Shawkānī gives information about his education, teachers, licenses, students, writings, and so on.

205. Al-Shawkānī, *Al-Badr al-Ṭāliʿ*, 1:82–85.

206. Al-Shawkānī, *Al-Badr al-Ṭāliʿ*, 1:232–36.

207. Al-Shawkānī, *Al-Badr al-Ṭāliʿ*, 1:233.

208. Al-Shawkānī, *Al-Badr al-Ṭāliʿ*, 1:379–80.

209. Al-Shawkānī, *Al-Badr al-Ṭāliʿ*, 1:236.

210. ʿAbd al-Raḥmān al-Jabartī, *ʿAbd al-Raḥmān al-Jabartī's History of Egypt: ʿAjāʾib al-āthār fī ʾl-tarājim wa-ʾl-akhbār*, ed. Thomas Philipp and Moshe Perlmann (Stuttgart: Franz Steiner, 1994). On al-Jabartī's historical writings, see Robert L. Tignor, introduction to ʿAbd al-Raḥmān al-Jabarti, *Napoleon in Egypt: Al-Jabarti's Chronicle of the French Occupation* (Princeton, N.J.: M. Weiner, 1993); David Ayalon, "The Historian al-Jabarti and His Background," *Bulletin of the School of Oriental and African Studies* 23, no. 2 (1960): 217–49; Ismail K. Poonawala, "The Evolution of al-Gabartī's Historical Thinking as Reflected in the Muẓhir and the ʿAgāʾib," *Arabica* 15, no. 3 (1968): 270–88; and Thomas Philipp and Guido Schwald, *ʿAbd al-Raḥmān al-Jabartī's History of Egypt* (Stuttgart: Franz Steiner, 1994).

On Classical Islamic historiography, see H. A. R. Gibb, "Tarikh," in H. A. R. Gibb, *Studies on the Civilization of Islam*, ed. Stanford Shaw and William Polk (Boston: Beacon, 1968), 108–37; Albrecht Noth, with Lawrence Conrad, *The Early Arabic Historical Tradition: A Source Critical Study*, trans. Michael Bonner (Princeton, N.J.: Darwin, 1994); Tarif Khalidi, *Arabic Historical Thought in the Classical Period* (New York: Cambridge University Press, 1994); Franz Rosenthal, *A History of Muslim Historiography* (Leiden, the Netherlands: E. J. Brill, 1968); and Chase F. Robinson, *Islamic Historiography* (Cambridge: Cambridge University Press, 2003). See also the excellent study by Tayeb el-Hibri, *Reinterpreting Islamic Historiography* (Cambridge: Cambridge University Press, 1999). On biographical literature, see Hamilton Gibb, "Islamic Biographical Literature," in *Historians of the Middle East*, ed. B. Lewis and P. M. Holt (Oxford: Oxford University Press, 1962); Bushra Hamad, "History and Biography," *Arabica* 45 (1998): 215–32; M. J. L. Young, "Arabic Biographical Writing," in *Religion, Learning and Science in the ʿAbbasid Period* (Cambridge: Cambridge University Press, 1990), 170; and Michael Cooperson, *Classical Arabic Biography: The Heirs of the Prophets in the Age of al-Maʾmūn* (Cambridge: Cambridge University Press, 2000).

On Arabic historical writings in the eighteenth and nineteenth centuries, see Daniel Crecelius and ʿAbd al-Wahhab Bakr, trans., *Al-Damurdashi's Chronicle of Egypt, 1688–1755: Al-Durra al-Musana fi Akhbar al-Kinana* (Leiden, the Netherlands: E. J. Brill, 1991); Daniel Crecelius, ed., *Eighteenth Century Egypt: The Arabic Manuscript Sources* (Claremont, Calif.: Regina, 1990); Gamal el-Din el-Shayyal, *Historiography in Egypt in the Nineteenth Century*, ed. B. Lewis and P. M. Holt (Oxford: Oxford University Press, 1962), 403–21; and Jack Crabbs, *The Writing of History in Nineteenth-Century Egypt* (Cairo: American University of Cairo Press, 1994). See also the excellent article by Dana Sajdi, "'A Room of His Own': The 'History' of the Barber of Damascus (fl. 1762)," *MIT Electronic Journal of Middle East Studies* 3 (2003): 19–35.

211. Walī Allāh, *Ḥujjat*, 1:148–49; Walī Allāh, *Ḥujjat Allāh al-Bāligha*, 2 vols. (Cairo: Dār al-Turāth, 1936), 1:148–49 (the Cairo edition is cited as *Ḥujjat*; occasionally, the Beirut edition is used, in which case it is cited as *Ḥujjat Allāh*). See Shāh Walī Allāh al-Dehlawī, *Ḥujjat Allāh al-Bāligha*, ed. M. S. Hāshim, 2 vols. (Beirut: Dār al-Kutub al-ʿIlmiyya, 1995); and Shāh Walī Allāh, *Al-Inṣāf fī Bayān Sabab al-Ikhtilāf* (Lahore: Maṭbaʿat al-Maktaba al-ʿIlmiyya, 1971), 23.

212. Walī Allāh, *Ḥujjat*, 1:151–52; and *Inṣāf*, 33.

213. Walī Allāh, *Ḥujjat*, 1:159; and *Inṣāf*, 64.

214. Walī Allāh, *Ḥujjat*, 1, 120, 152–53; and *Inṣāf*, 57.

215. Walī Allāh, *Ḥujjat*, 1:153; and *Inṣāf*, 58.

216. Walī Allāh, *Ḥujjat*, 1:141–43; Shāh Walī Allāh, *ʿIqd al-Jīd fī Aḥkām al-Ijtihād wal-Taqlīd* (Cairo: Al-Maṭbaʿa al-Salafiyya, 1385 AH), 8–9; and *Inṣāf*, 6–11.

217. Walī Allāh, *ʿIqd*, 6; and *Inṣāf*, 6.

218. Walī Allāh, *ʿIqd*, 6–7.

219. Walī Allāh, *ʿIqd*, 11.

220. Walī Allāh, *Ḥujjat*, 1:154; and *ʿIqd*, 14–15.

221. Walī Allāh, *ʿIqd*, 13.

222. Al-Shawkānī, *Al-Badr al-Ṭāliʿ*, 1:478–85.

223. For biographies of teachers and students of al-Shawkānī, see al-Shijnī, *Kitāb al-Tiqṣār*, 249.

224. Al-Shawkānī, *Al-Badr al-Ṭāliʿ*, 2:224.

225. On the books he studied and transmitted, and their chains of transmission, see al-Shawkānī, *Itḥāf al-Akābir*. On al-Shawkānī's writings see, for example, ʿAbd Allāh al-Ḥibshī, "Thabat bi Muʾallafāt al-ʿAllāma Muḥammad b. ʿAlī al-Shawkānī," *Dirāsāt Yamāniyya* 3 (1979): 65–86. See also Hilāl's introduction to *Wilāyat Allāh*, where he lists 164 of al-Shawkānī's books (34–55).

226. See al-Shijnī, *Kitāb al-Tiqṣār*, 423–24; and al-Shawkānī, *Al-Badr al-Ṭāliʿ*, 1:464. Also see Haykel, *Revival and Reform*, 18–19.

227. Al-Shawkānī, *Al-Badr al-Ṭāliʿ*, 1:464. Al-Shijnī also says that al-Shawkānī was not personally known either to scholars or to rulers because he avoided contact with all who are affiliated with the state (*arbāb al-dawla*). Al-Shijnī, *Kitāb al-Tiqṣār*, 423–24.

228. See al-Shijnī, *Kitāb al-Tiqṣār*, for some of the earliest references to al-Shawkānī as the *mujtahid al-ʿaṣr* (the independent jurist of the time) and as *mujaddid al-ʿaṣr* (the reviver of the time); also see al-Ahdal, *Al-Nafas al-Yamanī* (176) where al-Shawkānī is referred to as the "leading scholar of the time in all disciplines" (*Imām al-ʿaṣr fī kāffat al-ʿulūm*). ʿAbd al-Raḥmān b. Sulaymān al-Ahdal (d. 1250/1835), was a Shāfiʿī scholar from Zabīd; he studied with ʿAbd al-Qādir b. Aḥmad al-Kawkabānī (d. 1207/1792), a student of al-Ṣanʿānī and a teacher of al-Shawkānī; al-Shawkānī sent his sons to obtain *ijāzas* from al-Ahdal, and this was the occasion for his writing of *Al-Nafas al-Yamanī fī Ijāzat Banī al-Shawkānī* (Sanaa: Markaz al-Dirāsāt waʾl Abḥāth al-Yamaniyya, 1979).

229. At the time of al-Shawkānī, there already existed a network of like-minded scholars who were predisposed to appreciate al-Shawkānī and his peculiar brand of scholarship.

230. Note that while Shāh Walī Allāh repeatedly referred to himself as the *mujaddid* of his cycle, al-Shawkānī does not make such a claim. To be sure, al-Shawkānī did call himself a *mujtahid* and acted as if he knew of no more knowledgeable living scholar than himself. However, al-Shawkānī was vehemently opposed to imitation and hence could not claim unquestioned legal authority, since such authority was not possible or acceptable in his view.

231. See al-Shijnī, *Kitāb al-Tiqṣār al-Badr al-Ṭāliʿ*, 1:75–76; Shāmī served under al-Manṣūr Ḥusayn (r. 1727–48) and through part of the reign of al-Mahdī ʿAbbās (r. 1748–75).

232. Al-Shawkānī, *Al-Badr al-Ṭāliʿ*, 2:334–38.

233. Al-Shawkānī, *Al-Badr al-Ṭāliʿ*, 2:336.

234. Al-Shawkānī, *Al-Badr al-Ṭāliʿ*, 2:334–35.

235. Al-Shawkānī, *Al-Badr al-Ṭāliʿ*, 2:335.

236. Al-Shawkānī, *Al-Badr al-Ṭāliʿ*, 1:459–67.

237. Al-Shawkānī, *Al-Badr al-Ṭāliʿ*, 1:464.

238. Al-Shawkānī, *Al-Badr al-Ṭāliʿ*, 1:464–45.

239. As, for example, the knowledge of secretaries (*kātib*s) would be.

240. Al-Shawkānī, *Al-Badr al-Ṭāliʿ*, 1:381–82.

241. On the students of al-Shawkānī, see the biography written by his student Muḥammad b. al-Ḥasan al-Shijnī, *Kitāb al-Tiqṣār*.

242. Al-Shawkānī, *Al-Badr al-Ṭāliʿ*, 2:40.

243. The reference here is to the famous political theorist Ibn Jamāʿa, who wrote on the justification of usurped rule.

244. Al-Shawkānī, *Al-Badr al-Ṭāliʿ*, 1:502–3.

245. Al-Shawkānī, *Nayl al-Awṭār*, 1.2:154–55.

246. Al-Shawkānī, *Nayl al-Awṭār*, 4.8:280.

247. Al-Shawkānī, *Al-Darārī al-Muḍiyya*, 411–17.

248. Al-Shawkānī, *Adab al-Ṭalab*, 52–55.

249. Al-Shawkānī, *Adab al-Ṭalab*, 91.

250. See, for example, ʿAbd Allāh al-ʿAmrī, *Al-Imām al-Shawkānī Rāʾid ʿAṣrih* (Damascus: Dār al-Fikr, 1990), 434.

251. Al-Shawkānī, *Al-Qawl al-Mufīd*, 131–33.

252. Al-Shawkānī, *Adab al-Ṭalab*, 129–32.

253. Al-Shawkānī, *Adab al-Ṭalab*, 130.

254. Al-Shawkānī, *Adab al-Ṭalab*, 131.

255. Al Shawkānī, *Adab al-Ṭalab*, 132.

256. Al-Shawkānī, *Adab al-Ṭalab*, 132–33.

257. Al-Shawkānī, *Adab al-Ṭalab*, 134.

258. Note that al-Shawkānī nonetheless advocates the right, even duty, of individuals to practice *ijtihād*. This confidence in the commoners' as well as the elites' ability to choose independently rules out an explanation of al-Shawkānī's views in terms of mere class bias and suggests instead a taxonomy informed by cultural imperatives.

259. Al-Shawkānī, *Al-Badr al-Ṭāliʿ*, 2:135–36.

260. Al-Shawkānī, *Nayl al-Awṭār*, 1.1:194–96.

261. A related and equally charged point of contention is the Shiʿi practice of wiping of the feet in ablution instead of washing them as the Sunnis do. Note that despite his remarkable openness, Walī Allāh considers this issue grave enough to warrant excluding a person from the straight path (*jādda qawīma*). Shāh Walī Allāh, *Al-Tafhīmāt al-Ilāhīya*, ed. G. M. Qāsimī,

2 vols. (Hyderabad: Ākādimyyat al-Shāh Walī Allāh al-Dihlawī, 1967), 1:153–56. Other such grave issues, according to Walī Allāh, include the legalization of temporary marriage and the legalization of intoxicating drinks.

262. Note that al-Shawkānī, like al-Ṣanʿānī before him, does not accept consensus as one of the sources of the law. See chapter 5 and the conclusion for more details.

263. Al-Shawkānī, *Nayl al-Awṭār*, 1.2:182.

264. Al-Shawkānī, *Nayl al-Awṭār*, 1.2:193.

265. Al-Shawkānī, *Nayl al-Awṭār*, 2.3:174.

266. Al-Shawkānī, *Nayl al-Awṭār*, 2.3:175.

267. Al-Shawkānī, *Nayl al-Awṭār*, 3.6:141.

268. Al-Shawkānī, *Nayl al-Awṭār*, 3.6:145–46.

269. Al-Shawkānī, *Nayl al-Awṭār*, 3.6:239.

270. Of course, the conflicts between Ibn Taymiyya and Ibn al-Qayyim, on the one hand, and the establishment religion, on the other, were complex and are not reducible to conflict on just this one question. Nonetheless, the symbolic significance of this debate continues to have echoes even today, as some Muslims go as far as accusing others of unbelief depending on their view on this matter.

271. Al-Shawkānī, *Nayl al-Awṭār*, 3.6:246.

272. For more on the same subject, see also al-Shawkānī, *Al-Darārī al-Muḍiyya*, 271–73.

273. Al-Shawkānī, *Nayl al-Awṭār*, 1.2:302.

274. Al-Shawkānī, "Al-ʿIqd al-Thamīn fī Ithbāt Waṣiyyat Amīr al-Muʾminīn," in *Majmūʿ al-Rasāʾil al-Yamaniyya* (Cairo: Dār al-Ṭibāʿa al-Munīriyya, 1348 AH).

275. Al-Shawkānī, "Al-ʿIqd al-Thamīn," 4.

276. Al-Shawkānī, "Al-ʿIqd al-Thamīn," 7.

277. Al-Shawkānī, "Al-ʿIqd al-Thamīn," 4.

278. Al-Shawkānī, "Al-ʿIqd al-Thamīn," 4–5.

279. Al-Shawkānī, "Al-ʿIqd al-Thamīn," 9.

280. Al-Shawkānī, "Al-ʿIqd al-Thamīn," 10.

281. Al-Ṣanʿānī, *Irshād al-Nuqqād*, 38–39.

282. Al-Ṣanʿānī, *Irshād al-Nuqqād*, 39–40.

283. Al-Shawkānī, *Al-Durr al-Naḍīd*, 95–97.

284. Al-Shawkānī, *Al-Durr al-Naḍīd*, 96–97.

285. Al-Shawkānī, *Al-Qawl al-Mufīd*, 144.

286. Al-Shawkānī, *Al-Qawl al-Mufīd*, 145–46.

287. Al-Shawkānī, *Al-Badr al-Ṭāliʿ*, 1:292.

288. See, for example, Mawlavi M. Hidayat Husain, "The Persian Autobiography of Shāh Walīullah Ibn ʿAbd al-Raḥīm al-Dihlavī: Its English Translation and a List of His Works," *Journal and Proceedings of the Asiatic Society of Bengal*, n.s., 8 (1912): 161–75; and al-Shawkānī, *Al-Badr al-Ṭāliʿ*, 1:292–93.

289. Thus, none of these scholars practiced *taqiyya* (dissimulation) despite the pressures they were exposed to. For contrast with an elaborate performance of *taqiyya* in the course of intellectual exchange in the earlier case of the Twelver Imami scholar Bahāʾ al-Dīn al-ʿĀmilī, see Devin J. Stewart, "Taqiyyah as Performance: The Travels of Bahāʾ al-Dīn al-ʿĀmilī in the Ottoman Empire (991–93/1583–85)," in Devin J. Stewart, Baber Johansen, and Amy Singer, *Law and Society in Islam* (Princeton, N.J.: Markus Wiener, 1996).

290. A parallel drive to forge new intellectual identities, although not as radical in its rejection of *madhhabs*, is Walī Allāh's attempt to generate a body of knowledge that cuts across

madhhab lines. As we have seen, Walī Allāh maintains that he was a Shāfiʿī for the purposes of *ijtihād*, a Ḥanafī by legal affiliation, and recognizes the *Muwaṭṭa'* of Mālik as the most authoritative book after the Qur'ān (see chapter 5 for more on this point). In an *ijāza* he wrote for one of his students, Walī Allāh refers to himself as a "Ḥanafī in practice, and a Shāfiʿī in teaching." Qtd. in ʿUbayd Allāh al-Sindī, *Al-Tamhīd li-Taʿrīf A'immat al-Tajdīd* (Haidarabad: Maṭbaʿat Jamiʿat al-Sind, 1976), 442. Also Walī Allāh repeatedly refers to visionary dreams in which it was revealed to him that the purpose of his efforts should be the unification of Muslims and their intellectual traditions. For example, Shāh Walī Allāh, *Fuyūḍ al-Ḥaramayn* (Delhi: Mālik Maṭbaʿ-e-Aḥmadī, n.d.).

291. Contrast with Messick, who argues that before the legislative codes of the Ottomans, and, 100 years later, the codes of the Yemen Republic, there were the "old manual texts relied upon by Shafiʿis and Zaidis"; Messick, *The Calligraphic State*, 53.

292. Messick, *The Calligraphic State*, 53.

293. This is true of not just Shāh Walī Allāh and the Yemeni reformers but also of al-Sanūsī, who wrote on hadith following the example of al-Shawkānī, and also of other works such as those of Muḥammad Ḥayāt al-Sindī, and Ṣāliḥ Ibn Nūḥ al-Fulānī; see chapter 5 for details.

Chapter 5

1. See, for example, Shāh Walī Allāh, *Al-Tafhīmāt al-Ilāhiyya*, 1:54, 169, and 2:145, where Walī Allāh refers to several visions in which it is revealed to him that he is the *mujaddid* of a millennial cycle.

2. See, for example, Muḥammad b. al-Ḥasan b. ʿAlī b. Aḥmad b. Nāṣir al-Shijanī (al-Shijnī) al-Ḥimyarī al-Dhamārī, *Ḥayāt al-Imām al-Shawkānī al-Musammā Kitāb al-Tiqṣār fī Jīd Zamān ʿAllāmat al-Aqālīm wal-Amṣār* (Sanaa: Maktabat al-Jīl al-Jadīd, 1990), where al-Shawkānī is referred to as the *mujaddid* of the time. Also, as we have seen above, such scholars as al-Sanūsī and Ṣiddīq Aḥmad Khān adopted al-Shawkānī's views on *ijtihād* and his hadith methodology; in fact, al-Shawkānī's views occupied center stage in al-Sanūsī's reform agenda. Al-Shawkānī was also recognized as the *mujaddid* of his century by people like ʿAbdu and Riḍā.

3. For classical Sunni formulations of the theory of hadith, see Ibn al-Ṣalāḥ al-Shahrazūrī, *Muqaddimat Ibn al-Ṣalāḥ fī ʿUlūm al-Ḥadīth* (Cairo: Maktabat al-Mutanabbī, 1985); Ibn Ḥajar al-ʿAsqalānī (d. 852/1449), *Al-Nukat ʿalā Kitāb Ibn al-Ṣalāḥ* (Beirut: Dār al-Kutub al-ʿIlmiyya, 1994); see also Ibn Ḥajar al-ʿAsqalānī, *Fatḥ al-Bārī bi-Sharḥ Ṣaḥīḥ al-Bukhārī* (Cairo: Maktabat al-Kulliyya al-Azhariyya, 1978). For overviews of the field of hadith, see J. Robson, "Ḥadīth," in *Encyclopedia of Islam*, 2nd ed., vol. 3 (Leiden, the Netherlands: E. J. Brill, 1971), 23–28; Alfred Guillaume, *The Traditions of Islam: An Introduction to the Study of the Hadith Literature* (Beirut: Khayats, 1966). For useful modern scholarship on various aspects of hadith, see Scott Lucas, *Constructive Critics: Ḥadīth Literature and the Articulation of Sunni Islam* (Leiden, the Netherlands: E. J. Brill, 2004); Joseph Schacht, "A Revaluation of Islamic Traditions," *Journal of the Royal Asiatic Society* 3–4 (1949): 143–54; Harald Motzki, "The Muṣannaf of ʿAbd al-Razzāq al-Ṣanʿānī as a Source of Authentic Aḥādīth of the First Century A.H.," *Journal of Near Eastern Studies* 50, no. 1 (1991): 1–21; Michael Cook, "The Opponents of the Writing of Tradition in Early Islam," *Arabica* 44 (1997): 437–530. For studies of *isnād* criticism, see J. Robson, "Al-Djarḥ wa'l-Taʿdīl," in *Encyclopedia of Islam*, 2nd ed., vol. 3 (Leiden, the Netherlands: E. J. Brill, 1965), 462; G. H. A. Juynboll, "Ridjāl," in *Encyclopedia of Islam*, 2nd ed., vol. 8 (Leiden, the Netherlands: E. J. Brill, 1995), 514–19; and Iftikhar Zaman, "The Science of Rijāl as a Method in the Study of Hadiths," *Journal of Islamic Studies* 5, no. 1 (1994): 1–34. For a useful

study of nineteenth- and twentieth-century debates over the authority of the *Sunna* and how these relate to larger notions of religious authority, see Daniel Brown, *Rethinking Tradition in Modern Islamic Thought* (Cambridge: Cambridge University Press, 1996).

4. Again, this does not mean that Ibn al-Wazīr became a Sunni; perhaps more than al-Shawkānī after him, Ibn al-Wazīr was an independent *mujtahid* firmly rooted in the Zaydi tradition. See chapter 4 for a detailed examination of the question of the Yemeni reformers' intellectual identities.

5. In fact, the emphasis on the use of the canonical compilations of hadith became a staple of Yemeni reform. Thus, for example, al-Shawkānī asserts, "there is no Sunna outside of what one finds in these (books)" (*Adab al-Ṭalab*, 50). Al-Shawkānī further maintains that "except for a few rulings which are clearly stated in the noble Qur'ān, the science of jurisprudence is (mostly) derived from the science of the Sunna. So what can a specialist in a field do with his skills if he is not knowledgeable of the science of hadith, and if he does not master it relying on the books which are compiled in it?" (*Adab al-Ṭalab*, 58).

6. Muḥammad b. Ibrāhīm al-Wazīr, *Al-ʿAwāṣim wa-l-Qawāṣim fī al-Dhabb ʿan Sunnat Abī al-Qāsim*, ed. Shuʿayb al-Arnaʾūṭ, 3 vols. (Amman: Dār al-Bashīr, 1985); Ibn al-Wazīr, *Al-Rawḍ al-Bāsim fī al-Dhabb ʿan Sunnat Abī al-Qāsim*, 2 parts in 1 vol. (Cairo: Al-Maṭbaʿa al-Salafiyya wa Maktabatuha, 1385 AH). See also Muḥammad Ibn Ibrāhīm al-Wazīr (775–840 AH), *Tarjīḥ Asālīb al-Qurʾān ʿalā Asālīb al-Yūnān* (Beirut: Dār al-Kutub al-ʿIlmiyya, 1984).

7. For detailed references, see al-Ṣanʿānī's commentary on Ibn al-Wazīr's work, Muḥammad b. Ismāʿīl al-Amīr al-Ṣanʿānī, *Tawḍīḥ al-Afkār li-Maʿānī Tanqīḥ al-Anẓār*, ed. M. ʿAbd al-Ḥamīd (Cairo: Maktabat al-Khānjī, 1366 AH).

8. See, for example, Ibn al-Wazīr, *Tarjīḥ Asālīb al-Qurʾān ʿalā Asālīb al-Yūnān*.

9. An example of the technical problems he gets into is his comparison of the conventions of the scholars of principles of jurisprudence and those of the scholars of the principles of hadith; see the discussion of Ibn al-Wazīr's views in al-Ṣanʿānī, *Tawḍīḥ al-Afkār*, esp. 1:14.

10. For the bold assertion that none of the traditions transmitted by Muʿāwiya are questionable, see Ibn al-Wazīr, *Al-ʿAwāṣim*, 3:159, and *Al-Rawḍ al-Bāsim*, part 2, 260.

11. To be sure, there are many such technical elaborations and minor corrections by al-Ṣanʿānī; for example, in a discussion of the conditions for declaring a hadith sound by traditionalists, al-Ṣanʿānī maintains that these include a continuous chain of transmission, probity of transmitters, accuracy or precision, and absence of irregularity (or deviation [*shudhūdh*]) and of defect (*ʿilla*); according to the principles of *uṣūl al-fiqh* a hadith that has a nondisqualifying defect (*ʿilla ghayr qādiḥa*) is acceptable as a basis for action; according to *uṣūl al-ḥadīth* scholars, however, such a hadith is not sound; as a general rule, the conventions of the *uṣūl al-fiqh* scholars are more encompassing (al-Ṣanʿānī, *Tawḍīḥ al-Afkār*, 1:14–17). Such elaborations, however, are not the main purpose of this book.

12. Muḥammad Ibn Ibrāhīm al-Wazīr, *Īthār al-Ḥaqq ʿalā al-Khalq fī Radd al-Khilāfāt ilā al-Madhhab al-Ḥaqq min Uṣūl al-Tawḥīd*, ed. A. M. Ḥ. Ṣāliḥ (Sanaa: Al-Dār al-Yamaniyya lil-Nashr wal-Tawzīʿ, 1985).

13. Al-Ṣanʿānī, *Tawḍīḥ al-Afkār*.

14. Al-Ṣanʿānī, *Tawḍīḥ al-Afkār*.

15. Al-Ṣanʿānī, *Tawḍīḥ al-Afkār*, 1:24, 64.

16. Al-Ṣanʿānī, *Tawḍīḥ al-Afkār*, 1:90.

17. Al-Ṣanʿānī, *Tawḍīḥ al-Afkār*, 1:86–90.

18. Al-Ṣanʿānī, *Tawḍīḥ al-Afkār*, 1:89.

19. Al-Ṣanʿānī, *Tawḍīḥ al-Afkār*, 1:112.

20. Note that both Ibn al-Wazīr and al-Shawkānī accept this notion of favorable reception.

Ibn al-Wazīr says, "We have shown that the traditions in al-Bukhārī and Muslim are characterized by a kind of superiority [*tarjīḥ*] that is lacking in other books, namely, the favorable reception by the community. We have also shown that *ahl al-bayt*, as well as the Zaydi imams are among those who favorably received their traditions" (*Al-Rawḍ al-Bāsim*, 81). In a book titled *Tuḥfat al-Dhākirīn bi-ʿUddat al-Ḥiṣn al-Ḥasīn*, in which al-Shawkānī studies the traditions of the collection of prayers called *Al-Ḥiṣn al-Ḥaṣīn*, al-Shawkānī says (7) that he will only list the various transmission chains, and will provide details about the reporters of various versions of each tradition, when such a tradition is not reported in one of the two *ṣaḥīḥ*s; if it is in one of the two books, then, according to al-Shawkānī, he need only state that without going into further details. This is because the traditions of the two compilations are not questionable "due to the consensus by all the Muslim groups regarding the reception of all their traditions with acceptance [*talaqqī al-umma bil-qabūl*]." Al-Shawkānī adds that this acceptance, "according to scholars of the rational as well as the traditional sciences, endows the two works with a rank that is higher than simple soundness." Moreover, they have collected in their books the highest kinds of sound traditions, and later scholars of hadith who dealt with the question of soundness and wrote independent books on it have followed the model of their hadiths as well as their transmitters. Therefore, any hadith that appears in the two sound collections needs no further authentication. See Muḥammad b. ʿAlī al-Shawkānī, *Tuḥfat al-Dhākirīn bi-ʿUddat al-Ḥiṣn al-Ḥasīn min Kalām Sayyid al-Mursalīn* (Beirut: Dār al-Qalam, 1984), 7. Unlike al-Ṣanʿānī, therefore, al-Shawkānī questions neither the two *ṣaḥīḥ*s nor the arguments for their authority. Moreover, he does not object anywhere in his extensive work on hadith to the notion that a hadith that fulfills the conditions of al-Bukhārī and Muslim (*ʿalā sharṭ al-shaykhayn*) is sound. Occasionally, al-Shawkānī maintains that a certain hadith should not be considered fabricated based on the fact that "the men of its chain of transmission are either collectively or individually used as authorities in the two *ṣiḥāḥ*." See, for example, Muḥammad b. ʿAlī al-Shawkānī, *Al-Fawāʾid al-Majmūʿa fī al-Aḥādīth al-Mawḍūʿa* (Cairo: Maktabat al-Sunna al-Nabawiyya, 1960), 129, 149. Elsewhere, in reference to the hadith "innamā al-aʿmāl bil-niyyāt [actions are judged based on intentions]," al-Shawkānī responds to the claim that one of al-Bukhārī's conditions is that a tradition be reported by at least two Companions. This particular tradition, al-Shawkānī contends, is the first tradition reported by al-Bukhārī, and it does not satisfy this said condition. See Muḥammad b. ʿAlī al-Shawkānī, *Fāʾiq al-Kisā fī Jawāb ʿĀlim al-Ḥasā*, ed. M. Āl Ismāʿīl (Amman: Dār ʿAmmār, 1994), 54. Significantly, however, he does not deny the existence of such conditions as al-Ṣanʿānī does. In practice, therefore, al-Shawkānī recognizes the authoritativeness of the conditions of al-Bukhārī and Muslim, but he does not try to abstract the hypothetical conditions of authenticity according to these two compilers.

21. Al-Ṣanʿānī, *Tawḍīḥ al-Afkār*, 1:94.

22. Al-Ṣanʿānī, *Tawḍīḥ al-Afkār*, 1:94–95.

23. See, for example, Muḥammad b. Ismāʿīl al-Amīr al-Ṣanʿānī, *Thamarāt al-Nadhar fī ʿIlm al-Athar*, ed. R. Bin Abi ʿAlfa (Riyadh: Dār al-ʿĀṣima, 1996), esp. 137.

24. Al-Ṣanʿānī, *Tawḍīḥ al-Afkār*, 1:95.

25. Al-Ṣanʿānī, *Tawḍīḥ al-Afkār*, 1:42–45.

26. Al-Ṣanʿānī, *Tawḍīḥ al-Afkār*, 1:95.

27. Al-Ṣanʿānī, *Tawḍīḥ al-Afkār*, 1:42–45

28. Al-Ṣanʿānī, *Tawḍīḥ al-Afkār*, 1:42–45.

29. Al-Ṣanʿānī, *Tawḍīḥ al-Afkār*, 1:42–45.

30. The reference here is to Ibn Ḥajar al-Ḥāfiẓ (d. 852 AH). Note that these critical remarks are mostly in *Tawḍīḥ al-Afkār* and not in a separate work on the theory of hadith.

31. Al-Ṣanʿānī, *Tawḍīḥ al-Afkār*, 1:227–28.

32. Some scholars preferred the *Muwaṭṭa'* of Malik (d. 179/796) to Ibn Māja; see below on the difference between Yemeni scholars and Walī Allāh on this subject.

33. Al-Ṣanʿānī, *Tawḍīḥ al-Afkār*, 1:227–28.

34. Al-Ṣanʿānī, *Tawḍīḥ al-Afkār*, 1:101–3.

35. These are the doctrines of various Muslim sects. *Irjā'* is the creed attributed to the *Murji'a* who withheld judgment on the relative status of the first four caliphs, on the conflict between ʿAlī and his various opponents, and more generally on the status of Muslim sinners. Like many other sectarian identifications, the meaning of the term *murji'a* underwent its own historical evolution. *Naṣb* refers to hostility toward the family of the Prophet, which is manifested in cursing them. *Qadr* is the precursor of the doctrine of the Mu'tazilīs, which posits that Muslims, including rulers, are responsible and accountable for their actions. See, for example, Abū al-Ḥasan al-Ashʿarī, *Kitāb Maqālāt al-Islāmīyīn wa-Ikhtilāf al-Muṣallīn* (Cairo: Maktabat al-Nahḍa al-Miṣriyya, 1969–70). For a modern overview, see Binyamin Abrahamov, *Islamic Theology: Traditionalism and Rationalism* (Edinburgh: Edinburgh University Press, 1998).

36. Al-Ṣanʿānī, *Tawḍīḥ al-Afkār*, 1:103.

37. Al-Ṣanʿānī, *Tawḍīḥ al-Afkār*, 2:199.

38. The classic discussion of this subject in the Yemeni tradition is by Ibn al-Wazīr; see, for example, *Al-Rawḍ al-Bāsim*, 90, on accepting the report of Khārijites according to the opinion of the Zaydi imam al-Manṣūr bi-Allāh; also see *Al-Rawḍ al-Bāsim*, 237–65, on the general argument in favor of accepting the reports of *ahl al-ta'wīl*.

39. Al-Ṣanʿānī, *Tawḍīḥ al-Afkār*, 1:313.

40. Al-Ṣanʿānī, *Tawḍīḥ al-Afkār*, 1:96. See also *Tawḍīḥ al-Afkār*, 1:59, 78, where al-Ṣanʿānī says that accepting a report of a trustworthy person (*ʿadl*) is not *taqlīd* and that, according to principles of jurisprudence, its acceptance is obligatory (*khabar al-ʿadl yajibu qabūluhu*).

41. In his *Al-Qawl al-Mufīd* (123–24), al-Shawkānī responds to advocates of *taqlīd* who claim that imitation is involved every time we accept a report that implies a judgment of sorts. Such, for example, is a woman's report that she has her period, which implies a judgment, on her part, that she is ritually impure; or a muezzin's call to prayer, which implies his judgment that the time for prayer has commenced; or when a blind person accepts the information provided by a person concerning the direction of the *qibla*. Al-Shawkānī responds, however, that these things are of the category of witness testimony, or the information of a personality critic regarding the probity or lack thereof of transmitters of hadith; what is common to all of these cases is that only the report of the reporter is accepted and not his opinion, and therefore this is not imitation. The main difference between following (*ittibāʿ*) and imitating (*taqlīd*) is that in the first case one accepts an opinion because one accepts the tangible textual evidence behind it, whereas no such proof is provided in imitation.

42. Thus, for example, al-Shawkānī argues (*Nayl al-Awṭār*, 4.8:298) that a *ḥākim* (meaning either a judge or a ruler in executive office) should rule not on the basis of his knowledge but on the basis of external evidence (*bayyina khārijiyya*). See also *Al-Sayl al-Jarrār*, 4:213, where al-Shawkānī maintains that a *qāḍī* is commanded to pass God's rules, which are reached through confession, testimony, or oath and cannot be based on what is found in the judge's registers. Elsewhere (*Al-Sayl al-Jarrār*, 4:290–91), al-Shawkānī says that a judge can pass a ruling based on his knowledge, but it would seem that by knowledge he means the same sort of witness information that is allowed in court and not a judgment based on the judge's opinion.

43. Al-Ṣanʿānī, *Tawḍīḥ al-Afkār*, 1:24.

44. Al-Ṣanʿānī, *Tawḍīḥ al-Afkār*, 1:25, 310, 314. Also see *Tawḍīḥ al-Afkār*, 1:62–63, where al-Ṣanʿānī maintains that judging a hadith to be sound is no more than the reporting or testimony by a trustworthy person (*ikhbār min al-ʿadl*) that this hadith satisfies the formal requirements of soundness; this, and not the definite affirmation of the absolute soundness of the tradition, is the basis for acting upon the hadith.

45. Al-Ṣanʿānī, *Tawḍīḥ al-Afkār*, 2:263–64.

46. Muḥammad Ibn Ismāʿīl al-Amīr al-Ṣanʿānī, *Al-ʿUdda ʿalā Iḥkām al-Aḥkām Sharḥ ʿUmdat al-Aḥkām lil-ʿAllāma Ibn Daqīq al-ʿĪd*, ed. A. al-Hindī, 4 vols. (Cairo: Al-Maṭbaʿa al-Salafiyya, 1379 AH), 2:384.

47. Muḥammad b. Ismāʿīl al-Amīr al-Ṣanʿānī, *Subul al-Salām Sharḥ Bulūgh al-Marām min Jamʿ Adillat al-Aḥkām*, ed. Fawwāz Aḥmad Zamrlī and Ibrāhīm Muḥammad al-Jamal, 5 vols. (Beirut: Dār al-Kitāb al-ʿArabī, 1990), 4:227–30.

48. Al-Ṣanʿānī, *Subul al-Salām*, 4:229.

49. Al-Ṣanʿānī makes a similar argument in reference to the imams of the four Sunni schools of law; he maintains that "all expressions are [made up of] utterances that connote their meanings, so would he [the imitator] replace the utterances and meanings of his imam with those of the lawgiver, and would he derive rulings from the latter rather than deriving them from the opinion [*madhhad*] of his imam in matters where there is no text? . . . It is known with certainty that the words of God and the words of the Prophet are closer to understanding, and closer to hitting the target [that is, conveying the intended meaning]. . . . The reasoning with which the Companions understood the Divine word and the Prophetic discourse are similar to ours, and their discernment is like ours. If there were a discrepancy in understanding [between the Companions and later generations of Muslims], then such discrepancy would render the understanding of Divine utterances and Prophetic traditions impossible, in which case we would not be legally responsible, nor would we have been commanded, by way of either *ijtihād* or *taqlīd*." Al-Ṣanʿānī, *Irshād al-Nuqqād*, qtd. in Ibrāhīm Hilāl, *Al-Wijha al-Salafiyya ʿind al-Amīr al-Ṣanʿānī* (Cairo: Dār al-Nahḍa al-ʿArabiyya, 1984), 37–38.

50. For al-Shawkānī's definition of Companions, see Muḥammad b. ʿAlī al-Shawkānī, *Irshād al-Fuḥūl ilā Taḥqīq al-Ḥaqq min ʿIlm al-Uṣūl* (n.p.: Dār al-Fikr, n.d.), 70.

51. Al-Shawkānī, *Nayl al-Awṭār*, 4.8:325.

52. Al-Shawkānī, *Nayl al-Awṭār*, 4.8:326.

53. For other differentiations within the ranks of the Companions, despite their shared privilege of Companionship, see, for example, Muḥammad b. ʿAlī al-Shawkānī, *Wabl al-Ghamām ʿalā Shifāʾ al-Uwām*, ed. M. Ḥallāq, 2 vols. (Cairo: Maktabat Ibn Taymiyya, 1995), 1:26, 2:395, 4:495.

54. Al-Shawkānī, *Nayl al-Awṭār*, 4.8:326.

55. Al-Shawkānī, *Nayl al-Awṭār*, 4.8:327. Al-Ṣanʿānī makes a similar argument in his *Irshād al-Nuqqād ilā Taysīr al-Ijtihād* (30) with regard to the status of the followers of the imams of the four schools of law. In response to the claim that the followers of these imams are not capable of the kind of *ijtihād* the masters practiced, al-Ṣanʿānī maintains that "it is no secret to anyone who has intelligence that this is a baseless exaggeration and sheer skepticism the noise of which would not intimidate sharp, critical [minds]. It is as if, upon seeing the great numbers of followers of the imams, and the awe with which distinguished moderners have held them due to the knowledge and piety granted to them by God, skeptics thought that the early imams were not created of clay. Had these [skeptics] considered things with fairness, and had they reflected over the conditions of the early and modern scholars, they would have known with certainty that among the followers of the early imams there appeared some whose arms' reach in knowledge is longer, and who are more versed in the sciences of *ijtihād*

[than the early imams]. From among the multitude of people, God has endowed these [latter scholars] with sincere resolution and virtuous intention, in order to preserve the sciences of *ijtihād*. Thus, they facilitated them [the sciences] in every way and made them accessible to moderners."

56. Al-Shawkānī, *Al-Qawl al-Mufīd*, 113.

57. Al-Shawkānī, *Al-Qawl al-Mufīd*, 113–16.

58. Al-Shawkānī, *Al-Qawl al-Mufīd*, 117–18.

59. Al-Shawkānī, *Al-Qawl al-Mufīd*, 120.

60. Muḥammad b. ʿAlī al-Shawkānī, *Al-Badr al-Ṭāliʿ bi Maḥāsin man baʿd al-Qarn al-Sābiʿ*, 2 vols. (Beirut: Dār al-Maʿrifa, n.d.), 2:89. Also see al-Shawkānī, *Irshād al-Fuḥūl*, 267–70; and *Adab al-Ṭalab*.

61. Al-Shawkānī, *Al-Qawl al-Mufīd*, 121.

62. Ibn al-Wazīr, *Al-Rawḍ al-Bāsim*, esp. 237–65; and *Al-ʾAwāṣim*, 3:159.

63. Ibn al-Wazīr, *Al-Rawḍ al-Bāsim*, 260–66. Muʿāwiya, the governor of Syria, refused to recognize the legitimacy of the fourth caliph, ʿAlī, under the pretext that the legitimate caliph ought to bring the murderers of the third caliph, ʿUthmān, to justice. Arguably, the inconclusive war between Muʿāwiya's and ʿAlī's camps thwarted the latter's ability to establish his rule. Understandably, therefore, Muʿāwiya is vilified in the Shiʿi tradition.

64. Ibn al-Wazīr, *Al-Rawḍ al-Bāsim*, 265–66.

65. Al-Shawkānī, *Nayl al-Awṭār*, 1.1:194–96.

66. See, for example, al-Shawkānī, *Irshād al-Fuḥūl*, 70; *Adb al-Ṭalab*, 91; *Wabl al-Ghamām*, 1:58; and *Al-Sayl al-Jarrār*, 2:126.

67. See, for example, al-Shawkānī's reference to the Khārijīs as the "dogs of hell [*kilāb al-nār*]"; *Al-Sayl al-Jarrār*, 1:148, 2:126.

68. Al-Shawkānī, *Nayl al-Awṭār*, 4.7:178.

69. Al-Shawkānī, *Nayl al-Awṭār*, 4.7:50–51.

70. For references to such tribulations, see al-Shawkānī, *Al-Badr al-Ṭāliʿ*, 1:83, 233.

71. Al-Ṣanʿānī, *Tawḍīḥ al-Afkār*, 1:269–71.

72. Al-Ṣanʿānī, *Tawḍīḥ al-Afkār*, 1:271–72.

73. See, for example, al-Ṣanʿānī, *Tawḍīḥ al-Afkār*, 1:310–14.

74. Al-Ṣanʿānī, *Tawḍīḥ al-Afkār*, 2:149–50.

75. Al-Ṣanʿānī, *Tawḍīḥ al-Afkār*, 2:150.

76. See also the reference by al-Shawkānī in *Al-Badr al-Ṭāliʿ* (1:83) to a treatise on *Ḥadīth al-Firqa al-Nājiya* and the trouble he encountered because of it.

77. Muḥammad Ibn Ismāʿīl al-Amīr al-Ṣanʿānī, *Ḥadīth Iftirāq al-Umma ilā Nayyif wa Sabʿīn Firqa*, ed. S. Saʿdān (Riyadh: Dār al-ʿĀṣima, 1415 AH), 53.

78. Al-Ṣanʿānī, *Ḥadīth Iftirāq al-Umma*, 56.

79. Al-Ṣanʿānī, *Ḥadīth Iftirāq al-Umma*, 64.

80. Al-Ṣanʿānī, *Ḥadīth Iftirāq al-Umma*, 66.

81. Al-Ṣanʿānī, *Ḥadīth Iftirāq al-Umma*, 68–69.

82. Al-Ṣanʿānī, *Ḥadīth Iftirāq al-Umma*, 72.

83. Al-Ṣanʿānī, *Ḥadīth Iftirāq al-Umma*, 72.

84. Al-Ṣanʿānī, *Ḥadīth Iftirāq al-Umma*, 73–74.

85. Al-Ṣanʿānī, *Ḥadīth Iftirāq al-Umma*, 75.

86. Al-Ṣanʿānī, *Ḥadīth Iftirāq al-Umma*, 77–94.

87. Al-Ṣanʿānī, *Ḥadīth Iftirāq al-Umma*, 78.

88. Al-Ṣanʿānī, *Ḥadīth Iftirāq al-Umma*, 79. Contrast with Ibn ʿAbd al-Wahhāb's attempts to define *tawḥīd*, which invariably degenerate into negative definitions of its opposite, *shirk*.

89. Al-Ṣanʿānī, *Ḥadīth Iftirāq al-Umma*, 91, 93.

90. Much of Islamic reform thought, from the latter half of the nineteenth century till today, and in all varieties, provides a striking contrast to the eighteenth century. Reform in this later period does not translate into a systematic reworking of tradition; it is eclectic and relies on posturing as opposed to substantive scrutiny. For example, the reformers of the late nineteenth and early twentieth century regularly invoked *ijtihād* as the most fundamental need for reviving Islamic thinking, but they did not compose books on the actual theory of *ijtihād*. In contrast, most eighteenth-century thinkers wrote separate treatises on *ijtihād*. For a comparative study of eighteenth- and early twentieth-century reform, see Ahmad Dallal, "Appropriating the Past: Twentieth-Century Reconstruction of Pre-modern Islamic Thought," *Islamic Law and Society* 7, no. 1 (2000): 325–58.

91. Witness, for example, the teaching in al-Azhar and elsewhere in Islamic universities of such Yemeni works as al-Ṣanʿānī's *Subul al-Salām*, and al-Shawkānī's *Irshaād al-Fuḥūl*.

92. See ʿAbd al-Ḥayy al-Ḥasanī, *Al-Thaqāfa al-Islāmiyya fī al-Hind: Maʿārif al-ʿAwārif fī Anwāʿ al-ʿUlūm wal-Maʿārif* (Damascus: Maṭbūʿāt al-Majmaʿ al-ʿIlmī al-ʿArabī, 1958), 12, 135–36.

93. Al-Ḥasanī, *Al-Thaqāfa al-Islāmiyya*, 136.

94. These are the collections of al-Bukhārī, Muslim, Abū Dāwūd, Tirmidhī, Nasāʾī, and Ibn Māja.

95. Al-Ḥasanī, *Al-Thaqāfa al-Islāmiyya*, 12, 14–15, 135–36. ʿUbayd Allāh al-Sindī, *Al-Tamhīd li-Taʿrīf Aʾimmat al-Tajdīd* (Hyderabad: Maṭbaʿat Jāmiʿat al-Sind, 1976).

96. Al-Ḥasanī, *Al-Thaqāfa al-Islāmiyya*, 15, 136; al-Ḥasanī names several of these scholars of hadith before ʿAbd al-Ḥaqq al-Dihlawī, 137.

97. Al-Ḥasanī, *Al-Thaqāfa al-Islāmiyya*, 137.

98. Al-Sindī, *Al-Tamhīd*, 400–401.

99. Al-Sindī, *Al-Tamhīd*, 400.

100. ʿAbd al-Ḥayy al-Luknawī quotes Rashīd Riḍā's introduction of *Miftāḥ Kunūz al-Sunna*, where Riḍā says that, despite its late start, India after the tenth century, and up to his own time, became the exclusive guardian for the discipline of hadith, to the point that were it not for the Indian hadith scholar, the art may have vanished. ʿAbd al-Ḥayy Bin Fakhr al-Dīn al-Ḥasanī al-Luknawī, *Nuzhat al-Khawāṭir wa Bahjat al-Masāmiʿ wal-Nawāẓir* (Hyderabad Deccan: Maṭbaʿat Dāʾirat al-Maʿārif al-ʿUthmāniyya, 1947–51), vi–viii. Also for names of Indian hadith scholars from the time of ʿAbd al-Ḥaqq, through Aḥmad Sirhindī and until the time of Shāh Walī Allāh, see al-Ḥasanī, *Al-Thaqāfa al-Islāmiyya*, 138–39.

101. Al-Sindī, *Al-Tamhīd*, 402. Also see ʿAbd al-Ḥaqq al-Dihlawī, *Muqaddima fī Uṣūl al-Ḥadīth*, ed. Salmān al-Ḥusaynī al-Nadawī (Lucknow: Dār al-ʿUlūm li-Nadwat al-ʿUlamāʾ, 1984). ʿAbd al-Ḥaqq states that the sound traditions are not located exclusively in al-Bukhārī and Muslim, and that these two sources do not account for all sound traditions (93, 110); he also gives a list of various other books where one can find sound and good hadiths such as, for example, the *Mustadrak* of Al-Ḥākim al-Nisābūrī and the *Ṣaḥīḥ* of Ibn Ḥibbān (94–103); he then concludes that "all of these books are specialized in *ṣaḥīḥ* traditions, and they were only criticized out of partisanship and lack of fairness" (103).

102. Al-Sindī, *Al-Tamhīd*, 402–3.

103. Al-Sindī, *Al-Tamhīd*, 404.

104. Al-Sindī, *Al-Tamhīd*, 414.

105. Shāh Walī Allāh, *Al-Musawwā Sharḥ al-Muwaṭṭaʾ*, ed. ʿAbd al-Wahhāb al-Dihlawī, 2 vols. (Beirut: Dār al-Kutub al-ʿIlmiyya, 1983). The Persian version is *Al-Muṣaffā Sharḥ al-Muwaṭṭaʾ*.

106. The Persian is essentially a translation of the Arabic, with an expanded theoretical

introduction; an Arabic translation of the Persian introduction is included in the printed edition of *Al-Musawwā*, 1:17–53.

107. Walī Allāh, *Al-Musawwā*, 1:17.

108. See, for example, the editors introduction to Walī Allāh, *Al-Musawwā*, 1:9.

109. Walī Allāh, *Al-Musawwā*, 1:17.

110. Walī Allāh, *Al-Musawwā*, 1:18.

111. Walī Allāh, *Al-Musawwā*, 1:18, 23.

112. Walī Allāh, *Al-Musawwā*, 1:18.

113. Walī Allāh, *Al-Musawwā*, 1:22–23.

114. Walī Allāh, *Al-Musawwā*, 1:18.

115. Walī Allāh, *Al-Musawwā*, 1:23.

116. Walī Allāh, *Al-Musawwā*, 1:23, 45.

117. Walī Allāh, *Al-Musawwā*, 1:45.

118. Walī Allāh, *Al-Musawwā*, 1:23. See also Walī Allāh, *Ḥujjat Allāh*, 1:249, where Walī Allāh repeats al-Shāfiʿī's assertion that the soundest book after the book of God is the *Muwaṭṭaʾ* of Mālik, and adds that experts on hadith agree that all the traditions of the *Muwaṭṭaʾ* are sound according to the opinions of Mālik and those who concurred with him. Other hadith scholars who do not agree with this opinion do concede that the interrupted hadiths (*mursal* or *munqaṭiʿ*) of the *Muwaṭṭaʾ* are always corroborated through other ones with continuous chains of transmission going all the way to the Prophet. Walī Allāh thus argues that the *Muwaṭṭaʾ* is sound even if some of its traditions seem to be interrupted.

119. Walī Allāh, *Al-Musawwā*, 1:37.

120. Walī Allāh, *Al-Musawwā*, 1:35. These include Saʿīd Ibn al-Musayyib, ʿUrwa Ibn al-Zubayr, al-Qāsim Ibn Muḥammad Ibn Abī Bakr al-Ṣiddīq, Khārija Ibn Zayd Ibn Thābit, ʿUbayd Allāh Ibn ʿAbd Allāh Ibn ʿUtba Ibn Masʿūd, and Sulaymān Ibn Yasār. There are differences of opinion over the identity of the seventh jurist.

121. Walī Allāh, *Al-Musawwā*, 1:37.

122. Walī Allāh, *Al-Musawwā*, 1:45.

123. Walī Allāh, *Al-Musawwā*, 1:24.

124. Walī Allāh, *Al-Musawwā*, 1:25.

125. Walī Allāh, *Ḥujjat Allāh*, 1:249.

126. Walī Allāh, *Al-Musawwā*, 1:25–26.

127. Walī Allāh, *Al-Musawwā*, 1:26.

128. Walī Allāh, *Al-Musawwā*, 1:25.

129. Walī Allāh, *Al-Musawwā*, 1:63.

130. Walī Allāh, *Al-Musawwā*, 1:22.

131. Walī Allāh, *Al-Musawwā*, 1:19–20.

132. Walī Allāh, *Ḥujjat Allāh*, 1:249.

133. Walī Allāh, *Al-Musawwā*, 1:63.

134. Walī Allāh, *Al-Musawwā*, 1:29.

135. Walī Allāh, *Al-Musawwā*, 1:29.

136. Walī Allāh, *Al-Musawwā*, 1:30.

137. Walī Allāh, *Al-Musawwā*, 1:30.

138. Walī Allāh, *Al-Musawwā*, 1:31, 63.

139. Walī Allāh, *Al-Musawwā*, 1:46.

140. Walī Allāh, *Al-Musawwā*, 1:46.

141. Walī Allāh, *Al-Musawwā*, 1:47.

142. Walī Allāh, *Al-Musawwā*, 1:47.

143. Walī Allāh, *Al-Musawwā*, 1:62–63.

144. Walī Allāh, *Al-Musawwā*, 1:63.

145. Walī Allāh, *Al-Musawwā*, 1:63.

146. Walī Allāh, *Al-Musawwā*, 1:73.

147. Walī Allāh, *Al-Musawwā*, 1:95–96.

148. Walī Allāh, *Al-Musawwā*, 1:336–37.

149. Walī Allāh, *Al-Musawwā*, 1:64.

150. Walī Allāh, *Al-Musawwā*, 1:64.

151. Shāh Walī Allāh, *Sharḥ Tarājim Abwāb Ṣaḥīḥ al-Bukhārī* (Hyderabad Deccan: Majlis Dā'irat al-Ma'ārif al-'Uthmāniyya, 1949).

152. Walī Allāh, *Sharḥ Tarājim*, 51–52.

153. Walī Allāh, *Sharḥ Tarājim*, 52.

154. Walī Allāh, *Sharḥ Tarājim*, 79.

155. Walī Allāh, *Sharḥ Tarājim*, 2–5.

156. Walī Allāh, *Sharḥ Tarājim*, 4.

157. For example, Walī Allāh, *Sharḥ Tarājim*, 127–28.

158. For example, Walī Allāh, *Sharḥ Tarājim*, 83.

159. Walī Allāh, *Al-Musawwā*, 1:64.

160. See, for example, Walī Allāh, *Ḥujjat Allāh*, 1:29.

161. See Marcia Hermansen's excellent translation of the first volume of this book: Shāh Walī Allāh, *The Conclusive Argument from God: Shāh Walī Allāh of Delhi's "Ḥujjat Allāh al-Bāligha,"* trans. Marcia K. Hermansen (Leiden, the Netherlands: E. J. Brill, 1996).

162. Walī Allāh, *Ḥujjat Allāh*, 1:3.

163. Walī Allāh, *Ḥujjat Allāh*, 1:4.

164. Walī Allāh, *Ḥujjat Allāh*, 1:4.

165. Walī Allāh, *Ḥujjat Allāh*, 1:4.

166. See chapter 3 for a fuller discussion of Walī Allāh's views on Sufism. Here, however, this subject will be discussed only inasmuch as it relates to Walī Allāh's conceptualization of hadith.

167. Walī Allāh, *Ḥujjat Allāh*, 1:6.

168. Walī Allāh, *Ḥujjat Allāh*, 1:9.

169. Walī Allāh, *Ḥujjat Allāh*, 1:9–11.

170. Walī Allāh, *Ḥujjat Allāh*, 1:12.

171. Walī Allāh, *Ḥujjat Allāh*, 1:13.

172. Walī Allāh, *Ḥujjat Allāh*, 1:13.

173. Walī Allāh, *Ḥujjat Allāh*, 1:15.

174. Walī Allāh, *Ḥujjat Allāh*, 1:15.

175. Walī Allāh, *Ḥujjat Allāh*, 1:15–16.

176. Compare to al-Shawkānī, who, when talking about logic recognizes its un-Islamic origins (*'ulūm kufriyya*) but goes on to assert that it is impossible to deal with any of the religious sciences in his days without knowledge of logic, simply because it informs the structures of all the current books on the various religious disciplines. See, for example, al-Shawkānī, *Adab al-Ṭalab*, 124–25.

177. Walī Allāh, *Ḥujjat Allāh*, 1:16.

178. Walī Allāh, *Ḥujjat Allāh*, 1:18.

179. Walī Allāh, *Ḥujjat Allāh*, 1:17.

180. Walī Allāh, *Ḥujjat Allāh*, 1:18–19.

181. Walī Allāh, *Ḥujjat Allāh*, 1:19.

182. Walī Allāh, *Ḥujjat Allāh*, 1:19.

183. Walī Allāh, *Ḥujjat Allāh*, 1:247–48, see also 1:243.

184. Walī Allāh, *Ḥujjat Allāh*, 1:248.

185. Walī Allāh, *Ḥujjat Allāh*, 1:250.

186. Walī Allāh, *Ḥujjat Allāh*, 1:251.

187. Walī Allāh, *Ḥujjat Allāh*, 1:252.

188. Walī Allāh, *Ḥujjat Allāh*, 1:252, 395.

189. Walī Allāh, *Ḥujjat Allāh*, 1:248.

190. Walī Allāh, *Ḥujjat Allāh*, 1:248.

191. Walī Allāh, *Ḥujjat Allāh*, 1:249–50.

192. Walī Allāh, *Ḥujjat Allāh*, 2:397.

193. Walī Allāh, *Ḥujjat Allāh*, 1:290.

194. Walī Allāh, *Ḥujjat Allāh*, 1:291–92.

195. Al-Ṣanʿānī, *Tawḍīḥ al-Afkār*, 1:37.

196. Al-Ṣanʿānī, *Al-ʿUdda*, 2:171.

197. Walī Allāh, *Al-Tafhīmāt al-Ilāhiyya*, 1:208.

198. Walī Allāh, *Al-Tafhīmāt al-Ilāhiyya*, 1:211.

199. Walī Allāh, *Al-Tafhīmāt al-Ilāhiyya*, 1:211–12.

200. Shāh Walī Allāh, *Fuyūḍ al-Ḥaramayn* (Delhi: Mālik Maṭbaʿ-e-Aḥmadī, n.d.), 62.

201. Walī Allāh, *Fuyūḍ al-Ḥaramayn*, 62–63.

202. Walī Allāh, *Fuyūḍ al-Ḥaramayn*, 30.

203. Walī Allāh, *Fuyūḍ al-Ḥaramayn*, 65.

204. Shāh Walī Allāh, *ʿIqd al-Jīd fī Aḥkām al-Ijtihād wal-Taqlīd* (Cairo: Al-Maṭbaʿa al-Salafiyya, 1385 AH), 13.

205. Note, for example, that in an *ijāza* that he issued for one of his students, Shāh Walī Allāh refers to himself as a Ḥanafī in practice (*ʿamalan*) and Shāfiʿī in teaching (*tadrīsan*). Qtd. in ʿUbayd Allāh al-Sindī, *Al-Tamhīd li-Taʿrīf Aʾimmat al-Tajdīd*, 442. Also see Walī Allāh, *Al-Tafhīmāt al-Ilāhiyya*, 1:279, where Walī Allāh maintains that the Ḥanafī and Shāfiʿī schools ought to be treated as one school.

206. Walī Allāh, *Fuyūḍ al-Ḥaramayn*, 32.

207. Walī Allāh, *Fuyūḍ al-Ḥaramayn*, 63.

208. For the use of the term *ʿālim rabbānī*, see Walī Allāh, *Al-Qawl al-Jamīl*, qtd. in al-Sindī, *Al-Tamhīd*, 376.

209. Walī Allāh, *Fuyūḍ al-Ḥaramayn*, 48–49.

210. Muḥammad ʿAlī al-Sanūsī, "Iqāẓ al-Wasnān fī al-ʿAmal bi al-Ḥadīth wal-Qurʾān," in *Al-Majmūʿa al-Mukhtāra*, ed. Muhammad ʿAbdū Ibn Ghalbūn (Manchester, 1990), 116.

211. Al-Sanūsī, "Kitāb al-Masāʾil al-ʿAshr," 112–29; and "Iqāẓ," 19, 57, 117.

212. Muḥammad Bin ʿAlī al-Sanūsī, "Al-Masāʾil al-ʿAshr al-Musammā Bughyat al-Maqāṣid fī Khulāṣat al-Marāṣid," in *Al-Majmūʿa al-Mukhtāra*, ed. Muhammad ʿAbdū Ibn Ghalbūn (Manchester, 1990), 12; and "Iqāẓ," 55–56.

213. Al-Sanūsī, "Iqāẓ," 76–78, 89–90.

214. Muḥammad b. ʿAlī al-Sanūsī, "Shifāʾ al-Ṣadr bi Arī al-Masāʾil al-ʿAshr," in *Al-Majmūʿa al-Mukhtāra*, ed. Muhammad ʿAbdū Ibn Ghalbūn (Manchester, 1990), 21.

215. Al-Sanūsī, "Iqāẓ," 12, 20.

216. Al-Sanūsī, "Iqāẓ," 15.

217. Al-Sanūsī, "Al-Masāʾil," 9–11; and "Iqāẓ," 12–13, 19.

218. Al-Sanūsī, "Al-Masāʾil," 36; and "Iqāẓ," 20.

219. Al-Sanūsī, "Al-Masāʾil," 13; and "Iqāẓ," 22.

220. Al-Sanūsī, "Al-Masā'il," 13; and "Iqāẓ," 22.

221. As such, transmission is a vocation or a skill, judged by its conformity with formal procedures. This approach, common in historical reporting, was applied systematically by al-Shawkānī and al-Ṣanʿānī to hadith. Of course, the scrutiny of transmission was not the only criterion applied by these scholars; other criteria include the comparison of the contents of various reports and the use of outside supporting evidence (*shawāhid*). Still, the vocation of hadith scholarship as a whole was primarily judged on the basis of its conformity with the formal procedures of reporting (*riwāya* and *ikhbār*).

222. Muḥammad b. ʿAlī al-Shawkānī, *Al-Fawā'id al-Majmūʿa fī al-Aḥādīth al-Mawḍūʿa*, ed. ʿAbd al-Raḥmān b. Yaḥyā al-Maʿlamī al-Yamānī and ʿAbd al-Wahhāb ʿAbd al-Laṭīf (Cairo: Maktabat al-Sunna al-Nabawiyya, 1960).

223. Al-Shawkānī, *Al-Fawā'id*, 3.

224. Al-Shawkānī, *Al-Fawā'id*, 115.

225. Al-Shawkānī, *Al-Fawā'id*, 365.

226. Most of these books, including the two *ṣaḥīḥ* collections of Muslim (d. 261/875) and al-Bukhārī (d. 256/870), were compiled in the third century of Hijra, or shortly thereafter.

227. Al-Ṣanʿānī, *Irshād al-Nuqqād*, 33–34. For other similar references by al-Ṣanʿānī, see *Irshād al-Nuqqād*, 36, 59; and *Tawḍīḥ al-Afkār*, 1:119, where al-Ṣanʿānī asserts that there is no need to concern oneself with the *isnād*s of famous books such as *Sunan al-Nasā'ī*. For similar arguments by al-Shawkānī on the ease of *ijtihād* for later generations of Muslims, and that only a limited number of books is needed for the exercise of *ijtihād*, see *Irshād al-Fuḥūl*, 254; *Adab al-Ṭalab*, 85; *Al-Qawl al-Mufīd*, 150; and *Wabl al-Ghamām*, 2:85. For similar arguments by Walī Allāh, see *Al-Tafhīmāt al-Ilāhiyya*, 211–12; *Musawwā*, 47; *ʿIqd al-Jīd*, 3–4; and *Ḥujjat Allāh*, 1:248. For similar arguments by al-Sanūsī, see "Iqāẓ," 48–50, 67–69.

228. In fact, al-Sanūsī explicitly states that with the writing of books of hadith there is no longer a need for continued uninterrupted transmission. Al-Sanūsī, "Iqāẓ," 50.

229. The availability of these books is taken for granted; in fact, al-Shawkānī maintains that there are even different selections of equally authoritative sets of books, in all fields, and for each region of the Muslim world, from which scholars can choose. See, for example, al-Shawkānī, *Adab al-Ṭalab*, 107. Also see Walī Allāh, *Ḥujjat Allāh*, 1:269, where Walī Allāh says that scholars are naturally inclined to follow the scholarly traditions of their own countries.

230. Al-Shawkānī, *Al-Badr al-Ṭāliʿ*, 2:86–88.

231. Messick asserts a paradigmatic use of memorization in connection with the authorial transmission of written materials; Brinkley Messick, *The Calligraphic State: Textual Domination and History in a Muslim Society* (Berkeley: University of California Press, 1996), 27. It is significant, however, that Messick quotes early authorities on this subject (mainly al-Shāfiʿī), while al-Shawkānī and other eighteenth-century reformers clearly stated that memorization is no longer needed for *ijtihād*. See, for example, al-Shawkānī, *Irshād al-Fuḥūl*, 251; and *Adab al-Ṭalab*. Also see Walī Allāh, *ʿIqd*, 3–4, 32–35; and al-Sanūsī, *Iqaẓ*, esp. 15.

232. As such, al-Shawkānī's emphasis on *isnād* was not a remnant of an early doctrinal system that gave priority to the oral over the written (oral residues), simply because the technologies of writing were neither widely available nor reliable enough to enable the preservation of the Qur'ān and hadith. For theories of orality that posit a linear evolution from the oral to the written, and hence argue that the oral is less developed than the written, see Walter Ong, *Orality and Literacy: The Technologizing of the Word* (London: Routledge, 1988); and Jack Goody, *Literacy in Traditional Societies* (Cambridge: Cambridge University Press, 1968). For a useful critique of these theories, see Messick, *The Calligraphic State*, 24–25.

Of course, even earlier Islamic understandings of the relationship between the oral and the written were diverse and changed over time. The earliest discussions of this subject pertain to the writing down of hadith; the sources preserve many accounts of scholars of hadith who wrote down their own collections but insisted on destroying them before they died. However, this reluctance to write down hadith has nothing to do with a supposed privileging of orality over writing; rather, these scholars feared that a written compilation of hadith might compete in claims of authoritativeness with the Qur'ānic text. Once the text of the Qur'ān was codified and published in its official 'Uthmanic format, such fears gradually subsided, and written hadith books were soon compiled in earnest. Also note here the difference between the meaning of orality as it pertains to the Qur'ān and to hadith: in the former, the recitation of the Qur'ān is primarily an act of ritual worship and has nothing to do with endowing the text with authority. In contrast, orality in hadith, in the form of *isnād*, is primarily intended to authenticate a small portion of a large corpus that is recognizably indefinite. Contrast with Messick, *The Calligraphic State*, 22–30, 269.

233. Thus, for example, whereas early works on law or history often contained the *isnād* of various *riwāyas* of particular legal views or accounts of historical events, later works dispensed with such *isnāds*.

234. See, for example, *Majmūʿat Ḥaydar Ābād* (Hyderabad: Dā'irat al-Maʿārif al-ʿUthmāniyya, 1328/1910), where five such treatises are published. These are (1) Ibrāhīm b. Ḥasan b. Shahāb al-Dīn al-Kurdī al-Kūrānī al-Sahrzūrī (d. 1102), *Al-Amam li-Iqāẓ al-Himam*; (2) Aḥmad al-Nakhlī al-Makkī (d. 1114), *Bughyat al-Ṭālibīn li-Bayān al-Mashā'ikh al-Muḥaqqiqīn*; (3) ʿAbd Allāh b. Sālim al-Baṣrī (d. 1134), *Kitāb al-Imdād bi-Maʿrifat ʿUlūm al-Isnād*; (4) Ṣāliḥ b. Muḥammad al-ʿUmarī al-Fulānī (d. 1218), *Qatf al-Thamar fī Rafʿ Asānīd al-Muṣannafāt fī al-Funūn wal-Athar*; and (5) Muḥammad b. ʿAlī al-Shawkānī, *Itḥāf al-Akābir bi-Isnād al-Dafātir*.

235. See, for example, Muḥammad b. ʿAlī al-Shawkānī, *Itḥāf al-Akābir bi-Isnād al-Dafātir* (Hyderabad Deccan: Maṭbaʿat Dā'irat al-Maʿārif al-Niẓāmiyya, 1328 AH), 5, 6, 30.

236. Contrast with Messick (*The Calligraphic State*, 30), who, following Michel Foucault (*The Order of Things*, qtd. 30), argues that a commentary must recognize the "sovereignty of an original text," or the authority of the *matn*; such a commentary makes a *matn* comprehensible and opens it up to "lengthy doctrinal elaborations." While this is no doubt true of many traditional commentaries, even a cursory look at the commentaries of the Yemeni scholars reveals the subversive purpose of these works. Note also that it is not just the interpretations that are contested but also the basic *matn*, which is not "settled" as Messick asserts (35). Thus, for example, in his *Wabl al-Ghamām* al-Shawkānī provides a thorough critical commentary on Ḥusayn b. Yaḥyā's *Shifā' al-Awām*, a standard Zaydi *matn*. Al-Shawkānī states his intention to criticize and correct (and occasionally corroborate) the opinions of Ḥusayn b. Yaḥyā, especially since many scholars in Yemen use this book and assume that everything in it is correct (*Wabl al-Ghamām*, 47–48). Similarly, the other major legal work by al-Shawkānī, *Al-Sayl al-Jarrār*, is a deliberate critical commentary on *Kitāb al-Azhār*, another standard Zaydi *matn* by Aḥmad b. Yaḥyā al-Murtaḍā.

237. Messick, *The Calligraphic State*, 26.

238. Al-Shawkānī, *Itḥāf al-Akābir*, 2.

239. Al-Shawkānī, *Itḥāf al-Akābir*, 2.

240. Al-Shawkānī, *Adab al-Ṭalab*, 122.

241. Al-Shawkānī, *Adab al-Ṭalab*, 122.

Conclusion

1. Contrast to the notion of "ordering multiplicity" in Michel Foucault, *Discipline and Punish: The Birth of the Prison* (New York: Vintage Books, 1979), 218–19.

2. As in attempts by Walī Allāh and al-Shawkānī to explain the historical contexts of *madhhab* partisanship.

3. Contrast to the widely accepted Orientalist notion that Islamic legal thought is characterized by the "casuistical method . . . which is . . . the outcome of an analogical, as opposed to an analytical, way of thinking." See Joseph Schacht, *An Introduction to Islamic Law* (Oxford, UK: Clarendon, 1964), 5.

4. On the use of *mutūn*, such as the Shāfiʿī texts of Muḥyī al-Dīn al-Nawawī (d. 1277), *Al-Minhāj*, and the twelfth-century text *Al-Mukhtaṣar* by Ibn Shujāʿ, see Brinkley Messick, *The Calligraphic State: Textual Domination and History in a Muslim Society* (Berkeley: University of California Press, 1996), 20–21. Both texts were fundamental for instruction and for court rulings and were used for purposes of instruction all over the Muslim world, including in Yemen, Egypt, Syria, Malaya, and Java. They were also translated into French and English for use in British-administered colonies. According to Messick, these bare-bones presentations of the doctrines of various *madhhab*s were derivative but creative synopses and abridgements of larger works and were the most influential texts precisely because of their convenience and utility in the process of teaching (18).

5. Such as Muḥammad b. Ismāʿīl al-Amīr al-Ṣanʿānī, *Subul al-Salām Sharḥ Bulūgh al-Marām min Jamʿ Adillat al-Aḥkām*, ed. Fawwāz Aḥmad Zamrlī and Ibrāhīm Muḥammad al-Jamal, 5 vols. (Beirut: Dār al-Kitāb al-ʿArabī, 1990); and al-Shawkānī, *Irshād al-Fuḥūl*. Both were popular among students.

6. Some scholars have suggested that, on account of the proximity and influence of Shāfiʿīs in Yemen, and as evidenced by his frequent reference to Shāfiʿī *mujtahid*s, al-Shawkānī's notion of *ijtihād* is suggestive of his leanings toward the Shāfiʿī *madhhab*. Al-Shawkānī, however, directly disabuses his readers of this notion, when he says (in the context of responding to a common argument that *ijtihād* is not possible for later generations) that since most of those who make this argument are Shāfiʿīs, he will list the names of Shāfiʿī scholars who have amassed knowledge that far supersedes what is needed for the exercise of *ijtihād*. Al-Shawkānī, *Irshād al-Fuḥūl*, 254.

7. This is not to be confused with the common assertion that "in Islam" written books carry no authority and are always dependent on an oral authentication process. In fact, al-Shawkānī says that because of *tadwīn*, the writing down of books, "it is not a secret to anyone who has the slightest intelligence that God made *ijtihād* much easier to later generations than it was for earlier ones." Al-Shawkānī, *Irshād al-Fuḥūl*, 254.

8. On the dichotomy of commoners and elites (*ʿawām* and *khawāṣ*), al-Shawkānī says that often the belief in the hearts [literally chests] of commoners is like anchored mountains (*kal-jibāl al-rawāsī*), while some who dwell on the science of *kalām* and wade through its contested questions have shaky belief, and the more they delve into this science, the weaker their belief gets; in fact it progressively "gets undone, one buttonhole at a time." Al-Shawkānī, *Irshād al Fuḥūl*, 266.

9. Muḥammad b. ʿAlī al-Shawkānī, *Wabl al-Ghamām ʿalā Shifāʾ al-Uwām*, ed. M. Ḥallāq, 2 vols. (Cairo: Maktabat Ibn Taymiyya, 1995), 2:305–9; "Irshād al-Sāʾil ilā Dalāʾil al-Masāʾil," in *Al-Rasāʾil al-Salafiyya fī Iḥyāʾ Sunnat Khayr al-Bariyya* (Beirut: Dār al-Kutub al-ʿIlmiyya, 1930), 39–51, esp. 39; *Sharḥ al-Ṣudūr fī Taḥrīm Rafʿ al-Qubūr*, 1–13, in *Al-Rasāʾil al-Salafiyya fī Iḥyāʾ Sunnat Khayr al-Bariyya*, 1–2.

10. Al-Shawkānī, *Irshād al-Fuḥūl*, 265. For a fuller discussion of *ijtihād* and *taqlīd*, and asking the *mujtahid* for evidence of a ruling and not for his or her opinion, see al-Shawkānī, *Irshād al-Fuḥūl*, 264–70.

11. Al-Shawkānī, *Adab al-Ṭalab*, 166.

12. To be sure, al-Shawkānī argues that it is normal to delegate a *mujtahid* and scholar to take charge of certain offices or responsibilities, but this does not give the *mujtahid* the authority to claim unchecked authority. Rather, this delegation is contingent on the scholar's ability to exercise *ijtihād*. Al-Shawkānī, *Irshād al-Fuḥūl*, 264.

13. See also al-Ṣanʿānī, *Al-ʿUdda*, 2:186–87, who argues that a *mujtahid*'s imitation is itself an *ijtihād*. Al-Ṣanʿānī gives the example of the blind Companion of the Prophet, Ibn Umm Maktūm, who performed the *adhān* for the morning prayers; other Companions who at the time were inside the mosque and could not have seen the dawn themselves performed the prayer on hearing his *adhān* and did not question his ability, as a blind man, to verify the break of dawn. According to al-Ṣanʿānī, the Companions exercised their own *ijtihād* based on the knowledge that Ibn Umm Maktūm was a trustworthy companion who could not have called for the prayers had he not been informed by equally trustworthy Companions that it was the right time. In all cases, the *ijtihād* and subsequent actions of the Companions are based on the act of reporting (*ikhbār*) by morally credible informers, and not on their judgments and opinions.

14. On the meaning of "every mujtahid is correct [*kull mujtahid muṣīb*]," al-Shawkānī maintains that it is abominable to claim that, on any one matter, God's rulings are contradictory or are as numerous as the number of *mujtahid*s reflecting on this matter; rather, there can only be one correct answer (*al-ḥaqq wāḥid*), but *ijtihād* itself is rewarded even when the correct answer is missed. As such, the *mujtahid* who goes through the process is rewarded (*maʾjūr*) on account of his *ijtihād*, even if it is mistaken. Al-Shawkānī, *Irshād al-Fuḥūl*, 259–62. See also al-Shawkānī, *Wilāyat Allāh*, 324–25; *Al-Sayl al-Jarrār*, 1:18–21.

15. Al-Shawkānī, *Adab al-Ṭalab*, 55.

16. Al-Shawkānī, *Al-Qawl al-Mufīd*, 121–22; my emphasis.

17. Contrast, for example, with the classical view of Ibn al-Muqaffaʿ, who asserts in his *Risala fī al-Ṣaḥāba* that "all matters are relegated to the people in charge, and common people have no say in these matters, except for giving advice when asked, or responding when called upon." Ibn al-Muqaffaʿ, *Risala fī al-Ṣaḥāba* (Beirut: Maktabat al-Bayān, 1964), 199. In contrast to this position, which limits the contribution of people in political decision-making to a limited unbinding consultation, al-Shawkānī has essentially a rational and civil understanding of politics, since he ultimately argues that each Muslim has to exercise *ijtihād* and make his or her own choice. In a way, therefore, the final authority is entrusted to Muslims who exercise *ijtihād* and make their own choices.

18. Muḥammad Bin ʿAlī al-Sanūsī, "Iqāẓ al-Wasnān fī al-ʿAmal bi-l-Ḥadīth wal-Qurʾān," in *Al-Majmūʿa al-Mukhtāra*, ed. Muhammad ʿAbdū Ibn Ghalbūn (Manchester, 1990), 51–54. On the possibility of having partial *ijtihād*, see al-Sanūsī, "Iqāẓ," 44.

19. Al-Sanūsī, "Iqāẓ," 22.

20. Al-Sanūsī, "Iqāẓ," 30.

21. Al-Sanūsī, "Iqāẓ," 72.

22. Muḥammad Bin ʿAlī al-Sanūsī, "Al-Masāʾil al-ʿAshr al-Musammā Bughyat al-Maqāṣid fī Khulāṣat al-Marāṣid," in *Al-Majmūʿa al-Mukhtāra*, ed. Muhammad ʿAbdū Ibn Ghalbūn (Manchester, 1990), 111.

23. Contrast to Bernd Radtke, John O'Kane, Knut S. Vikor, and R. S. O'Fahey, *The Exoteric Aḥmad Ibn Idrīs: A Sufi's Critique of the Madhāhib and the Wahhābis* (Leiden, the Netherlands:

E. J. Brill, 2000), 22, who suggest parallels between Ibn ʿAbd al-Wahhāb and al-Shawkānī on *uṣūl al-fiqh*, specifically in that they both reject "the authority and tradition of the madhāhib." This assertion is erroneous not just because *uṣūl* as a discipline is not articulated along *madhhab* lines, and thus is not primarily concerned with acceptance or rejection of *madhhabs*, but also because *madhhabs* and *uṣūl* were nonissues to Ibn ʿAbd al-Wahhāb, who offered no substantive discussion of either, and therefore had no views on these subjects that can be compared with al-Shawkānī's elaborate views.

24. The Akhbārīs appeared as a distinct traditionalist movement in Twelver Shiism in the seventeenth century, under the intellectual leadership of such figures as Muḥammad Amīn al-Astarabādī (d. 1626). Akhbārīs survived into the eighteenth century but eventually lost to the reemerging Uṣūlīs, including the influential Muḥammad Bāqir al-Bahbahānī (d. 1791). See, for example, Etan Kohlberg, "Aspects of Akhbari Thought in the Seventeenth and Eighteenth Centuries," in *Eighteenth-Century Renewal and Reform in Islam*, ed. Nehemia Levtzion and John Obert Voll (Syracuse, N.Y.: Syracuse University Press, 1987), 133–60. Also see Meir Litvak, *Shiʿi Scholars of Nineteenth-Century Iraq: The ʿUlama of Najaf and Karbalaʾ* (Cambridge: Cambridge University Press, 1998). Also see Said Amir Arjomand, *The Shadow of God and the Hidden Imām* (Chicago: University of Chicago Press, 1984), 13–14, 145–47, 152–53; Juan Cole, "Shiʿi Clerics in Iraq and Iran, 1722–1780," *Iranian Studies* 18 (1985): 3–34; and Hossein Modarressi, "Rationalism and Traditionalism in Shiʿi Jurisprudence," *Studia Islamica* (1984): 148–58.

25. See Devin Stewart, *Islamic Legal Orthodoxy: Twelver Shiʿite Responses to the Sunni Legal System* (Salt Lake City: University of Utah Press, 1998), esp. 176. Stewart argues that "the legal system functioned over the long run to create a large degree of similarity between disparate Islamic groups" (21). The influential Akhbārī, Muḥammad Amīn al-Astarabādī (d. 1626), author of the book *Al-Fawāʾid al-Madaniyya*, accuses Uṣūlīs of applying "Sunni methods of hadith criticism to Shiʿite hadith," and using such Sunni categories as *ṣaḥīḥ*, *ḥasan*, and *ḍaʿīf* (Stewart, *Islamic Legal Orthodoxy*, 191). However, despite such formal parallels between Sunni and Shiʿi works on *uṣūl*, ultimately the discipline serves different purposes in each of these traditions. Of course, it is abundantly clear that hadith in the Akhbārī tradition serves a very different role than it does for the *Ahl al-ḥadīth* reformers of the eighteenth century. For Akhbārīs, hadith undermines *ijtihād* and the legal pluralism that follows from it. For the Uṣūlīs, in contrast, *ijtihād* is offered as an alternative to the authority of traditionalists, but it attributes this exclusive authority to select *mujtahids* and asserts the obligation of the majority of Muslims to exercise *taqlīd* of these authorities.

26. As Stewart, *Islamic Legal Orthodoxy*, seems to suggest.

27. Al-Shawkānī, *Irshād al-Fuḥūl ilā Taḥqīq al-Ḥaqq min ʿIlm al-uṣūl* (Dār al-Fikr, n.p., n.d.), 2–3.

28. Al-Shawkānī, *Irshād al-Fuḥūl*, 5.

29. Al-Shawkānī, *Irshād al-Fuḥūl*, 5–6.

30. *Tawātur* is transmission through a multiplicity of sources of a certain report that leads to certitude on account of multiplicity of reporters and unbroken chains of transmission.

31. Al-Shawkānī, *Irshād al-Fuḥūl*, 13, 15–17.

32. Al-Shawkānī, *Irshād al-Fuḥūl*, 130.

33. Al-Shawkānī, *Irshād al-Fuḥūl*, 141. Additionally, al-Shawkānī argues that the *ijtihād* and interpretations of all or some of the Companions do not constitute binding proofs (*ḥujja*), especially since they disagree with each other. Al-Shawkānī, *Al-Sayl al-Jarrār*, 2:168, 226.

34. Al-Shawkānī, *Irshād al-Fuḥūl*, 155–57.

35. Al-Shawkānī, *Irshād al-Fuḥūl*, 157.

36. Al-Shawkānī, *Irshād al-Fuḥūl*, 162.

37. In fact, in all of his books, al-Shawkānī seizes every possible occasion to discuss similar questions related to principles of jurisprudence and their implications with regard to intellectual authority. For example, in the introduction to *Al-Sayl al-Jarrār*, a commentary on the standard Zaydi legal manual taught in Yemen, *Kitāb al-Azhār* by Aḥmad b. Yaḥyā Ibn al-Murtaḍā (d. 1432), al-Shawkānī says that, because of significant disagreement over many of its views, his aim is to serve as an arbitrator between the book and its various commentators. Al-Shawkānī further notes that he focuses primarily on rulings related to transactions (*muʿāmalāt*) and is brief in his discussion of rulings related to acts of worship (*ʿibādāt*) because their principles are well established (*Al-Sayl al-Jarrār*, 3). Then, without skipping a beat, al-Shawkānī offers his first criticism of *Azhār*, related to a general principle of jurisprudence and not so much to a specific legal ruling: *Al-Azhār*, al-Shawkānī maintains, asserts that imitation in the practical branches of law, both the probable and the definitive ones, is permissible for a commoner but not for a *mujtahid*. In response, al-Shawkānī says that *taqlīd* is specific to the branches of the law (*al-taqlīd yakhtaṣṣ bil-masāʾil al-farʿiyya*), while the introduction of *Al-Azhār*, and in fact the majority of the book, does not deal with branches of the law. As such, according to al-Shawkānī, one must be a *mujtahid* to qualify to read *Al-Azhār*, although a *mujtahid* is not allowed to imitate it. Still, despite this effective overarching dismissal of the rationale behind *Al-Azhār*, al-Shawkānī welcomes the opportunity not just to engage the whole Zaydi legal tradition but also, and more important, to theorize *uṣūl* for Zaydis and non-Zaydis alike. Muḥammad Ibn ʿAlī al-Shawkānī, *Al-Sayl al-Jarrār al-Mutadaffiq ʿalā Ḥadāʾiq al-Azhār*, 4 vols., ed. Maḥmūd Ibrāhīm Zāyid (Beirut: Dār al-Kutub al-ʿIlmiyya, 1985), 1:4. Another example in which al-Shawkānī discusses juristic principles on almost every page of a book is *Wabl al-Ghamām*. This is a glossary on *Shifāʾ Al-Uwām fī Aḥādīth al-Aḥkām* (by al-Ḥusayn Ibn Badr al-Harawī, d. 1263–64).

38. Al-Shawkānī, *Al-Sayl al-Jarrār*, 3:371.

39. Al-Shawkānī, *Adab al-Ṭalab*, 95.

40. Al-Shawkānī, *Adab al-Ṭalab*, 96.

41. Al-Shawkānī, *Al-Sayl al-Jarrār*, 3:376. Contrast to Haykel, who suggests that al-Shawkānī's exclusive dependence on hadith, especially the collections of Muslim and al-Bukhārī, "aims, at the level of *uṣūl* at more certainty." Bernard Haykel, *Revival and Reform in Islam: The Legacy of Muhammad al-Shawkānī* (Cambridge: Cambridge University Press, 2003), 106–7. As noted, *uṣūl* principles are invoked everywhere in al-Shawkānī's works, especially in his major books *Nayl al-Awṭār*, *Wabl al-Ghamām*, and *Al-Sayl al-Jarrār*, as well as in his *tafsīr*, and he uses every opportunity to articulate, elaborate, and demonstrate various legal principles. Nonetheless, as he clearly explains in *Irshād al-Fuḥūl* and elsewhere, the rules developed by *uṣūl* scholars are not certain and are often wrong. Furthermore, all legal knowledge is presumptive (*ẓannī*), even when based on valid indicants such as authentic hadith. As such, al-Shawkānī's discussions of *uṣūl* aim to undermine the notions of certainty attributed to this field and not to establish alternative rules of certitude.

42. There is general agreement among students of Islamic law that the first attempt to systematically articulate the fundamental principles of Islamic jurisprudence was in al-Shāfʿī's *Risāla*. See Muḥammad Ibn Idrīs al-Shāfiʿī, *Al-Risāla*, ed. Muḥammad Sayyid Kilānī (Cairo: Mustafa Bābī al-Ḥalabī, 1969). For an English translation, see *Al-Shāfiʿī's "Risāla": Treatise on the Foundations of Islamic Jurisprudence*, trans. Majid Khadduri, 3rd ed. (Cambridge: Islamic Text Society, 2008). However, Wael Hallaq has argued that al-Shāfiʿī's synthesis was not immediately accepted, and another century passed before the theory of *uṣūl* was fully developed. See Hallaq, *A History of Islamic Legal Theories: An Introduction to Sunni Uṣūl al-Fiqh* (Cambridge: Cambridge University Press, 1997), 21–35.

43. Al-Shawkānī, *Irshād al-Fuḥūl*, 32.

44. Al-Shawkānī, *Irshād al-Fuḥūl*, 176–77.

45. Including his famous *tafsīr*: Muḥammad Ibn ʿAlī al-Shawkānī, *Fatḥ al-Qadīr al-Jāmiʿ bayn Fannay al-Riwāya wal-Dirāya min ʿIlm al-Tafsīr*, 2 vols. (Beirut: Dār al-Kitāb al-ʿArabī, 2001).

46. Al-Shawkānī, *Irshād al-Fuḥūl*, 33.

47. Al-Shawkānī, *Irshād al-Fuḥūl*, 64.

48. A *mukallaf* is a person who meets the legal prerequisites, including reaching the age of discernment (*bulūgh*) and sanity, and is obligated by law to discharge his or her legal duties.

49. Or exactitude, that is, having precise and strong memory to enable the reporter to accurately transmit the hadith.

50. Al-Shawkānī, *Irshād al-Fuḥūl*, 50.

51. Al-Shawkānī, *Irshād al-Fuḥūl*, 52.

52. Al-Shawkānī, *Irshād al-Fuḥūl*, 53.

53. Al-Shawkānī, *Irshād al-Fuḥūl*, 66.

54. Al-Shawkānī, *Irshād al-Fuḥūl*, 67.

55. Al-Shawkānī, *Irshād al-Fuḥūl*, 53.

56. Al-Shawkānī, *Irshād al-Fuḥūl*, 51.

57. Al-Shawkānī, *Irshād al-Fuḥūl*, 68.

58. Al-Shawkānī, *Irshād al-Fuḥūl*, 68–69.

59. Al-Shawkānī, *Irshād al-Fuḥūl*, 69. On the argument that later generations of Muslims can perform better actions and have superior knowledge than the Companions, despite *fadīlat al-ṣuḥba*, see al-Shawkānī, *Nayl al-Awṭār*, vol. 4, part 8, 325.

60. Al-Shawkānī, *Irshād al-Fuḥūl*, 70.

61. Al-Shawkānī, *Irshād al-Fuḥūl*, 55.

62. Al-Shawkānī, *Irshād al-Fuḥūl*, 56.

63. Akin to modern references to a constitution or bill of rights.

64. Al-Shawkānī, *Al-Sayl al-Jarrār*, 1:167.

65. Al-Shawkānī, *Al-Sayl al-Jarrār*, 1:185–87.

66. Al-Shawkānī, *Al-Sayl al-Jarrār*, 1:6–7.

67. Al-Ḥasan Ibn Aḥmad al-Jalāl, *Ḍawʾ al-Nahār ʿalā Ṣafaḥāt al-Azhār*, published with Muḥammad Ibn Ismāʿīl al-Amīr al-Ṣanʿānī, *Minḥat al-Ghaffār Ḥāshiyat Ḍawʾ al-Nahar*, ed. Muḥammad Ṣubḥī Ḥasan Ḥallaq, 7 vols. (Sanaa: Al-Jīl al-Jadīd, 2009).

68. Al-Shawkānī, *Al-Sayl al-Jarrār*, 1:8.

69. Al-Shawkānī, *Al-Sayl al-Jarrār*, 1:9.

70. Al-Shawkānī, *Al-Sayl al-Jarrār*, 1:17.

71. Al-Shawkānī, *Al-Sayl al-Jarrār*, 1:25.

72. Al-Shawkānī, *Al-Sayl al-Jarrār*, 1:222.

73. Al-Shawkānī, *Al-Sayl al-Jarrār*, 1:15.

74. Al-Shawkānī, *Al Sayl al-Jarrār*, 1:12–13.

75. Al-Shawkānī, *Al-Sayl al-Jarrār*, 1:15.

76. Al-Shawkānī, *Al-Sayl al-Jarrār*, 1:104. See also *Wabl al-Ghamām*, 1:142–47, 164.

77. Al-Shawkānī, *Al-Sayl al-Jarrār*, 1:21–22.

78. Al-Shawkānī, *Al-Sayl al-Jarrār*, 1:22–24.

79. Al-Shawkānī, *Al-Sayl al-Jarrār*, 1:23–24.

80. Al-Shawkānī, *Al-Sayl al-Jarrār*, 1:24.

81. Al-Shawkānī, *Al-Sayl al-Jarrār*, 4:120.

82. Al-Shawkānī, *Al-Sayl al-Jarrār*, 4:139–40.

83. Al-Shawkānī, *Wabl al-Ghamām*, 1:240.

84. Al-Shawkānī, *Irshād al-Fuḥūl*, 77.

85. Al-Shawkānī, *Irshād al-Fuḥūl*, 81.

86. Al-Shawkānī, *Irshād al-Fuḥūl*, 83.

87. Reporting by a large number without substantial difference. Al-Shawkānī, *Irshād al-Fuḥūl*, 71.

88. Al-Shawkānī, *Irshād al-Fuḥūl*, 72.

89. Al-Shawkānī, *Irshād al-Fuḥūl*, 73.

90. Al-Shawkānī, *Adab al-Ṭalab*, 160. See also al-Shawkānī, *Al-Qawl al-Mufīd*, 133–34, where he argues that the silence of the scholars of *ijtihād* is often out of dissimulation and for fear of harm if they refute *taqlīd*. Also see al-Shawkānī, *Wilāyat Allāh*, 338, where he maintains that many scholars of every school are in fact opposed to *taqlīd* but do not profess their views openly out of fear of the common people and imitators.

91. Al-Shawkānī, *Adab al-Ṭalab*, 170.

92. Al-Shawkānī, *Adab al-Ṭalab*, 162–63.

93. This is a view held by al-Juwaynī. Al-Shawkānī, *Irshād al-Fuḥūl*, 73.

94. Al-Shawkānī, *Irshād al-Fuḥūl*, 76.

95. Al-Shawkānī, *Irshād al-Fuḥūl*, 81–90.

96. Al-Shawkānī, *Irshād al-Fuḥūl*, 78.

97. Al-Shawkānī, *Irshād al-Fuḥūl*, 81.

98. Al-Shawkānī, *Nayl a-Awṭār*, vol. 1, part 1, 78.

99. As he himself repeatedly indicates, for example, in his references to the Ẓāhirī rejection of *ijmāʿ*.

100. Al-Shawkānī, *Adab al-Ṭalab*, 18.

101. Al-Shawkānī, *Adab al-Ṭalab*, 19–20.

102. Al-Shawkānī, *Irshād al-Fuḥūl*, 17.

103. Al-Shawkānī, *Irshād al-Fuḥūl*, 160.

104. Al-Shawkānī, *Al-Sayl al-Jarrār*, 2:374.

105. Al-Shawkānī, *Irshād al-Fuḥūl*, 198.

106. Al-Shawkānī, *Irshād al-Fuḥūl*, 202.

107. Al-Shawkānī, *Irshād al-Fuḥūl*, 199.

108. Al-Shawkānī, *Irshād al-Fuḥūl*, 200.

109. *Al-barāʿa al-aṣliyya*: original innocence, or the principle that things are originally permissible and not regulated by the law until they are explicitly forbidden or obligated through a direct indicant. For more on this principle, see below.

110. Al-Shawkānī, *Irshād al-Fuḥūl*, 200–201. This is just one example of al-Shawkānī's dismissal of various arguments used to prove *qiyās*. See, for example, al-Shawkānī, *Irshād al-Fuḥūl*, 202, for additional criticism of arguments in support of *qiyās*, including some by Aḥmad Ibn Taymiyya, and for arguments against various kinds of *qiyās* that "boil down to nothing more than mere opinion and false conjecture."

111. Al-Shawkānī, *Irshād al-Fuḥūl*, 202.

112. Al-Shawkānī, *Irshād al-Fuḥūl*, 202–4.

113. Al-Shawkānī, *Irshād al-Fuḥūl*, 204.

114. Al-Shawkānī, *Al-Sayl al-Jarrār*, 3:63–74.

115. Al-Shawkānī, *Adab al-Ṭalab*, 164.

116. Contrast to al-Shawkānī's focus on the limits on the applicability of the *ʿilla* and his emphasis that the *ʿilla* cannot be applied without explicit scriptural evidence supporting this application.

117. Walī Allāh, *Musawwā*, 49–50.

118. Walī Allāh, *Musawwā*, 51–52.

119. Walī Allāh, *Musawwā*, 49–50.

120. Al-Shawkānī, *Al-Sayl al-Jarrār*, 1:244. See also al-Shawkānī, *Irshād al-Fuḥūl*, 240–43, where he rejects the use of *al-maṣāliḥ al-mursala*, that is, unrestricted public interests that are not explicitly stated in the scripture.

121. Concealed analogy: discretionary opinion in breach of what usually falls under strict analogy.

122. Al-Shawkānī, *Adab al-Ṭalab*, 95.

123. Al-Shawkānī, *Adab al-Ṭalab*, 165.

124. Al-Shawkānī, *Adab al-Ṭalab*, 165–66; and *Irshād al-Fuḥūl*, 240–41.

125. Al-Shawkānī, *Irshād al-Fuḥūl*, 236.

126. Al-Shawkānī, *Irshād al-Fuḥūl*, 238.

127. *Athbata fī hādhihi al-sharīʿa al-Islāmiyya sharʿan lam yaʾmur Allāh bihi.*

128. Al-Shawkānī, *Irshād al-Fuḥūl*, 243–44.

129. Al-Shawkānī discusses taxation in many of his works, clearly reflecting the volatility of this matter in Yemen at the time. On different kinds of taxes, see al-Shawkānī, *Al-Sayl al-Jarrār*, 2:100–104.

130. Al-Shawkānī, *Al-Sayl al-Jarrār*, 2:55. See also *Al-Sayl al-Jarrār*, 4:501–602, where he discusses the conditions, rights, and duties of the *imāma* in great detail. Al-Shawkānī interestingly aims to reconcile three clusters of reports related to the *imāma*: the collection of traditions asserting the obligation to obey the imam, another related to the obligation of every individual Muslim to command the right and forbid the wrong, and the group related to the principle that there should be no obedience to a human being when that entails disobedience to God.

131. Al-Shawkānī, *Al-Sayl al-Jarrār*, 2:98–99.

132. Al-Shawkānī, *Al-Sayl al-Jarrār*, 2:103.

133. Al-Shawkānī, *Al-Sayl al-Jarrār*, 6:312.

134. Al-Shawkānī, *Al-Sayl al-Jarrār*, 4:525.

135. Al-Shawkānī, *Al-Sayl al-Jarrār*, 6:187.

136. Al-Shawkānī, *Al-Sayl al-Jarrār*, 6:192.

137. Al-Shawkānī, *Al-Sayl al-Jarrār*, 6:195–200.

138. Al-Shawkānī, *Al-Sayl al-Jarrār*, 6:300.

139. Al-Shawkānī, *Al-Sayl al-Jarrār*, 6:311.

140. Al-Shawkānī, *Al-Sayl al-Jarrār*, 6:300.

141. Al-Shawkānī, *Al-Sayl al-Jarrār*, 6:302–3, 298.

142. Muḥammad b. ʿAlī al-Shawkānī, *Al-Darārī al-Muḍiyya Sharḥ al-Durar al-Bahiyya* (Cairo: Maktabat al-Turāth al-Islāmī, 1986), 411–17.

143. Al-Shawkānī, *Al-Sayl al-Jarrār*, 6:213.

144. Al-Shawkānī, *Nayl al-Awṭār*, vol. 4, part 8, 298.

145. Al-Shawkānī, *Wabl al-Ghamām*, 2:316–17.

146. Al-Shawkānī, *Wabl al-Ghamām*, 1:131–32.

147. Al-Shawkānī, *Wabl al-Ghamām*, 1:517–18. In a similar vein, without diminishing the virtues of *ahl al-bayt*, al-Shawkānī argues that the claim that they are absolved of punishment for their sins is baseless. He blames this fabricated claim on corrupt scholars who "seek to pander to officials attached to the heads of the noble family." See al-Shawkānī, "Irshād al-Sāʾil," 44.

148. Al-Shawkānī, *Al-Sayl al-Jarrār*, 2:343, 359–60.

149. Al-Shawkānī, *Al-Sayl al-Jarrār,* 2:372.

150. Al-Shawkānī, *Nayl al-Awṭār,* vol. 3, part 6, 239; and *Wabl al-Ghamām,* 2:75–79. See also Muḥammad Ibn Ismāʿīl al-Amīr al-Ṣanʿānī, *Subl al-Salam Sharḥ Bulūgh al-Marām min Jamʿ Adillat al-Aḥkām,* ed. Fawwāz Aḥmad Zumarlī and Ibrāhīm Muḥammad al-Jamal, 5 vols. (Beirut: Dār al-Kitāb al-ʿArabī, 1990), 3:366–67. Al-Ṣanʿānī, while allowing different opinions on this matter, strongly decries the attacks on Ibn Taymiyya and Ibn al-Qayyim, whose views on this matter he considers legitimate. The reason for these attacks is zeal and *madhhab* partisanship.

151. Al-Shawkānī, *Irshād al-Fuḥūl,* 244–45.

152. Al-Shawkānī, *Al-Sayl al-Jarrār,* 1:31.

153. Al-Shawkānī notes that the aim of the discussions of impurity is to legislate based on what is legally and not psychologically reprehensible (*makrūhāt sharʿīyya not nafsiyya*); legislating on the basis of the latter is claiming law without evidence. It is possible, therefore, to be averse to certain things, but this does not make them forbidden in the eyes of the law. Al-Shawkānī, *Al-Sayl al-Jarrār,* 1:68.

154. Al-Shawkānī, *Al-Sayl al-Jarrār,* 1:38.

155. Al-Shawkānī, *Al-Sayl al-Jarrār,* 1:35.

156. Thereby arguing that a dog's flesh, bones, sweat, hair, or blood are pure. See al-Shawkānī, *Al-Sayl al-Jarrār,* 1:37.

157. Al-Shawkānī, *Al-Sayl al-Jarrār,* 1:38. The reference to pigs as *rijs* means prohibited (*muḥarram*), thereby prohibiting eating them but not proving their impurity.

158. Al-Shawkānī, *Al-Sayl al-Jarrār,* 1:38. See also *Wabl al-Ghamām,* 1:191–93.

159. Al-Shawkānī, *Al-Sayl al-Jarrār,* 1:42, 50, 111–12.

160. Al-Shawkānī, *Al-Sayl al-Jarrār,* 1:120–21.

161. Al-Shawkānī, *Al-Sayl al-Jarrār,* 1:149.

162. Al-Shawkānī, *Al-Sayl al-Jarrār,* 2:142–43.

163. Al-Shawkānī, *Al-Sayl al-Jarrār,* 2:138.

164. Al-Shawkānī, *Al-Sayl al-Jarrār,* 2:228.

165. Almost all of volume 3 of *Al-Sayl al-Jarrār* is devoted to sales. See al-Shawkānī, *Al-Sayl al-Jarrār,* 3:128, 138.

166. Al-Shawkānī, *Al-Sayl al-Jarrār,* 1:47, 220.

167. Al-Shawkānī, *Al-Sayl al-Jarrār,* 1:61. Al-Shawkānī distinguishes between *ẓann,* which means likely *mā ghalab ʿalyhi al-ẓann* (probability) and *shakk* (doubt), where probability is equal to or less than definiteness.

168. Al-Shawkānī, *Adab al-Ṭalab,* 152, 156.

169. Al-Shawkānī, *Wilāyat Allāh,* 353.

170. Al-Shawkānī, *Al-Sayl al-Jarrār,* 1:44.

171. Al-Shawkānī, *Al-Sayl al-Jarrār,* 1:50. For a similar view, see al-Sanūsī, "Iqāẓ," 90, where he argues that silence means a license granted by God.

172. Shāh Walī Allāh, *ʿIqd al-Jīd fī Aḥkām al-Ijtihād wal-Taqlīd* (Cairo: Al-Maṭbaʿa al-Salafiyya, 1385 AH), 6; and *Inṣāf,* 6.

173. Walī Allāh, *ʿIqd,* 6–7.

174. Walī Allāh, *ʿIqd,* 11.

175. Walī Allāh, *Ḥujjat,* 1:154; and *ʿIqd,* 14–15.

176. Walī Allāh, *ʿIqd,* 13.

177. Walī Allāh, *ʿIqd,* 20.

178. Walī Allāh, *ʿIqd,* 36.

179. Walī Allāh, *Ḥujjat,* 1:111, 129.

180. Walī Allāh, *Ḥujjat*, 1:130.

181. Walī Allāh, *ʿIqd*, 12–13; *Inṣāf*, 62; and *Ḥujjat* 1:161.

182. Walī Allāh, *Ḥujjat*, 1:111, 129.

183. Walī Allāh, *Ḥujjat*, 1:130.

184. Walī Allāh, *Ḥujjat*, 1:120, 2:22.

185. Walī Allāh, *Ḥujjat*, 1:130.

186. Walī Allāh, *Ḥujjat*, 1:111; and *Al-Tafhīmāt al-Ilāhiyya*, 1:266.

187. On the following theory of *irtifāqāt*, see Walī Allāh, *Ḥujjat*, 1:39–47; and Shāh Walī Allāh, *Al-Budūr al-Bāzigha*, ed. Ṣaghīr Ḥasan al-Maʾṣūmī (Hyderabad: Shah Wali Allah al-Dihlawi Academy, n.d.), 61–64, 119–20.

188. Walī Allāh, *Ḥujjat*, 1:111–12.

189. Shāh Walī Allāh, *A Mystical Interpretation of Prophetic Tales by an Indian Muslim: Translation of "Taʾwīl al-Aḥādīth,"* trans. J. M. S. Baljon (Leiden, the Netherlands: E. J. Brill, 1973), 4.

190. Shāh Walī Allāh, *Sufism and the Islamic Tradition: The Lamahat and Sataʿat of Shah Waliullah: Translation of "Lamaḥāt wa Saṭaʿāt,"* trans. G. N. Jalbani, ed. D. B. Fry (London: Octagon, 1980), 56–57.

191. Walī Allāh, *Ḥujjat*, 2:206–7.

192. Walī Allāh, *Sufism and the Islamic Tradition*, 41. The translation "metaphysical man" was used by Fazlur Rahman; see Rahman, "The Thinker of Crisis: Shah Waliy-Ullah," *Pakistan Quarterly* 6, no. 2 (1956): 46.

193. Walī Allāh, *Sufism and the Islamic Tradition*, 16.

194. Walī Allāh, *Ḥujjat*, 1:111–12.

195. Walī Allāh, *Ḥujjat*, 1:2–3.

196. Walī Allāh's principle of *taṭbīq*, or the mutual application of the two categories of transmitted and rationally construed knowledge, should not be confused with an attempt to subjugate tradition to independent reasoning; he frequently indicates that while attempts to rationally explain the wisdom in what the law obligates are recommended, they are subordinate to, and only attainable through, strict abidance by the letter of the law. See Walī Allāh, *Ḥujjat*, 1:8; and *Al-Tafhīmāt al-Ilāhiyya*, 2:242–43; and compare with Rahman, "The Thinker of Crisis," 44.

197. Walī Allāh, *Sharḥ Trājim Abwāb Ṣaḥīḥ Bukhārī* (Hyderabad Deccan: Majlis Dāʾirat al-Maʿārif al-ʿUthmāniyya, 1949), 96.

198. Al-Shawkānī, *Al-Darārī al-Muḍiyya*, esp. 5.

199. Al-Shawkānī, *Al-Sayl al-Jarrār*, 3:31.

200. Al-Shawkānī, *Al-Sayl al-Jarrār*, 4:312.

201. Al-Shawkānī, *Al-Sayl al-Jarrār*, 4:355–56.

202. Al-Shawkānī, *Al-Sayl al-Jarrār*, 4:64–69.

203. Al-Shawkānī, *Al-Sayl al-Jarrār*, 4:92–93.

204. Al-Shawkānī, *Al-Sayl al-Jarrār*, 4:94.

205. Al-Shawkānī, *Al-Sayl al-Jarrār*, 4:114–15. See also al-Ṣanʿānī, *Subul al-Salām*, 1:62–63.

206. Al-Shawkānī, *Nayl al-Awṭār*, vol. 1, part 1, 78.

207. See al-Shawkānī, *Nayl al-Awṭār*, vol. 1, part 1, 78, where he cites the hadith that God likes that people have recourse to the licenses He legislated for them and suggests that abandoning a *rukhṣa* is akin to abandoning an act of obedience.

208. Al-Shawkānī, *Wilāyat Allāh*, 359.

209. Al-Shawkānī, *Irshād al-Fuḥūl*, 36. See also al-Shawkānī, *Nayl al-Awṭār*, vol. 1, part 1, 29.

210. Al-Shawkānī, *Irshād al-Fuḥūl*, 36.

211. Al-Shawkānī, *Adab al-Ṭalab*, 145–46. To illustrate, al-Shawkānī cites an instance when the Prophet realized that a certain person who had formally converted to Islam was indeed a hypocrite, an offense that, according to the exact rulings of the law, is punishable by death. However, the Prophet decided not to implement this penalty "lest people say Muhammad kills his Companions." He thus opted to suspend the execution of the penalty in order to bring about a common good that is of a higher benefit for the community, and to ward off a bigger harm than the one resulting from the suspension of the law. For similar arguments on ease and facility, see Walī Allāh, *ʿIqd*, 24, 29. Walī Allāh argues that a mufti should opt for the easier choices when ruling for other people, especially the weak among them.

212. Muḥammad b. ʿAlī al-Shawkānī, *Nayl al-Awṭār min Aḥādīth Sayyid al-Akhyār, Sharḥ Muntaqā al-Akhbār*, 8 parts in 4 vols. (Beirut: Dār al-Kutub al-Ilmiyya, 1995).

213. Not to be confused with his grandson Taqī al-Dīn Ibn Taymiyya.

214. Al-Shawkānī relies heavily on *Talkhīṣ al-Habīr fī Takhrīj Aḥādīth al-Sharḥ al-Kabīr* by Ibn Ḥajar al-ʿAsqalānī (d. 1449), and also on his *Fath al-Bārī Sharḥ al-Bukhārī*.

215. Al-Shawkānī, *Al-Darārī al-Muḍiyya*, 20, 25–26. Also see al-Shawkānī, *Nayl al-Awṭār*, vol. 1, part 1, 29.

216. Al-Shawkānī, *Al-Darārī al-Muḍiyya*, 26. See also al-Shawkānī, *Irshād al-Fuḥūl* (285–86), where he says, "That on which God is silent is part of what He has pardoned [*mā sakat Allāh ʿanhu fa huwa mimmā ʿafā ʿanhu*]."

217. Al-Shawkānī, *Al-Darārī al-Muḍiyya*, 26. Al-Shawkānī distinguishes between tangible/ritual (*ḥissiyya/sharʿiyya*) impurity and allegorical (*rijsiyya/ḥukmiyya*) impurity and maintains that the kind of impurity that is relevant to worshipping is the tangible one (*ḥissiyya*) (27). See also similar arguments in al-Ṣanʿānī, *Subul al-Salām*, for example, 1:137.

218. Al-Shawkānī, *Nayl al-Awṭār*, vol. 1, part 1, 61.

219. Al-Shawkānī, *Nayl al-Awṭār*, vol. 2, part 4, 148.

220. Muḥammad b. ʿAlī al-Shawkānī, *Al-Fawāʾid al-Majmūʿa fī al-Aḥādīth al-Mawḍūʿa*, ed. Abdulraḥmān Bin Yaḥā al-Maʿlamī al-Yamānī (Cairo: Maṭbaʿat al-Sunna al-Muḥammadiyya, n.d.), 278–83. See also *Al-Fawāʾid*, 430, where al-Shawkānī is less accommodating of Ibn Ḥanbal's reports.

221. Walī Allāh, *Ḥujjat Allāh*, 1:182.

222. Walī Allāh, *Ḥujjat Allāh*, 1:185.

223. Walī Allāh, *Ḥujjat Allāh*, 2:38.

224. Walī Allāh, *Ḥujjat Allāh*, 2:39.

Index

ʿAbd al-Ḥaqq al-Dihlawī, 245–48, 267
ʿAbdu, Muḥammad, 23, 135, 138, 324n10
Abū Ḥanīfa, 247, 250, 257, 274
Afghānī, Jamāl al-Dīn al-, 23, 138, 324n10
Ahl al-bayt, 49–50, 173, 176, 177–78, 208, 212, 239, 307. See also *ʿItra*
ʿĀʾisha, 212–14, 257
ʿAlfī, Ḥasan al-, 147, 162
ʿAlī Ibn Abī Ṭālib, 105, 159, 175, 176, 177–78, 179–80, 212–13, 214, 307
ʿAmmār Ibn Yāsir, 177, 178, 239–40
Analogy, 274, 286, 287, 291, 295, 298–303, 309, 312, 315, 320
Apostasy, 46, 51, 55, 115, 125, 208
Arabic language, 65–66, 72, 73–74, 277, 286
Aristotelianism, 332n7
Association. See *Shirk*
ʿAṭṭār, Ḥasan al-, 369n84
Authority, intellectual: challenges to exclusive claims to, 88, 89, 94, 104, 105, 107, 126–27, 129, 133, 215–16; expanded participation in, through *ijtihād*, 66, 68, 88, 94, 280; intermediary, 74–75, 91, 94–95, 96, 121, 126, 141, 279, 320. *See also* Scholars: vis-à-vis political authorities
Authority, political: duties of, 110–11, 153, 164, 315; legitimacy of, 23–24, 43–44, 131, 141, 147, 150, 153–54, 155, 164–66, 283, 304–5; limits on, 98, 163, 165, 283. *See also* Imams of Sanaa; Scholars: vis-à-vis political authorities; Shawkānī, Muḥammad Ibn ʿAlī al-: and political power
Authority of the present, 17, 18, 181, 182, 279, 320

Bakriyya, 368–69n84
Banū Hāshim, 35, 149–50, 212
Barāʾa (disassociation), 26, 51, 116, 316
Barāʾa (nonliability), 300, 304, 308, 310, 315, 316–18, 320
Barelvī, Sayyid Aḥmad, 57
Biographical dictionaries, 15, 168–69, 182
Bukhārī, al-, hadith compilation of, 224–30, 233–34, 238, 241, 252, 258–59, 266, 268, 270

Clancy-Smith, Julia, 326n15
Classical/postclassical dichotomy, 20
Commins, David Dean, 334n68
Commoners: as ignorant mob (*ʿawām*), 91, 191, 192, 205, 297; participation in *ijtihād* by, 74–75, 79–80, 84–85, 88, 89–92, 292, 293, 295, 355nn141–42, 408n37; as unsuited to scholarship, 31, 206–7, 293, 352–53n94, 355n132
Companions of the Prophet: authority of, 43, 98, 123, 175–77, 179–80, 210–11, 212–14, 216, 234–37, 250, 268, 279, 286–87, 291, 295, 406n13; cursing of, 49–50, 171, 175–76, 178–79, 181, 239; as hadith transmitters, 175, 209, 212–13, 234–41, 257, 290–91; as saints, 119
Consensus, 24, 71, 78, 111, 123, 143–44, 210, 226, 268, 287, 295–98, 314
Cook, Michael, 345n16
Corruption: of religious practices, 34, 42, 114, 121–22, 144, 220; of rulers, 35, 44, 122, 138, 142, 144, 150–52, 165, 206, 220; of scholars, 88, 92, 126, 131, 152, 196, 205, 206–7

Decline thesis, 2, 3, 5, 7–8, 20, 57, 138–39, 321, 332n7, 363n15
Dhamārī, al-Ḥusayn Ibn Yaḥyā Ibn Ibrāhīm al-, 193–94
Dihlawī, Muḥammad Ismāʿīl al-, 9, 248
Dihlawī, Shāh Walī Allāh. *See* Walī Allāh al-Dihlawī, Shāh
Divorce, 211, 307
Doumani, Beshara, 326n15
Dreams, 39, 98

Elitism in religion, eighteenth-century rejection of, 90–91, 94, 129–33, 140
El-Rouayheb, Khaled, 323n2
Europe, as impetus for Muslim thought, 2, 5, 15, 20–21, 135–38, 330n46

Fairness, 204–5
Farā'iḍī movement, 26, 28
Fāṭima, 177, 179
Fatwas, 30, 75, 76, 82, 87, 280, 292, 293
Following. See *Ittibāʿ*; *Taqlīd*
Friedmann, Yohanan, 365–66n56
Fulani jihad, 26, 41–44, 60, 362n13. *See also* Ibn Fūdī, ʿUthmān
Fundamentalism, Islamic, 6–7, 14–15, 27–28, 57–58, 67, 134. *See also* Wahhabi movement

Gellner, Ernest, 347n25
Ghālib Ibn Musāʿid, 46, 136–37
Ghazālī, Abū Ḥāmid al-, 53, 95, 101, 204, 239, 288, 359n206
Goody, Jack, 347–48n27
Gran, Peter, 351n66
Gunpowder empires, 3–4

Hādawī Zaydism, 159–60, 161–62, 170–71, 172, 176
Ḥadd penalties, 52–53, 306
Hadith: authority of, 36, 78–79, 107, 170, 173, 175, 178, 180, 217–18, 222, 228, 233, 240, 241, 266, 268, 270, 282, 288; centrality of, in eighteenth-century thought, 3, 13, 18, 56, 67, 107, 127, 175, 218, 220–21, 245, 260, 279; compilations of, 224–31, 233–34, 238, 247, 249–50, 251, 258–59, 266–68, 270, 276–77, 291–92, 394n5; and *ijtihād*, 68–69, 74, 76, 78–80, 81, 82, 173, 220, 226, 233, 241, 255–56, 274; Indian tradition of scholarship on, 245–74 passim; and jurisprudence, 246–48, 252–56, 257–59, 260–61, 267, 270–74; ranks/types of, 224–25, 228, 230, 231, 250, 251, 260, 266–67, 275–76, 289, 291, 395n20; socio-moral use of, 7, 15, 21, 67; transmitters of, 175, 209, 213, 225, 229–30, 231–33, 234, 238–43, 247, 269, 270, 275, 288–90, 305, 318; Yemeni tradition of scholarship on, 127, 149, 155, 161, 174, 175, 221–45 passim, 268–69, 270, 275
Ḥanafism and hadith, 246–48, 253–54, 267, 270, 272, 273–74
Ḥaramayn network of scholars, 15–16, 42, 57, 58–59, 62, 63, 64–65
Haykel, Bernard, 350n48, 350n50, 353n94, 358nn188–89, 359n202, 383n80
Hermansen, Marcia, 345n15
Ḥiyal, 310
Hourani, Albert, 5, 20–21, 325n15
Hypocrisy, 30, 39, 109–10, 414n211

Ibn ʿAbd al-Wahhāb, Muḥammad: apoliticism of, 6, 22, 23–24, 35, 55, 140; contemporaries' views on, 34–35, 36–38, 45, 47, 55, 59; on *ijtihād*, 23, 24; on *kufr* and *tawḥīd*, 23, 24–26, 27, 47; life of, 9, 10, 59; rejection of Sufism of, 16, 38–39, 114. *See also* Wahhabi movement
Ibn al-Wazīr, Muḥammad Ibn Ibrāhīm, 11, 67, 161, 168, 184, 188, 330n51, 359–60n1; on hadith, 149, 175, 221–23, 224–25, 228, 229, 230, 238–39, 240, 394–95n20; on *ijtihād*, 71, 222; and theology, 127, 174, 221–22
Ibn ʿArabī: critiques of, 13, 36, 39, 114–16, 248, 362n14, 370n96; defenses of, 29, 99, 102, 106, 323n2, 343n201, 343n208, 366n56; influence of, 14, 117, 119, 360n5, 369–70n95
Ibn Fūdī, ʿUthmān: life and influence of, 4, 9, 10–11, 12, 59, 62, 65; social agenda of, 42–44, 59, 60–61, 65, 132–33, 141, 197, 362n13; and Wahhabism, 26–27, 41–42, 43, 44, 58
Ibn Ḥazm, 80, 83, 174, 184–85, 187, 269
Ibn Idrīs, Aḥmad, 11, 54, 326n15, 343n208, 353–54n117, 360n2, 362n13, 377n242; critique of Wahhabism of, 342–43n201, 349n40; revelational *ijtihād* of, 349n40, 354n117, 361n10, 368n81, 369n86
Ibn Makhlūf, 185–86
Ibn Qayyim al-Jawziyya, 37, 47, 113, 187, 211
Ibn Saʿūd, ʿAbd al-ʿAzīz, 46, 47
Ibn Taymiyya: life and influence, 164, 174,

184, 185–87, 211, 214; on Sufism, 47, 118, 360n7, 371n100, 378n252; on *takfīr*, 54; on *taqlīd*, 37, 170
Ijtihād: closing of gates of, 8, 66, 83, 135, 172–73, 216, 332n7; differing results of, 87–88, 195–96, 213, 257, 406n14; in eighteenth-century thought, 8–9, 24, 66–68, 77, 81, 83–86, 90, 92–93, 94, 134–35, 142, 214, 219–20, 280, 281–82, 284, 320; and hadith, 68–69, 74, 76, 78–80, 81, 82, 173, 220, 226, 233, 241, 255–56, 274; in nineteenth and twentieth centuries, 8, 23, 66–68, 83–84, 134–35, 399n90; obligation of, 69–70, 77–80, 88, 89, 94–95, 129, 203, 235, 254–55, 282; ranks in, 71–72, 73, 75–76, 82–83; requirements of, 63–64, 68–69, 71, 72–74, 76, 81, 82, 128, 164, 206, 256, 293, 302, 354n117; and Sufism, 99, 119. See also *Ittibāʿ*; *Taqlīd*
Iltizām, 77, 352n75
Imams of Sanaa: criticism of, 35, 122, 144, 165; religious authority of, 159–60, 161, 165, 168, 170–71, 175–76, 198, 209–10, 214; as rulers, 34, 136, 144–47, 158–60, 162–64, 165–66, 191–92, 199–200, 202, 297
Īmān, 25, 39, 51–52
Imitation. See *Taqlīd*
Impurity, 257, 308–9, 317–18
Injustice, 24, 35, 42, 66, 94, 142, 152, 155, 165–66, 306
Innovations, negative, 37, 42, 43, 112, 122, 204, 231, 232
Inṣāf, 204–5
Intellectualism, extreme (*taʿammuq*), 130, 131–32, 267, 269
Intercession, 25, 43, 46–47, 96–97, 98, 103, 106, 109, 110, 117, 123, 244
Ismāʿīlīs, 171–72, 193
*Isnād*s, 169, 180, 212, 229, 250, 275–76, 277–79, 281, 288
Istiḥsān, 303
Istiṣḥāb, 303, 304
ʿItra, 159, 165, 209, 210, 239, 295, 307
Ittibāʿ, 74–75, 79, 89, 277, 396n141

Jabartī, ʿAbd al-Raḥmān al-, 5, 195
Jādda al-qawīma, al-, 271, 274, 391n261
Jāhiliyya, 25, 26, 40, 51
Jalāl, al-Ḥasan al-, 11, 67, 174, 184, 188–89, 242, 292–93, 352–53n94
Jarḥ and *taʿdīl*, 51, 213, 255, 289–90. *See also* Hadith: transmitters of
Jazāʾirī, ʿAbd al-Qādir al-, 97, 362n13
Judges: authority of opinions of, 81, 82, 87, 305–6; as complicit in state corruption, 35, 92, 152; knowledge of, as evidence, 233–34, 306; necessity of service as, 150–52, 201; refusals to serve as, 151, 156–57, 183, 387n151; requirements for, 156, 201, 204, 306
Jurisprudence, principles of. *See* Legal theory
Jurists: authority of, 32, 87–89, 94, 129, 282–83; competent vs. incompetent, 31–32, 33, 87, 92; differences among, 195–96, 257–58, 271; duties of, 105, 131, 255–56; and hadith, 246–47, 252–53, 259, 271; and Sufism, 94, 96, 99–100, 105. See also *Ijtihād*; Scholars
Juwaynī, Ḍiyāʾ al-Dīn al-, 204, 288, 294, 298

Kalām, 32–33, 71, 86–87, 127–29, 174, 221, 222, 286. *See also* Theology
Karāmāt, 43, 108, 117–19, 360n3, 372n151
Keddie, Nikki, 332n7
Kerr, Malcolm, 351n64
Khawārij, 45, 53, 231–32, 239, 288
Kufr: *al-taʾwīl*, 115, 175, 231–32, 238, 289; non-Wahhabi views on, 29–30, 38, 40–41, 42–44, 45, 46, 50–51, 52–55, 109, 113, 115; Wahhabi concept of, 22, 24–26, 43, 50–51. See also *Shirk*; *Takfīr*
Kūrānī, Ibrāhīm al-, 369–70n95
Kurdī, Ibrāhīm al-, 108, 117, 217
Kurdī, Muḥammad Ibn Sulaymān al-, 59, 64–65

Legal differences (*ikhtilāfāt*), 195–96, 208
Legal theory: basic principles of, 307–10, 312–13, 315–19, 320; in eighteenth-century thought, 3, 18–19, 56, 67, 220, 280–81, 291, 295, 298, 302, 311, 319–20; and *ijtihād*, 71, 82, 285–86; nonsectarianism of, 285;

techniques of, 286–88, 295–302, 303–4, 314. *See also* Analogy; Consensus; Hadith: transmitters of

Madhhabs. *See* Schools of law
Mālik's *Muwaṭṭa'*, 249–55, 256–57, 259, 270, 271, 275
Manṣūr, Imam al-, 147, 162
Maqbalī, Ṣāliḥ Ibn Mahdī al-, 11, 67, 144, 168, 174, 184, 189–90, 217
Marriage, temporary, 210–11
Martin, B. G., 362n13
Maṣlaḥa, 261, 264, 303, 305, 316
Merad, Ali, 377n241
Messick, Brinkley, 83–84, 383n80, 403n231, 404n236
Miracles, 43, 108, 117–19, 312–13, 360n3, 372n151
Mosques, 121–22, 204
Muʿāwiya, 149, 175–76, 238, 239, 240
Mujtahids. See *Ijtihād*
Mukāshafāt, 117, 118
Music, 30–31, 98
Muslim, hadith compilation of, 224–30, 233–34, 238, 266, 268, 270
Musnad compilations, 230–31, 266
Mutawakkil, Imam al- (Aḥmad), 145–46, 147, 162
Muʿtazilism, 86, 127, 174, 221, 222, 245, 262

Nābulsī, ʿAbd al-Ghanī al-, 28–33, 97–101, 323n2
Nāṣibīs, 49–50
Neo-Sufism, 13–14, 21, 39, 59, 97, 104, 135, 330n45, 362–63nn13–15, 377n242
Nihmī, ʿAbd Allāh Ibn Ismāʿīl al-, 194
Nomads, 46, 48–49, 137

Occult knowledge, 108, 117, 124
O'Fahey, R. S., 363n14
Orality, 403–4n232, 405n7
Orientalist historiography, 2, 3, 7–8, 20–21, 57, 134, 138–39
Ottoman Empire, 2, 3, 6, 323n2
Owen, Roger, 325n15

Padri movement, 26–28
Peters, Rudolph, 326n16, 351n62
Philosophy, 119, 129, 222
Poetry, 36, 182–83
Poverty, in Sufism, 94–95, 108–9
Prayer, legal disagreements concerning, 209–10, 258
Probity (*ʿadāla*), 210, 231, 232, 234, 242–43, 288–90, 292–93, 296, 305

Qanūjī, Ṣiddīq Khān al-, 8–9, 11
Qarāfī, Shahāb al-Dīn al-, 80
Qāsimī dynasty. *See* Imams of Sanaa
Qiyās. *See* Analogy
Qur'ān: interpretation of, 13, 24, 51, 69, 72, 74, 76, 287–88, 299; translation of, 65–66

Radicalism, Islamic, 6–7. *See also* Fundamentalism, Islamic
Radtke, Bernd, 353n104, 361n10, 369n86
Rāfiḍa, 171–72, 176, 178, 193. *See also* Shiʿis
Rahman, Fazlur, 13, 324n11, 329–30n45, 361–62n13
Reason and tradition, 264–66
Rebellion, 162, 165–66
Reform, Islamic: and European influence, 5, 15, 20–21, 135–38, 139, 330n46; and Islamic tradition, 17, 21, 23, 57, 61, 66, 121, 133–36, 195, 196–97, 216–18, 219, 221, 308, 320–21; and political power, in eighteenth century, 140–42, 145–47, 174; social priorities of, in eighteenth century, 56–57, 61, 66, 94, 133–35, 142, 220; socio-moral, 14, 15, 21, 42, 67, 324n11, 330n45, 361–62n13; and Sufism, 63, 94–97, 107, 361–62n13, 377n242, 378n252; in Zaydi Yemen, 60, 138, 167, 174–75, 176, 177, 187–93, 198, 214, 217, 219, 237–38, 330n51
Regional traditions, 16–18, 57, 59–65, 66, 68, 133, 139, 170, 219, 221, 403n229. *See also* Hadith: Indian tradition of scholarship on; Hadith: Yemeni tradition of scholarship on; Zaydism: Yemeni tradition of
Revisionist historiography, 7–8, 13–14, 18, 21–22, 67–68, 134
Riḍā, Rashīd, 9, 23, 135, 399n100
Riḍawī, Sayyid Murtaḍā al-, 336n105
Roff, William, 26–28, 337nn123–24, 339–40n158
Rulers. *See* Authority, political

Saḥūlī, Yaḥyā Bin Ṣāliḥ al-, 200
Saints: excessive veneration of, 24, 34, 46–47, 95, 103, 108–9, 110; special powers of, 95, 96, 98, 106, 108, 110, 113, 117–19; tombs of, 43, 103, 107, 110, 111–12. *See also* Tombs: cultic practices at
Samāʿ, 98
Ṣanʿānī, Muḥammad Ibn Ismāʿīl al-: on ʿAlī, 177–78; on Companions of the Prophet, 234–35, 406n13; on hadith, 174, 223–35, 240–45, 268–69, 270, 275, 276–77; on *ijtihād*, 63, 67, 68–70, 71, 77, 214–15, 235, 284, 293; on legal schools, 34, 60, 143–44, 174, 178; life and influence of, 9–10, 11, 12, 34–36, 48–49, 138, 144–45, 184, 190–93; social critique of, 34–35, 39, 138, 142–44, 157–58; on Sufism, 36, 107–13; on Wahhabism, 33–38, 45, 55
Sanūsī, Muḥammad Bin ʿAlī al-: on hadith, 274–75; on *ijtihād*, 78–80, 81–82, 274–75, 283–84, 351n68, 368n81, 393n2; life and influence of, 4, 9, 11, 12, 54–55, 61–62, 136, 141, 197; Sufism of, 61–62, 97, 105–7, 361n9; on *takfīr*, 54–55
Sanūsiyya, 11–12, 60, 61–62, 141, 362n13, 377n242
Scholars: corrupt/inferior, 31, 87, 88, 92, 122, 131, 152, 196, 205–8; ideal/virtuous, 156–57, 182–84, 186–87, 203, 204–5, 269, 273; role of, 79, 88, 89, 91, 110, 131–32, 150–53, 194; vis-à-vis political authorities, 43–44, 88, 141, 145, 150–58, 161–62, 163, 197–98, 200, 203–4, 207, 218, 246 (*see also* Shawkānī, Muḥammad Ibn ʿAlī al-: and political power). *See also* Consensus; Jurists
Schools of law: affirmations of legitimacy of, 80–81, 83, 254, 272–74; challenges to authority of, 77, 79, 83, 88, 107, 126–27, 172–73, 214–16, 218, 270, 293, 307, 387–88n164, 397–98n55; excessive partisanship for, 20, 56, 66, 121, 171, 172, 181, 207–8, 215, 297, 336n105; hadith as mediator among, 220, 257, 267, 270–71, 271–72, 274; *ijtihād* within, 72, 73, 76, 86, 254–55, 256, 293, 353n104; imams of, 69, 107, 126, 215–16, 237, 250, 274–75, 397n49, 397n55; rejection of exclusivity of, 34, 80–81, 172, 193, 196, 208, 253–55, 272, 273, 294, 311, 392–93n290
Schulze, Reinhard, 328–29n34, 329n41
Shādhilī, Abū al-Ḥasan al-, 106, 360–61n8
Shāfiʿīs in Yemen, 158, 160–61, 166, 200, 384n98, 405n6. *See also* Sunnism: in Yemen
Sharia, limits to scope of, 283, 300, 301, 305, 308–10, 312, 314–16, 317, 319–20
Shariat Allah, Hajji, 26, 28
Shawkānī, Muḥammad Ibn ʿAlī al-: on commoners, 88, 89–92, 125–26, 192, 205–7, 292, 295, 352–53n94, 386n129, 405n8; on Companions of the Prophet, 12, 49–50, 119, 171, 175–77, 178–80, 181, 193–94, 210–11, 212–14, 235–37, 238–40, 286–87, 290–91; on divine vs. human law, 155, 283, 300, 305, 314–16; on hadith, 173–74, 175, 180, 209, 217–18, 233–34, 238–40, 268–69, 270, 275–76, 277–78, 288–92, 318–19, 394–95n20; on *ijtihād*, 63–64, 70, 72–76, 77–78, 82–83, 85–90, 157, 213, 214, 215–16, 282–83, 284, 292–94, 311; on inferior scholars, 87, 88, 92, 122, 152, 205–8; on intellectual virtues, 156–58, 181–95 passim, 203–5, 384n92; on legal theory, 285–88, 295–302, 303–10, 313–14, 315–19; life and influence of, 9, 11, 12, 48–49, 59, 60, 64–65, 90, 136–38, 141, 145, 181, 193–94, 198–99, 202, 217, 219–20, 278, 310–11, 324n10; and political power, 90, 136, 138, 141, 145–66, 167–68, 174, 197–204, 207, 214, 216, 218, 283, 304–5; on religious disciplines, 86–87, 127–30, 401n176; on Sufism, 94, 107, 112–21, 126, 182, 378n252, 386nn145–46; on Sunni-Shiʿi points of contention, 171, 208–14; on *takfīr*, 49–54, 56; on tomb veneration, 107, 113, 121–22, 126; on Wahhabism, 45–48, 50–51, 55; and Zaydism, 11, 12, 60, 107, 159, 161–62, 163, 165–77, 179–80, 208–12, 214, 217, 294, 408n37
Shiʿis, 49, 50, 171–72, 173, 208–14, 215, 236, 285, 341–42n181, 386n129
Shirk, 24–26, 32–33, 40–41, 51, 55, 109–10, 114, 123–25
Shrines. *See* Tombs
Sindī, Muḥammad Ḥayāt al-, 9, 59, 64, 77, 116, 352n75

Sinful pleasures, 30, 98
Sinners, as hadith transmitters, 175, 209, 231–32, 238–39, 242–43, 289
Sirhindī, Aḥmad, 102–3, 248, 362n13, 377n242
Social status, 31, 89, 90–91, 92, 205–7. *See also* Commoners
Sokoto Caliphate, 10–11, 42, 60–61, 65
Sufism: eighteenth-century defenses of, 29, 32–33, 95–107, 117–20, 123, 248; institutional functions of, 61–63; and law, 54, 96, 99–101, 103–4, 105–6, 119–20, 273, 361n10; non-Wahhabi critiques of, 36, 48, 54, 94–96, 97, 100, 107–16, 119–20, 123, 366n56; and reformism, 63, 94–97, 107, 361–62n13, 377n242, 378n252; revisionist view of, 7, 13–14, 59, 363n15 (*see also* Neo-Sufism); Wahhabi hostility to, 16, 28, 38–39, 48, 58, 97, 107
Sunnism: points of contention with Shiʿism and Zaydism, 208–14, 236; in Yemen, 158–61, 163, 166, 167, 170, 172, 174 (*see also* Shāfiʿīs in Yemen)
Suyūṭī, Jalāl al-Dīn al-, 106, 108, 161, 388n166

Taʿammuq, 130, 131–32, 267, 269
Ṭāghūt, 332n16
Ṭahṭāwī, Rifāʿa al-, 5
Tajdīd, 8–9, 85, 130, 219–20
Takfīr: arguments against, 22, 29–30, 37–38, 39–40, 45, 48, 50–52, 53–55, 56, 112, 115–16, 124–25, 239; political, 44, 141; Wahhabi focus on, 20, 21, 46–47, 50, 55. See also *Kufr*
Taklīf, 69–70, 89, 235, 288
Tamadhhub, 20, 56, 66, 121, 171, 172, 181, 253, 336n105
Tankar (governor), 164
Taqiyya, 392n289
Taqlīd: eighteenth-century rejection of, 17, 23, 24, 66, 69–70, 76, 77–81, 87–88, 91, 112, 126, 128, 170–71, 208, 214–16, 236–37, 283, 284, 293–94; vs. legitimate following, 74–75, 77–78, 79, 277, 282, 292, 396n41; in neo-Sufism, 13–14; as permissible/obligatory, 77–78, 80–81, 82, 83, 283–84, 293, 294, 408n37
Ṭarīqa Muḥammadiyya, 13–14, 62–63, 120, 369n86, 377n242
Tawḥīd, 10, 21, 23–24, 25–26, 32–33, 37, 52, 109, 219
Taxes, illegal, 20, 35, 56, 66, 94, 142–43, 144, 150, 162–63, 165, 297, 305
Taysīr, 309, 310, 311, 312, 313, 316–17, 319–20, 343n207. See also *Barāʾa* (nonliability)
Theology, 32–33, 71, 86–87, 105, 127–29, 174, 221, 222, 245, 261–62, 265, 286
Tījāniyya, 62–63, 360n6
Tombs: cultic practices at, 25, 42–43, 56, 87, 103, 107, 110, 111–12, 113, 114, 121–22, 126, 142–44; permissibility of building, 50, 122–23, 124, 144
Traditionalists, 54, 107, 127, 196, 255, 259, 269, 271. *See also* Hadith
Transmission. *See* Hadith: transmitters of; *Isnāds*
Trimingham, J. Spencer, 349n38, 350n60, 362n13, 368n81

Umma: division of, 243–45; probity of, 242–43, 245, 289–90
Unbelief. See *Kufr*
Unity of being (*waḥdat al-wujūd*), 29, 36, 99, 100, 102–3, 248, 362n14, 367–68n80, 370n95
Unity of witness (*waḥdat al-shuhūd*), 102–3, 248, 362n14, 367–68n80
Uṣūl al-fiqh. *See* Legal theory
Uṣūl al-ḥadīth, 18–19, 220, 280. *See also* Hadith
Usury (*ribā*), 301

Vikor, Knut, 348n35, 348n37, 349n40
Voll, John O., 324n11, 329nn43–45, 345n13

Wahhabi movement: anti-Sufism of, 28, 97, 107; eighteenth-century critiques of, 20, 22, 33, 37–38, 45, 46–48, 50–51; focus on, in historiography, 5–7, 20, 21, 22–23, 57, 378n252; influence of, on Islamic thought, 22, 26–28, 41–42, 57–58, 134, 136, 139; *takfīr* in, 21, 22, 50–51. *See also* Ibn ʿAbd al-Wahhāb, Muḥammad
Walī Allāh al-Dihlawī: anti-elitism of, 130–32; on hadith, 248–55, 256, 257–61, 263,

266–71, 273–74; on *ijtihād*, 71–72, 80–81, 83, 195–96, 284, 302–3; on jurisprudence, 256–57, 259, 260–61; on legal differences, 195–96, 249, 257–58, 271–74, 311, 391–92n261; on legal theory, 311–13, 319; life and influence of, 9, 10, 12, 39, 55, 59, 60, 65–66, 136, 197, 217, 248, 392–93n290; on Mālik's *Muwaṭṭa'*, 249–55, 256–57, 259, 270, 271, 275; as *mujaddid*, 85, 130, 219; and political power, 141–42, 197; on reason and tradition, 264–66, 313; on secret religious knowledge, 260–63, 264; Sufism of, 16, 38–39, 59, 97, 101–5, 273, 359n1, 362n13; on *takfīr*, 39–41

Wiping of shoes, in ablution, 209, 238

Zabīdī, Murtaḍā al-, 346–47n21, 362n13

Ẓāhirī school, 184–85, 298, 301

Zakāt, 149–50, 382n62

Zaydism: and Companions of the Prophet, 175–76, 179–80; disagreements with Shiʿism and Sunnism of, 209–12, 236, 237; hadith in, 149, 161, 170, 173–74, 175, 192, 221–23; political theory of, 160, 161–62, 163, 165, 198; and Sufism, 107; and theology, 86, 127, 174, 221, 222; Yemeni tradition of, 11, 34, 67, 158–62, 166, 167–72, 173–74, 191–92, 221–22, 330n51

Zuhd, 117, 275

ISLAMIC CIVILIZATION AND MUSLIM NETWORKS

Ahmad Dallal, *Islam without Europe: Traditions of Reform in Eighteenth-Century Islamic Thought* (2018).

Irfan Ahmad, *Religion as Critique: Islamic Critical Thinking from Mecca to the Marketplace* (2017).

Scott Kugle, *When Sun Meets Moon: Gender, Eros, and Ecstasy in Urdu Poetry* (2016).

Kishwar Rizvi, *The Transnational Mosque: Architecture, Historical Memory, and the Contemporary Middle East* (2015).

Ebrahim Moosa, *What Is a Madrasa?* (2015).

Bruce Lawrence, *Who Is Allah?* (2015).

Edward E. Curtis IV, *The Call of Bilal: Islam in the African Diaspora* (2014).

Sahar Amer, *What Is Veiling?* (2014).

Rudolph T. Ware III, *The Walking Qur'an: Islamic Education, Embodied Knowledge, and History in West Africa* (2014).

Saʿdiyya Shaikh, *Sufi Narratives of Intimacy: Ibn ʿArabī, Gender, and Sexuality* (2012).

Karen G. Ruffle, *Gender, Sainthood, and Everyday Practice in South Asian Shiʿism* (2011).

Jonah Steinberg, *Ismaʿili Modern: Globalization and Identity in a Muslim Community* (2011).

Iftikhar Dadi, *Modernism and the Art of Muslim South Asia* (2010).

Gary R. Bunt, *iMuslims: Rewiring the House of Islam* (2009).

Fatemeh Keshavarz, *Jasmine and Stars: Reading More than "Lolita" in Tehran* (2007).

Scott Kugle, *Sufis and Saints' Bodies: Mysticism, Corporeality, and Sacred Power in Islam* (2007).

Roxani Eleni Margariti, *Aden and the Indian Ocean Trade: 150 Years in the Life of a Medieval Arabian Port* (2007).

Sufia M. Uddin, *Constructing Bangladesh: Religion, Ethnicity, and Language in an Islamic Nation* (2006).

Omid Safi, *The Politics of Knowledge in Premodern Islam: Negotiating Ideology and Religious Inquiry* (2006).

Ebrahim Moosa, *Ghazālī and the Poetics of Imagination* (2005).

miriam cooke and Bruce B. Lawrence, eds., *Muslim Networks from Hajj to Hip Hop* (2005).

Carl W. Ernst, *Following Muhammad: Rethinking Islam in the Contemporary World* (2003).